ARCTIC OCEAN

tsbergen
(Nor.)

RUSSIAN FEDERATION

FINLAND
Helsinki
Tallinn St. Petersburg
LIT. Nizhniy
Novgorod Yekaterinburg Omsk Novosibirsk
hagen Minsk Moscow
Warsaw Samara
LAND BELARUS
Bratislava Kiev Kharkov
Budapest MOL. Odessa
ROMANIA UKRAINE KAZAKHSTAN
H. Belgrade Bucharest MONGOLIA Ulan Bator Harbin
BULG. Black Sea Alma-Ata
YUGO. Tbilisi Tashkent KYRG. Shenyang
ALB. Sofia T. ARM. AZ. UZBEK. Bishkek Beijing N.KOREA
GREECE Ankara Yerevan Baku TURKMENISTAN TAJ. (Peking) Pyongyang JAPAN
Athens TURKEY Caspian Sea Ashkhabad Dushanbe CHINA Tientsin Dalian Seoul Tokyo
ean Sea CYPRUS SYRIA Tehran Kabul JAMMU & Lanchow S.KOREA Osaka
Damascus AFGHAN- KASHMIR Sian
ISRAEL IRAQ ISTAN Islamabad Chengdu Wuhan Nanking Shanghai
Jerusalem Amman Baghdad IRAN Lahore Chungking
JORDAN PAKISTAN Kathmandu BHUTAN Kunming Canton Taipei
BYA EGYPT KUWAIT NEPAL Delhi Calcutta Dacca TAIWAN
SAUDI BAHRAIN Karachi BANGLA. HONG KONG (U.K.)
Cairo Riyadh QATAR Hanoi
ARABIA U.A.E. Muscat INDIA MYANMAR
HAD SUDAN Bombay BURMA Vientiane
Khartoum ERIT. Sana OMAN Madras THAILAND Manila PHILIPPINES
N'Djamena REA Asmara YEMEN Rangoon Bangkok Ho Chi
DJIBOUTI CAMB. Minh City
NTRAL AFRICAN ETHIOPIA SRI Phnom
REPUBLIC Addis Ababa LANKA Penh
Colombo MALAYSIA BRUNEI
SOMALI REPUBLIC MALDIVES Kuala Lumpur
ZAIRE KENYA Mogadishu SINGAPORE
Kampala INDONESIA
Kigali RWANDA Nairobi Jakarta
Bujumbura BURUNDI TANZANIA SEYCHELLES PAPUA
Kinshasa Dodoma Dar es Salaam NEW
GUINEA Port
GOLA COMOROS Moresby
MALAWI INDIAN
ZAMBIA Lilongwe
Lusaka Harare ZIM- MADAGASCAR
BABWE Antananarivo OCEAN
BOTSWANA MOZAMBIQUE MAURITIUS
oek Gaborone Pretoria Maputo
BIA Johannesburg SWAZILAND AUSTRALIA Brisbane
REP. LESOTHO
OF Maseru Perth
SOUTH AFRICA Adelaide Sydney
wn Canberra Auckland
Melbourne NEW
ZEALAND Wellington

Prince Edward Is.
(R.S.A.) Kerguelen Is. SOUTHERN OCEAN
(Fr.)

Aleutian Islands
(U.S.A.)

International Date Line

PACIFIC
Bonin Is.
(Japan) Tropic of Cancer
Northern Mariana
Islands
(U.S.A.)
FED. STATES OF MICRONESIA MARSHALL ISLANDS
PALAU OCEAN
(BELAU)
Caroline
Islands
Equator
NAURU
KIRIBATI
SOLOMON
ISLANDS TUVALU
Wallis Is.
(Fr.)
VANUATU FIJI W.SAMOA
New TONGA
Caledonia
(Fr.) Tropic of Capricorn

Arctic Circle
80°
60°
40°
20°
0°
20°
40°
60°
80°

ica

NDENCY
AUSTRALIAN ANTARCTIC TERRITORY TERRE ADÉLIE (Fr.) ROSS
AUSTRALIAN ANTARCTIC DEPENDENCY
TERRITORY (N.Z.)

Antarctic Circle

Note: Under the Antarctic
Treaty of 1959 all territorial
claims in the region were held in
abeyance in the interest of
international cooperation for scientific
purposes. The treaty binds the 12 original,
and all subsequent signatory states to use the
region solely for peaceful purposes and scientific
research. A concensus is being sought with regard
to mineral rights and exploitation before the Treaty
expires.

0 500 1000 1500 2000 2500 Miles
0 1000 2000 3000 4000 Kms.
Flat Polar Equal Area Projection

© Collins

D1305342

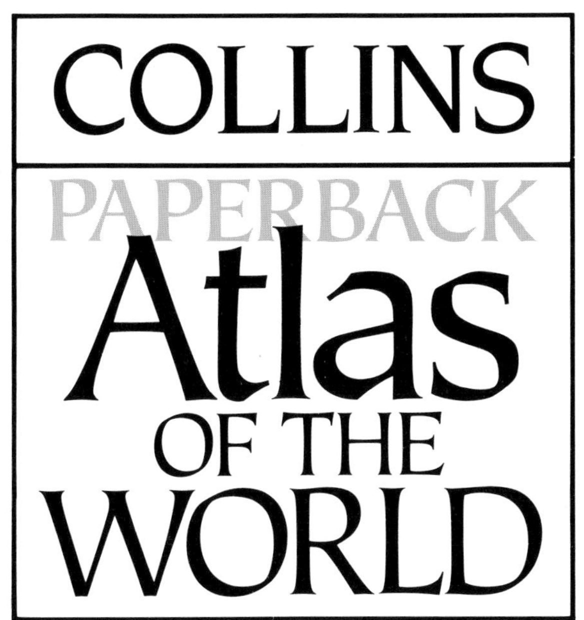

COLLINS
PAPERBACK
Atlas
OF THE
WORLD

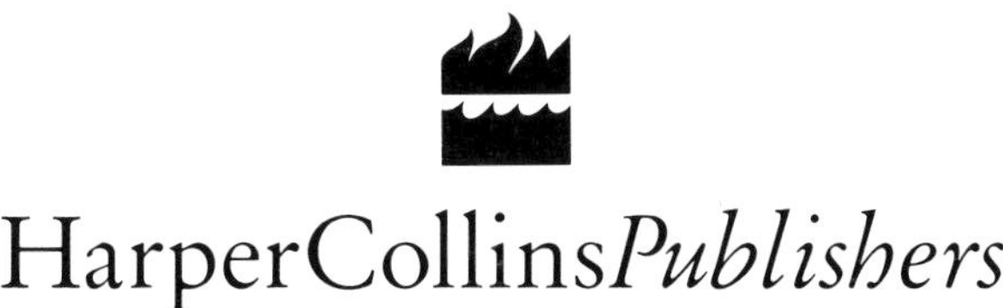

HarperCollins*Publishers*

Collins *Paperback* Atlas of the World
Published by
HarperCollins*Publishers*
77-85 Fulham Palace Road
Hammersmith
London W6 8JB

1st Edition 1988
2nd Edition 1992
New Edition 1993
Revised Edition 1994, 1995

Maps © HarperCollins*Publishers* and Collins-Longman Atlases
Illustrated section and statistics © HarperCollins*Publishers*

Produced by HarperCollins,Hong Kong

ISBN 0 00 448364 2

Photograph Credits
Credits read from top to bottom and left to right on each page.
XI Space Frontiers. VII Lockheed Solar Laboratory. XV NASA. XVI Robert Harding; Zefa; Grisewood &
Dempsey. XVII Pat Morris; Robert Harding; Zefa. XIX M. Borland. XX National Coal Board; Grisewood &
Dempsey (2). XXI Nasou; Atomic Energy Authority. XXII Photo Library International; Zefa; Daily Telegraph
Library. XXIII Picturepoint; US Environmental Protection Society.
XXIV NASA.

XXI Factfinder - B.P. Statistical Review of World Energy, 1993.

CONTENTS

GUIDE TO THE ATLAS

COLLINS PAPERBACK ATLAS OF THE WORLD consists of three self-contained but interrelated sections, as is clearly indicated in the preceding list of contents.

OUR PLANET EARTH

This concise encyclopaedia section, by use of stimulating illustration and informative text, brings together many of the latest scientific discoveries and conclusions about our world, our place in the universe, our neighbours in space, the origin, structure and dynamics of our planet, the distribution of peoples and resources, and the increasingly significant effects of man on his environment. Each double-page opening has been carefully designed to highlight an important facet of our world as we know it today. As a special feature, every subject presentation includes a factfinder panel, to which quick and easy reference can be made in order to find out particularly notable facts. All statistics quoted in this section are presented in metric terms in accordance with the System International d'Unites (S.I. units).

WORLD ATLAS

The main section of 64 pages of maps has been carefully planned and designed to meet the contemporary needs of the atlas user. Full recognition has been given to the many different purposes that currently call for map reference.

Map coverage Map coverage extends to every part of the world in a balanced scheme that avoids any individual country or regional bias. Map areas are chosen to reflect the social, economic, cultural or historical importance of a particular region. Each double spread or single page map has been planned deliberately to cover an entire physical or political unit. Generous map overlaps are included to maintain continuity. Each of the continents is treated systematically in a subsection of its own. As an aid to the reader in locating the required area, a postage stamp key map is incorporated into the title margin of each map page.

Map projections have been chosen to reflect the different requirements of particular areas. No map can be absolutely true on account of the impossibility of representing a spheroid accurately on a flat surface without some distortion in either area, distance, direction or shape. In a general world atlas it is the equal area property that is most important to retain for comparative map studies and feature size evaluation and this principle has been followed wherever possible in this map section. As a special feature of this atlas, the Global View projections used for each continental political map have been specially devised to allow for a realistic area comparison between the land areas of each continent and also between land and sea.

Map scales, as expressions of the relationship which the distance between any two points of the map bears to the corresponding distance on the ground, are in the context of this atlas grouped into three distinct categories.

Large scales, of between 1:2 000 000 (1 centimetre to 20 kilometres or 1 inch to 32 miles) and 1:3 000 000 (1 centimetre to 30 kilometres or 1 inch to 48 miles), are used to cover particularly dense populated areas of Western Europe and Japan.

Medium scales of between 1:3 000 000 and 1:10 000 000 are used for maps of important parts of Europe, North America, Australasia, etc.

Small scales of less than 1:10 000 000 (1 centimetre to 100 kilometres or 1 inch to 160 miles), are selected for maps of the complete world, continents, polar regions and many of the larger countries.

The actual scale at which a particular area is mapped therefore reflects its shape, size and density of detail, and as a basic principle the more detail required to be shown of an area, the greater its scale. However, throughout this atlas, map scales have been limited in number, as far as possible, in order to facilitate comparison between maps.

Map measurements give preference to the metric system which is now used in nearly every country throughout the world. All spot heights and ocean depths are shown in metres and the relief and submarine layer delineation is based on metric contour levels. However, all linear scalebar and height reference column figures are given in metric and Imperial equivalents to facilitate conversion of measurements for the non-metric reader.

Map symbols used are fully explained in the legend to be found on the first page of the World Atlas section. Careful study and frequent reference to this legend will aid in the reader's ability to extract maximum information.

Topography is shown by the combined means of precise spot heights, contouring, layer tinting and three-dimensional hill shading. Similar techniques are also used to depict the sea bed on the World Physical map and those of the oceans and polar regions.

Hydrographic features such as coastlines, rivers, lakes, swamps and canals are clearly differentiated.

Communications are particularly well represented with the contemporary importance of airports and road networks duly emphasized.

International boundaries and national capitals are fully documented and internal administrative divisions are shown with the maximum detail that the scale will allow. Boundary delineation reflects the 'de facto' rather than the 'de jure' political interpretation and where relevant an undefined or disputed boundary is distinguished. However there is no intended implication that the publishers necessarily endorse or accept the status of any political entity recorded on the maps.

Settlements are shown by a series of graded town stamps from major cities down to tiny villages.

Other features, such as notable ancient monuments, oases, national parks, oil and gas fields, are selectively included on particular maps that merit their identification.

Lettering styles used in the maps have been chosen with great care to ensure maximum legibility and clear distinction of named feature categories. The size and weight of the various typefaces reflect the relative importance of the features. Town names are graded to correspond with the appropriate town stamp.

Map place names have been selected in accordance with maintaining legibility at a given scale and at the same time striking an appropriate balance between natural and man-made features worthy of note. Name forms have been standardized according to the widely accepted principle, now well established in international reference atlases, of including place names and geographical terms in the local language of the country in question. In the case of non-Roman scripts (e.g. Arabic), transliteration and transcription have either been based on the rules recommended by the Permanent Committee on Geographical Names and the United States Board of Geographical Names, or as in the case of the adopted Pinyin transcription of Chinese names, a system officially proposed by the country concerned. The diacritical signs used in each language or transliteration have been retained on all the maps and throughout the index. However the English language reader's requirements have also been recognised in that the names of all countries, oceans, major seas and land features as well as familiar alternative name versions of important towns are presented in English.

Map sources used in the compilation of this atlas were many and varied, but always of the latest available information. At each stage of their preparation the maps were submitted to a thorough process of research and continual revision to ensure that on publication all data would be as accurate as practicable. A well-documented data bank was created to ensure consistency and validity of all information represented on the maps.

WORLD DATA

This detailed data section forms an appropriate complement to the preceding maps and illustrated texts. There are three parts, each providing a different type of essential geographical information.

World Facts and Figures Drawn from the latest available official sources, these tables present an easy reference profile of significant world physical, political and demographic as well as national data.

World Index This concluding part of the atlas lists in alphabetical order all individual place names to be found on the maps, which total about 20,000. Each entry in the index is referenced to the appropriate map page number, the country or region in which the name is located and the position of the name on the map, given by its co-ordinates of latitude and longitude. A full explanation of how to use the index is to be found on page 71.

World Maps Finally two summary maps giving separate coverage of the main political and physical features of the world are to be found on the front and back endpapers.

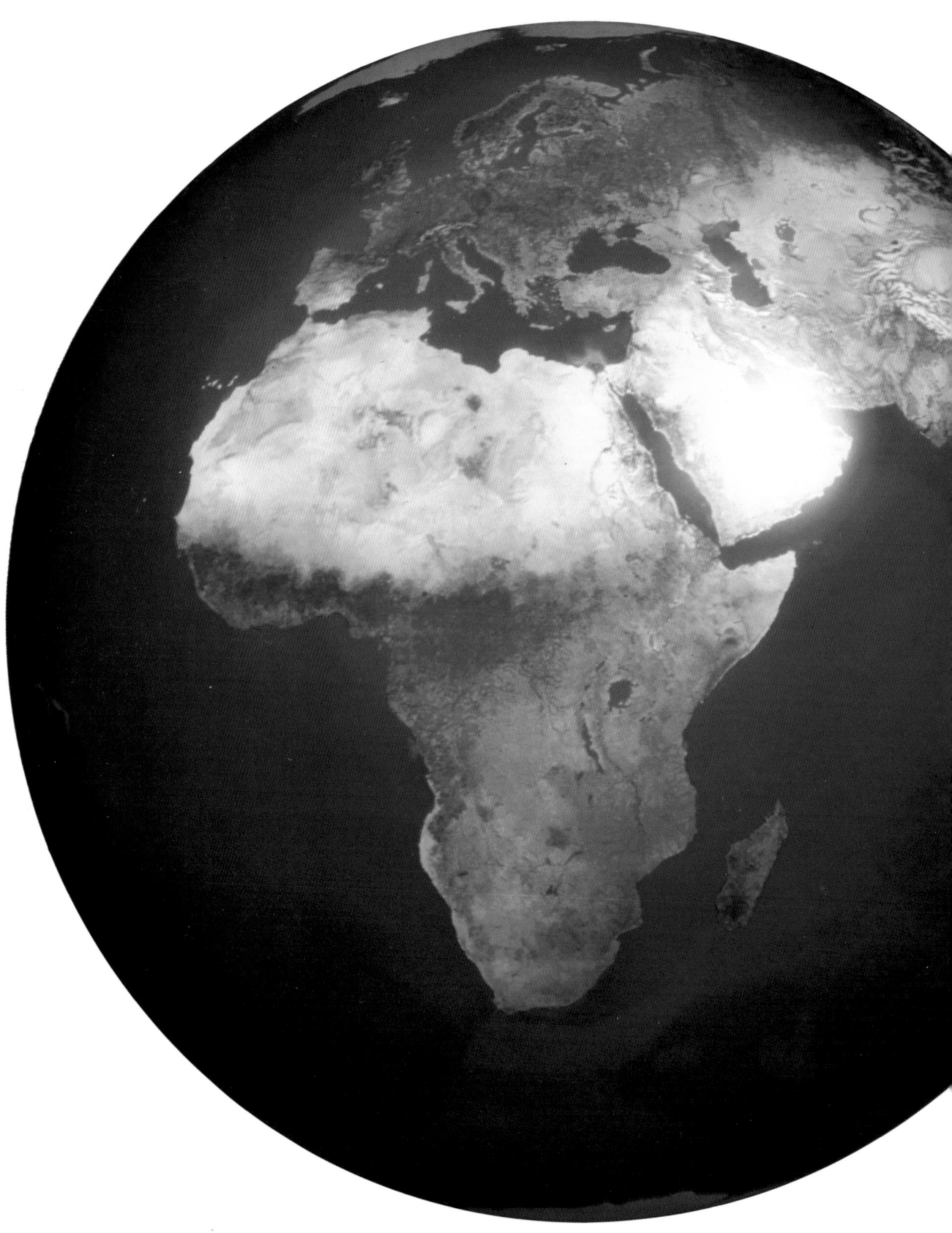

OUR PLANET EARTH

While the earth formed about 4500 million years ago, life as we know it today has only evolved gradually over the last 45 million years. Human beings have inhabited the earth for less than half a million years, and a couple of hundred generations takes us back to the dawn of history. Within this time people have conquered the animal kingdom, learnt how to harness the forces of nature, and proliferated in such numbers that they have colonised nearly every corner of the earth. Even more stunning are the changes which have taken place within living memory. The use of electricity, nuclear fission and modern technology have now given us the power to alter the balance of life on earth.

The first astronauts reported that the earth hangs "like a blue pearl in space". Their experience has helped dispel the dangerous notion that the world is boundless in extent, with limitless resources. Ecologists have also shown that the earth is a self enclosed system in which all forms of life are interconnected. Disruption in one part of the ecosystem can have serious consequences elsewhere. It follows that all human activity has an effect on the natural environment, and that we misuse this fragile planet at our peril.

In recent years people have been putting the environment under increasing stress. Raw materials such as timber, water and minerals are beginning to run short. Pollution and the disposal of wastes are becoming critical issues, and global warming has highlighted the dangers that we face. Environmental problems have been compounded by inequalities of wealth, where rich nations control and exploit the bulk of available resources in a world in which large numbers of people are struggling for survival. Decisive and concerted action will be needed to confront the growing ecological crisis.

Despite these threats there are encouraging signs. Over the past few decades food production has more than matched the growth in population. In industry there is scope for much greater efficiency and more careful use of resources. Sustainable development holds one of the keys to the future. Improvements in social justice also offer great possibilities.

These are exciting times in which we live. In the next decade the state of the environment is set to become the most pressing issue confronting us all. The way we respond to the challenge will have a profound effect on the earth and its life support systems. We will only make balanced decisions on the basis of detailed and careful research. This illustrated encyclopaedia seeks to provide up-to-date information on the issues that confront us all.

THE SOLAR SYSTEM

The Solar System rotates once around the centre of the Milky Way galaxy every 200 million years. The Solar System consists principally of the Sun and the nine planets that orbit around it, but it also includes moons and much debris, such as the spectacular rings of Saturn, and asteroids, which are called minor planets because they measure up to about 1000 km across. Other rocky matter and frozen gas form comets, which are even more numerous than asteroids. Comets have extremely elongated orbits, the farthest point of which may be in the vicinity of the outer planets. The path of one is shown by the red line in the diagram below. As the comets near the Sun, the frozen matter vaporizes to form a tail that is millions of kilometres long. If the orbit of a comet crosses that of the Earth, loose particles may be ejected into the atmosphere. There, they burn up in meteor showers. Fragments large enough to reach Earth are called meteorites.

Many solar systems probably exist in the Universe. In 1982 Russian astronomers

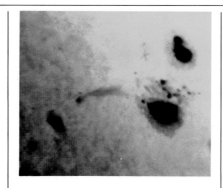

Groups of sunspots are dark areas on the Sun's surface that are around 1000° cooler than surrounding areas. The largest recorded sunspot covered 10,000 million km². Sunspots probably result from magnetic fields that cause local cooling. Sunspots may last for months, but small ones vanish after a few days.

estimated that 130 solar systems similar to our own lie within the observable part of the Milky Way galaxy. But their presence can only be inferred.

Our Sun probably began to form about 4600 million years ago from the solar nebula, a huge cloud of dust and gas. The planets formed somewhat later from the debris that was left over. The Sun consists mainly of hydrogen that is being turned into a central core of helium. The reactions involved in this process generate energy, giving the Sun a surface temperature of 6000°C. Prominences, eruptions of gas from the surface, may reach 50,000°C or more. They are often associated with sunspots, cooler patches possibly caused by strong magnetic fields that block the outward flow of heat. The Sun is surrounded by a thin atmosphere, the corona, which can be seen during a total eclipse. Eventually, the Sun, like all stars, will use up most of its hydrogen and will become a red giant star, engulfing the Solar System. But this will not occur for another 5000 million years.

The Inner Planets

The planets differ in many ways in their makeup, appearance, size and temperature. The four inner planets are the cratered Mercury, whose surface resembles that of our Moon; Venus, which is swathed by a cloudy atmosphere containing much carbon dioxide; Earth; and Mars, which also has a cratered surface. These four, comparatively small, rocky bodies are called terrestrial planets.

The Outer Planets

Most of the asteroids in the Solar System lie between Mars, the outermost of the terrestrial planets, and Jupiter, the innermost of the outer planets. The outer planets include three others – the ringed Saturn, Uranus and Neptune – which, like Jupiter, are huge balls of gas, mainly hydrogen and its compounds, with nitrogen (giving ammonia), carbon (giving methane) and helium. Rocky cores may exist beneath the gases. Pluto, which was discovered in 1930, is probably a rocky body with a methane-type atmosphere.

FACTFINDER

		Mean distance from the Sun (millions of km)	Equatorial diameter (km)	Period of rotation on axis	Surface °C temp- erature	Mass (Earth = 1)	Sidereal Period
1	Sun	–	1,392,000	25d 9h	6000°	333,400.00	–
2	Mercury	57.8	4,878	58d 15h	430°/-180°	0.055	88d
3	Venus	108.9	12,104	-243d*	480°	0.815	224d 16h
4	Earth	149.6	12,756	23h 56m	22°	1.00	1y
5	Mars	227.9	6,794	24h 37m	-120°/-20°	0.107	1y 332d
6	Jupiter	778.3	142,800	9h 50m	-150°	317.80	11y 313d
7	Saturn	1427	120,000	10h 14m	-180°	95.20	29y 167d
8	Uranus	2870	52,000	-17h 45m*	-210°	14.50	84y 6d
9	Neptune	4497	49,400	16h 10m	-220°	17.20	164y 292d
10	Pluto	5900	2,303	-6d 9h*	-230°?	0.003	247y 255d
				*(retrograde)			

Number of satellites: Mercury and Venus – 0; Earth – 1; Mars – 2; Jupiter – 16; Saturn – 17; Uranus – 15; Neptune – 8; Pluto – 1.

Orbital inclination: Mercury – 7°; Venus – 3°23'; Mars – 1°51'; Jupiter – 1°18'; Saturn – 2°29'; Uranus – 0°46'; Neptune – 1°46'; Pluto – 17°08'.

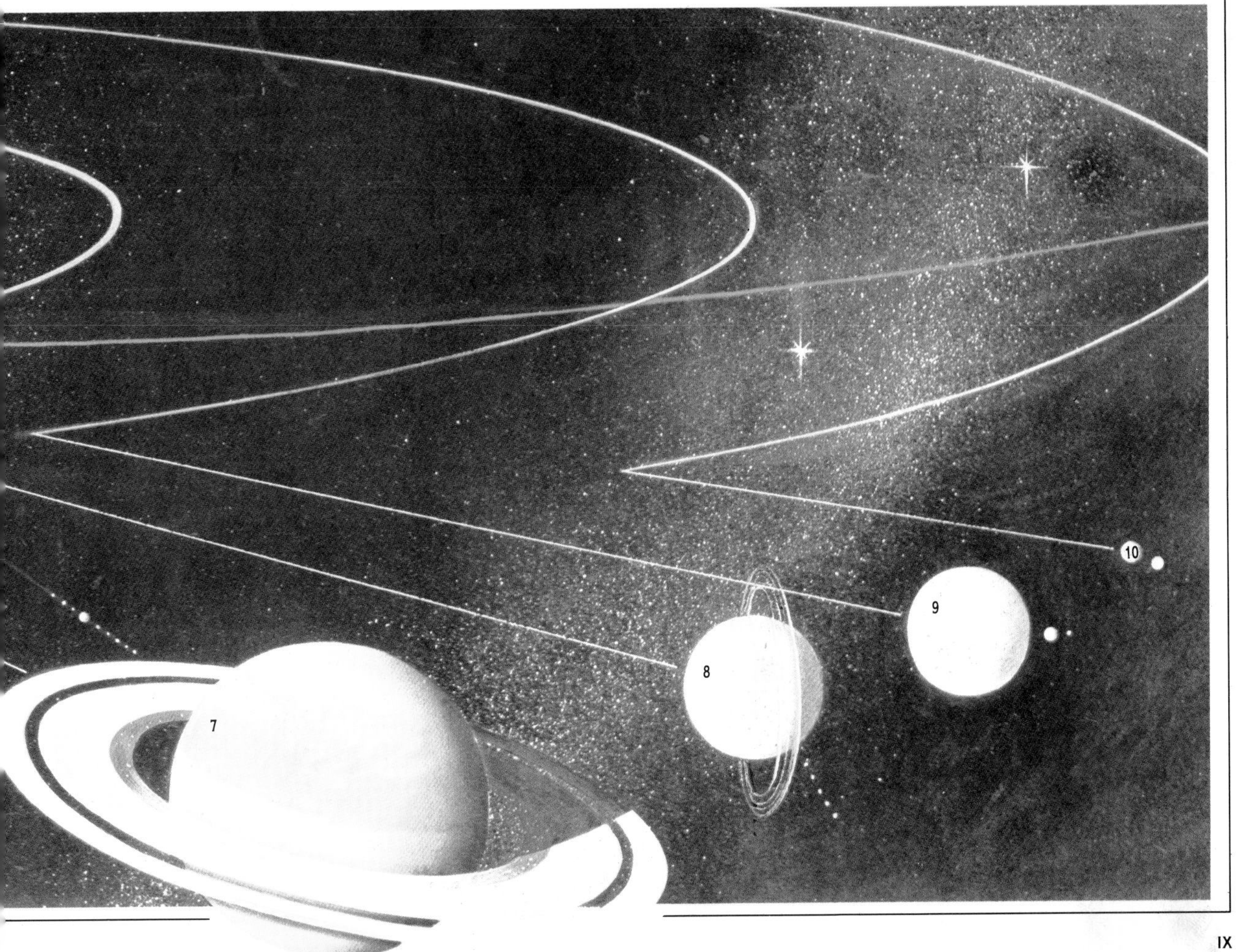

THE WHIRLING EARTH

The Earth moves in three ways: it spins on its axis; it orbits the Sun; and it moves around the Milky Way galaxy with the rest of the Solar System. As it spins on its axis, the Sun appears to move around the sky once every 24 hours. This, the mean solar day, is slightly longer than the sidereal day of 23 hours, 56 minutes and 4 seconds. The difference between the two is explained by the fact that the Earth is orbiting the Sun while it spins on its axis, with the effect that it must rotate 1/365th of a revolution more than a sidereal day in order that the same meridian exactly faces the Sun again.

As the Earth spins on its axis, the time at any point on the surface is calculated from the position of the Sun in the sky. This is called the local or apparent time. Because the Earth rotates 360° in 24 hours, local time changes by one hour for every 15° of longitude or 4 minutes for every 1° of longitude. For practical purposes, however, we use standard or zone time, so that the times are fixed over extensive north-south zones that also take account of national boundaries. By an international agreement in 1884, time zones are measured east and west of the prime meridian (0° longitude) which passes through Greenwich, London. Because clocks are advanced by 12 hours 180° east of Greenwich, but put back by 12 hours 180° west of Greenwich, there is a time difference of 24 hours at the International Date Line. This is approximately 180°W or E, although internationally agreed deviations prevent confusion of dates in island groups and land areas.

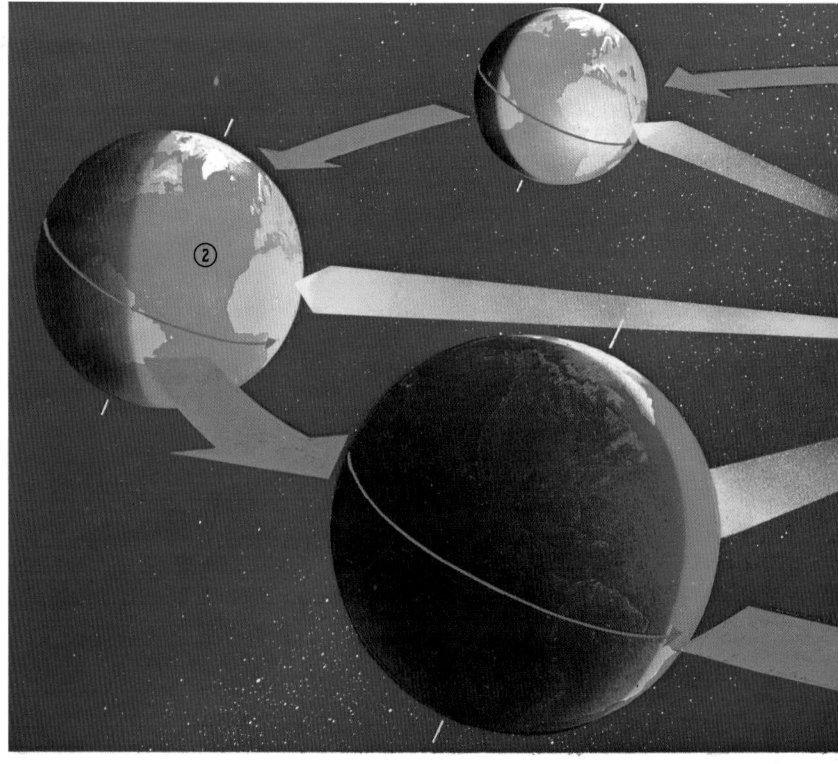

People crossing the International Date Line from west to east gain a day. Those going from east to west lose a day.

The Seasons

Because the Earth's axis is tilted by 23½°, the Sun appears to travel in a higher or lower path across the sky at various times of the year, giving differing lengths of daylight. The diagram at the top of the page shows that, at the spring equinox in the northern hemisphere (March 21), the Sun is overhead at the Equator. After March 21, the overhead Sun moves northwards as the northern hemisphere tilts towards the Sun. On June 21, the summer solstice in the northern hemisphere, the Sun is overhead at the Tropic of Cancer (latitude 23½° North). By September 23, the Sun is again overhead at the Equator. By about December 21, the Sun is overhead at the Tropic of Capricorn (23½° S). This is the winter solstice in the northern hemisphere. The seasons are reversed in the southern hemisphere.

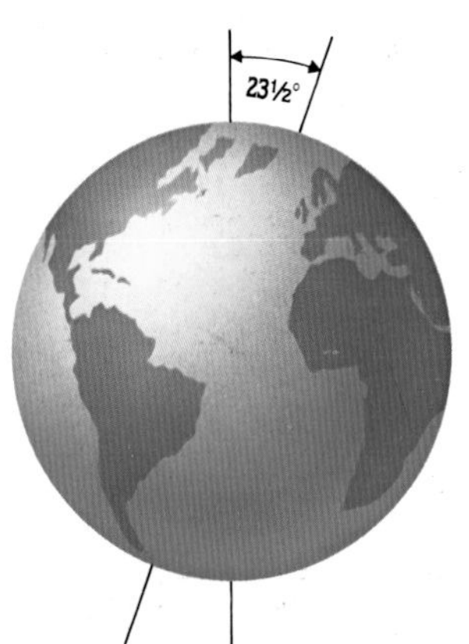

Above: The Earth's axis (joining the North and South poles via the centre of the Earth) is tilted by 23½°. The Earth rotates on its axis once every 23 hours, 56 minutes and 4 seconds. The tilt of the axis remains constant as the Earth orbits the Sun.

Right: The path of the Sun across the sky is highest on Midsummer Day, the longest day, and lowest at midwinter (December 21), the shortest day. The total variation in altitude is 47°, which is twice the angle by which the Earth's axis is tilted.

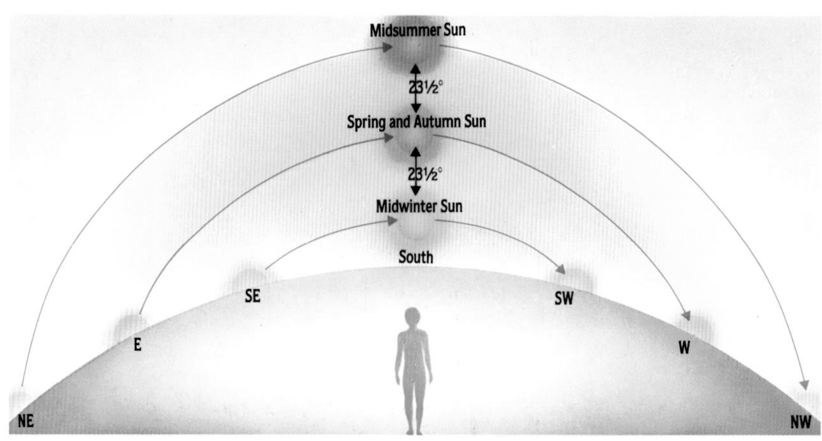

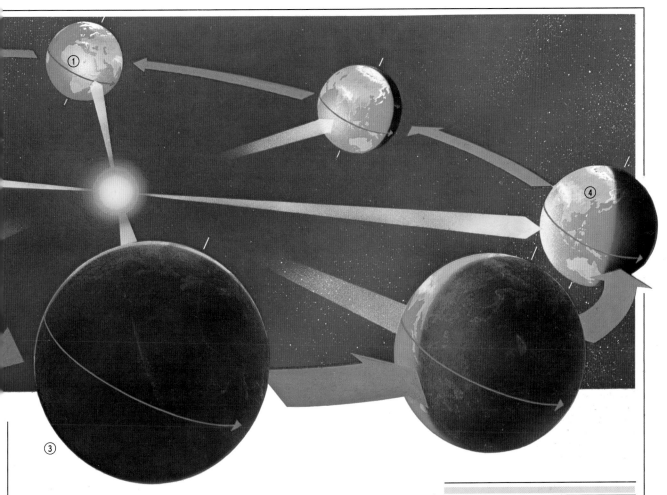

Above: On March 21, the spring or vernal equinox in the northern hemisphere, the Sun is overhead at the equator (1). On June 21, it is overhead at the Tropic of Cancer, the summer solstice (2). On September 23, it is overhead at the Equator, the autumn equinox (3). On December 21, it is overhead at the Tropic of Capricorn, the winter solstice (4).

Below; Zones Times (given in bold figures at the top of the map) are the Standard Times kept on land and sea compared with 12 hours (noon) Greenwich Mean Time. Daylight Saving Time (normally one hour in advance of Local Standard Time), which is observed by certain countries for part of the year, is not shown on the map.

FACTFINDER

Length of day: Mean solar day, 24 hours. Sidereal day (measured against fixed stars) 23·93 hours.

Speed of the Earth's rotation on its axis: At the Equator, it is rotating at 1660 km/h. It is less away from the Equator: at 30°N and S, it is 1438 km/h; at 60° N and S, it is 990 km/h.

Equinoxes: The vernal equinox is on March 21, and the autumn equinox on September 23 in the northern hemisphere. The equinoxes are reversed in the southern hemisphere.

Solstices: In the northern hemisphere, the summer solstice is on June 21 and the winter solstice on December 21. The reverse applies in the southern hemisphere.

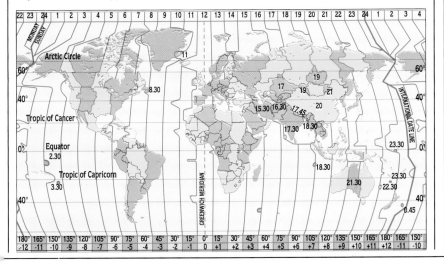

THE EARTH'S STRUCTURE

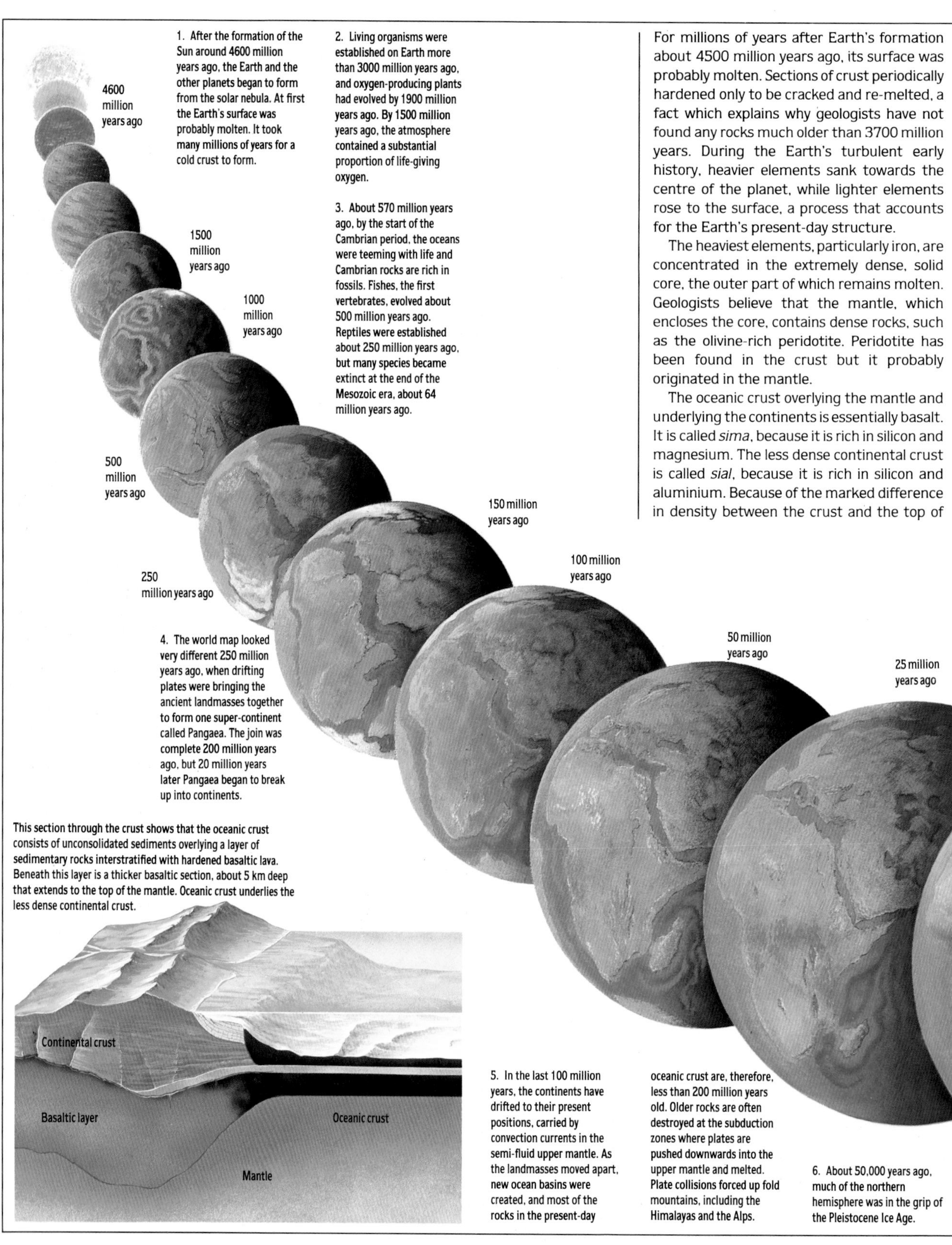

1. After the formation of the Sun around 4600 million years ago, the Earth and the other planets began to form from the solar nebula. At first the Earth's surface was probably molten. It took many millions of years for a cold crust to form.

2. Living organisms were established on Earth more than 3000 million years ago, and oxygen-producing plants had evolved by 1900 million years ago. By 1500 million years ago, the atmosphere contained a substantial proportion of life-giving oxygen.

3. About 570 million years ago, by the start of the Cambrian period, the oceans were teeming with life and Cambrian rocks are rich in fossils. Fishes, the first vertebrates, evolved about 500 million years ago. Reptiles were established about 250 million years ago, but many species became extinct at the end of the Mesozoic era, about 64 million years ago.

4600 million years ago

1500 million years ago

1000 million years ago

500 million years ago

250 million years ago

150 million years ago

100 million years ago

50 million years ago

25 million years ago

4. The world map looked very different 250 million years ago, when drifting plates were bringing the ancient landmasses together to form one super-continent called Pangaea. The join was complete 200 million years ago, but 20 million years later Pangaea began to break up into continents.

This section through the crust shows that the oceanic crust consists of unconsolidated sediments overlying a layer of sedimentary rocks interstratified with hardened basaltic lava. Beneath this layer is a thicker basaltic section, about 5 km deep that extends to the top of the mantle. Oceanic crust underlies the less dense continental crust.

Continental crust

Basaltic layer

Oceanic crust

Mantle

For millions of years after Earth's formation about 4500 million years ago, its surface was probably molten. Sections of crust periodically hardened only to be cracked and re-melted, a fact which explains why geologists have not found any rocks much older than 3700 million years. During the Earth's turbulent early history, heavier elements sank towards the centre of the planet, while lighter elements rose to the surface, a process that accounts for the Earth's present-day structure.

The heaviest elements, particularly iron, are concentrated in the extremely dense, solid core, the outer part of which remains molten. Geologists believe that the mantle, which encloses the core, contains dense rocks, such as the olivine-rich peridotite. Peridotite has been found in the crust but it probably originated in the mantle.

The oceanic crust overlying the mantle and underlying the continents is essentially basalt. It is called *sima*, because it is rich in silicon and magnesium. The less dense continental crust is called *sial*, because it is rich in silicon and aluminium. Because of the marked difference in density between the crust and the top of

5. In the last 100 million years, the continents have drifted to their present positions, carried by convection currents in the semi-fluid upper mantle. As the landmasses moved apart, new ocean basins were created, and most of the rocks in the present-day oceanic crust are, therefore, less than 200 million years old. Older rocks are often destroyed at the subduction zones where plates are pushed downwards into the upper mantle and melted. Plate collisions forced up fold mountains, including the Himalayas and the Alps.

6. About 50,000 years ago, much of the northern hemisphere was in the grip of the Pleistocene Ice Age.

FACTFINDER

The Earth's crust: The oceanic crust averages 6 km thick; density, 3·0 g/cm³. The continental crust averages 35—40 km, reaching 60—70 km under high mountains; density 2·7 g/cm³.

Mantle: About 2900 km thick; density, 3·4—4·5 g/cm³.

Core: Diameter 6740 km. Outer core 2000 km thick, molten iron and nickel. Inner core, a solid metal ball, 1370 km thick. Density of core, 10—13 g/cm³. Temperature at 2700°C, under pressure of 3800 tonnes per sq cm.

Surface area of the Earth: 510,066,000 km². About 148,326,000 km², or just over 29 per cent of the Earth's surface, is land.

Mass: 5976 million million million tonnes.

Shape and size: Oblate spheroid, slightly flattened at the poles and bulging at the Equator. So, at sea level, the diameter of the Earth between the poles is 12,713 km, as compared with a diameter of 12,756 km, across the plane of the Equator. Similarly, the equatorial circumference of 40,075 km is greater than the polar circumference of 40,007 km.

the mantle, the crust cannot sink. It is split into large, rigid plates that 'float' on the denser mantle. Plate movements cause earthquakes, mountain building and volcanic activity — occurrences that remind us of the restless nature of our world.

About 85 per cent of the top 16 km of the crust are either igneous rocks (rocks formed from molten magma) or metamorphic rocks

(igneous or sedimentary rocks that have been changed by heat, pressure or, sometimes, chemical action). However, sedimentary rocks cover 75 per cent of the surface of landmasses. Many sedimentary rocks are clastic (formed from eroded rock fragments), some, such as coal, are organic, and some are formed by chemical action, such as rock salt precipitated from water.

Below are eight rocks found in the Earth's crust. There are three main kinds of rocks: igneous, sedimentary and metamorphic. Igneous rocks, including obsidian and granite, are forms of hardened magma. Many sedimentary rocks, such as sandstone and conglomorate, are composed of worn fragments of other rocks, while coal is compressed plant remains. Metamorphic rocks, such as marble and slate, are formed when great heat and pressure alter igneous or sedimentary rocks.

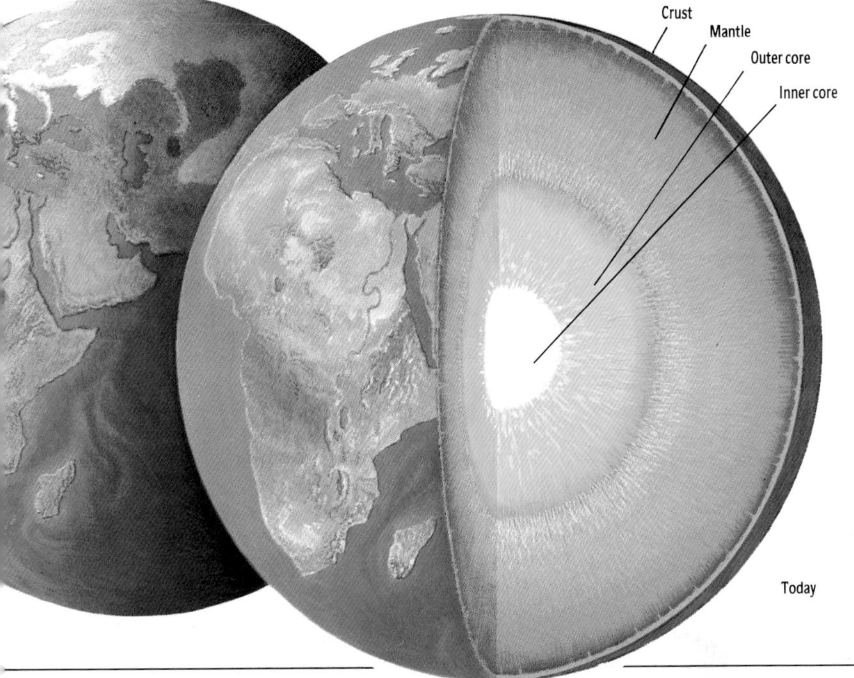

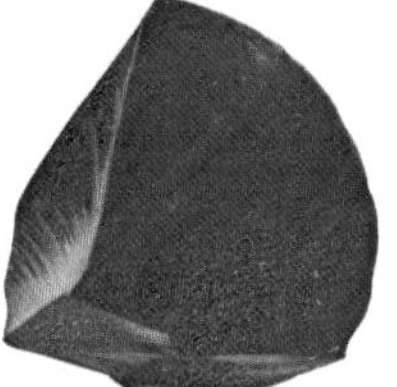

Obsidian is a glassy, extrusive igneous rock, formed on the surface.

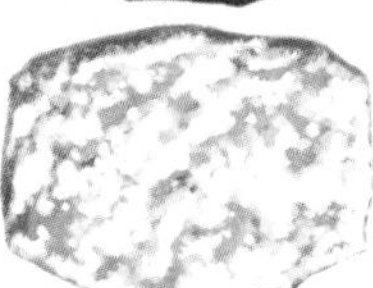

Granite is a coarse-grained, intrusive igneous rock, which forms in huge underground masses.

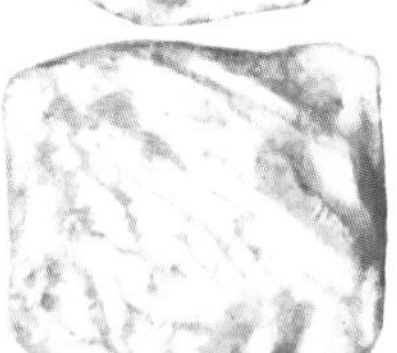

Marble is formed by the action of great heat and pressure on limestone.

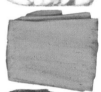

Slate is usually formed by the metamorphism of shale.

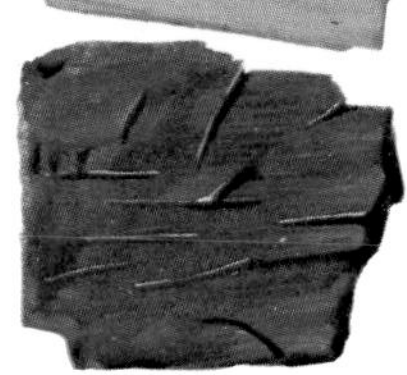

Coal is a fossil fuel formed in ancient swamps.

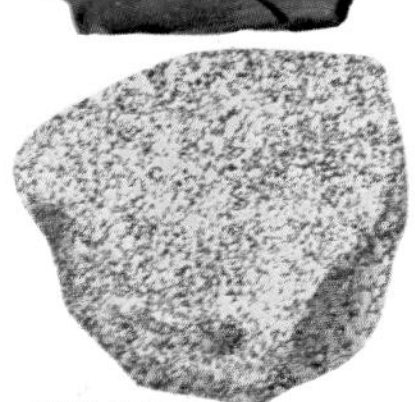

Limestones are sedimentary rocks composed mainly of calcium carbonate.

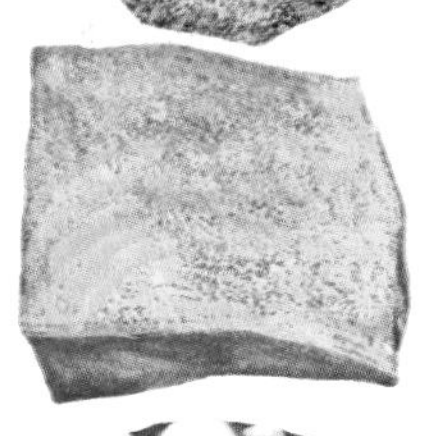

Sandstone contains grains of quartz and other minerals bound together by tough mineral cements.

Conglomerates contain pebbles cemented in a fine silt or sand matrix.

50,000 years ago

Crust
Mantle
Outer core
Inner core

Today

THE ATMOSPHERE AND CLOUDS

The atmosphere is a thin skin of gases, chiefly nitrogen and life-giving oxygen, that encircles and protects the Earth. It moderates temperatures, preventing enormous diurnal changes in heating that would destroy life on Earth. And, in the stratosphere, one of the five main layers of the atmosphere, is a belt of ozone that absorbs most of the Sun's dangerous ultraviolet radiation. The depth of the atmosphere cannot be defined precisely, because it becomes increasingly rarefied with height. But more than 99 per cent of its mass is within 40 km of the surface.

Air Pressure

Air has weight and the total weight of the atmosphere is about 5000 million million tonnes. However, we do not feel the constant pressure of about one tonne of air on our shoulders, because there is an equal air pressure inside our bodies. Air pressure varies, a major factor in weather. Generally, pressures are lower in warm, expanding air which tends to rise, as at the doldrums. It is higher in cold, dense air which sinks downwards, as at the high pressure horse latitudes.

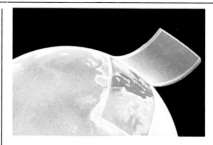

The Earth is surrounded by a thin layer of gases, known as the atmosphere.

This section through the atmosphere shows its five main layers.

EXOSPHERE, which begins at about 500 km above the surface, is extremely rarefied and composed mainly of hydrogen and helium. The exosphere merges into space.

IONOSPHERE, between 80 and 500 km, contains gas molecules that are ionized, or electrically charged, by cosmic or solar rays. Disturbances in the ionosphere cause glowing lights, called aurorae. Temperatures rise steadily with height from −92°C at 80 km to 2200°C at 400 km.

MESOSPHERE, between 50 and 80 km, is marked by a fall in temperature from 10°C at 50 km to −92°. at 80 km. (Temperatures as low as −170°C have been recorded in this layer in the presence of noctilucent clouds, thought to be composed of ice-covered meteoric dust.)

STRATOSPHERE, stretches above the tropopause (the name for the upper boundary of the troposphere) to 50 km height. It has a layer of ozone (oxygen with three rather than two atoms) that filters out most of the Sun's ultraviolet rays. Temperatures rise from −55°C to 10°C at 50 km.

TROPOSPHERE is the lowest 18 km of the atmosphere over the Equator, the lowest 10 to 11 km in the middle latitudes, and the lowest 8 km over the poles. It contains most of the atmosphere's mass. Temperatures fall with height, but stabilize at the tropopause.

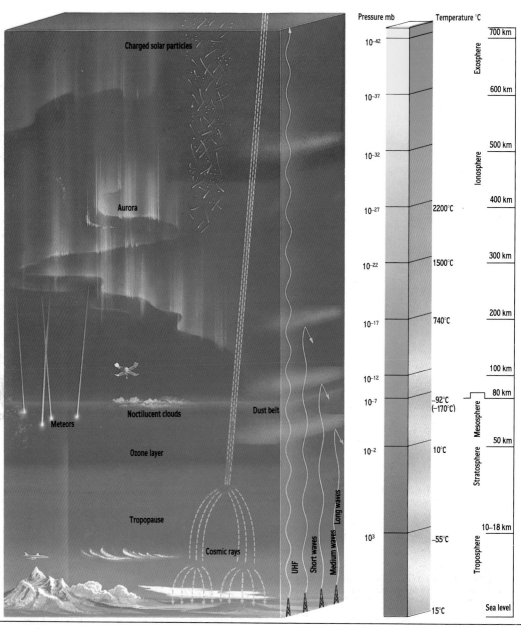

Charged solar particles

Aurora

Meteors

Noctilucent clouds

Dust belt

Ozone layer

Tropopause

Cosmic rays

UHF

Short waves

Medium waves

Long waves

Pressure mb	Temperature °C	
10^{-42}		700 km
		Exosphere
10^{-37}		600 km
		500 km
10^{-32}		Ionosphere
10^{-27}	2200°C	400 km
10^{-22}	1500°C	300 km
10^{-17}	740°C	200 km
10^{-12}		100 km
10^{-7}	−92°C (−170°C)	80 km
		Mesosphere 50 km
10^{-2}	10°C	Stratosphere
		10–18 km
10^{3}	−55°C	Troposphere
	−15°C	Sea level

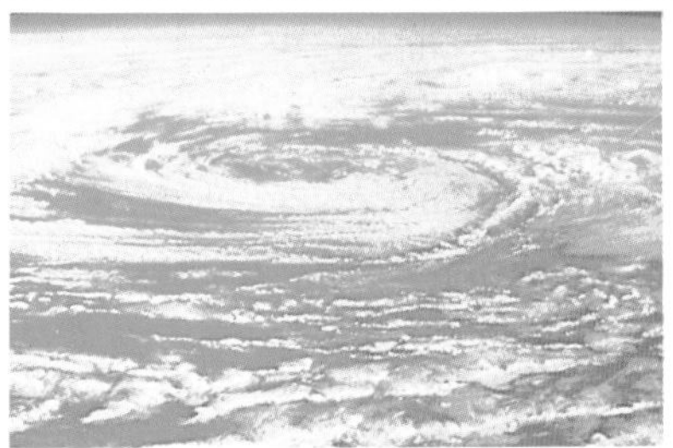

The clouds on this photograph reveal a hurricane, a rotating low pressure air system.

Cloud Formation

All air contains water vapour, but warm air holds much more than cold air. When air is cooled it can hold less water vapour. At dew point, it is saturated, containing all the water vapour it can at that temperature. Further cooling causes water vapour to condense around specks of dust or salt in the air to form tiny, visible water droplets or ice crystals, masses of which form clouds.

Circulation of Air

Air is invisible but, powered by energy from the Sun, it is always moving. Generally, winds blow from areas of high air pressure, such as the horse latitudes, towards areas of low pressure, such as the doldrums. Winds are deflected by the Coriolis effect, which is caused by the Earth's rotation. Local factors, such as mountains, also affect winds. Monsoons are seasonal reversals of winds. For example, over northern India in winter, cold, dense air masses develop, from which winds blow outwards. But heating in summer creates low air pressure and moist winds are sucked on to the land.

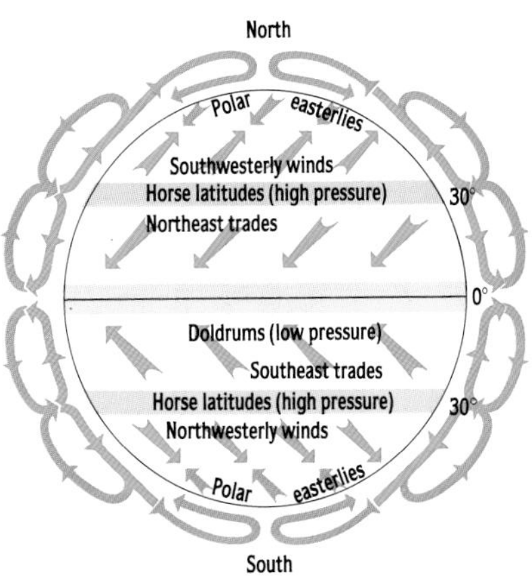

Above: The diagram shows the main movements of air in the atmosphere and across the surface in the prevailing wind systems. Winds generally blow towards low pressure regions, such as the doldrums, and outwards from high pressure systems at the horse latitudes and the poles.

FACTFINDER

Composition of the air: Nitrogen (78·09 per cent); oxygen (20·95 per cent); argon (0·93 per cent).
Other gases include carbon dioxide, helium, hydrogen, krypton, methane, neon, ozone, and xenon.

Average surface pressure: 1013 mb.

Atmospheric level reached by radio waves (frequency in kilohertz)
Long waves (below 500 kHz)	: 50 km
Medium waves (500 – 1500 kHz)	: 95 km
Short (1500 – 30,000 kHz by day)	: 200 km
waves (1500 – 30,000 kHz by night)	: 280 km

Very short wavelengths (UHF) penetrate all layers.

Cloud Types

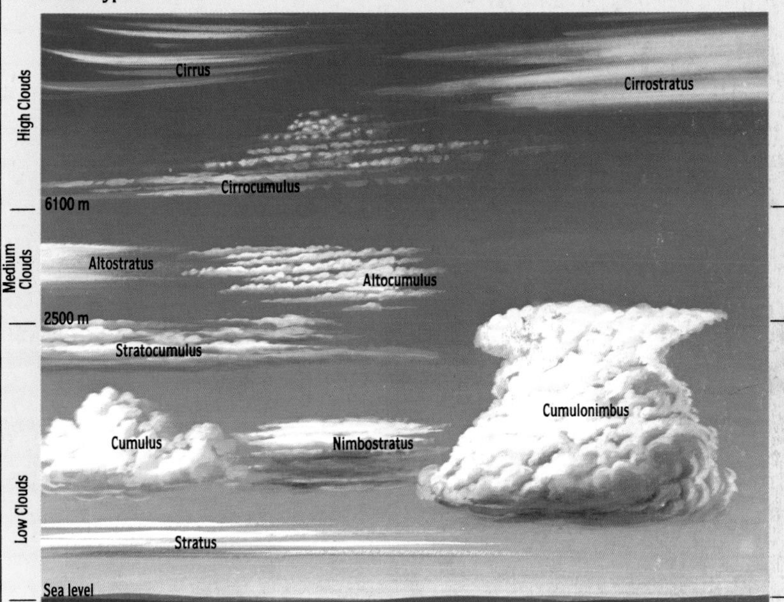

High Clouds
High clouds form above 6100 metres above ground level, as follows:
CIRRUS is a delicate feathery cloud, sometimes called mares' tails or ice banners. It is often the first sign of an approaching depression.
CIRROSTRATUS is a thin layer cloud, with ripples and rounded masses. It veils but does not block out the Sun.
CIRROCUMULUS is a patchy cloud composed of small white balls. Formed from ice crystals, it is often called mackerel sky.

Medium Clouds
Medium clouds occur between about 2500 and 6100 metres, as follows:
ALTOSTRATUS is a greyish or bluish layer cloud that may become so thick that it blocks out the Sun. It is a sign of an advancing depression.
ALTOCUMULUS resembles a mass of tiny clouds. It indicates unsettled weather.

Low Clouds
Low clouds form below 2500 metres above ground level as follows:
STRATOCUMULUS is a greyish-white cloud, consisting of rounded masses.
NIMBOSTRATUS is a dark cloud, associated with rain and snow, which often occurs along the warm fronts of depressions.
CUMULUS is a white, heap cloud, usually with a flat base and a dome-shaped top. In summer, fluffy cumulus is a feature of fine weather. Heavy cumulus can develop into cumulonimbus cloud.
STRATUS is a grey layer cloud that often forms ahead of warm fronts in depressions where warm air is rising fairly slowly over cold air. Such clouds bring drizzle, rain and snow.
CUMULONIMBUS is a dark, heavy cloud. It may rise 4500 metres or more from its ragged base to its often anvil-shaped top. It is associated with thunder, lightning, rain and snow.

Cloud Classification. There are three main types of cloud shapes: feathery cirrus; heap or cumuliform clouds; and layer or stratiform clouds.

THE WATER OF LIFE

In some countries, people take their regular supply of fresh water for granted, while elsewhere, in desert lands, it is a prized commodity. Water reaches us, in one way or another, through the hydrological, or water, cycle, whereby land areas are supplied with precipitation that originates in the saline oceans, where more than 97 per cent of the world's water is found.

Another vital resource, also taken for granted in many places, is the soil, the character of which is largely determined by the climate. The delicate balance between climate, water, and plant life is something that we disturb at our peril.

Soil is the thin layer of loose material derived from and overlying the bedrock. Soils vary in thickness. Mineral grains, the product of weathering, make up more than 90 per cent of most dry soils. Soil also contains humus, including the remains of dead plants and animals. About 40 per cent of moist soils is made up of spaces, occupied by air or water. Soils vary according to the climate, for example, soils in tropical rainy regions are leached by heavy rain. By contrast, some soils in arid regions contain mineral salts deposited by water rising *upwards* towards the surface.

Plant life shows remarkable adaptations to a vast variety of environments. The main vegetation zones are largely determined by climate. But, like climatic regions, vegetation zones have no marked boundaries; they merge imperceptibly with one another.

Vegetation zones usually refer to the original plant cover, or optimum growth, before it was altered by human activity. Human interference with nature can be disastrous. For example, semi-arid grasslands have been ploughed up. Prolonged droughts have reduced the exposed soil to a powdery dust which is removed by the wind, creating dust bowls and encouraging the spread of deserts. The destruction of tropical forests, such as in Brazil, is a matter of concern today. Plants that have never been identified are being destroyed for ever, when they might be sources of new drugs. A massive forest clearance might change world climates.

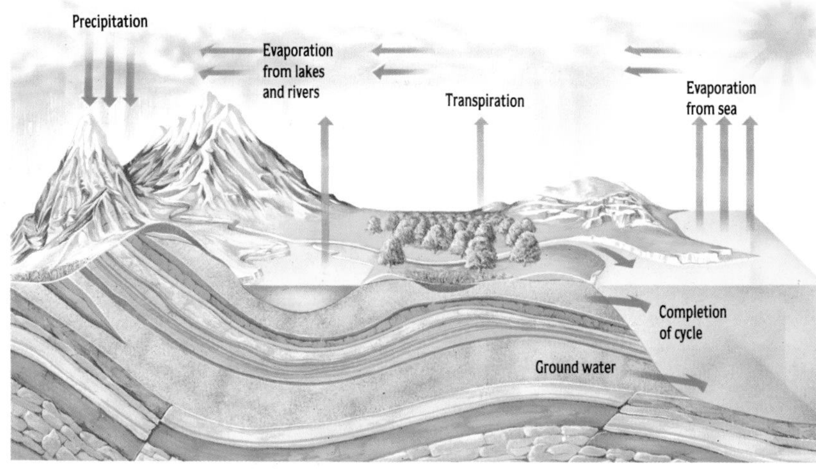

Above: The water cycle provides landmasses with fresh water. The water comes mainly from moisture evaporated from the oceans, to which the water eventually returns.

Right: The map shows the world's chief vegetation zones.

Below: The photographs show major vegetation regions:
1. Tundra is the name for treeless regions near the poles and near the tops of high mountains that are snow-covered for most of the year. But mosses, lichens and some flowering plants flourish in the short summer.
2. Coniferous forests, or taiga, cover a broad belt south of the tundra in the northern hemisphere. The shapes of conifers prevent their being overloaded by snow. The needle-like leaves reduce transpiration, while the thick bark and pitch-like sap reduce evaporation.
3. Broadleaf, or deciduous, forests grow in warm temperate regions. By shedding their leaves, deciduous trees are better able to survive the winter.
4. Scrub and semi-arid grasslands cover large areas of the world. They are highly susceptible to soil erosion if the vegetation cover is removed. Scrub, called maquis, fynbos, chaparral and mallee scrub, are typical of Mediterranean lands where the original forest cover has been destroyed.
5. Tropical grassland includes the llanos of Venezuela. The palm trees in the photograph are growing in a swamp. Tropical grassland is also called campos or savanna.
6. Evergreen tropical rain forest flourishes in regions which are hot and have ample rain throughout the year.

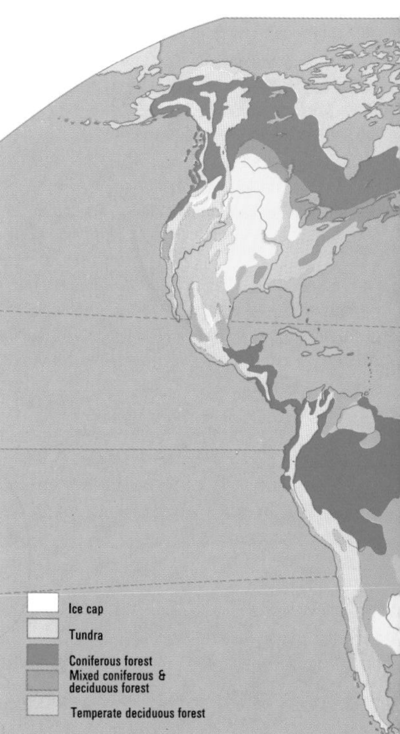

Ice cap
Tundra
Coniferous forest
Mixed coniferous & deciduous forest
Temperate deciduous forest

1
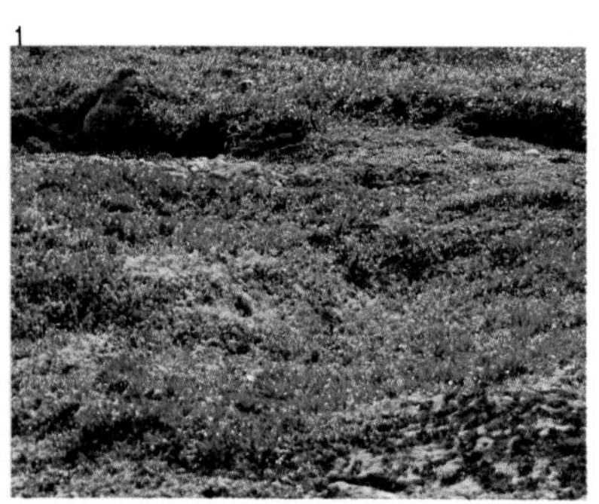

2
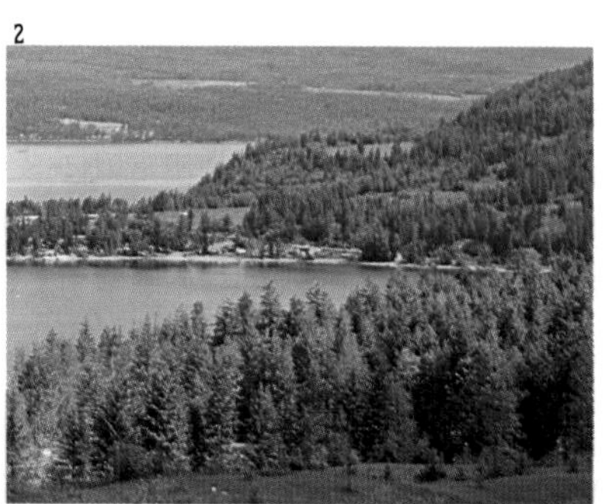

3
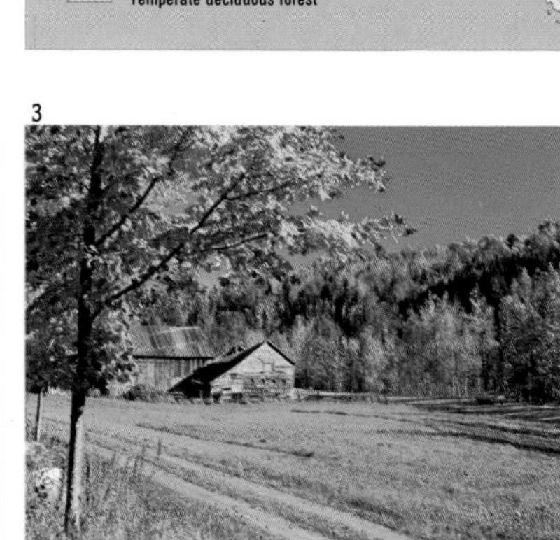

FACTFINDER

Water distribution: 97·2% is in the oceans (about 1360 million km³); 2·15% is frozen in bodies of ice; 0·625% is ground water; 0·171% is in rivers and lakes; 0·001 is water vapour in the atmosphere.

Average daily water consumption: In the United States: about 200 litres (flushing toilet, washing and bathing, 78%; kitchen use, 6%; drinking, 5%; other, 11%). In many hot countries, the daily per capita water consumption is less than 4 litres.

Common soils: Laterites (leached soils in tropical rainy regions); grey marginal soils (deserts); chestnut-brown soils (arid grasslands); brown forest earths (Mediteranean lands); podsols (cold temperate regions).

Vegetation: Ice covers about 10% of the world's land surfaces and hot deserts 20%. The largest forest is the coniferous forest of Northern Asia, which covers 1100 million hectares – 27% of the world's total forests.

Below: Well-developed soils have three layers, called the A, B and C horizons, overlying the parent rock.

Right: Prairie soils occur in regions that are wet enough in places to support woodland. The A horizon contains much humus, but it is also much leached by seeping water.

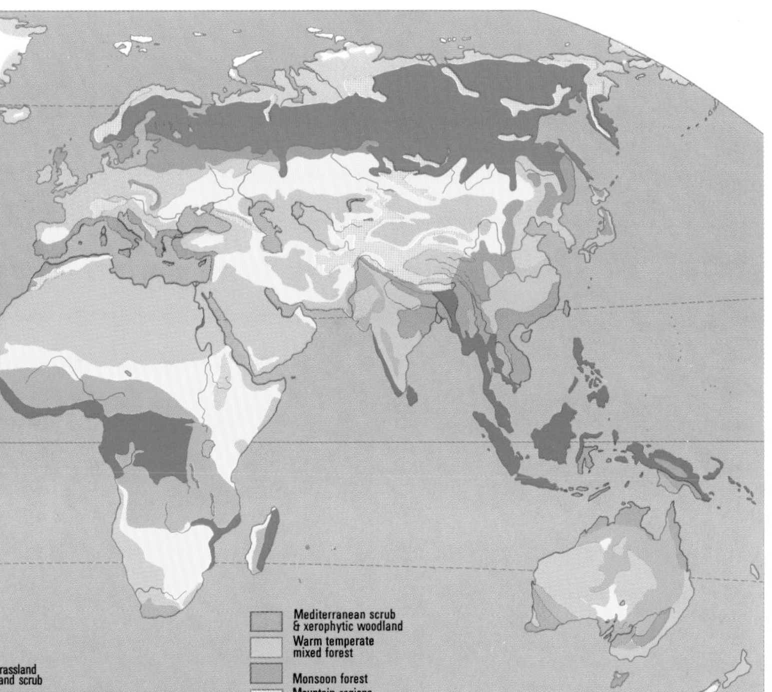

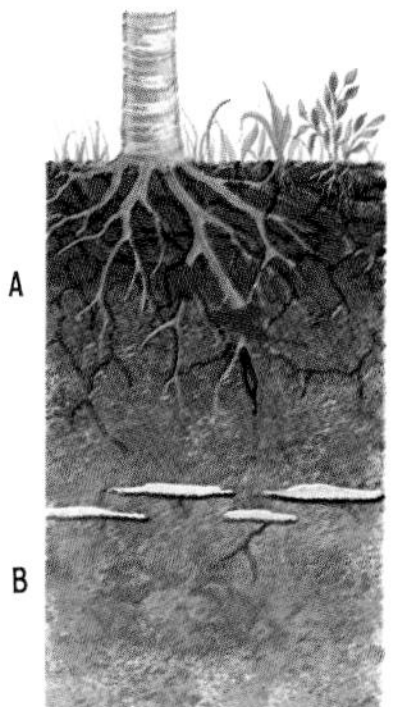

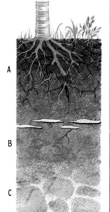

Woodland and mixed grasses

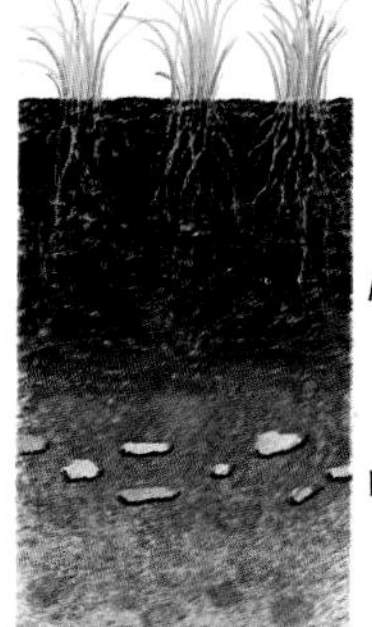

Tall bunch grass

Chernozem soils, sometimes called black earths, contain much humus (mainly decomposed grass). They occur in steppelands which have less rainfall than prairies.

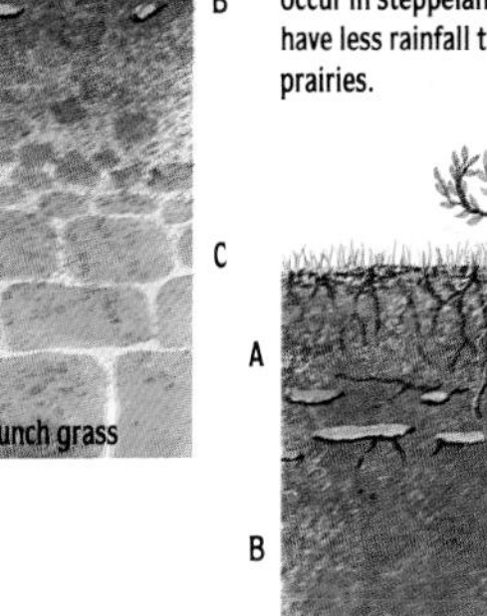

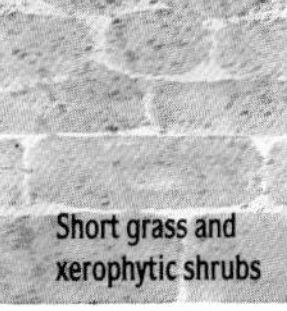

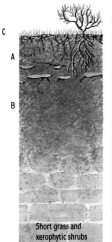

Chestnut-brown soils are typical of particularly arid grasslands. They occur south of the Russian steppes and in the drier parts of Argentina, South Africa and the United States.

Short grass and xerophytic shrubs

Desert

Grassland

Savanna - grassland with trees and scrub

Tropical rain forest

Mediterranean scrub & xerophytic woodland

Warm temperate mixed forest

Monsoon forest

Mountain regions - little vegetation

4

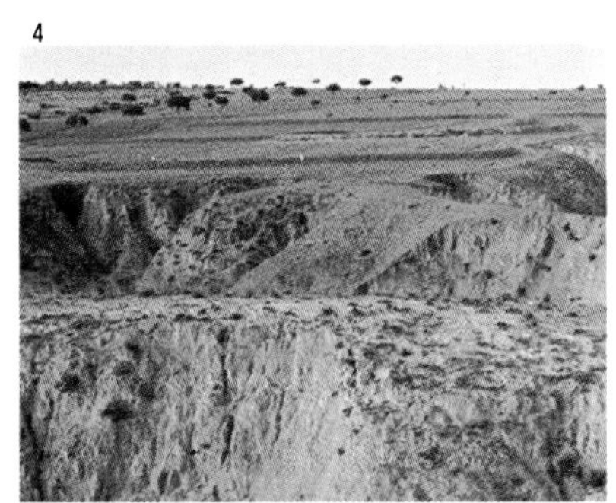

5

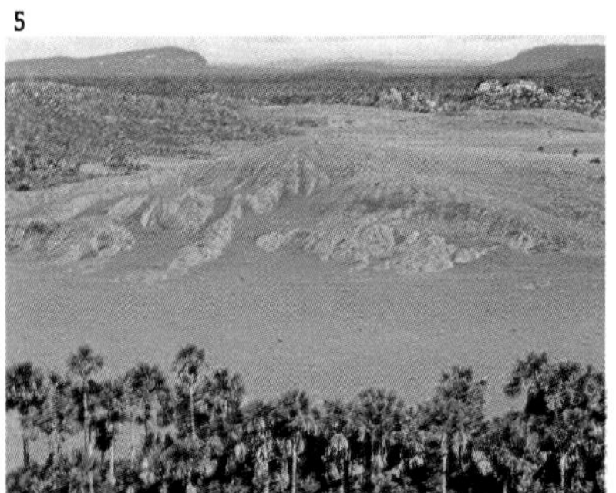

6

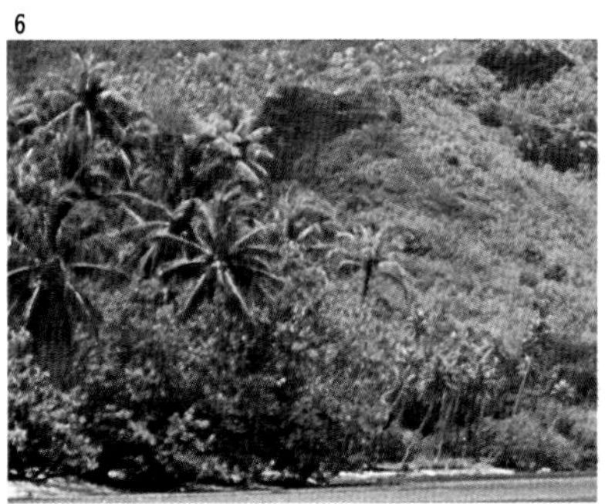

THE POPULATION EXPLOSION

One of the world's most serious problems is the population explosion and the difficulties that can be foreseen in feeding the people of the world in the future. Assuming present growth rates of 1.7 per cent continue, the UN estimates that total world population will increase from 5.5 billion in mid 1992 to around 6.2 billion by the turn of the century. The problems arising from the population explosion are most marked in the developing world and least in the industrial nations where people see advantages in population control.

Population explosions occur when average birth rates far exceed death rates. In recent years, death rates have everywhere declined mainly because of improved medical care. In industrial countries birth rates have also fallen so that a growing proportion of people is in the senior age groups. But while such countries must finance retirement pensions, developing nations have the highest expenditures on health and other children's services, because 40 per cent or more of their population is under 15. This contrast between developing and developed nations is also illustrated by the average life expectancies of 42 years in Sierra Leone and 79 years in Japan.

The distribution of people throughout the world is uneven, because few people live in the vast hot and cold deserts, mountain regions and rain forests. In the world's most densely populated areas, the proportions of urban dwellers is increasing quickly. Urban growth is also a problem in developing nations where unqualified youngsters flock to the cities only to become unemployed occupants of shanty towns.

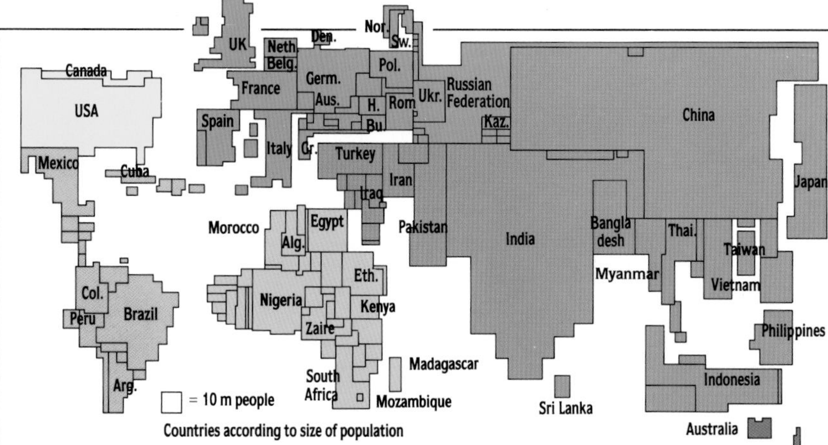

Countries according to size of population

= 10 m people

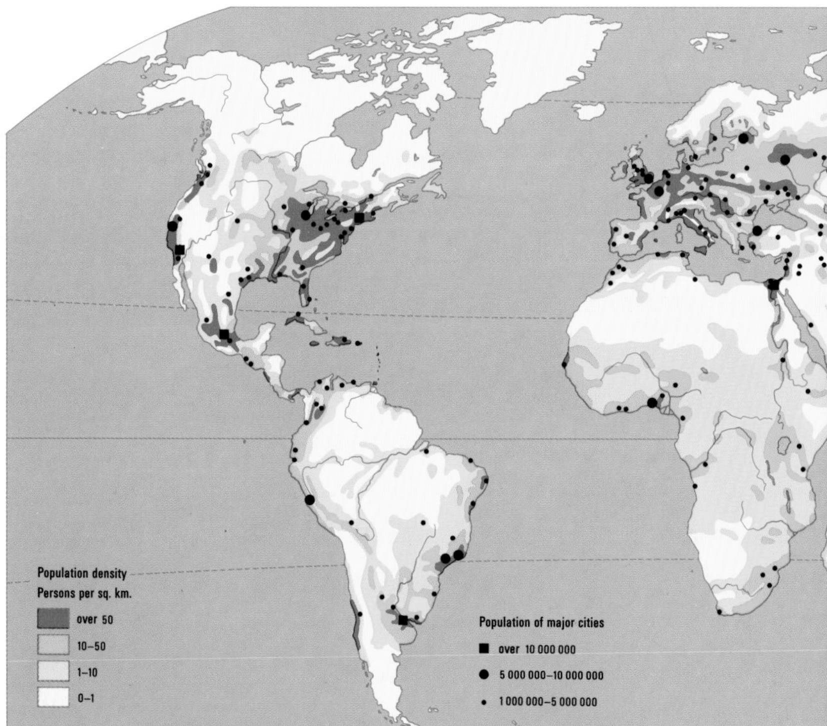

Population density
Persons per sq. km.

- over 50
- 10–50
- 1–10
- 0–1

Population of major cities

- ■ over 10 000 000
- ● 5 000 000–10 000 000
- ・ 1 000 000–5 000 000

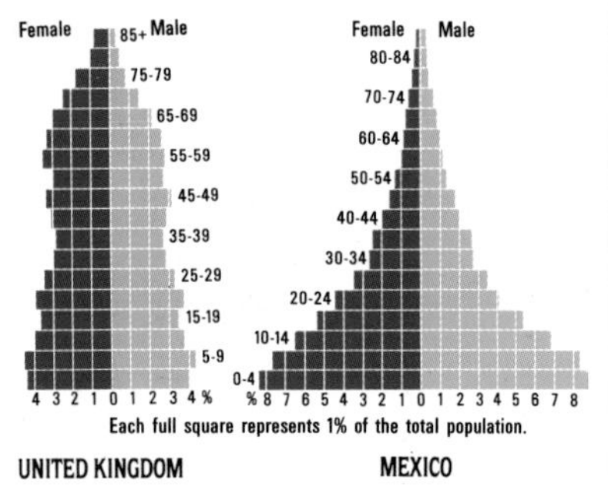

Each full square represents 1% of the total population.

UNITED KINGDOM   MEXICO

Left: The graphs depict the population structures of two nations according to sex and age. Developed nations, such as the United Kingdom (left), have a high proportion of older people, while developing nations such as Mexico (right) have a young population, with as many as 40 per cent of the people being under 15 years of age.

Above: The map shows the uneven distribution of the world's population, a feature that is emphasized by the cartogram, top, which represents the size of nations by their populations rather than by their areas.

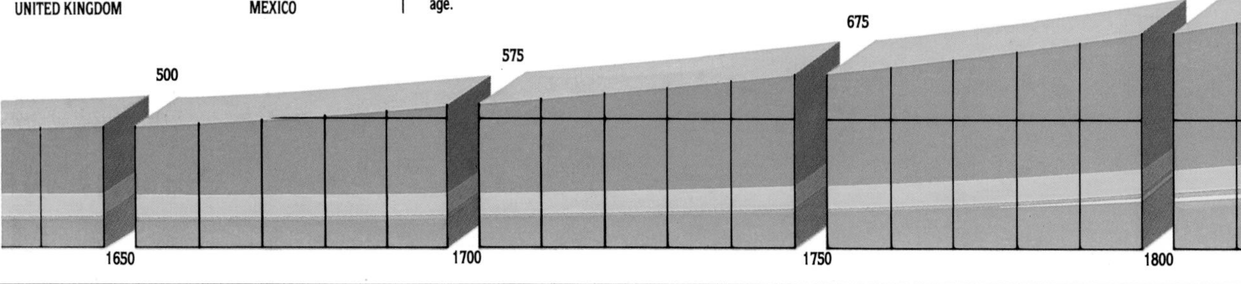

500   575   675   825

1650   1700   1750   1800

FACTFINDER

Population distribution: The mainly developed continents of North America, Europe, Oceania and Northern Asia contain 23% of the world's people. The rest live in the mainly developing continents of Africa, Latin America and Southern Asia.

Urbanization: Ranges from 6% in Nepal to 100% in Kuwait (1992).

Population density: Hong Kong had 5,600 people per square km. in 1992, as compared to 2 people per square km. in Australia.

Largest country: Russian Federation (by area): China (by population).

Largest metropolitan area: Mexico City 18,748,000

The world's population was around 300 million in AD 1000. It passed the 1000 million mark around 1850, but the Industrial Revolution led to an acceleration of population growth. The 2000 million mark was passed in the 1920s and 4000 million mark by the 1970s. By the year 2000, if the present growth rates of 1.7% per year continue, there will be more than 6200 million people on Earth. (for the purposes of this graph, the Americas have been divided into Anglo-Saxon – and Spanish-speaking America).

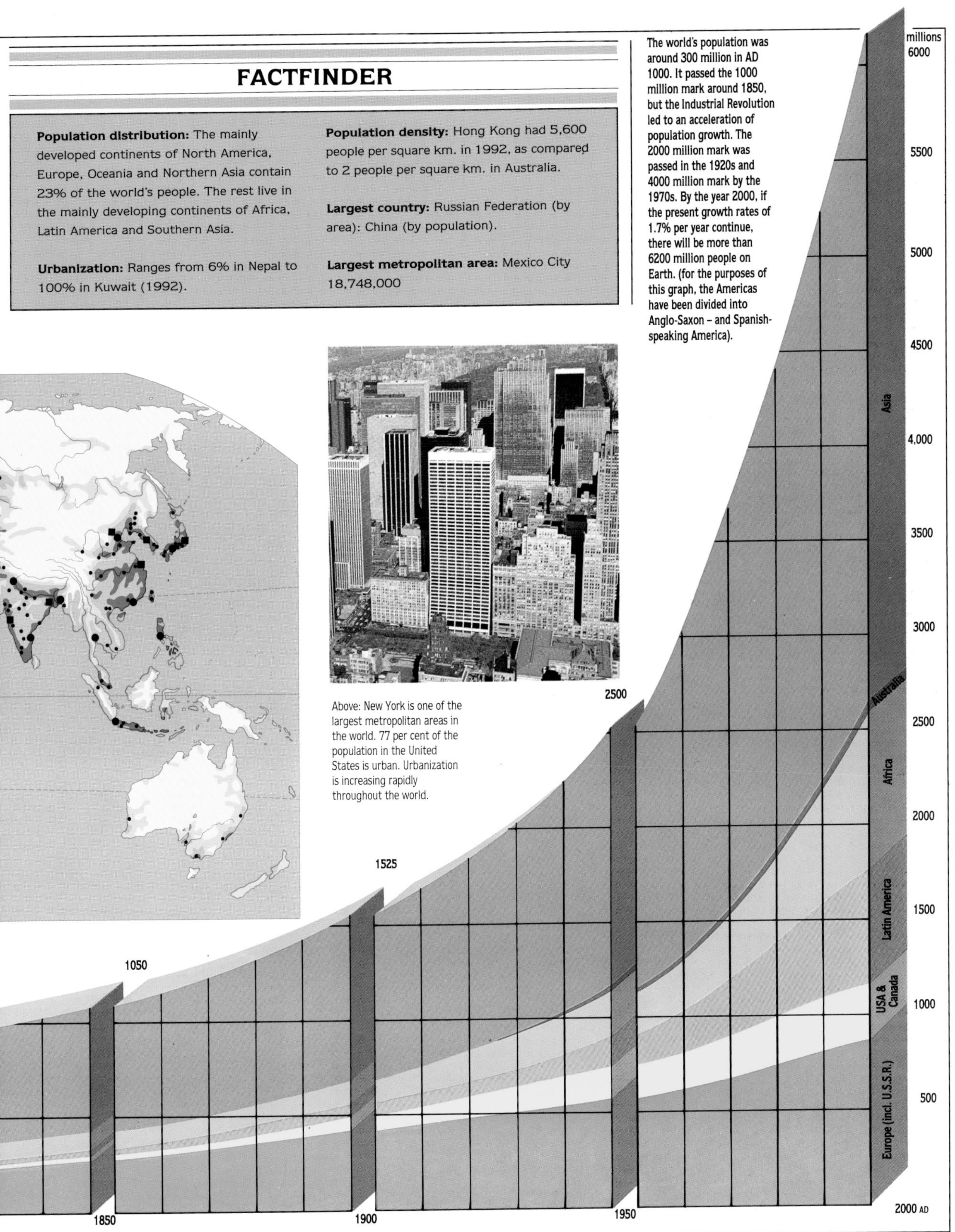

Above: New York is one of the largest metropolitan areas in the world. 77 per cent of the population in the United States is urban. Urbanization is increasing rapidly throughout the world.

ALTERNATIVE ENERGY

All forms of energy come directly or indirectly from the Sun. Prehistoric people had only their own labour, but as life styles changed and technology developed, draught animals, the burning of wood, windmills, waterwheels and sails to propel ships were all employed. With the onset of the Industrial Revolution, another abundant source of energy, the fossil fuel coal, was used to power 'the age of steam'. And recently, oil and natural gas have become the main fossil fuels, chiefly because they are fairly cheap to extract, easy to transport, and weight for weight they are more heat-efficient than coal. In consequence, world coal production has remained roughly stable over the last thirty years, although in some industrial nations, such as France, West Germany and the United Kingdom, it has declined. And yet coal may again become important if the existing reserves of oil start to run out, as predicted on current levels of consumption, in the early 21st century.

Despite the recent pre-eminence of oil and natural gas, alternative forms of energy that could replace fossil fuels have been successfully developed, notably hydro-electricity and, in the last thirty years, nuclear power. Hydro-electricity is now the chief form of electrical energy in such countries as Norway, where it supplies 100 per cent of the nation's electrical supply, Brazil (93 per cent), Switzerland (61 per cent) and Canada (61 per cent). But hydro-electricity is clearly unsuited to flat nations, such as the Netherlands.

Nuclear power, using the heat of nuclear fission, can be generated anywhere and, in several Western nations, including the United States and the United Kingdom, it already supplies more than one tenth of the total electrical supply. Uranium, the raw material used in nuclear fission, is generally abundant, and is produced in the West by the United States, South Africa and Canada.

But nuclear power is surrounded by controversy, particularly concerning the disposal of radioactive nuclear wastes. This factor, together with the finite nature of fossil fuel reserves, have led conservationists to explore many other possible forms of energy, employing the latest modern technology. The diagram, right, summarizes the main possibilities that are currently under investigation, including the harnessing of solar radiation, the power of winds and moving water, and the exploitation of the heat that exists not far beneath the Earth's surface.

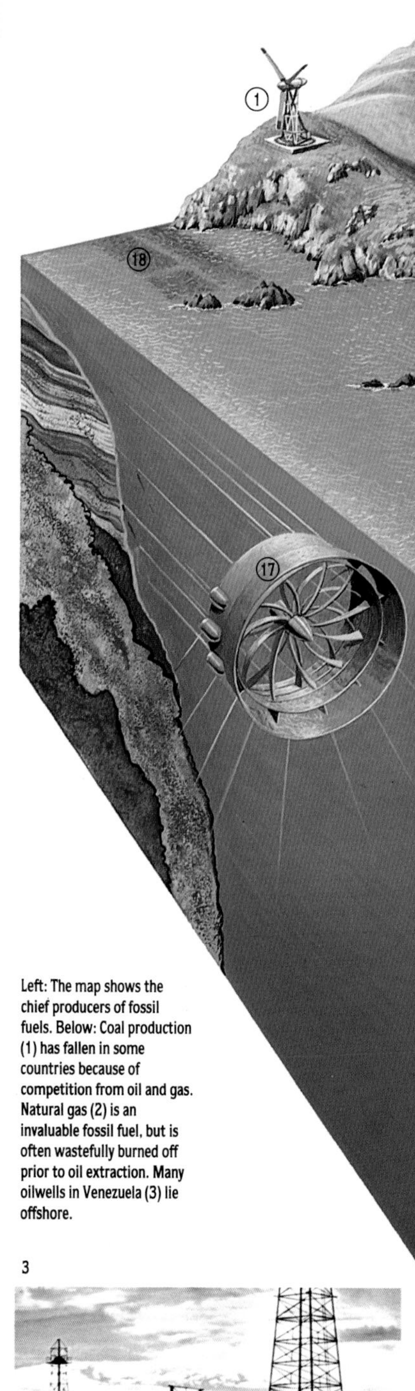

Left: The map shows the chief producers of fossil fuels. Below: Coal production (1) has fallen in some countries because of competition from oil and gas. Natural gas (2) is an invaluable fossil fuel, but is often wastefully burned off prior to oil extraction. Many oilwells in Venezuela (3) lie offshore.

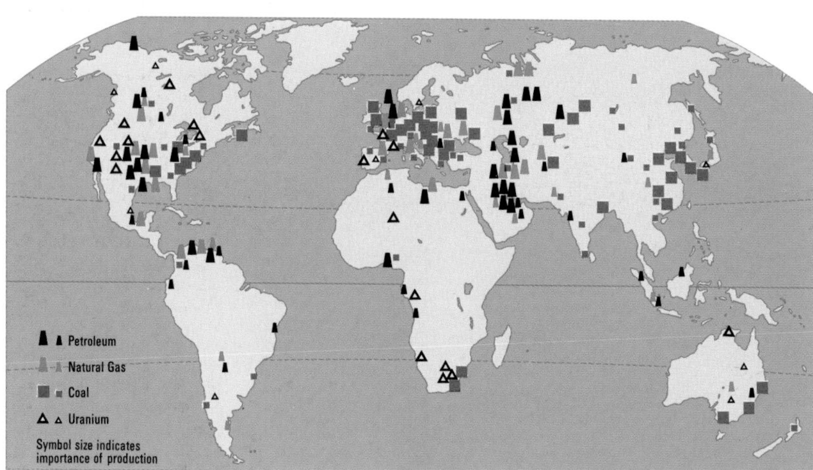

▲ ▴ Petroleum
△ ▵ Natural Gas
■ ▪ Coal
△ ▵ Uranium
Symbol size indicates importance of production

1

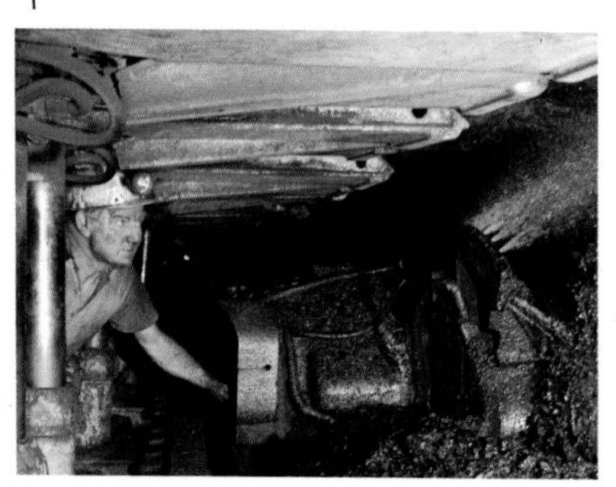

2

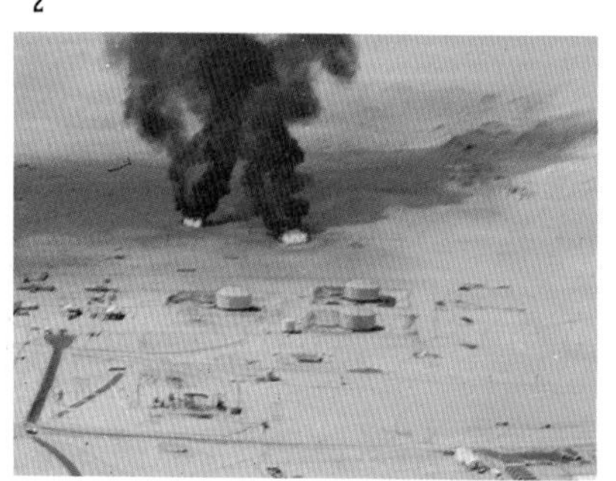

3

FACTFINDER

Energy consumption (in million tonnes oil equivalent, 1992): Africa 217; South America 272; Middle East 254; Western Europe 1407; Oceania 100; North America 2275.

Largest oil producers (1992): United States (13 per cent of world production); Saudi Arabia (13 per cent); Russia (12 per cent); China (5 per cent); Mexico (5 per cent); Iran (5 per cent); Venezuela (4 per cent); United Kingdom (3 per cent).

Oil reserves (1992): Saudi Arabia (26 per cent); Iraq (10 per cent); United Arab Emirates (10 per cent); Kuwait (9 per cent); Iran (9 per cent); Venezuela (6 per cent); Russia and Mexico (5 per cent each).

Nuclear power: France (75 per cent of its electrical energy production in 1990); Belgium (66 per cent); Sweden (47 per cent); Hungary (46 per cent); United Kingdom (20 per cent).

Left: Alternative energy sources include improved windmills (1) and pump storage reservoirs (2), into which water is pumped when energy is abundant and then used to drive turbine generators. Hydro-electric stations (3) are important in many countries, while solar power stations, powered by concentrated sunlight, could get microwave energy beamed from a satellite (4) or from banks of angled mirrors or heliostats (5). Decaying waste (6) is a source of heat, as are geysers (7) in volcanic areas. Mud (8) can be used to store heat, while greenhouses (9) are familiar ways of utilizing solar energy. Shallow solar ponds (10) produce heated water to drive generators, and solar houses (11) are self-supporting. Geothermal energy (12) comes from heat inside the Earth. Tidal power stations (13) have much potential, and wave power (14) could be harnessed by moving floats ('bobbing ducks'). Ordinary powered ships might use aluminium sails (15) as an extra form of energy. Floating thermal stations (16) could tap heat under the sea, while huge underwater turbines (17) could be driven by ocean currents. Even kelp (18), a seaweed, could be cultivated as a plant fuel. Solar furnaces (19) can produce temperatures of 4000°C by concentrating the Sun's rays with a paraboloid mirror.

Below: Hydro-electricity is a major alternative to fossil fuels in upland areas with abundant rivers that can be dammed (4). Nuclear power stations (5), a recent development, now supply a substantial proportion of the total electrical energy in several developed nations.

4

5

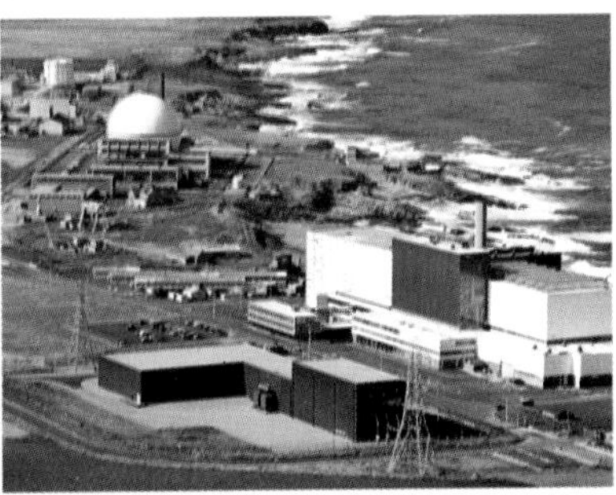

ENVIRONMENT IN DANGER

Because of the population explosion and the industrial and technological developments of the last 200 years, great damage has been done to the environment in many areas by the disruption of the balance of nature.

Pollution has become a major problem particularly in modern industrial societies. For example, air pollution in the form of smog has made cities unpleasant and unhealthy. It causes bronchitis and various other respiratory diseases – the London smog of 1952 killed an estimated 4000 people.

Water pollution by sewage and industrial wastes has fouled rivers, lakes and even seas, notably parts of the almost tideless Mediterranean. The flora and fauna have been destroyed and people's health has been directly affected as at Minamata in Japan in the 1950s. Here perhaps as many as 10,000 people suffered death, deformity or acute illness after eating fish poisoned by acetaldehyde waste pumped into the sea by a chemical company.

The land, too, has been polluted in many ways. For example, the pesticide DDT was once regarded as a means of raising food production. But it has also wiped out large populations of birds and, because of its persistence, it has damaged the fragile ecology of soils by weakening the micro-organisms in it.

Steps have been taken in many places to control the dangers of smog, Minamata disease and DDT. But many other, perhaps even more serious, problems lie ahead if the balance of nature is disturbed. For example, if jet airliners and rocket discharges damage the ozone layer in the stratosphere, it could expose the Earth to the Sun's broiling ultraviolet rays. And no one is sure of the consequences of the rising content in the air of carbon dioxide, which increased by nine per cent between 1958 and 1990. One estimate is that it could double by the year 2030. The atmosphere would then increasingly block long-wave radiation from the Earth, like the glass roof of a greenhouse, and temperatures would rise by an average of 3°C. Climatic zones would change and ice sheets would melt, submerging coastal plains and cities.

Radioactive fallout from nuclear weapons' tests (1) pollutes the air, as do kerosene combustion products, soot and unburned fuel expelled by aircraft (2). The build-up of carbon dioxide in the air (3), caused mainly by the burning of fossil fuels and the cutting down of forests may have a greenhouse effect, causing the atmosphere to overheat.

Aerial crop spraying (4) can introduce poisons into the soil that can disturb its ecology for years, while nuclear power stations (5) may discharge radioactive coolants, and thermal power stations (6) and city air conditioning systems may cause thermal and chemical pollution.

Below: Rubbish dumps for cars (1), open-cast mines (2) and oil spillages (3) that foul beaches are all examples of pollution.

1

2

3

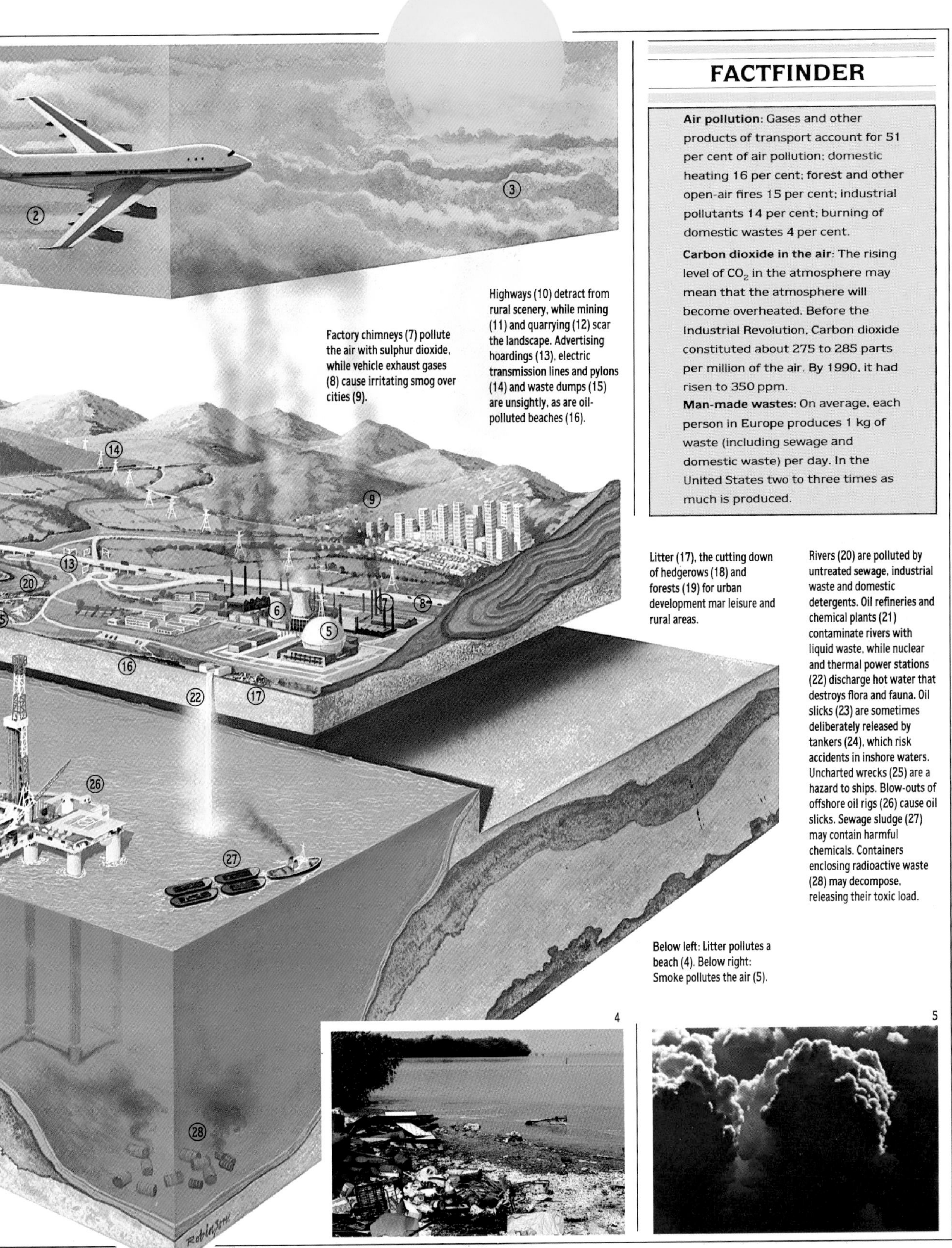

Air pollution: Gases and other products of transport account for 51 per cent of air pollution; domestic heating 16 per cent; forest and other open-air fires 15 per cent; industrial pollutants 14 per cent; burning of domestic wastes 4 per cent.

Carbon dioxide in the air: The rising level of CO_2 in the atmosphere may mean that the atmosphere will become overheated. Before the Industrial Revolution, Carbon dioxide constituted about 275 to 285 parts per million of the air. By 1990, it had risen to 350 ppm.

Man-made wastes: On average, each person in Europe produces 1 kg of waste (including sewage and domestic waste) per day. In the United States two to three times as much is produced.

Factory chimneys (7) pollute the air with sulphur dioxide, while vehicle exhaust gases (8) cause irritating smog over cities (9).

Highways (10) detract from rural scenery, while mining (11) and quarrying (12) scar the landscape. Advertising hoardings (13), electric transmission lines and pylons (14) and waste dumps (15) are unsightly, as are oil-polluted beaches (16).

Litter (17), the cutting down of hedgerows (18) and forests (19) for urban development mar leisure and rural areas.

Rivers (20) are polluted by untreated sewage, industrial waste and domestic detergents. Oil refineries and chemical plants (21) contaminate rivers with liquid waste, while nuclear and thermal power stations (22) discharge hot water that destroys flora and fauna. Oil slicks (23) are sometimes deliberately released by tankers (24), which risk accidents in inshore waters. Uncharted wrecks (25) are a hazard to ships. Blow-outs of offshore oil rigs (26) cause oil slicks. Sewage sludge (27) may contain harmful chemicals. Containers enclosing radioactive waste (28) may decompose, releasing their toxic load.

Below left: Litter pollutes a beach (4). Below right: Smoke pollutes the air (5).

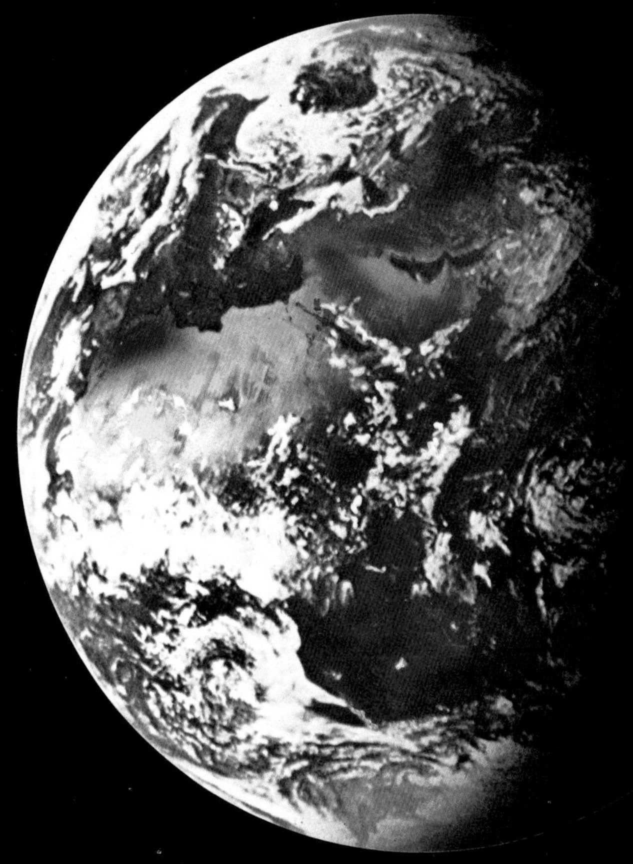

The problems that face mankind are truly monumental. According to the United Nations Environment Programme (UNEP), a recently established agency, soil erosion and soil degradation were still widespread in the early 1990s, and one third of the world's arable land was at risk of becoming desert because of human misuse. Tropical forests were disappearing at an estimated rate of 50 hectares a minute – a rate that, if it continues, will eliminate all tropical forests in forty years. One plant or animal species was also being lost per day – a rate that was accelerating. And in human terms, UNEP estimated that every day some 40,000 infants and young children were dying from hunger or from pollution-related disease.

Disease and malnutrition are features of everyday life in the developing world and, despite all the aid that goes to developing nations, the economic gap between them and the developed world is enormous and increasing. In 1988, the per capita gross national products of the United Kingdom, United States and Switzerland were, respectively, US $12,800, $19,780 and $27,260. By contrast, the per capita GNPs of Chad, Burma and India were $160, $200 and $330. A world split into two sectors – one rich and one poor – is a world fraught with danger. And the population explosion, which is most marked in the poorest countries, could cause global chaos.

The world's problems must be tackled with a real understanding of all the factors involved. People once talked of 'taming' Nature, as if Nature were hostile towards and separate from them. However, in recent years, we have begun to realize that the key to our future lies not in 'taming' but in comprehending Nature, particularly the highly complex ecological relationships that exist between us, the Earth and the millions of animals and plant species that the Earth supports. A view from space has made us realize that damage has been and is still being done. But hopefully it is not too late for us to heal the wounds we have inflicted.

WORLD ATLAS

SYMBOLS

Relief

Symbol	Name
⬭	Land contour
▲ 8848	Spot height (metres)
⤬	Pass
▭	Permanent ice cap

Feet	Relief	Metres
16404		5000
9843		3000
6562		2000
3281		1000
1640		500
656		200
0	Land Dep.	Sea Level
656		200
13123		4000
22966		7000

Hydrography

Symbol	Name
⬭	Submarine contour
▼ 11034	Ocean depth (metres)
(217)	Lake level (metres)
∼∼∼∼	Reef
∼	River
∼ ∼	Intermittent river
∼	Falls
⌐∼	Dam
⌇	Gorge
⊢⊢⊢⊢	Canal
⬭	Lake/Reservoir
⬭	Intermittent lake
∼∼∼	Marsh/Swamp

Communications

Symbol	Name
—Tunnel—	Main railway
⊕	Main airport
– – – –	Track

Road representation varies with the scale category.

Symbol	Road	Scale
═══	Principal road	Large scale
———	Other main road	
———	Principal road	Medium scale
———	Other main road	
———	Principal road	Small scale

Administration

Symbol	Name
———	International boundary
– – –	Undefined/Disputed international boundary
–·–·–	Internal division : First order
·······	Internal division : Second order
▨ ◉ ▣ / ◎ ◻ ■	National capitals

Settlement

Each settlement is given a town stamp according to its relative importance and scale category.

	Large Scale	Medium Scale	Small Scale
▨	Major City	Major City	Major City
◉	City	City	City
◎	Large Town	Large Town	Large Town
⊙	Town	Town	Town
○	Small Town	Small Town	–
·	Village	–	–
⬙	Urban area (Large scale only)		

The size of type used for each settlement is graded to correspond with the appropriate town stamp.

Other features

Symbol	Name
∴	Ancient monument
◡	Oasis
⬭	National Park
▲	Oil field
△	Gas field
—▲—	Oil/Gas pipeline

Lettering

Various styles of lettering are used - each one representing a different type of feature.

ALPS	Physical feature	KENYA	Country name
Red Sea	Hydrographic feature	IOWA	Internal division
Paris	Settlement name	*(Fr.)*	Territorial administration

© Collins

EUROPE

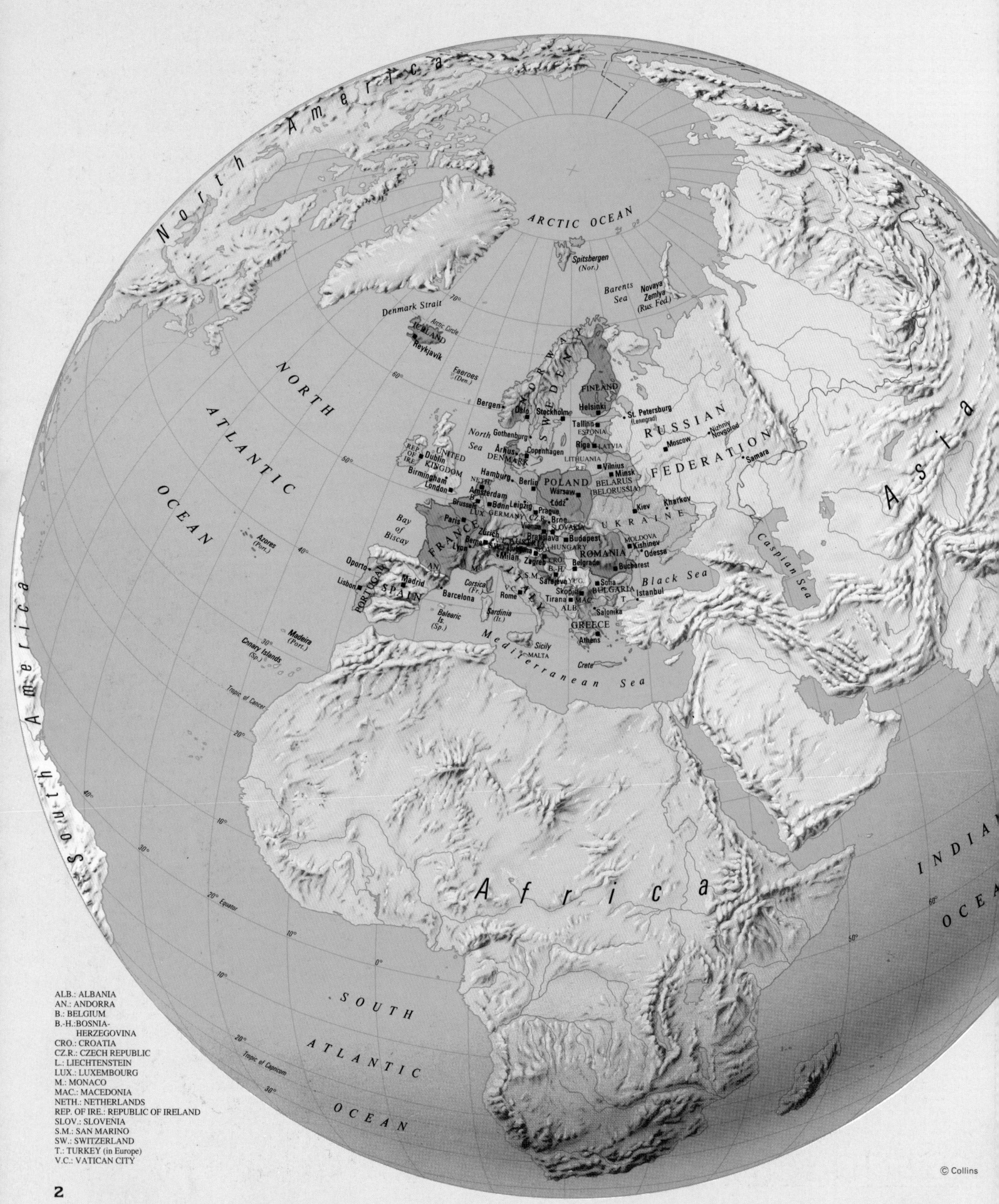

North America

Arctic Ocean

Spitsbergen (Nor.)

Barents Sea

Novaya Zemlya (Rus. Fed.)

Denmark Strait

Arctic Circle

ICELAND
Reykjavik

Faeroes (Den.)

NORTH

ATLANTIC

OCEAN

Bergen
Oslo
Stockholm

NORWAY
SWEDEN

FINLAND
Helsinki

RUSSIAN

St. Petersburg (Leningrad)

North Sea
Gothenburg
Arhus
Copenhagen
DENMARK

Tallinn
ESTONIA
Riga
LATVIA

Moscow

Nizhniy Novgorod

FEDERATION

REP. OF IRE.
Dublin
UNITED KINGDOM
Birmingham
London

Hamburg
NETH.
Amsterdam
Brussels
Leipzig
Berlin

LITHUANIA
Vilnius
Minsk
BELARUS (BELORUSSIA)

Samara

Kharkov

Bonn
GERMANY
Prague
POLAND
Warsaw
Łódź

Paris
LUX.
B.
Zürich
SLOVAKIA
Bratislava
Brno

Kiev
UKRAINE

Bay of Biscay
FRANCE
Bern
SW.
AN.
Lyon
Milan
Vienna
Budapest
HUNGARY
MOLDOVA
Kishinev
Odessa

Azores (Port.)

Oporto
Madrid
SPAIN
Barcelona
S.M.
Rome
Zagreb
CRO.
B.-H.
Sarajevo
Belgrade
Y.G.
ROMANIA
Bucharest

Black Sea

Lisbon
PORTUGAL

Corsica (Fr.)
Sardinia (It.)
V.C.
Tirana
ALB.
Skopje
MAC.
Sofia
BULGARIA
Salonika
Istanbul

Caspian Sea

Madeira (Port.)

Canary Islands (Sp.)

Balearic Is. (Sp.)

Sicily
MALTA

Mediterranean Sea

GREECE
Athens

Crete

Tropic of Cancer

Africa

Asia

INDIAN OCEAN

South America

SOUTH

ATLANTIC

OCEAN

Equator

Tropic of Capricorn

ALB.: ALBANIA
AN.: ANDORRA
B.: BELGIUM
B.-H.: BOSNIA-HERZEGOVINA
CRO.: CROATIA
CZ.R.: CZECH REPUBLIC
L.: LIECHTENSTEIN
LUX.: LUXEMBOURG
M.: MONACO
MAC.: MACEDONIA
NETH.: NETHERLANDS
REP. OF IRE.: REPUBLIC OF IRELAND
SLOV.: SLOVENIA
S.M.: SAN MARINO
SW.: SWITZERLAND
T.: TURKEY (in Europe)
V.C.: VATICAN CITY

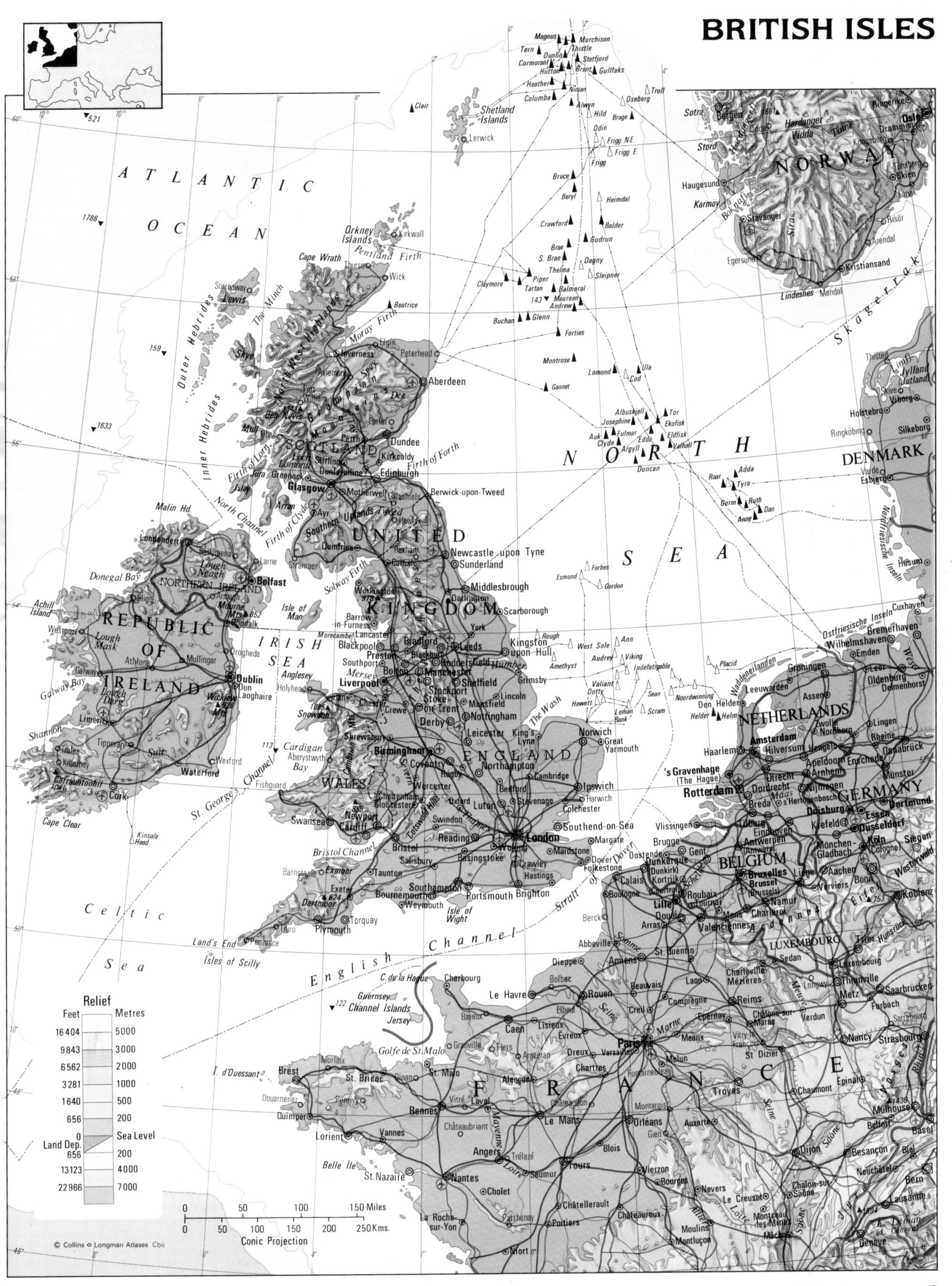

BRITISH ISLES

ATLANTIC OCEAN

NORWAY

NORTH SEA

DENMARK

UNITED KINGDOM

SCOTLAND

ENGLAND

WALES

REPUBLIC OF IRELAND

NORTHERN IRELAND

IRISH SEA

NETHERLANDS

GERMANY

BELGIUM

LUXEMBOURG

FRANCE

Celtic Sea

English Channel

Shetland Islands

Orkney Islands

Outer Hebrides

Inner Hebrides

The Minch

West Highlands

Relief

Feet	Metres
16 404	5000
9843	3000
6562	2000
3281	1000
1640	500
656	200
0	Sea Level
Land Dep.	
656	200
13 123	4000
22 966	7000

0   50   100   150 Miles

0   50   100   150   200   250 Kms.

Conic Projection

© Collins ● Longman Atlases Cbii

3

ENGLAND AND WALES

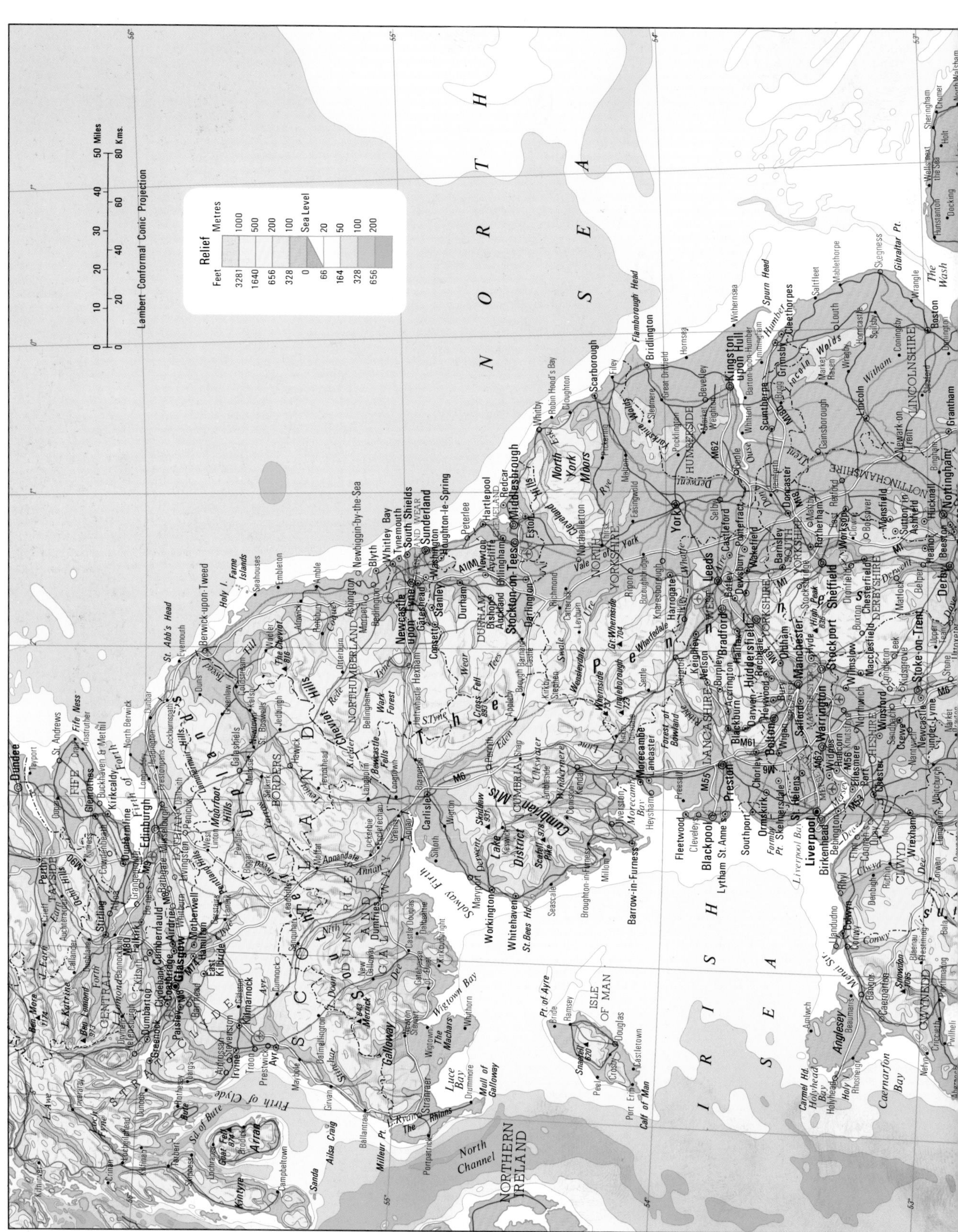

0 10 20 30 40 50 Miles
0 20 40 60 80 Kms.
Lambert Conformal Conic Projection
Relief
Feet Metres
3281 1000
1640 500
656 200
328 100
0 Sea Level
66 20
164 50
328 100
656 200
NORTH SEA
IRISH SEA
NORTHERN IRELAND
North Channel
ISLE OF MAN
SCOTLAND

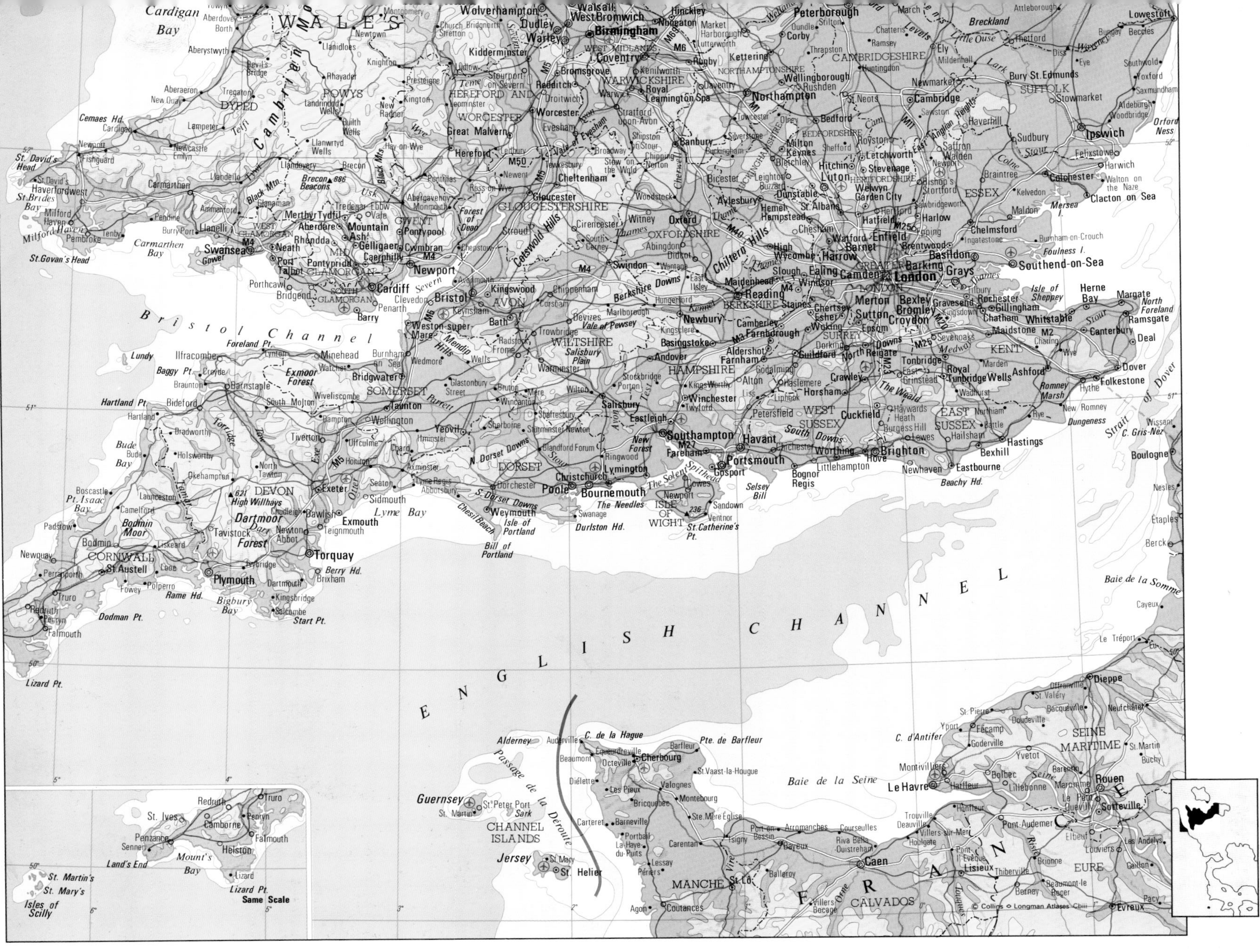

ENGLISH CHANNEL
Bristol Channel
WALES
London
Birmingham
Bristol
Cardiff
Southampton
Portsmouth
Plymouth
Brighton
Oxford
Reading
Cambridge
Ipswich
Dover
Swansea
Newport
Exeter
Torquay
Bournemouth
Poole
Dartmoor Forest
Cornwall
Devon
Dorset
Hampshire
Wiltshire
Somerset
Kent
Essex
Suffolk
Isle of Wight
Channel Islands
Jersey
Guernsey
Alderney
Sark
Cherbourg
Le Havre
Caen
Rouen
Dieppe
Boulogne
Baie de la Seine
Baie de la Somme
Strait of Dover
Lyme Bay
Cardigan Bay
Carmarthen Bay
Lizard Pt.
Land's End
Isles of Scilly
Same Scale
© Collins • Longman Atlases

SCOTLAND

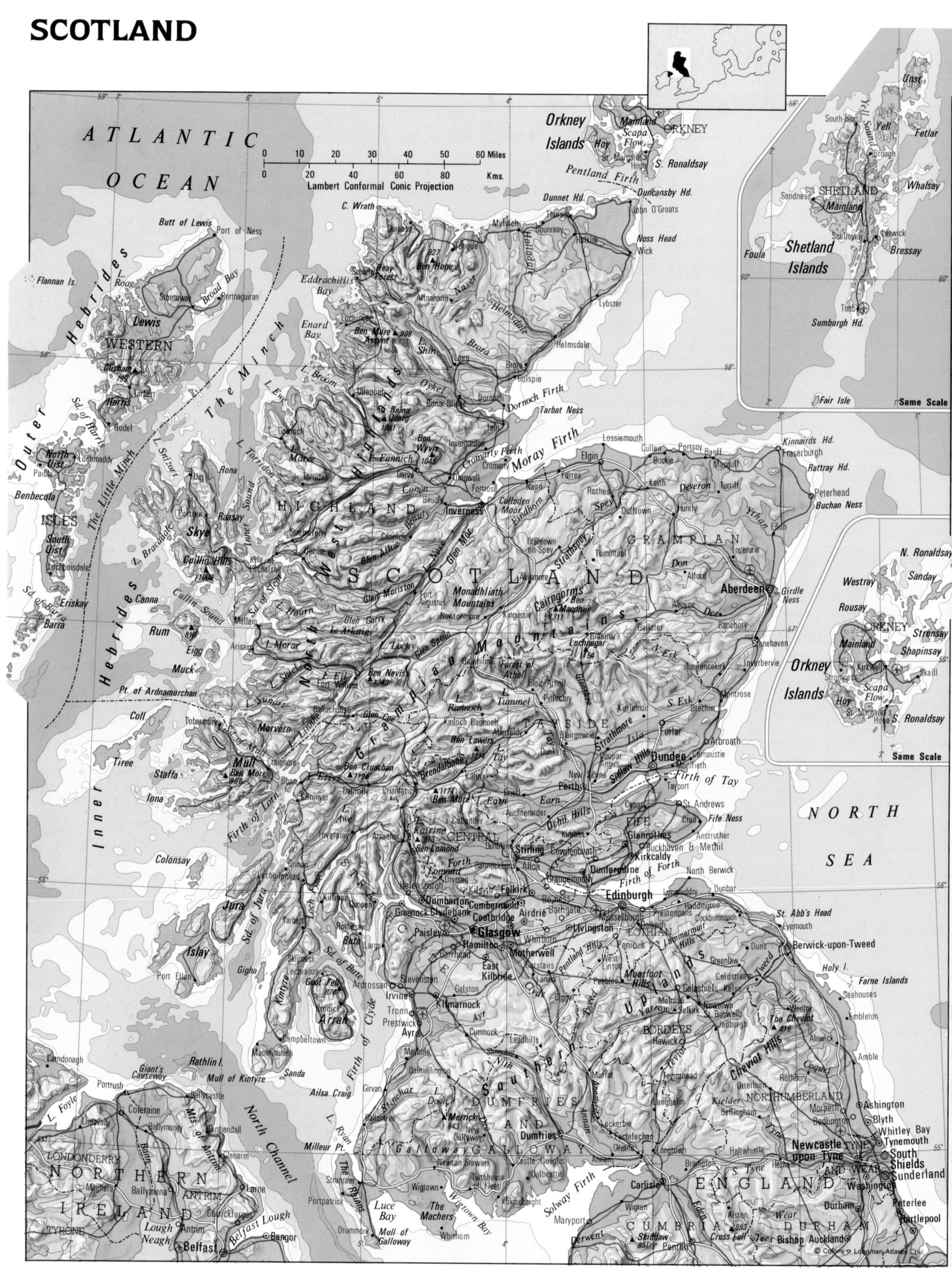

ATLANTIC OCEAN
NORTH SEA
Lambert Conformal Conic Projection
SCOTLAND
HIGHLAND
GRAMPIAN
TAYSIDE
CENTRAL
FIFE
LOTHIAN
BORDERS
DUMFRIES AND GALLOWAY
WESTERN ISLES
NORTHERN IRELAND
ENGLAND
Orkney Islands
Shetland Islands
Outer Hebrides
Inner Hebrides
The Minch
Moray Firth
Firth of Forth
Firth of Clyde
North Channel
Solway Firth
Pentland Firth
Edinburgh
Glasgow
Aberdeen
Dundee
Inverness
Perth
Stirling
Same Scale

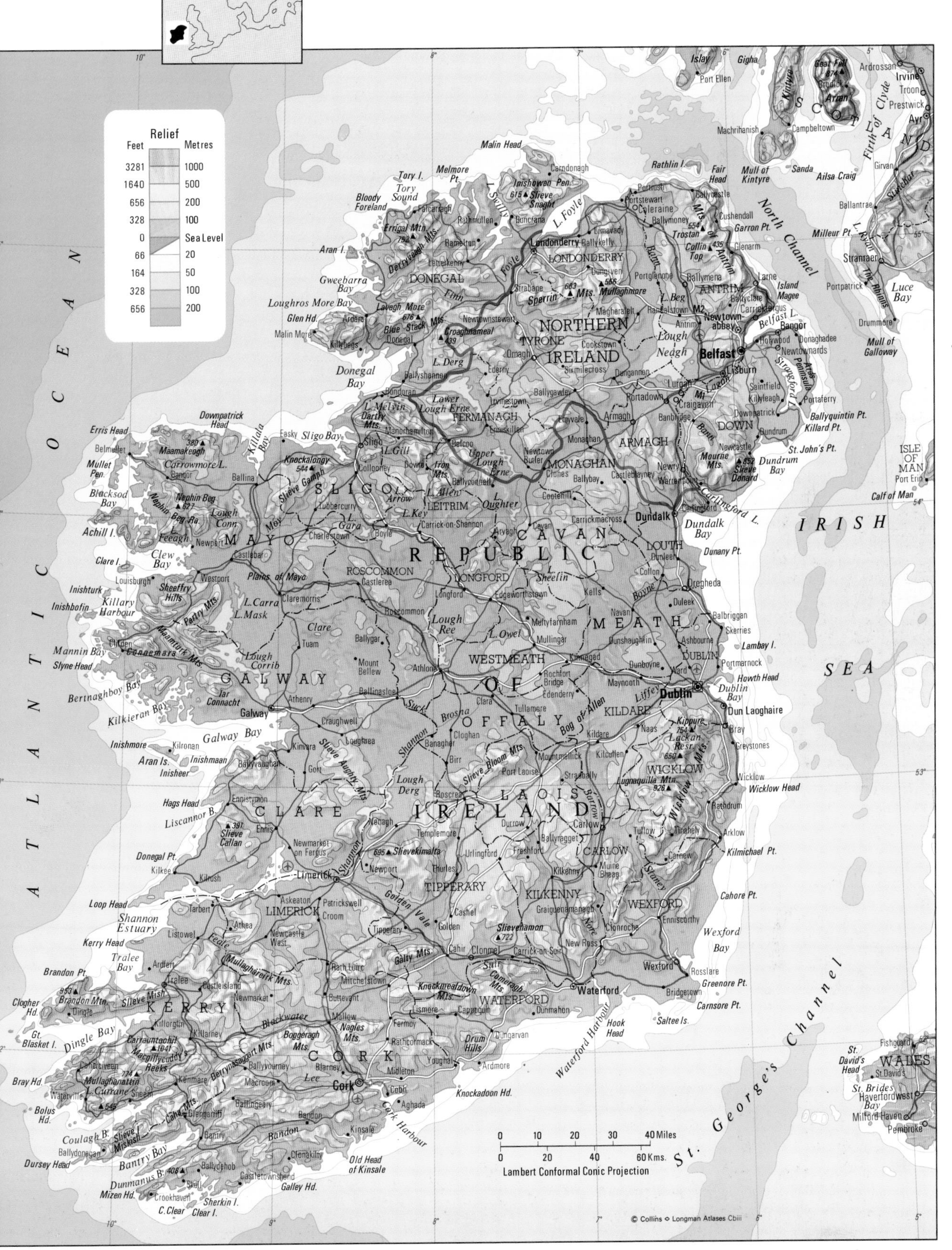

Relief

Feet		Metres
3281		1000
1640		500
656		200
328		100
0		Sea Level
66		20
164		50
328		100
656		200

ATLANTIC OCEAN

IRISH SEA

NORTH CHANNEL

St. George's Channel

SCOTLAND

WALES

ISLE OF MAN

REPUBLIC OF IRELAND

NORTHERN IRELAND

| 0 | 10 | 20 | 30 | 40 Miles |
| 0 | 20 | 40 | | 60 Kms. |

Lambert Conformal Conic Projection

© Collins ◊ Longman Atlases Cbiii

THE LOW COUNTRIES

Scale

0 10 20 30 40 50 60 Miles
0 20 40 60 80 Kms.
Conic Projection

Relief

Feet		Metres
16 404		5000
9843		3000
6562		2000
3281		1000
1640		500
656		200
0	Sea Level	
656	Land Dep.	200
13 123		4000
22 966		7000

NORTH

SEA

NETHERLANDS

BELGIUM

GERMANY

FRANCE

LUXEMBOURG

Ostfriesische Inseln

Waddeneilanden

Waddenzee

IJsselmeer

GRONINGEN

FRIESLAND

DRENTHE

NIEDERSACHSEN

NOORD HOLLAND

Amsterdam

Haarlem

ZUID HOLLAND

's Gravenhage (The Hague)

Rotterdam

OVERIJSSEL

FLEVOLAND

GELDERLAND

UTRECHT

Utrecht

ZEELAND

NOORD BRABANT

LIMBURG

Eindhoven

NORDRHEIN WESTFALEN

Düsseldorf

Essen

Dortmund

Köln (Cologne)

Bonn

Duisburg

Münster

Osnabrück

Oldenburg

Wilhelmshaven

Emden

Antwerpen

Bruxelles (Brussel) Brussels

WEST VLAANDEREN

OOST VLAANDEREN

Gent

VLAANDEREN

BRABANT

HAINAUT

Liège

LIEGE

NAMUR

LUXEMBOURG

Maastricht

Aachen

RHEINLAND-PFALZ

Koblenz

Trier

Eifel

Ardenne

Ardennes

SAARLAND

Kaiserslautern

NORD

PICARDIE

FLANDRE

ARTOIS

CHAMPAGNE

Lille

Dunkerque (Dunkirk)

© Collins ● Longman Atlases Cbm

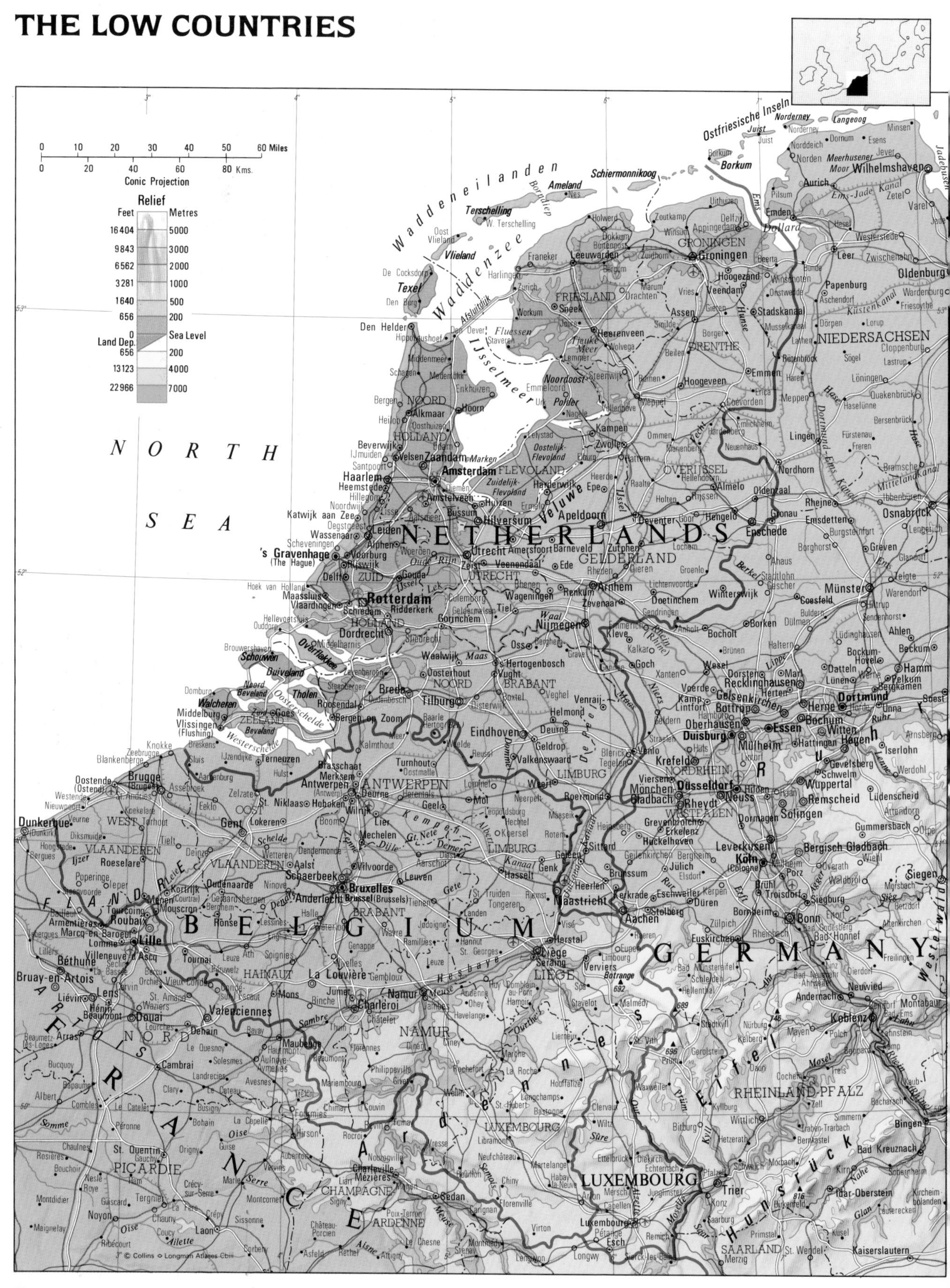

PARIS BASIN AND PO VALLEY

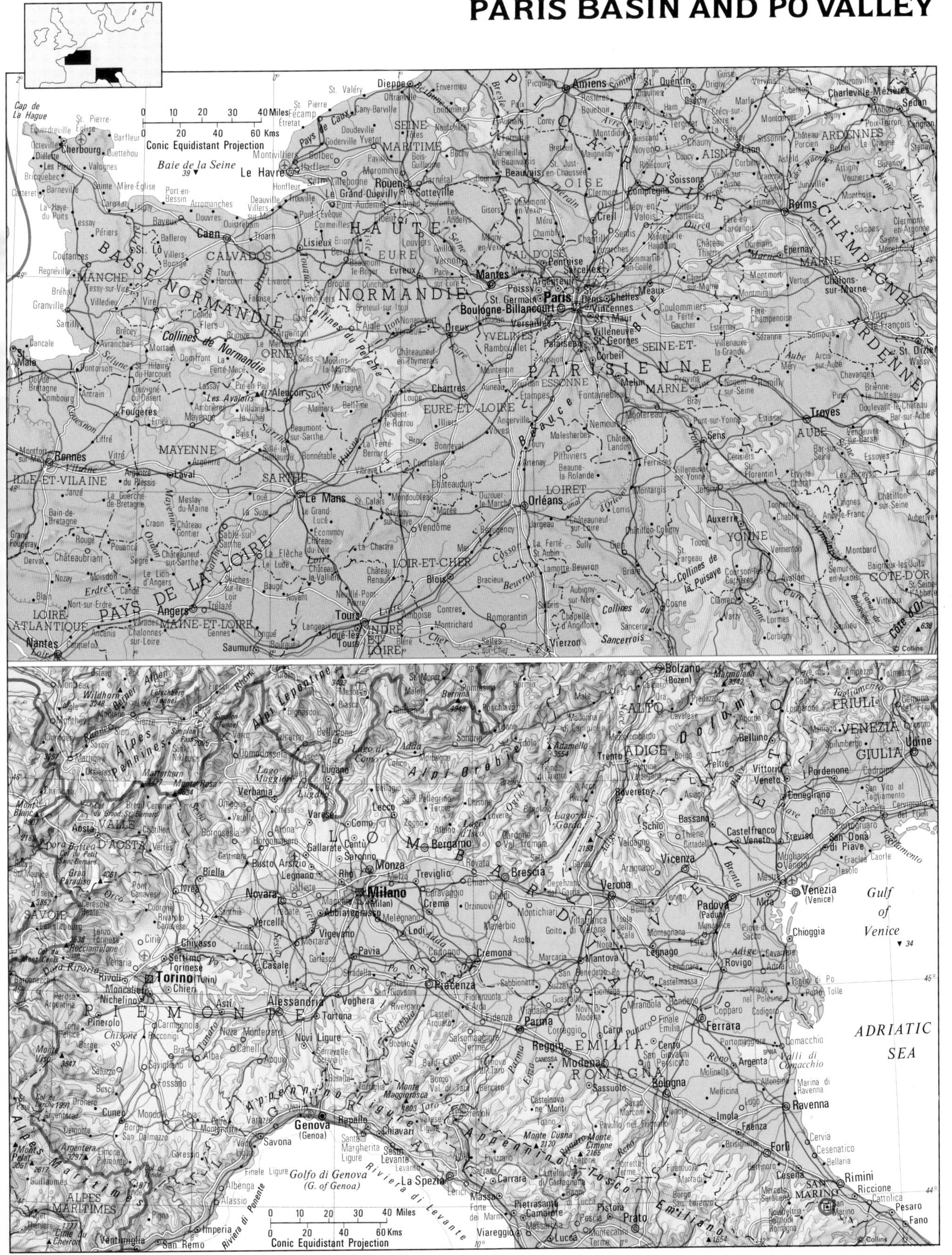
Cap de La Hague
Cherbourg
Baie de la Seine
Le Havre
Caen
CALVADOS
BASSE-NORMANDIE
MANCHE
Collines de Normandie
ORNE
HAUTE
NORMANDIE
SEINE-MARITIME
EURE
Rouen
Dieppe
Amiens
PICARDIE
St. Quentin
Charleville-Mézières
Sedan
ARDENNES
AISNE
OISE
Reims
CHAMPAGNE
ARDENNE
MARNE
Châlons-sur-Marne
Paris
Boulogne-Billancourt
Versailles
YVELINES
ESSONNE
SEINE-ET-MARNE
PARISIENNE
Chartres
EURE-ET-LOIRE
Orléans
LOIRET
Troyes
AUBE
Auxerre
YONNE
CÔTE-D'OR
Rennes
ILLE-ET-VILAINE
MAYENNE
Laval
Le Mans
SARTHE
PAYS DE LA LOIRE
Angers
MAINE-ET-LOIRE
LOIRE-ATLANTIQUE
Nantes
Tours
INDRE-ET-LOIRE
Blois
LOIR-ET-CHER
Vierzon
Collines du Sancerrois
Conic Equidistant Projection
Miles
Kms
Bolzano (Bozen)
ALTO ADIGE
Dolomiti
FRIULI-VENEZIA GIULIA
Udine
Trento
VENETO
Alpi Orobie
Lago Maggiore
Lago di Como
Lago di Garda
Alpi Lepontine
Alpes Pennines
Matterhorn
Monte Rosa
Mont Blanc
VALLE D'AOSTA
Aosta
Gran Paradiso
LOMBARDIA
Milano (Milan)
Bergamo
Brescia
Monza
Verona
Vicenza
Padova (Padua)
Venezia (Venice)
Gulf of Venice
Treviso
Torino (Turin)
PIEMONTE
Novara
Vercelli
Alessandria
Pavia
Piacenza
Cremona
Mantova
Parma
Reggio EMILIA-ROMAGNA
Modena
Bologna
Ferrara
Ravenna
Forlì
Rimini
SAN MARINO
ADRIATIC SEA
Genova (Genoa)
Golfo di Genova (G. of Genoa)
LIGURIA
Appennino Ligure
Appennino Tosco-Emiliano
Riviera di Ponente
Riviera di Levante
La Spezia
Savona
Cuneo
Alpes Maritimes
ALPES MARITIMES
SAVOIE
Sanremo
Imperia
Prato
Pistoia
Lucca
Viareggio
Pesaro
Fano
Collins

SPAIN AND PORTUGAL

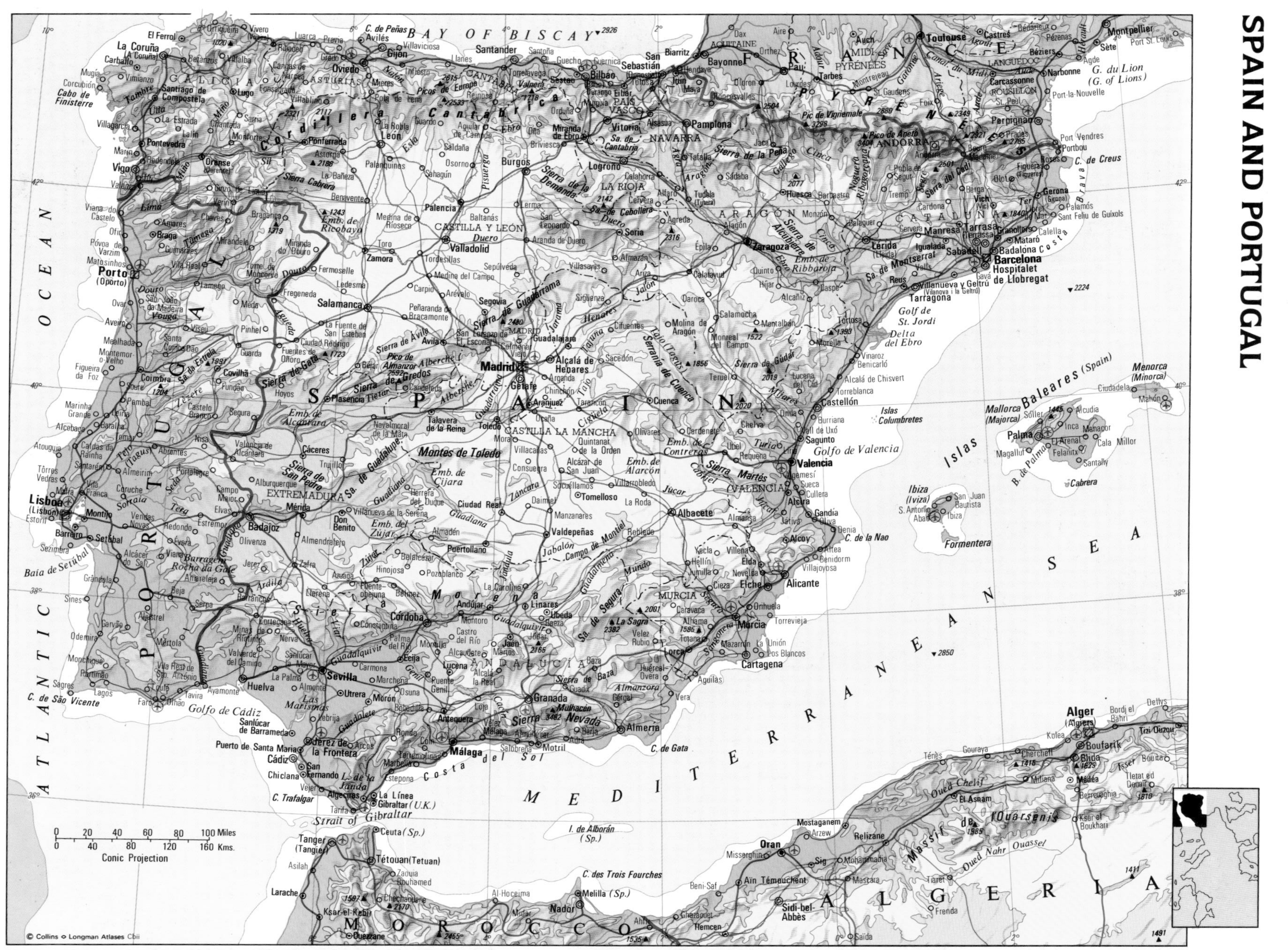
BAY OF BISCAY
ATLANTIC OCEAN
MEDITERRANEAN SEA
FRANCE
SPAIN
PORTUGAL
ALGERIA
MOROCCO
PYRENEES
Cordillera Cantábrica
Islas Baleares (Spain)
Mallorca (Majorca)
Menorca (Minorca)
Ibiza (Iviza)
Formentera
Golfo de Valencia
Golf de St. Jordi
Golfo de Cádiz
Strait of Gibraltar
Gibraltar (U.K.)
C. de São Vicente
Cabo de Finisterre
Madrid
Lisboa (Lisbon)
Porto (Oporto)
Barcelona
Valencia
Sevilla
Málaga
Zaragoza
Bilbao
Granada
Córdoba
Alicante
Murcia
Cartagena
Almería
Cádiz
Salamanca
Valladolid
Burgos
Toledo
Badajoz
Vigo
La Coruña
Oviedo
Gijón
Santander
Pamplona
Alger (Algiers)
Oran
Tanger (Tangier)
Tétouan (Tetuan)
Melilla (Sp.)
Ceuta (Sp.)
Toulouse
Montpellier
Perpignan
Andorra
0 20 40 60 80 100 Miles
0 40 80 120 160 Kms.
Conic Projection
© Collins ○ Longman Atlases Cbii

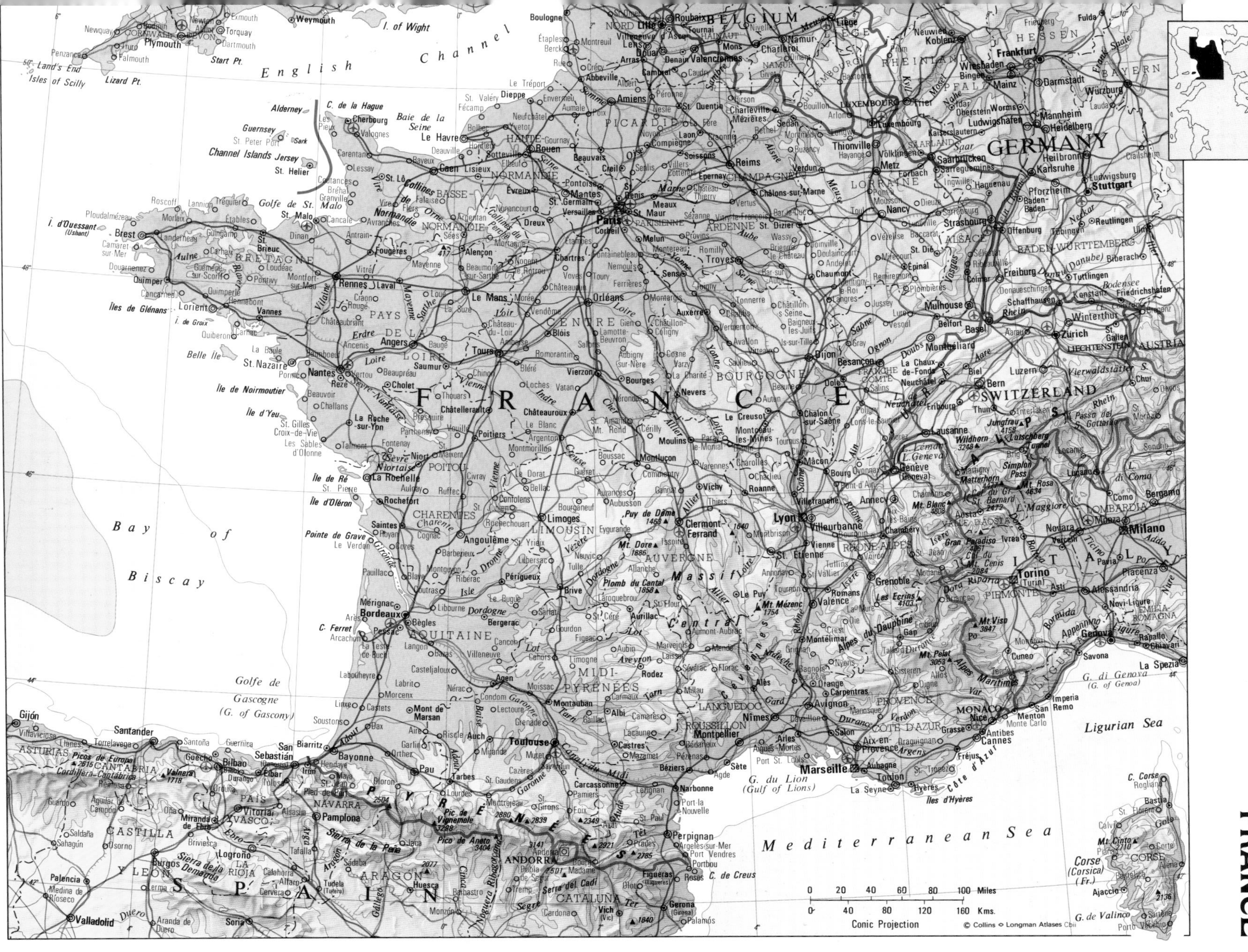
FRANCE
GERMANY
SWITZERLAND
ITALIA
BELGIUM
SPAIN
AUSTRIA
English Channel
Bay of Biscay
Golfe de Gascogne (G. of Gascony)
Mediterranean Sea
Ligurian Sea
G. du Lion (Gulf of Lions)
G. di Genova (G. of Genoa)
Channel Islands Jersey
Corse (Corsica) (Fr.)
Massif Central
PYRÉNÉES
Paris
Lyon
Marseille
Bordeaux
Toulouse
Nantes
0 20 40 60 80 100 Miles
0 40 80 120 160 Kms.
Conic Projection
© Collins ◇ Longman Atlases

ITALY AND THE BALKANS

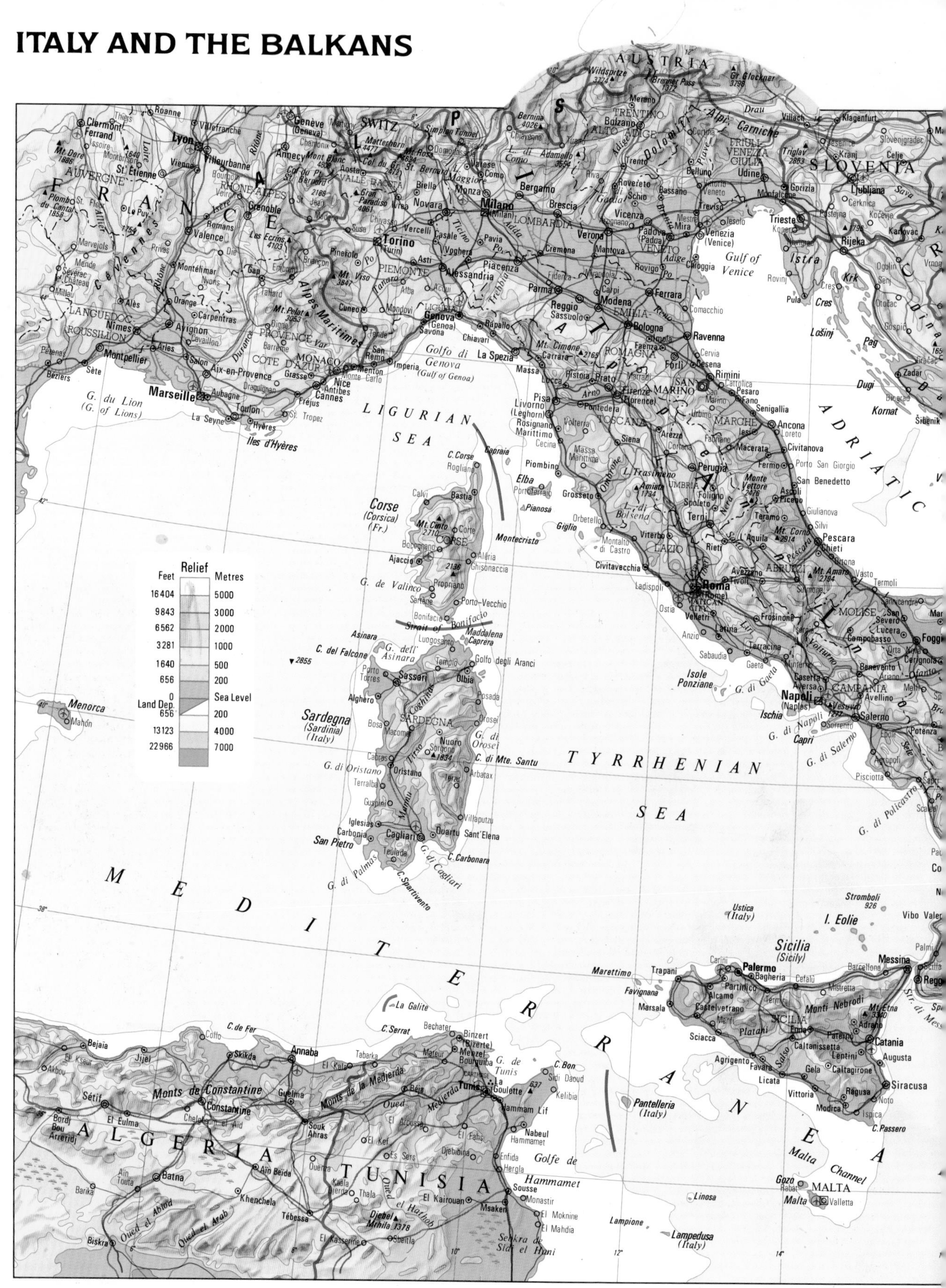

Relief
Feet
Metres
16404
5000
9843
3000
6562
2000
3281
1000
1640
500
656
200
0
Sea Level
Land Dep.
656
200
13123
4000
22966
7000
AUSTRIA
SWITZ.
SLOVENIA
FRANCE
ALGERIA
TUNISIA
MALTA
LIGURIAN SEA
TYRRHENIAN SEA
MEDITERRANEAN SEA
ADRIATIC
Gulf of Venice
Golfo di Genova (Gulf of Genoa)
G. du Lion (G. of Lions)
Strait of Bonifacio
Malta Channel
Golfe de Hammamet
Corse (Corsica) (Fr.)
Sardegna (Sardinia) (Italy)
Sicilia (Sicily)
I. Eolie
Ustica (Italy)
Pantelleria (Italy)
Lampedusa (Italy)
Linosa
Lampione
Menorca
Elba
Capraia
Pianosa
Montecristo
Giglio
Isole Ponziane
Ischia
Capri
Iles d'Hyères
La Galite
Marettimo
Favignana
Asinara
San Pietro
Gozo
Malta
Milano (Milan)
Torino (Turin)
Genova (Genoa)
Venezia (Venice)
Firenze (Florence)
Roma (Rome)
Napoli (Naples)
Palermo
Messina
Catania
Siracusa
Cagliari
Sassari
Ajaccio
Bastia
Marseille
Lyon
Nice
Monaco
Trieste
Ljubljana
Bologna
Verona
Padova (Padua)
Pisa
Livorno (Leghorn)
Ancona
Pescara
Perugia
Tunis
Annaba
Constantine
Valletta
Mt. Blanc
Matterhorn 4477
Gran Paradiso 4061
Mt. Viso 3847
Mt. Etna 3340
Vesuvio 1277
Mt. Corno 2914
Mt. Amaro 2794
Mt. Cimone 2165
Gr. Glockner 3798
Triglav 2863
Alpes Maritimes
Alpi Carniche
Dolomiti
Monti Nebrodi
Monts de Constantine

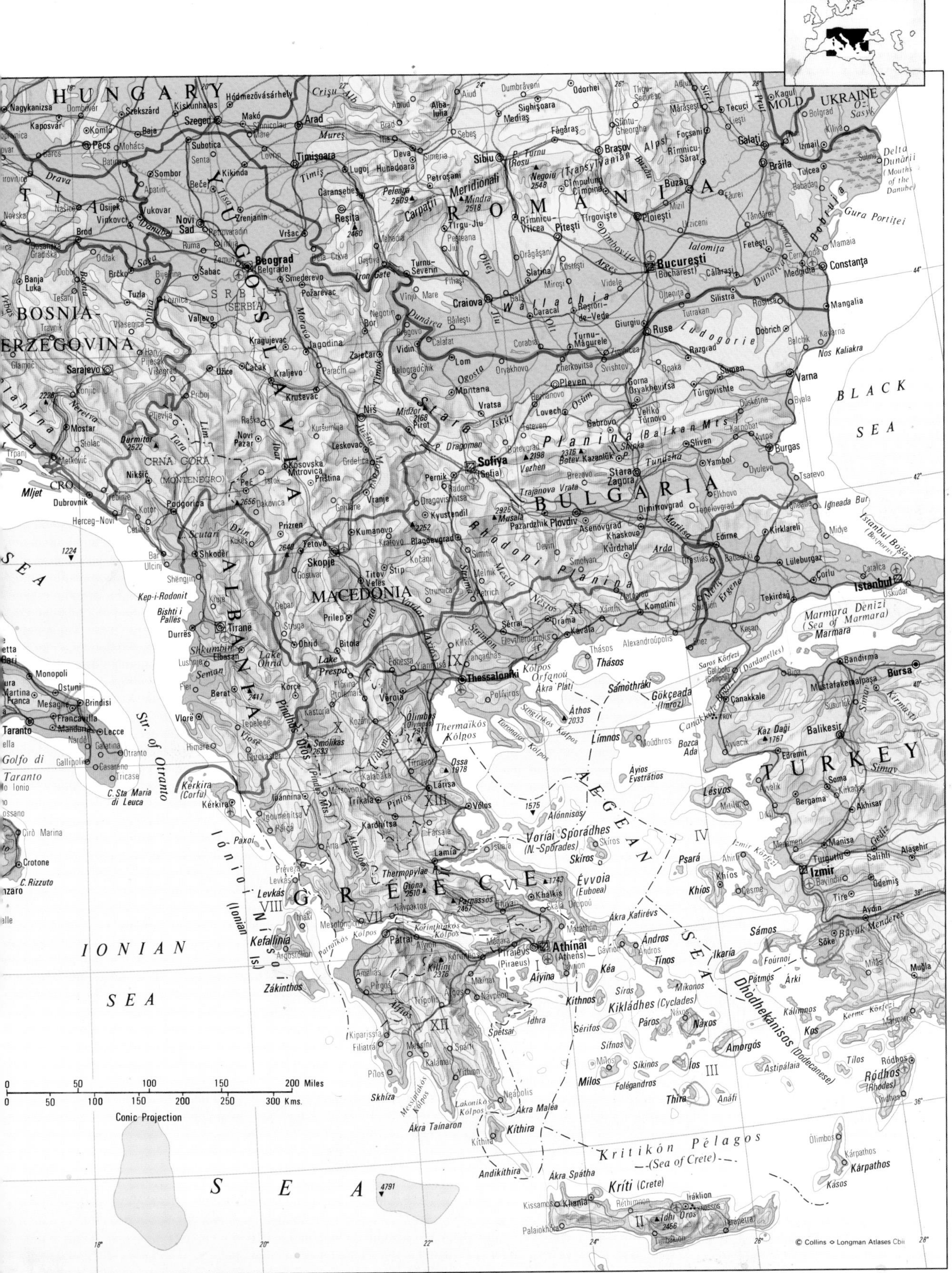
HUNGARY
ROMANIA
YUGOSLAVIA
BOSNIA-HERZEGOVINA
BULGARIA
MACEDONIA
ALBANIA
GREECE
TURKEY
UKRAINE
MOLD
BLACK SEA
AEGEAN SEA
IONIAN SEA
Beograd (Belgrade)
Bucureşti (Bucharest)
Sofiya (Sofia)
Skopje
Tiranë
Athínai (Athens)
Istanbul
Thessaloníki
Conic Projection
© Collins ◇ Longman Atlases Cbii

CENTRAL EUROPE

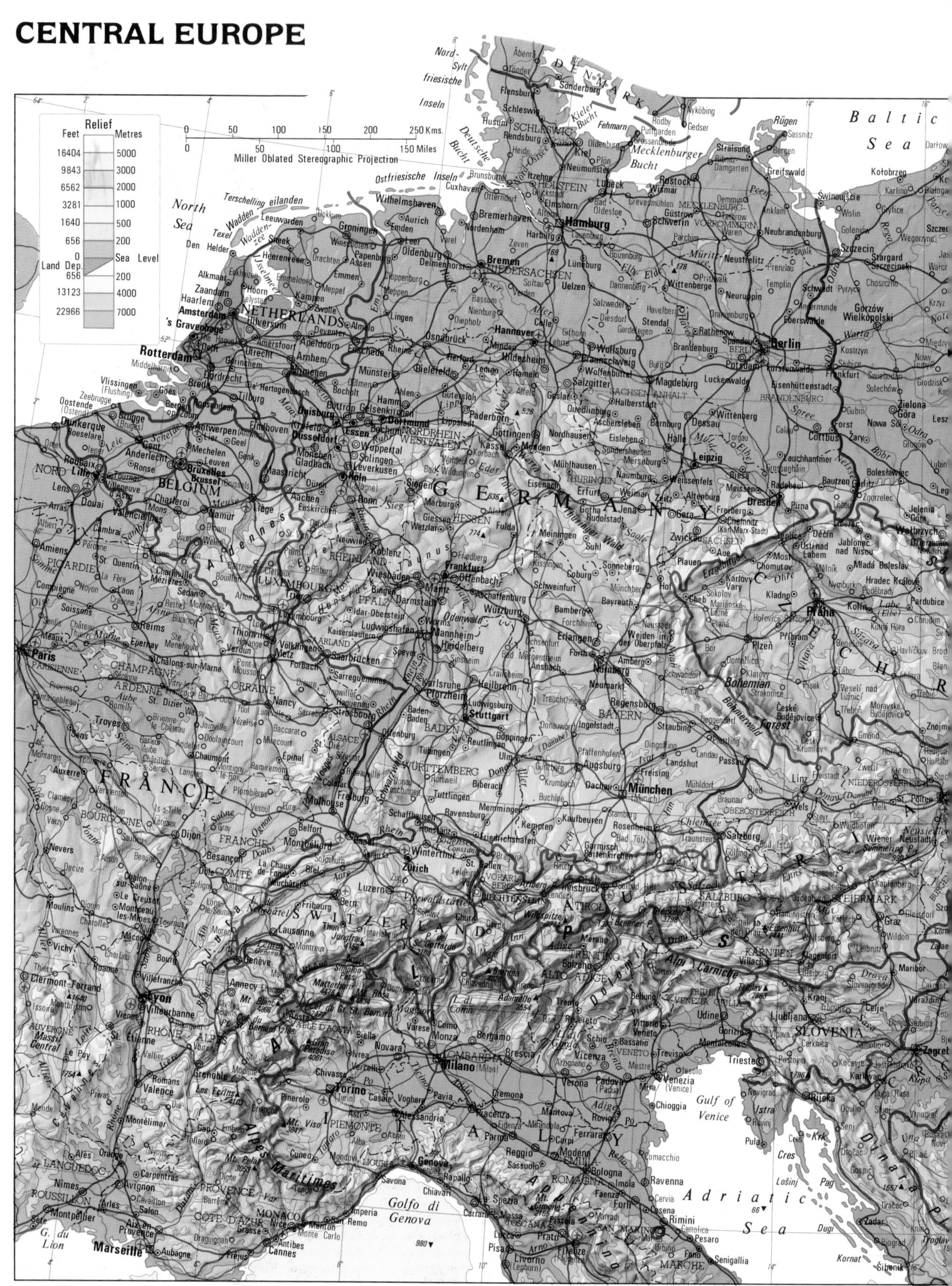

Relief
Feet
Metres
16404
5000
9843
3000
6562
2000
3281
1000
1640
500
656
200
0
Sea Level
Land Dep.
656
200
13123
4000
22966
7000
0
50
100
150
200
250 Kms.
0
50
100
150 Miles
Miller Oblated Stereographic Projection
North Sea
Baltic Sea
Nord-friesische Inseln
Deutsche Bucht
Ostfriesische Inseln
Terschelling
Wadden eilanden
Kieler Bucht
Mecklenburger Bucht
DENMARK
NETHERLANDS
BELGIUM
LUXEMBOURG
GERMANY
FRANCE
SWITZERLAND
AUSTRIA
ITALY
SLOVENIA
CZECH REPUBLIC
Gulf of Venice
Golfo di Genova
Adriatic Sea
G. du Lion
Amsterdam
Rotterdam
's Gravenhage
Den Helder
Groningen
Hamburg
Bremen
Hannover
Berlin
Rostock
Kiel
Lübeck
Magdeburg
Leipzig
Dresden
Essen
Dortmund
Düsseldorf
Köln
Bonn
Frankfurt
Stuttgart
München
Nürnberg
Bruxelles
Antwerpen
Lille
Paris
Reims
Nancy
Strasbourg
Dijon
Lyon
Marseille
Genève
Bern
Zürich
Basel
Innsbruck
Salzburg
Linz
Graz
Praha
Plzeň
Milano
Torino
Genova
Venezia
Bologna
Trieste
Ljubljana
Zagreb
Szczecin
Ardennes
Eifel
Taunus
Schwarzwald
Thüringer Wald
Erzgebirge
Bohemian Forest
Alpes Maritimes
Alpi Carniche
Apennino
Massif Central
Jura
Rhein
Elbe
Donau
Po
Rhône
Oder
14

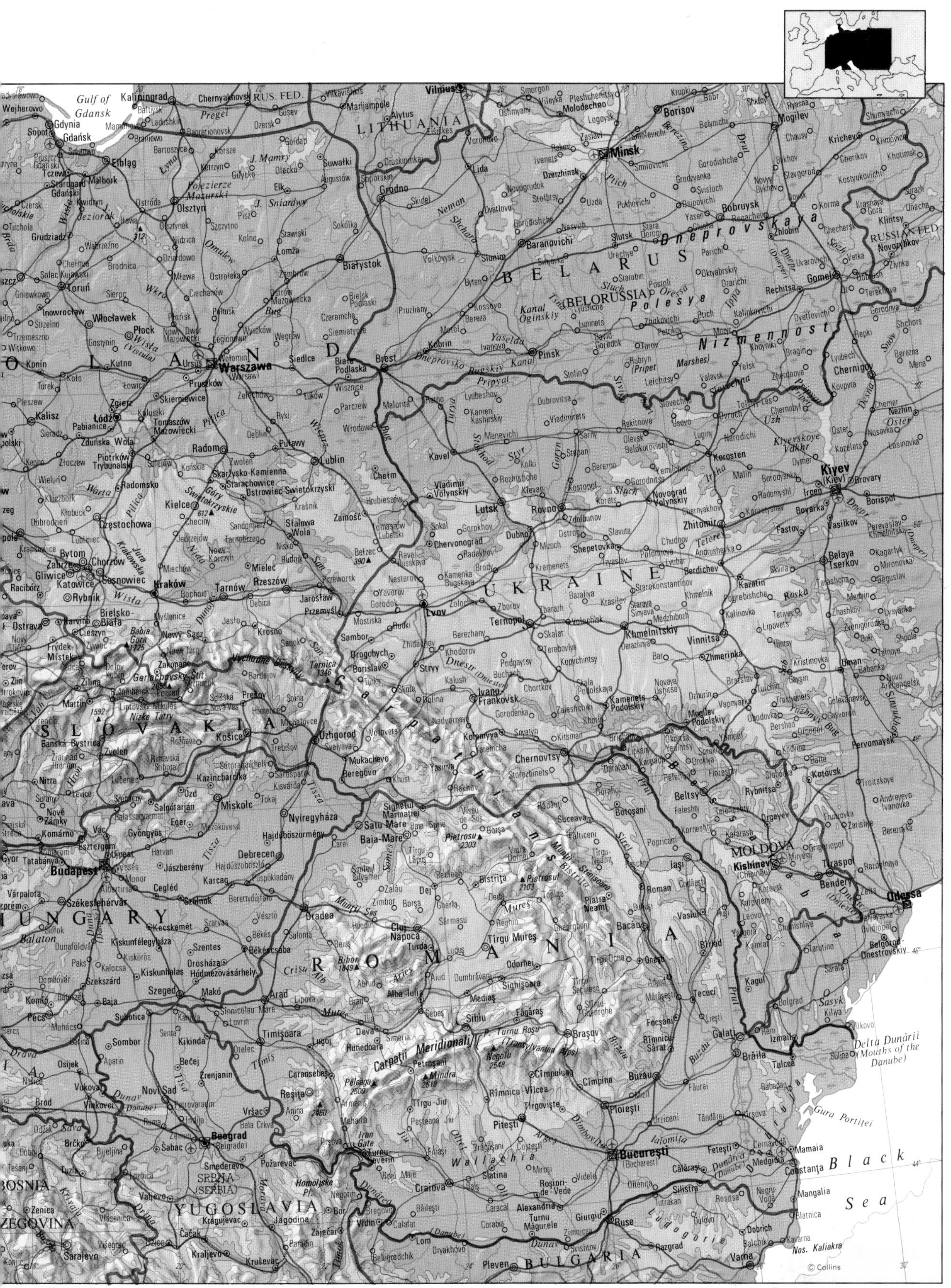
Gulf of Gdansk
Kaliningrad
RUS. FED.
LITHUANIA
Vilnius
Minsk
Borisov
Mogilev
Gdynia
Gdańsk
Elbląg
Olsztyn
Grodno
Białystok
Baranovichi
BELARUS
(BELORUSSIA)
Dneprovskaya
Polesye
Nizmennost
Gomel
RUSSIAN FED.
Toruń
Włocławek
Płock
POLAND
Warszawa
(Warsaw)
Brest
Pinsk
Pripet Marshes
Łódź
Radom
Lublin
Chernigov
Kiyev
(Kiev)
Częstochowa
Kielce
Lutsk
Rovno
Zhitomir
Katowice
Kraków
Tarnów
Rzeszów
Lvov
Ternopol
UKRAINE
Khmelnitskiy
Vinnitsa
Belaya Tserkov
Ostrava
Carpathians
SLOVAKIA
Košice
Uzhgorod
Chernovtsy
Kishinev
MOLDOVA
Odessa
Miskolc
Budapest
Debrecen
HUNGARY
Balaton
Cluj-Napoca
ROMANIA
Iaşi
Szeged
Arad
Timişoara
Braşov
Galaţi
Delta Dunării
(Mouths of the Danube)
Novi Sad
Beograd
(Belgrade)
Carpaţii Meridionali
Ploieşti
Bucureşti
(Bucharest)
Constanţa
Black Sea
SRBIJA
(SERBIA)
YUGOSLAVIA
BOSNIA-
-ZEGOVINA
Sarajevo
Craiova
Ruse
Varna
BULGARIA
Pleven
Dunav
Nos. Kaliakra
© Collins

SCANDINAVIA AND BALTIC LANDS

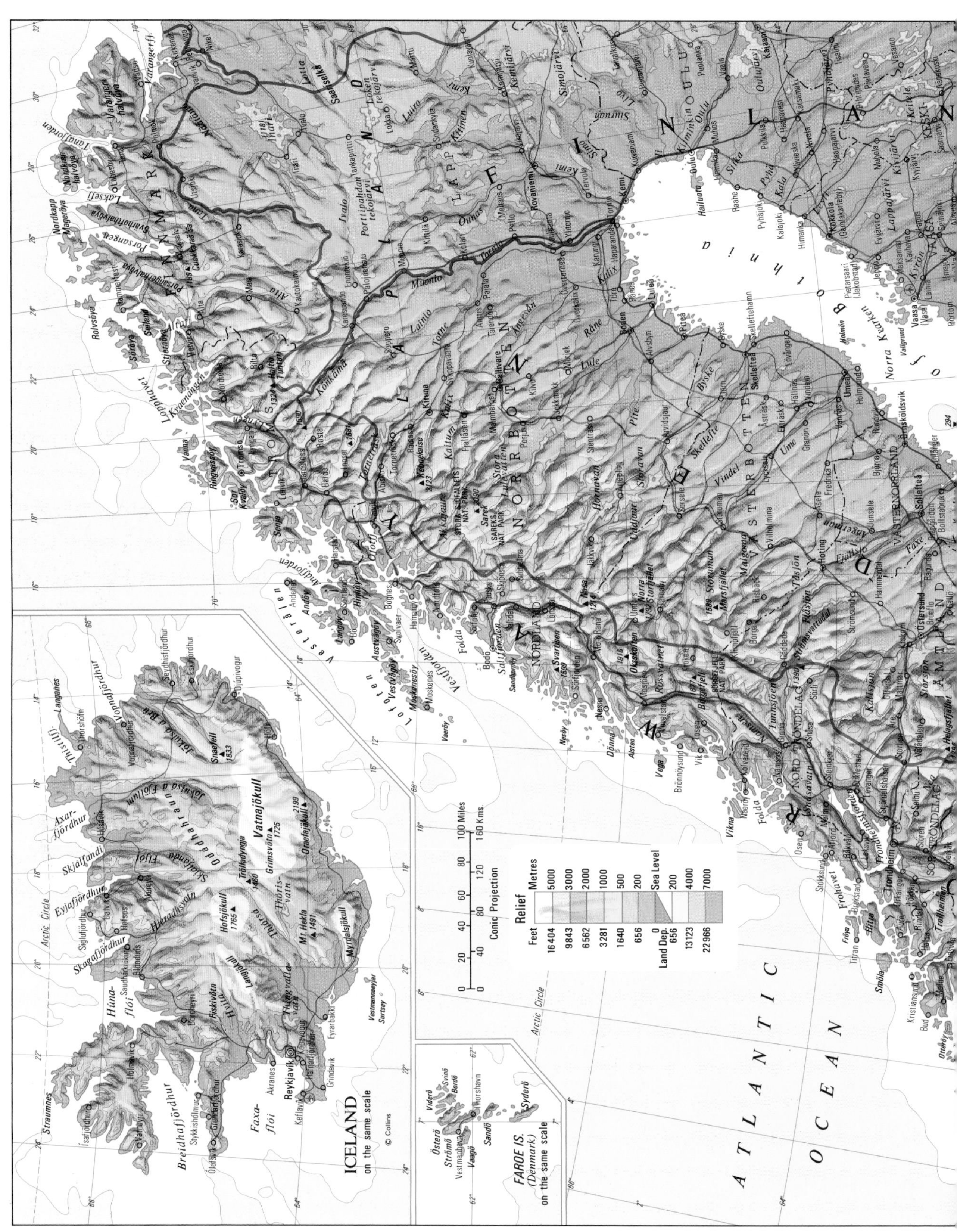

ICELAND
on the same scale

© Collins

FAROE IS.
(Denmark)
on the same scale

Relief
Feet	Metres
16 404	5000
9843	3000
6562	2000
3281	1000
1640	500
656	200
	Sea Level

Land Dep.
656	200
13 123	4000
22 966	7000

100 Miles
160 Kms.

Conic Projection

ATLANTIC OCEAN

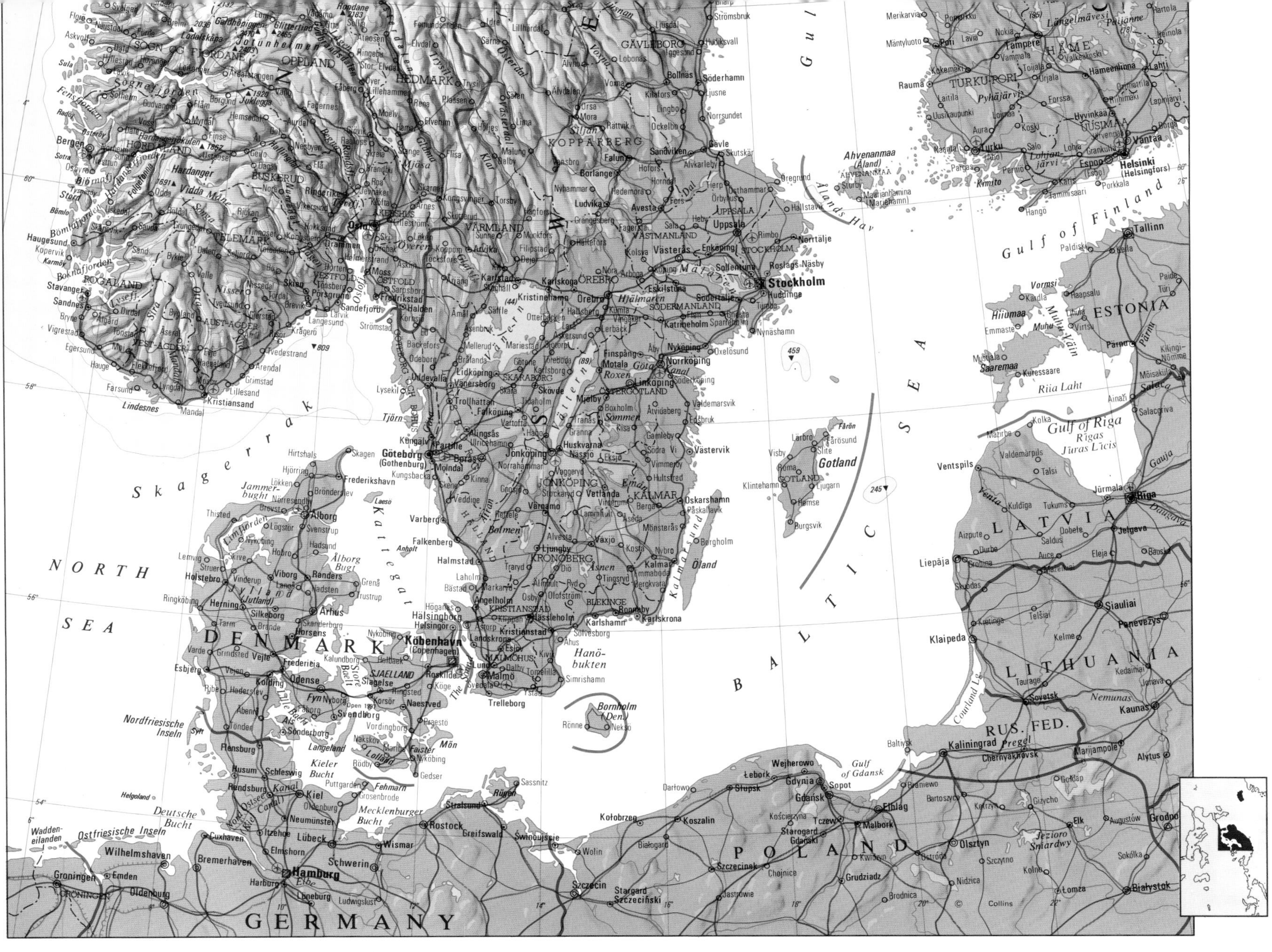
NORTH SEA
Skagerrak
Kattegat
BALTIC SEA
Gulf of Finland
Gulf of Riga
Gulf of Gdansk
Ålands Hav
DENMARK
GERMANY
POLAND
LITHUANIA
LATVIA
ESTONIA
RUS. FED.
Gotland
Öland
Bornholm (Den.)
Stockholm
København (Copenhagen)
Helsinki (Helsingfors)
Tallinn
Riga
Göteborg (Gothenburg)
Hamburg
Kaliningrad
Gdańsk
Szczecin
Collins

RUSSIAN FEDERATION, WEST & UKRAINE

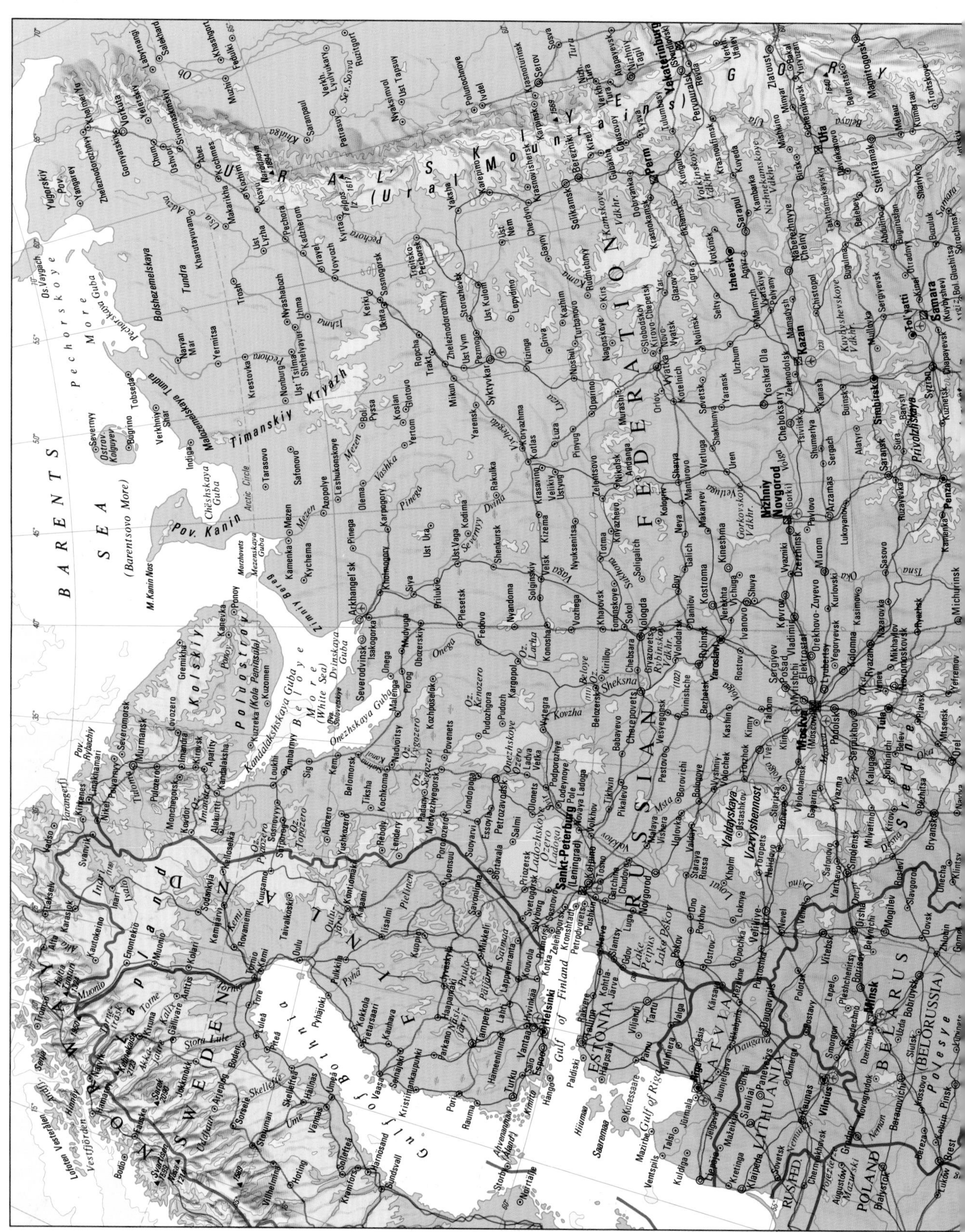
BARENTS SEA
(Barentsovo More)
Pechorskoye More
Pov. Kanin
Timanskiy Kryazh
Beloye More
(White Sea)
Kol'skiy Poluostrov
(Kola Peninsula)
URAL MOUNTAINS
RUSSIAN FEDERATION
FINLAND
SWEDEN
NORWAY
ESTONIA
LATVIA
LITHUANIA
BELARUS
(BELORUSSIA)
POLAND
Gulf of Finland
Gulf of Riga
Gulf of Bothnia
Arctic Circle
Ladozhskoye Ozero
(Ladoga)
Onezhskoye Ozero
Sankt-Peterburg
(Leningrad)
Moskva
Helsinki
Minsk
Vilnius
Riga
Tallinn
Arkhangel'sk
Murmansk
Nizhniy Novgorod
Kazan
Perm
Samara
Ufa
Yekaterinburg

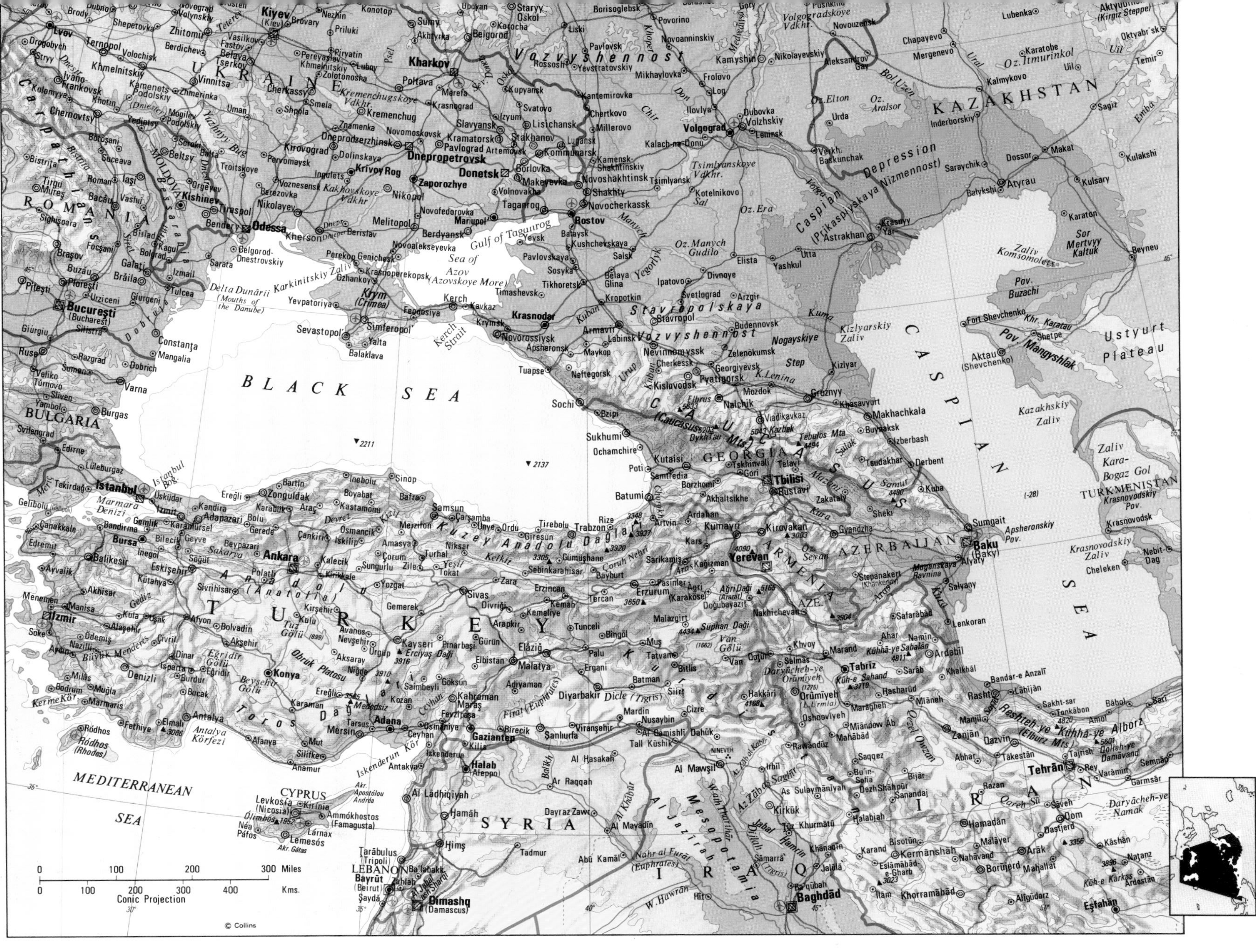
BLACK SEA
CASPIAN SEA
MEDITERRANEAN SEA
KAZAKHSTAN
UKRAINE
ROMANIA
BULGARIA
MOLDOVA
GEORGIA
ARMENIA
AZERBAIJAN
TURKMENISTAN
TURKEY
SYRIA
IRAQ
IRAN
LEBANON
CYPRUS
Caspian Depression
Ustyurt Plateau
Mesopotamia
Sea of Azov
Kharkov
Kiyev
Odessa
Volgograd
Rostov
Astrakhan
Baku
Tbilisi
Yerevan
Istanbul
Ankara
Bucureşti
Tehrān
Baghdād
Dimashq
0 100 200 300 Miles
0 100 200 300 400 Kms.
Conic Projection
© Collins

NORTH ASIA

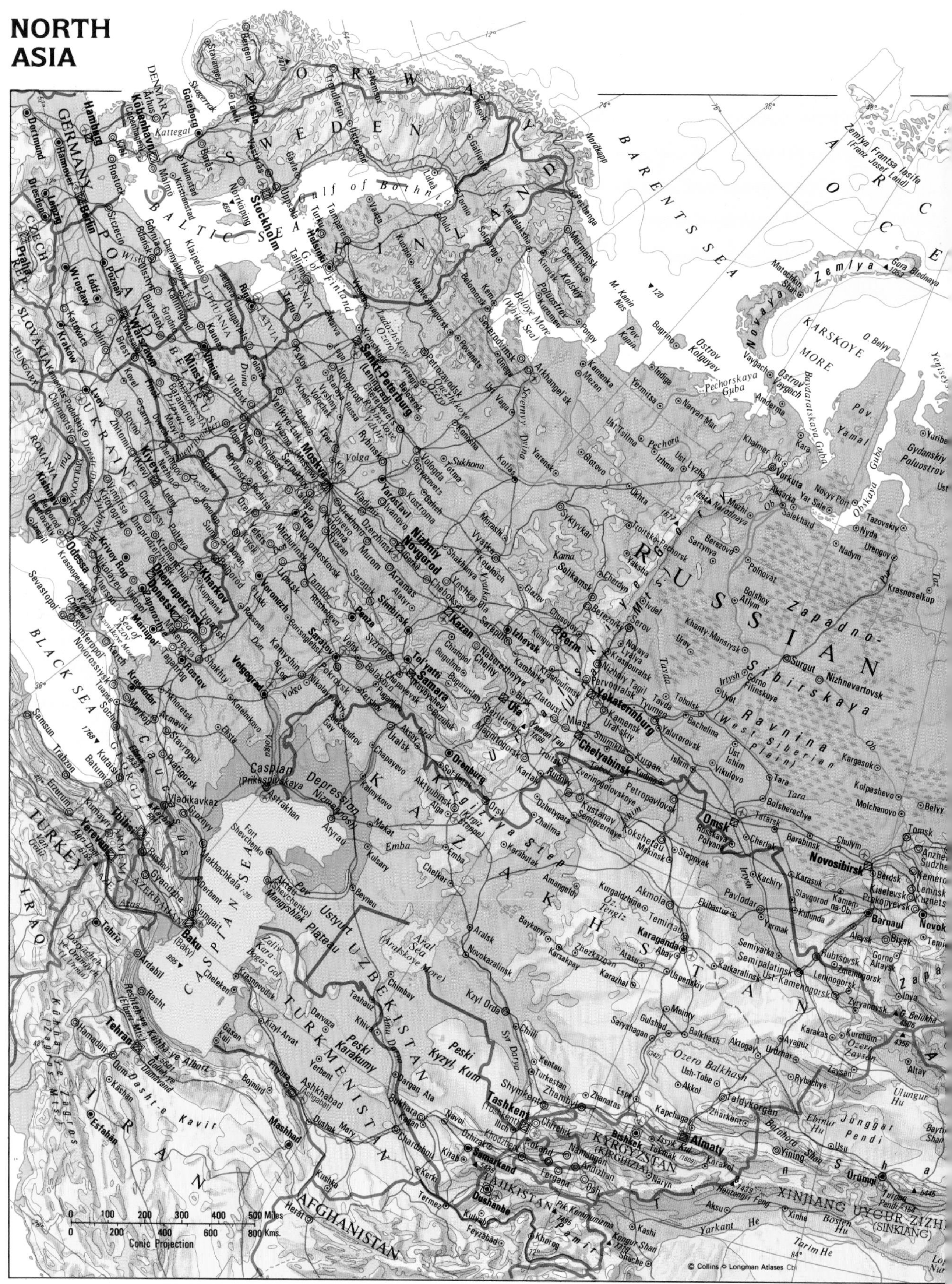
NORWAY
SWEDEN
FINLAND
DENMARK
GERMANY
POLAND
CZECH REP.
SLOVAKIA
HUNGARY
ROMANIA
UKRAINE
BELARUS
LITHUANIA
LATVIA
ESTONIA
MOLDOVA
RUSSIAN
KAZAKHSTAN
UZBEKISTAN
TURKMENISTAN
KYRGYZSTAN
TAJIKISTAN
AFGHANISTAN
IRAN
IRAQ
TURKEY
GEORGIA
ARMENIA
AZERBAIJAN
BARENTS SEA
KARSKOYE MORE
BALTIC SEA
Gulf of Bothnia
G. of Finland
BLACK SEA
CASPIAN SEA
Sea of Azov
Aral Sea
Ozero Balkhash
Novaya Zemlya
Zemlya Frantsa Iosifa (Franz Josef Land)
Zapadno-Sibirskaya Ravnina (West Siberian Plain)
Caspian Depression
Ustyurt Plateau
Peski Karakumy
Peski Kyzyl Kum
XINJIANG UYGUR ZIZHIQU (SINKIANG)
Moskva
Sankt-Peterburg (Leningrad)
Kiyev
Minsk
Warszawa
Berlin
Stockholm
Helsinki
Oslo
Kobenhavn
Praha
Riga
Vilnius
Tallinn
Nizhniy Novgorod
Kazan
Samara
Volgograd
Rostov
Kharkov
Odessa
Perm
Yekaterinburg
Chelyabinsk
Omsk
Novosibirsk
Ufa
Orenburg
Tbilisi
Yerevan
Baku
Tehran
Tashkent
Almaty
Bishkek
Dushanbe
Ashkhabad
Samarkand
Karaganda
Akmola
Urumqi
Mashhad
Esfahan
0 100 200 300 400 500 Miles
0 200 400 600 800 Kms.
Conic Projection

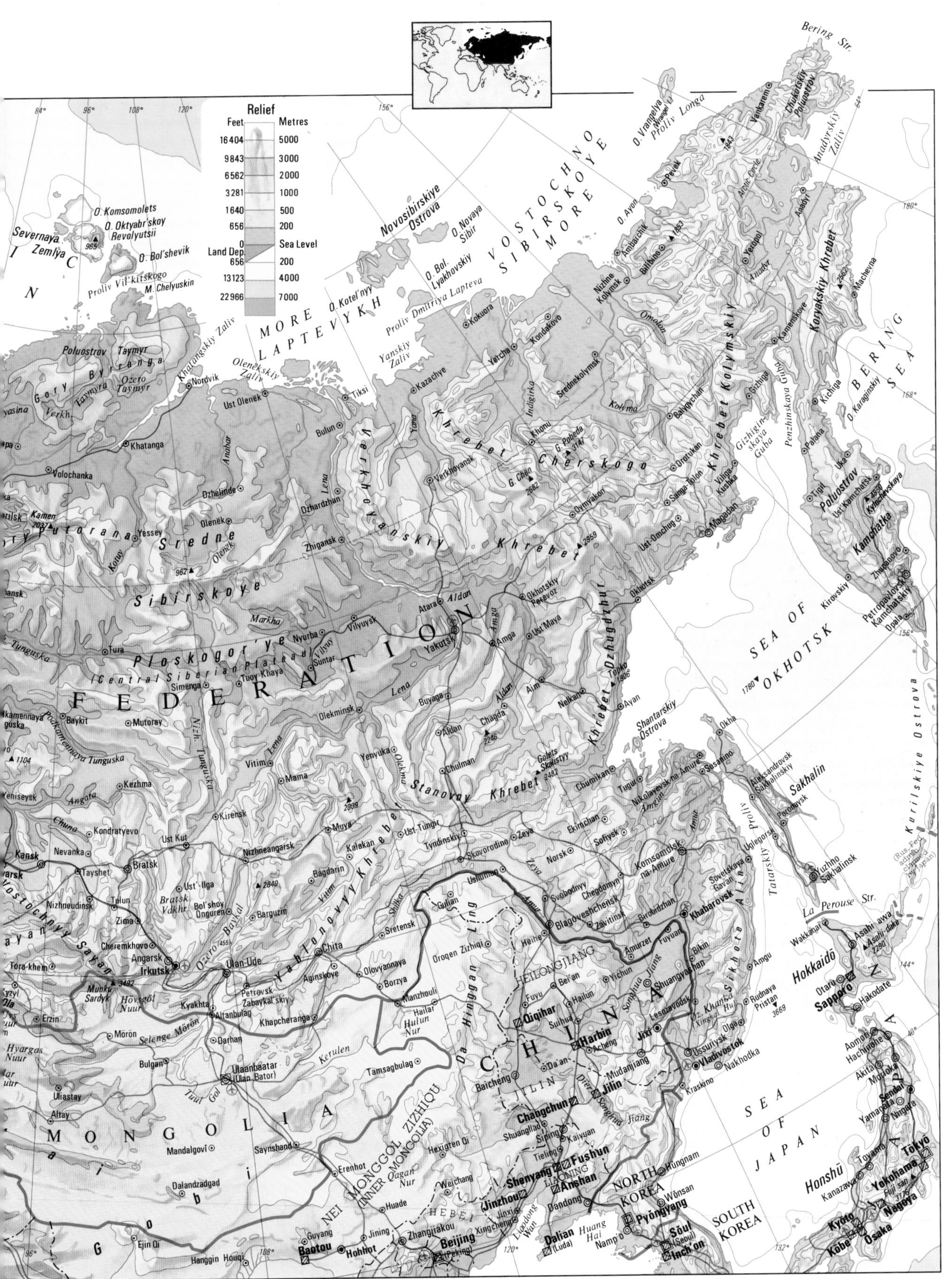

ASIA

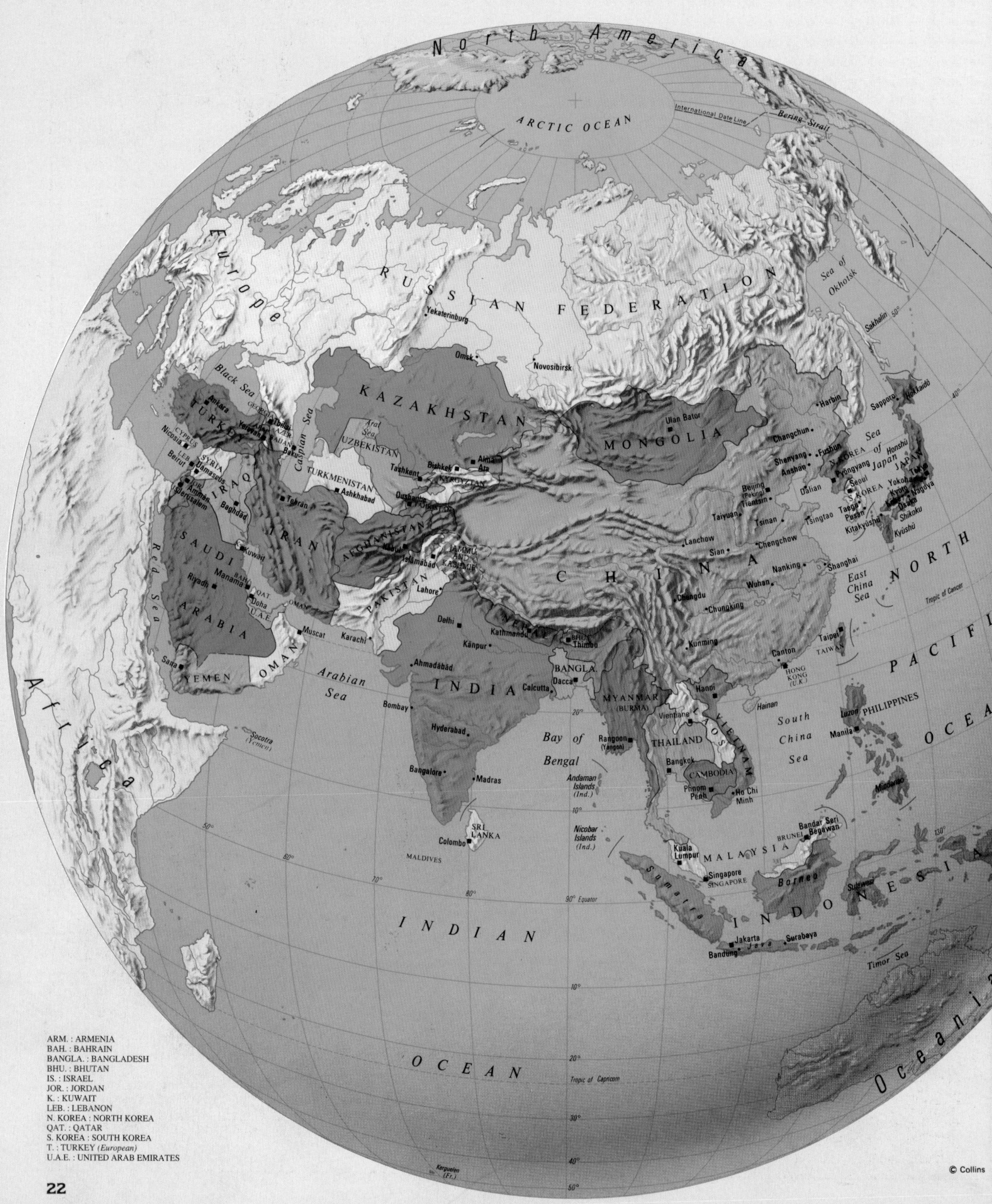

North America

ARCTIC OCEAN

International Date Line

Bering Strait

Europe

RUSSIAN FEDERATION

Yekaterinburg

Omsk

Novosibirsk

Sea of Okhotsk

Sakhalin

Black Sea

KAZAKHSTAN

Aral Sea

Caspian Sea

TURKEY

GEORGIA

Ankara

Nicosia

CYPRUS

Yerevan

ARM.

AZER.

Baku

Beirut

SYRIA

Damascus

LEB.

IS.

Amman

JOR.

Jerusalem

IRAQ

Baghdad

Tehran

IRAN

SAUDI

ARABIA

Riyadh

Manama

BAH.

QAT.

Doha

U.A.E.

OMAN

Muscat

YEMEN

Sada

Red Sea

Africa

Socotra (Yemen)

UZBEKISTAN

Tashkent

Bishkek

Almaty

Alma-Ata

TURKMENISTAN

Ashkhabad

Dushanbe

KYRGYZSTAN

TAJIKISTAN

AFGHANISTAN

Islamabad

PAKISTAN

Lahore

Kuwait

K.

Karachi

Delhi

Kanpur

Ahmadābād

INDIA

Bombay

Hyderabad

Bangalore

Madras

Colombo

SRI LANKA

MALDIVES

Arabian Sea

MONGOLIA

Ulan Bator

Changchun

Sheyang

Anshou

Beijing

Hohhot

Huhehot

Dalian

Taiyuan

Tsinan

CHINA

Lanchow

Sian

Chengchow

Chengdu

Chunking

Wuhan

Nanking

Shanghai

Kunming

Canton

HONG KONG (U.K.)

Harbin

Sapporo

Hokkaido

Sea of Japan

N. KOREA

Pyongyang

Seoul

S. KOREA

Pusan

Taegu

Honshu

Tokyo

Yokohama

Kyoto

Nagoya

Osaka

JAPAN

Kitakyūshū

Shikoku

Kyushu

East China Sea

Tsingtao

Taipei

TAIWAN

NORTH

PACIFIC

OCEAN

Tropic of Cancer

Kathmandu

NEPAL

Thimbu

BHU.

BANGLA.

Dacca

Calcutta

MYANMAR (BURMA)

Rangoon (Yangon)

Bay of Bengal

Andaman Islands (Ind.)

Nicobar Islands (Ind.)

Hanoi

Vientiane

LAOS

THAILAND

Bangkok

CAMBODIA

Phnom Penh

VIETNAM

Ho Chi Minh

Hainan

South China Sea

Luzon

PHILIPPINES

Manila

Mindoro

Kuala Lumpur

MALAYSIA

BRUNEI

Bandar Seri Begawan

Borneo

Singapore

SINGAPORE

Sumatra

Sulawesi

INDONESIA

Jakarta

Bandung

Java

Surabaya

Timor Sea

Oceania

Equator

INDIAN

OCEAN

Tropic of Capricorn

Kerguélen (Fr.)

© Collins

JAPAN

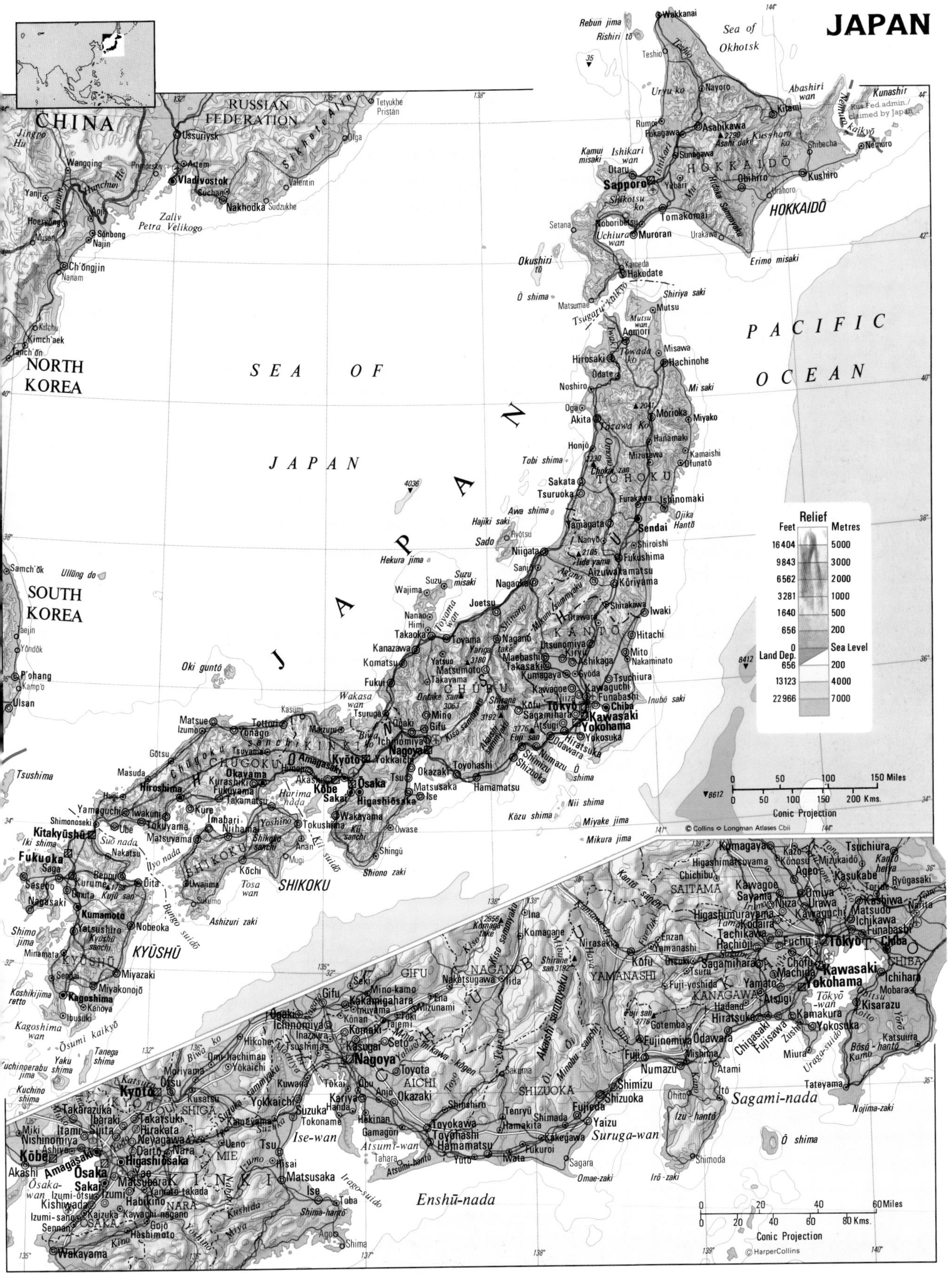

RUSSIAN FEDERATION
CHINA
NORTH KOREA
SOUTH KOREA
SEA OF JAPAN
PACIFIC OCEAN
Sea of Okhotsk
JAPAN
HOKKAIDŌ
SHIKOKU
KYŪSHŪ
TŌHOKU
KANTŌ
CHŪBU
KINKI
CHŪGOKU
Vladivostok
Nakhodka
Ussuriysk
Ch'ŏngjin
Wakkanai
Asahikawa
Sapporo
Otaru
Muroran
Tomakomai
Kushiro
Nemuro
Kitami
Hakodate
Aomori
Hachinohe
Hirosaki
Akita
Morioka
Miyako
Sendai
Yamagata
Fukushima
Niigata
Sado
Toyama
Kanazawa
Fukui
Nagano
Utsunomiya
Mito
Tōkyō
Chiba
Kawasaki
Yokohama
Yokosuka
Kōfu
Shizuoka
Hamamatsu
Nagoya
Gifu
Kyōto
Ōsaka
Kōbe
Sakai
Wakayama
Okayama
Hiroshima
Matsue
Tottori
Matsuyama
Kōchi
Tokushima
Kitakyūshū
Fukuoka
Nagasaki
Kumamoto
Ōita
Miyazaki
Kagoshima
Tsushima
Oki guntō
Relief
Feet
Metres
16404
5000
9843
3000
6562
2000
3281
1000
1640
500
656
200
0
Sea Level
Land Dep.
656
200
13123
4000
22966
7000
0
50
100
150 Miles
0
50
100
150
200 Kms.
Conic Projection
© Collins ⊙ Longman Atlases Cbii
Sagami-nada
Suruga-wan
Ise-wan
Enshū-nada
Tōkyō-wan
0
20
40
60 Miles
0
20
40
60
80 Kms.
Conic Projection
© HarperCollins

EAST ASIA

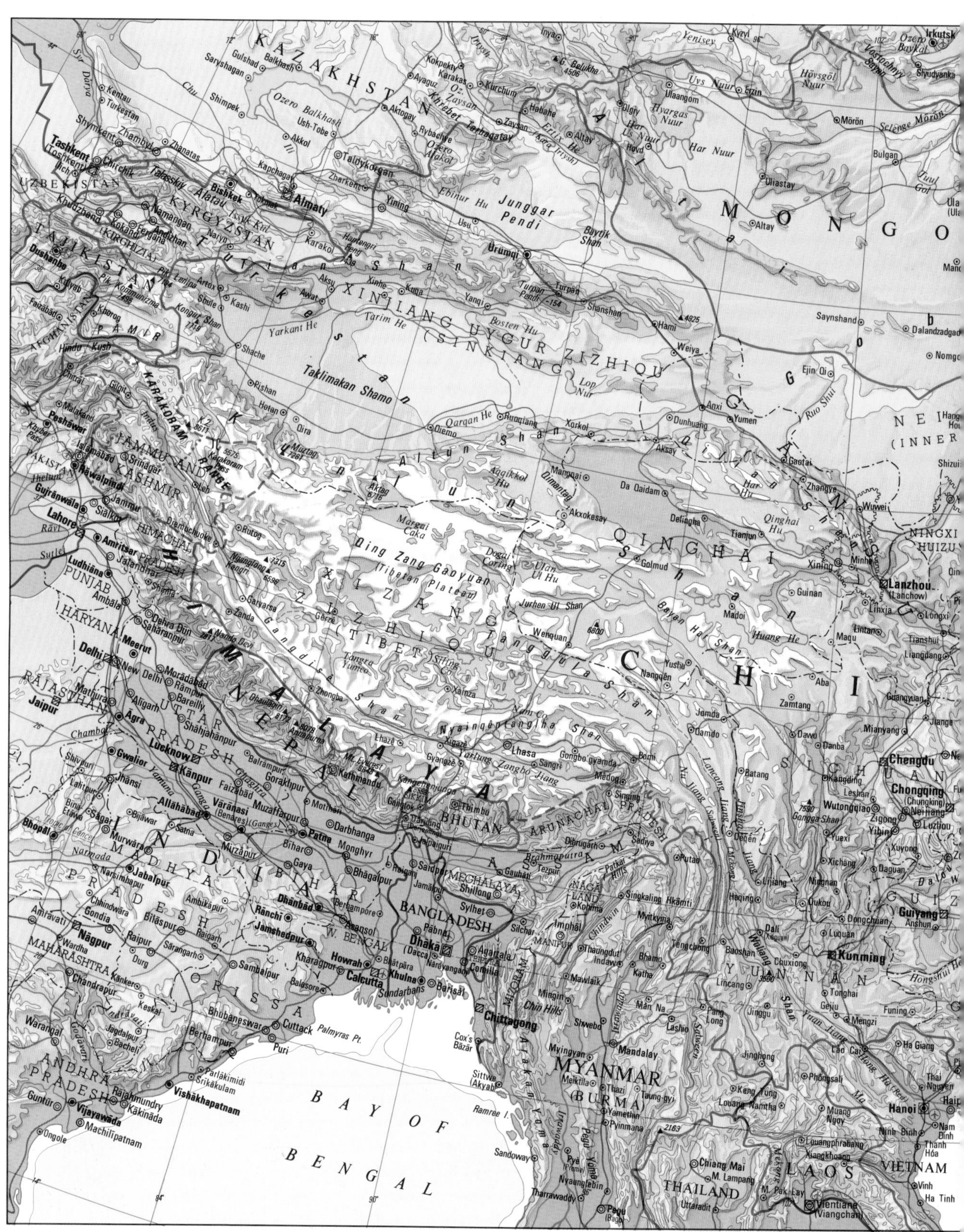

KAZAKHSTAN
Ozero Balkhash
Almaty
Bishkek
KYRGYZSTAN
(KIRGHIZIA)
Tashkent
(Toshkent)
UZBEKISTAN
TAJIKISTAN
Dushanbe
AFGHANISTAN
PAMIR
Hindu Kush
KARAKORAM
JAMMU AND KASHMIR
PAKISTAN
Islamabad
Rawalpindi
Lahore
Peshawar
Amritsar
HIMACHAL PRADESH
PUNJAB
HARYANA
Delhi
New Delhi
RAJASTHAN
Jaipur
UTTAR PRADESH
Agra
Lucknow
Kanpur
Gwalior
Allahabad
Varanasi
(Benares)
MADHYA PRADESH
Bhopal
Jabalpur
Nagpur
MAHARASHTRA
ORISSA
ANDHRA PRADESH
Vishakhapatnam
Vijayawada
Cuttack
Calcutta
Howrah
W. BENGAL
BIHAR
Patna
Ranchi
Jamshedpur
INDIA
NEPAL
Kathmandu
Mt. Everest
BHUTAN
Thimbu
BANGLADESH
Dhaka
(Dacca)
Khulna
Chittagong
MEGHALAYA
ASSAM
ARUNACHAL PRADESH
NAGALAND
MANIPUR
MIZORAM
MYANMAR
(BURMA)
Mandalay
Pegu
(Bago)
BAY OF BENGAL
THAILAND
Chiang Mai
LAOS
Vientiane
(Viangchan)
VIETNAM
Hanoi
HIMALAYA
XIZANG ZIZHIQU
(TIBET)
Lhasa
Qing Zang Gaoyuan
(Tibetan Plateau)
Kunlun Shan
XINJIANG UYGUR ZIZHIQU
(SINKIANG)
Taklimakan Shamo
Tarim He
Tian Shan
Junggar Pendi
Ürümqi
Turpan Pendi
QINGHAI
Qinghai Hu
Xining
Lanzhou
(Lanchow)
SICHUAN
Chengdu
Chongqing
(Chungking)
YUNNAN
Kunming
Guiyang
Altai
MONGOLIA
Gobi
Irkutsk
Ozero Baykal
NEI MONGOL
(INNER
NINGXIA HUIZU
CHINA
Bay of Bengal

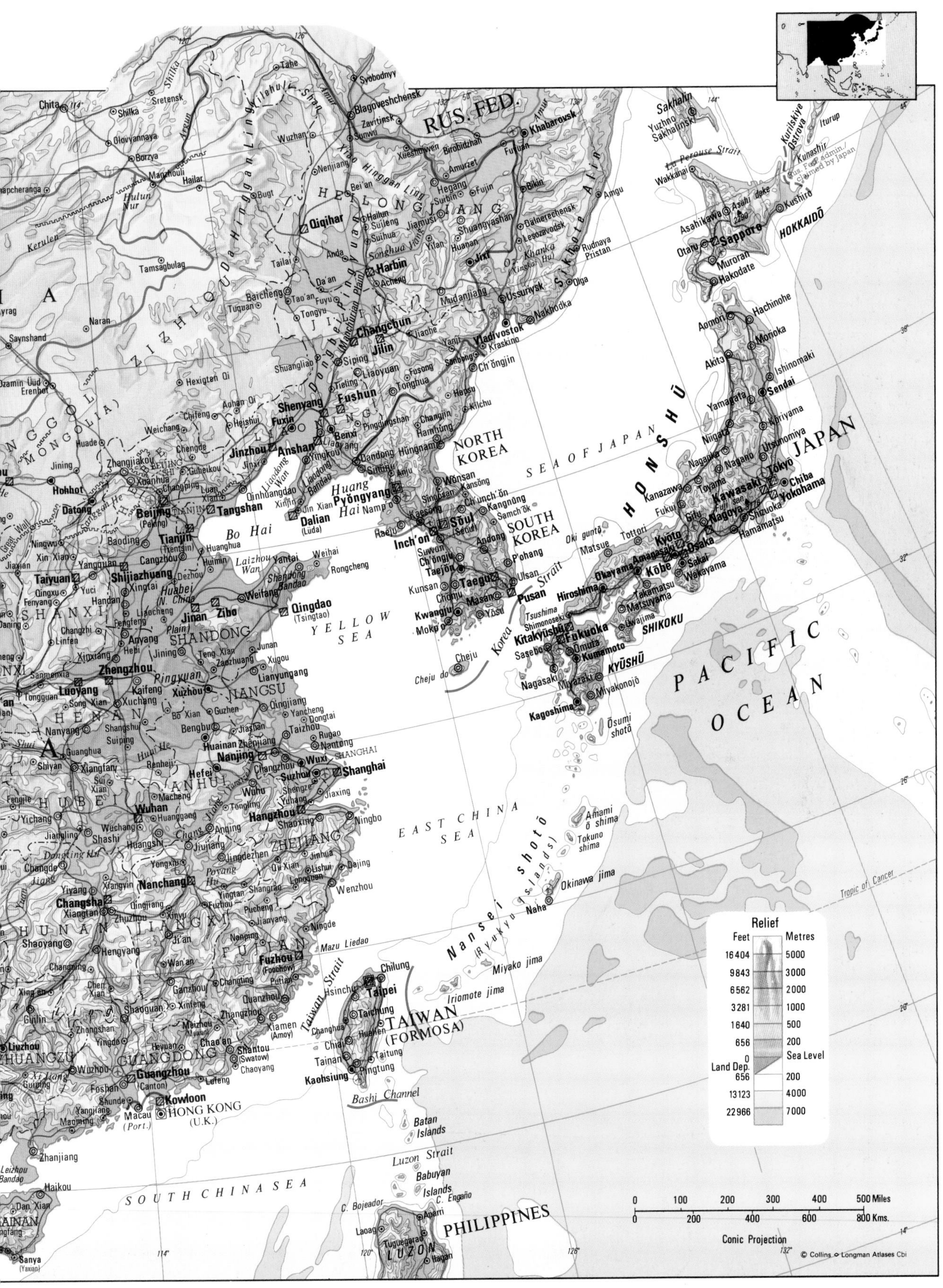

RUS. FED.

HEILONGJIANG

Chita
Shilka
Sretensk
Olovyannaya
Borzya
Tamsagbulag
Hailar
Hulun Nur
Kerulen
Saynshand
Zamin Uud
Erenhot
(MONGOLIA)
Jining
Naran
Hohhot
Datong
BEIJING
Zhangjiakou
Baoding
Tianjin (Tientsin)
Tangshan
Taiyuan
SHANXI
Shijiazhuang
Cangzhou
Jinan
Zibo
SHANDONG
Qingdao (Tsingtao)
Zhengzhou
HENAN
Luoyang
Kaifeng
Xuzhou
JIANGSU
Nanjing
Hefei
ANHUI
Wuhan
HUBEI
Wuxi
Suzhou
SHANGHAI
Shanghai
Hangzhou
ZHEJIANG
Ningbo
EAST CHINA SEA
Nanchang
Changsha
HUNAN
JIANGXI
FUJIAN
Fuzhou (Foochow)
Xiamen (Amoy)
TAIWAN STRAIT
Taipei
Taichung
TAIWAN (FORMOSA)
Kaohsiung
Liuzhou
GUANGDONG
Guangzhou (Canton)
Kowloon
HONG KONG (U.K.)
Macau (Port.)
Zhanjiang
Haikou
HAINAN
Sanya (Yaxian)
SOUTH CHINA SEA
PHILIPPINES
LUZON
Luzon Strait
Babuyan Islands
Batan Islands
Bashi Channel

Qiqihar
Harbin
Changchun
Jilin
JILIN
Shenyang
Fushun
Fuxin
Anshan
Jinzhou
LIAONING
Dalian (Lüda)
Bo Hai
YELLOW SEA
Huang Hai
Weifang
Yantai

Khabarovsk
Vladivostok
Ussuriysk
SIKHOTE ALIN
SEA OF JAPAN

NORTH KOREA
Pyongyang
Namp'o
SOUTH KOREA
Seoul
Inch'on
Suwon
Taejon
Taegu
Kwangju
Mokp'o
Pusan
Masan
Cheju do
Korea Strait

Sakhalin
Yuzhno-Sakhalinsk
La Perouse Strait
Wakkanai
HOKKAIDO
Asahikawa
Sapporo
Otaru
Muroran
Hakodate
Aomori
HONSHU
Akita
Sendai
Niigata
Nagano
Tokyo
Kawasaki
Yokohama
Nagoya
Kyoto
Osaka
Kobe
Hiroshima
SHIKOKU
Fukuoka
Kitakyushu
Nagasaki
KYUSHU
Kumamoto
Kagoshima
Osumi shoto
JAPAN
PACIFIC OCEAN
Nansei shoto (Ryukyu Islands)
Okinawa jima
Naha
Amami o shima
Tropic of Cancer

Relief

Feet		Metres
16 404		5000
9843		3000
6562		2000
3281		1000
1640		500
656		200
0		Sea Level
Land Dep.		
656		200
13123		4000
22966		7000

Scale:
0 100 200 300 400 500 Miles
0 200 400 600 800 Kms.

Conic Projection

25

SOUTHEAST ASIA

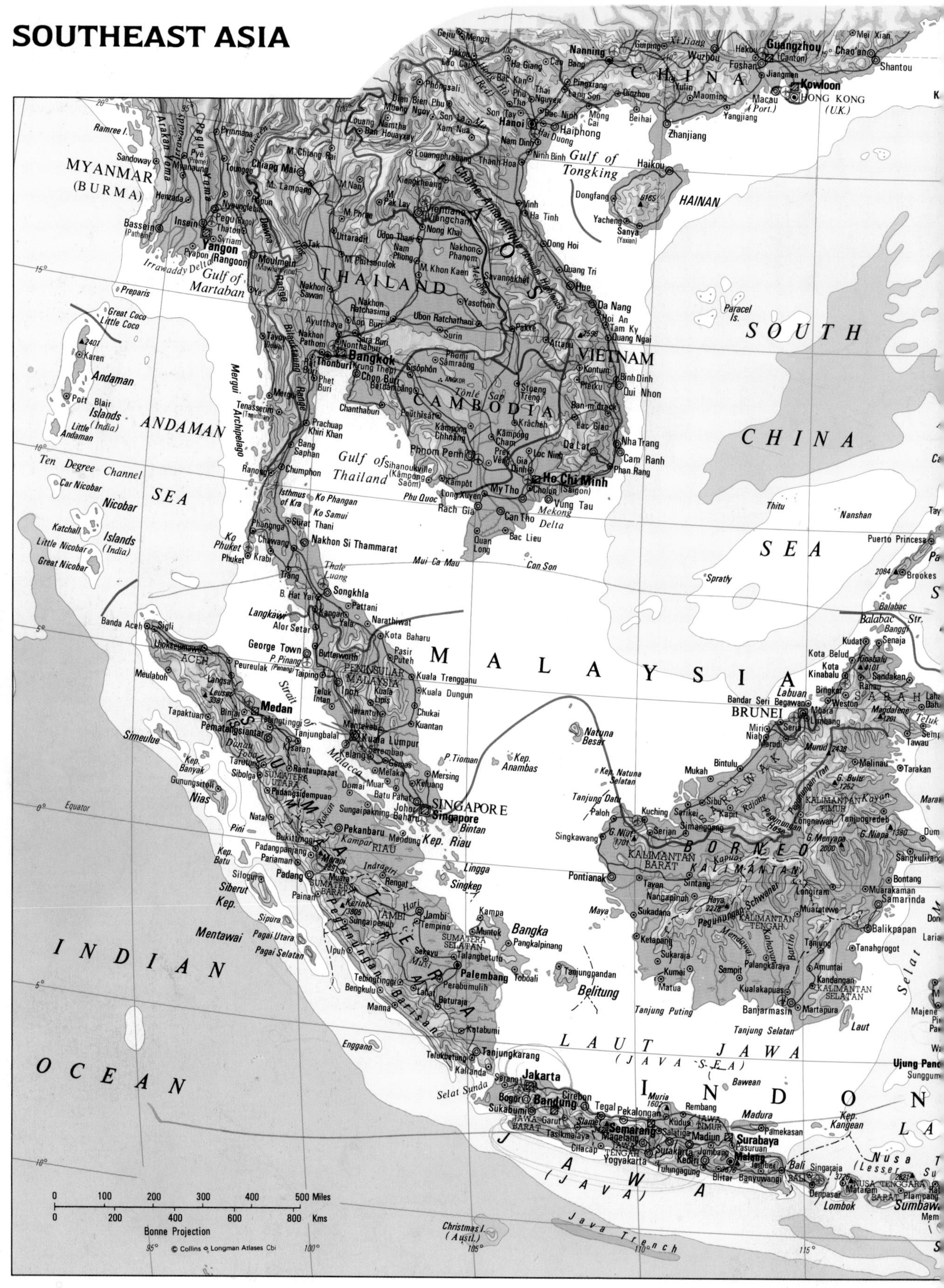
CHINA
Nanning
Guangzhou (Canton)
Kowloon
HONG KONG (U.K.)
Macau (Port.)
Shantou
Zhanjiang
Haikou
HAINAN
Gulf of Tongking
Hanoi
Haiphong
LAOS
Vientiane (Viangchan)
MYANMAR (BURMA)
Yangon (Rangoon)
Bassein (Pathein)
Moulmein
Gulf of Martaban
Irrawaddy Delta
THAILAND
Chiang Mai
Bangkok
Thonburi
Nakhon Ratchasima
Ubon Ratchathani
VIETNAM
Hue
Da Nang
Qui Nhon
Nha Trang
Da Lat
Ho Chi Minh (Saigon)
Mekong Delta
CAMBODIA
Phnom Penh
Gulf of Thailand
Paracel Is.
SOUTH CHINA SEA
Spratly
ANDAMAN SEA
Andaman Islands (India)
Port Blair
Nicobar Islands (India)
Ten Degree Channel
Mergui Archipelago
Phuket
Songkhla
MALAYSIA
PENINSULAR MALAYSIA
George Town
Kuala Lumpur
SINGAPORE
Singapore
Strait of Malacca
BRUNEI
Bandar Seri Begawan
SABAH
SARAWAK
Kuching
Kota Kinabalu
Labuan
Natuna Besar
BORNEO
KALIMANTAN
Pontianak
Banjarmasin
Balikpapan
Samarinda
SUMATERA
Medan
Padang
Pekanbaru
Palembang
Jambi
Bengkulu
Tanjungkarang
Nias
Siberut
Mentawai Kep.
Bangka
Belitung
Singkep
Lingga
Kep. Riau
LAUT JAWA (JAVA SEA)
JAWA (JAVA)
Jakarta
Bandung
Semarang
Surabaya
Yogyakarta
Malang
Madura
Bali
Lombok
Sumbawa
Nusa Tenggara (Lesser Sunda)
INDONESIA
Selat Sunda
Christmas I. (Austl.)
Java Trench
INDIAN OCEAN
Equator
0 100 200 300 400 500 Miles
0 200 400 600 800 Kms
Bonne Projection
© Collins - Longman Atlases Cbi

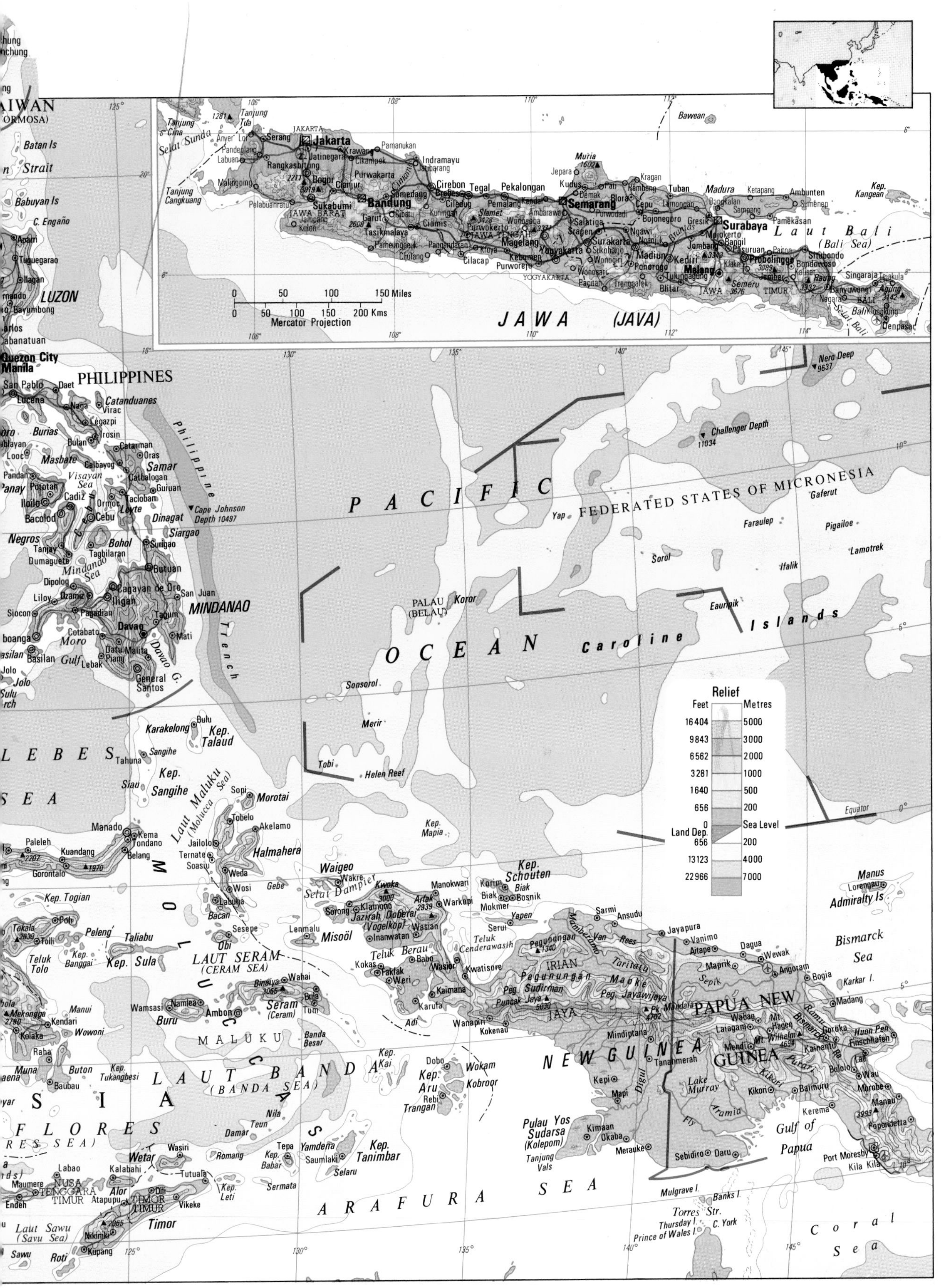

TAIWAN
(FORMOSA)

Batan Is

Strait

Babuyan Is

C. Engaño

Aparri
Tuguegarao
Ilagan
LUZON
Bayombong
Bambang

Quezon City
Manila
San Pablo
Lucena
Daet
Naga
Virac
Catanduanes
Légazpi
Irosin
Sorsogon
Burias
Masbate
Catarman
Samar
Catbalogan
Guiuan

*Visayan
Sea*
Iloilo
Cadiz
Cebu
Tacloban
Ormoc
Leyte
Negros
Tanjay
Bohol
Tagbilaran
Surigao
Siargao
Dinagat
Dumaguete
Butuan
*Mindanao
Sea*
Cagayan de Oro
Dipolog
Ozamiz
Iligan
San Juan
MINDANAO
Pagadian
Tagum
Cotabato
Davao
Moro
Datu Piang
Mati
Gulf
General G.
Santos
Zamboanga
Basilan
Jolo
Sulu
Arch

CELEBES

SEA

Tahuna

Kep.
Talaud

Karakelong

Bulu

Sangihe
Siau
Kep.
Sangihe

Manado
Tondano
Kema
Tobelo
Akelamo
Palaleh
Kuandang
Belang
Gorontalo

Sopi
Morotai

Halmahera
Jailolo
Ternate
Soasiu
Weda
Gebe

Kep.
Togian

Poso
Peleng
Taliabu

Tokala
Tolli
Teluk
Tolo

*Teluk
Banggai*
Manui
Kep. Sula
LAUT SERAM
(CERAM SEA)

Wamsasi
Namlea
Buru

Wowoni
Ambon

Mekongga
Kolaka
Kendari

M
O
L
U
C
C
A

S

Obi
Bacan
Sesepe

Misoöl

Lenmalu
Inanwatan

LAUT BANDA
(BANDA SEA)

Wasiri
Romang
Tepa
Yamdena

FLORES
(RES SEA)

Wetar

Labao
Kalabahi
Maumere
**NUSA
TENGGARA
TIMUR**
Alor
Atapupu
Dili
**TIMOR
TIMUR**
Vikeke
Timor

*Laut Sawu
(Savu Sea)*
Kupang
Sawu
Roti

PHILIPPINES

JAWA (JAVA)

Tanjung Tua
1281
JAKARTA
Anyer
Serang
Jakarta
Pamanukan
Labuan
Jatinegara
Krawang
Indramayu
Rangkasbitung
Cikampek
Bogor
Cianjur
Cirebon
Tegal
Pekalongan
Malingping
Sukabumi
Bandung
Cifebon
Pemalang
Kudus
Pati
Kragan
Tuban
Madura
Ketapang
Ambunten
Kep.
Kangean
JAWA BARAT
Garut
Ciamis
Purwokerto
Wonosobo
Salatiga
Blora
Cepu
Bojonegoro
Gresik
Bangkalan
Pamekasan
Sumenep
Pelabuanratu
Tjampuhan
Kroya
Purwokerto
**JAWA
TENGAH**
Magelang
Semarang
Sragen
Surakarta
Ngawi
Jombang
Surabaya
Pandangaran
Cilacap
YOGYAKARTA
Wonogiri
Madiun
Kediri
Sidoarjo
Probolinggo
Bondowoso
Situbondo
Banyuwangi
Purworejo
Pacitan
Ponorogo
Tulungagung
Malang
Jember
**JAWA
TIMUR**
Semeru
3676
Agung
3142
Denpasar
Blitar
Trenggalek
Negara
Singaraja
Bali

*Laut Bali
(Bali Sea)*

PACIFIC

OCEAN

Challenger Depth
11034

FEDERATED STATES OF MICRONESIA
Yap
Gaferut
Faraulep
Pigailoe
Sorol
Ifalik
Lamotrek
Eauripik

PALAU
(BELAU)
Koror

Sonsorol
Caroline *Islands*

Merir

Tobi
Helen Reef

Equator

Waigeo
Wakre
Manokwari
**Kep.
Schouten**
Biak
Bosnik
Mokmer
Manus
Lorengau
Admiralty Is

Selat Dampier
Sorong
Klamono
Arfak
2939
Warkopi
Yapen
Sarmi
Ansudu
**Bismarck
Sea**
Karkar I.

Jazirah Doberai
(Vogelkop)
Wasian
Serui
Teluk
Cenderawasih
Jayapura
Vanimo
Dagua
Wewak
Angoram
Bogia
Madang

Kokas
Teluk Berau
Babo
Wasior
Pegunungan
1340
Van Rees
Aitape
Maprik
Sepik

Faktak
Weri
Kaimana
IRIN
Karufa
Wanapiri
JAYA
Nabire
Pegunungan
Sudirman
Puncak Jaya
5030
Mandala
4700
Wabag
Mt.
Wilhelm
4694
Goroka
Kainantu
PAPUA NEW

Binaiya
3055
Wahai
Bula
Tum
Seram
(Ceram)
Banda
Besar
Adi
Kokenau

Kep.
Kai
Dobo
Wokam
Kimaan
Mindiptanah
Tanahmerah
Mt.
Hagen
Mendi
GUINEA
Bulolo
Lae
Huon Pen.
Finschhafen
Wau
Morobe

M
A
L
U
K
U

Kep.
Aru
Rebi
Trangan
Kepi
Mapi
Lake
Murray
Kikori
Balimuru

Nila
Damar
Teun
Kep.
Tanimbar
Pulau Yos
Sudarsa
(Kolepom)
Okaba
Merauke
Digul
NEW GUINEA
Kerema
Aramia
Fly
Popondetta

Saumlaki
Kep.
Babar
Kep.
Leti
Sermata
Tanjung
Vals
Sebidiro
Daru
**Gulf of
Papua**
Port Moresby
Kila Kila

Mulgrave I.
Banks I.
Torres Str.
Thursday I.
C. York
Prince of Wales I.
**Coral
Sea**

ARAFURA SEA

Relief

Feet		Metres
16 404		5000
9843		3000
6562		2000
3281		1000
1640		500
656		200
0	Sea Level	
Land Dep.		
656		200
13123		4000
22 966		7000

SOUTH ASIA

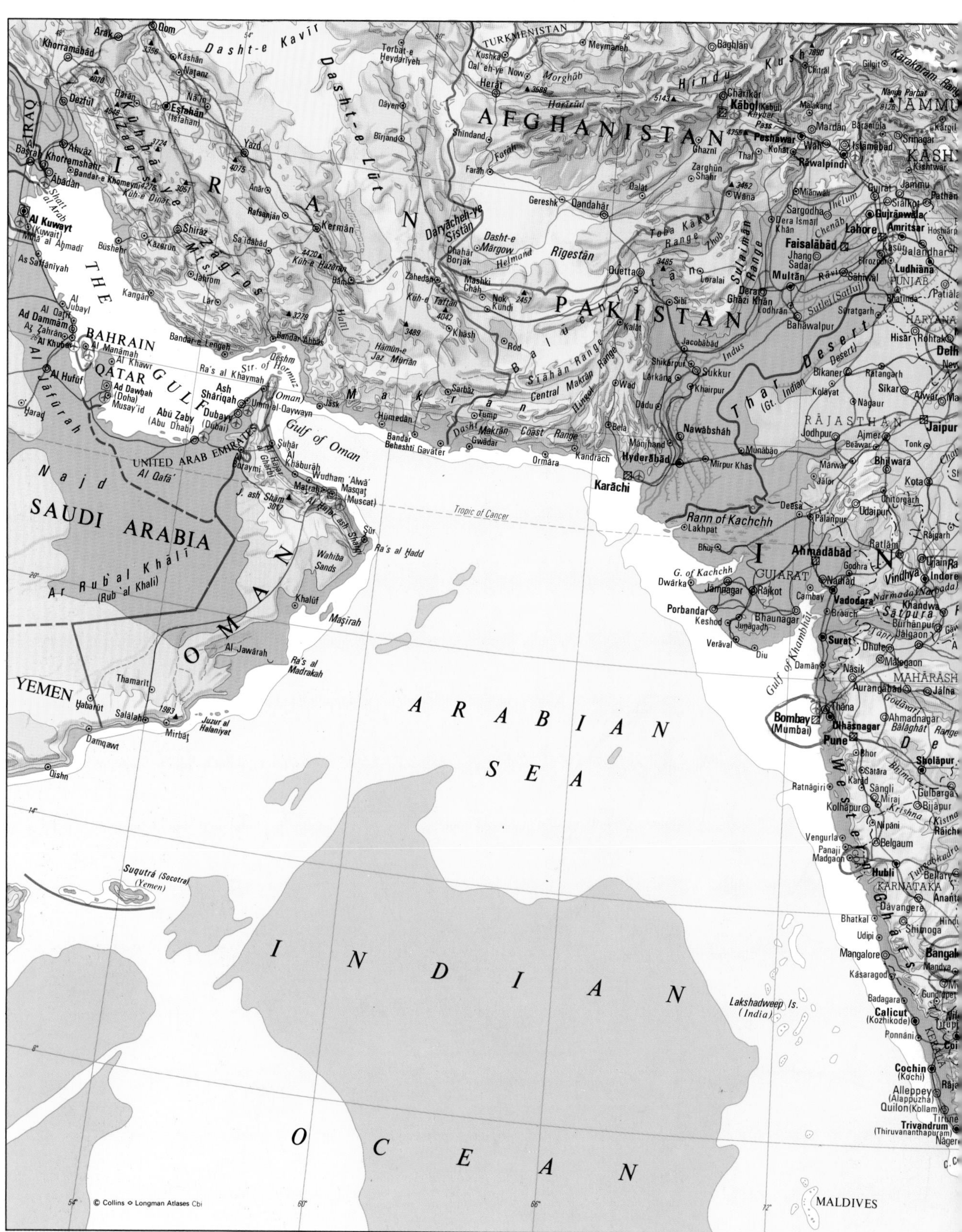

Qom
Arāk
Khorramābād
Kāshān
Naţanz
Dasht-e Kavīr
Dasht-e Lūt
Torbat-e Heydarīyeh
TURKMENISTAN
Meymaneh
Baghlān
Kushka
Qal'eh-ye Now
Morghāb
Herāt
Harīrūd
Hindu Kush
Chitral
Gilgit
Karakoram Range
Nanga Parbat
Chārīkār
Kābol (Kabul)
Khyber Pass
Malakand
Mardān
Bāramūla
Srinagar
JAMMU
KASH
Kishtwar
Kārgil
Dezfūl
IRAQ
Ahvāz
Basrah
Khorramshahr
Ābādān
Bandar-e Khomeynī
Dārān
Eşfahān (Isfahan)
Nā'īn
Yazd
Qāyen
Bīrjand
Shīndand
Farāh
AFGHANISTAN
Ghaznī
Peshawar
Kohāt
Thal
Wah
Islāmābād
Rāwalpindi
Zarghūn Shahr
Wāna
Qalāt
Gereshk
Qandahār
Mianwāli
Gujrāt
Jammu
Pathān
Sargodha
Jhelum
Sialkot
Gujrānwāla
Dera Ismāīl Khān
Chenāb
Lahore
Amritsar
Faisalābād
Jhang Sadar
Kasur
Jalandhar
Multān
Rāvi
Sāhīwāl
Ludhiāna
PUNJAB
Firozpur
Bhatinda
Patiāla
Al Kuwayt (Kuwait)
Shatt al Arab
Mīnā' al Aḩmadī
Būshehr
Kāzerūn
Shīrāz
Zagros Mts.
Kūh-e Dīnār
Zāgros
Kūhhā-ye
Rafsanjān
Anār
Kermān
Sa'īdābād
Kūh-e Hazārān
Bam
IRAN
Daryācheh-ye Sīstān
Chahār Borjak
Dasht-e Mārgow
Helmand
Rīgestān
Quetta
Toba Kākar Range
Zhob
Loralai
Sulaiman Range
Dera Ghāzi Khān
Lodhrān
Bahāwalpur
Sutlej (Satluj)
Suratgarh
HARYANA
As Saffānīyah
THE
Jahrom
Kangān
Lār
Zāhedān
Mashki Chāh
Nok Kundi
Kūh-e Taftān
Sibi
PAKISTAN
Balūchistān
Kalāt
Jacobābād
Hisār
Rohtak
Delh
Al Jubayl
Al Qaţīf
Ad Dammām
Az Zahrān
Al Khubar
BAHRAIN
Al Manāmah
Al Khawr
QATAR
Ad Dawḩah (Doha)
Musay'īd
Al Hufūf
Al Jāfūrah
Ḩaraḑ
Bandar-e Lengeh
Bandar Abbās
Qeshm
Str. of Hormuz
Ra's al Khaymah
Ash Shāriqah
Umm al Qaywayn
Dubayy (Dubai)
Abū Zaby (Abu Dhabi)
GULF
Jāsk
Hāmūn-e Jaz Mūrīān
Khāsh
Rod
Siāhān Range
Central Makrān Range
Hingol
Wad
Shikārpur
Sukkur
Khairpur
Lārkāna
Thar Desert (Gt. Indian Desert)
Indus
Bikaner
Ratangarh
Sikar
Alwar
Kolāyat
Nāgaur
RĀJASTHĀN
Jaipur
Dādu
Nawābshāh
Jodhpur
Ajmer
Beāwar
Tonk
Sarbāz
Makrān
Tump
Humedān
Dasht
Makrān Coast Range
Gwādar
Bandar Beheshtī
Gavāter
Ormāra
Kandrāch
Bela
Manjhand
Hyderābād
Mīrpur Khās
Munābāo
Karāchi
Mārwār
Bhīlwara
Kota
Jālor
Chitorgarh
Udaipur
Deesa
Pālanpur
Rann of Kachchh
Lakhpat
Bhuj
UNITED ARAB EMIRATES
Al Qafā'
Najd
SAUDI ARABIA
Al Buraymī
Şuḩār
Al Khābūrah
Gulf of Oman
Wudham 'Alwā'
Maţraḩ
Masqaţ (Muscat)
J. ash Shām
Ṣūr
Ra's al Ḩadd
Tropic of Cancer
Wahiba Sands
Ar Rub' al Khālī (Rub 'al Khali)
OMAN
Khalūf
Maşīrah
Al Jawārah
Ra's al Madrakah
YEMEN
Thamarīt
Ḩabarūt
Şalālah
Mirbāţ
Juzur al Ḩalāniyāt
Damqawt
Qishn
Ahmadābād
Godhra
Vindhya
Indore
G. of Kachchh
GUJARAT
Dwārka
Jāmnagar
Rājkot
Nadiad
Cambay
Vadodara
Narmada
Khandwa
Sātpura
Porbandar
Keshod
Junāgadh
Bhaunagar
Broach
Burhānpur
Jalgaon
Verāval
Diu
Gulf of Khambhāt
Surat
Dhule
Mālegaon
Damān
Nāsik
MAHĀRĀSH
Aurangābād
Jālna
Godāvari
Thāna
Ahmadnagar
Bālāghāt Range
Bombay (Mumbai)
Ulhāsnagar
Pune
Bhor
Sholāpur
Sātāra
Karād
Sāngli
Miraj
Gulbarga
Bījāpur
Ratnāgiri
Kolhāpur
Krishna
Nipāni
Rāichur
Vengurla
Belgaum
Panaji
Madgaon
Western Ghats
Hubli
Tungabhadra
Bellary
KARNATAKA
Anant
Dāvangere
Bhatkal
Shimoga
Udipi
Mangalore
Bangal
Mandya
Kāsaragod
Badagara
Calicut (Kozhikode)
Ponnāni
KERALA
Cochin (Kochi)
Alleppey (Alappuzha)
Quilon (Kollam)
Trivandrum (Thiruvananthapuram)
Nāger
ARABIAN SEA
Suquṭrá (Socotra) (Yemen)
Lakshadweep Is. (India)
INDIAN OCEAN
MALDIVES
© Collins ◇ Longman Atlases Cbi

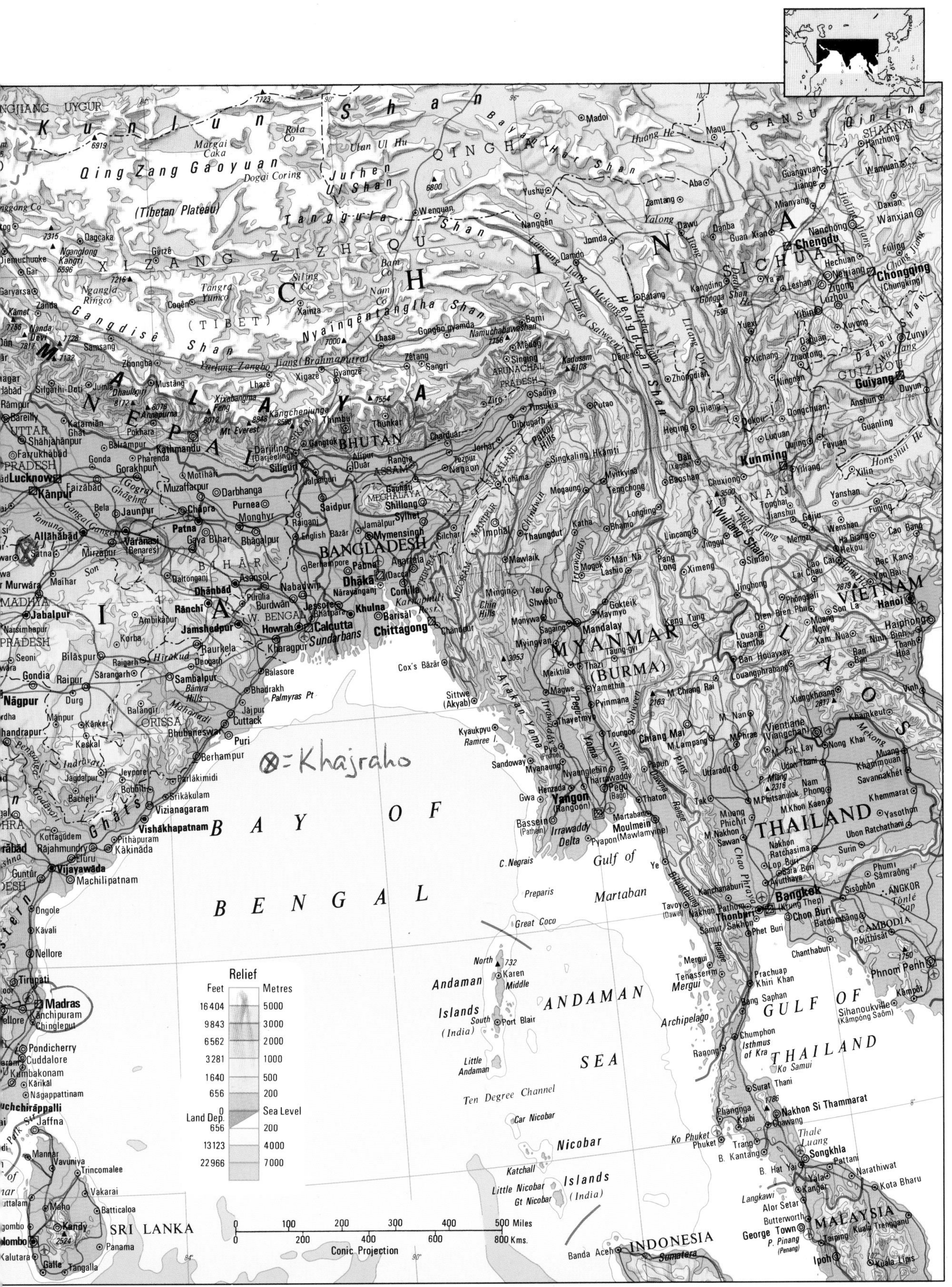

K u n l u n S h a n
Qing Zang Gaoyuan
(Tibetan Plateau)
Tanggula Shan
XIZANG ZIZHIQU
(TIBET)
Gangdisê Shan
Nyainqêntanglha Shan
QINGHAI
Bayan Har Shan
GANSU
Qinling
SHAANXI
SICHUAN
C H I N A
GUIZHOU
YUNNAN
Hengduan Shan
Lhasa
Chengdu
Chongqing (Chungking)
Kunming
Guiyang
H I M A L A Y A
Mt Everest 8848
Kangchenjunga 8598
Annapurna 8078
NEPAL
Kathmandu
BHUTAN
Thimbu
ARUNACHAL PRADESH
ASSAM
MEGHALAYA
NAGALAND
MANIPUR
MIZORAM
TRIPURA
BANGLADESH
Dhākā (Dacca)
Chittagong
Khulna
Sundarbans
I N D I A
UTTAR PRADESH
MADHYA PRADESH
BIHĀR
W. BENGAL
ORISSA
Lucknow
Kānpur
Allāhābād
Vārānasi (Benares)
Patna
Calcutta
Howrah
Jamshedpur
Rānchi
Jabalpur
Nāgpur
Cuttack
Bhubaneswar
Vishākhapatnam
Vijayawāda
Madras
Pondicherry
Jaffna
Trincomalee
Kandy
Colombo
Galle
SRI LANKA
Eastern Ghats
MYANMAR (BURMA)
Mandalay
Yangon (Rangoon)
Moulmein (Mawlamyine)
Sittwe (Akyab)
Irrawaddy Delta
Arakan Yoma
Pegu Yoma
VIETNAM
Hanoi
Haiphong
L A O S
Vientiane (Viangchan)
THAILAND
Bangkok (Krung Thep)
Chiang Mai
CAMBODIA
Phnom Penh
ANGKOR
Tonlé Sap
MALAYSIA
George Town
Kuala Lipis
Ipoh
INDONESIA
Sumatera
Banda Aceh
B A Y O F B E N G A L
Gulf of Martaban
A N D A M A N S E A
Andaman Islands (India)
Port Blair
Ten Degree Channel
Nicobar Islands (India)
G U L F O F T H A I L A N D
Isthmus of Kra
Mergui Archipelago
Relief
Feet
Metres
16404
5000
9843
3000
6562
2000
3281
1000
1640
500
656
200
0
Sea Level
Land Dep.
656
200
13123
4000
22966
7000
0 100 200 300 400 500 Miles
0 200 400 600 800 Kms.
Conic Projection
⊗=Khajraho

SOUTHWEST ASIA

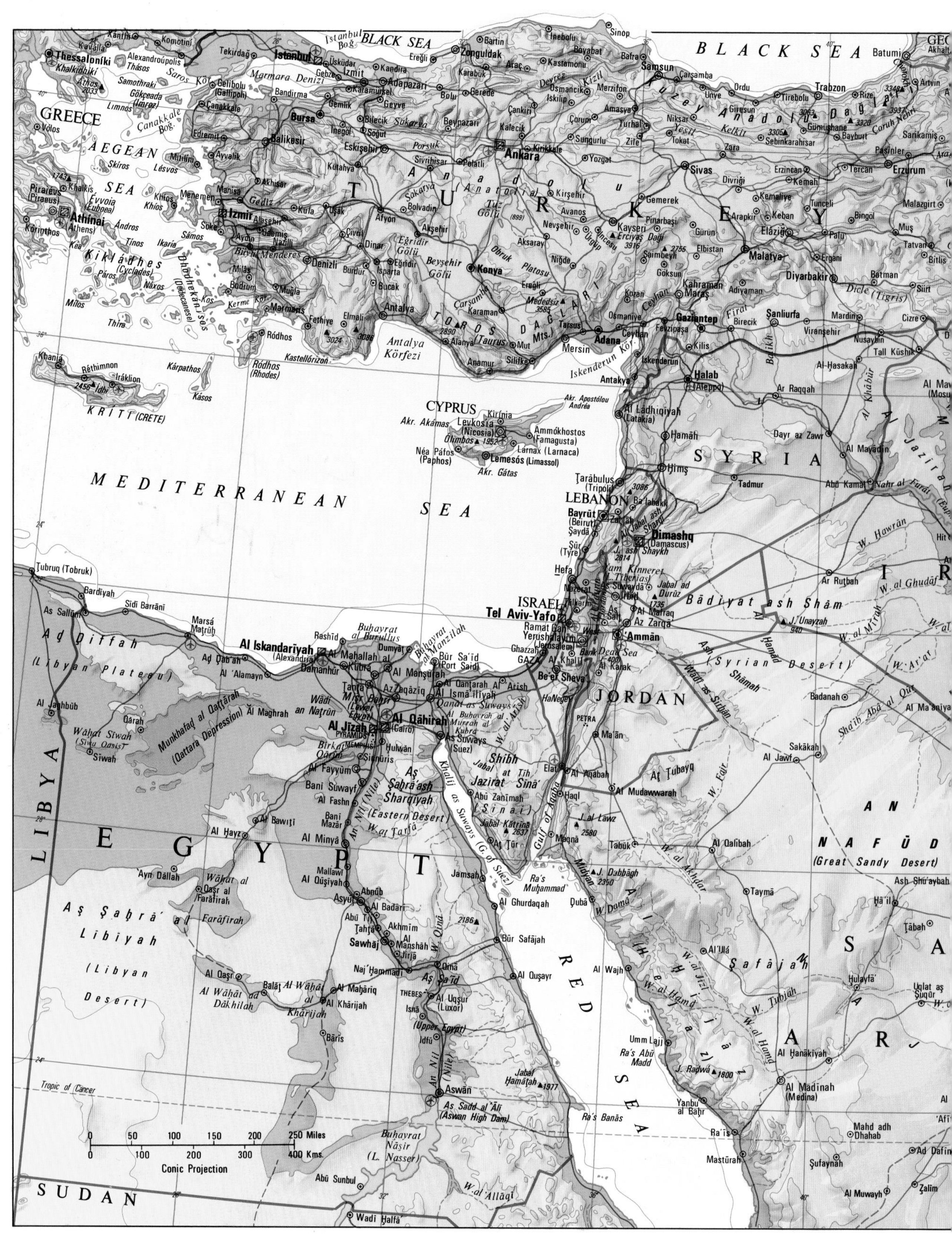

BLACK SEA
GREECE
Thessaloniki
Khalkidhikí
Kavála
Xánthi
Komotiní
Alexandroúpolis
Thásos
Samothráki
Límnos
Gökçeada (İmroz)
Áthos 2033
Vólos
AEGEAN SEA
Skíros
Lésvos
Khíos
Évvoia (Euboea)
Khalkís
Piraiévs (Piraeus)
Athínai (Athens)
Kórinthos
Kéa
Ándros
Tínos
Síros
Ikaría
Sámos
Kikládhes (Cyclades)
Páros
Náxos
Mílos
Thíra
Dhodhekánisos (Dodecanese)
Kos
Ródhos
Ródhos (Rhodes)
Kárpathos
Kásos
Kastellórizon
Khaniá
Réthimnon
Iráklion
2456 Ídhi
KRÍTI (CRETE)
Istanbul Boğ.
İstanbul
Üsküdar
Tekirdağ
Saros Kör.
Gelibolu (Gallipoli)
Marmara Denizi
Çanakkale
Çanakkale Boğ.
Bandırma
Gemlik
Bursa
İzmit
Gebze
Kandıra
Adapazarı
Karamürsel
Geyve
İnegöl
Bilecik
Söğüt
Sakarya
Balıkesir
Edremit
Ayvalık
Mitilini
Eskişehir
Kütahya
Akhisar
Manisa
Menemen
Gediz
İzmir
Alaşehir
Kula
Uşak
Söke
Aydın
Ödemiş
Nazilli
Büyük Menderes
Denizli
Milâs
Bodrum
Muğla
Kerme Kör.
Marmaris
Fethiye
Elmalı
3024
3086
Antalya
Antalya Körfezi
Burdur
Isparta
Bucak
Eğirdir
Eğirdir Gölü
Beyşehir Gölü
Dinar
Çivril
Afyon
Akşehir
Bolvadin
Sivrihisar
Polatlı
Porsuk
Ereğli
Zonguldak
Bartın
Karabük
Bolu
Gerede
Beypazarı
Ankara
Kırıkkale
Kalecik
Çankırı
İnebolu
Araç
Kastamonu
Boyabat
Sinop
Bafra
Samsun
Çarşamba
Devrez
Kızıl
Osmancık
İskilip
Merzifon
Çorum
Amasya
Turhal
Sungurlu
Zile
Yozgat
Niksar
Yeşil
Tokat
Ünye
Ordu
Giresun
Tirebolu
Trabzon
Rize
Artvin
Batumi
Akhalt
Kuzey Anadolu Dağları
Kelkit
Gümüşhane
Sebinkarahisar
Bayburt
Çoruh Nehri
Zara
Sivas
Divriği
Erzincan
Kemah
Tercan
Erzurum
Sarıkamış
Pasinler
Kemaliye
Tunceli
Malazgirt
Bingöl
Muş
Tatvan
Bitlis
Anadolu (Anatolia)
TURKEY
Tuz Gölü
Kırşehir
Avanos
Nevşehir
Ürgüp
Aksaray
Kayseri
Erciyaş Dağı 3916
Gemerek
Pınarbaşı
Gürün
Arapkir
Keban
Elâzığ
Palu
Malatya
Ergani
Diyarbakır
Batman
Siirt
Dicle (Tigris)
Kozan
Kahramanmaraş
Adıyaman
Elbistan
Göksun
Şaimbeyli
2755
Niğde
Konya
Obruk Platosu
Karaman
Ereğli
Çarşamba
Medetsiz 3585
TOROS DAĞLARI (Taurus Mts.)
2890
Alanya
Anamur
Silifke
Mut
Tarsus
Mersin
Adana
Ceyhan
Osmaniye
İskenderun Kör.
İskenderun
Antakya
Gaziantep
Fevzipaşa
Kilis
Fırat
Birecik
Şanlıurfa
Mardin
Viranşehir
Cizre
Nusaybin
Tall Kūshik
Al Ḩasakah
Balikh
Al Khābūr
Ḩalab (Aleppo)
Ar Raqqah
Al Mawşil (Mosul)
Al Jazīrah
Dayr az Zawr
Al Mayādīn
Abū Kamāl
Nahr al Furāt (Euphrates)
SYRIA
Tadmur
Ḩamāh
Ḩimş
Al Lādhiqīyah (Latakia)
CYPRUS
Kirínia
Akr. Apostólou Andréa
Lefkosía (Nicosia)
Ammókhostos (Famagusta)
Lárnax (Larnaca)
Lemesós (Limassol)
Ólimbos 1952
Akr. Akámas
Néa Páfos (Paphos)
Akr. Gátas
MEDITERRANEAN SEA
Ţarābulus (Tripoli)
3086
LEBANON
Ba'labakk
Bayrūt (Beirut)
Zahlah
Şaydā
Şūr (Tyre)
Dimashq (Damascus)
J. ash Shaykh 2814
Ḩefa
Yam Kinneret (L. Tiberias)
Nazerat
Jabal ad Durūz 1735
Suwaydā
Al Mafraq
Bādiyat ash Shām
Ar Ruţbah
W. Ḩawrān
W. al Ghudāf
ISRAEL
Tel Aviv-Yafo
Ramat Gan
Yerushalayim (Jerusalem)
Ghazzah
GAZA
Al Khalīl
Dead Sea
Be'er Sheva
HaNegev
'Ammān
Az Zarqā'
Al Karak
JORDAN
PETRA
Ma'ān
Al 'Aqabah
Elat
Gulf of Aqaba
Al Mudawwarah
Ḩaql
J. 'Unayzah 940
W. al Mirah
Ash Shāmah (Syrian Desert)
Wādī as Sirḩān
Badanah
Sha'ib Abā al Qūr
Al Ma'āniya
Sakākah
Al Jawf
W. Fajr
AN NAFŪD (Great Sandy Desert)
Tubruq (Tobruk)
Bardīyah
As Sallūm
Sīdī Barrānī
Marsá Maţrūḩ
Ad Diffah (Libyan Plateau)
Al Jaghbūb
Qārah
Wāḩat Sīwah (Siwa Oasis)
Sīwah
Munkhafad al Qaţţārah (Qattara Depression)
Al Maghrah
Ad Dab'ah
Al 'Alamayn
Al Iskandarīyah (Alexandria)
Rashīd
Buḩayrat al Burullus
Dumyāţ
Buḩayrat al Manzilah
Būr Sa'īd (Port Said)
Damanhūr
Al Maḩallah al Kubrá
Ţanţā
Al Manşūrah
Az Zaqāzīq
Al Qanţarah
Al Ismā'īlīyah
Al 'Arīsh
Qanāt as Suways
Buḩayrah al Murrah al Kubrá
Wādī an Naţrūn
Mişr Baḩrī (Lower Egypt)
Al Qāhirah (Cairo)
Al Jīzah
PYRAMIDS
MEMPHIS
Ḩulwān
As Suways (Suez)
Birkat Qārūn
Al Fayyūm
Sinnūris
Bani Suwayf
Al Fashn
Aş Şaḩrā' ash Sharqīyah (Eastern Desert)
An Nīl (Nile)
Shibh Jazīrat Sīnā' (Sinai)
Jabal at Tīh
W. al 'Arīsh
Abū Zanīmah
Jabal Kātrīnā 2637
Aţ Ţūr
Khalīj as Suways (G. of Suez)
Ra's Muḩammad
Bani Mazār
Al Minyā
Al Bawīţī
Al Ḩayz
W. aţ Ţarfā
EGYPT
LIBYA
Mallawī
Al Qūşīyah
'Ayn Dallah
Wāḩāt al Farāfirah
Qaşr al Farāfirah
Aş Şaḩrā' al Lībīyah (Libyan Desert)
Asyūţ
Abnūb
Al Badārī
Abū Tīj
Ţahţā
Akhmīm
Sawhāj
Al Manshāh
Jirjā
Jamsah
Al Ghurdaqah
2186
W. Qinā
Būr Safājah
Qinā
Naj' Ḩammādī
Aş Şa'īd
Al Quşayr
Al Qaşr
Balāţ
Al Wāḩāt ad Dākhilah
Al Wāḩāt al Khārijah
Al Mahāriq
Al Khārijah
THEBES
Al Uqşur (Luxor)
Isnā
(Upper Egypt)
Idfū
Bārīs
An Nīl (Nile)
Jabal Ḩamāţah 1977
Aswān
As Sadd al 'Ālī (Aswan High Dam)
Buḩayrat Nāşir (L. Nasser)
Abū Sunbul
W. al 'Allāqī
Wādī Ḩalfā
SUDAN
RED SEA
Ra's Banās
J. al Lawz 2580
Maqnā
Tabūk
Al Qalībah
J. Dabbāgh 2350
Ḑubā
Al Wajh
W. Damā
Al Ḩijāz
Taymā
Al 'Ulā
Şafājah
W. al Jizl
W. al Ḩamḑ
W. Tubjah
Umm Lajj
Ra's Abū Madd
J. Raḑwā 1800
Yanbu' al Baḩr
Al Ḩanākīyah
Al Madīnah (Medina)
Ra'īs
Mastūrah
Mahd adh Dhahab
Şufaynah
Ad Dafīnah
Al Muwayh
Z̧alim
Ash Shu'aybah
Ḩā'il
Ţābah
Ḩulayfā'
Uqlat aş Şuqūr
Tropic of Cancer
0 50 100 150 200 250 Miles
0 100 200 300 400 Kms.
Conic Projection

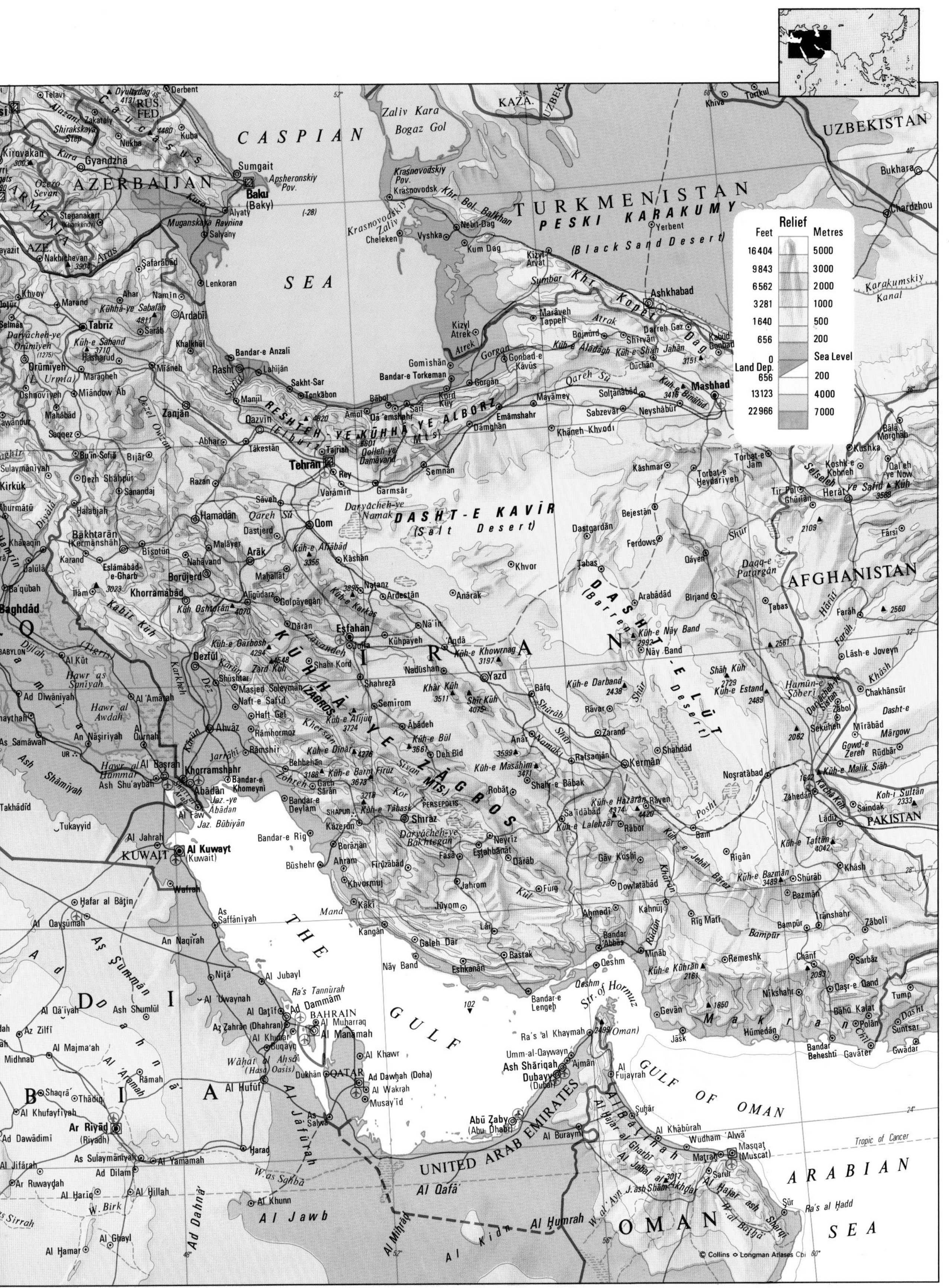

CASPIAN

SEA

AZERBAIJAN

UZBEKISTAN

TURKMENISTAN

PESKI KARAKUMY

(Black Sand Desert)

RUS. FED.

KAZA.

Baku (Baky)

Ashkhabad

Mashhad

AFGHANISTAN

DASHT-E KAVIR

(Salt Desert)

DASHT-E LŪT (Barren Desert)

Tehrān

KŪHHĀ-YE ALBORZ Mts.

RESHTEH-YE KŪHHĀ-YE ALBORZ

I R A N

KŪHHĀ-YE ZĀGROS Mts.

PAKISTAN

Eşfahān

Shīrāz

PERSEPOLIS

Baghdād

IRAQ

KUWAIT

Al Kuwayt (Kuwait)

BAHRAIN

Al Manāmah

QATAR

Ad Dawḥah (Doha)

UNITED ARAB EMIRATES

Abū Ẓaby (Abu Dhabi)

Dubayy (Dubai)

Ar Riyāḍ (Riyadh)

S A U D I   A R A B I A

THE GULF

Strs. of Hormuz

GULF OF OMAN

OMAN

Masqaṭ (Muscat)

Tropic of Cancer

ARABIAN

SEA

© Collins • Longman Atlases

Relief

Feet		Metres
16 404		5000
9843		3000
6562		2000
3281		1000
1640		500
656		200
0		Sea Level
Land Dep.		200
656		4000
13 123		4000
22 966		7000

THE LEVANT

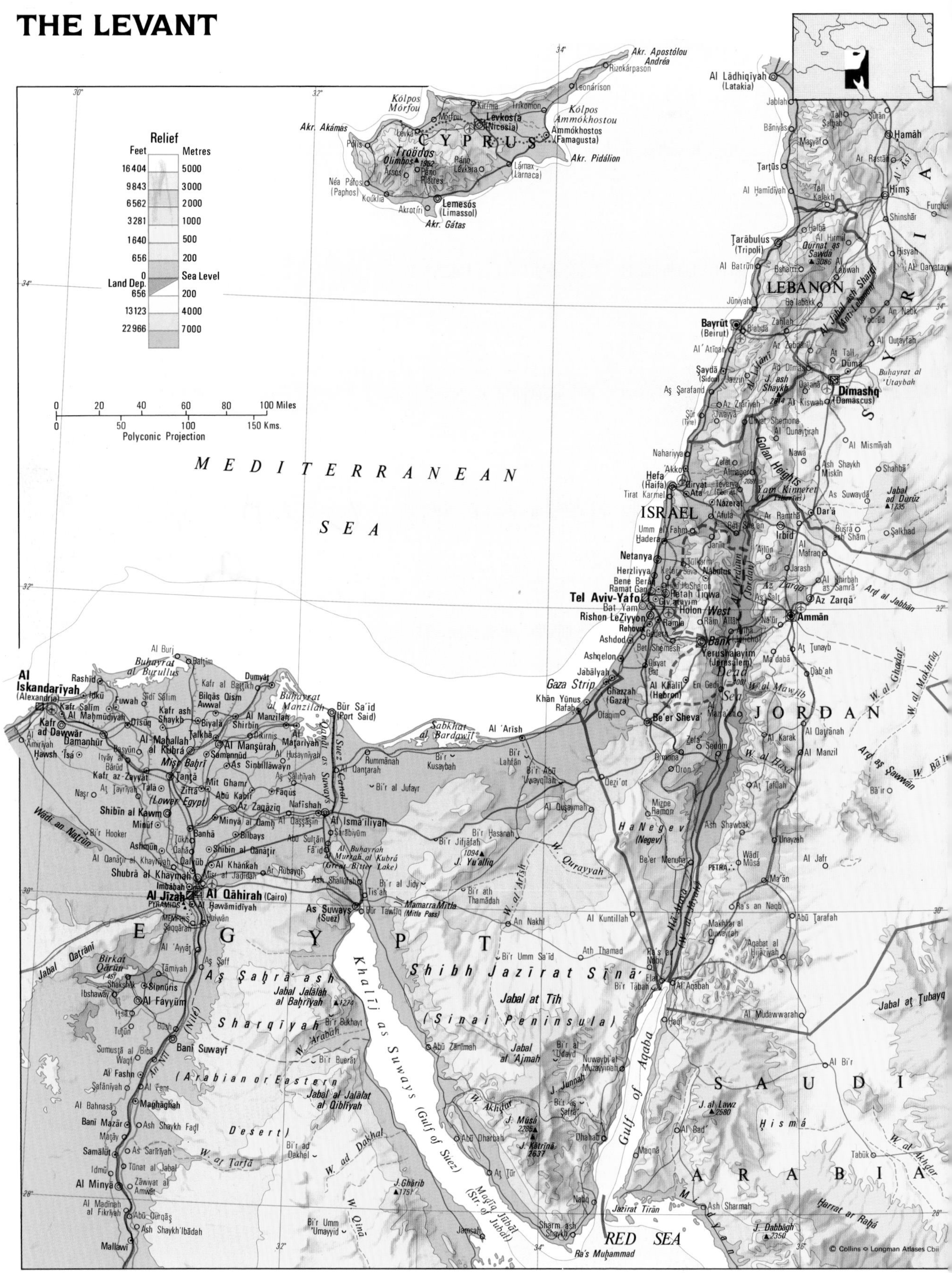

Relief

Feet	Metres
16 404	5000
9843	3000
6562	2000
3281	1000
1640	500
656	200
0	Sea Level
Land Dep.	
656	200
13 123	4000
22 966	7000

0   20   40   60   80   100 Miles
0   50   100   150 Kms.
Polyconic Projection

MEDITERRANEAN

SEA

CYPRUS

Kólpos
Mórfou

Akr. Akámas

Akr. Apostólou
Andréa
Rizokárpason

Leonárison

Akr. Pidálion

Kólpos
Ammókhostou

Ammókhostos
(Famagusta)

Levkosía
(Nicosia)

Tróodos
Olimbos

Néa Pátos
(Paphos)

Lemesós
(Limassol)

Akr. Gátas

Al Lādhiqīyah
(Latakia)

Jablah

Bāniyās

Tall Şalḥab

Şūrān

Hamāh

Ar Rastān

Furuqlus

Ḥimş

Shinshār

LEBANON

Ţarābulus
(Tripoli)

Qurnat as
Sawda

Baalbek

Bayrūt
(Beirut)

An Nabk

Al 'Qutayfah

At Tall

Dūmā

Buḥayrat al
'Utaybah

Dimashq
(Damascus)

SYRIA

Golan Heights

ISRAEL

Ḥefa
(Haifa)

Yam Kinneret

As Suwaydā

Jabal
ad Durūz

Netanya

Herzliyya

Tel Aviv-Yafo

Rishon LeZiyyon

Ashdod

West
Bank

Yerushalayim
(Jerusalem)

'Ammān

Az Zarqā'

JORDAN

Ashqelon

Gaza Strip

Ghazzah
(Gaza)

Al Khalīl
(Hebron)

Dead
Sea

Be'er Sheva

Al Karak

H a   N e g e v
(Negev)

PETRA

Wādī
Mūsā

Ma'ān

Al 'Arīsh

Sabkhat
al Bardawīl

Al Iskandarīyah
(Alexandria)

Rashīd

Buḥayrat
al Burullus

Dumyāţ

Būr Sa'īd
(Port Said)

Kafr ash
Shaykh

Buḥayrat
al Manzilah

Al Manşūrah

Kafr ad Dawwār

Damanhūr

Al Maḥallah
al Kubrá

Ţanţā

Az Zaqāzīq

Banhā

Ismā'īlīyah

Al Buḥayrat
Murrah al Kubrá
(Great Bitter Lake)

Shibīn al Kawm

Minūf

EGYPT

Al Jīzah
Al Qāhirah (Cairo)

PYRAMIDS

MEMPHIS

Saqqārah

Al Fayyūm

Birkat
Qārūn

As Suways
(Suez)

Mitla Pass

An Nakhl

Shibh Jazīrat Sīnā'

Jabal at Tīh
(Sinai Peninsula)

Al Minyā

Al 'Aqabah

Gulf of Aqaba

SAUDI

ARABIA

Khalīj as Suways (Gulf of Suez)
(Sir. of Suez)

(Arabian or Eastern
Desert)

Banī Suwayf

J. Mūsá

J. Kātrīnā

Aţ Ţūr

RED SEA

Ra's Muḥammad

© Collins · Longman Atlases Cbii

AFRICA

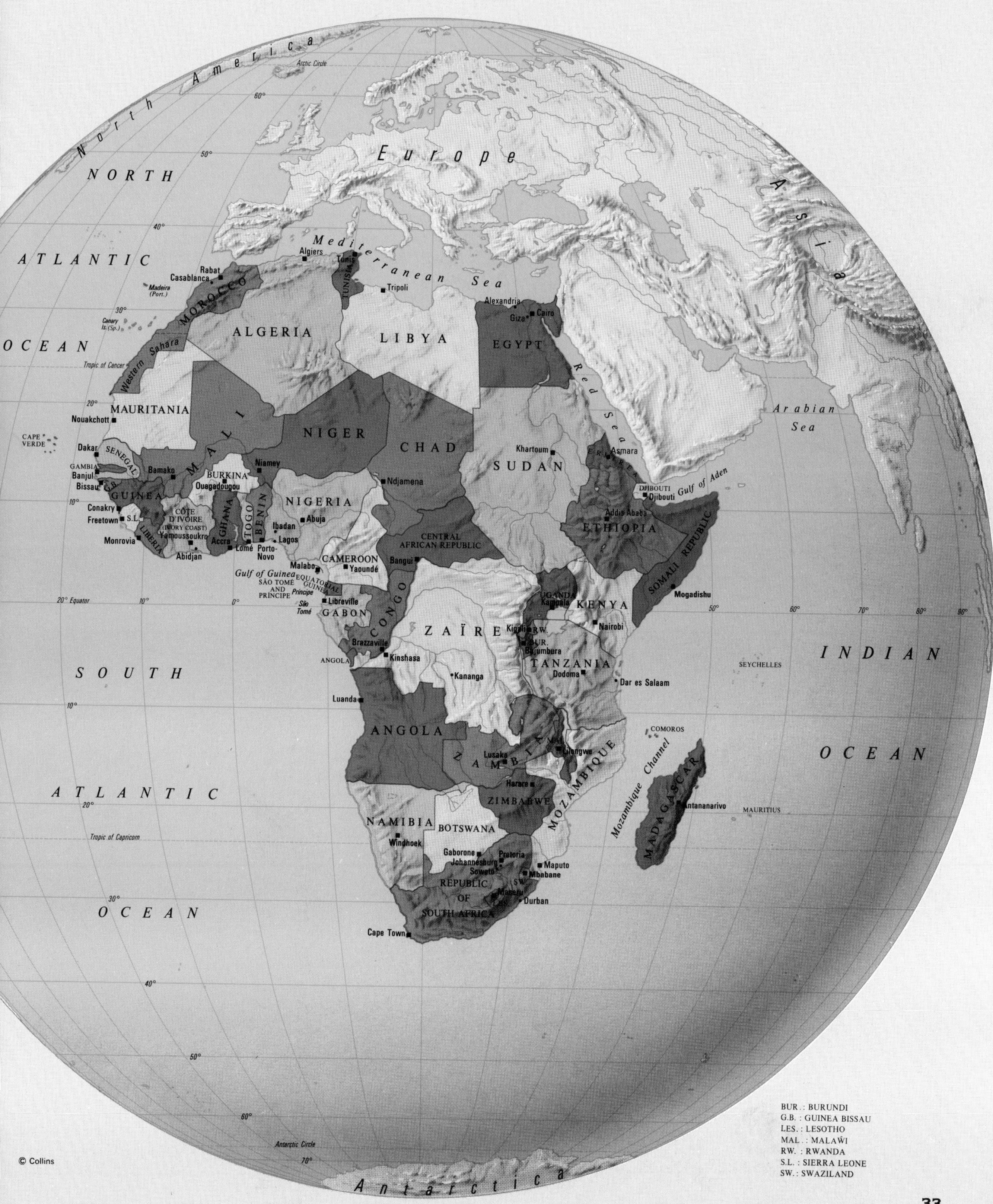

North America

Arctic Circle

Europe

60°

Asia

50°

NORTH

40°

Mediterranean Sea

Algiers Tunis

Rabat

ATLANTIC

Casablanca

Tripoli

MOROCCO

Madeira
(Port.)

30°

Alexandria

Giza Cairo

OCEAN

Canary
Is.(Sp.)

ALGERIA

LIBYA

EGYPT

Tropic of Cancer

Western Sahara

20°

MAURITANIA

NIGER

CHAD

Red Sea

Arabian
Sea

Nouakchott

Khartoum Asmara

CAPE
VERDE

Dakar

SENEGAL

Niamey

SUDAN

DJIBOUTI

Gulf of Aden

GAMBIA
Banjul

Bamako

BURKINA

Djibouti

Bissau

G.B.

Ouagadougou

Ndjamena

10°

GUINEA

NIGERIA

CENTRAL
AFRICAN REPUBLIC

Addis Ababa

Conakry

CÔTE
D'IVOIRE
(IVORY COAST)

GHANA

TOGO

Ibadan

Abuja

ETHIOPIA

SOMALI REPUBLIC

Freetown S.L.

Lagos

Monrovia

LIBERIA

Yamoussoukro

Accra

BENIN

Porto-
Novo

Abidjan

Lomé

CAMEROON

Bangui

Gulf of Guinea

Malabo

EQUATORIAL
GUINEA

Yaoundé

UGANDA

Mogadishu

SÃO TOME
AND
PRINCIPE

Príncipe

Kampala

KENYA

São
Tomé

Libreville

RW.

Nairobi

20° Equator

10°

0°

GABON

CONGO

ZAÏRE

Kigali

BUR.

Bujumbura

Brazzaville

Kinshasa

TANZANIA

Dar es Salaam

ANGOLA

Kananga

Doudoma

SEYCHELLES

INDIAN

Luanda

10°

SOUTH

COMOROS

ANGOLA

ZAMBIA

OCEAN

ATLANTIC

Lusaka

Lilongwe

MOZAMBIQUE

Mozambique Channel

MADAGASCAR

20°

Harare

MAURITIUS

Tropic of Capricorn

NAMIBIA

BOTSWANA

ZIMBABWE

Antananarivo

Windhoek

Gaborone Pretoria

Johannesburg

Maputo

OCEAN

Soweto

Mbabane

SW.

REPUBLIC
OF
SOUTH AFRICA

LES.

Durban

30°

OCEAN

Cape Town

40°

50°

Antarctic Circle

60°

70°

© Collins

Antarctica

BUR.: BURUNDI
G.B.: GUINEA BISSAU
LES.: LESOTHO
MAL.: MALAŴI
RW.: RWANDA
S.L.: SIERRA LEONE
SW.: SWAZILAND

33

NORTHERN AFRICA

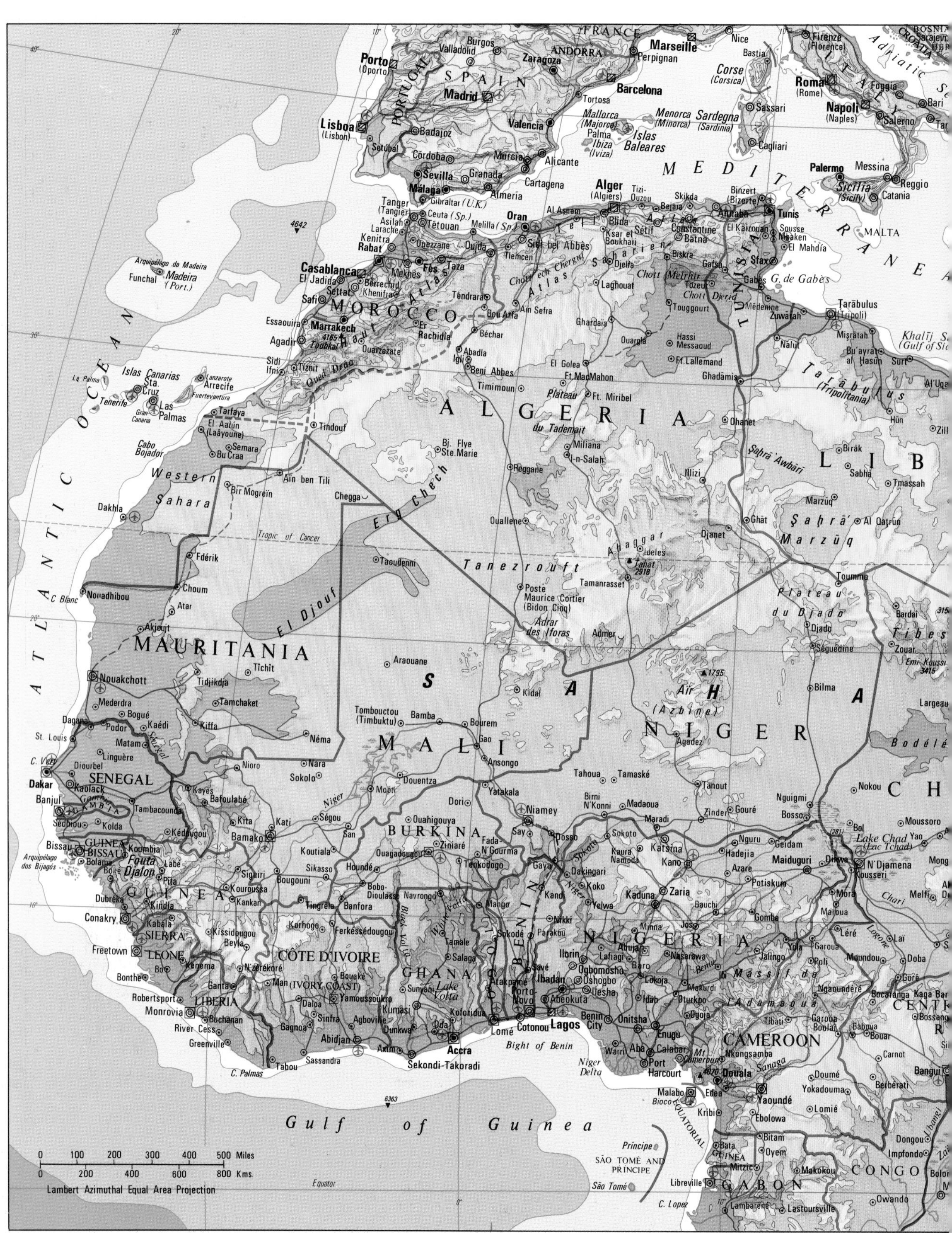
FRANCE
Marseille
Nice
Perpignan
ANDORRA
Burgos
Valladolid
Zaragoza
Porto
(Oporto)
PORTUGAL
SPAIN
Madrid
Barcelona
Tortosa
Corse
(Corsica)
Bastia
Sassari
Sardegna
(Sardinia)
Cagliari
Lisboa
(Lisbon)
Setúbal
Badajoz
Valencia
Mallorca
(Majorca)
Palma
Ibiza
(Iviza)
Menorca
(Minorca)
Islas
Baleares
Córdoba
Murcia
Alicante
Sevilla
Granada
Málaga
Almería
Cartagena
Gibraltar (U.K.)
ITALY
Firenze
(Florence)
Roma
(Rome)
Napoli
(Naples)
Foggia
Bari
Salerno
Palermo
Messina
Sicilia
(Sicily)
Reggio
Catania
MALTA
Adriatic
MEDITERRANEAN
Tanger
(Tangier)
Ceuta (Sp.)
Asilah
Tétouan
Larache
Kenitra
Rabat
Melilla (Sp.)
Oran
Alger
(Algiers)
Tizi-Ouzou
Bejaïa
Skikda
Annaba
Bizerte
Binzert
Tunis
Sousse
Meaken
El Mahdia
Sfax
Gabès
G. de Gabès
Blida
Sétif
Constantine
Batna
Biskra
Ksar el Boukhari
Sidi bel Abbès
Tlemcen
Oujda
Ouezzane
Fès
Taza
Meknès
Casablanca
El Jadida
Settat
Berrechid
Khenifra
Safi
MOROCCO
Essaouira
Marrakech
Toubkal
4165
Ouarzazate
Agadir
Er Rachidia
Tendrara
Bou Arfa
Aïn Sefra
Béchar
Laghouat
Ghardaïa
Touggourt
Ouargla
Hassi Messaoud
Ft. Lallemand
Ghadāmis
Chott Melrhir
Chott Djerid
Tozeur
Médenine
Zuwārah
Tarābulus
(Tripoli)
Misrātah
Nālūt
TUNISIA
Tarābulus
(Tripolitania)
Khalīj Surt
Hūn
Arquipélago da Madeira
Funchal
Madeira
(Port.)
Islas Canarias
Sta. Cruz
Las Palmas
Lanzarote
Arrecife
Fuerteventura
Tenerife
Gran Canaria
La Palma
Tarfaya
Tindouf
El Aaiún
(Laâyoune)
Semara
Bu Craa
Cabo Bojador
Western Sahara
Dakhla
Aïn ben Tili
Bir Mogreïn
Tiznit
Sidi Ifni
Abadla
Igli
Beni Abbes
Timimoun
El Golea
Ft. MacMahon
Plateau du Tademaït
Ft. Miribel
ALGERIA
Bj. Flye Ste. Marie
Miliana
I-n-Salah
Reggane
Illizi
Chegga
Erg Chech
Ouallene
Djanet
Ghāt
Ahaggar
Ideles
Tahat
2918
Tamanrasset
Tanezrouft
Tropic of Cancer
Fdérik
Taoudenni
El Djouf
Choum
Nouadhibou
C. Blanc
Atar
Akjoujt
MAURITANIA
Tichît
Nouakchott
Tidjikja
Tamchaket
Poste Maurice Cortier
(Bidon Cinq)
Adrar des Iforas
Araouane
SAHARA
Kidal
Aïr
(Azbine)
1795
Agadez
NIGER
Tahoua
Tamaské
Mederdra
Bogué
Kaédi
Dagana
Podor
St. Louis
Matam
Linguère
Kiffa
Néma
Tombouctou
(Timbuktu)
Bamba
Bourem
Gao
MALI
Ansongo
C. Vert
Dakar
Diourbel
Kaolack
SENEGAL
Banjul
GAMBIA
Tambacounda
Kolda
Kayes
Bafoulabé
Nioro
Nara
Sokolo
Douentza
Mopti
Niger
Ségou
Kita
Kati
Bamako
Kédougou
Bissau
GUINEA BISSAU
Bolama
Koumbia
Arquipélago dos Bijagós
Fouta Djalon
Labé
Boké
Pita
GUINEA
Dubréka
Kindia
Conakry
Kouroussa
Kankan
Siguiri
Bougouni
Sikasso
Koutiala
San
Ouahigouya
BURKINA
Ouagadougou
Ziniaré
Fada-N'Gourma
Tenkodogo
Houndé
Bobo-Dioulasso
Banfora
Navrongo
Tingréla
Dori
Yatakala
Niamey
Say
Dosso
Gaya
Kandi
BENIN
TOGO
Birni N'Konni
Madaoua
Maradi
Zinder
Gouré
Tanout
Nguigmi
Bosso
Nokou
Sokoto
Kaura Namoda
Katsina
Kano
Nguru
Hadejia
Geidam
Maiduguri
Azare
Potiskum
Dikwa
Lake Chad
(Lac Tchad)
N'Djamena
Kousseri
Mora
Maroua
Dakingari
Koko
Yelwa
Kaduna
Zaria
Bauchi
Jos
Gombe
Minna
Abuja
Lafiagi
Nikki
Parakou
NIGERIA
Ilorin
Ogbomosho
Oshogbo
Ilesha
Ibadan
Abeokuta
Porto-Novo
Lagos
Cotonou
Lomé
Atakpamé
Sokodé
Savé
Mango
Tamale
Salaga
GHANA
Lake Volta
Black Volta
White Volta
Kumasi
Koforidua
Sunyani
Oda
Accra
Sekondi-Takoradi
Bight of Benin
Benin City
Onitsha
Enugu
Aba
Warri
Calabar
Port Harcourt
Niger Delta
Lokoja
Makurdi
Oturkpo
Ogoja
Nasarawa
Benue
Yola
Jalingo
Garoua
Poli
Ngaoundéré
Massif de l'Adamaoua
Tibati
CAMEROON
Nkongsamba
Mt. Cameroun
4070
Douala
Sanaga
Yaoundé
Edéa
Kribi
Ebolowa
Bitam
Oyem
Malabo
Bioco
EQUATORIAL GUINEA
Bata
Mitzic
Libreville
GABON
Lambaréné
Lastoursville
Makokou
Príncipe
SÃO TOMÉ AND PRÍNCIPE
São Tomé
C. Lopez
Equator
Korhogo
Ferkéssédougou
Kissidougou
Beyla
Kabala
SIERRA LEONE
Freetown
Kenema
Bo
Bonthe
N'Zérékoré
Man
CÔTE D'IVOIRE
(IVORY COAST)
Bouaké
Yamoussoukro
Daloa
Sinfra
Agboville
Dunkwa
Gagnoa
Abidjan
Axim
Sassandra
Tabou
C. Palmas
Ganta
LIBERIA
Robertsport
Monrovia
Buchanan
River Cess
Greenville
Gulf of Guinea
6363
4642
ATLANTIC OCEAN
CHAD
Bodélé
Largeau
Tibesti
Emi Koussi
3415
Bardai
Zouar
Bilma
Séguédine
Djado
Plateau du Djado
Toummo
LIBYA
Ṣaḥrā' Awbārī
Ṣaḥrā' Marzūq
Marzūq
Sabhā
Birāk
Tmassah
Al Qaṭrūn
Ohanet
Moussoro
Mongo
Melfi
Chari
Logone
Léré
Laï
Moundou
Doba
Goré
Kaga Bandoro
Bossangoa
Bocaranga
Bouar
Baboua
Garoua Boulaï
Carnot
Berbérati
Bangui
Doumé
Yokadouma
Lomié
Dongou
Impfondo
Ubangi
CONGO
Ouesso
Owando
0
100
200
300
400
500 Miles
0
200
400
600
800 Kms.
Lambert Azimuthal Equal Area Projection

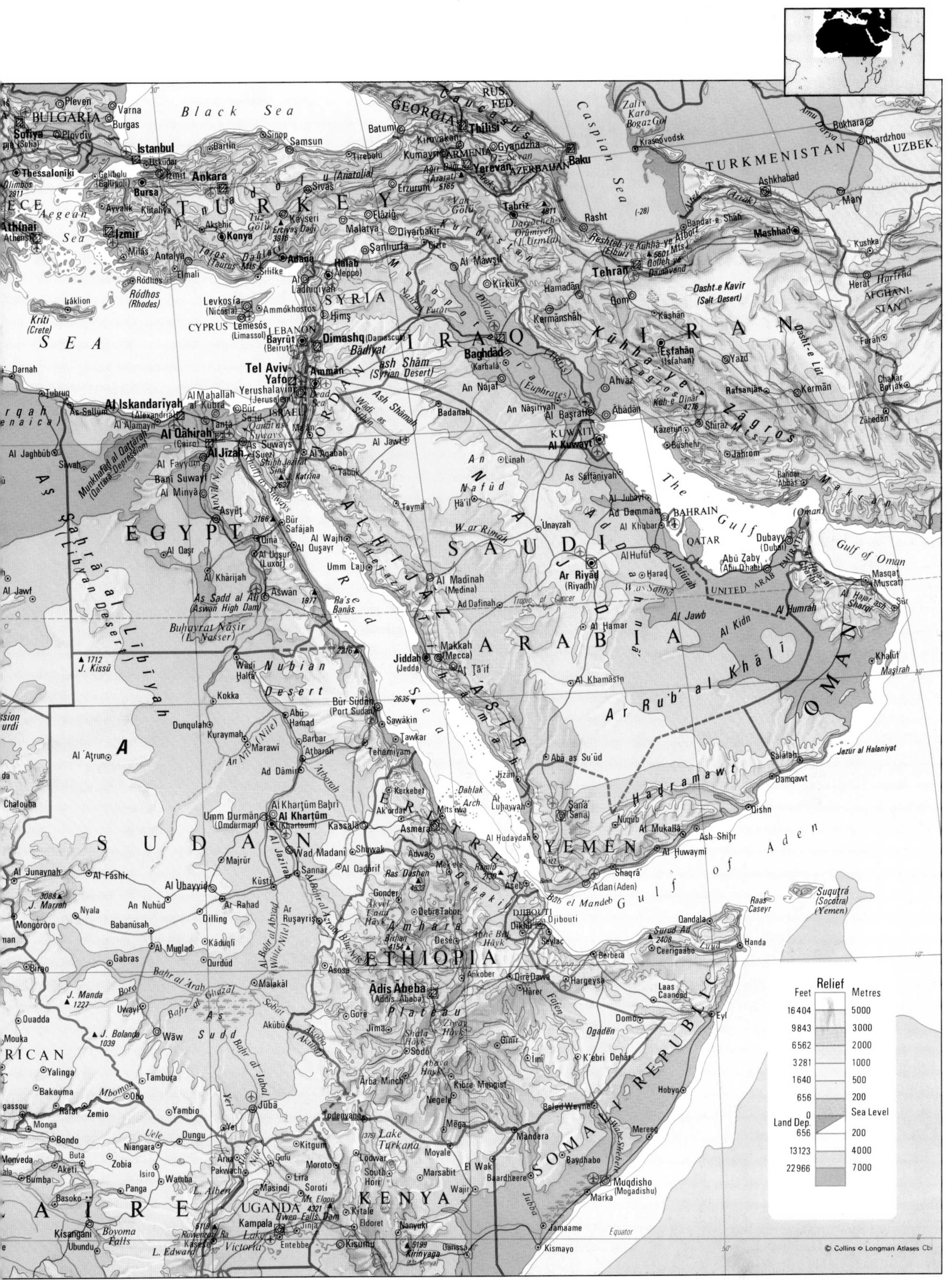

Black Sea
BULGARIA
Varna
Burgas
Sofiya (Sofia)
Plovdiv
Istanbul
Üsküdar
İzmit
Ankara
Bursa
Samsun
Sinop
Bartin
Trabzon
Tirebolu
Sivas
Erzurum
Kayseri
Konya
Aksehir
Antalya
Adana
Silifke
Mersin
İzmir
Aydın
Ayvalık
Kütahya
Thessaloníki
Athínai (Athens)
Aegean Sea
TURKEY
Anatolia
Elazığ
Malatya
Diyarbakır
Şanlıurfa
Cizre
Van Gölü
Kurdistan
GEORGIA
Batumi
Tbilisi
Caucasus
RUS. FED.
Kirovakan
Kumayri
ARMENIA
Gyandzha
Oz. Sevan
Yerevan
AZERBAIJAN
Baku
Ağrı Dağı (Ararat) 5165
Caspian Sea
(-28)
Zaliv Kara-Bogaz Gol
Krasnovodsk
TURKMENISTAN
Ashkhabad
Amu Darya
Bukhara
Chardzhou
UZBEK.
Mary
Atrek
Tabriz
4811
Daryācheh-ye Orūmīyeh (L. Urmia)
Rasht
Bandar-e Shāh
Mashhad
Reshteh-ye Kūhhā-ye Alborz (Elburz Mts.)
5601 Qolleh-ye Damāvand
Tehrān
Qom
Kāshān
Dasht-e Kavīr (Salt Desert)
Kushka
Herāt
Harīrūd
AFGHANISTAN
Farāh
Hamadān
Kermānshāh
IRAN
Kūhhā-ye Zāgros
Eşfahān (Isfahan)
Yazd
Dasht-e Lūt
Kermān
Rafsanjān
Chahar Borjak
Zāhedān
Ahvāz
Ābādān
Kūh-e Dīnār 4276
Zāgros Mts.
Shīrāz
Kāzerūn
Būshehr
Jahrom
Bandar-e 'Abbās
Makran
Kirkūk
Al Mawşil
Dijlah (Tigris)
Al Furāt (Euphrates)
Mesopotamia
IRAQ
Baghdād
Karbalā'
An Najaf
An Nāşirīyah
Al Başrah
KUWAIT
Al Kuwayt
Badanah
Ḩalab (Aleppo)
Al Lādhiqīyah
SYRIA
Ḩimş
Dimashq (Damascus)
Bādiyat ash Shām (Syrian Desert)
Ash Shāmah
Wādī as Sirḩān
LEBANON
Bayrūt (Beirut)
Tel Aviv-Yafo
'Ammān
Yerushalayim (Jerusalem)
Dead Sea
ISRAEL
JORDAN
Ma'ān
CYPRUS
Levkosía (Nicosia)
Ammókhostos
Lemesós (Limassol)
Ródhos (Rhodes)
Iráklion
Kríti (Crete)
SEA
Darnah
Tubruq
As Sallūm
Al Iskandarīyah (Alexandria)
Al 'Alamayn
Al Maḩallah al Kubrá
Ţanţā
Būr Sa'īd
Qanāt as Suways
Al Qāhirah (Cairo)
Al Jīzah
As Suways (Suez)
Al Jaghbūb
Sīwah
Munkhafaḑ al Qaţţārah (Qattara Depression)
Al Fayyūm
Banī Suwayf
Al Minyā
Asyūţ
Shibh Jazīrat Sīnā'
Jabal Katrīnā 2637
Al 'Aqabah
Tabūk
EGYPT
Al Qaşr
Al Khārijah
Al Uqşur (Luxor)
Qinā
Aswān
As Sadd al Ālī (Aswan High Dam)
Buḩayrat Nāşir (L. Nasser)
Aş Şaḩrā' al Lībīyah (Libyan Desert)
Al Jawf
Būr Safājah
Al Quşayr
Al Wajh
Ra's Banās
Umm Lajj
Taymā'
An Nafūd
Ḩā'il
Līnah
Al Jawf
W. ar Rimah
AL HIJAZ
Al Madīnah (Medina)
Ad Dafīnah
Tropic of Cancer
SAUDI ARABIA
'Unayzah
Ad Dahnā'
As Saffānīyah
Al Jubayl
Ad Dammām
Al Khubar
BAHRAIN
QATAR
The Gulf
Al Hufūf
Ar Riyāḑ (Riyadh)
Ḩaraḑ
W. as Sahba
Al Jafūrah
Dubayy (Dubai)
Abū Ẓaby (Abu Dhabi)
UNITED ARAB EMIRATES
Gulf of Oman
Masqaţ (Muscat)
Şūr
Al Ḩajar ash Sharqī
Al Ḩumrah
Al Jawb
Al Kidn
Ar Rub' al Khālī
OMAN
Khalūf
Maşīrah
Jazur al Halaniyat
Şalālah
Makkah (Mecca)
Jiddah (Jedda)
Aţ Ţā'if
Al Khamāsīn
Al Ḩamar
'ASIR
Tihāmah
Red Sea
Abā as Su'ūd
Jīzān
Şan'ā' (Sana)
YEMEN
Ḩaḑramawt
Damqawt
Qishn
Al Mukallā
Ash Shiḩr
Al Ḩuwaymī
Shaqrā'
Adan (Aden)
Gulf of Aden
Bāb el Mandeb
Ta'izz
Al Ḩudaydah
Al Luḩayyah
Dahlak Arch.
Suquţrá (Socotra) (Yemen)
Raas Caseyr
Qandala
Surud Ad 2408
Ceerigaabo
Handa
Berbera
Hargeysa
Laas Caanood
Eyl
Dooi
Ogadēn
Gīnīr
K'ebri Dehar
Hobyo
SOMALI REPUBLIC
Beled Weyne
Mereeg
Webi Shabeelle
Jubba
Muqdisho (Mogadishu)
Marka
Baydhabo
Baardheere
Kismayo
Jamaame
Equator
Mandera
El Wak
Wajir
Moyale
Marsabit
KENYA
Nanyuki
Kirinyaga 5199 (Mt. Kenya)
Garissa
Kisumu
Eldoret
Kitale
Mt. Elgon 4321
Soroti
Moroto
Lodwar
South Horr
Lake Turkana
(375)
Todenyang
Mēga
Negelē
Kibre Mengist
Ārba Minch
Abaya Hāyk'
Sodo
Shala Hāyk'
Ziway Hāyk'
Jīma
Gore
Plateau
Ādīs Ābeba (Addis Ababa)
Ankober
Dirē Dawa
Hārer
Fafen
Ēmī
ETHIOPIA
Amhara
Bīrhan 4154
Dese
Debre Tabor
Gonder
Ras Dashen 4533
T'ana Hāyk'
Āk'ele
Mek'ele
Āsmera
ERITREA
Keren
Āk'ordat
Mits'iwa
Ramlu 2130
Aseb
Denakil
DJIBOUTI
Djibouti
Dikhil
Seylac
Ādwa
Kassalā
Al Qaḑārif
Ash Shuwak
Wad Madanī
Sannār
Al Jazīrah
Kūstī
Ar Rusayriş
Al Baḩr al Azraq (Blue Nile)
Al Baḩr al Abyaḑ (White Nile)
Umm Durmān (Omdurman)
Al Khartūm (Khartoum)
Al Khartūm Baḩrī
Ad Dāmir
'Aţbarah
Barbar
Abū Ḩamad
Kuraymah
Marawī
An Nīl (Nile)
Dunqulah
Kokka
Wādī Ḩalfā'
Nubian Desert
2216
2635
Būr Sūdān (Port Sudan)
Sawākin
Tawkar
Al 'Aţrūn
SUDAN
Al Fāshir
Al Junaynah
3088 J. Marrah
Nyala
An Nuhūd
Al Ubayyiḑ
Ar Rahad
Mongororo
Babanūsah
Dilling
Kāduglī
Al Muglad
Gabras
Dūrdud
Malakāl
Bahr al 'Arab
Bahr al Ghazāl
Sobat
As Sudd
J. Manda 1227
Uwayl
J. Bolanda 1039
Wāw
Akūbū
Akobo
Bahr al Jabal
Yei
Jūbā
Yambio
Tambura
Zemio
Rafai
Mbomou
Obo
Bakouma
Yalinga
Ouadda
Birao
Mouka
CENTRAL AFRICAN
Monga
Bondo
Uele
Niangara
Dungu
Kitgum
Gulu
Arua
Pakwach
Lira
Masindi
L. Albert
UGANDA
Kampala
Owen Falls Dam
Jinja
Entebbe
Lake Victoria
Kasese
Ruwenzori Ra 5118
L. Edward
Kisangani
Boyoma Falls
Ubundu
ZAIRE
Basoko
Bumba
Aketi
Buta
Zobia
Isiro
Wamba
Panga
Chalouba
Kissū J. 1712
Relief
Feet
Metres
16404 5000
9843 3000
6562 2000
3281 1000
1640 500
656 200
0 Sea Level
Land Dep.
656 200
13123 4000
22966 7000
© Collins Longman Atlases

CENTRAL AND SOUTHERN AFRICA

Relief

Feet	Metres
16 404	5000
9843	3000
6562	2000
3281	1000
1640	500
656	200
0	Sea Level
656	200
13123	4000

0 100 200 300 400 500 Miles
0 200 400 600 800 Kms.
Lambert Azimuthal Equal Area Projection

© Collins · Longman Atlases Cbi

same scale

NIGERIA · CHAD · CENTRAL AFRICAN REPUBLIC · SUDAN · ETHIOPIA · SOMALI REPUBLIC · CAMEROON · EQUATORIAL GUINEA · GABON · CONGO · ZAÏRE · UGANDA · KENYA · RWANDA · BURUNDI · TANZANIA · COMOROS · ANGOLA · ZAMBIA · MALAWI · MOZAMBIQUE · NAMIBIA · BOTSWANA · ZIMBABWE · REPUBLIC OF SOUTH AFRICA · LESOTHO · SWAZILAND · MADAGASCAR

ATLANTIC OCEAN · INDIAN OCEAN · Mozambique Channel · Tropic of Capricorn

Lake Turkana · Lake Victoria · Lake Tanganyika · Lake Malawi · L. Kariba · L. Mweru · L. Bangweulu · Etosha Pan · Okavango Basin · Kalahari Desert · Great Karoo · Namib Desert

Douala · Yaoundé · Libreville · Brazzaville · Kinshasa · Luanda · Lusaka · Harare · Nairobi · Dar es Salaam · Maputo · Pretoria · Johannesburg · Bloemfontein · Cape Town · Durban · Port Elizabeth · Windhoek · Gaborone · Antananarivo (Tananarive)

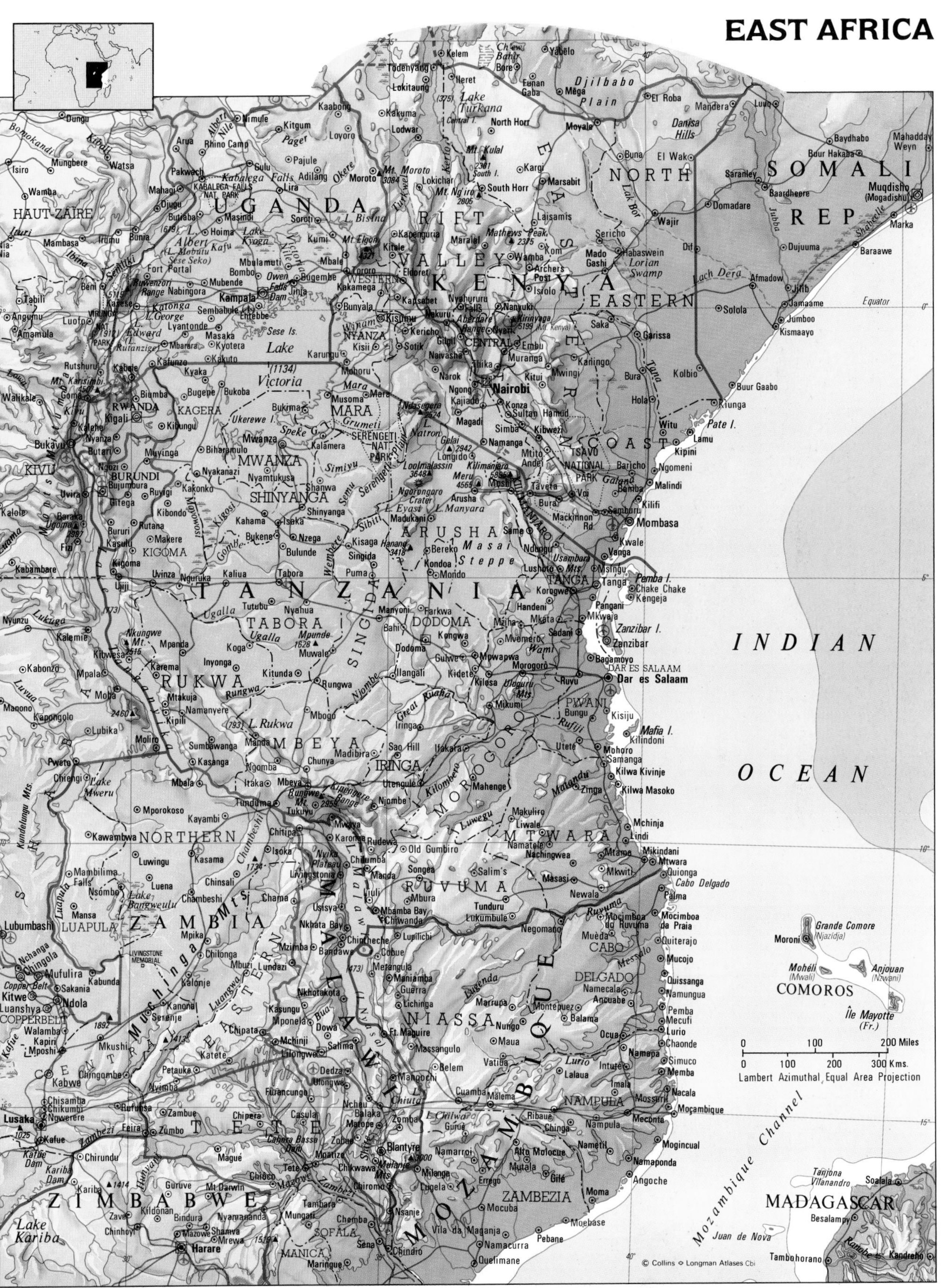

INDIAN

OCEAN

SOMALI

REP

NORTH

KENYA

EASTERN

COAST

UGANDA

RWANDA

BURUNDI

TANZANIA

MWANZA

SHINYANGA

TABORA

ARUSHA

DODOMA

MOROGORO

PWANI

MTWARA

RUVUMA

RUKWA

MBEYA

IRINGA

ZAMBIA

MALAWI

NIASSA

CABO DELGADO

COMOROS

MOZAMBIQUE

ZAMBEZIA

MADAGASCAR

ZIMBABWE

HAUT-ZAIRE

KIVU

KIGOMA

KAGERA

MARA

NYANZA

WESTERN

CENTRAL

Nairobi

Dar es Salaam

Mozambique Channel

Grande Comore
(Njazidja)
Moroni

Mohéli
(Mwali)

Anjouan
(Nzwani)

Île Mayotte
(Fr.)

Nairobi

Dodoma

Lusaka

Harare

Lake
Turkana

Lake
Victoria

Lake
Kariba

Equator

0   100   200 Miles
0   100   200   300 Kms.
Lambert Azimuthal Equal Area Projection

© Collins ● Longman Atlases Cbi

WEST AFRICA – EAST

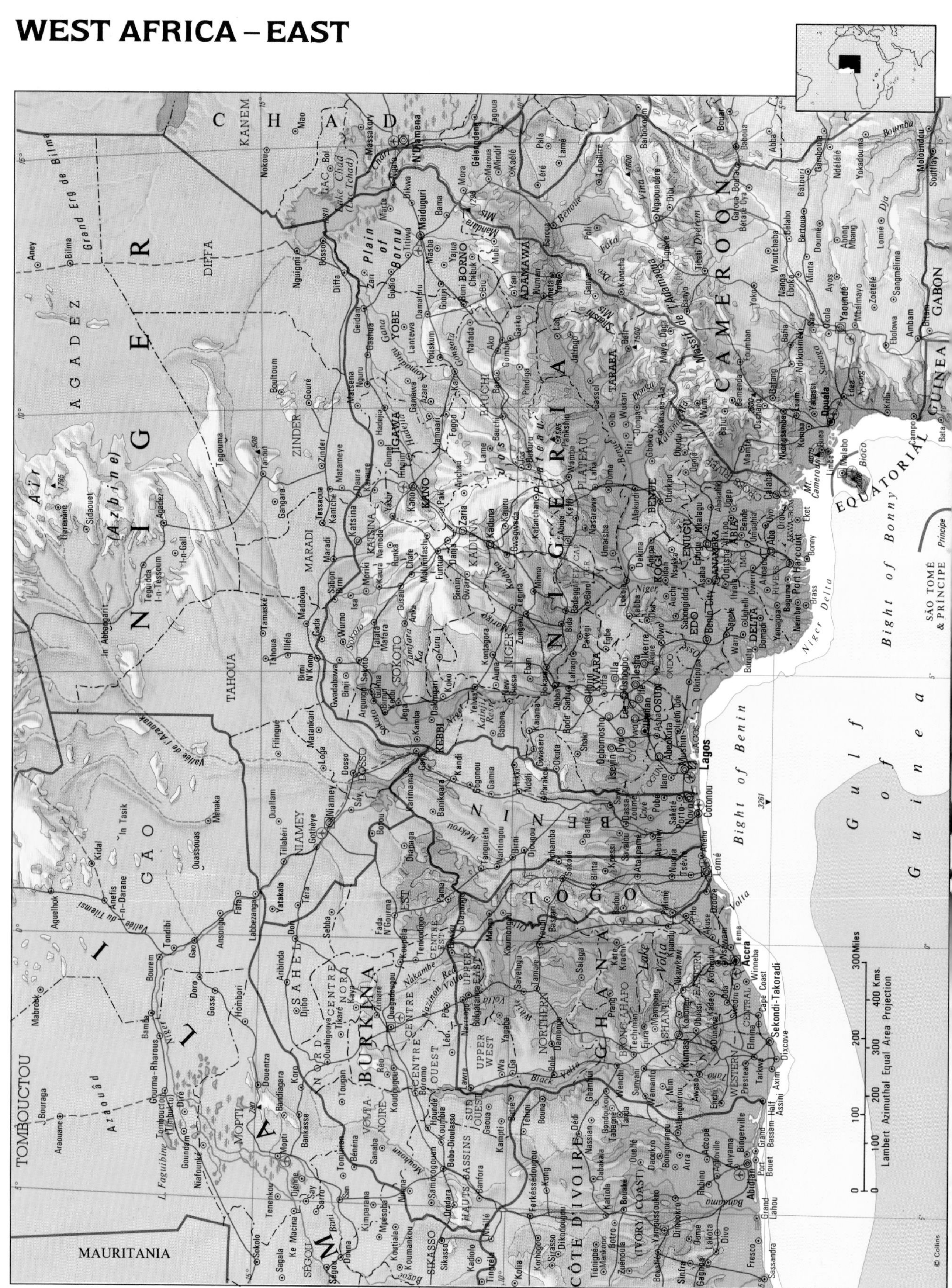

CHAD
NIGER
MALI
BURKINA
NIGERIA
CAMEROON
GHANA
TOGO
BENIN
CÔTE D'IVOIRE (IVORY COAST)
MAURITANIA
EQUATORIAL GUINEA
GABON
SÃO TOMÉ & PRÍNCIPE
Gulf of Guinea
Bight of Benin
Bight of Bonny
Plain of Bornu
Lake Chad
Lagos
Accra
Niamey
Yaoundé
0 100 200 300 Miles
0 100 200 300 400 Kms
Lambert Azimuthal Equal Area Projection
© Collins

SOUTH AFRICA

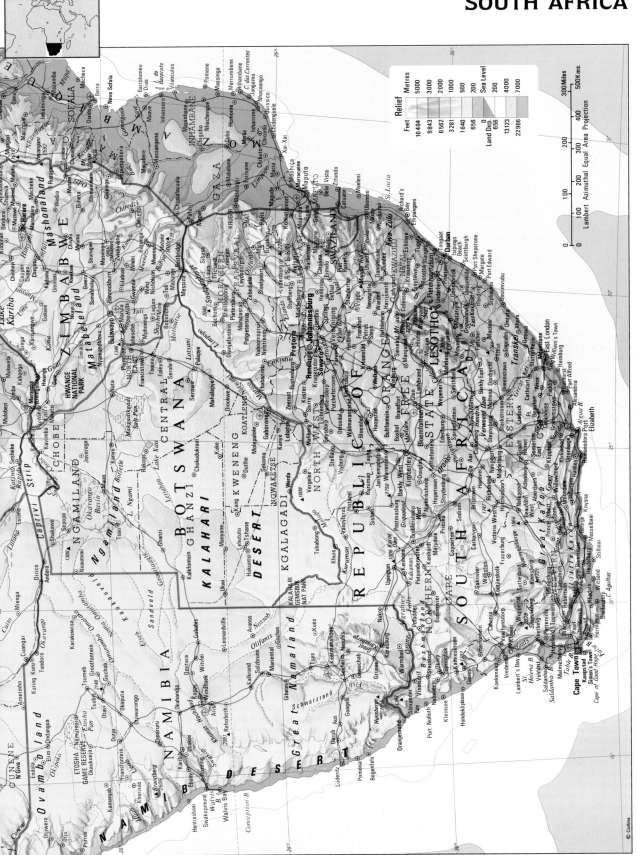

OCEANIA

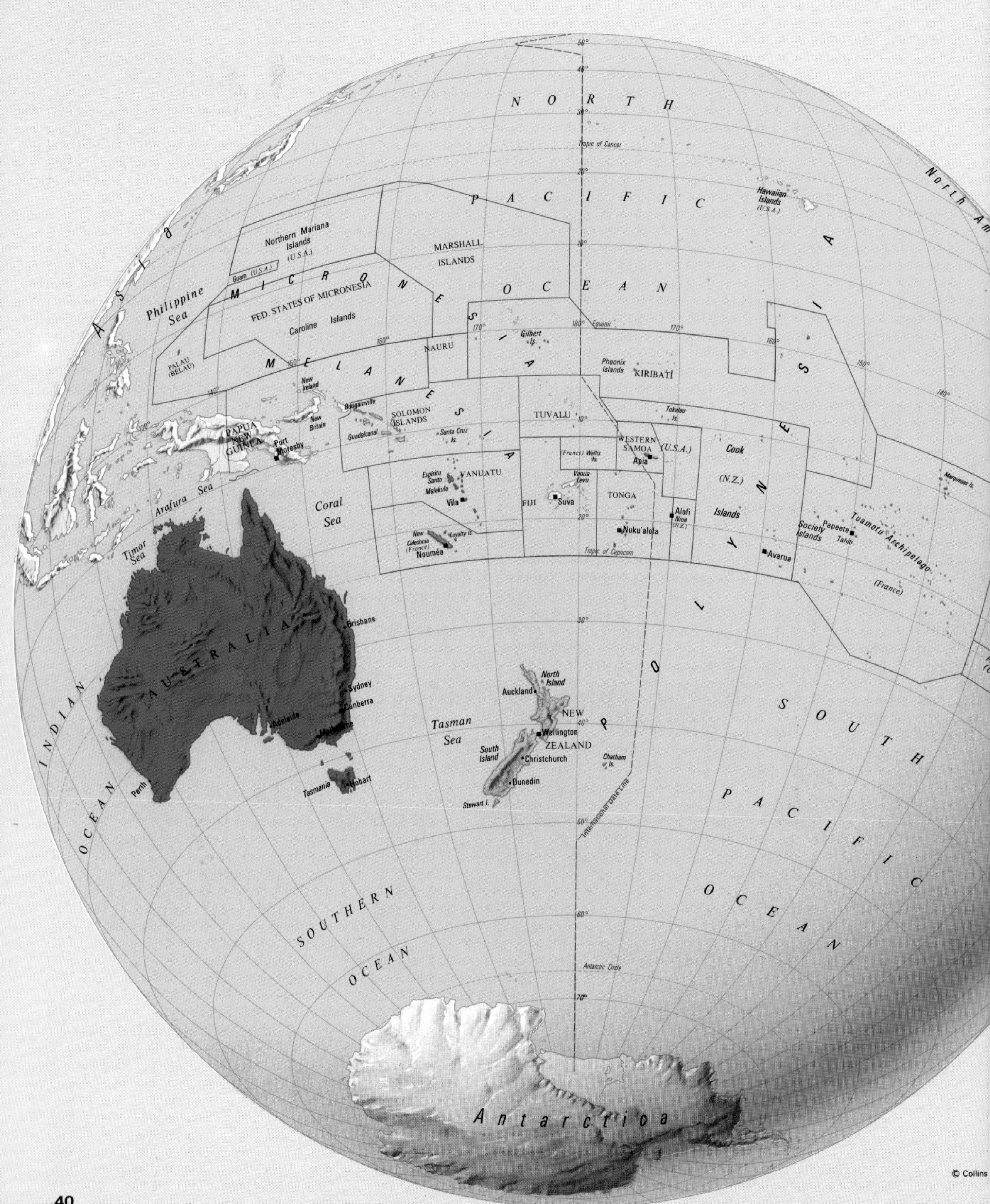

© Collins

NORTH PACIFIC OCEAN
Tropic of Cancer
Hawaiian Islands (U.S.A.)
North America
Asia
Northern Mariana Islands (U.S.A.)
Guam (U.S.A.)
MARSHALL ISLANDS
MICRONESIA
FED. STATES OF MICRONESIA
Caroline Islands
Philippine Sea
PALAU (BELAU)
NAURU
Gilbert Is.
Equator
Pheonix Islands
KIRIBATI
MELANESIA
POLYNESIA
New Ireland
New Britain
Bougainville
SOLOMON ISLANDS
Guadalcanal
Santa Cruz Is.
TUVALU
Tokelau Is.
PAPUA NEW GUINEA
Port Moresby
WESTERN SAMOA
Apia
(U.S.A.)
(France) Wallis Is.
Cook (N.Z.) Islands
Marquesas Is.
Espiritu Santo
Malekula
VANUATU
Vila
FIJI
Vanua Levu
Suva
TONGA
Nuku'alofa
Alofi
Niue (N.Z.)
Tropic of Capricorn
Avarua
Society Islands
Papeete
Tahiti
Tuamotu Archipelago (France)
Arafura Sea
Timor Sea
Coral Sea
New Caledonia (France)
Loyalty Is.
Nouméa
AUSTRALIA
Brisbane
Sydney
Canberra
Adelaide
Melbourne
Perth
Tasmania
Hobart
INDIAN OCEAN
Tasman Sea
North Island
Auckland
NEW ZEALAND
Wellington
South Island
Christchurch
Dunedin
Stewart I.
Chatham Is.
International Date Line
SOUTH PACIFIC OCEAN
SOUTHERN OCEAN
Antarctic Circle
Antarctica

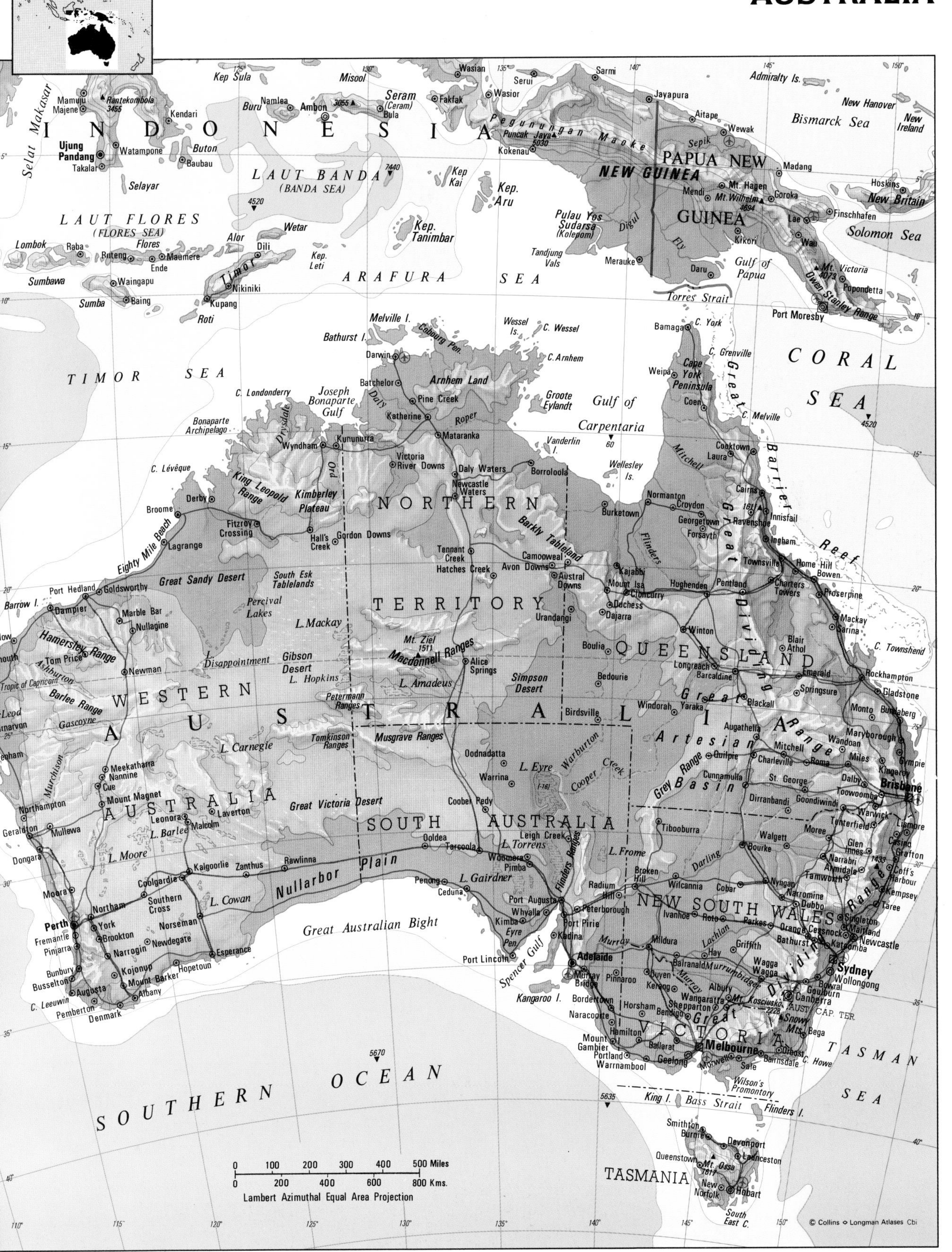

INDONESIA

Selat Makasar

Mamuju
Majene
Rantekombola 3455
Kendari

Ujung Pandang
Watampone
Takalar
Buton
Baubau

Selayar

LAUT FLORES
(FLORES SEA)

Lombok
Raba
Binteng
Flores
Alor
Wetar
Kep.
Tanimbar

Sumbawa
Waingapu
Ende
Maumere
Dili
Timor
Kep.
Leti

Sumba
Baing
Kupang
Roti
Nikiniki

Kep Sula

Buru
Namlea
Ambon
Seram
(Ceram)
Bula

Misool

Serui

Fakfak

Wasian
Wasior

LAUT BANDA
(BANDA SEA)

7440
4520

Kep
Kai

Kep.
Aru

ARAFURA **SEA**

Sarmi

Jayapura
Aitape
Wewak

Pegunungan Maoke
Puncak Jaya
5030
Kokenau

Sepik

PAPUA NEW

NEW GUINEA

GUINEA

Mendi
Mt. Hagen
Mt.Wilhelm
4694
Goroka

Madang
Hoskins

Bismarck Sea

New Hanover
New
Ireland

New Britain

Solomon Sea

Lae
Wau
Kikori

Digul

Fly

Daru

Merauke

Gulf of
Papua

Mt. Victoria
4070
Popondetta

Owen Stanley Range

Port Moresby

TIMOR **SEA**

C. Londonderry

Bonaparte
Archipelago

C. Lévêque

Joseph
Bonaparte
Gulf

Melville I.

Bathurst I.

Darwin
Batchelor
Pine Creek

Daly

Arnhem Land

Cobourg Pen.

C. Arnhem

Wessel
Is.
C. Wessel

Groote
Eylandt

Gulf of
Carpentaria

Vanderlin
I.

60

Wellesley
Is.

Torres Strait

Bamaga
C. York

C. Grenville

Weipa

Cape
York
Peninsula

Coen
C. Melville

4520

CORAL

SEA

C. York

Great

Barrier

Reef

Broome

Derby

Fitzroy
Crossing

King Leopold
Range

Kimberley
Plateau

Wyndham
Kununurra

Victoria
River Downs

Katherine
Mataranka

Roper

Daly Waters

Newcastle
Waters

Borroloola

Hall's
Creek
Gordon Downs

NORTHERN

Tennant
Creek
Hatches Creek

Camooweal
Avon Downs

Barkly Tableland

Austral
Downs

Burketown

Normanton
Croydon

Georgetown
Forsayth

Cairns
Innisfail

Mitchell

Laura

Conkton

Ravenshoe

Ingham
Home Hill
Bowen

Townsville

Charters
Towers

Proserpine

Great

Eighty Mile Beach

Lagrange

Port Hedland
Goldsworthy

Barrow I.
Dampier

Marble Bar
Nullagine

Hamersley Range

Tom Price
Newman

Ashburton

Great Sandy Desert

South Esk
Tablelands

Percival
Lakes

L. Mackay

TERRITORY

Kajabbi
Mount Isa
Cloncurry

Hughenden
Pentland

Dajarra

Duchess

Urandangi

Boulia

QUEENSLAND

Winton

Longreach

Blair
Athol

Mackay
Sarina

C. Townshend

Dividing

Rockhampton

Barrow I.

slow.

mouth

Carnarvon

L.McLeod

Tropic of Capricorn

Barlee Range

Gascoyne

Murchison

WESTERN

Meekatharra
Nannine
Cue

Mount Magnet

Laverton

Disappointment

Gibson
Desert

L. Hopkins

Mt. Ziel
1511
Macdonnell Ranges

Alice
Springs

Petermann
Ranges

L. Amadeus

AUSTRALIA

Simpson
Desert

Birdsville

AUSTRALIA

Windorah
Yaraka

Bedourie

Barcaldine

Emerald

Blackall

Springsure

Monto
Bundaberg

Maryborough

Wandoan

Gympie

L. Carnegie

Tomkinson
Ranges

Musgrave Ranges

Warburton

Cooper

Creek

Great

Range

Artesian

Augathella

Mitchell

Charleville
Roma

Miles

Grey
Range

Quilpie

Cunnamulla

St. George

Dirranbandi

Dalby
Toowoomba

Kingaroy

Brisbane

Warwick

Oodnadatta

Warrina

L. Eyre
(-16)

Coober Pedy

SOUTH

AUSTRALIA

Basin

Goondiwindi

Tenterfield

Lismore

Casino

Grafton

Geraldton
Mullewa

Northampton

Dongara

Moora

L. Moore

L. Barlee
Malcolm

Leonora

Meekatharra

Coolgardie
Kalgoorlie
Zanthus

Southern
Cross

L. Cowan

Norseman

Rawlinna

Nullarbor **Plain**

Oldea
Tarcoola

Penong
Ceduna

Leigh Creek

L. Torrens

Woomera
Pimba

L. Gairdner

L. Frome

Tibooburra

Broken
Hill

Wilcannia
Cobar

Bourke

Nyngan

Walgett
Moree

Narrabri

Glen
Innes

Armidale

Inverell

Coff's
Harbour

Kempsey

Taree

NEW SOUTH WALES

Dividing

Perth
Fremantle
York
Brookton
Pinjarra
Narrogin

Bunbury
Busselton
Augusta

C. Leeuwin
Pemberton
Denmark

Northam
Newdegate

Kojonup
Mount Barker
Hopetoun

Albany

Esperance

Great Australian Bight

Kimba

Eyre
Pen.

Port Augusta
Peterborough

Whyalla
Port Pirie
Kadina

Port Lincoln

Spencer Gulf

Radium
Hill

Murray

Ivanhoe

Hay

Griffith

Lachlan

Condobolin

Parkes

Orange
Bathurst

Dubbo

Wellington

Mudgee

Cessnock
Maitland
Newcastle

Sydney
Wollongong

Range

SOUTHERN **OCEAN**

5670

Kangaroo I.

Adelaide

Murray
Bridge

Pinnaroo

Bordertown

Naracoorte

Mount
Gambier

Portland
Warrnambool

Buyen
Kerang

Wangaratta
Shepparton

Bendigo

Hamilton
Ballarat

Geelong

VICTORIA

Melbourne

Wilson's
Promontory

King I.

5635

Bass Strait

Flinders I.

Mildura

Balranald
Murrumbidgee

Albury

Wagga
Wagga

Mt. Kosciusko
2228

AUST. CAP. TER.

Canberra

Great

Snowy

Mts.

Bega

C. Howe

Bairnsdale

Morwell

Sale

TASMAN

SEA

Smithton
Burnie
Queenstown
Mt. Ossa

Devonport
Launceston

New
Norfolk

Hobart

South
East C.

TASMANIA

Lambert Azimuthal Equal Area Projection

© Collins ◇ Longman Atlases Cbi

0	100	200	300	400	500 Miles
0	200	400	600	800 Kms.	

WESTERN AUSTRALIA

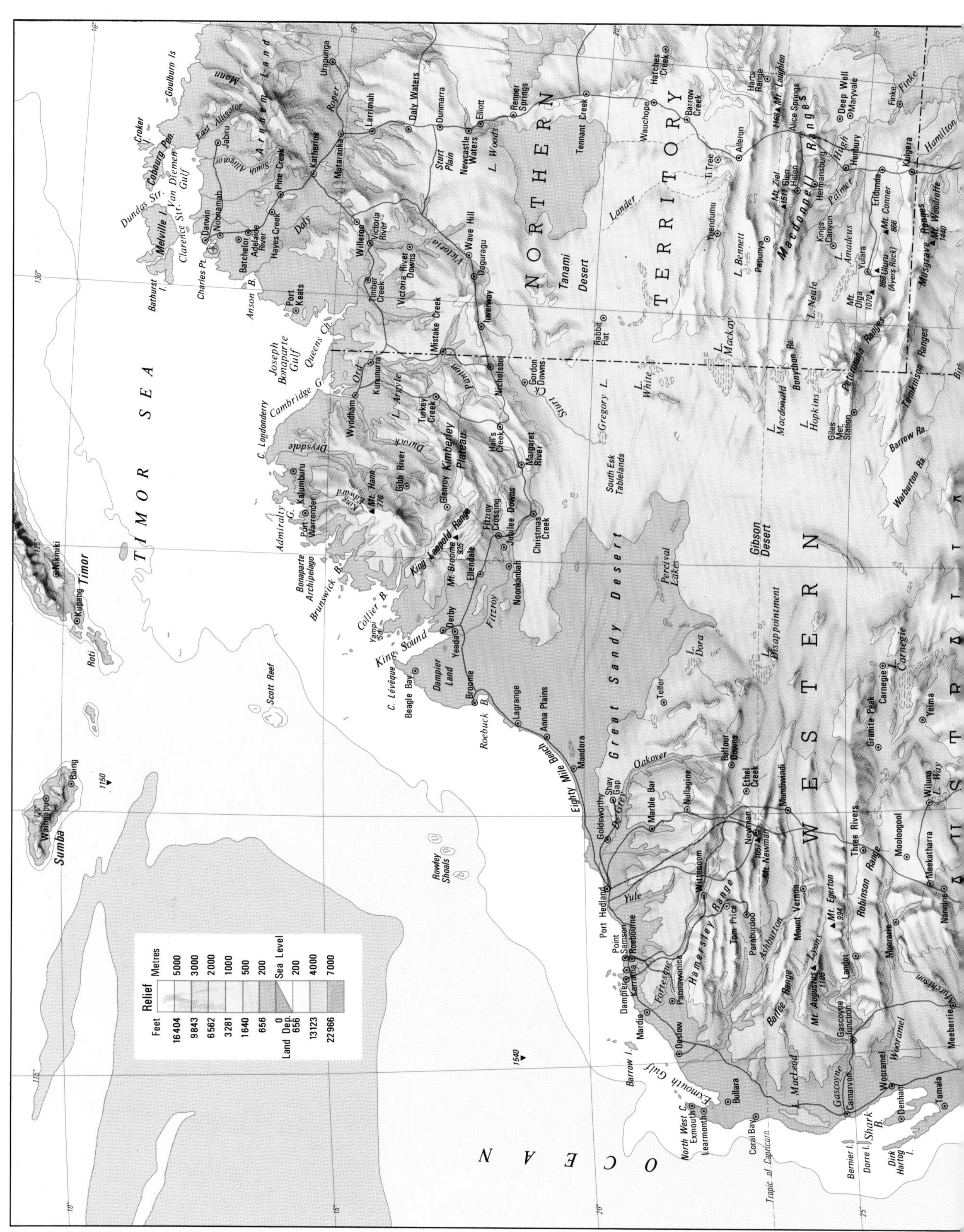

Relief
Feet
Metres
16404
5000
9843
3000
6562
2000
3281
1000
1640
500
656
200
0
Sea Level
Land Dep.
656
200
13123
4000
22966
7000
TIMOR SEA
OCEAN
NORTHERN TERRITORY
WESTERN AUSTRALIA
Timor
Kupang
Roti
Sumba
Waingapu
Scott Reef
Rowley Shoals
Joseph Bonaparte Gulf
Queens Ch.
Cambridge G.
C. Londonderry
Admiralty G.
Bonaparte Archipelago
Brunswick B.
Collier B.
King Sound
C. Lévêque
Beagle Bay
Dampier Land
Derby
Broome
Roebuck B.
Lagrange
Anna Plains
Mandora
Eighty Mile Beach
Great Sandy Desert
Gibson Desert
Tanami Desert
Kimberley Plateau
King Leopold Range
Fitzroy Crossing
Hall's Creek
Wyndham
Kununurra
L. Argyle
Ord
Port Hedland
Roebourne
Dampier
Karratha
Onslow
Barrow I.
Exmouth Gulf
North West C.
Exmouth
Learmonth
Coral Bay
Carnarvon
Shark B.
Dirk Hartog I.
Denham
Hamersley Range
Mt. Newman
Newman
Tom Price
Paraburdoo
Wittenoom
Marble Bar
Nullagine
Meekatharra
Wiluna
L. Disappointment
L. Mackay
L. Macdonald
L. Hopkins
Tropic of Capricorn
Darwin
Katherine
Alice Springs
Macdonnell Ranges
Tennant Creek
Melville I.
Bathurst I.
Dundas Str.
Cobourg Pen.
Arnhem Land
Uluru (Ayers Rock)
Petermann Ranges
Musgrave Ranges
Giles Met. Station
Warburton Ra.

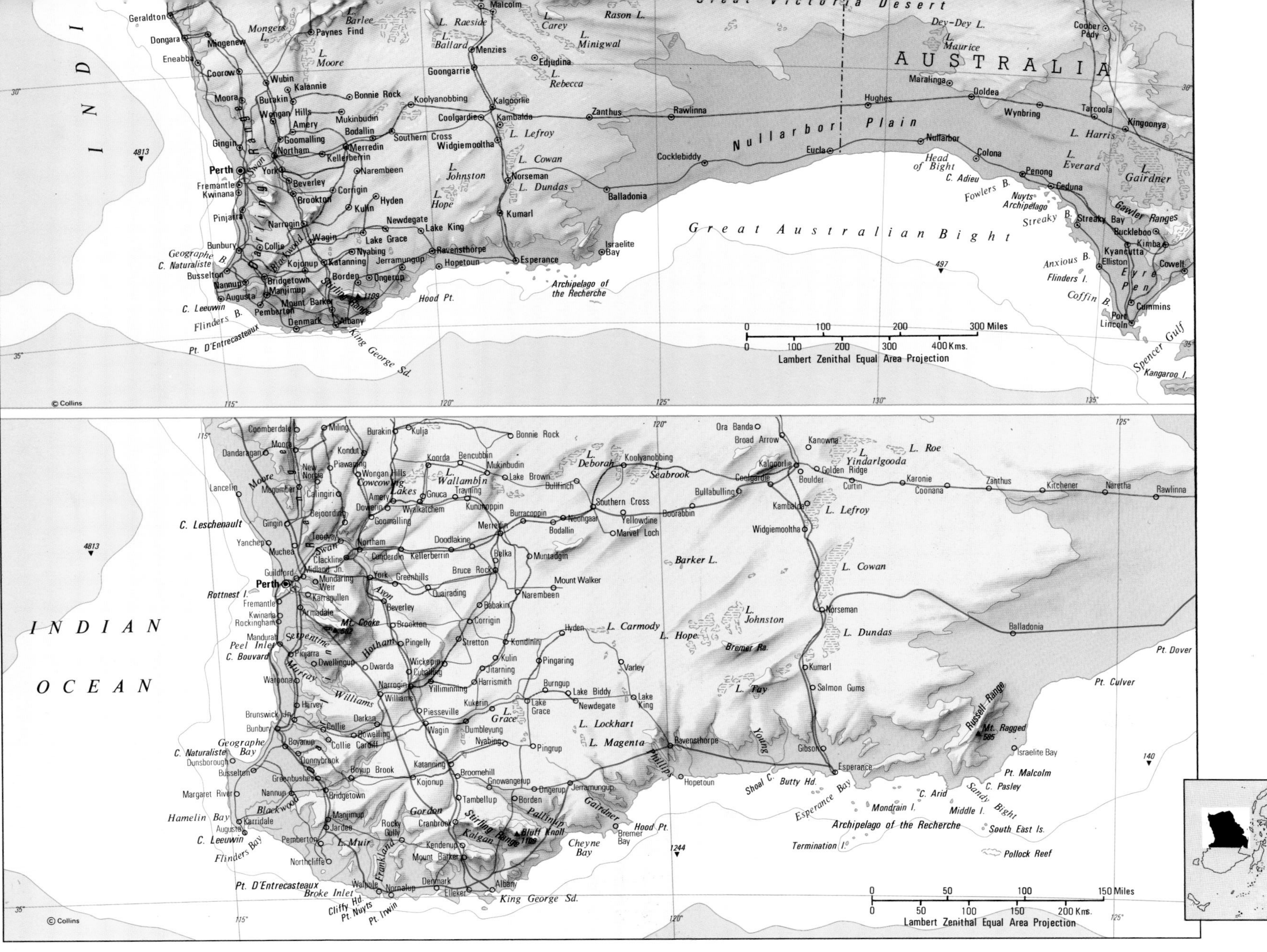

AUSTRALIA
INDIAN OCEAN
Great Australian Bight
Nullarbor Plain
Great Victoria Desert
Perth
Kalgoorlie
Coolgardie
Esperance
Albany
Geraldton
Bunbury
Fremantle
Norseman
Eucla
Ceduna
Port Lincoln
Spencer Gulf
Archipelago of the Recherche
King George Sd.
C. Leeuwin
C. Naturaliste
Geographe B.
Rottnest I.
Stirling Range
Russell Range
L. Lefroy
L. Cowan
L. Dundas
L. Johnston
L. Grace
L. Magenta
L. Barlee
L. Moore
Gawler Ranges
Eyre Pen.
Lambert Zenithal Equal Area Projection
0 100 200 300 Miles
0 100 200 300 400 Kms.
0 50 100 150 Miles
0 50 100 150 200 Kms.
© Collins

EASTERN AUSTRALIA

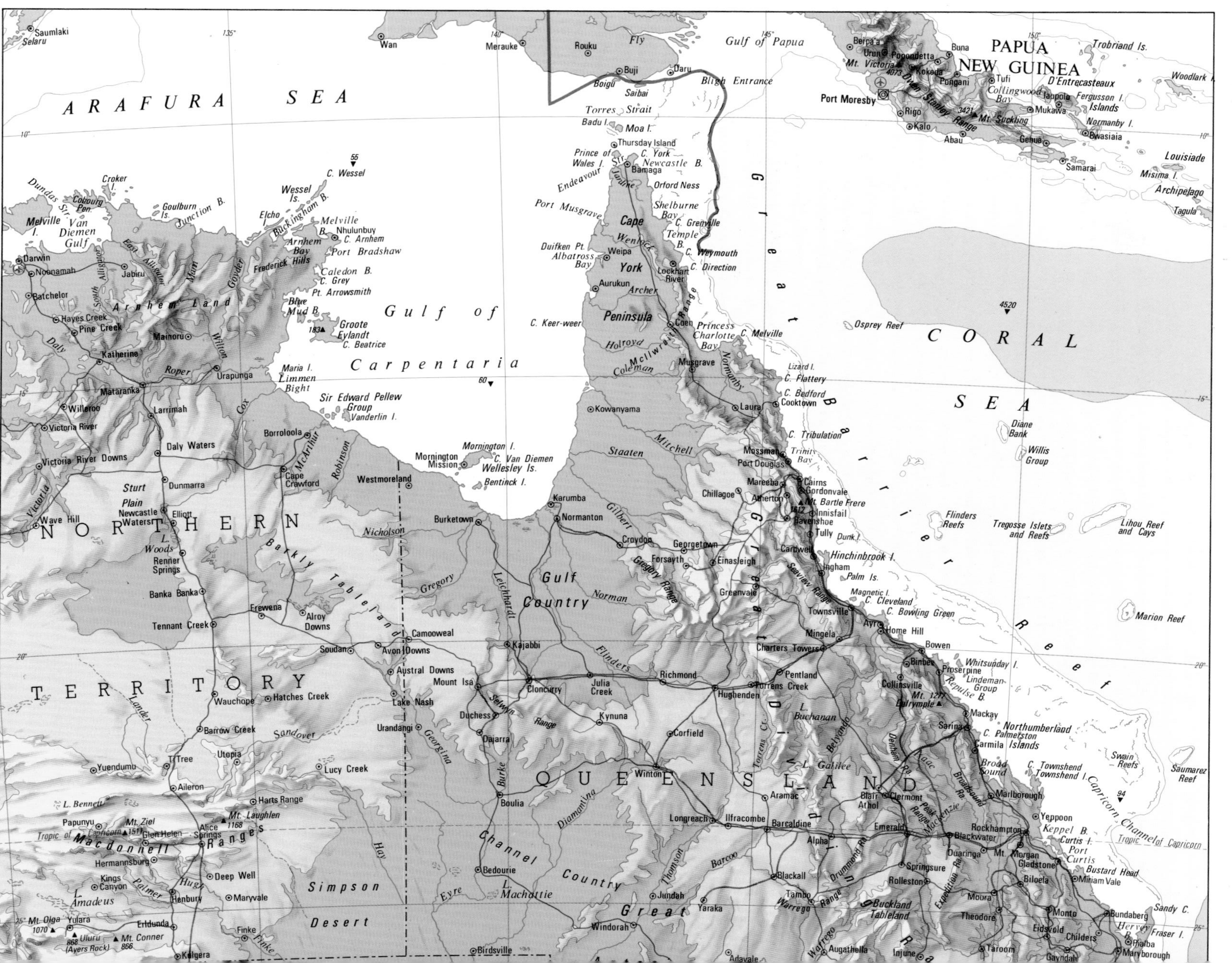

PAPUA NEW GUINEA
Port Moresby
Gulf of Papua
Owen Stanley Range
Trobriand Is.
D'Entrecasteaux Islands
Louisiade Archipelago
ARAFURA SEA
CORAL SEA
Great Barrier Reef
Gulf of Carpentaria
Torres Strait
Thursday Island
Cape York Peninsula
Weipa
Cooktown
Cairns
Townsville
Mackay
Rockhampton
Bundaberg
Maryborough
Gladstone
Charters Towers
Hughenden
Richmond
Julia Creek
Cloncurry
Mount Isa
Winton
Longreach
Barcaldine
Emerald
Normanton
Karumba
Burketown
Gulf Country
Channel Country
Great Dividing Range
QUEENSLAND
NORTHERN TERRITORY
Darwin
Katherine
Mataranka
Daly Waters
Tennant Creek
Alice Springs
Macdonnell Ranges
Barkly Tableland
Arnhem Land
Groote Eylandt
Simpson Desert
Uluru (Ayers Rock)
Tropic of Capricorn
Birdsville
Boulia
Windorah
Capricorn Channel

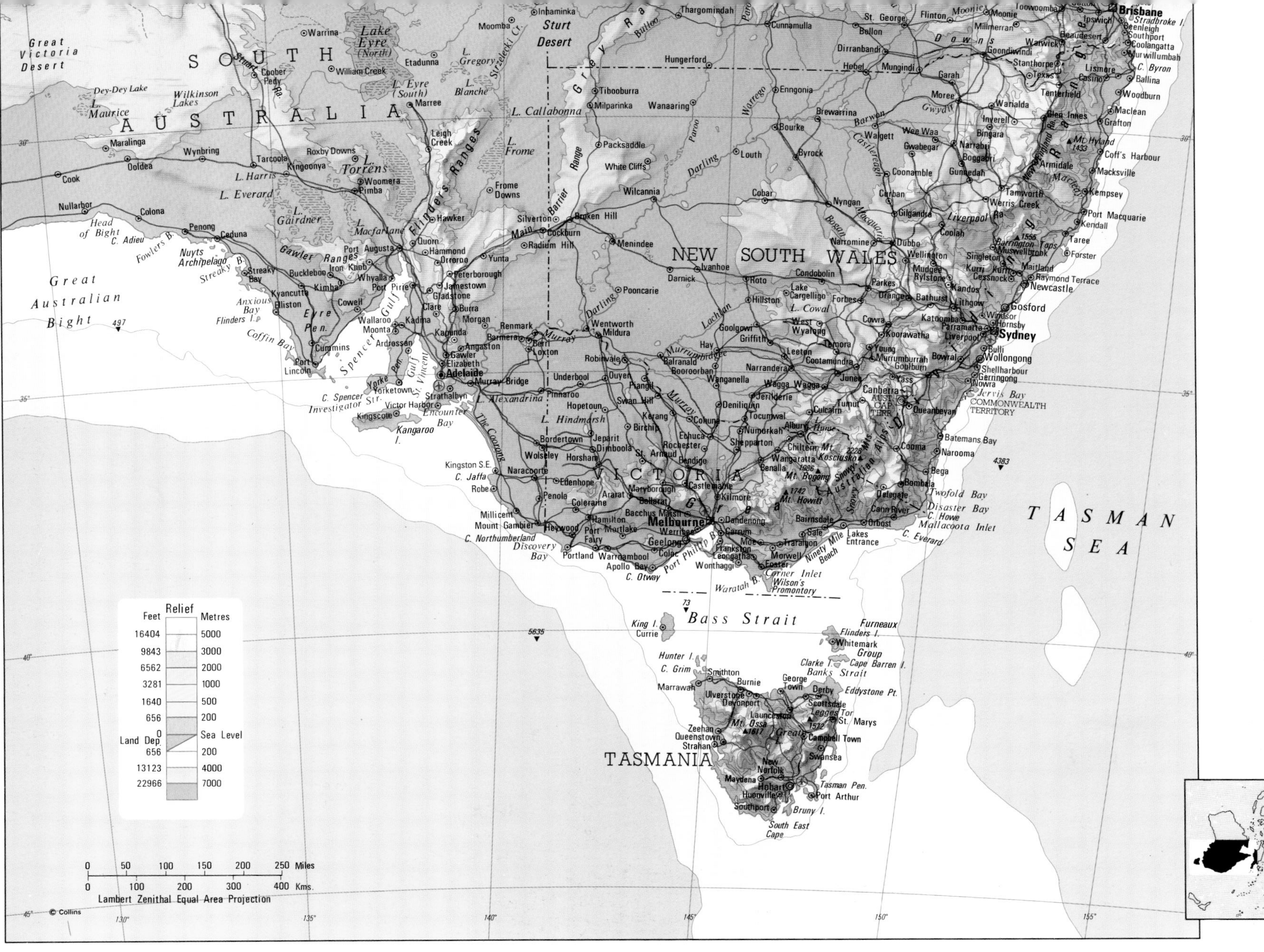

SOUTH AUSTRALIA
NEW SOUTH WALES
VICTORIA
TASMANIA
TASMAN SEA
Great Australian Bight
Bass Strait
Banks Strait
Spencer Gulf
Gulf St. Vincent
Sturt Desert
Great Victoria Desert
Flinders Ranges
Grey Range
Barrier Range
Gawler Ranges
Eyre Pen.
Kangaroo I.
King I.
Flinders I.
Furneaux Group
Lake Eyre (North)
L. Eyre (South)
L. Torrens
L. Gairdner
L. Frome
L. Callabonna
Darling
Murray
Murrumbidgee
Lachlan
Adelaide
Melbourne
Sydney
Brisbane
Canberra
Hobart
Launceston
Newcastle
Wollongong
Geelong
Ballarat
Bendigo
Broken Hill
Port Augusta
Port Lincoln
Whyalla
Mt. Kosciusko 2228
Australian Alps
COMMONWEALTH TERRITORY
Relief
Feet | Metres
16404 | 5000
9843 | 3000
6562 | 2000
3281 | 1000
1640 | 500
656 | 200
0 | Sea Level
Land Dep. 656 | 200
13123 | 4000
22966 | 7000
0 50 100 150 200 250 Miles
0 100 200 300 400 Kms.
Lambert Zenithal Equal Area Projection
© Collins

SOUTHEAST AUSTRALIA

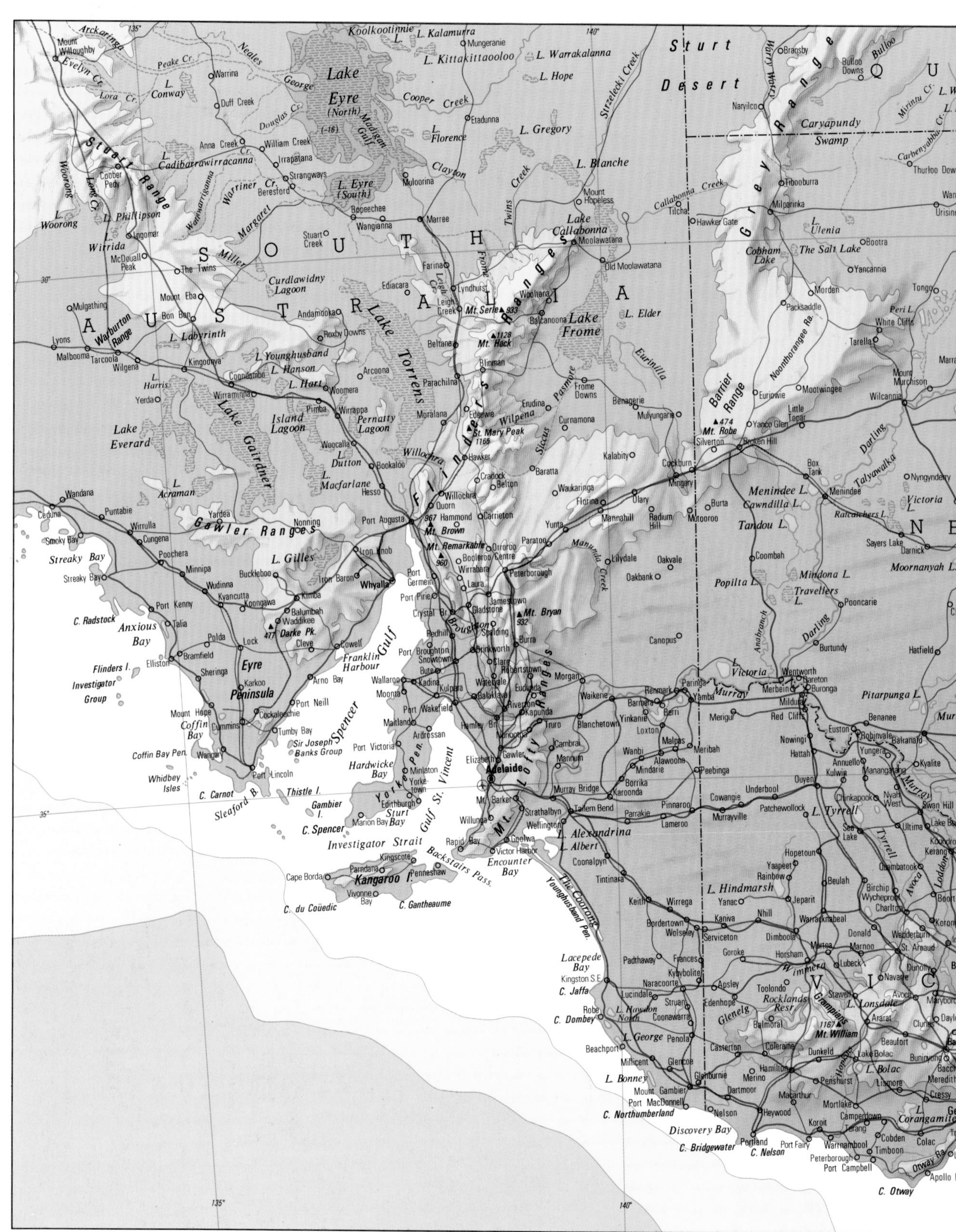

SOUTH AUSTRALIA
Sturt Desert
Lake Eyre (North)
L. Eyre (South)
Lake Torrens
Lake Gairdner
Lake Frome
Lake Callabonna
L. Blanche
L. Gregory
Cooper Creek
Strzelecki Creek
Stuart Range
Flinders Ranges
Gawler Ranges
Grey Range
Barrier Range
Mt. Lofty Ranges
Eyre Peninsula
Spencer Gulf
Gulf St. Vincent
Yorke Pen.
Kangaroo I.
Investigator Strait
Backstairs Pass.
Encounter Bay
L. Alexandrina
L. Albert
The Coorong
Younghusband Pen.
Lacepede Bay
Discovery Bay
C. Northumberland
C. Bridgewater
C. Nelson
C. Otway
Streaky Bay
Anxious Bay
Coffin Bay
C. Radstock
C. Carnot
C. Spencer
C. du Couëdic
C. Gantheaume
Sleaford B.
Thistle I.
Gambier I.
Flinders I.
Investigator Group
Whidbey Isles
Sir Joseph Banks Group
Hardwicke Bay
Sturt Bay
Franklin Harbour
Murray
Darling
Menindee L.
Cawndilla L.
Tandou L.
L. Victoria
L. Tyrrell
L. Hindmarsh
Wimmera
Grampians
Glenelg
Mt. William 1167
Mt. Brown 967
Mt. Remarkable 960
Mt. Bryan 932
St. Mary Peak 1165
Mt. Serle 933
Mt. Robe 474
Darke Pk. 477
Adelaide
Port Augusta
Port Pirie
Whyalla
Port Lincoln
Ceduna
Mount Gambier
Broken Hill
Mildura
Renmark
Murray Bridge
Woomera
Coober Pedy
Marree
Hawker
Quorn
Peterborough
Kadina
Wallaroo
Moonta
Kingscote
Victor Harbor
Naracoorte
Penola
Bordertown
Keith
Horsham
Hamilton
Portland
Warrnambool
Port Fairy
Ararat
Stawell
135°
140°
30°
35°

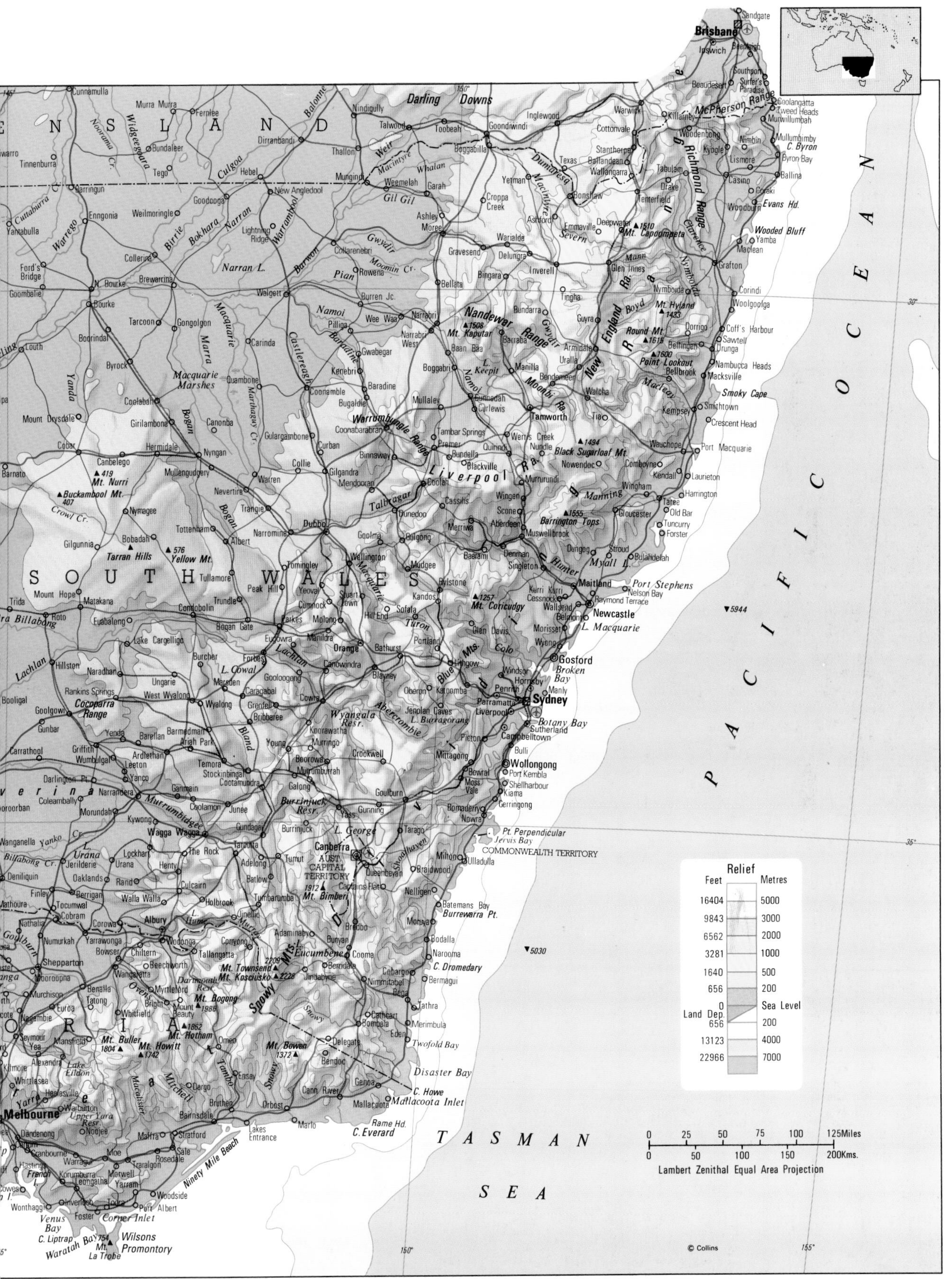

Brisbane
Ipswich
Darling Downs
McPherson Range
Richmond Range
New England Ra.
Nandewar Range
Warrumbungle Range
Liverpool Ra.
Barrington Tops
Blue Mts.
Snowy Mts.
Sydney
Newcastle
Wollongong
Gosford
Canberra
AUST. CAPITAL TERRITORY
COMMONWEALTH TERRITORY
Jervis Bay
Melbourne
Dubbo
Orange
Bathurst
Tamworth
Goulburn
Wagga Wagga
Albury
Port Macquarie
Port Stephens
Botany Bay
Broken Bay
L. Macquarie
L. George
Mt. Kosciusko
Mt. Townsend
C. Howe
Wilsons Promontory
Ninety Mile Beach
Corner Inlet
Mallacoota Inlet
Smoky Cape
C. Byron
Evans Hd.
Wooded Bluff
C. Dromedary
Disaster Bay
Twofold Bay
Rame Hd.
C. Everard
Murrumbidgee
Lachlan
Macquarie
Bogan
Castlereagh
Namoi
Gwydir
Barwon
Darling
Warrego
Culgoa
Narran L.
Macquarie Marshes
Riverina
SOUTH WALES
QUEENSLAND
VICTORIA
PACIFIC OCEAN
TASMAN SEA
Relief
Feet
Metres
16404 5000
9843 3000
6562 2000
3281 1000
1640 500
656 200
0 Sea Level
Land Dep.
656 200
13123 4000
22966 7000
0 25 50 75 100 125Miles
0 50 100 150 200Kms.
Lambert Zenithal Equal Area Projection
© Collins

NEW ZEALAND

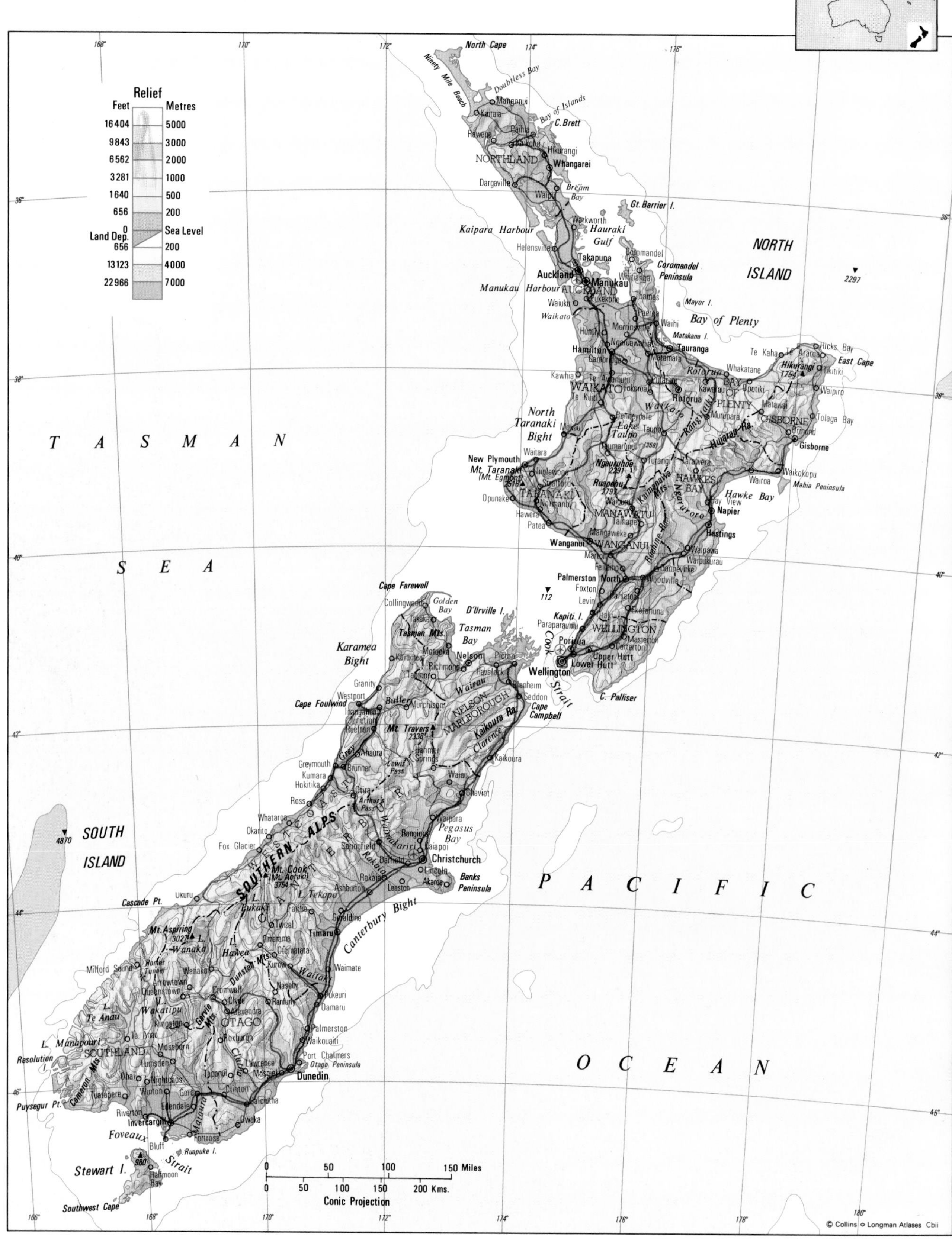

Relief

Feet	Metres
16 404	5000
9 843	3000
6 562	2000
3 281	1000
1 640	500
656	200
0 Land Dep.	Sea Level
656	200
13 123	4000
22 966	7000

0   50   100   150 Miles

0   50   100   150   200 Kms.

Conic Projection

© Collins · Longman Atlases Cbii

NORTH AMERICA

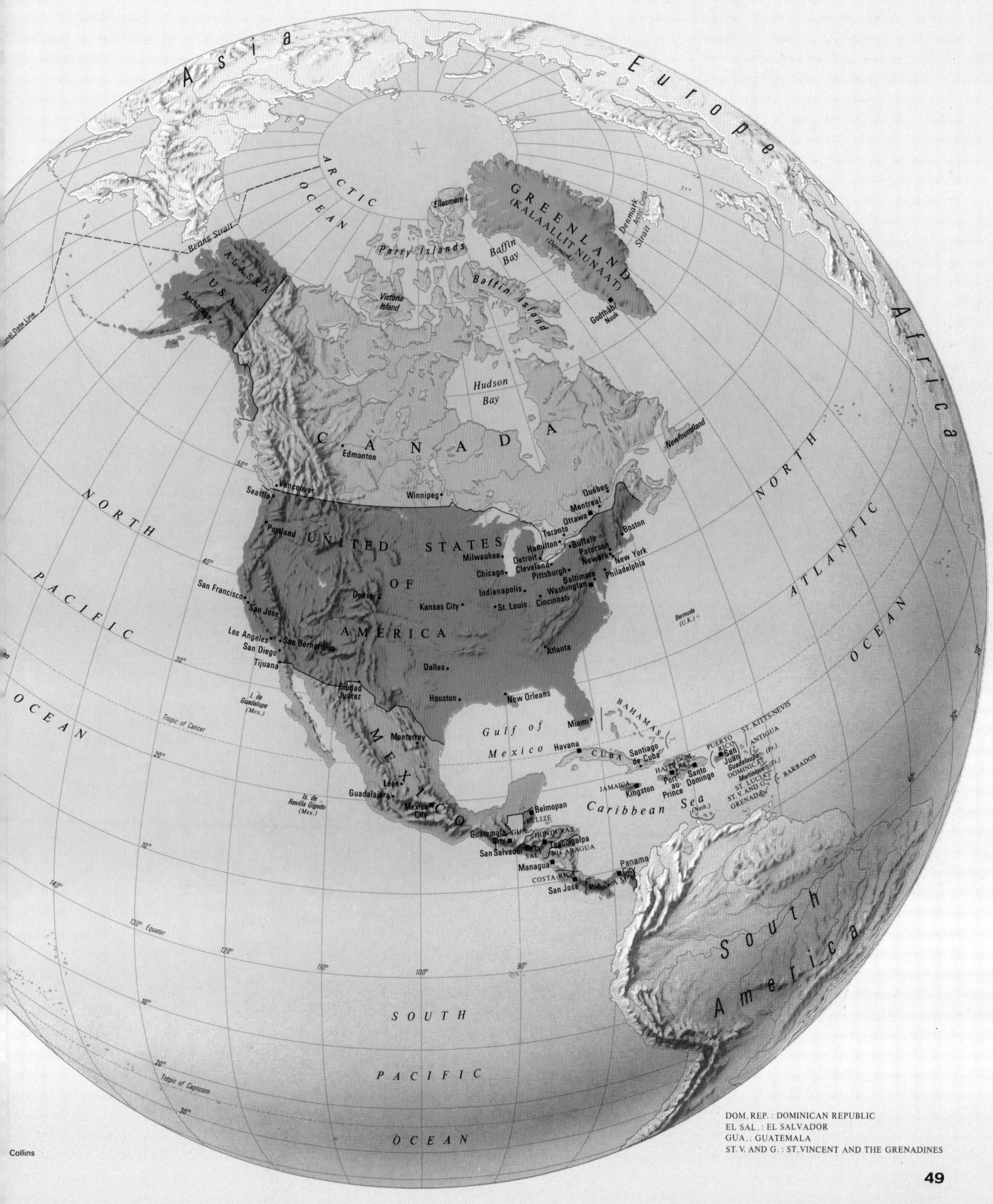

Asia

Europe

Africa

ARCTIC OCEAN

Bering Strait

A L A S K A
U.S.A
Anchorage

International Date Line

Ellesmere

GREENLAND
(KALAALLIT NUNAAT)
(Denmark)

Parry Islands

Baffin Bay

Denmark Strait

Victoria Island

Baffin Island

Goothåb
Nuuk

Hudson Bay

N O R T H

P A C I F I C

O C E A N

50°

Edmonton

C A N A D A

Newfoundland

Seattle
Vancouver

Winnipeg

Quebec

Montreal

N O R T H

Portland

U N I T E D   S T A T E S

Ottawa

Toronto

Hamilton
Detroit
Cleveland
Buffalo
Paterson
Newark

Boston

40°

San Francisco
San José

Omaha

O F

Milwaukee
Chicago

Pittsburgh
Baltimore
Washington

New York
Philadelphia

A T L A N T I C

Kansas City

Indianapolis
St. Louis
Cincinnati

A M E R I C A

Bermuda
(U.K.)

O C E A N

Los Angeles
San Bernardino
San Diego
Tijuana

30°

Dallas

Atlanta

Tropic of Cancer

I. de Guadalupe
(Mex.)

Ciudad Juárez

Houston

New Orleans

Miami

BAHAMAS

20°

Is. de Revilla Gigedo
(Mex.)

Guadalajara

León

M E X I C O

Monterrey

Gulf of Mexico

Havana

CUBA

Santiago
de Cuba

PUERTO
RICO

ST. KITTS-NEVIS

San
Juan

ANTIGUA

Guadeloupe (Fr.)
DOMINICA

140°

Mexico City

BELIZE

Belmopan

Caribbean Sea

JAMAICA
Kingston

HAITI
Port-
au-
Prince

DOM.
REP.
Santo
Domingo

Martinique (Fr.)
ST. LUCIA
ST. V. AND G.
BARBADOS

(Neth.)

GRENADA

O C E A N

130° Equator

Guatemala
City
San Salvador

GUA.
SAL.

Tegucigalpa
HONDURAS

NICARAGUA

10°

Managua

Panama
City

120°

110°

100°

San José
COSTA RICA

90°

S o u t h

10°

SOUTH

A m e r i c a

20° Tropic of Capricorn

PACIFIC

30°

OCEAN

Collins

DOM. REP. : DOMINICAN REPUBLIC
EL SAL. : EL SALVADOR
GUA. : GUATEMALA
ST. V. AND G. : ST. VINCENT AND THE GRENADINES

49

CANADA AND ALASKA

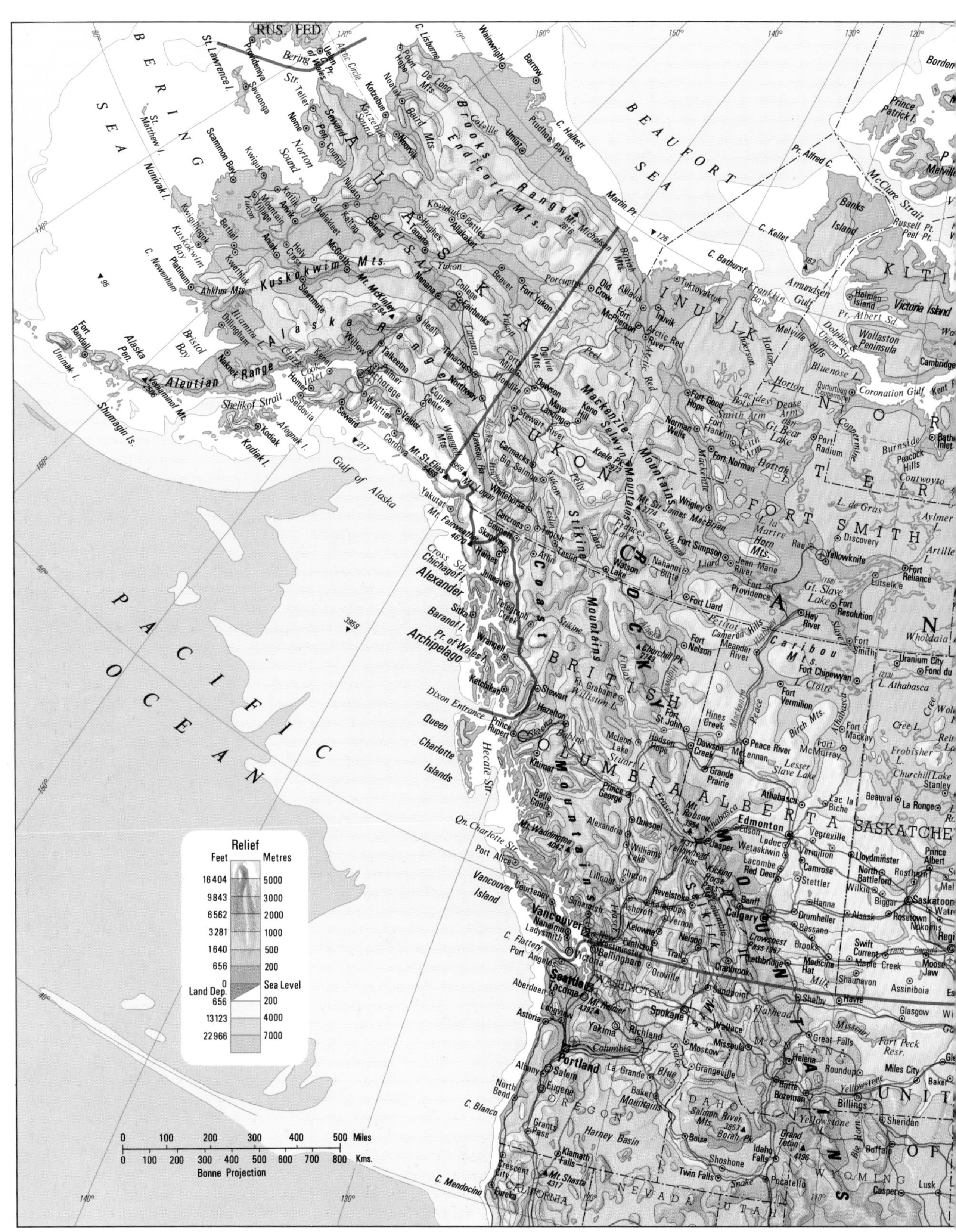

RUS. FED.
BERING SEA
BEAUFORT SEA
PACIFIC OCEAN
Gulf of Alaska
ALASKA (U.S.A.)
YUKON
BRITISH COLUMBIA
ALBERTA
SASKATCHE
INUVIK
FORT SMITH
WASHINGTON
OREGON
IDAHO
MONTANA
WYOMING
CALIFORNIA
NEVADA
UTAH
Brooks Range
Alaska Range
Kuskokwim Mts.
Aleutian Range
Mackenzie Mountains
Selwyn Mountains
Coast Mountains
ROCKY MOUNTAINS
Queen Charlotte Islands
Vancouver Island
Alexander Archipelago
Anchorage
Fairbanks
Juneau
Whitehorse
Dawson
Yellowknife
Edmonton
Calgary
Vancouver
Victoria
Seattle
Portland
Spokane
Saskatoon
Relief
Feet
Metres
16404
5000
9843
3000
6562
2000
3281
1000
1640
500
656
200
0
Sea Level
Land Dep.
656
200
13123
4000
22966
7000
0
100
200
300
400
500 Miles
0
100
200
300
400
500
600
700
800 Kms.
Bonne Projection

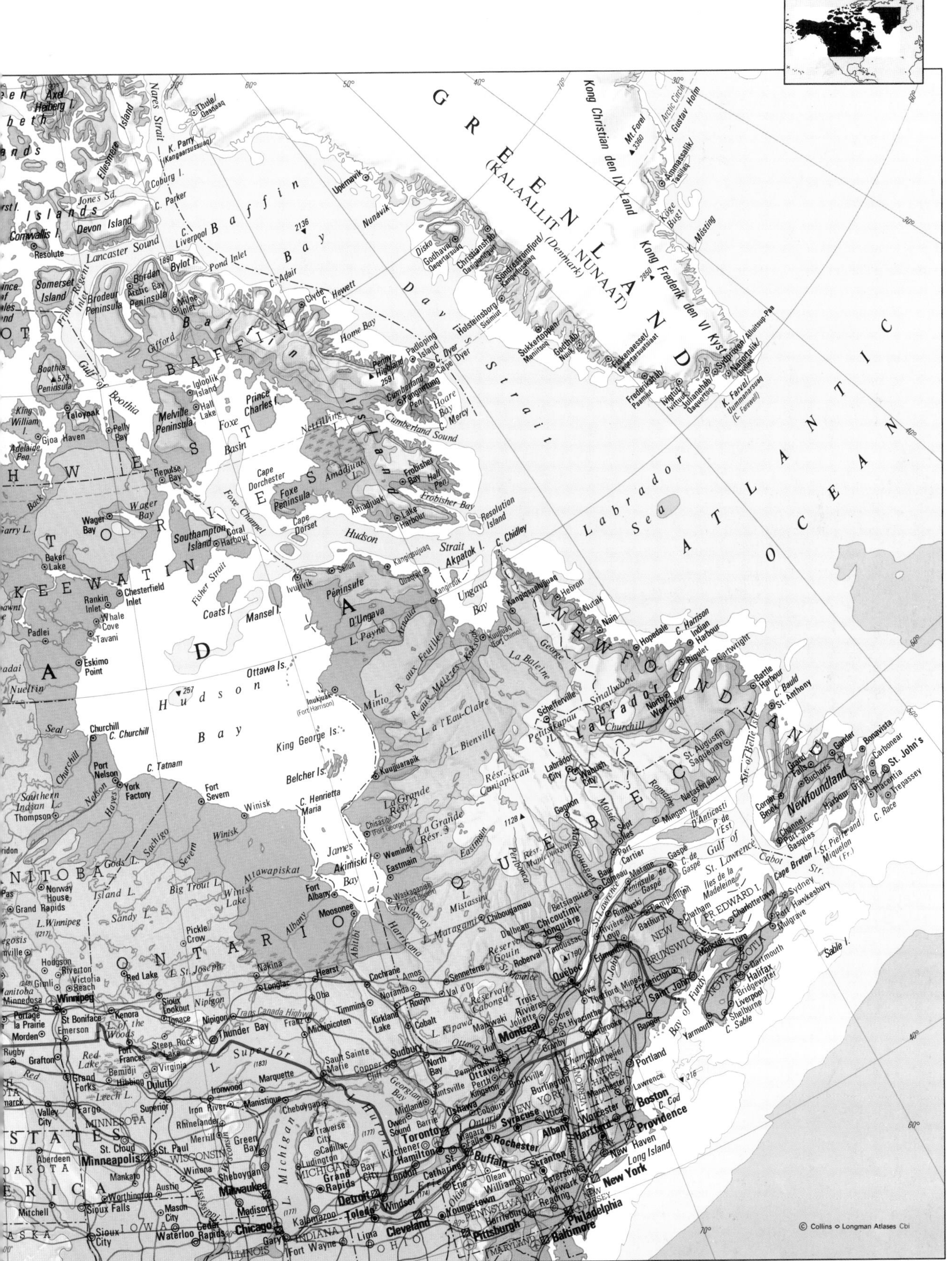

GREENLAND
(KALAALLIT NUNAAT)
(Denmark)
Baffin Bay
Davis Strait
Labrador Sea
ATLANTIC OCEAN
Hudson Bay
Hudson Strait
Ungava Bay
James Bay
NEWFOUNDLAND
QUEBEC
ONTARIO
MANITOBA
KEEWATIN
BAFFIN
Baffin Island
Foxe Basin
Newfoundland
New York
Boston
Montreal
Toronto
Chicago
Detroit
Philadelphia
Winnipeg
Québec
Halifax
St. John's
Ottawa
Cleveland
Pittsburgh
Buffalo
Baltimore
Minneapolis
© Collins · Longman Atlases Cbi

UNITED STATES

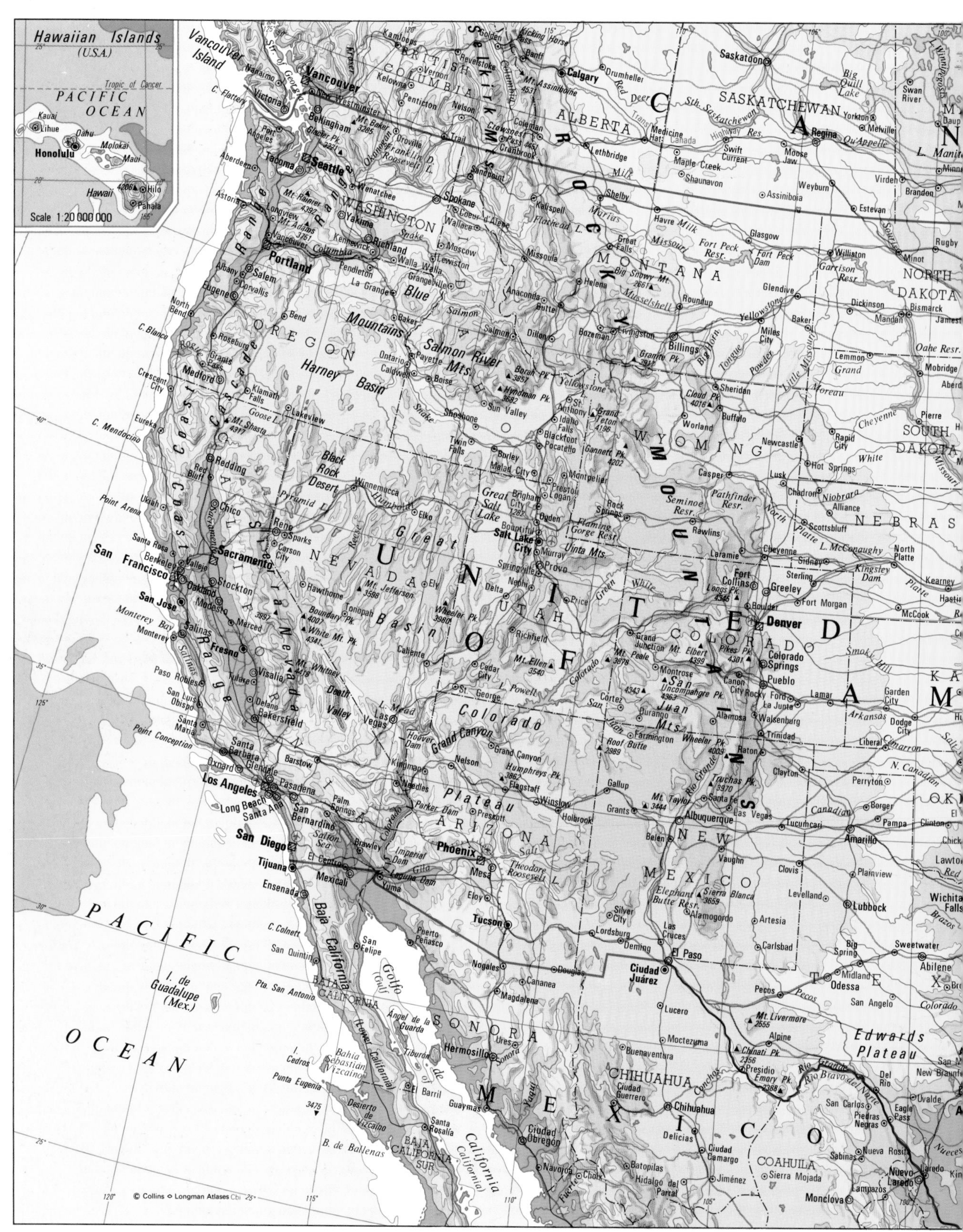

Hawaiian Islands
(U.S.A.)

Tropic of Cancer

PACIFIC
OCEAN

Kauai
Lihue
Oahu
Honolulu
Molokai
Maui
Hawaii
Hilo
Pahala

Scale 1:20 000 000

Vancouver
Island

C. Flattery

PACIFIC

OCEAN

I. de
Guadalupe
(Mex.)

© Collins ○ Longman Atlases

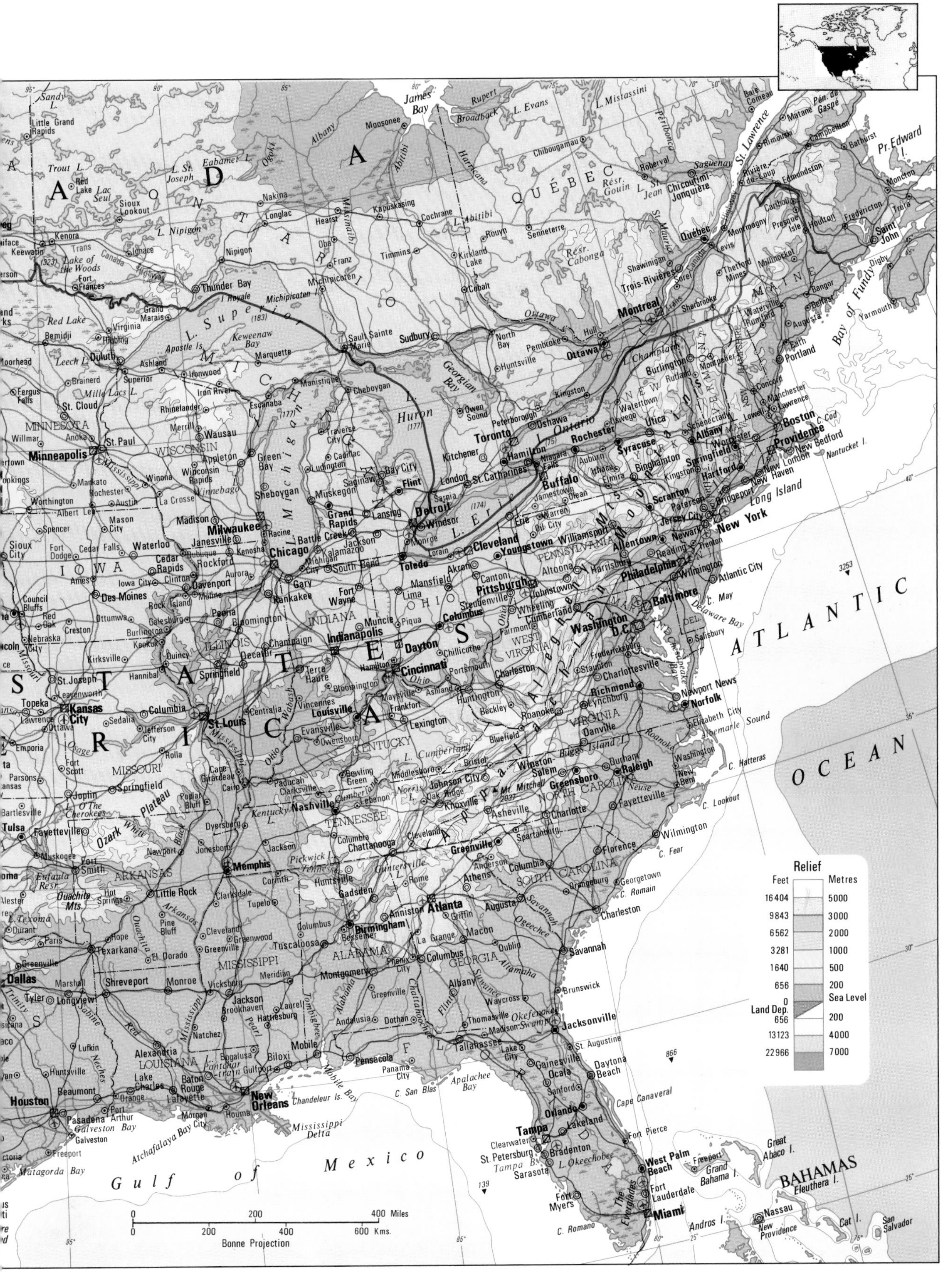

CANADA
ONTARIO
QUÉBEC
UNITED STATES OF AMERICA
ATLANTIC OCEAN
Gulf of Mexico
BAHAMAS
James Bay
L. Superior
L. Michigan
L. Huron
L. Erie
L. Ontario
Bay of Fundy
Long Island
Chicago
Detroit
Cleveland
Toronto
Montreal
Ottawa
Québec
Boston
New York
Philadelphia
Baltimore
Washington D.C.
Pittsburgh
Buffalo
Milwaukee
Minneapolis
St. Paul
St. Louis
Kansas City
Cincinnati
Indianapolis
Louisville
Nashville
Memphis
Atlanta
Birmingham
New Orleans
Houston
Dallas
Jacksonville
Tampa
Orlando
Miami
Nassau
Relief
Feet
Metres
16404
5000
9843
3000
6562
2000
3281
1000
1640
500
656
200
0
Sea Level
Land Dep.
656
200
13123
4000
22966
7000
0
200
400 Miles
0
200
400
600 Kms.
Bonne Projection

WESTERN UNITED STATES

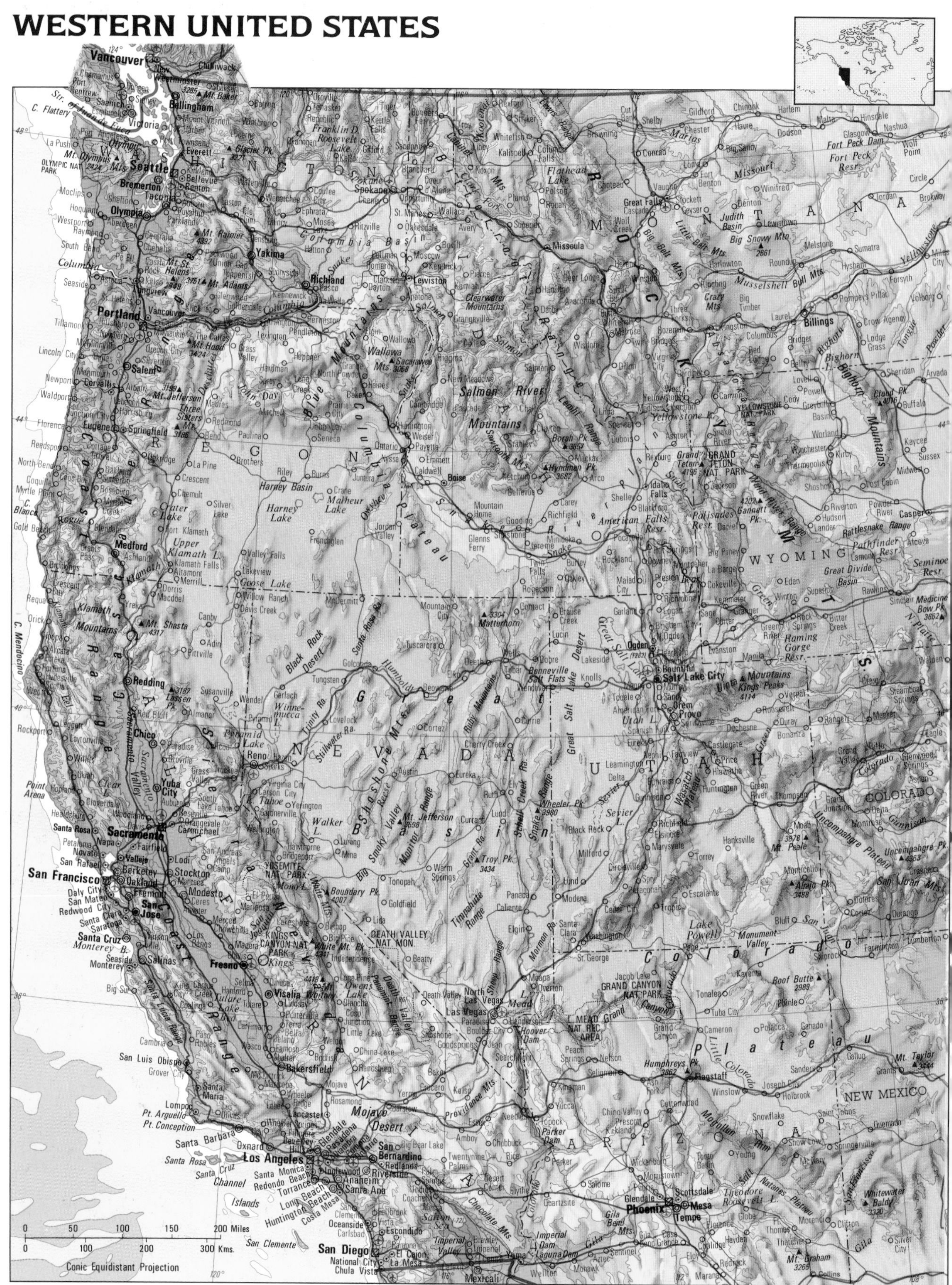

Vancouver
Victoria
Bellingham
Mt. Baker
Seattle
Bremerton
Tacoma
Olympia
Mt. Olympus
Olympic Mts.
Mt. Rainier
Mt. St. Helens
Mt. Adams
Yakima
Richland
Spokane
Lewiston
Portland
Mt. Hood
Salem
Eugene
Springfield
Mt. Jefferson
Three Sisters
Medford
Crater Lake
Upper Klamath L.
Harney Basin
Malheur Lake
Harney Lake
Goose Lake
Boise
Salmon River Mountains
Clearwater Mountains
Wallowa Mts.
Blue Mountains
Columbia Basin
Columbia Plateau
Snake River Plain
Idaho Falls
Pocatello
American Falls Resr.
Missoula
Great Falls
Helena
Butte
Billings
Bozeman
Big Snowy Mts.
Little Belt Mts.
Big Belt Mts.
Crazy Mts.
Musselshell
Missouri
Yellowstone
Yellowstone L.
Yellowstone Nat. Park
Grand Teton
Grand Teton Nat. Park
Bighorn Mountains
Cloud Pk.
Wind River Range
Gannett Pk.
Casper
Rattlesnake Range
Pathfinder Resr.
Seminoe Resr.
Medicine Bow Pk.
Great Divide Basin
Flaming Gorge Resr.
Rock Springs
Uinta Mountains
Kings Peaks
Salt Lake City
Ogden
Great Salt Lake
Great Salt Lake Desert
Bonneville Salt Flats
Provo
Utah L.
Wasatch Plateau
Sevier L.
Wheeler Pk.
Matterhorn
Ruby Mountains
Great Basin
Humboldt
Black Rock Desert
Pyramid Lake
Reno
Carson City
Lake Tahoe
Walker L.
Shoshone Mts.
Toiyabe Range
Mt. Jefferson
Troy Pk.
Boundary Pk.
Tonopah
Goldfield
Death Valley Nat. Mon.
Las Vegas
Lake Mead
Hoover Dam
Lake Mead Nat. Rec. Area
Grand Canyon
Grand Canyon Nat. Park
Colorado
Lake Powell
Monument Valley
Colorado Plateau
Little Colorado
Humphreys Pk.
Flagstaff
Mogollon Rim
Phoenix
Mesa
Tempe
Scottsdale
Gila
Gila Bend Mts.
Theodore Roosevelt L.
Mt. Graham
Yuma
Imperial Dam
Imperial Valley
Salton Sea
Chocolate Mts.
Mexicali
San Diego
El Cajon
Chula Vista
Los Angeles
Long Beach
Santa Ana
Anaheim
Riverside
San Bernardino
Mojave Desert
Bakersfield
Santa Barbara
Santa Barbara Channel
Santa Cruz
Santa Rosa
San Clemente
Channel Islands
Pt. Conception
Pt. Arguello
San Luis Obispo
Santa Lucia Range
Coast Range
Fresno
Visalia
Mt. Whitney
Tulare Lake
Kings Canyon Nat. Park
Yosemite Nat. Park
Sierra Nevada
White Mt. Pk.
Owens Lake
Panamint Range
San Francisco
Oakland
Berkeley
San Jose
Stockton
Modesto
Sacramento
Sacramento Valley
Monterey B.
Salinas
Point Arena
Clear L.
Chico
Redding
Lassen Pk.
Mt. Shasta
Klamath Mountains
C. Mendocino
C. Blanco
Cascade Range
Coast Ranges
Str. of Juan de Fuca
C. Flattery
WASHINGTON
OREGON
IDAHO
MONTANA
WYOMING
NEVADA
UTAH
COLORADO
ARIZONA
NEW MEXICO
Bitterroot Range
Rocky Mountains
Uncompahgre Plateau
San Juan Mts.
Roof Butte
Mt. Taylor
Whitewater Baldy
0 50 100 150 200 Miles
0 100 200 300 Kms.
Conic Equidistant Projection

NORTHEAST U.S.A. – SOUTH CENTRAL CANADA

Relief

Metres	
5000	
3000	
2000	
1000	
500	
200	
Sea Level	
200	Land Dep.
4000	
7000	

Feet	
16404	
9843	
6562	
3281	
1640	
656	
0	
656	
13123	
22966	

© Collins

200 Miles
300 Kms.

Conic Equidistant Projection

CENTRAL AMERICA AND THE CARIBBEAN

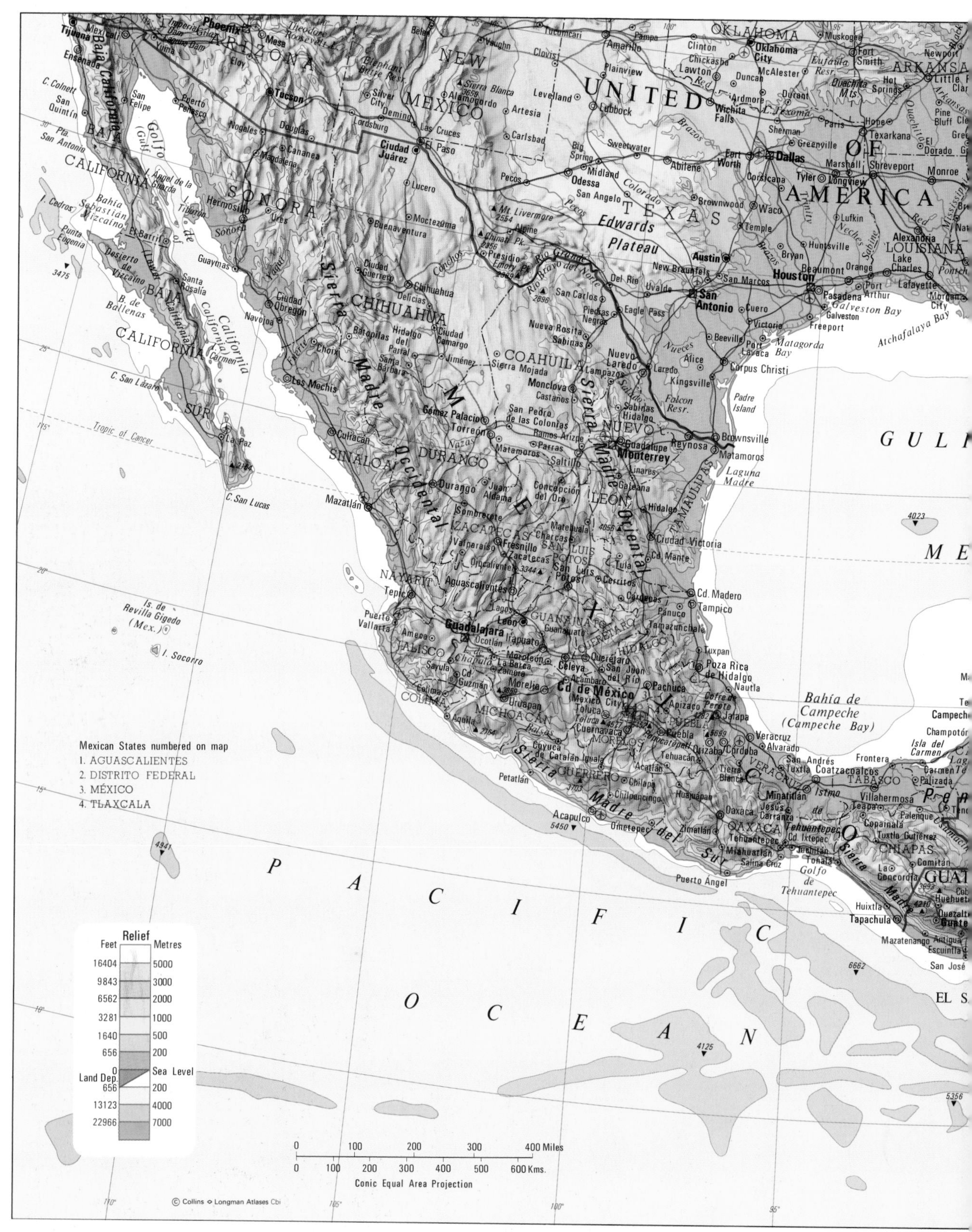

Mexican States numbered on map
1. AGUASCALIENTES
2. DISTRITO FEDERAL
3. MÉXICO
4. TLAXCALA

Relief

Feet		Metres
16404		5000
9843		3000
6562		2000
3281		1000
1640		500
656		200
0	Land Dep.	Sea Level
656		200
13123		4000
22966		7000

0   100   200   300   400 Miles
0   100   200   300   400   500   600 Kms.
Conic Equal Area Projection

© Collins ◆ Longman Atlases Cbi

56

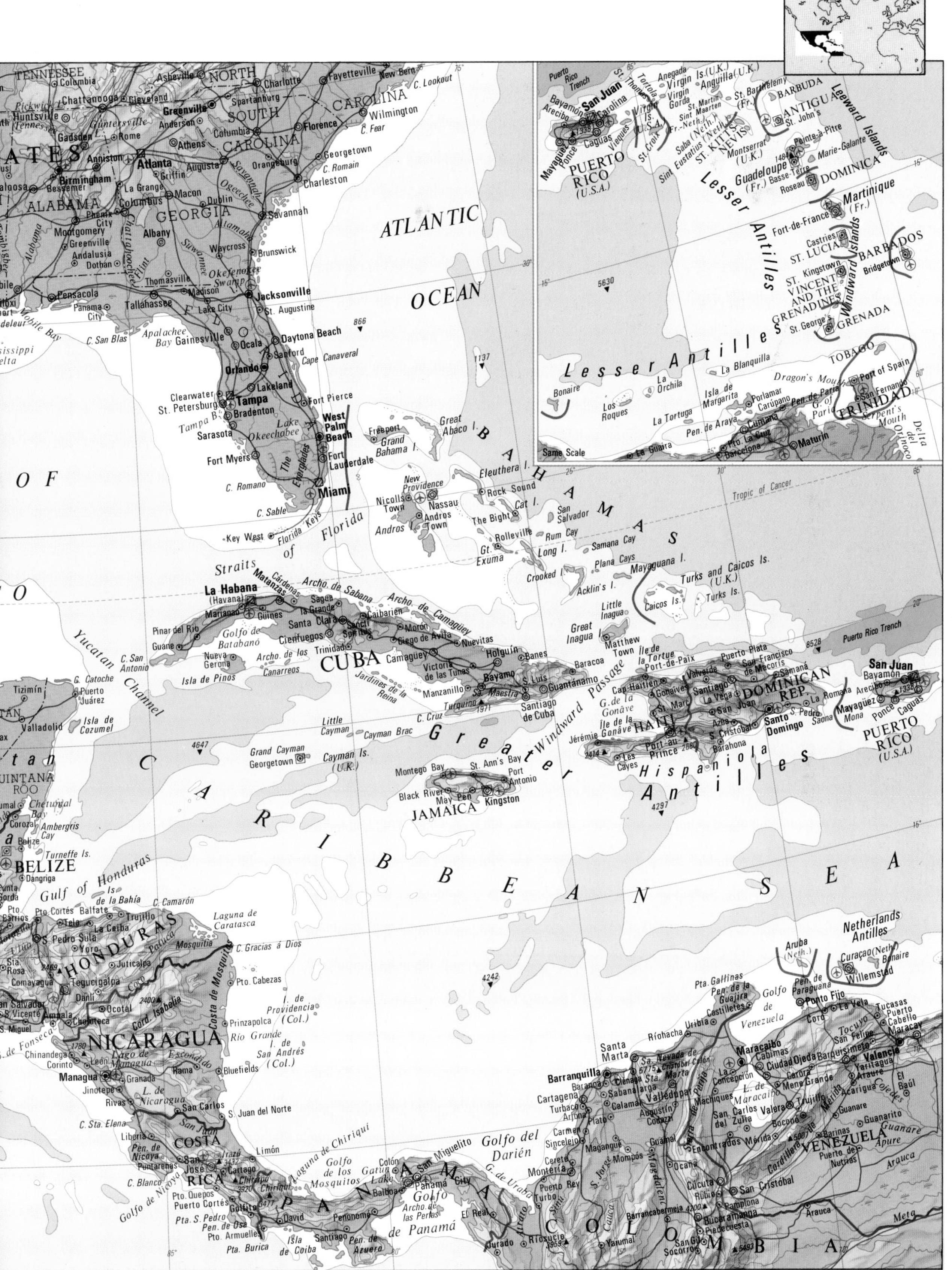

TENNESSEE
Columbia
Chattanooga
Cleveland
NORTH
CAROLINA
Asheville
Charlotte
Fayetteville
New Bern
C. Lookout
Pickwick
L.
Huntsville
Gadsden
Rome
SOUTH
CAROLINA
Spartanburg
Greenville
Anderson
Columbia
Florence
Wilmington
Athens
Augusta
Orangeburg
Georgetown
C. Fear
Birmingham
Bessemer
Atlanta
Griffin
Macon
GEORGIA
Savannah
Charleston
ALABAMA
Montgomery
Columbus
Albany
Waycross
Brunswick
ATLANTIC
OCEAN
Pensacola
Tallahassee
Jacksonville
St. Augustine
Panama City
Daytona Beach
Sanford
Ocala
Gainesville
Orlando
Cape Canaveral
Clearwater
St. Petersburg
Tampa
Lakeland
Bradenton
Fort Pierce
Sarasota
Lake
Okeechobee
West Palm Beach
Fort Myers
Fort Lauderdale
Miami
BAHAMAS
Freeport
Grand Bahama I.
Great Abaco I.
Eleuthera I.
New Providence
Nassau
Rock Sound
Cat I.
San Salvador
Nicolls Town
Andros Town
Andros
The Bight
Rolleville
Rum Cay
Long I.
Gt. Exuma
Samana Cay
Key West
Florida Keys
Straits of Florida
Crooked I.
Acklin's I.
Plana Cays
Mayaguana I.
Turks and Caicos Is. (U.K.)
La Habana (Havana)
Matanzas
Cárdenas
Archo. de Sabana
Archo. de Camaguey
Little Inagua
Caicos Is.
Turks Is.
Pinar del Rio
Marianao
Güines
Sagua la Grande
Caibarién
Great Inagua
Santa Clara
Golfo de Batabanó
Cienfuegos
Sancti Morón
Diego de Avila
Nuevitas
Matthew Town
Guane
Nueva Gerona
Archo. de los Canarreos
CUBA
Trinidad
Camaguey
Holguín
Banes
Baracoa
Isla de Pinos
Jardines de la Reina
Victoria de las Tunas
Bayamo
S. Luis
Guantánamo
Turquino 1974
Manzanillo
Maestra
Santiago de Cuba
C. Cruz
CARIBBEAN
Little Cayman
Cayman Brac
Greater
Windward Passage
HAITI
DOMINICAN REP.
Santiago
Grand Cayman
Georgetown
Cayman Is. (U.K.)
Montego Bay
St. Ann's Bay
Port Antonio
Santo Domingo
Black River
May Pen
JAMAICA
Kingston
Hispaniola
Antilles
BELIZE
Gulf of Honduras
Is. de la Bahía
C. Camarón
Laguna de Caratasca
Netherlands Antilles
Aruba (Neth.)
Curaçao(Neth.)
Bonaire
HONDURAS
Tegucigalpa
Mosquitia
C. Gracias á Dios
Pta. Gallinas
Willemstad
NICARAGUA
Managua
Granada
Río Grande
I. de Providencia (Col.)
Pto. Cabezas
Bluefields
I. de San Andrés (Col.)
Maracaibo
Barquisimeto
Valencia
VENEZUELA
COSTA RICA
Limón
Laguna de Chiriquí
Golfo del Darién
Barranquilla
Cartagena
L. de Maracaibo
Valera
PANAMA
Panamá
Golfo de Panamá
COLOMBIA

SEA

57

SOUTH AMERICA

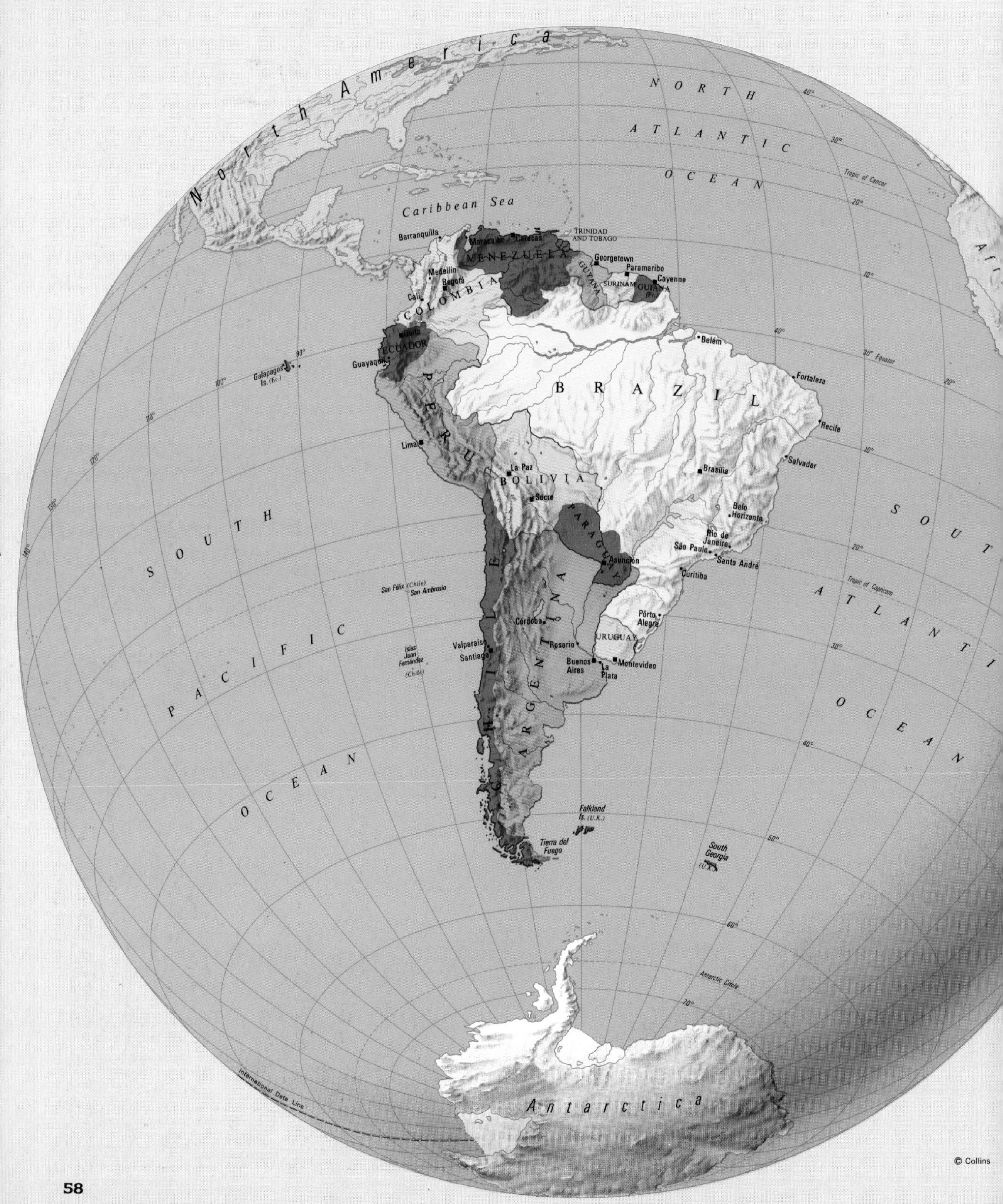

North America

NORTH

ATLANTIC

OCEAN

Tropic of Cancer

Caribbean Sea

Barranquilla

TRINIDAD
AND TOBAGO

Maracaibo · Caracas

VENEZUELA

Georgetown

Medellín

Paramaribo

Cayenne

Bogotá

GUYANA

SURINAM

GUIANA
(Fr.)

Cali

COLOMBIA

Quito

ECUADOR

Belém

Galápagos
Is. (Ec.)

Guayaquil

BRAZIL

Fortaleza

Equator

PERU

Recife

Lima

La Paz

BOLIVIA

Brasília

Salvador

Sucre

Belo
Horizonte

PARAGUAY

Rio de
Janeiro

SOUTH

São Paulo

Santo André

Asunción

Curitiba

San Félix (Chile)

Tropic of Capricorn

San Ambrosio

Córdoba

Pôrto
Alegre

PACIFIC

Islas
Juan
Fernández
(Chile)

Valparaíso

ARGENTINA

CHILE

Rosario

URUGUAY

ATLANTIC

Santiago

Buenos
Aires

Montevideo

La
Plata

OCEAN

OCEAN

Falkland
Is. (U.K.)

Tierra del
Fuego

South
Georgia
(U.K.)

International Date Line

Antarctic Circle

Antarctica

© Collins

TOCANTINS

Planalto do Mato Grosso

Serra dos Parecis

MATO GROSSO

Cuiabá

Cáceres

San Javier
San Ignacio
San Matías

SANTA CRUZ

BOLIVIA

Santa Cruz
Montero
Bañados de Izozog (Izozog Marshes)

Corumbá

MATO GROSSO DO SUL

Campo Grande
Três Lagoas

Ponta Porã
Dourados

PARAGUAY

FORMOSA

Asunción
Paraguari
Villarrica
Formosa

CHACO

Resistencia
Corrientes
Barranqueras

CORRIENTES

ARGENTINA

Santa Fé
Paraná
Rosario

ENTRE RÍOS

URUGUAY

Buenos Aires
La Plata
Montevideo

Río de la Plata (R. Plate)

Bahía Samborombón

Punta Norte

BUENOS AIRES

Mar del Plata

Bahía Blanca
Bahía Blanca

BRAZIL

GOIÁS

Goiânia
Brasília
DISTRITO FEDERAL
Anápolis

MINAS GERAIS

Uberlândia
Uberaba
Belo Horizonte
Divinópolis

SÃO PAULO

São José do Rio Prêto
Araçatuba
Marília
Presidente Prudente
Londrina
Maringá

PARANÁ

Curitiba
Ponta Grossa
Paranaguá
Guarapuava

SANTA CATARINA

Joinville
Blumenau
Itajaí
Florianópolis
Lajes

RIO GRANDE DO SUL

Caxias do Sul
Novo Hamburgo
São Leopoldo
Pôrto Alegre
Santa Maria
Rio Grande
Pelotas

Lagoa dos Patos

L. Mirim
L. Mangueira

São Paulo
Santos
São Vicente
Santo André
Campinas
Sorocaba
Rio de Janeiro
Niterói
Volta Redonda
Juiz de Fora
Barbacena
Campos

Tropic of Capricorn

Relief

Feet	Metres
16 404	5000
9843	3000
6562	2000
3281	1000
1640	500
656	200
0	Sea Level
Land Dep.	
656	200
13123	4000

0   100   200   300   400 Miles
0 100 200 300 400 500 600 Kms.

Lambert Azimuthal Equal Area Projection

(Inset map)

Belo Horizonte
Divinópolis
MINAS GERAIS
Franca
Passos
Ribeirão Prêto
Araraquara
São Carlos
Rio Claro
Limeira
Piracicaba
Campinas
Americana
SÃO PAULO
São Paulo
Mogi das Cruzes
Santo André
São Caetano do Sul
Santos
São Vicente
Jundiaí
Sorocaba
Juiz de Fora
Barbacena
Volta Redonda
Barra Mansa
Petrópolis
Nova Friburgo
Teresópolis
Duque de Caxias
Magé
Niterói
Rio de Janeiro
RIO DE JANEIRO
Cabo Frio
Campos
Cachoeiro
Itapemirim
Tropic of Capricorn

0   40   80 Miles
0 40 80 120 Kms.

© Collins

© Collins · Longman Atlases Cbi

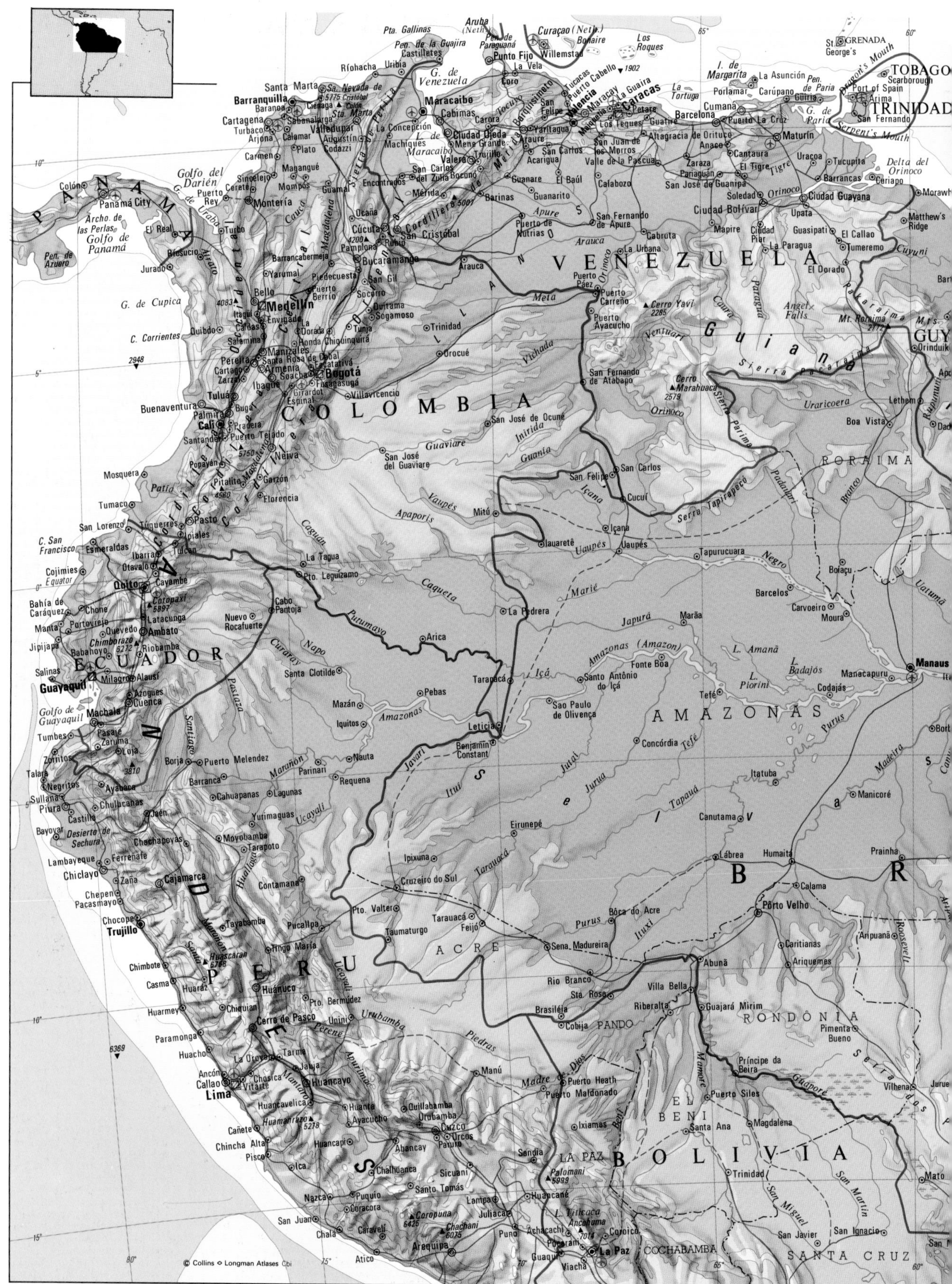

GRENADA
TOBAGO
TRINIDAD

VENEZUELA

COLOMBIA

Delta del Orinoco

Guiana

GUY

RORAIMA

PANAMA

Golfo del Darién
Golfo de Panamá
Pen. de Azuero

Medellín

Bogotá

Cali

ECUADOR

Quito

Guayaquil

Golfo de Guayaquil

Equator

AMAZONAS

Manaus

B R

PERU

ACRE

Lima

BOLIVIA

RONDÔNIA

EL BENI

LA PAZ

La Paz
COCHABAMBA

SANTA CRUZ

60

Collins ◇ Longman Atlases Cbi

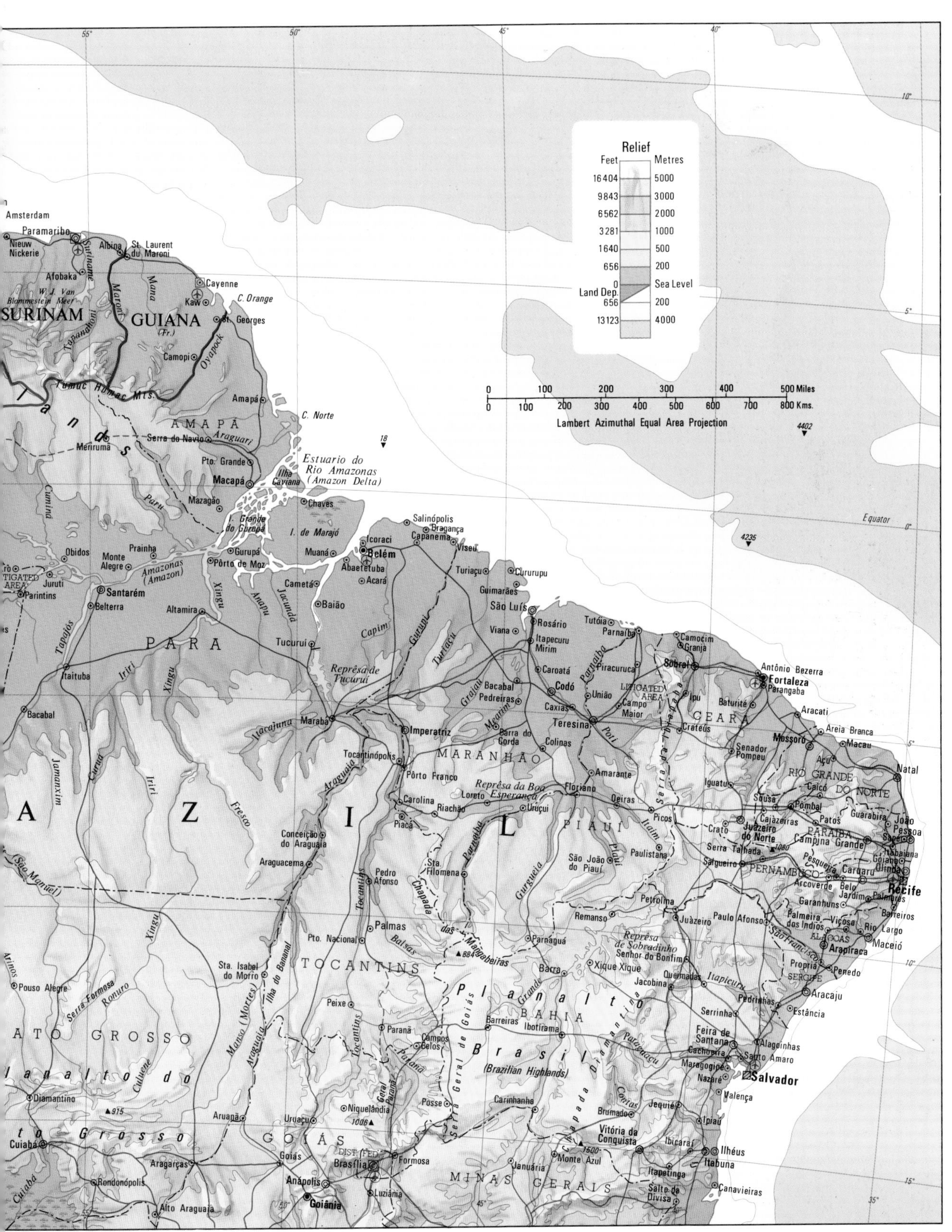

Relief

Feet		Metres
16 404		5000
9843		3000
6562		2000
3281		1000
1640		500
656		200
0		Sea Level
Land Dep.		
656		200
13 123		4000

0	100	200	300	400	500 Miles
0	100 200	300 400	500 600	700	800 Kms.

Lambert Azimuthal Equal Area Projection

Amsterdam
Paramaribo
Nieuw Nickerie
Afobaka
W. J. Van Blommestein Meer
SURINAM
Albina St. Laurent du Maroni
Cayenne
Kaw
C. Orange
St. Georges
GUIANA (Fr.)
Camopi
Tumuc Humac Mts.
Meriruma
Amapá
AMAPÁ
Serra do Navio
Araguari
Pto. Grande
C. Norte
Macapá
Mazagão
Estuario do Rio Amazonas (Amazon Delta)
Ilha Caviana
Chaves
I. Grande do Gurupá
I. de Marajó
Salinópolis
Bragança
Capanema
Viseu
Icoraci
Muaná
Belém
Abaetetuba
Acará
Cametá
Baião
Turiaçu
Cururupu
Guimarães
São Luís
Rosário
Viana
Tutóia
Parnaíba
Camocim
Obidos
Monte Alegre
Prainha
Juruti
Parintins
Santarém
Belterra
Altamira
Gurupá
Pôrto de Moz
Amazonas (Amazon)
Capim
Xingu
Tocantins
Tucuruí
PARÁ
Itaituba
Bacabal
Imperatriz
Marabá
Tocantinópolis
MARANHÃO
Pôrto Franco
Carolina
Riachão
Serra do Gorda
Caxias
Teresina
Colinas
Amarante
Floriano
Codó
Pedreiras
União
Campo Maior
Caroatá
Piracuruca
Ipu
Baturité
Sobral
Antônio Bezerra
Fortaleza
Parangaba
Aracati
Crateús
CEARÁ
Senador Pompeu
Iguatu
Açu
Mossoró
Areia Branca
Macau
RIO GRANDE DO NORTE
Caicó
Natal
Piauí
Conceição do Araguaia
Araguacema
Pedro Afonso
Sta. Filomena
Piacá
Uruçui
São João do Piauí
Paulistana
PIAUÍ
Picos
Crato
Juàzeiro do Norte
Serra Talhada
Salgueiro
Cajàzeiras
Patos
Pombal
Guarabira
João Pessoa
PARAÍBA
Campina Grande
Caruaru
Recife
Olinda
PERNAMBUCO
Arcoverde
Belo Jardim
Garanhuns
Barreiros
Palmas
Palmeira dos Indios
ALAGOAS
Maceió
TOCANTINS
Pto. Nacional
Peixe
Paraná
Campos Belos
Posse
Niquelândia
Uruaçu
GOIÁS
Goiás
Brasília
Formosa
Luziânia
Anápolis
Goiânia
Aragarças
Rondonópolis
Alto Araguaia
Cuiabá
Diamantino
MATO GROSSO
Planalto do Mato Grosso
Pouso Alegre
Sta. Isabel do Morro
BRAZIL
Remanso
Juàzeiro
Paulo Afonso
Petrolina
Xique Xique
Barra
Parnaguá
Represa de Sobradinho
Senhor do Bonfim
Jacobina
Queimadas
Serrinha
Feira de Santana
BAHIA
Barreiras
Ibotirama
Carinhanha
Brumado
Vitória da Conquista
Januária
Monte Azul
MINAS GERAIS
Ibicaraí
Itapetinga
Salto da Divisa
Canavieiras
Itabuna
Ilhéus
Ipiaú
Jequié
Valença
Nazaré
Maragogipe
Cachoeira
Santo Amaro
Alagoinhas
Salvador
Estância
Aracaju
SERGIPE
Propriá
Penedo
Arapiraca
Rio Largo
Viçosa
(Brazilian Highlands)

Equator

4402
4235

18

61

SOUTH AMERICA – SOUTH

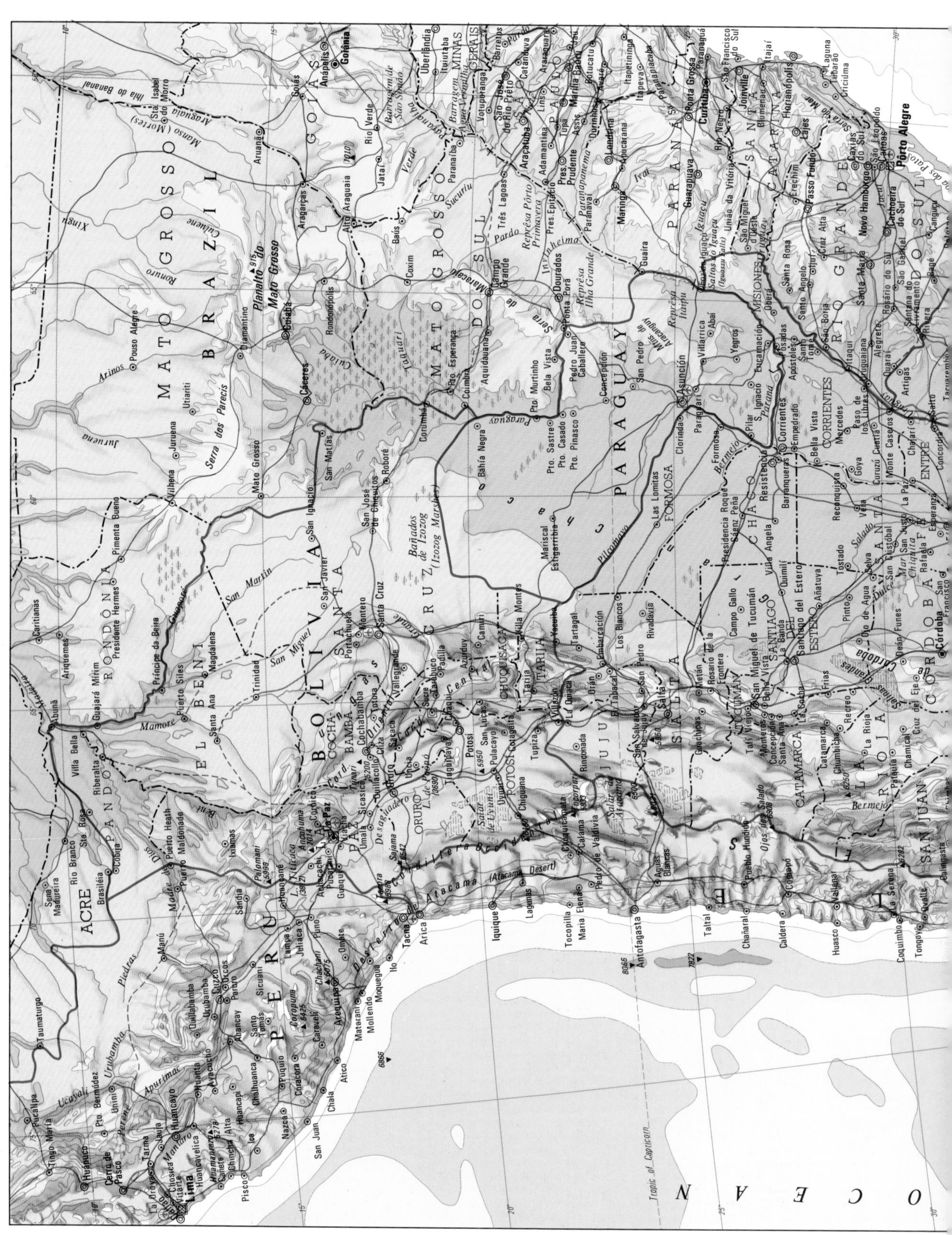
MATO GROSSO
BRAZIL
GOIÁS
MATO GROSSO DO SUL
PARANÁ
SANTA CATARINA
RIO GRANDE DO SUL
RONDÔNIA
ACRE
PERU
BOLIVIA
PARAGUAY
OCEAN
Tropic of Capricorn
Lima
La Paz
Asunción
Curitiba
Pôrto Alegre
Córdoba
Goiânia
Antofagasta
Arica
Iquique
Arequipa
Cuzco
Cochabamba
Santa Cruz
Sucre
Potosí
Campo Grande
Corrientes
Resistencia
Londrina
Florianópolis
Atacama Desert
Planalto do Mato Grosso
Serra dos Parecis
Bañados de Izozog
L. Titicaca
L. de Poopó
Salar de Uyuni

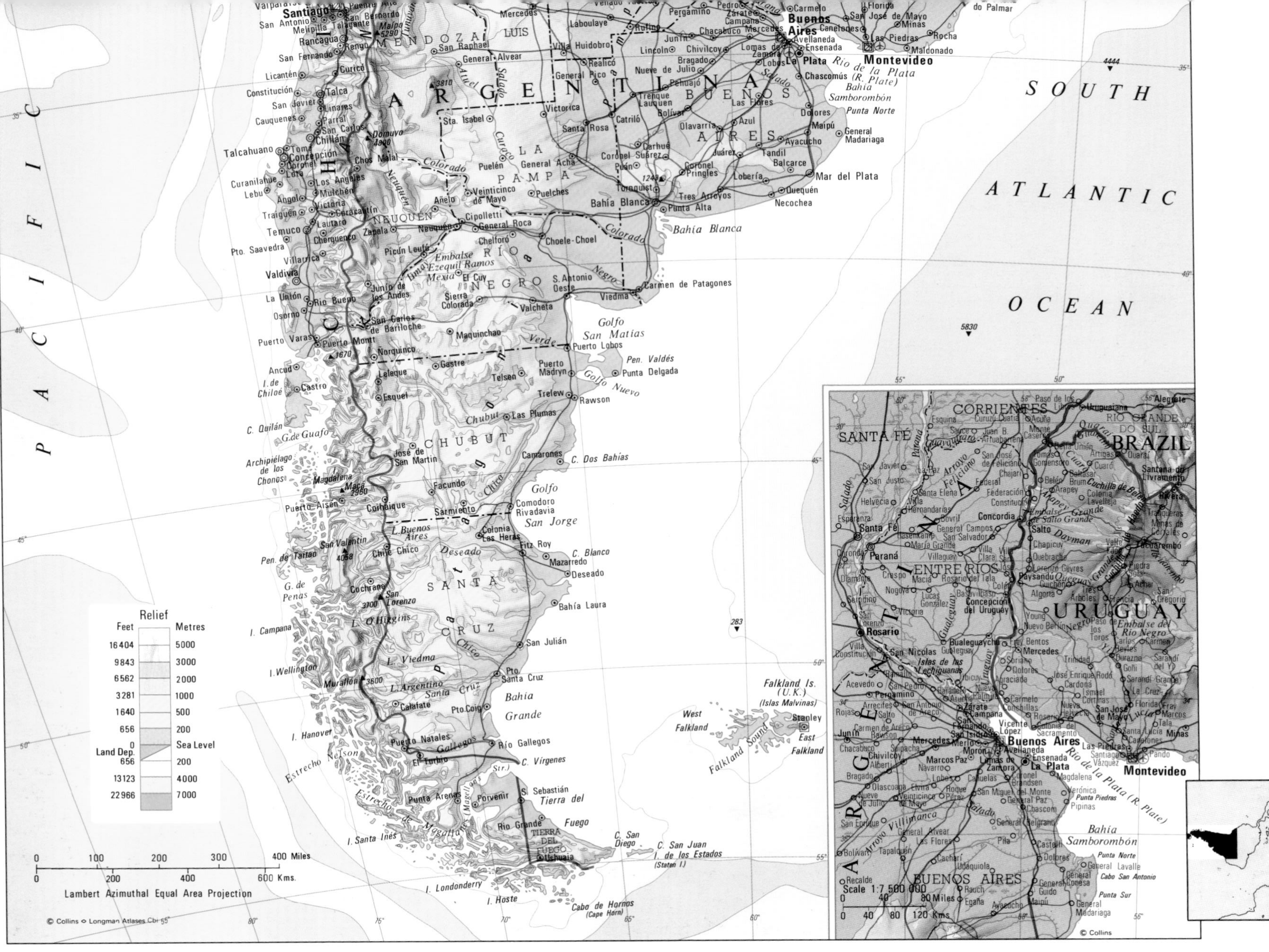

SOUTH

ATLANTIC

OCEAN

BRAZIL

URUGUAY

Montevideo

Buenos Aires

La Plata

Río de la Plata (R. Plate)

CORRIENTES

ENTRE RIOS

SANTA FE

Rosario

Paraná

ARGENTINA

Scale 1:7 500 000

0   40   80   120 Kms.
0   40   80 Miles

Falkland Is.
(Islas Malvinas)

East
Falkland

Falkland Sound

West
Falkland

Stanley

ATLANTIC

OCEAN

Montevideo

San José de Mayo

Buenos Aires
La Plata
Río de la Plata (R. Plate)

Maldonado

Punta Norte

General
Madariaga

Samborombón

Mar del Plata

BUENOS AIRES

Bahía Blanca

Carmen de Patagones

Pen. Valdés
Punta Delgada

Golfo
San Matías

Golfo Nuevo

Puerto Madryn

Rawson

C. Dos Bahías

Golfo
San Jorge

Comodoro
Rivadavia

C. Blanca

Deseado

Bahía Laura

San Julián

Pto.
Santa Cruz

Bahía
Grande

Río Gallegos

C. Vírgenes

C. San Diego
C. San Juan
de los Estados
(Staten I.)

Fuego
TIERRA
DEL
FUEGO

Cabo de Hornos
(Cape Horn)

I. Hoste

I. Londonderry

ARGENTINA

LA
PAMPA

RIO
NEGRO

NEUQUEN

CHUBUT

SANTA
CRUZ

MENDOZA

SAN
LUIS

Santiago

Valdivia

CHILE

Pto. Montt

Ancud
I. de Chiloé

Archipiélago
de los
Chonos

PACIFIC

OCEAN

Relief
Feet   Metres
16404   5000
9843   3000
6562   2000
3281   1000
1640   500
656   200
        Sea Level
Land Dep.
656   200
13123   4000
22966   7000

0   100   200   300   400   600 Kms.
0   100   200   300   400 Miles

Lambert Azimuthal Equal Area Projection

© Collins ○ Longman Atlases CbI-55°

63

POLAR REGIONS

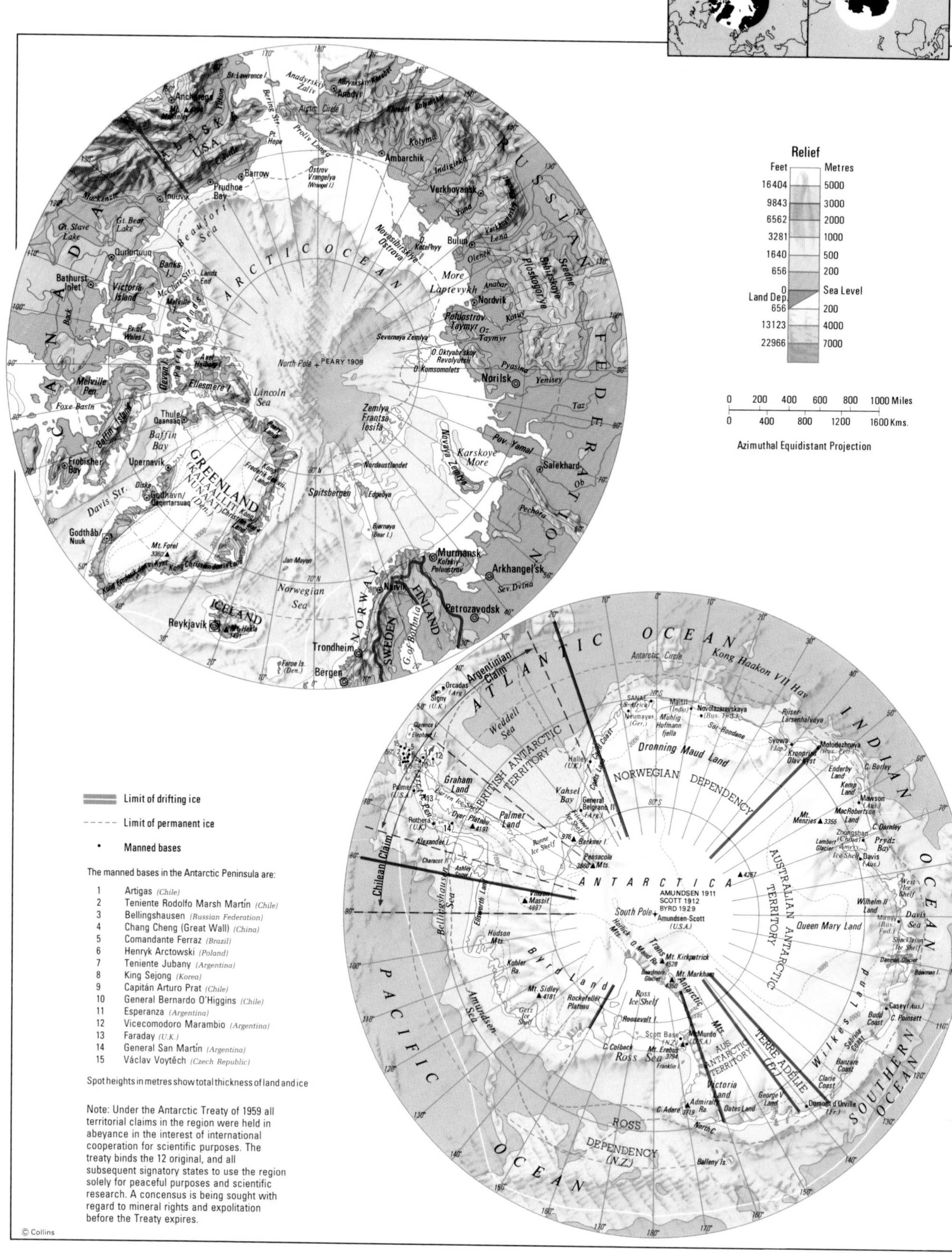

Relief

Feet		Metres
16404		5000
9843		3000
6562		2000
3281		1000
1640		500
656		200
0	Sea Level	
Land Dep.		
656		200
13123		4000
22966		7000

0   200   400   600   800   1000 Miles
0   400   800   1200   1600 Kms.

Azimuthal Equidistant Projection

━━━━ Limit of drifting ice

- - - - - Limit of permanent ice

• Manned bases

The manned bases in the Antarctic Peninsula are:

1   Artigas *(Chile)*
2   Teniente Rodolfo Marsh Martin *(Chile)*
3   Bellingshausen *(Russian Federation)*
4   Chang Cheng (Great Wall) *(China)*
5   Comandante Ferraz *(Brazil)*
6   Henryk Arctowski *(Poland)*
7   Teniente Jubany *(Argentina)*
8   King Sejong *(Korea)*
9   Capitán Arturo Prat *(Chile)*
10 General Bernardo O'Higgins *(Chile)*
11 Esperanza *(Argentina)*
12 Vicecomodoro Marambio *(Argentina)*
13 Faraday *(U.K.)*
14 General San Martín *(Argentina)*
15 Václav Voytěch *(Czech Republic)*

Spot heights in metres show total thickness of land and ice

Note: Under the Antarctic Treaty of 1959 all territorial claims in the region were held in abeyance in the interest of international cooperation for scientific purposes. The treaty binds the 12 original, and all subsequent signatory states to use the region solely for peaceful purposes and scientific research. A concensus is being sought with regard to mineral rights and expoitation before the Treaty expires.

© Collins

WORLD DATA

Part 1

WORLD FACTS AND FIGURES 66-70

Part 2

WORLD INDEX 71-112

Part 3

WORLD MAPS–ENDPAPERS

WORLD PHYSICAL DATA

Earth's Dimensions

Superficial area	196 936 679 miles²	510 066 000 km²
Land surface	57 268 725 miles²	148 326 000 km²
Water surface	139 667 953 miles²	361 740 000 km²
Equatorial circumference	24 902 miles	40 075 km
Meridional circumference	24 859 miles	40 007 km
Volume	259 902x10⁶ miles³	1 083 230x10⁶ km³
Mass	5.882x10²¹ tons	5.976x10²¹ tonnes

The Continents

Asia	16 837 065 miles²	43 608 000 km²
Africa	11 720 077 miles²	30 355 000 km²
North America	9 787 258 miles²	25 349 000 km²
South America	6 799 613 miles²	17 611 000 km²
Antarctica	5 150 000 miles²	13 338 500 km²
Europe	4 053 281 miles²	10 498 000 km²
Oceania	3 300 000 miles²	8 547 000 km²

Oceans and Sea Areas

Pacific Ocean	63 854 826 miles²	165 384 000 km²
Atlantic Ocean	31 744 015 miles²	82 217 000 km²
Indian Ocean	28 371 042 miles²	73 481 000 km²
Arctic Ocean	5 427 027 miles²	14 056 000 km²
Mediterranean Sea	967 181 miles²	2 505 000 km²
South China Sea	894 980 miles²	2 318 000 km²
Bering Sea	876 061 miles²	2 269 000 km²
Caribbean Sea	750 193 miles²	1 943 000 km²
Gulf of Mexico	596 138 miles²	1 544 000 km²
Okhotskoye More	589 961 miles²	1 528 000 km²
East China Sea	481 853 miles²	1 248 000 km²
Hudson Bay	476 061 miles²	1 233 000 km²
Sea of Japan	389 189 miles²	1 008 000 km²
North Sea	222 007 miles²	575 000 km²
Black Sea	177 992 miles²	461 000 km²

Island Areas

Greenland; Arctic / Atlantic Ocean	839 998 miles²	2 175 597 km²
New Guinea; Indonesia / P. N. G.	312 166 miles²	808 510 km²
Borneo; Malaysia / Indonesia / Brunei	292 297 miles²	757 050 km²
Madagascar; Indian Ocean	229 413 miles²	594 180 km²
Sumatera (Sumatra) ; Indonesia	202 355 miles²	524 100 km²
Baffin Island; Canada	183 810 miles²	476 068 km²
Honshū; Japan	88 978 miles²	230 455 km²
Great Britain; United Kingdom	88 751 miles²	229 867 km²
Ellesmere Island; Canada	82 118 miles²	212 688 km²
Victoria Island; Canada	81 930 miles²	212 199 km²
Sulawesi (Celebes) ; Indonesia	72 988 miles²	189 040 km²
South Island; New Zealand	58 093 miles²	150 461 km²
Jawa (Java) ; Indonesia	51 754 miles²	134 045 km²
North Island; New Zealand	44 281 miles²	114 688 km²
Cuba; Caribbean Sea	44 218 miles²	114 525 km²

River Lengths

An Nīl (Nile) ; Africa	4160 miles	6695 km
Amazonas (Amazon) ; South America	4048 miles	6516 km
Chang Jiang (Yangtze) ; Asia	3964 miles	6380 km
Mississippi - Missouri; North America	3740 miles	6020 km
Ob-Irtysh; Asia	3461 miles	5570 km
Huang He (Hwang Ho) ; Asia	3395 miles	5464 km
Zaïre; Africa	2900 miles	4667 km
Mekong; Asia	2749 miles	4425 km
Amur; Asia	2744 miles	4416 km
Lena; Asia	2734 miles	4400 km
Mackenzie; North America	2640 miles	4250 km
Yenisey; Asia	2541 miles	4090 km
Niger; Africa	2504 miles	4030 km
Murray - Darling; Oceania	2330 miles	3750 km
Volga; Europe	2291 miles	3688 km

Mountain Heights (Selected)

Everest; Nepal / China	29 028 feet	8848 m
K2; Jammu & Kashmir / China	28 251 feet	8611 m
Kāngchenjunga; Nepal / India	28 208 feet	8598 m
Dhaulāgiri; Nepal	26 811 feet	8172 m
Annapurna; Nepal	26 502 feet	8078 m
Aconcagua; Argentina	22 834 feet	6960 m
Ojos del Salado; Argentina / Chile	22 664 feet	6908 m
McKinley; Alaska, U.S.A.	20 321 feet	6194 m
Logan; Canada	19 551 feet	5959 m
Kilimanjaro; Tanzania	19 340 feet	5895 m
Elbrus; Russian Federation	18 480 feet	5633 m
Kirinyaga (Mt. Kenya); Kenya	17 057 feet	5199 m
Puncak Jaya; Indonesia	16 502 feet	5030 m
Vinson Massif; Antarctica	16 066 feet	4897 m
Blanc; France / Italy	15 774 feet	4808 m

Lake and Inland Sea Areas

Some areas are subject to seasonal variations.

Caspian Sea; Central Asia	143 550 miles²	371 795 km²
Lake Superior; U.S.A. / Canada	32 150 miles²	83 270 km²
Lake Victoria; East Africa	26 828 miles²	69 485 km²
Lake Huron; U.S.A. / Canada	23 436 miles²	60 700 km²
Lake Michigan; U.S.A.	22 400 miles²	58 016 km²
Aral Sea; Central Asia	14 092 miles²	36 500 km²
Lake Tanganyika; East Africa	12 700 miles²	32 893 km²
Great Bear Lake; Canada	12 274 miles²	31 792 km²
Ozero Baikal (Lake Baykal) ; Rus. Fed.	11 779 miles²	30 510 km²
Great Slave Lake; Canada	11 169 miles²	28 930 km²
Lake Erie; U.S.A. / Canada	9910 miles²	25 667 km²
Lake Winnipeg; Canada	9464 miles²	24 514 km²
Lake Malaŵi; Malaŵi / Mozambique	8683 miles²	22 490 km²
Lake Ontario; U.S.A. / Canada	7540 miles²	19 529 km²
Ladozhskoye Ozero (Lake Ladoga) ; Rus. Fed.	7100 miles²	18 390 km²

Volcanoes (Selected)

	Last Eruption	Height	Height
Cameroun; Cameroon	1922	13 353 feet	4070 m
Cotopaxi; Ecuador	1975	19 347 feet	5897 m
Elbrus; Russian Federation	extinct	18 510 feet	5642 m
Erebus; Antarctica	1979	12 447 feet	3794 m
Etna; Sicilia, Italy	1983	10 958 feet	3340 m
Fuji san (Fujiyama) ; Japan	extinct	12 388 feet	3776 m
Hekla; Iceland	1981	4891 feet	1491 m
Kilimanjaro; Tanzania	extinct	19 340 feet	5895 m
Mauna Loa; Hawaii	1978	13 684 feet	4171 m
Ngauruhoe; New Zealand	1975	7516 feet	2291 m
Popocatépetl; Mexico	1920	17 887 feet	5452 m
St. Helens; U.S.A.	1981	9675 feet	2949 m
Stromboli; Italy	1975	3038 feet	926 m
Tristan da Cunha; Atlantic Ocean	1962	7086 feet	2160 m
Vesuvio (Vesuvius) ; Italy	1944	4189 feet	1277 m

National Areas

Russian Federation; Asia / Europe	6 592 849 miles^2	17 075 400 km^2
Canada; North America	3 849 674 miles^2	9 970 610 km^2
China; Asia	3 691 484 miles^2	9 560 900 km^2
United States; North America	3 618 785 miles^2	9 372 610 km^2
Brazil; South America	3 286 488 miles^2	8 511 965 km^2
Australia; Oceania	2 966 153 miles^2	7 682 300 km^2
India; Asia	1 269 219 miles^2	3 287 263 km^2
Argentina; South America	1 068 302 miles^2	2 766 889 km^2
Sudan; Africa	967 500 miles^2	2 505 813 km^2
Algeria; Africa	919 595 miles^2	2 381 741 km^2
Zaïre; Africa	905 568 miles^2	2 345 410 km^2
Saudi Arabia; Asia	849 425 miles^2	2 200 000 km^2
Greenland; North America	840 000 miles^2	2 175 600 km^2
Mexico; North America	761 604 miles^2	1 972 545 km^2
Indonesia; Asia	741 102 miles^2	1 919 445 km^2
Libya; Africa	679 362 miles^2	1 759 540 km^2
Iran; Asia	636 296 miles^2	1 648 000 km^2
Mongolia; Asia	604 250 miles^2	1 565 000 km^2
Peru; South America	496 222 miles^2	1 285 216 km^2
Chad; Africa	495 755 miles^2	1 284 000 km^2

National Populations

China; Asia	1 196 360 000
India; Asia	901 459 000
United States; North America	258 233 000
Indonesia; Asia	189 921 000
Brazil; South America	151 534 000
Russian Federation; Asia / Europe	147 760 000
Japan; Asia	124 536 000
Pakistan; Asia	122 802 000
Bangladesh; Asia	115 203 000
Nigeria; Africa	105 264 000
Mexico; North America	91 261 000
Germany; Europe	81 409 530
Vietnam; Asia	71 324 000
Philippines; Asia	65 649 000
Iran; Asia	64 169 000
Turkey; Asia / Europe	60 227 000
Thailand; Asia	58 584 000
United Kingdom; Europe	58 191 000
France; Europe	57 660 000
Italy; Europe	57 057 000

World Cities

Ciudad de México (Mexico City) ; Mexico	20 200 000
Tōkyō; Japan	18 100 000
São Paulo; Brazil	17 400 000
New York; United States	16 200 000
Shanghai; China	13 400 000
Chicago; United States	11 900 000
Calcutta; India	11 800 000
Buenos Aires; Argentina	11 500 000
Bombay; India	11 200 000
Sŏul (Seoul) ; South Korea	11 000 000
Beijing (Peking) ; China	10 800 000
Rio de Janeiro; Brazil	10 700 000
Tianjin; China	9 400 000
Jakarta; Indonesia	9 300 000
Al Qāhirah (Cairo) ; Egypt	9 000 000

Major International Organisations

United Nations - in August 1995 the United Nations had 185 members. The only independent states not represented are Kiribati, Nauru, Switzerland, Taiwan, Tonga, Tuvalu and the Vatican City.

Commonwealth

Antigua	Australia	Bahamas	Bangladesh
Barbados	Belize	Botswana	Brunei
Canada	Cyprus	Dominica	Fiji
Gambia	Ghana	Grenada	Guyana
India	Jamaica	Kenya	Kiribati
Lesotho	Malaŵi	Malaysia	Maldives
Malta	Mauritius	Namibia	Nauru
New Zealand	Nigeria	Pakistan	Papua New Guinea
St. Kitts & Nevis	St. Lucia	St. Vincent	Seychelles
Sierra Leone	Singapore	Solomon Islands	South Africa
Sri Lanka	Swaziland	Tanzania	Tonga
Trinidad & Tobago	Tuvalu	Uganda	United Kingdom
Vanuatu	Western Samoa	Zambia	Zimbabwe

OAU - Organisation of African Unity

Algeria	Angola	Benin	Botswana
Burkina	Burundi	Cameroon	Cape Verde
Central African Rep.	Chad	Comoros	Congo
Côte d'Ivoire	Djibouti	Egypt	Equatorial Guinea
Eritrea	Ethiopia	Gabon	Gambia
Ghana	Guinea	Guinea Bissau	Kenya
Lesotho	Liberia	Libya	Madagascar
Malaŵi	Mali	Mauritania	Mauritius
Mozambique	Namibia	Niger	Nigeria
Rwanda	São Tomé & Príncipe	Senegal	Seychelles
Sierra Leone	Somali Rep.	South Africa	Sudan
Swaziland	Tanzania	Togo	Tunisia
Uganda	Western Sahara	Zaïre	Zambia
Zimbabwe			

OAS - Organisation of American States

Antigua	Argentina	Bahamas	Barbados
Belize	Bolivia	Brazil	Canada
Chile	Colombia	Costa Rica	Dominica
Dominican Rep.	Ecuador	El Salvador	Grenada
Guatemala	Guyana	Haiti	Honduras
Jamaica	Mexico	Nicaragua	Panama
Paraguay	Peru	St. Kitts & Nevis	St. Lucia
St. Vincent	Surinam	Trinidad & Tobago	United States
Venezuela			

EU - European Union

Austria	Belgium	Denmark	Finland
France	Germany	Greece	Ireland
Italy	Luxembourg	Netherlands	Portugal
Spain	Sweden	United Kingdom	

EFTA - European Free Trade Association

Iceland	Liechtenstein	Norway	Switzerland

ASEAN - Association of Southeast Asian Nations

Brunei	Indonesia	Malaysia	Philippines
Singapore	Thailand	Vietnam	

ECOWAS - Economic Community of West African States

Benin	Burkina	Cape Verde	Côte d'Ivoire
Gambia	Ghana	Guinea	Guinea Bissau
Liberia	Mali	Mauritania	Niger
Nigeria	Senegal	Sierra Leone	Togo

CARICOM - Caribbean Community and Common Market

Antigua	Bahamas	Barbados	Belize
Dominica	Grenada	Guyana	Jamaica
Montserrat	St. Kitts & Nevis	St. Lucia	St. Vincent
Surinam	Trinidad & Tobago		

NATIONS OF THE WORLD

COUNTRY	AREA miles²	AREA km²	POPULATION total	density per mile²	density per km²	FORM OF GOVERNMENT	CAPITAL CITY	MAIN LANGUAGES	CURRENCY
AFGHANISTAN	251,825	652,225	17,691,000	70	27	republic	Kâbol	Pushtu,Dari	afghani
ALBANIA	11,100	28,748	3,389,000	305	118	republic	Tiranë	Albanian	lek
ALGERIA	919,595	2,381,741	26,722,000	29	11	republic	Alger (Algiers)	Arabic	dinar
ANDORRA	180	465	61,000	339	131	principality	Andorra	Catalan	French franc,Spanish peseta
ANGOLA	481,354	1,246,700	10,276,000	21	8	republic	Luanda	Portuguese	kwanza
ANTIGUA & BARBUDA	171	442	65,000	380	147	constitutional monarchy	St John's	English	East Caribbean dollar
ARGENTINA	1,068,302	2,766,889	32,322,000	30	12	federal republic	Buenos Aires	Spanish	peso
ARMENIA	11,506	29,800	3,732,000	324	125	republic	Yerevan	Armenian,Russian	rouble
AUSTRALIA	2,966,153	7,682,300	17,663,000	6	2	monarchy (federal)	Canberra	English	dollar
AUSTRIA	32,376	83,855	7,988,000	239	95	federal republic	Wien (Vienna)	German	schilling
AZERBAIJAN	33,436	86,600	7,392,000	221	85	republic	Baku	Azerbaijani,Russian	rouble
BAHAMAS	5382	13,939	269,000	50	19	constitutional monarchy	Nassau	English	dollar
BAHRAIN	267	691	539,000	2019	780	emirate	Al Manãmah	Arabic	dinar
BANGLADESH	55,598	143,998	115,203,000	2072	800	republic	Dhaka	Bengali	taka
BARBADOS	166	430	260,000	1536	605	constitutional monarchy	Bridgetown	English	dollar
BELARUS (BELORUSSIA)	80,155	207,600	10,188,000	127	49	republic	Minsk	Belorussian	rouble
BELGIUM	11,784	30,520	10,046,000	853	329	constitutional monarchy	Bruxelles (Brussels) Brussel	French,Dutch, German	franc
BELIZE	8867	22,965	205,000	23	9	constitutional monarchy	Belmopan	English	dollar
BENIN	43,483	112,620	5,215,000	120	46	republic	Porto-Novo	French	CFA franc
BHUTAN	18,000	46,620	1,596,000	89	34	constitutional monarchy	Thimbu	Dzongkha	Indian rupee,ngultrum
BOLIVIA	424,164	1,098,581	7,065,000	17	6	republic	La Paz / Sucre	Spanish,Aymara	boliviano
BOSNIA-HERZEGOVINA	19,741	51,130	3,707,000	188	73	republic	Sarajevo	Serbo-Croat	dinar
BOTSWANA	224,468	581,370	1,443,000	6	2	republic	Gaborone	English,Tswana	pula
BRAZIL	3,286,473	8,511,965	151,534,000	46	18	federal republic	Brasília	Portuguese	cruzeiro
BRUNEI	2226	5,765	274,000	123	48	sultanate	Bandar Seri Begawan	Malay	dollar
BULGARIA	42,855	110,994	8,469,000	198	76	republic	Sofiya (Sofia)	Bulgarian	lev
BURKINA	105,869	274,200	9,682,000	91	35	republic	Ouagadougou	French	CFA franc
BURUNDI	10,747	27,834	5,958,000	554	214	republic	Bujumbura	French,Kirundi	franc
CAMBODIA	69,884	181,000	9,308,000	133	51	republic	Phnom Penh	Cambodian (Khmer)	riel
CAMEROON	183,591	475,500	11,834,000	64	25	republic	Yaoundé	French,English	CFA franc
CANADA	3,849,674	9,970,610	28,436,000	7	3	monarchy (federal)	Ottawa	English,French	dollar
CAPE VERDE	1558	4,035	370,000	237	92	republic	Praia	Portuguese,Creole	escudo
CENTRAL AFRICAN REPUBLIC	240,324	622,436	3,156,000	13	5	republic	Bangui	French,Sango	CFA franc
CHAD	495,755	1,284,000	6,098,000	12	5	republic	N'Djamena	French,Arabic	CFA franc
CHILE	292,258	756,945	13,813,000	47	18	republic	Santiago	Spanish	peso
CHINA	3,691,484	9,560,900	1,196,360,000	324	125	people's republic	Beijing (Peking)	Mandarin	yuan
COLOMBIA	440,831	1,141,748	33,951,000	77	28	republic	Bogotá	Spanish	peso
COMOROS	719	1,862	607,000	844	326	federal republic	Moroni	Comoran,Arabic,French	CFA franc
CONGO	132,047	342,000	2,443,000	19	7	republic	Brazzaville	French	CFA franc
COSTA RICA	19,730	51,100	3,199,000	162	63	republic	San José	Spanish	colón
CÔTE D'IVOIRE (IVORY COAST)	124,504	322,463	13,316,000	107	41	republic	Yamoussoukro	French	CFA franc
CROATIA	21,829	56,538	4,511,000	207	80	republic	Zagreb	Serbo-Croat	Dinar
CUBA	42,803	110,860	10,905,000	255	98	republic	La Habana (Havana)	Spanish	peso
CYPRUS	3572	9,251	726,000	203	78	republic	Levkosía (Nicosia)	Greek	pound
CZECH REPUBLIC	30,450	78,864	10,328,000	339	131	republic	Praha (Prague)	Czech	koruna
DENMARK	16,631	43,075	5,189,000	312	120	constitutional monarchy	Köbenhavn (Copenhagen)	Danish	krone
DJIBOUTI	8958	23,200	557,000	62	24	republic	Djibouti	French,Somali,Afar	franc
DOMINICA	290	750	71,000	245	95	republic	Roseau	English,French	East Caribbean dollar
DOMINICAN REPUBLIC	18,704	48,442	7,608,000	407	157	republic	Santo Domingo	Spanish	peso
ECUADOR	105,037	272,045	10,981,000	105	40	republic	Quito	Spanish	sucre
EGYPT	386,199	1,000,250	56,488,000	146	56	republic	Al Qãhirah (Cairo)	Arabic	pound
EL SALVADOR	8124	21,041	5,517,000	679	262	republic	San Salvador	Spanish	colón
EQUATORIAL GUINEA	10,831	28,051	379,000	35	14	republic	Malabo	Spanish	CFA franc
ERITREA	45,328	117,400	3,345,000	74	28	republic	Äsmera (Asmara)	Tigrinya, Arabic, English	Ethiopian birr
ESTONIA	17,452	45,200	1,517,000	87	34	republic	Tallinn	Estonian,Russian	kroon
ETHIOPIA	437,794	1,133,880	51,859,000	118	46	republic	Ãdïs Ãbeba (Addis Ababa)	Amharic	birr
FEDERATED STATES OF MICRONESIA	271	701	105,000	387	150	federal republic	Palikir on Pohnpei	English,Kosrean,Yapese, Pohnpeian,Trukese	US dollar
FIJI	7077	18,330	762,000	108	42	republic	Suva	English,Fiji,Hindustani	dollar
FINLAND	130,559	338,145	5,067,000	39	15	republic	Helsinki	Finnish,Swedish	markka
FRANCE	210,026	543,965	57,660,000	275	106	republic	Paris	French	franc
GABON	103,347	267,667	1,012,000	10	4	republic	Libreville	French	CFA franc
GAMBIA	4361	11,295	1026,000	235	91	republic	Banjul	English	dalasi
GEORGIA	26,911	69,700	5,493,000	204	79	republic	Tbilisi	Georgian,Russian	coupon
GERMANY	138,174	357,868	81,409,530	589	227	federal republic	Berlin,Bonn	German	mark
GHANA	92,100	238,537	16,446,000	179	69	republic	Accra	English	cedi

COUNTRY	AREA		POPULATION			FORM OF GOVERNMENT	CAPITAL CITY	MAIN LANGUAGES	CURRENCY
	miles²	km²	total	density per mile²	km²				
GREECE	50,949	131,957	10,350,000	203	78	republic	Athinai (Athens)	Greek	drachma
GRENADA	146	378	92,000	630	243	constitutional monarchy	St George's	English	East Caribbean dollar
GUATEMALA	42,043	108,890	10,029,000	239	92	republic	Guatemala	Spanish	quetzal
GUINEA	94,926	245,857	6,306,000	66	26	republic	Conakry	French	franc
GUINEA-BISSAU	13,948	36,125	1,028,000	74	28	republic	Bissau	Portuguese	peso
GUYANA	83,000	214,969	816,000	10	4	republic	Georgetown	English	dollar
HAITI	10,714	27,750	6,903,000	644	249	republic	Port-au-Prince	French, Creole	gourde
HONDURAS	43,277	112,088	5,595,000	129	50	republic	Tegucigalpa	Spanish	lempira
HUNGARY	35,919	93,030	10,294,000	287	111	republic	Budapest	Magyar	forint
ICELAND	39,699	102,820	263,000	7	3	republic	Reykjavík	Icelandic	króna
INDIA	1,269,219	3,287,263	901,459,000	710	274	republic	New Delhi	Hindi, English	rupee
INDONESIA	741,102	1,919,445	189,921,000	256	99	republic	Jakarta	Bahasa Indonesia	rupiah
IRAN	636,296	1,648,000	64,169,000	101	39	Islamic republic	Tehrān	Persian	rial
IRAQ	169,235	438,317	19,454,000	115	44	republic	Baghdād	Arabic, Kurdish	dinar
IRELAND, REPUBLIC OF	27,136	70,282	3,563,000	131	51	republic	Dublin	English, Irish	punt
ISRAEL	8019	20,770	5,256,000	655	253	republic	Yerushalayim (Jerusalem)	Hebrew	shekel
ITALY	116,311	301,245	57,057,000	491	189	republic	Roma (Rome)	Italian	lira
JAMAICA	4244	10,991	2,411,000	568	219	constitutional monarchy	Kingston	English	dollar
JAPAN	145,841	377,727	124,536,000	854	330	monarchy	Tōkyō	Japanese	yen
JORDAN	34,443	89,206	4,936,000	143	55	monarchy	Ammān	Arabic	dinar
KAZAKHSTAN	1,049,155	2,717,300	16,956,000	16	6	republic	Almaty	Kazakh, Russian	rouble
KENYA	224,961	582,646	28,113,000	125	48	republic	Nairobi	Kiswahili, English	shilling
KIRIBATI	277	717	77,000	278	107	republic	Bairiki on Tarawa Atoll	English, Gilbertese, I-Kiribati	Australian dollar
KUWAIT	6880	17,818	1,433,000	208	80	emirate	Al Kuwayt (Kuwait)	Arabic	dinar
KYRGYZSTAN (KIRGHIZIA)	76,641	198,500	4,528,000	59	23	republic	Bishkek	Kirghiz, Russian	rouble
LAOS	91,429	236,800	4,605,000	50	19	republic	Vientiane (Viangchan)	Lao	kip
LATVIA	24,595	63,700	2,586,000	105	41	republic	Rīga	Latvian, Russian	Latvian rouble
LEBANON	4036	10,452	2,806,000	695	268	republic	Bayrūt (Beirut)	Arabic	pound
LESOTHO	11,720	30,355	1,943,000	166	64	monarchy	Maseru	English, Sesotho	loti
LIBERIA	43,000	111,369	2,640,000	61	24	republic	Monrovia	English	dollar
LIBYA	679,362	1,759,540	4,700,000	7	3	socialist state	Tarābulus (Tripoli)	Arabic	dinar
LIECHTENSTEIN	62	160	30,000	484	188	constitutional monarchy	Vaduz	German	Swiss franc
LITHUANIA	25,174	65,200	3,730,000	148	57	republic	Vilnius	Lithuanian	rouble, Litas prop.
LUXEMBOURG	998	2,586	395,000	396	153	constitutional monarchy	Luxembourg	Letzeburgish, French, German	franc
MACEDONIA	9,928	25,713	2,060,000	207	80	republic	Skopje	Macedonian	denar
MADAGASCAR	226,658	587,041	13,854,000	61	24	republic	Antananarivo	Malagasy, French	franc
MALAWI	45,747	118,484	9,135,000	200	77	republic	Lilongwe	English, Chichewa	kwacha
MALAYSIA	128,442	332,665	19,247,000	150	58	constitutional monarchy	Kuala Lumpur	Bahasa Malay	ringgit
MALDIVES	115	298	238,000	2070	799	republic	Malé	Divehi	rufiyaa
MALI	478,821	1,240,140	10,135,000	21	8	republic	Bamako	French, Bambara	CFA franc
MALTA	122	316	361,000	2959	1142	republic	Valletta	Maltese, English	lira
MARSHALL ISLANDS	70	181	52,000	743	287	republic	Dalap-Uliga-Darrit	Marshallese, English	US dollar
MAURITANIA	397,955	1,030,700	2,161,000	5	2	republic	Nouakchott	Arabic, French	ouguiya
MAURITIUS	788	2,040	1,098,000	1393	538	republic	Port Louis	English, Creole	rupee
MEXICO	761,604	1,972,545	91,261,000	120	46	federal republic	Ciudad de México (Mexico City)	Spanish	peso
MOLDOVA (MOLDAVIA)	13,012	33,700	4,356,000	335	129	republic	Kishinev	Romanian, Russian	rouble
MONACO	1	2	31,000	31,000	15500	constitutional monarchy	Monaco	French	French franc
MONGOLIA	604,250	1,565,000	2,318,000	4	2	republic	Ulaanbaatar (Ulan Bator)	Khalka Mongol	tugrik
MOROCCO	172,414	446,550	26,069,000	151	58	monarchy	Rabat	Arabic	dirham
MOZAMBIQUE	308,642	799,380	15,583,000	50	19	republic	Maputo	Portuguese	metical
MYANMAR (BURMA)	261,228	676,577	44,596,000	171	66	military regime	Yangon (Rangoon)	Burmese	kyat
NAMIBIA	318,261	824,292	1,461,000	5	2	republic	Windhoek	Afrikaans, English	dollar
NAURU	8	21	10,000	1250	476	republic	Yaren	Nauruan, English	Australian dollar
NEPAL	56,827	147,181	20,812,000	366	141	monarchy	Kathmandu	Nepali	rupee
NETHERLANDS	16,033	41,526	15,287,000	953	368	constitutional monarchy	Amsterdam	Dutch	guilder
NEW ZEALAND	104,454	270,534	3,451,000	33	13	constitutional monarchy	Wellington	English, Maori	dollar
NICARAGUA	50,193	130,000	4,265,000	85	33	republic	Managua	Spanish	córdoba
NIGER	489,191	1,267,000	8,361,000	17	7	republic	Niamey	French	CFA Franc
NIGERIA	356,699	923,768	105,264,000	295	114	federal republic	Abuja	English	naira
NORTH KOREA	46,540	120,538	23,048,000	495	191	people's republic	Pyŏngyang	Korean	won
NORWAY	125,050	323,878	4,312,000	34	13	constitutional monarchy	Oslo	Norwegian	krone
OMAN	105,000	271,950	1,992,000	19	7	sultanate	Masqaṭ (Muscat)	Arabic	rial
PAKISTAN	310,403	803,940	122,802,000	396	153	federal Islamic republic	Islāmābād	Urdu, Punjabi, English	rupee
PALAU (BELAU)	192	497	16,000	83	32	republic	Koror	Palauan, English	dollar
PANAMA	29,762	77,082	2,563,000	86	33	republic	Panamá City	Spanish	balboa

NATIONS OF THE WORLD

COUNTRY	AREA		POPULATION			FORM OF	CAPITAL CITY	MAIN	CURRENCY
	miles²	km²	total	density per mile²	km²	GOVERNMENT		LANGUAGES	
PAPUA NEW GUINEA	178,704	462,840	3,922,000	22	8	constitutional monarchy	Port Moresby	English,Pidgin,Motu	kina
PARAGUAY	157,048	406,752	4,643,000	25	10	republic	Asunción	Spanish,Guarani	guaraní
PERU	496,225	1,285,216	22,454,000	45	17	republic	Lima	Spanish,Quechua	sol
PHILIPPINES	115,831	300,000	65,649,000	567	219	republic	Manila	Pilipino,English	peso
POLAND	120,728	312,683	38,459,000	319	123	republic	Warszawa (Warsaw)	Polish	zloty
PORTUGAL	34,340	88,940	9,860,000	287	111	republic	Lisboa (Lisbon)	Portuguese	escudo
QATAR	4416	11,437	559,000	127	49	emirate	Ad Dawḥaḥ (Doha)	Arabic	riyal
ROMANIA	91,699	237,500	22,755,000	248	96	republic	Bucureşti (Bucharest)	Romanian	leu
RUSSIAN FEDERATION	6,592,849	17,075,400	147,760,000	22	9	republic	Moskva (Moscow)	Russian	rouble
RWANDA	10,169	26,338	7,554,000	743	287	republic	Kigali	Kinyarwanda,French	franc
ST KITTS-NEVIS	101	261	42,000	416	161	constitutional monarchy	Basseterre	English	East Caribbean dollar
ST LUCIA	238	616	139,000	584	226	constitutional monarchy	Castries	English,French	East Caribbean dollar
ST VINCENT & THE GRENADINES	150	389	110,000	733	283	constitutional monarchy	Kingstown	English	East Caribbean dollar
SAN MARINO	24	61	24,000	1000	393	republic	San Marino	Italian	Italian lira
SÃO TOMÉ & PRÍNCIPE	372	964	122,000	328	127	republic	São Tomé	Portuguese,Creole	dobra
SAUDI ARABIA	849,425	2,200,000	17,119,000	20	8	monarchy	Ar Riyāḍ (Riyadh)	Arabic	riyal
SENEGAL	75,954	196,720	7,902,000	104	40	republic	Dakar	French	CFA franc
SEYCHELLES	176	455	72,000	409	158	republic	Victoria	English,French,Creole	rupee
SIERRA LEONE	27,699	71,740	4,297,000	155	60	republic	Freetown	English	leone
SINGAPORE	247	639	2,874,000	11,636	4498	republic	Singapore	Bahasa Malay,English, Chinese,Tamil	dollar
SLOVAKIA	18,933	49,035	5,318,000	281	108	republic	Bratislava	Slovak	koruna
SLOVENIA	7819	20,251	1,990,000	255	98	republic	Ljubljana	Slovene	dinar
SOLOMON ISLANDS	10,954	28,370	355,000	32	13	constitutional monarchy	Honiara	English	dollar
SOMALI REPUBLIC	246,201	637,657	8,954,000	36	14	republic	Muqdisho (Mogadishu)	Arabic,Somali,Italian, English	shilling
SOUTH AFRICA,REPUBLIC OF	473,290	1,225,815	39,659,000	84	32	republic	Pretoria/ Cape Town (Kaapstad)	Afrikaans,English	rand
SOUTH KOREA	38,330	99,274	44,056,000	1149	444	republic	Sŏul (Seoul)	Korean	won
SPAIN	194,897	504,782	39,143,000	201	78	constitutional monarchy	Madrid	Spanish	peseta
SRI LANKA	25,332	65,610	17,619,000	696	269	republic	Colombo	Sinhala,Tamil	Rupee
SUDAN	967,500	2,505,813	28,129,000	29	11	republic	Al Kharṭūm (Khartoum)	Arabic	dinar
SURINAM	63,251	163,820	414,000	7	3	republic	Paramaribo	Dutch,English	guilder
SWAZILAND	6704	17,364	809,000	121	47	monarchy	Mbabane	English,Siswati	lilangeni
SWEDEN	173,732	449,964	8,716,000	50	19	constitutional monarchy	Stockholm	Swedish	krona
SWITZERLAND	15,943	41,293	6,938,000	435	168	federal republic	Bern (Berne)	German,French,Italian, Romansh	franc
SYRIA	71,498	185,180	13,393,000	187	72	republic	Dimashq (Damascus)	Arabic	pound
TAIWAN	13,969	36,179	20,300,000	1453	561	republic	Taipei	Mandarin	dollar
TAJIKISTAN	55,251	143,100	5,767,000	104	40	republic	Dushanbe	Tajik,Russian	rouble
TANZANIA	364,900	945,087	28,019,000	77	30	republic	Dodoma	Kiswahili,English	shilling
THAILAND	198,115	513,115	58,584,000	296	114	monarchy	Bangkok (Krung Thep)	Thai	baht
TOGO	21,925	56,785	3,885,000	177	68	republic	Lomé	French	CFA franc
TONGA	289	748	98,000	339	131	constitutional monarchy	Nuku'alofa	English,Tongan	pa'anga
TRINIDAD AND TOBAGO	1981	5,130	1,260,000	636	246	republic	Port of Spain	English	dollar
TUNISIA	63,379	164,150	8,570,000	135	52	republic	Tunis	Arabic	dinar
TURKEY	300,948	779,452	60,227,000	200	77	republic	Ankara	Turkish	lira
TURKMENISTAN	188,456	488,100	3,921,000	21	8	republic	Ashkhabad	Turkmenian	rouble
TUVALU	10	25	9000	900	360	constitutional monarchy	Funafuti	English,Tuvaluan	Australian dollar
UGANDA	93,065	241,038	19,940,000	214	83	republic	Kampala	Kiswahili,English	shilling
UKRAINE	233,090	603,700	52,179,000	224	86	republic	Kiyev	Ukrainian,Russian	rouble
UNITED ARAB EMIRATES	30,000	77,700	1,910,000	64	25	federation of emirates	Abū Ẓaby (Abu Dhabi)	Arabic	dirham
UNITED KINGDOM	93,643	242,534	58,191,000	621	240	constitutional monarchy	London	English	pound
UNITED STATES OF AMERICA	3,618,785	9,372,610	258,233,000	71	28	federal republic	Washington	English	dollar
URUGUAY	68,037	176,215	3,149,000	46	18	republic	Montevideo	Spanish	peso
UZBEKISTAN	172,742	447,400	21,860,000	127	49	republic	Tashkent	Uzbek,Russian	rouble
VANUATU	4707	12,190	156,000	33	13	republic	Vila	English,French,Bislama	vatu
VATICAN CITY	0.17	0.44	1000	5882	2273	ecclesiastical state	Vatican City	Italian	lira
VENEZUELA	352,144	912,050	20,712,000	59	23	federal republic	Caracas	Spanish	bolívar
VIETNAM	127,246	329,565	71,324,000	561	216	republic	Hanoi	Vietnamese	dong
WESTERN SAMOA	1093	2831	163,000	149	58	constitutional monarchy	Apia	Samoan,English	tala
YEMEN	203,850	527,968	12,302,000	60	23	republic	San'a	Arabic	rial,dinar
YUGOSLAVIA	39,449	102,173	10,485,000	266	103	federal republic	Beograd (Belgrade)	Serbo-Croat, Macedonian,Albanian	dinar
ZAÏRE	905,568	2,345,410	41,231,000	46	18	republic	Kinshasa	French,Lingala	zaïre
ZAMBIA	290,586	752,614	8,936,000	31	12	republic	Lusaka	English	kwacha
ZIMBABWE	150,873	390,759	10,739,000	71	27	republic	Harare	English	dollar

Introduction to World Index

The index includes an alphabetical list of all names appearing on the maps in the World Atlas section. Each entry indicates the country or region of the world in which the name is located. This is followed by a page reference and finally the name's location on the map, given by latitude and longitude co-ordinates. Most features are indexed to the largest scale map on which they appear, however when the name applies to countries or other extensive features it is generally indexed to the map on which it appears in its entirety. Areal features are generally indexed using co-ordinates

which indicate the centre of the feature. The latitude and longitude indicated for a point feature gives the location of the point on the map. In the case of rivers the mouth or confluence is always taken as the point of reference.

Names in the index are generally in the local language and where a conventional English version exists, this is cross referenced to the entry in the local language. Names of features which extend across the boundaries of more than one country are usually named in English if no single official name exists. Names in languages not

written in the Roman alphabet have been transliterated using the official system of the country if one exists, e.g. Pinyin system for China, otherwise the systems recognised by the United States Board on Geographical Names have been used.

Names abbreviated on the maps are given in full in the Index. Abbreviations are used for both geographical terms and administrative names in the Index. All abbreviations used in the Index are listed below.

Abbreviations of Geographical Terms

b., B.	bay, Bay	**f.**	physical feature e.g. valley, plain, geographic district or region	**mts., Mts.**	mountains, Mountains
c., C.	cape, Cape			**pen., Pen.**	peninsula, Peninsula
d.	internal division e.g county, region, state	**g., G.**	gulf, Gulf	Pt.	Point
des.	desert	**i., I., is., Is.**	island, Island, islands, Islands	**r.**	river
est.	estuary	I., L.	lake, Lake	**resr., Resr.**	reservoir, Reservoir
		mtn., Mtn.	mountain, Mountain	Sd.	Sound
				str., Str.	strait, Strait

Abbreviations of Country / Administrative Names

Afghan.	Afghanistan	Man.	Manitoba	Raj.	Rājasthān
A.H. Prov.	Alpes de Haut Provence	Mass.	Massachusetts	Rep. of Ire.	Republic of Ireland
Ala.	Alabama	Md.	Maryland	Rhein.-Pfalz	Rheinland-Pfalz
Alas.	Alaska	Mich.	Michigan	R.I.	Rhode Island
Alta.	Alberta	Minn.	Minnesota	R.S.A.	Republic of South Africa
Ariz.	Arizona	Miss.	Mississippi	Russian Fed.	Russian Federation
Ark.	Arkansas	Mo.	Missouri	S.A.	South Australia
Baja Calif.	Baja California	Mont.	Montana	Sask.	Saskatchewan
Baja Calif. Sur	Baja California Sur	M.-Pyr.	Midi-Pyrénées	S.C.	South Carolina
Bangla.	Bangladesh	N.B.	New Brunswick	Sch.-Hol.	Schleswig-Holstein
B.C.	British Columbia	N.C.	North Carolina	S. Dak.	South Dakota
Bos.-Her.	Bosnia-Herzegovina	N. Dak.	North Dakota	S. Korea	South Korea
B.-Würt	Baden-Württemberg	Nebr.	Nebraska	S. Mar.	Seine Maritime
Calif.	California	Neth.	Netherlands	Sogn og Fj.	Sogn og Fjordane
C.A.R.	Central African Republic	Nev.	Nevada	Somali Rep.	Somali Republic
Char. Mar.	Charente Maritime	Nfld.	Newfoundland	Switz.	Switzerland
Colo.	Colorado	N.H.	New Hampshire	Tas.	Tasmania
Conn.	Connecticut	N. Ireland	Northern Ireland	Tenn.	Tennessee
C.P.	Cape Province	N.J.	New Jersey	Tex.	Texas
D.C.	District of Columbia	N. Korea	North Korea	T.G.	Tarn-et-Garonne
Del.	Delaware	N. Mex	New Mexico	Trans.	Transvaal
Dom. Rep.	Dominican Republic	Nschn.	Niedersachsen	U.A.E.	United Arab Emirates
Equat. Guinea	Equatorial Guinea	N.S.W.	New South Wales	U.K.	United Kingdom
Eth.	Ethiopia	N. Trönd.	North Tröndelag	U.S.A.	United States of America
Fla.	Florida	N.T.	Northern Territory	Uttar P.	Uttar Pradesh
Ga.	Georgia	N.-Westfalen	Nordrhein-Westfalen	Va.	Virginia
Guang. Zhuang	Guangxi Zhuangzu	N.W.T.	Northwest Territories	Vic.	Victoria
H.-Gar.	Haute Garonne	N.Y.	New York State	Vt.	Vermont
Himachal P.	Himachal Pradesh	O.F.S.	Orange Free State	W.A.	Western Australia
H. Zaïre	Haut Zaïre	Okla.	Oklahoma	Wash.	Washington
Ill.	Illinois	Ont.	Ontario	W. Bengal	West Bengal
Ind.	Indiana	Oreg.	Oregon	Wisc.	Wisconsin
Kans.	Kansas	P.E.I.	Prince Edward Island	W. Sahara	Western Sahara
K. Occidental	Kasai Occidental	Penn.	Pennsylvania	W. Va.	West Virginia
K. Oriental	Kasai Oriental	Phil.	Philippines	Wyo.	Wyoming
Ky.	Kentucky	P.N.G.	Papua New Guinea	Xin. Uygur	Xinjiang Uygur Zizhiqu
La.	Louisiana	Poit.-Char.	Poitou-Charente	Yugo.	Yugoslavia
Liech.	Liechtenstein	Pyr. Or.	Pyrénées Orientales		
Lux.	Luxembourg	Qld.	Queensland		
Madhya P.	Madhya Pradesh	Que.	Québec		

A

Aachen Germany 8 50.46N 6.06E
Aalsmeer Neth. 8 52.17N 4.46E
Aalst Belgium 8 50.57N 4.03E
Äänekoski Finland 16 62.36N 25.44E
Aarau Switz. 14 47.24N 8.04E
Aardenburg Neth. 8 51.16N 3.26E
Aare r. Switz. 14 47.37N 8.13E
Aarschot Belgium 8 50.59N 4.50E
Aba China 29 32.55N 101.42E
Aba Nigeria 38 5.06N 7.21E
Abā as Su'ūd Saudi Arabia 35 17.28N 44.06E
Ābādān Iran 31 30.21N 48.15E
Abadan, Jazīreh-ye i. Iran 31 30.10N 48.30E
Ābādeh Iran 31 31.10N 52.40E
Abadla Algeria 34 31.01N 2.45W
Abaetetuba Brazil 61 1.45S 48.54W
Abaí Paraguay 62 26.01S 55.57W
Abajo Peak mtn. U.S.A. 54 37.51N 109.28W
Abakaliki Nigeria 38 6.17N 8.04E
Abakan Russian Fed. 21 53.43N 91.25E
Abancay Peru 62 13.35S 72.55W
Abau P.N.G. 44 10.10S 148.40E
Abay Kazakhstan 20 49.40N 72.47E
Ābaya Hāyk' l. Ethiopia 35 6.20N 38.00E
Abayḑ, Al Baḩr al r. Sudan 35 15.45N 32.25E
Abba C.A.R. 38 5.20N 15.11E
Abbeville France 11 50.06N 1.51E
Abbiategrasso Italy 9 45.24N 8.54E
Abbotsbury U.K. 5 50.40N 2.36W
Abdulino Russian Fed. 18 53.42N 53.40E
Abéché Chad 35 13.49N 20.49E
Abengourou Côte d'Ivoire 38 6.42N 3.27W
Åbenrå Denmark 17 55.02N 9.26E
Abeokuta Nigeria 38 7.10N 3.26E
Aberayron U.K. 5 52.15N 4.16W
Abercrombie r. Australia 47 33.50S 149.10E
Aberdare U.K. 5 51.43N 3.27W
Aberdare Range mts. Kenya 37 0.20S 36.40E
Aberdeen Australia 47 32.10S 150.54E
Aberdeen R.S.A. 39 32.28S 24.03E
Aberdeen U.K. 6 57.08N 2.07W
Aberdeen Md. U.S.A. 55 39.30N 76.10W
Aberdeen Ohio U.S.A. 55 38.39N 83.46W
Aberdeen S. Dak. U.S.A. 52 45.28N 98.30W
Aberdeen Wash. U.S.A. 54 46.59N 123.50W
Aberdovey U.K. 5 52.33N 4.03W
Aberfeldy U.K. 6 56.37N 3.54W
Abergavenny U.K. 5 51.49N 3.01W
Abersoch U.K. 4 52.50N 4.31W
Aberystwyth U.K. 5 52.25N 4.06W
Abetone Italy 9 44.08N 10.40E
Abez Russian Fed. 18 66.33N 61.51E
Abhar Iran 31 36.09N 49.13E
Ābhē Bid Hāyk' l. Ethiopia 35 11.06N 41.50E
Abia d. Nigeria 38 5.45N 7.40E
Abidjan Côte d'Ivoire 38 5.19N 4.01W
Abilene Tex. U.S.A. 52 32.27N 99.45W
Abingdon U.K. 5 51.40N 1.17W
Abisko Sweden 16 68.20N 18.51E
Abitibi r. Canada 55 51.03N 80.55W
Abitibi, L. Canada 55 48.42N 79.45W
Abnūb Egypt 30 27.16N 31.09E
Åbo see Turku Finland 17
Abomey Benin 38 7.14N 2.00E
Abong Mbang Cameroon 38 3.59N 13.12E
Abou Deïa Chad 34 11.20N 19.20E
Aboyne U.K. 6 57.05N 2.48W
Abrantes Portugal 10 39.28N 8.12W
Abrud Romania 15 46.17N 23.04E
Abruzzi d. Italy 12 42.05N 13.45E
Absaroka Range mts. U.S.A. 54 44.45N 109.50W
Abu Dhabi see Abū Ẓaby U.A.E. 31
Abū Dharbah Egypt 32 28.29N 33.20E
Abū Ḩamad Sudan 35 19.32N 33.20E
Abuja Nigeria 38 9.12N 7.11E
Abū Kabīr Egypt 32 30.44N 31.40E
Abū Kamāl Syria 30 34.27N 40.55E
Abū Madd, Ra's c. Saudi Arabia 30 24.50N 37.07E
Abunã Brazil 60 9.41S 65.20W
Abū Qurqāş Egypt 32 27.56N 30.50E
Abū Sulţān Egypt 32 30.25N 32.19E
Abū Sunbul Egypt 30 22.18N 31.40E
Abū Ţarafah Jordan 32 30.00N 35.56E
Abū Tīj Egypt 30 27.06N 31.17E
Abū Ẓaby U.A.E. 31 24.27N 54.23E
Abū Zanīmah Egypt 32 29.03N 33.06E
Åby Sweden 17 58.40N 16.11E
Acámbaro Mexico 56 20.01N 101.42W
Acapulco Mexico 56 16.51N 99.56W
Acará Brazil 61 1.57S 48.11W
Acarigua Venezuela 60 9.35N 69.12W
Acatlán Mexico 56 18.12N 98.02W
Accra Ghana 38 5.33N 0.15W
Accrington U.K. 4 53.46N 2.22W
Aceh d. Indonesia 26 4.00N 97.30E
Acevedo Argentina 63 33.46S 60.27W
Achacachi Bolivia 62 16.03S 68.43W
Achar Uruguay 63 32.25S 56.10W
Acheng China 25 45.32N 126.59E
Achill I. Rep. of Ire. 7 53.57N 10.00W
Achinsk Russian Fed. 20 56.10N 90.10E
Acklin's I. Bahamas 57 22.30N 74.10W
Aconcagua mtn. Argentina 62 32.39S 70.00W
A Coruña see La Coruña Spain 10
Acqui Italy 9 44.41N 8.28E
Acraman, L. Australia 46 32.02S 135.26E
Acre d. Brazil 60 8.50S 71.30W
Açu Brazil 61 5.35S 36.57W
Acuña Argentina 63 29.54S 57.57W
Adair, C. Canada 51 71.24N 71.13W
Adamantina Brazil 59 21.42S 51.04W
Adamaoua, Massif de l' mts. Cameroon/Nigeria 38 7.05N 12.00E
Adamawa d. Nigeria 38 9.55N 12.30E
Adamello mtn. Italy 9 46.10N 10.35E
Adaminaby Australia 47 36.04S 148.42E
Adamintina Brazil 62 21.42S 51.04W
Adams N.Y. U.S.A. 55 43.49N 76.01W
Adams, Mt. U.S.A. 54 46.12N 121.28W
'Adan Yemen 35 12.50N 45.00E
Adana Turkey 30 37.00N 35.19E
Adapazari Turkey 30 40.45N 30.23E
Adare, C. Antarctica 64 71.30S 171.00E
Adavale Australia 44 25.55S 144.36E
Adda r. Italy 9 45.08N 9.55E
Aḑ Ḑab'ah Egypt 30 31.02N 28.26E
Ad Dafīnah Saudi Arabia 30 23.18N 41.58E
Ad Dahnā' des. Saudi Arabia 31 26.00N 47.00E
Ad Dāmir Sudan 35 17.37N 33.59E
Ad Dammām Saudi Arabia 31 26.23N 50.08E
Ad Dawādimī Saudi Arabia 31 24.29N 44.23E
Ad Dawḩah Qatar 31 25.15N 51.34E
Aḑ Ḑiffah f. Africa 30 30.45N 26.00E
Ad Dilam Saudi Arabia 31 23.59N 47.10E
Ad Dīmās Syria 32 33.35N 36.05E
Addis Ababa see Ādīs Ābeba Ethiopia 35
Ad Dīwānīyah Iraq 31 31.59N 44.57E
Adelaide Australia 46 34.56S 138.36E
Adelaide Pen. Canada 51 68.09N 97.45W
Adelaide River town Australia 42 13.14S 131.06E
Adelong Australia 47 35.21S 148.04E
Aden see 'Adan Yemen 35
Adendorp R.S.A. 39 32.18S 24.31E
Aden, G. of Indian Oc. 35 13.00N 50.00E
Adi i. Indonesia 27 4.10S 133.10E
Adieu, C. Australia 43 31.59S 132.09E
Adige r. Italy 9 45.10N 12.20E
Adilang Uganda 37 2.44N 33.28E
Adin U.S.A. 54 41.12N 120.57W
Adirondack Mts. U.S.A. 55 44.00N 74.00W
Ādīs Ābeba Ethiopia 35 9.03N 38.42E
Adiyaman Turkey 30 37.46N 38.15E
Adjud Romania 15 46.04N 27.11E
Admer well Algeria 34 20.23N 5.27E
Admiralty G. Australia 42 14.20S 125.50E
Admiralty Is. P.N.G. 27 2.30S 147.20E
Admiralty Range mts. Antarctica 64 72.00S 164.00E
Adour r. France 11 43.28N 1.35W
Adra Spain 10 36.43N 3.03W
Adrano Italy 12 37.39N 14.49E
Adrar des Iforas mts. Algeria/Mali 34 20.00N 2.30E
Adria Italy 9 45.03N 12.03E
Adrian Mich. U.S.A. 55 41.55N 84.01W
Adriatic Sea Med. Sea 12 42.30N 16.00E
Ādwa Ethiopia 35 14.12N 38.56E
Adzopé Côte d'Ivoire 38 6.07N 3.49W
Adzva r. Russian Fed 18 66.30N 59.30E
Aegean Sea Med. Sea 13 39.00N 25.00E
Afghanistan Asia 28 34.00N 65.30E
'Afif Saudi Arabia 30 23.53N 42.59E
Afikpo Nigeria 38 5.53N 7.55E
Afjord Norway 16 63.57N 10.12E
Afmadow Somali Rep. 37 0.27N 42.05E
Afobaka Surinam 61 5.00N 55.05W
Afognak I. U.S.A. 50 58.15N 152.30W
Afonso Cláudio Brazil 59 20.05S 41.06W
Afsluitdijk f. Neth. 8 53.04N 5.11E
'Afula Israel 32 32.36N 35.17E
Afyon Turkey 30 38.46N 30.32E
Agadez Niger 38 17.00N 7.56E
Agadez d. Niger 38 19.25N 11.00E
Agadir Morocco 34 30.26N 9.36W
Agapa Russian Fed. 21 71.29N 86.16E
Agartala India 29 23.49N 91.15E
Agboville Côte d'Ivoire 38 5.55N 4.15W
Agde France 11 43.19N 3.28E
Agen France 11 44.12N 0.38E
Ageo Japan 23 35.58N 139.36E
Agger r. Germany 8 50.45N 7.06E
Aghada Rep. of Ire. 7 51.50N 8.13W
Aginskoye Russian Fed. 21 51.10N 114.32E
Agnew Australia 43 28.01S 120.30E
Ago Japan 23 34.17N 136.48E
Agordo Italy 9 46.17N 12.02E
Āgra India 29 27.09N 78.00E
Agra r. Spain 10 42.12N 1.43W
Agraciada Uruguay 63 33.48S 58.15W
Agreda Spain 10 41.51N 1.55W
Agri r. Italy 13 40.13N 16.45E
Ağri Turkey 30 39.44N 43.04E
Ağri Daği mtn. Turkey 31 39.45N 44.15E
Agrigento Italy 12 37.19N 13.36E
Agropoli Italy 12 40.21N 15.00E
Agryz Russian Fed. 18 56.30N 53.00E
Aguas Blancas Chile 62 24.13S 69.50W
Aguascalientes Mexico 56 21.51N 102.18W
Aguascalientes d. Mexico 56 22.00N 102.00W
Agudos Brazil 59 22.27S 49.03W
Águeda r. Spain 10 41.00N 6.56W
Aguelhok Mali 38 19.28N 0.52E
Aguilar de Campóo Spain 10 42.47N 4.15W
Águilas Spain 10 37.25N 1.35W
Agulhas, C. R.S.A. 39 34.50S 20.00E
Agulhas Negras mtn. Brazil 59 22.20S 44.43W
Ahaggar mts. Algeria 34 24.00N 5.50E
Ahar Iran 31 38.25N 47.07E
Ahaura New Zealand 48 42.21S 171.33E
Ahaus Germany 8 52.04N 7.01E
Ahklun Mts. U.S.A. 50 59.15N 161.00W
Ahlen Germany 8 51.47N 7.52E
Ahmadābād India 28 23.03N 72.40E
Aḩmadī Iran 31 27.56N 56.42E
Ahmadnagar India 28 19.08N 74.48E
Ahoada Nigeria 38 5.06N 6.39E
Ahr r. Germany 8 50.34N 7.16E
Ahram Iran 31 28.52N 51.16E
Aḩsā', Wāḩat al oasis Saudi Arabia 31 25.37N 49.40E
Ähtäri Finland 16 62.34N 24.06E
Åhus Sweden 17 55.55N 14.17E
Ahvāz Iran 31 31.17N 48.44E
Ahvenanmaa d. Finland 17 60.15N 20.00E
Ahvenanmaa is. Finland 17 60.15N 20.00E
Aichi d. Japan 23 35.02N 137.15E
Aigle Switz. 9 46.19N 6.58E
Aigues-Mortes France 11 43.34N 4.11E
Aileron Australia 44 22.38S 133.20E
Ailette r. France 8 49.35N 3.09E
Ailsa Craig i. U.K. 6 55.15N 5.07W
Aim Russian Fed. 21 58.50N 134.15E
Aimorés Brazil 59 19.30S 41.04W
Ain r. France 11 45.47N 5.12E
Ainaži Estonia 17 57.52N 24.21E
Aïn ben Tili Mauritania 34 26.00N 9.32W
Aïn Sefra Algeria 34 32.45N 0.35W
Aïr mts. Niger 38 18.30N 8.30E
Airdrie U.K. 6 55.52N 3.59W
Aire France 11 43.39N 0.15W
Aire r. France 9 49.19N 4.49E
Aire r. U.K. 4 53.42N 0.54W
Aisne d. France 9 49.30N 3.30E
Aisne r. France 9 49.27N 2.51E
Aitape P.N.G. 27 3.10S 142.17E
Aiud Romania 15 46.19N 23.44E
Aix-en-Provence France 11 43.31N 5.27E
Aix-les-Bains France 11 45.42N 5.55E
Aíyina i. Greece 13 37.43N 23.30E
Aíyion Greece 13 38.15N 22.05E
Aizpute Latvia 17 56.43N 21.38E
Ajaccio France 11 41.55N 8.43E
Ajdābiyā Libya 34 30.48N 20.15E
'Ajlūn Jordan 32 32.20N 35.45E
'Ajmah, Jabal al f. Egypt 32 29.12N 33.58E
'Ajmān U.A.E. 31 25.23N 55.26E
Ajmer India 28 26.29N 74.40E
Akaishi sammyaku mts. Japan 23 35.20N 138.10E
Akámas, Akrotírion c. Cyprus 32 35.06N 32.17E
Akaroa New Zealand 48 43.50S 172.59E
Akashi Japan 23 34.38N 134.59E
Akbulak Russian Fed. 19 51.00N 55.40E
Akelamo Indonesia 27 1.35N 129.40E
Akershus d. Norway 17 60.00N 11.10E
Aketi Zaïre 36 2.46N 23.51E
Akhaltsikhe Georgia 30 41.37N 42.59E
Akhḑar, Al Jabal al mts. Libya 35 32.10N 22.00E
Akhḑar, Al Jabal al mts. Oman 31 23.10N 57.25E
Akhḑar, Wādī r. Egypt 32 28.42N 33.41E
Akhḑar, Wādī al r. Saudi Arabia 32 28.30N 36.48E
Akhelóös Greece 13 38.20N 21.04E
Akhisar Turkey 13 38.54N 27.49E
Akhmīm Egypt 30 26.34N 31.44E
Akhtyrka Ukraine 19 50.19N 34.54E
Akimiski I. Canada 51 53.00N 81.20W
Akita Japan 25 39.44N 140.05E
Akjoujt Mauritania 34 19.44N 14.26W
Akkajaure l. Sweden 16 67.40N 17.30E
'Akko Israel 32 32.55N 35.04E
Akkol Kazakhstan 24 45.04N 75.39E
Aklavik Canada 50 68.12N 135.00W
Akmola Kazakhstan 20 51.10N 71.28E
Ako Nigeria 38 10.19N 10.48E
Ākobo r. Ethiopia 35 8.30N 33.15E
Akola India 28 20.44N 77.00E
Āk'ordat Eritrea 35 15.35N 37.55E
Akpatok I. Canada 51 60.30N 68.30W
Akranes Iceland 16 64.19N 22.05W
Akron Ohio U.S.A. 55 41.04N 81.31W
Akrotíri Cyprus 32 34.36N 32.57E
Aksaray Turkey 30 38.22N 34.02E
Aksarka Russian Fed. 20 66.31N 67.50E
Aksay China 24 39.28N 94.15E
Aksay Kazakhstan 19 51.24N 52.11E
Akşehir Turkey 30 38.22N 31.24E
Aksu China 24 42.10N 80.00E
Aktag mtn. China 24 36.45N 84.40E
Aktau Kazakhstan 19 43.37N 51.11E
Aktogay Kazakhstan 24 46.59N 79.42E
Aktyubinsk Kazakhstan 19 50.16N 57.13E
Akūbū Sudan 36 7.47N 33.01E
Akūbū r. see Ākobo r. Sudan 36
Akure Nigeria 38 7.14N 5.08E
Akureyri Iceland 16 65.41N 18.04W
Akuse Ghana 38 6.04N 0.12E
Akwa-Ibom d. Nigeria 38 4.45N 7.50E
Akxokesay China 24 36.48N 91.06E
Akyab see Sittwe Myanmar 29
Ål Norway 17 60.38N 8.34E
Alabama d. U.S.A. 53 33.00N 87.00W
Alabama r. U.S.A. 53 31.05N 87.55W
Alādāgh, Kūh-e mts. Iran 31 37.15N 57.30E
Alagoas d. Brazil 61 9.30S 37.00W
Alagoinhas Brazil 61 12.09S 38.21W
Alagón Spain 10 41.46N 1.12W
Alakol, Ozero l. Kazakhstan 24 46.00N 81.40E
Alakurtti Russian Fed. 18 67.00N 30.23E
Al 'Alamayn Egypt 30 30.49N 28.57E
Al 'Amārah Iraq 31 31.52N 47.50E
Al Āmirīyah Egypt 32 31.01N 29.48E
Alamogordo U.S.A. 52 32.54N 105.57W
Alamosa U.S.A. 52 37.28N 105.52W
Åland is. see Ahvenanmaa is. Finland 17
Ålands Hav sea Finland 17 60.00N 19.30E
Alanya Turkey 30 36.32N 32.02E
Alapayevsk Russian Fed. 18 57.55N 61.42E
Alappuzha India 28 9.30N 76.22E
Al 'Aqabah Jordan 32 29.32N 35.00E
Al 'Aramah f. Saudi Arabia 31 25.30N 46.30E
Alarcón, Embalse de resr. Spain 10 39.36N 2.10W
Al 'Arīsh Egypt 32 31.08N 33.48E
Alaşehir Turkey 13 38.22N 28.29E
Alaska d. U.S.A. 50 65.00N 153.00W
Alaska, G. of U.S.A. 50 58.45N 145.00W
Alaska Pen. U.S.A. 50 56.00N 160.00W
Alaska Range mts. U.S.A. 50 62.10N 152.00W
Alassio Italy 9 44.00N 8.10E
Al 'Atīqah Lebanon 32 33.42N 35.27E
Al 'Aţrun Sudan 35 18.11N 26.36E
Alatyr Russian Fed. 18 54.51N 46.35E
Alausí Ecuador 60 2.00S 78.50W
Alavus Finland 16 62.35N 23.37E
Alawoona Australia 46 34.44S 140.33E
Al 'Ayyāţ Egypt 32 29.37N 31.15E
Alazani r. Georgia 31 41.06N 46.40E
Alba Italy 9 44.42N 8.02E
Albacete Spain 10 39.00N 1.52W
Al Bad' Saudi Arabia 32 28.29N 35.02E
Al Badārī Egypt 30 26.59N 31.25E
Al Bahnasā Egypt 32 28.32N 30.39E
Alba-Iulia Romania 15 46.04N 23.33E
Albania Europe 13 41.00N 20.00E
Albany Australia 43 34.57S 117.54E
Albany r. Canada 51 52.10N 82.00W
Albany Ga. U.S.A. 53 31.37N 84.10W
Albany N.Y. U.S.A. 55 42.39N 73.45W
Albany Oreg. U.S.A. 54 44.38N 123.06W
Al Başrah Iraq 31 30.33N 47.50E
Al Bāţinah f. Oman 31 24.25N 56.50E
Albatross B. Australia 44 12.45S 141.43E
Al Batrūn Lebanon 32 34.16N 35.40E
Al Bawīţī Egypt 30 28.21N 25.52E
Al Bayḑā' Libya 35 32.50N 21.50E
Albemarle Sd. U.S.A. 53 36.10N 76.00W
Albenga Italy 9 44.03N 8.13E
Alberche r. Spain 10 40.00N 4.45W
Alberga Australia 45 27.12S 135.28E
Alberga r. Australia 45 27.12S 135.28E
Albert Australia 47 32.21S 147.33E
Albert France 8 50.02N 2.38E
Alberta d. Canada 50 55.00N 115.00W
Alberti Argentina 63 35.01S 60.16W
Albertirsa Hungary 15 47.15N 19.38E
Albert Kanaal canal Belgium 8 51.00N 5.15E
Albert, L. Australia 46 35.38S 139.17E
Albert, L. Uganda/Zaïre 37 1.45N 31.00E
Albert Lea U.S.A. 53 43.38N 93.16W
Albert Nile r. Uganda 37 3.30N 32.00E
Albi France 11 43.56N 2.08E
Albina Surinam 61 5.30N 54.03W
Albino Italy 9 45.46N 9.47E
Albion Mich. U.S.A. 55 42.14N 84.45W
Albion Penn. U.S.A. 55 41.53N 80.22W
Al Bi'r Saudi Arabia 32 28.52N 36.15E
Alborán, Isla de i. Spain 10 35.55N 3.10W
Ålborg Denmark 17 57.03N 9.56E
Ålborg Bugt b. Denmark 17 56.45N 10.30E
Alborz, Reshteh-ye Kūhhā-ye mts. Iran 31 36.00N 52.30E
Albuquerque U.S.A. 52 35.05N 106.40W
Al Buraymī U.A.E. 31 24.15N 55.45E
Al Burj Egypt 32 31.35N 30.59E
Alburquerque Spain 10 39.13N 6.59W
Albury Australia 47 36.03S 146.53E
Alby Sweden 16 62.30N 15.25E
Alcácer do Sal Portugal 10 38.22N 8.30W
Alcalá de Chisvert Spain 10 40.19N 0.13E
Alcalá de Henares Spain 10 40.28N 3.22W
Alcalá la Real Spain 10 37.28N 3.55W
Alcamo Italy 12 37.59N 12.58E
Alcañiz Spain 10 41.03N 0.09W
Alcántara, Embalse de resr. Spain 10 39.45N 6.25W
Alcaudete Spain 10 37.35N 4.05W
Alcázar de San Juan Spain 10 39.24N 3.12W
Alcira Spain 10 39.10N 0.27W
Alcobaça Portugal 10 39.33N 8.59W
Alcova U.S.A. 54 42.35N 106.34W
Alcoy Spain 10 38.42N 0.29W
Alcubierre, Sierra de mts. Spain 10 41.40N 0.20W
Alcudia Spain 10 39.51N 3.09E
Aldan Russian Fed. 21 58.44N 125.22E
Aldan r. Russian Fed. 21 63.30N 130.00E
Aldeburgh U.K. 5 52.09N 1.35E
Alderney i. U.K. 5 49.42N 2.11W
Aldershot U.K. 5 51.15N 0.47W
Aldridge U.K. 5 52.36N 1.55W
Alegre Brazil 59 20.44S 41.30W
Alegrete Brazil 63 29.46S 55.46W
Aleksandrov Gay Russian Fed. 19 50.08N 48.34E
Aleksandrovsk Sakhalinskiy Russian Fed. 21 50.55N 142.12E
Além Paraíba Brazil 59 21.49S 42.36W
Alençon France 9 48.25N 0.05E
Aleppo see Ḩalab Syria 30
Aléria France 11 42.05N 9.30E
Alès France 11 44.08N 4.05E
Alessandria Italy 9 44.54N 8.37E
Ålesund Norway 16 62.28N 6.11E
Aleutian Range mts. U.S.A. 50 58.00N 156.00W
Alexander Archipelago is. U.S.A. 50 56.30N 134.30W
Alexander Bay town R.S.A. 39 28.36S 16.26E
Alexander I. Antarctica 64 72.00S 70.00W
Alexandra Australia 47 37.12S 145.14E
Alexandra New Zealand 48 45.14S 169.26E
Alexandria B.C. Canada 50 52.38N 122.27W
Alexandria Ont. Canada 55 45.18N 74.39W
Alexandria see Al Iskandarīyah Egypt 32
Alexandria Romania 15 43.58N 25.20E
Alexandria R.S.A. 39 33.39S 26.24E
Alexandria La. U.S.A. 53 31.19N 92.29W
Alexandria Va. U.S.A. 55 38.48N 77.03W
Alexandrina, L. Australia 46 35.26S 139.10E
Alexandroúpolis Greece 13 40.50N 25.53E
Aleysk Russian Fed. 20 52.32N 82.45E
Al Fant Egypt 32 28.46N 30.53E
Alfaro Spain 10 42.11N 1.45W
Al Fāshir Sudan 35 13.37N 25.22E
Al Fashn Egypt 32 28.49N 30.54E
Al Fāw Iraq 31 29.57N 48.30E
Al Fayyūm Egypt 32 29.19N 30.50E
Alfeld Germany 14 51.59N 9.50E
Alfenas Brazil 59 21.28S 45.48W
Alfiós r. Greece 13 37.37N 21.27E
Alfonsine Italy 9 44.30N 12.03E
Alford U.K. 6 57.14N 2.42W
Al Fujayrah U.A.E. 31 25.10N 56.20E
Alga Kazakhstan 20 49.49N 57.16E
Ålgård Norway 17 58.46N 5.51E
Algeciras Spain 10 36.08N 5.27W
Algemesí Spain 10 39.11N 0.27W
Alger Algeria 34 36.50N 3.00E
Algeria Africa 34 28.00N 2.00E
Al Ghayl Saudi Arabia 31 22.36N 46.19E
Alghero Italy 12 40.33N 8.20E
Al Ghurdaqah Egypt 30 27.14N 33.50E
Algiers see Alger Algeria 34
Algoa B. R.S.A. 39 33.50S 26.00E
Algonquin Prov. Park Canada 55 45.27N 78.26W
Algorta Uruguay 63 32.25S 57.23W
Al Ḩajar al Gharbī mts. Oman 31 24.00N 56.30E
Al Ḩajar ash Sharqī mts. Oman 31 22.45N 58.45E
Alhama Spain 10 37.51N 1.25W
Al Ḩamād des. Saudi Arabia 30 31.45N 39.00E
Al Ḩamar Saudi Arabia 31 22.26N 46.12E
Alhambra U.S.A. 54 34.06N 118.08W
Al Ḩamīdīyah Syria 32 34.43N 35.56E
Al Ḩanākīyah Saudi Arabia 30 24.53N 40.30E
Al Ḩarīq Saudi Arabia 31 23.37N 46.31E
Al Ḩasakah Syria 30 36.29N 40.45E
Al Ḩawāmidīyah Egypt 32 29.54N 31.15E
Al Ḩayz Egypt 30 28.02N 28.39E
Al Ḩijāz f. Saudi Arabia 30 26.00N 37.30E
Al Ḩillah Iraq 31 32.28N 44.29E
Al Ḩillah Saudi Arabia 31 23.30N 46.51E
Al Hirmil Lebanon 32 34.25N 36.23E
Al Ḩudaydah Yemen 35 14.50N 42.58E
Al Hufūf Saudi Arabia 31 25.20N 49.34E
Al Ḩumrah des. U.A.E. 31 22.45N 55.10E
Al Ḩusaynīyah Egypt 32 30.52N 31.55E
Al Ḩuwaymī Yemen 35 14.05N 47.44E
Alīābād, Kūh-e mtn. Iran 31 34.09N 50.48E
Aliákmon r. Greece 13 40.30N 22.38E
Alicante Spain 10 38.21N 0.29W
Alice R.S.A. 39 32.47S 26.49E
Alice U.S.A. 52 27.45N 98.06W
Alice Springs town Australia 44 23.42S 133.52E
Alīgarh India 29 27.54N 78.04E
Alīgūdarz Iran 31 33.25N 49.38E
'Alījūq, Kūh-e mtn. Iran 31 31.27N 51.43E
Alingsås Sweden 17 57.56N 12.31E
Alīpur Duār India 29 26.29N 89.44E
Aliquippa U.S.A. 55 40.38N 80.16W
Al Iskandarīyah Egypt 32 31.13N 29.55E
Al Ismā'īlīyah Egypt 32 30.36N 32.15E
Aliwal North R.S.A. 39 30.41S 26.41E
Al Jafr Jordan 32 30.16N 36.11E
Al Jāfūrah des. Saudi Arabia 31 24.40N 50.20E
Al Jaghbūb Libya 35 29.42N 24.38E
Al Jahrah Kuwait 31 29.20N 47.41E
Al Jawārah Oman 28 18.55N 57.17E
Al Jawb f. Saudi Arabia 31 23.00N 50.00E
Al Jawf Libya 35 24.09N 23.19E
Al Jawf Saudi Arabia 30 29.49N 39.52E
Al Jazīrah f. Iraq 30 35.00N 41.00E
Al Jazīrah f. Sudan 35 14.30N 33.00E
Al Jifārah Saudi Arabia 31 23.59N 45.11E
Al Jīzah Egypt 32 30.01N 31.12E
Al Jubayl Saudi Arabia 31 27.59N 49.40E
Al Junaynah Sudan 35 13.27N 22.30E
Aljustrel Portugal 10 37.55N 8.10W
Al Karak Jordan 32 31.11N 35.42E
Al Khābūr r. Syria 30 35.07N 40.30E
Al Khābūrah Oman 31 23.58N 57.10E
Al Khalīl Jordan 32 31.32N 35.06E
Al Khamāsīn Saudi Arabia 35 20.29N 44.49E
Al Khānkah Egypt 32 30.12N 31.21E
Al Khārijah Egypt 30 25.26N 30.33E
Al Kharţūm Sudan 35 15.33N 32.35E
Al Kharţūm Baḩrī Sudan 35 15.39N 32.34E
Al Khawr Qatar 31 25.39N 51.32E
Al Khirbah as Samrā' Jordan 32 32.11N 36.10E
Al Khubar Saudi Arabia 31 26.18N 50.06E
Al Khufayfīyah Saudi Arabia 31 24.55N 44.42E
Al Khunn Saudi Arabia 31 23.18N 49.15E
Al Kidn des. Saudi Arabia 35 22.30N 54.00E
Al Kiswah Syria 32 33.21N 36.14E
Alkmaar Neth. 8 52.37N 4.44E
Al Kuntillah Egypt 32 30.00N 34.41E
Al Kūt Iraq 31 32.30N 45.51E
Al Kuwayt Kuwait 31 29.20N 48.00E
Al Labwah Lebanon 32 34.11N 36.21E
Al Lādhiqīyah Syria 32 35.31N 35.47E
Allāhābād India 29 25.57N 81.50E
Allakaket U.S.A. 50 66.30N 152.45W
Allanche France 11 45.14N 2.56E
'Allāqī, Wādī al r. Egypt 30 22.55N 33.02E
Allegheny r. U.S.A. 55 40.27N 80.00W
Allegheny Mts. U.S.A. 53 38.30N 80.00W
Allen, Lough Rep. of Ire. 7 54.07N 8.04W
Allentown U.S.A. 55 40.37N 75.30W
Aller r. Germany 14 52.57N 9.11E
Alliance Nebr. U.S.A. 52 42.06N 102.52W
Allier r. France 11 46.58N 3.04E
Al Līţānī r. Lebanon 32 33.22N 35.14E
Alloa U.K. 6 56.07N 3.49W
Allos France 11 44.14N 6.38E
Al Luḩayyah Yemen 35 15.43N 42.42E
Alluitsup-Paa see Sydpröven Greenland 51
Alma Canada 55 48.32N 71.40W
Alma Mich. U.S.A. 55 43.23N 84.40W
Al Ma'ānīyah well Iraq 30 30.44N 43.00E
Almadén Spain 10 38.47N 4.50W
Al Madīnah Saudi Arabia 30 24.30N 39.35E
Al Madīnah al Fikrīyah Egypt 32 27.56N 30.49E
Al Mafraq Jordan 32 32.20N 36.12E
Al Maghrah well Egypt 30 30.14N 28.56E
Almagor Israel 32 32.55N 35.36E
Al Maḩallah al Kubrá Egypt 32 30.59N 31.12E
Al Maḩāriq Egypt 30 25.37N 30.39E
Al Maḩmūdīyah Egypt 32 31.10N 30.30E
Al Majma'ah Saudi Arabia 31 25.52N 45.25E
Al Manāmah Bahrain 31 26.12N 50.36E

anor U.S.A. 54 40.15N 121.08W
ansa Spain 10 38.52N 1.06W
Manshāh Egypt 30 26.28N 31.48E
Manşūrah Egypt 32 31.03N 31.23E
Manzil Jordan 32 31.03N 36.01E
Manzilah Egypt 32 31.10N 31.56E
anzora r. Spain 10 37.16N 1.49W
anzor, Pico de mtn. Spain 10 40.20N 5.22W
Maţarīyah Egypt 32 31.12N 32.02E
aty Kazakhstan 24 43.19N 76.55E
Mawşil Iraq 30 36.21N 43.08E
Mayādīn Syria 30 35.01N 40.28E
nazán Spain 10 41.29N 2.31W
Mazra'ah Jordan 32 31.16N 35.31E
eirim Portugal 10 39.12N 8.37W
nelo Neth. 8 52.21N 6.40E
nendralejo Spain 10 38.41N 6.26W
nería Spain 10 36.50N 2.26W
hult Sweden 17 56.33N 14.08E
Midhnab Saudi Arabia 31 25.52N 44.15E
Miḩrāḑ des. Saudi Arabia 31 20.00N 52.30E
Minyā Egypt 32 28.06N 30.45E
Mismīyah Syria 32 33.08N 36.24E
nonte Spain 10 37.16N 6.31W
Mudawwarah Jordan 32 29.20N 36.00E
Muglad Sudan 35 11.01N 27.50E
Muḩarraq Bahrain 31 26.16N 50.38E
Mukallā Yemen 35 14.34N 49.09E
nuñécar Spain 10 36.44N 3.41W
Muwayh Saudi Arabia 30 22.41N 41.37E
wick U.K. 4 55.25N 1.41W
fi Niue 40 19.03S 169.55W
nnisos i. Greece 13 39.08N 23.50E
r i. Indonesia 27 8.20S 124.30E
r Setar Malaysia 26 6.06N 100.23E
zero Russian Fed. 18 65.02N 31.10E
ena U.S.A. 55 45.04N 83.27W
es Maritimes mts. France 11 44.07N 7.08E
ha Australia 44 23.39S 146.38E
hen Neth. 8 52.08N 4.40E
ine U.S.A. 52 30.22N 103.40W
s mts. Europe 11 46.00N 7.30E
Qaḑārif Sudan 35 14.02N 35.24E
Qafā' des. U.A.E. 31 23.30N 53.30E
Qāhirah Egypt 32 30.03N 31.15E
Qā'īyah Saudi Arabia 30 24.18N 43.30E
Qā'īyah well Saudi Arabia 31 26.27N 45.35E
Qalībah Saudi Arabia 30 28.24N 37.42E
Qanāţir al Khayrīyah Egypt 32 30.12N 31.08E
Qanţarah Egypt 32 30.52N 32.20E
Qaryatayn Syria 32 34.13N 37.13E
Qaşr Egypt 30 25.43N 28.54E
Qaşşāşīn Egypt 32 30.34N 31.56E
Qaţīf Saudi Arabia 31 26.31N 50.00E
Qaţrānah Jordan 32 31.15N 36.03E
Qaţrūn Libya 34 24.55N 14.38E
Qayşūmah Saudi Arabia 31 28.20N 46.07E
Qunayţirah Syria 32 33.08N 35.49E
Qurnah Iraq 31 31.00N 47.26E
Quşaymah Egypt 32 30.40N 34.22E
Quşayr Egypt 30 26.06N 34.17E
Qūşīyah Egypt 30 27.26N 30.49E
Quţayfah Syria 32 33.44N 36.36E
roy Downs town Australia 44 19.18S 136.04E
s i. Denmark 17 54.59N 9.55E
sace d. France 11 48.25N 7.40E
sask Canada 50 51.23N 109.59W
sasua Spain 10 42.54N 2.10W
sborg d. Sweden 17 58.00N 12.20E
sfeld Germany 14 50.45N 9.16E
sten i. Norway 16 65.55N 12.35E
ston U.K. 6 54.48N 2.26W
a Norway 16 70.00N 23.15E
a r. Norway 16 69.50N 23.30E
afjorden est. Norway 16 70.10N 23.00E
a Gracia Argentina 62 31.40S 64.26W
agracia de Orituco Venezuela 60 9.54N 6.24W
ai mts. Mongolia 24 46.30N 93.30E
amaha r. U.S.A. 53 31.15N 81.23W
amira Brazil 61 3.12S 52.12W
amont Oreg. U.S.A. 54 42.12N 121.44W
amura Italy 13 40.50N 16.32E
ay China 24 47.48N 88.07E
ay Mongolia 24 46.20N 97.00E
ea Spain 10 38.37N 0.03W
enburg Germany 14 50.59N 12.27E
enkirchen Germany 8 50.41N 7.40E
naharra U.K. 6 58.16N 4.26W
to Araguaia Brazil 61 17.19S 53.10W
to Molocue Mozambique 37 15.38S 37.42E
ton U.K. 5 51.08N 0.59W
tona Germany 14 53.32N 9.56E
toona U.S.A. 55 40.30N 78.24W
tun Shan mts. China 24 38.10N 87.50E
Ubayyiḑ Sudan 35 13.11N 30.10E
'Ulá Saudi Arabia 30 26.39N 37.58E
Uqaylah Libya 34 30.15N 19.12E
Uqşur Egypt 30 25.41N 32.24E
Urduun r. Asia 32 31.47N 35.31E
'Uwaynah well Saudi Arabia 31 26.46N 48.13E
'Uyūn Saudi Arabia 31 26.32N 43.41E
va U.S.A. 52 36.48N 98.40W
varado Mexico 56 18.49N 95.46W
vdalen Sweden 17 61.14N 14.02E
vesta Sweden 17 56.54N 14.33E
vho Sweden 17 61.30N 14.46E
vkarleby Sweden 17 60.34N 17.27E
vsbyn Sweden 16 65.39N 20.59E
Wajh Saudi Arabia 30 26.16N 36.28E
Wakrah Qatar 31 25.09N 51.36E
war India 28 27.32N 76.35E
Yamāmah Saudi Arabia 31 24.11N 47.21E
yaty Azerbaijan 31 39.59N 49.20E
ytus Lithuania 15 54.24N 24.03E
zette r. Lux. 8 49.52N 6.07E
madeus, L. Australia 42 24.50S 130.45E
madjuak Canada 51 64.00N 72.50W
madjuak L. Canada 51 65.00N 71.00W
Amagasaki Japan 23 34.43N 135.25E
Åmål Sweden 17 59.03N 12.42E
Amaliás Greece 13 37.48N 21.21E
Amami ō shima i. Japan 25 28.20N 129.30E
Amamula Zaïre 37 0.17S 27.49E
Amanã, L. Brazil 60 2.35S 64.40W
Amangeldy Kazakhstan 20 50.12N 65.11E
Amapá Brazil 61 2.00N 50.50W
Amapá d. Brazil 61 2.00N 52.00W
Amarante Brazil 61 6.14S 42.51W
Amareleja Portugal 10 38.12N 7.13W
Amares Portugal 10 41.38N 8.21W
Amarillo U.S.A. 52 35.14N 101.50W
Amaro, Monte mtn. Italy 12 42.06N 14.04E
Amasya Turkey 30 40.37N 35.50E
Amazon r. see Amazonas r. Brazil 61
Amazonas d. Brazil 60 4.50S 64.00W
Amazonas r. Brazil 61 2.00S 52.00W
Amazonas, Estuario do Rio f. Brazil 61 0.00 50.30W
Amazon Delta see Amazonas, Estuario do Rio f. Brazil 61
Ambāla India 28 30.19N 76.49E
Ambam Cameroon 38 2.25N 11.16E
Ambarchik Russian Fed. 21 69.39N 162.27E
Ambarnyy Russian Fed. 18 65.59N 33.53E
Ambato Ecuador 60 1.18S 78.36W
Ambato-Boeni Madagascar 36 16.28S 46.43E
Ambatondrazaka Madagascar 36 17.50S 48.25E
AmLerg Germany 14 49.27N 11.52E
Ambergris Cay i. Belize 57 18.00N 87.58W
Ambikāpur India 29 23.07N 83.12E
Ambilobe Madagascar 36 13.12S 49.04E
Amble U.K. 4 55.20N 1.34W
Ambleside U.K. 4 54.26N 2.58W
Amboise France 9 47.25N 1.00E
Ambon Indonesia 27 4.50S 128.10E
Ambovombe Madagascar 36 25.11S 46.05E
Amboy U.S.A. 54 34.33N 115.44W
Ambrières France 9 48.24N 0.38W
Ambriz Angola 36 7.54S 13.12E
Amderma Russian Fed. 20 69.44N 61.35E
Ameca Mexico 56 20.33N 104.02W
Ameland i. Neth. 8 53.28N 5.48E
Americana Brazil 59 22.44S 47.19W
American Falls Resr. U.S.A. 54 43.00N 113.00W
American Fork U.S.A. 54 40.23N 111.48W
Amersfoort Neth. 8 52.10N 5.23E
Amery Australia 43 31.09S 117.05E
Ames U.S.A. 53 42.02N 93.39W
Ameson Canada 55 49.49N 84.34W
Ametinho Angola 39 17.20S 17.20E
Amga Russian Fed. 21 60.51N 131.59E
Amga r. Russian Fed. 21 62.40N 135.20E
Amgu Russian Fed. 25 45.48N 137.36E
Amgun r. Russian Fed. 21 53.10N 139.47E
Amhara Plateau f. Ethiopia 35 10.00N 37.00E
Amiata mtn. Italy 12 42.53N 11.37E
Amiens France 9 49.54N 2.18E
Åmli Norway 17 58.47N 8.30E
Amlwch U.K. 4 53.24N 4.21W
'Ammān Jordan 32 31.57N 35.56E
Ammanford U.K. 5 51.48N 4.00W
Ammassalik Greenland 51 65.40N 38.00W
Ammókhostos Cyprus 32 35.07N 33.57E
Ammókhostou, Kólpos b. Cyprus 32 35.12N 34.05E
Āmol Iran 31 36.26N 52.24E
Amorgós i. Greece 13 36.50N 25.55E
Amos Canada 55 48.34N 78.07W
Amoy see Xiamen China 25
Ampala Honduras 57 13.16N 87.39W
Amparo Brazil 59 22.44S 46.44W
Ampezzo Italy 9 46.25N 12.48E
Ampotaka Madagascar 36 25.03S 44.41E
Amqui Canada 55 48.28N 67.27W
Amrāvati India 28 20.58N 77.50E
Amritsar India 28 31.35N 74.56E
Amstelveen Neth. 8 52.18N 4.51E
Amsterdam Neth. 8 52.22N 4.54E
Amsterdam N.Y. U.S.A. 55 42.57N 74.11W
Am Timan Chad 35 11.02N 20.17E
Amu Darya r. Uzbekistan 20 43.50N 59.00E
Amundsen G. Canada 50 70.30N 122.00W
Amundsen Sea Antarctica 64 72.00S 120.00W
Amuntai Indonesia 26 2.24S 115.14E
Amur r. Russian Fed. 21 53.17N 140.00E
Amurzet Russian Fed. 25 47.50N 131.05E
Anabar r. Russian Fed. 21 72.40N 113.30E
Anabranch r. Australia 46 34.08S 141.46E
Anaco Venezuela 60 9.27N 64.28W
Anaconda U.S.A. 54 46.08N 112.57W
Anadolu f. Turkey 30 38.00N 35.00E
Anadyr Russian Fed. 21 64.40N 177.32E
Anadyr r. Russian Fed. 21 65.00N 176.00E
Anadyrskiy Zaliv g. Russian Fed. 21 64.30N 177.50W
Anáfi i. Greece 13 36.21N 25.50E
Anaheim U.S.A. 54 33.51N 117.57W
Analalava Madagascar 36 14.38S 47.45E
Anambas, Kepulauan is. Indonesia 26 3.00N 106.10E
Anambra d. Nigeria 38 6.20N 7.25E
Anamur Turkey 30 36.06N 32.49E
Anantapur India 28 14.41N 77.36E
Anápolis Brazil 61 16.19S 48.58W
Anapú r. Brazil 61 1.53S 50.53W
Anār Iran 31 30.54N 55.18E
Anārak Iran 31 33.20N 53.42E
Anatolia f. see Anadolu f. Turkey 30
Anatone U.S.A. 54 46.08N 117.09W
Añatuya Argentina 62 28.26S 62.48W
Ancenis France 9 47.21N 1.10W
Anchau Nigeria 38 11.00N 8.23E
Anchorage U.S.A. 50 61.10N 150.00W
Ancohuma mtn. Bolivia 62 16.05S 68.36W
Ancón Peru 60 11.50S 77.10W
Ancona Italy 12 43.37N 13.33E
Ancuabe Mozambique 37 13.00S 39.50E
Ancud Chile 63 41.05S 73.50W
Ancy-le-Franc France 9 47.46N 4.10E
Anda China 25 46.25N 125.20E
Andalsnes Norway 16 62.33N 7.43E
Andalucía d. Spain 10 37.36N 4.30W
Andalusia U.S.A. 53 31.20N 86.30W
Andaman Is. India 29 12.00N 93.00E
Andaman Sea Indian Oc. 29 11.15N 95.30E
Andamooka Australia 46 30.27S 137.12E
Andanga Russian Fed. 18 59.11N 45.44E
Andara Namibia 39 18.04S 21.26E
Andelot France 11 48.15N 5.18E
Andenes Norway 16 69.18N 16.10E
Andenne Belgium 8 50.29N 5.04E
Anderlecht Belgium 8 50.51N 4.18E
Andernach Germany 8 50.25N 7.24E
Anderson r. Canada 50 69.45N 129.00W
Anderson Ind. U.S.A. 55 40.05N 85.41W
Anderson S.C. U.S.A. 53 34.30N 82.39W
Andes mts. S. America 63 32.40S 70.00W
Andevoranto Madagascar 36 18.57S 49.06E
Andfjorden est. Norway 16 69.10N 16.00E
Andhra Pradesh d. India 29 17.00N 79.00E
Andikíthira i. Greece 13 35.52N 23.18E
Andizhan Uzbekistan 24 40.48N 72.23E
Andong S. Korea 25 36.37N 128.44E
Andorra town Andorra 11 42.30N 1.31E
Andorra Europe 11 42.30N 1.32E
Andover U.K. 5 51.13N 1.29W
Andöy i. Norway 16 69.05N 15.40E
Andreyevo-Ivanovka Ukraine 15 47.28N 30.29E
Andria Italy 12 41.13N 16.18E
Ándros Greece 13 37.50N 24.57E
Ándros i. Greece 13 37.50N 24.50E
Andros I. Bahamas 57 24.30N 78.00W
Andros Town Bahamas 57 24.43N 77.47W
Andrushevka Ukraine 15 50.00N 28.59E
Andújar Spain 10 38.02N 4.03W
Anefis I-n-Darane Mali 38 17.57N 0.35E
Anegada i. B.V.Is. 57 18.46N 64.24W
Aného Togo 38 6.17N 1.40E
Añelo Argentina 63 38.20S 68.45W
Aneto, Pico de mtn. Spain 10 42.40N 0.19E
Aney Niger 38 19.24N 12.56E
Angara r. Russian Fed. 21 58.00N 93.00E
Angarsk Russian Fed. 21 52.31N 103.55E
Angaston Australia 45 34.30S 139.03E
Angatuba Brazil 59 23.27S 48.25W
Ånge Sweden 16 62.31N 15.40E
Ángel de la Guarda, Isla i. Mexico 56 29.20N 113.25W
Angel Falls f. Venezuela 60 5.55N 62.30W
Ängelholm Sweden 17 56.15N 12.50E
Angels Camp U.S.A. 54 38.04N 120.32W
Ångerman r. Sweden 16 63.00N 17.43E
Angermünde Germany 14 53.01N 14.00E
Angers France 9 47.29N 0.32W
Angerville France 9 48.19N 2.00E
Ångesån r. Sweden 16 66.22N 22.58E
Angkor ruins Cambodia 26 13.26N 103.50E
Anglesey i. U.K. 4 53.16N 4.25W
Angoche Mozambique 37 16.10S 39.57E
Angol Chile 63 37.48S 72.43W
Angola Africa 36 12.00S 18.00E
Angola Ind. U.S.A. 55 41.38N 85.01W
Angola N.Y. U.S.A. 55 42.39N 79.02W
Angoram P.N.G. 27 4.04S 144.04E
Angoulême France 11 45.40N 0.10E
Angra dos Reis Brazil 59 22.59S 44.17W
Anguilla i. Leeward Is. 57 18.14N 63.05W
Angumu Zaïre 37 0.10S 27.38E
Anholt i. Denmark 17 56.42N 11.34E
Anholt Germany 8 51.51N 6.26E
Anhui d. China 25 31.30N 116.45E
Aniak U.S.A. 50 61.32N 159.40W
Anina Romania 15 45.05N 21.51E
Anjō Japan 23 34.57N 137.05E
Anjouan i. Comoros 37 12.12S 44.28E
Anju N. Korea 25 39.36N 125.42E
Anka Nigeria 38 12.06N 5.56E
Ankara Turkey 30 39.55N 32.50E
Anklam Germany 14 53.51N 13.41E
Ānkober Ethiopia 35 9.32N 39.43E
Ankpa Nigeria 38 7.26N 7.38E
Annaba Algeria 34 36.55N 7.47E
An Nabk Syria 32 34.02N 36.43E
Anna Creek town Australia 46 28.50S 136.07E
An Nafūd des. Saudi Arabia 30 28.40N 41.30E
An Najaf Iraq 31 31.59N 44.19E
An Nakhl Egypt 32 29.55N 33.45E
Annam Highlands see Annamitique, Chaîne mts. Laos/Vietnam 26
Annamitique, Chaîne mts. Laos/Vietnam 26 17.40N 105.30E
Annan U.K. 6 54.59N 3.16W
Annan r. U.K. 6 54.58N 3.16W
Annandale f. U.K. 6 55.12N 3.25W
Anna Plains Australia 42 19.18S 121.34E
Annapolis U.S.A. 55 38.59N 76.30W
Annapurna mtn. Nepal 29 28.34N 83.50E
An Naqīrah well Saudi Arabia 31 27.53N 48.15E
Ann Arbor U.S.A. 55 42.18N 83.43W
An Nāşirīyah Iraq 31 31.04N 46.16E
Annecy France 11 45.54N 6.07E
Anniston U.S.A. 53 33.58N 85.50W
Annonay France 11 45.15N 4.40E
Annuello Australia 46 34.52S 142.54E
An Nuhūd Sudan 35 12.41N 28.28E
Anoka U.S.A. 53 45.11N 93.20W
Anqing China 25 30.20N 116.50E
Ansbach Germany 14 49.18N 10.36E
Anshan China 25 41.05N 122.58E
Anshun China 29 26.02N 105.57E
Anson B. Australia 42 13.10S 130.00E
Ansongo Mali 38 15.40N 0.30E
Anstruther U.K. 6 56.14N 2.42W
Ansudu Indonesia 27 2.11S 139.22E
Antakya Turkey 30 36.12N 36.10E
Antalya Turkey 30 36.53N 30.42E
Antalya Körfezi g. Turkey 30 36.38N 31.00E
Antananarivo Madagascar 36 18.55S 47.31E
Antarctica 64
Antas Brazil 61 10.20S 38.20W
Antequera Spain 10 37.01N 4.34W
Antibes France 11 43.35N 7.07E
Anticosti, Île d' i. Canada 51 49.20N 63.00W
Antifer, Cap d' c. France 9 49.41N 0.10E
Antigua Guatemala 56 14.33N 90.42W
Antigua i. Leeward Is. 57 17.09N 61.49W
Anti-Lebanon mts. see Sharqī, Al Jabal ash mts. Lebanon 32
Antofagasta Chile 62 23.39S 70.24W
Antônio Bezerra Brazil 61 3.44S 38.35W
Antônio Carlos Brazil 59 21.18S 43.48W
Antrain France 9 48.28N 1.30W
Antrim U.K. 7 54.43N 6.14W
Antrim d. U.K. 7 54.58N 6.20W
Antrim, Mts. of U.K. 7 55.00N 6.10W
Antsiranana Madagascar 36 12.16S 49.17E
Anttis Sweden 16 67.16N 22.52E
Antwerp see Antwerpen Belgium 8
Antwerpen Belgium 8 51.13N 4.25E
Antwerpen d. Belgium 8 51.16N 4.45E
Anvik U.S.A. 50 62.38N 160.20W
Anxi Gansu China 24 40.32N 95.57E
Anxious B. Australia 46 33.25S 134.35E
Anyama Côte d'Ivoire 38 5.30N 4.03W
Anyang China 25 36.04N 114.20E
Anzhero-Sudzhensk Russian Fed. 20 56.10N 86.10E
Anzio Italy 12 41.27N 12.37E
Aohan Qi China 25 42.23N 119.59E
Aomori Japan 25 40.50N 140.43E
Aosta Italy 9 45.43N 7.19E
Apalachee B. U.S.A. 53 29.30N 84.00W
Apaporis r. Colombia 60 1.40S 69.20W
Aparri Phil. 27 18.22N 121.40E
Apatin Yugo. 13 45.40N 18.59E
Apatity Russian Fed. 18 67.32N 33.21E
Apeldoorn Neth. 8 52.13N 5.57E
Apia W. Samoa 40 13.48S 171.45W
Apizaco Mexico 56 19.25N 98.09W
Apollo Bay town Australia 46 38.45S 143.40E
Apostle Is. U.S.A. 53 47.00N 90.30W
Apóstoles Argentina 62 27.55S 55.45W
Apostólou Andréa, Akrotírion c. Cyprus 32 35.40N 34.35E
Apoteri Guyana 60 4.02N 58.32W
Appalachian Mts. U.S.A. 53 39.30N 78.00W
Appennino mts. Italy 12 42.00N 13.30E
Appennino Ligure mts. Italy 9 44.30N 9.00E
Appennino Tosco-Emiliano mts. Italy 9 44.05N 11.00E
Appiano Italy 9 46.28N 11.15E
Appingedam Neth. 8 53.18N 6.52E
Appleby U.K. 4 54.35N 2.29W
Appleton U.S.A. 53 44.17N 88.24W
Apsheronsk Russian Fed. 19 44.26N 39.45E
Apsheronskiy Poluostrov pen. Azerbaijan 31 40.28N 50.00E
Apsley Australia 46 36.58S 141.08E
Apsley Canada 55 44.45N 78.06W
Apucarana Brazil 59 23.34S 51.28W
Apure r. Venezuela 60 7.40N 66.30W
Apurimac r. Peru 60 10.43S 73.55W
Aqaba, G. of Asia 32 28.45N 34.45E
Aqabat al Ḩijāzīyah Jordan 32 29.40N 35.55E
'Aqdā Iran 31 32.25N 33.38E
Aqqikkol Hu l. China 24 35.44N 81.34E
Aquidauana Brazil 62 20.27S 55.45W
Aquila Mexico 56 18.30N 103.50W
Aquitaine d. France 11 44.40N 0.00
Arabādād Iran 31 33.02N 57.41E
'Arabah, Wādī r. Egypt 32 29.07N 32.40E
'Arab, Baḩr al r. Sudan 35 9.02N 29.28E
Arabian Sea Asia 28 16.00N 65.00E
Araç Turkey 30 41.14N 33.20E
Aracaju Brazil 61 10.54S 37.07W
Aracanguy, Montañas de mts. Paraguay 62 24.00S 55.50W
Aracati Brazil 61 4.32S 37.45W
Araçatuba Brazil 59 21.12S 50.24W
Arad Romania 15 46.12N 21.19E
Arafura Sea Austa. 44 9.00S 133.00E
Aragarças Brazil 61 15.55S 52.12W
Aragats mtn. Armenia 31 40.32N 44.11E
Aragón d. Spain 10 41.25N 1.00W
Aragón r. Spain 10 42.20N 1.45W
Araguacema Brazil 61 8.50S 49.34W
Araguaia r. Brazil 61 5.20S 48.30W
Araguari Brazil 59 18.38S 48.13W
Araguari r. Brazil 61 1.15N 50.05W
Arāk Iran 31 34.06N 49.44E
Arakan Yoma mts. Myanmar 29 20.00N 94.00E
Araks r. Azerbaijan 31 40.00N 48.28E
Aral Sea sea Asia 20 45.00N 60.00E
Aralsk Kazakhstan 20 46.56N 61.43E
Aralskoye More see Aral Sea sea Asia 20
Aralsor, Ozero l. Kazakhstan 19 49.00N 48.40E
Aramac Australia 44 22.59S 145.14E
Aramia r. P.N.G. 27 8.00S 143.20E
Aranda de Duero Spain 10 41.40N 3.41W
Aran I. Rep. of Ire. 7 53.07N 9.38W
Aran Is. Rep. of Ire. 7 53.07N 9.38W
Aranjuez Spain 10 40.02N 3.37W
Aranos Namibia 39 24.09S 19.09E
Araouane Mali 38 18.53N 3.31W
Arapey Uruguay 63 30.58S 57.30W
Arapey Grande r. Uruguay 63 30.55S 57.49W
Arapiraca Brazil 61 9.45S 36.40W
Arapkir Turkey 30 39.03N 38.29E
Araraquara Brazil 59 21.46S 48.08W
Araras Brazil 59 22.20S 47.23W
Ararat Australia 46 37.20S 143.00E
Ararat mtn. see Ağri Daği mtn. Turkey 31
'Ar'ar, Wādī r. Iraq 30 32.00N 42.30E
Aras r. see Araks r. Turkey 30
Arauca Colombia 60 7.04N 70.41W
Arauca r. Venezuela 60 7.05N 70.45W
Araure Venezuela 60 9.36N 69.15W
Araxá Brazil 59 19.37S 46.50W
Araxes r. Iran see Araks r. Iran 31
Ārba Minch' Ethiopia 35 6.02N 37.40E
Arbatax Italy 12 39.56N 9.41E
Arboga Sweden 17 59.24N 15.50E
Arbroath U.K. 6 56.34N 2.35W
Arcachon France 11 44.40N 1.11W
Arcata U.S.A. 54 40.52N 124.05W
Archer r. Australia 44 13.28S 141.41E
Archers Post Kenya 37 0.42N 37.40E
Arcis-sur-Aube France 9 48.32N 4.08E
Arckaringa r. Australia 46 27.56S 134.45E
Arco Italy 9 45.55N 10.53E
Arco U.S.A. 54 43.38N 113.18W
Arcoona Australia 46 31.06S 137.19E
Arcos Brazil 59 20.12S 45.30W
Arcos Spain 10 36.45N 5.45W
Arcoverde Brazil 61 8.23S 37.00W
Arctic Bay town Canada 51 73.05N 85.20W
Arctic Ocean 64
Arctic Red r. Canada 50 67.26N 133.48W
Arctic Red River town Canada 50 67.27N 133.46W
Arda r. Greece 13 41.39N 26.30E
Ardabīl Iran 31 38.15N 48.18E
Ardahan Turkey 30 41.08N 42.41E
Årdalstangen Norway 17 61.14N 7.43E
Ardara Rep. of Ire. 7 54.46N 8.25W
Arḑ aş Şawwān f. Jordan 32 30.45N 37.15E
Ardèche r. France 11 44.31N 4.40E
Ardennes mts. Belgium 8 50.10N 5.30E
Ardennes d. France 9 49.40N 4.40E
Ardennes, Canal des France 9 49.26N 4.02E
Ardestān Iran 31 33.22N 52.25E
Ardfert Rep. of Ire. 7 52.20N 9.48W
Ardila r. Portugal 10 38.10N 7.30W
Ardlethan Australia 47 34.20S 146.53E
Ardmore Rep. of Ire. 7 51.58N 7.43W
Ardmore Okla. U.S.A. 53 34.11N 97.08W
Ardnamurchan, Pt. of U.K. 6 56.44N 6.14W
Ardrossan Australia 46 34.25S 137.55E
Ardrossan U.K. 6 55.38N 4.49W
Ards Pen. U.K. 7 54.30N 5.30W
Åre Sweden 16 63.25N 13.05E
Arecibo Puerto Rico 57 18.29N 66.44W
Areia Branca Brazil 61 4.56S 37.07W
Arena, Pt. U.S.A. 52 38.58N 123.44W
Arendal Norway 17 58.27N 8.48E
Arequipa Peru 60 16.25S 71.32W
Arès France 11 44.47N 1.08W
Arévalo Spain 10 41.03N 4.43W
Arezzo Italy 12 43.27N 11.52E
Arfak mtn. Indonesia 27 1.30S 133.50E
Arganda Spain 10 40.19N 3.26W
Argelès-sur-Mer France 11 42.33N 3.01E
Argens r. France 11 43.10N 6.45E
Argenta Italy 9 44.37N 11.50E
Argentan France 9 48.45N 0.01W
Argentera Italy 9 44.24N 6.57E
Argentera mtn. Italy 9 44.10N 7.18E
Argenteuil France 9 48.57N 2.15E
Argentina S. America 63 36.00S 63.00W
Argentino, L. Argentina 63 50.15S 72.25W
Argenton France 11 46.36N 1.30E
Argentré France 9 48.05N 0.39W
Argentré du Plessis France 9 48.03N 1.08W
Argeş r. Romania 13 44.13N 26.22E
Árgos Greece 13 37.37N 22.45E
Argostólion Greece 13 38.10N 20.30E
Arguello, Pt. U.S.A. 54 34.35N 120.39W
Argun r. Russian Fed. 25 53.30N 121.48E
Argungu Nigeria 38 12.45N 4.35E
Århus Denmark 17 56.09N 10.13E
Ariah Park town Australia 47 34.20S 147.10E
Ariano Italy 12 41.04N 15.00E
Ariano nel Polesine Italy 9 44.56N 12.07E
Aribinda Burkina 38 14.17N 0.52W
Arica Chile 62 18.29S 70.20W
Arica Colombia 60 2.07S 71.46W
Arid, C. Australia 43 33.58S 123.05E
Arieş r. Romania 15 46.26N 23.59E
Arīḩā Al Quds Jordan 32 31.51N 35.27E
Arima Trinidad 60 10.38N 61.17W
Arinos r. Brazil 61 10.20S 57.35W
Aripuanã Brazil 60 9.10S 60.38W
Aripuanã r. Brazil 60 5.05S 60.30W
Ariquemes Brazil 60 9.56S 63.04W
Aris Namibia 39 22.48S 17.10E
Arisaig U.K. 6 56.55N 5.51W
'Arīsh, Wādī al r. Egypt 32 31.09N 33.49E
Ariza Spain 10 41.19N 2.03W
Arizona d. U.S.A. 52 34.00N 112.00W
Årjäng Sweden 17 59.23N 12.08E
Arjeplog Sweden 16 66.00N 17.58E
Arjona Colombia 60 10.14N 75.22W
Arkaig, Loch U.K. 6 56.58N 5.08W
Arkansas d. U.S.A. 53 35.00N 92.00W
Arkansas r. U.S.A. 53 33.50N 91.00W
Arkansas City U.S.A. 53 37.03N 97.02W
Arkhangel'sk Russian Fed. 18 64.32N 41.10E
Árki i. Greece 13 37.22N 26.45E
Arklow Rep. of Ire. 7 52.47N 6.10W
Arkville U.S.A. 55 42.09N 74.37W
Arlberg Pass Austria 14 47.00N 10.05E
Arles France 11 43.41N 4.38E
Arlington Oreg. U.S.A. 54 45.16N 120.13W
Arlington Va. U.S.A. 55 38.52N 77.05W
Arlon Belgium 8 49.41N 5.49E
Armadale Australia 43 32.10S 115.57E
Armagh U.K. 7 54.21N 6.41W
Armagh d. U.K. 7 54.16N 6.35W
Armançon r. France 9 47.57N 3.30E
Armavir Russian Fed. 19 44.59N 41.10E
Armenia Colombia 60 4.32N 75.40W
Armenia Europe 31 40.00N 45.00E
Armenia f. Iran/Turkey/Armenia 31 40.00N 44.30E

74

Benin, Bight of Africa **38** 5.30N 3.00E
Benin City Nigeria **38** 6.19N 5.41E
Benjamin Constant Brazil **60** 4.22S 70.02W
Ben Lawers *mtn.* U.K. **6** 56.33N 4.14W
Ben Lomond *mtn.* U.K. **6** 56.12N 4.38W
Ben Macdhui *mtn.* U.K. **6** 57.04N 3.40W
Ben More *mtn.* Central U.K. **6** 56.23N 4.31W
Ben More *mtn.* Strath. U.K. **6** 56.26N 6.02W
Ben More Assynt *mtn.* U.K. **6** 58.07N 4.52W
Bennett Canada **50** 59.49N 135.01W
Bennett, L. Australia **44** 22.50S 131.01E
Ben Nevis *mtn.* U.K. **6** 56.48N 5.00W
Benneydale New Zealand **48** 38.31S 175.21E
Benoni R.S.A. **39** 26.12S 28.18E
Bénoué *r.* Cameroon *see* Benue *r.* Nigeria **38**
Bentinck I. Australia **44** 17.04S 139.30E
Benton Harbor U.S.A. **55** 42.07N 86.27W
Benue *d.* Nigeria **38** 7.20N 8.00E
Benue *r.* Nigeria **38** 7.52N 6.45E
Ben Wyvis *mtn.* U.K. **6** 57.40N 4.35W
Benxi China **25** 41.21N 123.45E
Beograd Yugo. **15** 44.49N 20.28E
Beowawe U.S.A. **54** 40.35N 116.29W
Berat Albania **13** 40.42N 19.59E
Berau, Teluk *b.* Indonesia **27** 2.20S 133.00E
Berbera Somali Rep. **35** 10.28N 45.02E
Berbérati C.A.R. **36** 4.19N 15.51E
Berceto Italy **9** 44.31N 9.59E
Berchem Belgium **8** 50.48N 3.32E
Berck France **11** 50.25N 1.36E
Bercu France **8** 50.32N 3.15E
Berdichev Ukraine **15** 49.54N 28.39E
Berdsk Russian Fed. **20** 54.51N 82.51E
Berdyansk Ukraine **19** 46.45N 36.47E
Beregovo Ukraine **15** 48.13N 22.39E
Bereko Tanzania **37** 4.27S 35.43E
Beresford Australia **46** 29.14S 136.40E
Berettyóújfalu Hungary **15** 47.14N 21.32E
Bereza Belarus **15** 52.32N 25.00E
Berezhany Ukraine **15** 49.27N 24.56E
Berezina *r.* Belarus **15** 54.10N 28.10E
Berezna Ukraine **15** 51.34N 31.46E
Berezniki Russian Fed. **18** 59.26N 56.49E
Berezno Ukraine **15** 51.00N 26.41E
Berezovka Ukraine **15** 47.12N 30.56E
Berezovo Russian Fed. **20** 63.58N 65.00E
Berga Spain **10** 42.06N 1.48E
Berga Sweden **17** 57.14N 16.03E
Bergama Turkey **13** 39.08N 27.10E
Bergamo Italy **9** 45.42N 9.40E
Bergen Germany **14** 54.25N 13.26E
Bergen Neth. **8** 52.40N 4.41E
Bergen Norway **17** 60.23N 5.20E
Bergen op Zoom Neth. **8** 51.30N 4.17E
Bergerac France **11** 44.50N 0.29E
Bergheim Germany **8** 50.58N 6.39E
Berghem Neth. **8** 51.46N 5.32E
Bergisch Gladbach Germany **8** 50.59N 7.10E
Bergkamen Germany **8** 51.35N 7.39E
Bergkvara Sweden **17** 56.23N 16.05E
Bergland U.S.A. **55** 46.36N 89.33W
Bergues France **8** 50.58N 2.21E
Bergum Neth. **8** 53.14N 5.59E
Berhampore India **29** 24.06N 88.18E
Berhampur India **29** 19.21N 84.51E
Bering Sea N. America/Asia **50** 65.00N 170.00W
Bering Str. Russian Fed./U.S.A **50** 65.00N 170.00W
Berislav Ukraine **19** 46.51N 33.26E
Berja Spain **10** 36.50N 2.56W
Berkåk Norway **16** 62.48N 10.03E
Berkel *r.* Neth. **8** 52.10N 6.12E
Berkeley U.S.A. **54** 37.57N 122.18W
Berkner I. Antarctica **64** 79.30S 50.00W
Berkshire *d.* U.K. **5** 51.25N 1.03W
Berkshire Downs *hills* U.K. **5** 51.32N 1.36W
Berlin Germany **14** 52.32N 13.25E
Berlin *d.* Germany **14** 52.30N 13.20E
Berlin N.H. U.S.A. **55** 44.29N 71.10W
Bermagui Australia **47** 36.28S 150.03E
Bermejo *r.* San Juan Argentina **62** 31.40S 67.15W
Bermejo *r.* Tucumán Argentina **62** 26.47S 58.30W
Bern Switz. **14** 46.57N 7.26E
Bernard L. Canada **55** 45.44N 79.24W
Bernay France **9** 48.06N 0.36E
Bernburg Germany **14** 51.48N 11.44E
Berne *see* Bern Switz. **11**
Bernier I. Australia **42** 24.51S 113.09E
Bernina *mtn.* Italy/Switz. **9** 46.22N 9.57E
Bernkastel Germany **8** 49.55N 7.05E
Beroun Czech Republic **14** 49.58N 14.04E
Berrechid Morocco **34** 33.17N 7.35W
Berri Australia **46** 34.17S 140.36E
Berridale Australia **47** 36.21S 148.51E
Berrigan Australia **47** 35.41S 145.48E
Berry Head U.K. **5** 50.24N 3.28W
Bersenbrück Germany **8** 52.36N 7.58E
Bershad Ukraine **15** 48.20N 29.30E
Berté, Lac *l.* Canada **55** 50.47N 68.30W
Bertinoro Italy **9** 44.09N 12.08E
Bertoua Cameroon **38** 4.34N 13.42E
Bertraghboy B. Rep. of Ire. **7** 53.23N 9.52W
Berwick-upon-Tweed U.K. **4** 55.46N 2.00W
Besalampy Madagascar **37** 16.45S 44.30E
Besançon France **11** 47.14N 6.02E
Bessarabia *f.* Moldova **15** 46.30N 28.40E
Bessemer U.S.A. **53** 33.22N 87.00W
Betanzos Spain **10** 43.17N 8.13W
Bétaré Oya Cameroon **38** 5.34N 14.09E
Bethal R.S.A. **39** 26.26S 29.27E
Bethany Beach *town* U.S.A. **55** 38.31N 75.04W
Bethel Alas. U.S.A. **50** 60.48N 161.46W
Bethlehem R.S.A. **39** 28.13S 28.18E
Bethlehem U.S.A. **55** 40.36N 75.22W
Béthune France **8** 50.32N 2.38E
Béthune *r.* France **9** 49.53N 1.09E
Betim Brazil **59** 19.55S 44.07W
Betroka Madagascar **36** 23.16S 46.06E
Bet She'an Israel **32** 32.30N 35.30E
Bet Shemesh Israel **32** 31.45N 35.00E
Betsiamites Canada **55** 48.56N 68.38W
Bettles U.S.A. **50** 66.53N 151.51W
Betzdorf Germany **8** 50.48N 7.54E
Beulah Australia **46** 35.59S 142.26E
Beuvron *r.* France **9** 47.29N 3.31E
Beverley Australia **43** 32.06S 116.56E
Beverley U.K. **4** 53.52N 0.26W
Beverley Hills *town* U.S.A. **54** 34.04N 118.26W
Beverly Mass. U.S.A. **55** 42.33N 70.53W
Beverwijk Neth. **8** 52.29N 4.40E
Bewcastle Fells *hills* U.K. **4** 55.05N 2.50W
Bexhill U.K. **5** 50.51N 0.29E
Bexley U.K. **5** 51.26N 0.10E
Beyla Guinea **34** 8.42N 8.39W
Beyneu Kazakhstan **19** 45.16N 55.04E
Beypazari Turkey **30** 40.10N 31.56E
Beyşehir Gölü *l.* Turkey **30** 37.47N 31.30E
Bezhanovo Bulgaria **13** 43.13N 24.26E
Bezhetsk Russian Fed. **18** 57.49N 36.40E
Bezhitsa Russian Fed. **18** 53.19N 34.17E
Béziers France **11** 43.21N 3.13E
Bhadrakh India **29** 21.04N 86.30E
Bhāgalpur India **29** 25.14N 86.59E
Bhamo Myanmar **29** 24.15N 97.15E
Bhatinda India **28** 30.12N 74.57E
Bhatkal India **28** 13.58N 74.34E
Bhātpāra India **29** 22.51N 88.31E
Bhaunagar India **28** 21.46N 72.14E
Bhīlwāra India **28** 25.21N 74.38E
Bhima *r.* India **28** 16.30N 77.10E
Bhopāl India **28** 23.17N 77.28E
Bhor India **28** 18.12N 73.53E
Bhubaneswar India **29** 20.15N 85.50E
Bhuj India **28** 23.12N 69.54E
Bhutan Asia **29** 27.25N 89.50E
Biak Indonesia **27** 1.10S 136.05E
Biak *i.* Indonesia **27** 0.55S 136.00E
Biała Podlaska Poland **15** 52.02N 23.06E
Białogard Poland **14** 54.00N 16.00E
Białystok Poland **15** 53.09N 23.10E
Biarritz France **11** 43.29N 1.33W
Biasca Switz. **9** 46.22N 8.58E
Bibā Egypt **32** 28.56N 30.59E
Biberach Germany **14** 48.20N 9.30E
Bic Canada **55** 48.23N 68.43W
Bicas Brazil **59** 21.44S 43.04W
Bicester U.K. **5** 51.53N 1.09W
Bida Nigeria **38** 9.06N 5.59E
Bīdar India **28** 17.54N 77.33E
Biddeford U.S.A. **55** 43.30N 70.26W
Bideford U.K. **5** 51.01N 4.13W
Biel Switz. **11** 47.09N 7.16E
Bielefeld Germany **14** 52.02N 8.32E
Biella Italy **9** 45.34N 8.03E
Bielsko-Biała Poland **15** 49.49N 19.02E
Bielsk Podlaski Poland **15** 52.47N 23.12E
Bienville, Lac *l.* Canada **51** 55.05N 72.40W
Bié Plateau *f.* Angola **36** 13.00S 16.00E
Big Bald Mtn. Canada **55** 47.12N 66.25W
Big Bear Lake *town* U.S.A. **54** 34.15N 116.53W
Big Belt Mts. U.S.A. **54** 46.40N 111.25W
Bigbury B. U.K. **5** 50.15N 3.56W
Biggar Canada **50** 52.04N 107.59W
Biggar U.K. **6** 55.38N 3.31W
Bighorn *r.* U.S.A. **54** 46.09N 107.28W
Bighorn L. U.S.A. **54** 45.06N 108.08W
Bighorn Mts. U.S.A. **54** 44.00N 107.30W
Bight, Head of *b.* Australia **45** 31.29S 131.16E
Bignasco Switz. **9** 46.20N 8.36E
Big Pine U.S.A. **54** 37.10N 118.17W
Big Piney U.S.A. **54** 42.32N 110.07W
Big Salmon Canada **50** 61.53N 134.55W
Big Sandy U.S.A. **54** 48.11N 110.07W
Big Smoky Valley *f.* U.S.A. **54** 38.30N 117.15W
Big Snowy Mtn. U.S.A. **54** 46.50N 109.30W
Big Spring *town* U.S.A. **52** 32.15N 101.30W
Big Sur U.S.A. **54** 36.15N 121.48W
Big Timber U.S.A. **54** 45.50N 109.57W
Big Trout L. Canada **51** 53.45N 90.00W
Bihać Bosnia-Herzegovina **12** 44.49N 15.53E
Bihar India **29** 25.13N 85.31E
Bihar *d.* India **29** 24.15N 86.00E
Biharamulo Tanzania **37** 2.34S 31.20E
Bihor *mtn.* Romania **15** 46.26N 22.43E
Bijagós, Arquipélago dos *is.* Guinea Bissau **34** 11.30N 16.00W
Bījāpur India **28** 16.52N 75.47E
Bījār Iran **31** 35.52N 47.39E
Bījāwar India **29** 24.36N 79.30E
Bijeljina Bosnia-Herzegovina **13** 44.45N 19.13E
Bīkaner India **28** 28.01N 73.22E
Bikin Russian Fed. **25** 46.52N 134.15E
Bilāspur India **29** 22.03N 82.12E
Bilauktaung Range *mts.* Myanmar **29** 13.20N 99.30E
Bilbao Spain **10** 43.15N 2.56W
Bilbays Egypt **32** 30.25N 31.34E
Bilbo *see* Bilbao Spain **10**
Bilecik Turkey **30** 40.10N 29.59E
Bilibino Russian Fed. **21** 68.02N 166.15E
Billabong Creek *r.* Australia **46** 35.04S 144.06E
Billingham U.K. **4** 54.36N 1.18W
Billings U.S.A. **54** 45.47N 108.27W
Bill of Portland *c.* U.K. **5** 50.32N 2.28W
Bilma Niger **38** 18.46N 12.50E
Biloela Australia **44** 24.24S 150.30E
Biloxi U.S.A. **53** 30.30N 88.53W
Bilqās Qism Awwal Egypt **32** 31.14N 31.22E
Bilto Norway **16** 69.26N 21.35E
Bimberi, Mt. Australia **47** 35.40S 148.47E
Bīna-Etāwa India **29** 24.09N 78.10E
Binaiya *mtn.* Indonesia **27** 3.10S 129.30E
Bīnālūd, Kūh-e *mts.* Iran **31** 36.15N 59.00E
Binbee Australia **44** 20.20S 147.55E
Binche Belgium **8** 50.25N 4.10E
Bindura Zimbabwe **39** 17.18S 31.20E
Binga Zimbabwe **39** 17.38S 27.19E
Binga, Mt. Zimbabwe **39** 19.47S 33.03E
Bingara Australia **47** 29.51S 150.38E
Bingen Germany **8** 49.58N 7.55E
Bingerville Côte d'Ivoire **38** 5.20N 3.53W
Bingham U.K. **4** 52.57N 0.57W
Bingham U.S.A. **55** 45.03N 69.53W
Binghamton U.S.A. **55** 42.08N 75.54W
Bingkor Malaysia **26** 5.26N 116.15E
Bingöl Turkey **19** 38.54N 40.29E
Bingol Dağlari *mtn.* Turkey **30** 39.21N 41.22E
Binh Dinh Vietnam **26** 13.55N 109.07E
Binjai Indonesia **26** 3.37N 98.25E
Binji Nigeria **38** 13.12N 4.55E
Binnaway Australia **47** 31.32S 149.23E
Bintan *i.* Indonesia **26** 1.10N 104.30E
Bintulu Malaysia **26** 3.12N 113.01E
Binzert Tunisia **34** 37.17N 9.51E
Biograd Croatia **12** 43.56N 15.27E
Bioko I. Equat. Guinea **38** 3.25N 8.45E
Bi'r Abū 'Uwayqīlah *well* Egypt **32** 30.50N 34.07E
Bi'r ad Dakhal *well* Egypt **32** 28.40N 32.24E
Birāk Libya **34** 27.32N 14.17E
Bi'r al Jidy *well* Egypt **32** 30.13N 33.03E
Bi'r al Jufayr *well* Egypt **32** 30.49N 32.40E
Bi'r al 'Udayd *well* Egypt **32** 28.59N 34.05E
Birao C.A.R. **35** 10.17N 22.47E
Bi'r aş Şafrā' *well* Egypt **32** 28.46N 34.20E
Bi'r ath Thamadah *well* Egypt **32** 30.10N 33.28E
Bi'r Buerāt *well* Egypt **32** 28.59N 32.10E
Bi'r Bukhayt *well* Egypt **32** 29.13N 32.17E
Birchip Australia **46** 35.59S 142.59E
Birch Mts. Canada **50** 57.30N 112.30W
Birdsville Australia **44** 25.54S 139.22E
Birecik Turkey **30** 37.03N 37.59E
Birhan *mtn.* Ethiopia **35** 11.00N 37.50E
Bi'r Ḩasanah *well* Egypt **32** 30.29N 33.47E
Bi'r Hooker *well* Egypt **32** 30.23N 30.20E
Bīrjand Iran **31** 32.54N 59.10E
Bi'r Jifjafah *well* Egypt **32** 30.28N 33.11E
Birkenfeld Rhein.-Pfalz Germany **8** 49.39N 7.10E
Birkenhead U.K. **4** 53.24N 3.01W
Birksgate Range *mts.* Australia **42** 27.10S 129.45E
Bi'r Kusaybah *well* Egypt **32** 22.41N 29.55E
Birk, Wādī *r.* Saudi Arabia **31** 24.08N 47.35E
Bîrlad Romania **15** 46.14N 27.40E
Bi'r Lahfān *well* Egypt **32** 31.01N 33.52E
Birmingham U.K. **5** 52.30N 1.55W
Birmingham Ala. U.S.A. **53** 33.30N 86.55W
Bir Mogreïn Mauritania **34** 25.14N 11.35W
Birni Benin **38** 9.59N 1.34E
Birnin Gwari Nigeria **38** 11.02N 6.47E
Birnin Kebbi Nigeria **38** 12.30N 4.11E
Birni N'Konni Niger **38** 13.49N 5.19E
Birobidzhan Russian Fed. **25** 48.49N 132.54E
Birr Rep. of Ire. **7** 53.06N 7.56W
Birrie *r.* Australia **47** 29.43S 146.37E
Birsk Russian Fed. **18** 55.28N 55.31E
Bi'r Tābah *well* Egypt **32** 29.30N 34.53E
Bi'r Umm Sa'īd *well* Egypt **32** 29.40N 33.34E
Bi'r Umm 'Umayyid *well* Egypt **32** 27.53N 32.30E
Biržai Lithuania **18** 56.10N 24.48E
Biscay, B. of France **11** 45.30N 4.00W
Bisceglie Italy **13** 41.14N 16.31E
Bishkek Kyrgyzstan **24** 42.53N 74.46E
Bishop Calif. U.S.A. **54** 37.22N 118.24W
Bishop Auckland U.K. **4** 54.40N 1.40W
Bishop's Stortford U.K. **5** 51.53N 0.09E
Bisina, L. Uganda **37** 1.35N 34.08E
Biskra Algeria **34** 34.48N 5.40E
Bismarck U.S.A. **52** 46.50N 100.48W
Bismarck Range *mts.* P.N.G. **27** 6.00S 145.00E
Bismarck Sea Pacific Oc. **27** 4.00S 146.30E
Bīsotūn Iran **31** 34.22N 47.29E
Bispgården Sweden **16** 63.02N 16.40E
Bissau Guinea Bissau **34** 11.52N 15.39W
Bistriţa Romania **15** 47.08N 24.30E
Bistriţa *r.* Romania **15** 46.30N 26.54E
Bitam Gabon **36** 2.05N 11.30E
Bitburg Germany **8** 49.58N 6.31E
Bitlis Turkey **30** 38.23N 42.04E
Bitola Macedonia **13** 41.02N 21.21E
Bitter Creek *town* U.S.A. **54** 41.31N 109.27W
Bitterfontein R.S.A. **39** 31.02S 18.14E
Bitterroot Range *mts.* U.S.A. **54** 47.06N 115.10W
Biu Nigeria **38** 10.36N 12.11E
Biumba Rwanda **37** 1.38S 30.02E
Biwa ko *l.* Japan **23** 35.10N 136.00E
Biyalā Egypt **32** 31.11N 31.13E
Biysk Russian Fed. **20** 52.35N 85.16E
Bizerte *see* Binzert Tunisia **34**
Bjelovar Croatia **13** 45.54N 16.51E
Bjorli Norway **17** 62.16N 8.13E
Björna Sweden **16** 63.32N 18.36E
Bjørnafjorden *est.* Norway **17** 60.06N 5.22E
Bjørnøya *i.* Arctic Oc. **64** 74.30N 19.00E
Black *r.* Ark. U.S.A. **53** 35.30N 91.20W
Blackall Australia **44** 24.25S 145.28E
Blackburn U.K. **4** 53.44N 2.30W
Blackfoot U.S.A. **54** 43.11N 112.20W
Black Mtn. U.K. **5** 51.52N 3.50W
Black Mts. U.K. **5** 51.52N 3.09W
Blackpool U.K. **4** 53.48N 3.03W
Black River *town* Jamaica **57** 18.02N 77.52W
Black River *town* Mich. U.S.A. **55** 44.51N 83.21W
Black Rock *town* U.S.A. **54** 38.41N 112.59W
Black Rock Desert U.S.A. **54** 41.10N 119.00W
Black Sand Desert *see* Karakumy, Peski Turkmenistan **31**
Black Sea Europe **15** 44.00N 30.00E
Blacksod B. Rep. of Ire. **7** 54.04N 10.00W
Black Sugarloaf Mt. Australia **47** 31.24S 151.34E
Blackville Australia **47** 31.34S 150.10E
Black Volta *r.* Ghana **38** 8.14N 2.11w
Blackwater Australia **44** 23.34S 148.53E
Blackwater *r.* Waterford Rep. of Ire. **7** 51.58N 7.52W
Blackwood *r.* Australia **43** 34.15S 115.10E
Blaenau Ffestiniog U.K. **4** 53.00N 3.57W
Blagoevgrad Bulgaria **13** 42.02N 23.04E
Blagoveshchensk Russian Fed. **25** 50.19N 127.30E
Blain France **9** 47.29N 1.46W
Blair Athol Australia **44** 22.42S 147.33E
Blair Atholl U.K. **6** 56.46N 3.51W
Blairgowrie U.K. **6** 56.36N 3.21W
Blanca, Bahía *b.* Argentina **63** 39.20S 62.00W
Blanca, Sierra *mtn.* U.S.A. **52** 33.23N 105.48W
Blanc, Cap *c.* Mauritania **34** 20.44N 17.05W
Blanchard U.S.A. **54** 48.01N 116.59W
Blanche, L. Australia **46** 29.15S 139.40E
Blanchetown Australia **46** 34.21S 139.38E
Blanc, Mont *mtn.* Europe **11** 45.50N 6.52E
Blanco, C. Argentina **63** 47.12S 65.20W
Blanco, C. Costa Rica **57** 9.36N 85.06W
Blanco, C. U.S.A. **54** 42.50N 124.34W
Bland *r.* Australia **47** 33.42S 147.30E
Blandford Forum U.K. **5** 50.52N 2.10W
Blankenberge Belgium **8** 51.18N 3.08E
Blansko Czech Republic **14** 49.22N 16.39E
Blantyre Malaŵi **37** 15.46S 35.00E
Blarney Rep. of Ire. **7** 51.56N 8.34W
Blatnica Bulgaria **15** 43.42N 28.31E
Blavet *r.* France **11** 47.43N 3.18W
Blaye France **11** 45.08N 0.40W
Blayney Australia **47** 33.32S 149.19E
Blednaya, Gora *mtn.* Russian Fed. **20** 76.23N 65.08E
Bleiburg Austria **14** 46.35N 14.48E
Blekinge *d.* Sweden **17** 56.20N 15.00E
Blenheim New Zealand **48** 41.32S 173.58E
Bléré France **9** 47.20N 0.59E
Blerick Neth. **8** 51.22N 6.08E
Bletchley U.K. **5** 51.59N 0.45W
Blida Algeria **34** 36.30N 2.50E
Bligh Entrance Australia **44** 9.18S 144.10E
Blind River *town* Canada **55** 46.16N 82.58W
Blinman Australia **46** 31.05S 138.11E
Blitar Indonesia **26** 8.06S 112.12E
Blitta Togo **38** 8.23N 1.06E
Bloemfontein R.S.A. **39** 29.07S 26.14E
Bloemhof R.S.A. **39** 27.37S 25.34E
Blois France **9** 47.36N 1.20E
Blönduós Iceland **16** 65.39N 20.18W
Bloody Foreland *c.* Rep. of Ire. **7** 55.09N 8.17W
Bloomington Ill. U.S.A. **53** 40.29N 89.00W
Bloomington Ind. U.S.A. **55** 39.10N 86.31W
Bloomsburg U.S.A. **55** 41.00N 76.27W
Bluefield U.S.A. **53** 37.14N 81.17W
Bluefields Nicaragua **57** 12.00N 83.49W
Blue Mts. Australia **47** 33.16S 150.19E
Blue Mts. U.S.A. **54** 45.30N 118.15W
Blue Mud B. Australia **44** 13.26S 135.56E
Blue Nile *r. see* Azraq, Al Baḩr al *r.* Sudan **35**
Bluenose L. Canada **50** 68.30N 119.35W
Blue Stack Mts. Rep. of Ire. **7** 54.44N 8.09W
Bluff New Zealand **48** 46.38S 168.21E
Bluff U.S.A. **54** 37.17N 109.33W
Bluff Knoll *mtn.* Australia **43** 34.25S 118.15E
Blumenau Brazil **59** 26.55S 49.07W
Blyth Northum. U.K. **4** 55.07N 1.29W
Blythe U.S.A. **54** 33.37N 114.36W
Bö Nordland Norway **16** 68.38N 14.35E
Bö Telemark Norway **17** 59.25N 9.04E
Bo Sierra Leone **34** 7.58N 11.45W
Boa Esperança Brazil **59** 21.03S 45.37W
Boa Esperança, Represa da *resr.* Brazil **61** 6.45S 44.15W
Boane Mozambique **39** 26.02S 32.19E
Boa Vista Brazil **60** 2.51N 60.43W
Bobadah Australia **47** 32.18S 146.42E
Bobadilla Spain **10** 37.02N 4.44W
Bobbili India **29** 18.34N 83.22E
Bobbio Italy **9** 44.46N 9.23E
Bobo-Dioulasso Burkina **38** 11.11N 4.18W
Bobonong Botswana **39** 21.59S 28.29E
Bobr Belarus **15** 54.19N 29.18E
Bóbr *r.* Poland **14** 52.04N 15.04E
Bobruysk Belarus **15** 53.08N 29.10E
Bôca do Acre Brazil **60** 8.45S 67.23W
Bocaranga C.A.R. **36** 7.01N 15.35E
Bochnia Poland **15** 49.58N 20.26E
Bocholt Germany **8** 51.49N 6.37E
Bochum Germany **8** 51.28N 7.11E
Bochum R.S.A. **39** 23.12S 29.12E
Bockum-Hövel Germany **8** 51.42N 7.41E
Boconó Venezuela **60** 9.17N 70.17W
Bodalla Australia **47** 36.05S 150.03E
Bodallin Australia **43** 31.22S 118.52E
Bodélé *f.* Chad **34** 16.50N 17.10E
Boden Sweden **16** 65.50N 21.42E
Bodensee *l.* Europe **14** 47.40N 9.30E
Bode Sadu Nigeria **38** 8.57N 4.49E
Bodfish U.S.A. **54** 35.36N 118.30W
Bodmin U.K. **5** 50.28N 4.44W
Bodmin Moor U.K. **5** 50.53N 4.35W
Bodö Norway **16** 67.18N 14.26E
Bodrum Turkey **30** 37.03N 27.28E
Boende Zaïre **36** 0.15S 20.49E
Bogalusa U.S.A. **53** 30.56N 89.53W
Bogan *r.* Australia **47** 30.00S 146.20E
Bogan Gate *town* Australia **47** 33.08S 147.50E
Bogenfels Namibia **39** 27.26S 15.22E
Boggabilla Australia **47** 28.36S 150.21E
Boggabri Australia **47** 30.42S 150.02E
Boggeragh Mts. Rep. of Ire. **7** 52.03N 8.53W
Bogia P.N.G. **27** 4.16S 145.00E
Bognes Norway **16** 68.15N 16.00E
Bognor Regis U.K. **5** 50.47N 0.40W
Bog of Allen *f.* Rep. of Ire. **7** 53.17N 7.00W
Bogong, Mt. Australia **47** 36.45S 147.21E
Bogor Indonesia **26** 6.34S 106.45E
Bogotá Colombia **60** 4.38N 74.05W
Bogué Mauritania **34** 16.40N 14.10W
Boguslav Ukraine **15** 49.32N 30.52E
Bo Hai *b.* China **25** 38.30N 119.30E
Bohain France **8** 49.59N 3.28E
Bohemian Forest *see* Böhmerwald *mts.* Germany **14**
Böhmerwald *mts.* Germany **14** 49.20N 13.10E
Bohol *i.* Phil. **27** 9.45N 124.10E
Boiaçu Brazil **60** 0.27S 61.46W
Boigu *i.* Australia **44** 9.16S 142.12E
Boise U.S.A. **54** 43.37N 116.13W
Bois-Guillaume France **9** 49.28N 1.08E
Bois, Lac des *l.* Canada **50** 66.40N 125.15W
Boizenburg Germany **14** 53.22N 10.43E
Bojador, Cabo *c.* W. Sahara **34** 26.08N 14.30W
Bojeador, C. Phil. **27** 18.30N 120.50E
Bojnūrd Iran **31** 37.28N 57.20E
Bokani Nigeria **38** 9.27N 5.13E
Boké Guinea **34** 10.57N 14.13W
Bokhara *r.* Australia **47** 29.55S 146.42E
Boknafjorden *est.* Norway **17** 59.10N 5.35E
Bol Chad **38** 13.27N 14.40E
Bolama Guinea Bissau **34** 11.35N 15.30W
Bolanda, Jabal *mtn.* Sudan **35** 7.44N 25.28E
Bolbec France **9** 49.34N 0.28E
Bole Ghana **38** 9.03N 2.23W
Bolesławiec Poland **14** 51.16N 15.34E
Bolgatanga Ghana **38** 10.42N 0.52W
Bolgrad Ukraine **15** 45.42N 28.40E
Bolívar Argentina **63** 36.14S 61.07W
Bolivia S. America **62** 17.00S 65.00W
Bollnäs Sweden **17** 61.21N 16.25E
Bollon Australia **45** 28.02S 147.28E
Bollstabruk Sweden **16** 62.59N 17.42E
Bolmen *l.* Sweden **17** 56.55N 13.40E
Bologna Italy **9** 44.30N 11.20E
Bologoye Russian Fed. **18** 57.58N 34.00E
Bolomba Zaïre **36** 0.30N 19.13E
Bolsena, Lago di *l.* Italy **12** 42.36N 11.55E
Bolshaya Glushitsa Russian Fed. **18** 52.28N 50.30E
Bolshaya Pyssa Russian Fed. **18** 64.11N 48.44E
Bolsherechye Russian Fed. **20** 56.07N 74.40E
Bol'shevik, Ostrov *i.* Russian Fed. **21** 78.30N 102.00E
Bolshezemelskaya Tundra *f.* Russian Fed. **18** 67.00N 56.10E
Bolshoy Atlym Russian Fed. **20** 62.17N 66.30E
Bol'shoy Balkhan, Khrebet *mts.* Turkmenistan **31** 39.38N 54.30E
Bol'shoy Irgiz *r.* Russian Fed. **18** 52.00N 47.20E
Bol'shoy Lyakhovskiy, Ostrov *i.* Russian Fed. **21** 73.30N 142.00E
Bol'shoy Onguren Russian Fed. **21** 53.40N 107.40E
Bolshoy Uzen *r.* Kazakhstan **19** 49.00N 49.40E
Bolsover U.K. **4** 53.14N 1.18W
Bolton U.K. **4** 53.35N 2.26W
Bolu Turkey **30** 40.45N 31.38E
Bolus Head Rep. of Ire. **7** 51.47N 10.20W
Bolvadin Turkey **30** 38.43N 31.02E
Bolzano Italy **9** 46.30N 11.20E
Boma Zaïre **36** 5.50S 13.03E
Bomaderry Australia **47** 34.21S 150.34E
Bomadi Nigeria **38** 5.13N 6.01E
Bombala Australia **47** 36.55S 149.16E
Bombay India **28** 18.56N 72.51E
Bombo Uganda **37** 0.34N 32.32E
Bom Despacho Brazil **59** 19.46S 45.15W
Bomi China **24** 29.50N 95.45E
Bømlafjorden *est.* Norway **17** 59.39N 5.20E
Bømlo *i.* Norway **17** 59.46N 5.13E
Bomokandi *r.* Zaïre **37** 3.37N 26.09E
Bonaire *i.* Neth. Antilles **60** 12.15N 68.27W
Bonanza U.S.A. **54** 40.01N 109.11W
Bonaparte Archipelago *is.* Australia **42** 14.17S 125.18E
Bonar-Bridge *town* U.K. **6** 57.53N 4.21W
Bonavista Canada **51** 48.38N 53.08W
Bon Bon Australia **46** 30.26S 135.28E
Bondeno Italy **9** 44.53N 11.25E
Bondo Zaïre **36** 3.47N 23.45E
Bondoukou Côte d'Ivoire **38** 8.03N 2.15W
Bo'ness U.K. **6** 56.01N 3.36W
Bone, Teluk *b.* Indonesia **27** 4.00S 120.50E
Bongouanou Côte d'Ivoire **38** 6.44N 4.10W
Bonifacio, Str. of Med. Sea **12** 41.18N 9.10E
Bonn Germany **8** 50.44N 7.06E
Bonners Ferry U.S.A. **54** 48.41N 116.18W
Bonnétable France **9** 48.11N 0.26E
Bonneval France **9** 48.11N 1.24E
Bonneville Salt Flats *f.* U.S.A. **54** 40.45N 113.52W
Bonney, L. Australia **46** 37.47S 140.23E
Bonnie Rock *town* Australia **43** 30.32S 118.21E
Bonny Nigeria **38** 4.25N 7.10E
Bonny, Bight of Africa **38** 2.58N 7.00E
Bonshaw Australia **47** 29.08S 150.53E
Bontang Indonesia **26** 0.05N 117.31E
Bonthe Sierra Leone **34** 7.32N 12.30W
Bonython Range *mts.* Australia **42** 23.51S 129.00E
Bookaloo Australia **46** 31.56S 137.21E
Booleroo Centre Australia **46** 32.53S 138.21E
Booligal Australia **47** 33.54S 144.54E
Boom Belgium **8** 51.07N 4.21E
Boomrivier R.S.A. **39** 29.34S 20.26E
Boonville N.Y. U.S.A. **55** 43.29N 75.20W
Boorabbin Australia **43** 31.14S 120.21E
Boorindal Australia **47** 30.23S 146.11E
Booroorban Australia **47** 34.56S 144.46E
Boorowa Australia **47** 34.26S 148.48E
Boort Australia **46** 36.08S 143.46E
Boothia, G. of Canada **51** 70.00N 90.00W
Boothia Pen. Canada **51** 70.30N 95.00W
Bootra Australia **46** 30.00S 143.00E
Bopeechee Australia **46** 29.36S 137.23E
Boppard Germany **8** 50.13N 7.35E
Bor Czech Republic **14** 49.43N 12.47E
Bor Yugo. **13** 44.05N 22.07E
Borah Peak *mtn.* U.S.A. **54** 44.08N 113.38W
Borås Sweden **17** 57.43N 12.55E

ján Iran **31** 29.14N 51.12E
Brazil **60** 4.24S 59.35W
aux France **11** 44.50N 0.34W
n Australia **43** 34.05S 118.16E
n I. Canada **50** 78.30N 111.00W
n Pen. Canada **51** 73.00N 83.00W
rs *d.* U.K. **6** 55.30N 2.53W
rtown Australia **46** 36.18S 140.49E
eyri Iceland **16** 65.12N 21.06W
ghera Italy **9** 43.46N 7.39E
Flye Sainte Marie Algeria **34** 27.17N 2.59E
i. Faroe Is. **16** 62.10N 7.13W
Finland **17** 60.24N 25.40E
Sweden **16** 64.49N 15.05E
efjell *mtn.* Norway **16** 65.20N 13.45E
efjell Nat. Park Norway **16** 65.00N 13.58E
er Neth. **8** 52.57N 6.46E
er U.S.A. **52** 35.39N 101.24W
olm Sweden **17** 56.53N 16.39E
orst Germany **8** 52.08N 7.27E
Italy **9** 46.03N 11.27E
manero Italy **9** 45.42N 8.28E
San Dalmazzo Italy **9** 44.20N 7.30E
San Lorenzo Italy **9** 43.57N 11.23E
sesia Italy **9** 45.43N 8.16E
Val di Taro Italy **9** 44.29N 9.46E
nd Norway **17** 61.03N 7.49E
av Ukraine **15** 49.18N 23.28E
oglebsk Russian Fed. **19** 51.23N 42.02E
ov Belarus **15** 54.09N 28.30E
ol Ukraine **15** 50.21N 30.59E
Peru **60** 4.20S 77.40W
n Germany **8** 51.50N 6.52E
m Germany **8** 53.34N 6.41E
m *i.* Germany **8** 53.35N 6.45E
nge Sweden **17** 60.29N 15.25E
, C. Antarctica **64** 66.15S 55.00E
o Italy **9** 46.28N 10.22E
iep *g.* Neth. **8** 53.28N 5.35E
o *i.* Asia **26** 1.00N 114.00E
eim Germany **8** 50.45N 7.00E
olm *i.* Denmark **17** 55.10N 15.00E
d. Nigeria **38** 11.20N 12.40E
, Plain of *f.* Nigeria **38** 12.30N 13.00E
r. Sudan **35** 8.50N 28.00E
yanka Ukraine **15** 50.38N 29.59E
mo Burkina **38** 11.43N 2.53W
ghbridge U.K. **4** 54.06N 1.23W
ichi Russian Fed. **18** 58.22N 34.00E
a Australia **46** 35.00S 140.05E
loola Australia **44** 16.04S 136.17E
Romania **15** 46.56N 23.40E
Romania **15** 47.39N 24.40E
U.K. **5** 52.29N 4.03W
erd Iran **31** 33.54N 48.47E
Tucholskie *f.* Poland **15** 53.45N 17.30E
omi Georgia **19** 41.49N 43.23E
a Ukraine **19** 51.15N 32.25E
a Russian Fed. **21** 50.24N 116.35E
Italy **12** 40.18N 8.29E
nska Gradiška Croatia **13** 45.09N 17.15E
nski Novi Bosnia-Herzegovina **14** 45.03N
3E
astle U.K. **5** 50.42N 4.42W
of R.S.A. **39** 28.32S 25.12E
a *r.* Bosnia-Herzegovina **13** 45.04N 18.27E
ia-Herzegovina Europe **13** 44.00N 18.10E
ik Indonesia **27** 1.09S 136.14E
-hantō *pen.* Japan **23** 35.08N 140.00E
orus *str. see* Istanbul Boğazi *str.* Turkey **13**
angoa C.A.R. **36** 6.27N 17.21E
o Niger **38** 13.43N 13.19E
n Hu *l.* China **24** 42.00N 87.00E
n U.K. **4** 52.59N 0.02W
n U.S.A. **55** 42.21N 71.04W
y B. Australia **47** 34.04S 151.08E
mtn. Bulgaria **13** 42.43N 24.55E
grad Bulgaria **13** 42.55N 23.57E
nia, G. of Europe **16** 63.30N 20.30E
tle *r.* Botswana **39** 21.06S 24.47E
ani Romania **15** 47.44N 26.41E
Burkina **38** 12.47N 2.02E
nge *mtn.* Belgium **8** 50.30N 6.04E
Côte d'Ivoire **38** 7.51N 5.19W
wana Africa **39** 22.00S 24.15E
op Germany **8** 51.31N 6.55E
catu Brazil **59** 22.52S 48.30W
flé Côte d'Ivoire **38** 7.01N 5.47W
aké Côte d'Ivoire **38** 7.42N 5.00W
r C.A.R. **38** 5.58N 15.35E
Arfa Morocco **34** 32.30N 1.59W
choir France **9** 49.45N 2.41E
gainville *i.* Pacific Oc. **40** 6.00S 155.00E
gouni Mali **34** 11.25N 7.28W
llon Belgium **8** 49.48N 5.03E
der Australia **43** 30.55S 121.32E
der U.S.A. **52** 40.01N 105.17W
der City U.S.A. **54** 35.59N 114.50W
ia Australia **44** 22.54S 139.54E
ogne France **11** 50.43N 1.37E
ogne-Billancourt France **9** 48.50N 2.15E
toum Niger **38** 14.45N 10.25E
mba *r.* Cameroon **38** 2.00N 15.10E
na Côte d'Ivoire **38** 9.19N 2.53W
ndary Peak *mtn.* U.S.A. **54** 37.51N 118.21W
ntiful U.S.A. **54** 40.53N 111.53W
aga *well* Mali **38** 19.00N 3.36W
em Mali **38** 16.59N 0.20W
g France **11** 46.12N 5.13E
ganeuf France **11** 45.57N 1.44E
ges France **11** 47.05N 2.23E
g Madame France **11** 42.26N 1.55E
gogne *d.* France **11** 47.10N 4.20E
gogne, Canal de France **9** 47.58N 3.30E
goin France **11** 45.35N 5.17E
gueil France **9** 47.17N 0.10E
ke Australia **47** 30.09S 145.59E
nemouth U.K. **5** 50.43N 1.53W
ssac France **11** 46.22N 2.13E
Bouvard, C. Australia **43** 32.40S 115.34E
Bovill U.S.A. **54** 46.51N 116.24W
Bovril Argentina **63** 31.22S 59.25W
Bowelling Australia **43** 33.25S 116.27E
Bowen Australia **44** 20.00S 148.15E
Bowen, Mt. Australia **47** 37.11S 148.34E
Bowling Green U.S.A. **53** 37.00N 86.29W
Bowling Green, C. Australia **44** 19.19S 146.25E
Bowman I. Antarctica **64** 65.00S 104.00E
Bowral Australia **47** 34.30S 150.24E
Bowser Australia **47** 36.19S 146.23E
Boxholm Sweden **17** 58.12N 15.03E
Bo Xian China **25** 33.40N 115.50E
Box Tank Australia **46** 32.13S 142.17E
Boxtel Neth. **8** 51.36N 5.20E
Boyabat Turkey **30** 41.27N 34.45E
Boyanup Australia **43** 33.29S 115.40E
Boyarka Ukraine **15** 50.20N 30.26E
Boyd *r.* Australia **47** 29.51S 152.25E
Boyle Rep. of Ire. **7** 53.58N 8.19W
Boyne *r.* Rep. of Ire. **7** 53.43N 6.17W
Boyoma Falls *f.* Zaïre **36** 0.18N 25.30E
Boyup Brook Australia **43** 33.50S 116.22E
Bozca Ada *i.* Turkey **13** 39.49N 26.03E
Bozeman U.S.A. **54** 45.41N 111.02W
Bozen *see* Bolzano Italy **9**
Bra Italy **9** 44.42N 7.51E
Brabant *d.* Belgium **8** 50.47N 4.30E
Brač *i.* Croatia **13** 43.20N 16.38E
Bracadale, Loch U.K. **6** 57.22N 6.30W
Bracebridge Canada **55** 45.02N 79.19W
Bracieux France **9** 47.33N 1.33E
Bräcke Sweden **16** 62.44N 15.30E
Brad Romania **13** 46.06N 22.48E
Bradano *r.* Italy **13** 40.23N 16.52E
Bradenton U.S.A. **53** 27.29N 82.33W
Bradford Canada **55** 44.07N 79.34W
Bradford U.K. **4** 53.47N 1.45W
Bradford Penn. U.S.A. **55** 41.58N 78.39W
Bradworthy U.K. **5** 50.54N 4.22W
Braemar U.K. **6** 57.01N 3.24W
Braga Portugal **10** 41.32N 8.26W
Bragado Argentina **63** 35.10S 60.30W
Bragança Brazil **61** 1.03S 46.46W
Bragança Portugal **10** 41.47N 6.46W
Bragança Paulista Brazil **59** 22.59S 46.32W
Bragin Belarus **15** 51.49N 30.16E
Brahmaputra *r.* Asia **29** 23.50N 89.45E
Braidwood Australia **47** 35.27S 149.50E
Brăila Romania **15** 45.18N 27.58E
Brainerd U.S.A. **53** 46.20N 94.10W
Braintree U.K. **5** 51.53N 0.32E
Brålanda Sweden **17** 58.34N 12.22E
Bramfield Australia **46** 33.37S 134.59E
Brampton Canada **55** 43.41N 79.46W
Brampton U.K. **4** 54.56N 2.43W
Bramsche Germany **8** 52.26N 7.59E
Branco *r.* Brazil **60** 1.00S 62.00W
Brandberg *mtn.* Namibia **39** 21.08S 14.35E
Brandbu Norway **17** 60.28N 10.30E
Brande Denmark **17** 55.57N 9.07E
Brandenburg Germany **14** 52.25N 12.34E
Brandenburg *d.* Germany **14** 52.15N 13.10E
Brandfort R.S.A. **39** 28.41S 26.27E
Brandon Canada **51** 49.50N 99.57W
Brandon Mtn. Rep. of Ire. **7** 52.14N 10.15W
Brandon Pt. Rep. of Ire. **7** 52.17N 10.11W
Braniewo Poland **15** 54.24N 19.50E
Bransby Australia **46** 28.40S 142.00E
Brasiléia Brazil **60** 11.00S 68.44W
Brasília Brazil **61** 15.45S 47.57W
Brasil, Planalto *mts.* Brazil **61** 17.02S 50.00W
Braşov Romania **15** 45.40N 25.35E
Brass Nigeria **38** 4.20N 6.15E
Brasschaat Belgium **8** 51.18N 4.28E
Bratislava Slovakia **15** 48.10N 17.10E
Bratsk Russian Fed. **21** 56.20N 101.15E
Bratsk Vodokhranilishche *resr.* Russian Fed. **21** 54.40N 103.00E
Bratslav Ukraine **15** 48.49N 28.51E
Braunau Austria **14** 48.15N 13.02E
Braunschweig Germany **14** 52.15N 10.30E
Braunton U.K. **5** 51.06N 4.09W
Bravo del Norte, Rio *r.* Mexico *see* Rio Grande *r.* Mexico/U.S.A. **56**
Brawley U.S.A. **54** 32.59N 115.31W
Bray France **9** 48.25N 3.14E
Bray Rep. of Ire. **7** 53.12N 6.07W
Bray Head Kerry Rep. of Ire. **7** 51.53N 10.26W
Brazilian Highlands *see* Brasil, Planalto *mts.* Brazil **61**
Brazos *r.* U.S.A. **53** 28.55N 95.20W
Brazzaville Congo **36** 4.14S 15.14E
Brčko Bosnia-Herzegovina **15** 44.53N 18.48E
Brda *r.* Poland **15** 53.07N 18.08E
Breadalbane *f.* U.K. **6** 56.30N 4.20W
Bream B. New Zealand **48** 36.00S 174.30E
Brécey France **9** 48.44N 1.10W
Brechin U.K. **6** 56.44N 2.40W
Breckland *f.* U.K. **5** 52.28N 0.40E
Břeclav Czech Republic **14** 48.46N 16.53E
Brecon U.K. **5** 51.57N 3.23W
Brecon Beacons *mts.* U.K. **5** 51.53N 3.27W
Breda Neth. **8** 51.35N 4.46E
Bredasdorp R.S.A. **39** 34.31S 20.03E
Bredbo Australia **47** 35.57S 149.10E
Bregenz Austria **14** 47.31N 9.46E
Bregovo Bulgaria **13** 44.08N 22.39E
Bréhal France **9** 48.53N 1.30W
Breidhafjördhur *est.* Iceland **16** 65.15N 23.00W
Breim Norway **17** 61.44N 6.25E
Brekstad Norway **16** 63.42N 9.40E
Bremangerland *i.* Norway **17** 61.51N 5.02E
Bremen Germany **14** 53.05N 8.48E
Bremer Bay *town* Australia **43** 34.21S 119.20E
Bremerhaven Germany **14** 53.33N 8.35E
Bremer Range *mts.* Australia **43** 32.40S 120.55E
Bremerton U.S.A. **54** 47.34N 122.38W
Brenner Pass Italy/Austria **14** 47.00N 11.30E
Breno Italy **9** 45.57N 10.18E
Brent Canada **55** 46.02N 78.29W
Brenta *r.* Italy **9** 45.25N 12.15E
Brentwood U.K. **5** 51.38N 0.18E
Brescia Italy **9** 45.33N 10.12E
Breskens Neth. **8** 51.24N 3.34E
Bressay *i.* U.K. **6** 60.08N 1.05W
Bressuire France **11** 46.50N 0.28W
Brest Belarus **15** 52.08N 23.40E
Brest France **11** 48.23N 4.30W
Bretagne *d.* France **11** 48.15N 2.30W
Breteuil France **9** 49.38N 2.18E
Breteuil-sur-Iton France **9** 48.50N 0.55E
Brett, C. New Zealand **48** 35.15S 174.20E
Breuil-Cervinia Italy **9** 45.56N 7.38E
Brevik Norway **17** 59.04N 9.42E
Brewarrina Australia **47** 29.57S 147.54E
Brewer U.S.A. **55** 44.48N 68.46W
Brezovo Bulgaria **13** 42.20N 25.06E
Bria C.A.R. **35** 6.32N 21.59E
Briançon France **11** 44.53N 6.39E
Briare France **9** 47.38N 2.44E
Bribbaree Australia **47** 34.07S 147.51E
Brichany Moldova **15** 48.20N 27.01E
Bricquebec France **9** 49.28N 1.38W
Bride I.o.M Europe **4** 54.23N 4.24W
Bridgend U.K. **5** 51.30N 3.35W
Bridgeport Calif. U.S.A. **54** 38.10N 119.13W
Bridgeport Conn. U.S.A. **55** 41.12N 73.12W
Bridger U.S.A. **54** 45.18N 108.55W
Bridgetown Australia **43** 33.57S 116.08E
Bridgetown Barbados **57** 13.06N 59.37W
Bridgetown Rep. of Ire. **7** 52.14N 6.33W
Bridgewater Canada **51** 44.23N 64.31W
Bridgewater, C. Australia **46** 38.25S 141.28E
Bridgnorth U.K. **5** 52.33N 2.25W
Bridgwater U.K. **5** 51.08N 3.00W
Bridlington U.K. **4** 54.06N 0.11W
Brie *f.* France **9** 48.40N 3.20E
Brienne-le-Château France **9** 48.24N 4.32E
Brig Switz. **9** 46.19N 8.00E
Brigg U.K. **4** 53.33N 0.30W
Brigham City U.S.A. **54** 41.31N 112.01W
Bright Australia **47** 36.42S 146.58E
Brighton U.K. **5** 50.50N 0.09W
Brindisi Italy **13** 40.38N 17.57E
Brinkworth Australia **46** 33.42S 138.24E
Brionne France **9** 49.12N 0.43E
Briouze France **9** 48.42N 0.22W
Brisbane Australia **47** 27.30S 153.00E
Brisighella Italy **9** 44.13N 11.46E
Bristol U.K. **5** 51.26N 2.35W
Bristol Tenn. U.S.A. **53** 36.35N 82.12W
Bristol B. U.S.A. **50** 58.00N 158.50W
Bristol Channel U.K. **5** 51.17N 3.20W
British Antarctic Territory Antarctica **64** 70.00S 50.00W
British Columbia *d.* Canada **50** 55.00N 125.00W
British Mts. Canada **50** 69.00N 140.20W
British Virgin Is. C. America **57** 18.30N 64.30W
Britstown R.S.A. **39** 30.34S 23.30E
Britt Canada **55** 45.46N 80.35W
Brive France **11** 45.09N 1.32E
Briviesca Spain **10** 42.33N 3.19W
Brixham U.K. **5** 50.24N 3.31W
Brno Czech Republic **14** 49.11N 16.39E
Broach India **28** 21.42N 72.58E
Broad Arrow Australia **43** 30.32S 121.20E
Broad B. U.K. **6** 58.15N 6.15W
Broadback *r.* Canada **55** 51.20N 78.50W
Broadford Australia **47** 37.16S 145.03E
Broadmere Australia **44** 25.30S 149.30E
Broad Sd. Australia **44** 22.20S 149.50E
Broadsound Range *mts.* Australia **44** 22.30S 149.30E
Broadway U.K. **5** 52.02N 1.51W
Brochet Canada **51** 57.53N 101.40W
Brockton U.S.A. **55** 42.05N 71.01W
Brockville Canada **55** 44.35N 75.41W
Brockway Mont. U.S.A. **54** 47.15N 105.45W
Brod Croatia **15** 45.09N 18.02E
Brodeur Pen. Canada **51** 73.00N 88.00W
Brodick U.K. **6** 55.34N 5.09W
Brodnica Poland **15** 53.16N 19.23E
Brody Ukraine **15** 50.05N 25.08E
Broglie France **9** 49.01N 0.32E
Broke Inlet Australia **43** 34.55S 116.25E
Broken B. Australia **47** 33.34S 151.18E
Broken Hill *town* Australia **46** 31.57S 141.30E
Bromley U.K. **5** 51.24N 0.02E
Bromsgrove U.K. **5** 52.20N 2.03W
Brönderslev Denmark **17** 57.16N 9.58E
Brong-Ahafo *d.* Ghana **38** 7.45N 1.30W
Brönnöysund Norway **16** 65.30N 12.10E
Brooke's Point *town* Phil. **26** 8.50N 117.52E
Brookhaven U.S.A. **53** 31.36N 90.28W
Brookings Oreg. U.S.A. **54** 42.03N 124.17W
Brookings S.Dak. U.S.A. **53** 44.19N 96.47W
Brooks Canada **50** 50.35N 111.53W
Brooks Range *mts.* U.S.A. **50** 68.50N 152.00W
Brookton Australia **43** 32.22S 117.01E
Broome Australia **42** 17.58S 122.15E
Broomehill *town* Australia **43** 33.50S 117.35E
Broome, Mt. Australia **42** 17.21S 125.23E
Broom, Loch U.K. **6** 57.52N 5.07W
Brora U.K. **6** 58.01N 3.52W
Brora *r.* U.K. **6** 58.00N 3.51W
Brosna *r.* Rep. of Ire. **7** 53.13N 7.58W
Brothers U.S.A. **54** 43.49N 120.36W
Brou France **9** 48.13N 1.11E
Brough England U.K. **4** 54.32N 2.19W
Brough Scotland U.K. **6** 60.29N 1.12W
Broughton *r.* Australia **46** 33.21S 137.46E
Broughton in Furness U.K. **4** 54.17N 3.12W
Brouwershaven Neth. **8** 51.44N 3.53E
Brovary Ukraine **15** 50.30N 30.45E
Brovst Denmark **17** 57.06N 9.32E
Browning U.S.A. **54** 48.34N 113.01W
Brown, Mt. Australia **46** 32.33S 138.02E
Brownwood U.S.A. **52** 31.42N 98.59W
Bruay-en-Artois France **8** 50.29N 2.36E
Bruce Pen. Canada **55** 44.50N 81.20W
Bruce Rock *town* Australia **43** 31.52S 118.09E
Bruges *see* Brugge Belgium **8**
Brugge Belgium **8** 51.13N 3.14E
Brühl Germany **8** 50.50N 6.55E
Brumadinho Brazil **59** 20.09S 44.11W
Brumado Brazil **61** 14.13S 41.40W
Brunei Asia **26** 4.56N 114.58E
Brünen Germany **8** 51.45N 6.41E
Brunflo Sweden **16** 63.04N 14.50E
Brunner New Zealand **48** 42.28S 171.12E
Brunsbüttel Germany **14** 53.44N 9.05E
Brunssum Neth. **8** 50.57N 5.59E
Brunswick Ga. U.S.A. **53** 31.09N 81.21W
Brunswick Maine U.S.A. **55** 43.55N 69.58W
Brunswick B. Australia **42** 15.05S 125.00E
Brunswick Junction Australia **43** 33.15S 115.45E
Bruny I. Australia **45** 43.15S 147.16E
Brusilovka Kazakhstan **19** 50.39N 54.59E
Brussel *see* Bruxelles Belgium **8**
Brussels *see* Bruxelles Belgium **8**
Bruthen Australia **47** 37.44S 147.49E
Bruton U.K. **5** 51.06N 2.28W
Bruxelles Belgium **8** 50.50N 4.23E
Bryan Ohio U.S.A. **55** 41.30N 84.34W
Bryan Tex. U.S.A. **53** 30.41N 96.24W
Bryan, Mt. Australia **46** 33.26S 138.27E
Bryansk Russian Fed. **18** 53.15N 34.09E
Bryne Norway **17** 58.44N 5.39E
Bryson Canada **55** 45.41N 76.37W
Bryson, Lac *l.* Canada **55** 46.19N 77.27W
Brzeg Poland **15** 50.52N 17.27E
Bsharrī Lebanon **32** 34.15N 36.00E
Bua *r.* Malaŵi **37** 12.42S 34.15E
Bu'ayrāt al Ḩasūn Libya **34** 31.24N 15.44E
Būbiyān, Jazīrat *i.* Kuwait **31** 29.45N 48.15E
Bubye *r.* Zimbabwe **39** 22.18S 31.00E
Bucak Turkey **30** 37.28N 30.36E
Bucaramanga Colombia **60** 7.08N 73.10W
Buchach Ukraine **15** 49.09N 25.20E
Buchanan Liberia **34** 5.57N 10.02W
Buchanan, L. Australia **44** 21.28S 145.52E
Buchan Ness *c.* U.K. **6** 57.28N 1.47W
Buchans Canada **51** 48.49N 56.52W
Bucharest *see* Bucureşti Romania **15**
Buchloe Germany **14** 48.02N 10.44E
Buchy France **9** 49.35N 1.22E
Buckambool Mt. Australia **47** 31.55S 145.40E
Buckhaven and Methil U.K. **4** 56.11N 3.03W
Buckie U.K. **6** 57.40N 2.58W
Buckingham U.K. **5** 52.00N 0.59W
Buckingham B. Australia **44** 12.10S 135.46E
Buckinghamshire *d.* U.K. **5** 51.50N 0.48W
Buckland Tableland *f.* Australia **44** 25.00S 148.00E
Buckleboo Australia **46** 32.55S 136.12E
Bucquoy France **8** 50.09N 2.43E
Bu Craa W. Sahara **34** 26.21N 12.57W
Bucureşti Romania **15** 44.25N 26.06E
Bucyrus U.S.A. **55** 40.47N 82.57W
Bud Norway **16** 62.54N 6.56E
Budapest Hungary **15** 47.30N 19.03E
Budaun India **29** 28.02N 79.07E
Budda Australia **46** 31.12S 144.16E
Budd Coast *f.* Antarctica **64** 67.00S 112.00E
Bude U.K. **5** 50.49N 4.33W
Bude B. U.K. **5** 50.50N 4.40W
Budennovsk Russian Fed. **19** 44.50N 44.10E
Buea Cameroon **38** 4.09N 9.13E
Buenaventura Colombia **60** 3.54N 77.02W
Buenaventura Mexico **56** 29.51N 107.29W
Buenos Aires Argentina **63** 34.40S 58.25W
Buenos Aires *d.* Argentina **63** 36.30S 59.00W
Buenos Aires, L. Argentina/Chile **63** 46.35S 72.00W
Buffalo N.Y. U.S.A. **55** 42.52N 78.55W
Buffalo Wyo. U.S.A. **54** 44.21N 106.42W
Bug *r.* Poland **15** 52.29N 21.11E
Buga Colombia **60** 3.53N 76.17W
Bugaldie Australia **47** 31.02S 149.08E
Bugembe Uganda **37** 0.26N 33.16E
Bugene Tanzania **37** 1.34S 31.07E
Buggs Island *l.* U.S.A. **53** 36.35N 78.20W
Bugrino Russian Fed. **18** 68.45N 49.15E
Bugt China **25** 48.45N 121.58E
Bugulma Russian Fed. **18** 54.32N 52.46E
Buguma Nigeria **38** 4.43N 6.53E
Buguruslan Russian Fed. **18** 53.36N 52.30E
Buhera Zimbabwe **39** 19.21S 31.25E
Buhuşi Romania **15** 46.43N 26.41E
Builth Wells U.K. **5** 52.09N 3.24W
Buinsk Russian Fed. **18** 54.58N 48.15E
Bu'in-Sofiā Iran **31** 35.51N 46.02E
Buitenpost Neth. **8** 53.15N 6.09E
Buji P.N.G. **44** 9.07S 142.26E
Bujumbura Burundi **37** 3.22S 29.21E
Bukavu Zaïre **37** 2.30S 28.49E
Bukene Tanzania **37** 4.13S 32.52E
Bukhara Uzbekistan **31** 39.47N 64.26E
Buki Ukraine **15** 49.02N 30.29E
Bukima Tanzania **37** 1.48S 33.25E
Bukittinggi Indonesia **26** 0.18S 100.20E
Bukoba Tanzania **37** 1.20S 31.49E
Bukuru Nigeria **38** 9.48N 8.52E
Bula Indonesia **27** 3.07S 130.27E
Bulahdelah Australia **47** 32.25S 152.13E
Bulan Phil. **27** 12.40N 123.53E
Bulawayo Zimbabwe **39** 20.10S 28.43E
Buldern Germany **8** 51.52N 7.21E
Bulgan Mongolia **24** 48.34N 103.12E
Bulgaria Europe **13** 42.30N 25.00E
Būl, Kūh-e *mtn.* Iran **31** 30.48N 52.45E
Bullabulling Australia **43** 31.05S 120.52E
Bullara Australia **42** 22.40S 114.03E
Buller *r.* New Zealand **48** 41.45S 171.35E
Buller, Mt. Australia **47** 37.11S 146.26E
Bullfinch Australia **43** 30.59S 119.06E
Bulli Australia **47** 34.20S 150.55E
Bull Mts. U.S.A. **54** 46.05N 109.00W
Bulloo *r.* Australia **46** 28.43S 142.27E
Bulloo Downs *town* Australia **46** 28.30S 142.45E
Bulolo P.N.G. **27** 7.13S 146.35E
Bultfontein R.S.A. **39** 28.17S 26.09E
Bulu Indonesia **27** 4.34N 126.45E
Bulu, Gunung *mtn.* Indonesia **26** 3.00N 116.00E
Bulun Russian Fed. **21** 70.50N 127.20E
Bulunde Tanzania **37** 4.19S 32.57E
Bumba Zaïre **35** 2.15N 22.32E
Buna Kenya **37** 2.49N 39.27E
Buna P.N.G. **44** 8.40S 148.25E
Bunbury Australia **43** 33.20S 115.34E
Buncrana Rep. of Ire. **7** 55.08N 7.27W
Bundaberg Australia **44** 24.50S 152.21E
Bundaleer Australia **47** 28.39S 146.31E
Bundarra Australia **47** 30.11S 151.04E
Bünde Germany **8** 53.12N 7.16E
Bundella Australia **47** 31.35S 149.59E
Bundoran Rep. of Ire. **7** 54.28N 8.17W
Bungay U.K. **5** 52.27N 1.26E
Bungu Tanzania **37** 7.37S 39.07E
Buni Nigeria **38** 11.20N 11.59E
Bunia Zaïre **37** 1.30N 30.10E
Buninyong Australia **46** 37.41S 143.58E
Bunyala Kenya **37** 0.07N 34.00E
Bunyan Australia **47** 36.11S 149.09E
Buol Indonesia **27** 1.12N 121.28E
Buqayq Saudi Arabia **31** 25.55N 49.40E
Bura Coast Kenya **37** 1.09S 39.55E
Bura Coast Kenya **37** 3.30S 38.19E
Burakin Australia **43** 30.30S 117.08E
Buraydah Saudi Arabia **31** 26.18N 43.58E
Burcher Australia **47** 33.32S 147.18E
Burdur Turkey **19** 37.44N 30.17E
Burdwān India **29** 23.15N 87.52E
Burg Germany **14** 52.17N 11.51E
Burgas Bulgaria **13** 42.30N 27.29E
Burgenland *d.* Austria **14** 47.30N 16.20E
Burgess Hill U.K. **5** 50.57N 0.07W
Burgos Spain **10** 42.21N 3.41W
Burgsteinfurt Germany **8** 52.09N 7.21E
Burgsvik Sweden **17** 57.03N 18.16E
Burhānpur India **28** 21.18N 76.08E
Buri Brazil **59** 23.46S 48.39W
Burias *i.* Phil. **27** 12.50N 123.10E
Burica, Punta *c.* Panama **57** 8.05N 82.50W
Burke *r.* Australia **44** 23.12S 139.33E
Burketown Australia **44** 17.44S 139.22E
Burkina Africa **38** 12.30N 2.00W
Burley U.S.A. **54** 42.32N 113.48W
Burlington Canada **55** 43.19N 79.48W
Burlington Iowa U.S.A. **53** 40.50N 91.07W
Burlington Vt. U.S.A. **55** 44.29N 73.13W
Burma *see* Myanmar Asia **29**
Burngup Australia **43** 33.00S 118.39E
Burnham-on-Crouch U.K. **5** 51.37N 0.50E
Burnham-on-Sea U.K. **5** 51.15N 3.00W
Burnie Australia **45** 41.03S 145.55E
Burnley U.K. **4** 53.47N 2.15W
Burns Oreg. U.S.A. **54** 43.35N 119.03W
Burnside *r.* Canada **50** 66.51N 108.04W
Buronga Australia **46** 34.08S 142.11E
Burra Australia **46** 33.40S 138.57E
Burracoppin Australia **43** 31.22S 118.30E
Burragorang, L. Australia **47** 33.58S 150.27E
Burren Junction Australia **47** 30.08S 148.59E
Burrewarra Pt. Australia **47** 35.56S 150.12E
Burriana Spain **10** 39.54N 0.05W
Burrinjuck Australia **47** 35.01S 148.33E
Burrinjuck Resr. Australia **47** 35.00S 148.40E
Burry Port U.K. **5** 51.41N 4.17W
Bursa Turkey **13** 40.11N 29.04E
Būr Safājah Egypt **30** 26.44N 33.56E
Būr Sa'īd Egypt **32** 31.17N 32.18E
Būr Sūdān Sudan **35** 19.39N 37.01E
Burta Australia **46** 32.30S 141.05E
Būr Tawfīq Egypt **32** 29.57N 32.34E
Burton upon Trent U.K. **4** 52.58N 1.39W
Burtundy Australia **46** 33.45S 142.22E
Buru *i.* Indonesia **27** 3.30S 126.30E
Burullus, Buḩayrat al *l.* Egypt **32** 31.30N 30.45E
Burundi Africa **37** 3.00S 30.00E
Bururi Burundi **37** 3.58S 29.35E
Burutu Nigeria **38** 5.20N 5.31E
Bury G.M. U.K. **4** 53.36N 2.19W
Bury St. Edmunds U.K. **5** 52.15N 0.42E
Busalla Italy **9** 44.34N 8.57E
Busca Italy **9** 44.31N 7.29E
Būsh Egypt **32** 29.09N 31.07E
Būshehr Iran **31** 28.57N 50.52E
Bushmanland *f.* R.S.A. **39** 29.25S 19.40E
Busigny France **8** 50.03N 3.29E
Buskerud Norway **17** 60.20N 9.00E
Buşrá ash Shām Syria **32** 32.30N 36.29E
Busselton Australia **43** 33.43S 115.15E
Bussum Neth. **8** 52.17N 5.10E
Bustard Head *c.* Australia **44** 24.02S 151.48E
Busto Arsizio Italy **9** 45.37N 8.51E
Buta Zaïre **35** 2.49N 24.50E
Butari Rwanda **37** 2.38S 29.43E
Bute Australia **46** 33.24S 138.01E
Bute *i.* U.K. **6** 55.51N 5.07W
Bute, Sd. of U.K. **6** 55.44N 5.10W
Butiaba Uganda **37** 1.48N 31.15E
Buton *i.* Indonesia **27** 5.00S 122.50E
Butte Mont. U.S.A. **54** 46.00N 112.32W
Butterworth Malaysia **26** 5.24N 100.22E
Buttevant Rep. of Ire. **7** 52.14N 8.41W
Butt of Lewis *c.* U.K. **6** 58.31N 6.15W
Butty Head Australia **43** 33.52S 121.35E
Butuan Phil. **27** 8.56N 125.31E
Buur Gaabo Somali Rep. **37** 1.10S 41.50E
Buur Hakaba Somali Rep. **37** 2.43N 44.10E
Buxton U.K. **4** 53.16N 1.54W
Buy Russian Fed. **18** 58.23N 41.27E
Buyaga Russian Fed. **21** 59.42N 126.59E

tre Ouest d. Burkina 38 12.00N 2.20W
am i. see Seram i. Indonesia 27
am Sea see Seram, Laut sea Pacific Oc. 27
s U.S.A. 54 37.35N 120.57W
sole Reale Italy 9 45.26N 7.15E
té Colombia 60 8.54N 75.51W
gnola Italy 12 41.17N 15.53E
lly France 11 46.37N 2.50E
siers France 9 48.08N 3.29E
nica Slovenia 12 45.48N 14.22E
avodă Romania 15 44.20N 28.02E
itos Mexico 56 22.26N 100.17W
o de Pasco Peru 60 10.43S 76.15W
era Lérida Spain 10 41.40N 1.16E
ia Italy 9 44.15N 12.22E
ignano del Friuli Italy 9 45.49N 13.20E
na Italy 9 44.08N 12.15E
natico Italy 9 44.12N 12.24E
s Latvia 18 57.18N 25.18E
ké Budějovice Czech Republic 14 49.00N 30E
ký Krumlov Czech Republic 14 48.49N 19E
snock Australia 47 32.51S 151.21E
nje Yugo. 13 42.24N 18.55E
ta Spain 10 35.53N 5.19W
a Italy 9 44.23N 8.01E
ennes mts. France 11 44.25N 4.05E
han Turkey 30 37.02N 35.48E
han r. Turkey 30 36.54N 34.58E
lis France 9 47.47N 3.48E
cabuco Argentina 63 34.38S 60.29W
chani mtn. Peru 60 16.12S 71.32W
chapoyas Peru 60 6.13S 77.54W
co d. Argentina 62 26.30S 60.00W
d Africa 34 13.00N 19.00E
d, L. Africa 38 13.30N 14.00E
dron U.S.A. 52 42.50N 103.02W
fe Nigeria 38 11.56N 6.55E
gda Russian Fed. 21 58.44N 130.38E
hār Borjak Afghan. 28 30.17N 62.03E
jarí Argentina 63 30.45S 57.59W
ke Chake Tanzania 37 5.13S 39.46E
khānsūr Afghan. 31 31.10N 62.02E
la Peru 60 15.48S 74.20W
leur B. Canada 55 48.00N 65.45W
lhuanca Peru 60 14.20S 73.10W
lans France 11 46.51N 1.52W
llenger Depth Pacific Oc. 27 11.19N 142.15E
llis U.S.A. 54 44.30N 114.14W
onnes-sur-Loire France 9 47.21N 0.46W
ons-sur-Marne France 9 48.58N 4.22E
lon-sur-Saône France 11 46.47N 4.51E
m Germany 14 49.13N 12.41E
ma Zambia 37 11.09S 33.10E
mbal r. India 29 26.30N 79.20E
mbersburg U.S.A. 55 39.56N 77.39W
mbéry France 11 45.34N 5.55E
mbeshi Zambia 37 10.57S 31.04E
mbeshi r. Zambia 37 11.15S 30.37E
mbly France 9 49.10N 2.15E
mical Argentina 62 30.22S 66.19W
monix France 11 45.55N 6.52E
mpagne-Ardenne d. France 8 49.42N 4.30E
mpaign U.S.A. 53 40.07N 88.14W
mpéry Switz. 9 46.10N 6.52E
mplain, L. U.S.A. 55 44.45N 73.15W
mpotón Mexico 56 19.21N 90.43W
ñaral Chile 62 26.21S 70.37W
ndeleur Is. U.S.A. 53 29.50N 88.50W
ndīgarh India 28 30.44N 76.54E
ndpur Bangla. 29 22.08N 91.55E
ndrapur India 29 19.58N 79.21E
nf Iran 31 26.40N 60.31E
ngchun China 25 43.50N 125.20E
ngde China 25 29.03N 111.35E
ng Jiang r. China 25 31.40N 121.15E
ngjin N. Korea 25 40.21N 127.20E
ngning China 25 26.24N 112.24E
ngping China 25 40.12N 116.12E
ngsha China 25 28.10N 113.00E
ngting China 25 25.47N 116.17E
ngzhi China 25 36.09N 113.12E
ngzhou China 25 31.45N 119.57E
nnel Is. Europe 5 49.28N 2.13W
nnel Is. U.S.A. 54 34.00N 120.00W
nnel-Port-aux-Basques town Canada 51 .35N 59.10W
nning Mich. U.S.A. 55 46.08N 88.06W
ntada Spain 10 42.36N 7.46W
nthaburi Thailand 29 12.38N 102.12E
ntilly France 9 49.12N 2.28E
o'an China 25 23.43N 116.35E
onde Mozambique 37 13.43S 40.31E
o Phraya r. Thailand 29 13.30N 100.25E
oyang Guangdong China 25 23.17N 116.33E
pada das Mangabeiras mts. Brazil 61 10.00S .30W
pada Diamantina Brazil 59 13.30S 42.30W
pala, Lago de l. Mexico 56 20.00N 103.00W
payevo Kazakhstan 19 50.12N 51.09E
payevsk Russian Fed. 18 52.58N 49.44E
pelle-d'Angillon France 9 47.22N 2.26E
picuy Uruguay 63 31.39S 57.54W
pleau Canada 55 47.50N 83.24W
pra India 29 25.46N 84.45E
qui Bolivia 62 19.36S 65.32W
racot I. Antarctica 64 70.00S 75.00W
rcas Mexico 56 23.08N 101.07W
rd U.K. 5 50.52N 2.59W
rduār India 29 26.52N 92.46E
rdzhou Turkmenistan 31 39.09N 63.34E
rente r. France 11 45.57N 1.00W
ri r. Chad 38 13.00N 14.30E
rīkār Afghan. 28 35.02N 69.13E
ring U.K. 5 51.12N 0.49E
rleroi Belgium 8 50.25N 4.27E
rlesbourg Canada 55 46.53N 71.16W
rles Pt. Australia 42 12.23S 130.37E
Charleston S.C. U.S.A. 53 32.48N 79.58W
Charleston W.Va. U.S.A. 55 38.23N 81.40W
Charlestown Rep. of Ire. 7 53.57N 8.48W
Charlestown Ind. U.S.A. 55 38.28N 85.40W
Charleville Australia 44 26.25S 146.13E
Charleville-Mézières France 9 49.46N 4.43E
Charlieu France 11 46.10N 4.10E
Charlotte N.C. U.S.A. 53 35.05N 80.50W
Charlottesville U.S.A. 53 38.02N 78.29W
Charlottetown Canada 51 46.14N 63.09W
Charlton Australia 46 36.18S 143.27E
Charly-sur-Marne France 9 48.58N 3.17E
Charolles France 11 46.26N 4.17E
Charters Towers Australia 44 20.05S 146.16E
Chartres France 9 48.27N 1.30E
Chascomús Argentina 63 35.35S 58.00W
Châteaubriant France 9 47.43N 1.22W
Château-du-Loir France 9 47.42N 0.25E
Châteaudun France 9 48.04N 1.20E
Château Gontier France 9 47.50N 0.42W
Château Landon France 9 48.09N 2.42E
Château-la-Vallière France 9 47.33N 0.19E
Châteauneuf-en-Thymerais France 9 48.35N 1.15E
Châteauneuf-sur-Loire France 9 47.52N 2.14E
Chateauneuf-sur-Sarthe France 9 47.41N 0.30W
Château-Porcien France 9 49.32N 4.15E
Château Renault France 9 47.35N 0.55E
Châteauroux France 11 46.49N 1.41E
Château-Thierry France 9 49.03N 3.24E
Châtelet Belgium 8 50.24N 4.32E
Châtellerault France 11 46.49N 0.33E
Chatham N.B. Canada 55 47.02N 65.30W
Chatham Ont. Canada 55 42.24N 82.11W
Chatham U.K. 5 51.23N 0.32E
Chatham Is. Pacific Oc. 40 44.00S 176.35W
Châtillon Italy 9 45.45N 7.37E
Châtillon-Coligny France 9 47.50N 2.51E
Châtillon-sur-Seine France 9 47.52N 4.35E
Chattahoochee r. U.S.A. 53 30.52N 84.57W
Chattanooga U.S.A. 53 35.01N 85.18W
Chatteris U.K. 5 52.27N 0.03E
Chaulnes France 9 49.49N 2.48E
Chaumont France 11 48.07N 5.08E
Chaumont-en-Vexin France 9 49.16N 1.53E
Chauny France 9 49.37N 3.13E
Chausy Belarus 15 53.49N 30.57E
Chavanges France 9 48.31N 4.34E
Chaves Brazil 61 0.10S 49.55W
Chaves Portugal 10 41.44N 7.28W
Chawang Thailand 29 8.25N 99.32E
Cheb Czech Republic 14 50.04N 12.20E
Cheboksary Russian Fed. 18 56.08N 47.12E
Cheboygan U.S.A. 55 45.40N 84.28W
Chebsara Russian Fed. 18 59.14N 38.59E
Chech, Erg des. Africa 34 25.00N 2.15W
Chechersk Belarus 15 52.54N 30.54E
Checiny Poland 15 50.48N 20.28E
Chegdomyn Russian Fed. 21 51.09N 133.01E
Chegga well Mauritania 34 25.30N 5.46W
Chegutu Zimbabwe 39 18.09S 30.07E
Chehalis U.S.A. 54 46.40N 122.58W
Cheiron, Cime du mtn. France 9 43.49N 6.58E
Cheju S. Korea 25 33.31N 126.29E
Cheju do i. S. Korea 25 33.20N 126.30E
Cheleken Turkmenistan 31 39.26N 53.11E
Chelforó Argentina 63 39.04S 66.33W
Chelkar Kazakhstan 20 47.48N 59.39E
Chelles France 9 48.53N 2.36E
Chełm Poland 15 51.10N 23.28E
Chelmsford U.K. 5 51.44N 0.28E
Chełmża Poland 15 53.12N 18.37E
Cheltenham U.K. 5 51.53N 2.07W
Chelva Spain 10 39.45N 1.00W
Chelyabinsk Russian Fed. 20 55.10N 61.25E
Chelyuskin, Mys c. Russian Fed. 21 77.20N 106.00E
Chemainus Canada 54 48.55N 123.48W
Chemba Mozambique 37 17.11S 34.53E
Chemnitz Germany 14 50.50N 12.55E
Chemult U.S.A. 54 43.13N 121.47W
Chenāb r. Asia 28 29.26N 71.09E
Cheney U.S.A. 54 47.29N 117.34W
Chengde China 25 40.48N 118.06E
Chengdu China 29 30.37N 104.06E
Chēn, Gora mtn. Russian Fed. 21 65.30N 141.20E
Chen Xian China 25 25.48N 113.02E
Chepen Peru 60 7.15S 79.20W
Chepstow U.K. 5 51.38N 2.40W
Cher r. France 9 47.12N 2.04E
Cherbourg France 9 49.38N 1.37W
Cherdyn Russian Fed. 18 60.25N 55.22E
Cheremkhovo Russian Fed. 21 53.08N 103.01E
Cherepovets Russian Fed. 18 59.05N 37.55E
Cherikov Belarus 15 53.35N 31.23E
Cherkassy Ukraine 19 49.27N 32.04E
Cherkessk Russian Fed. 19 44.14N 42.05E
Cherkovitsa Bulgaria 13 43.41N 24.49E
Cherlak Russian Fed. 20 54.10N 74.52E
Chernigov Ukraine 15 51.30N 31.18E
Chernikovsk Russian Fed. 18 54.51N 56.06E
Chernobyl Ukraine 15 51.17N 30.15E
Chernovtsy Ukraine 15 48.19N 25.52E
Chernyakhov Ukraine 15 50.30N 28.38E
Chernyakhovsk Russian Fed. 17 54.38N 21.49E
Cherquenco Chile 63 38.41S 72.00W
Cherry Creek town Nev. U.S.A. 54 39.54N 113.53W
Cherskogo, Khrebet mts. Russian Fed. 21 65.50N 143.00E
Chertkovo Russian Fed. 19 49.22N 40.12E
Chertsey U.K. 5 51.23N 0.27W
Chervonograd Ukraine 15 50.25N 24.10E
Cherwell r. U.K. 5 51.44N 1.15W
Chesapeake B. U.S.A. 53 38.40N 76.25W
Chesham U.K. 5 51.43N 0.38W
Cheshire d. U.K. 4 53.14N 2.30W
Chëshskaya Guba g. Russian Fed. 18 67.20N 46.30E
Chesil Beach f. U.K. 5 50.37N 2.33W
Chester U.K. 4 53.12N 2.53W
Chester Mont. U.S.A. 54 48.31N 110.58W
Chester Penn. U.S.A. 55 39.51N 75.21W
Chesterfield U.K. 4 53.14N 1.26W
Chesterfield Inlet town Canada 51 63.00N 91.00W
Chesuncook L. U.S.A. 55 46.00N 69.20W
Chetumal Mexico 57 18.30N 88.17W
Chetumal B. Mexico 57 18.30N 88.00W
Cheviot New Zealand 48 42.49S 173.16E
Cheviot U.S.A. 55 39.10N 84.32W
Cheyenne r. U.S.A. 52 44.40N 101.15W
Cheyenne Wyo. U.S.A. 52 41.08N 104.49W
Cheyne B. Australia 43 34.35S 118.50E
Chhindwāra India 29 22.04N 78.58E
Chiang Mai Thailand 29 18.48N 98.59E
Chiapas d. Mexico 56 16.30N 93.00W
Chiari Italy 9 45.32N 9.56E
Chiavari Italy 9 44.19N 9.19E
Chiavenna Italy 9 46.19N 9.24E
Chiba Japan 23 35.36N 140.07E
Chiba d. Japan 23 35.10N 140.00E
Chibemba Angola 36 15.43S 14.07E
Chibougamau Canada 55 49.53N 74.24W
Chibougamau Lac l. Canada 55 49.50N 74.19W
Chibougamau Prov. Park Canada 55 49.24N 73.48W
Chibuk Nigeria 38 10.52N 12.50E
Chibuto Mozambique 39 24.41S 33.32E
Chicago U.S.A. 53 41.50N 87.45W
Chichagof I. U.S.A. 50 57.55N 135.45W
Chichester U.K. 5 50.50N 0.47W
Chichibu Japan 23 35.59N 139.05E
Chickasha U.S.A. 52 35.03N 97.57W
Chiclana Spain 10 36.26N 6.09W
Chiclayo Peru 60 6.47S 79.47W
Chico r. Chubut Argentina 63 43.45S 66.10W
Chico r. Santa Cruz Argentina 63 50.03S 68.35W
Chico U.S.A. 54 39.44N 121.50W
Chicomo Mozambique 39 24.33S 34.11E
Chicoutimi-Jonquière Canada 55 48.26N 71.04W
Chicualacuala Mozambique 39 22.06S 31.42E
Chidambarum India 29 11.24N 79.42E
Chidenguele Mozambique 39 24.54S 34.13E
Chidley, C. Canada 51 60.30N 65.00W
Chiemsee l. Germany 14 47.55N 12.30E
Chiengi Zambia 37 8.42S 29.07E
Chieri Italy 9 45.01N 7.49E
Chieti Italy 12 42.22N 14.12E
Chifeng China 25 41.17N 118.56E
Chigasaki Japan 23 35.19N 139.24E
Chiguana Bolivia 62 21.05S 67.58W
Chigubo Mozambique 39 22.38S 33.18E
Chihuahua Mexico 56 28.38N 106.05W
Chihuahua d. Mexico 56 28.40N 106.00W
Chiili Kazakhstan 20 44.10N 66.37E
Chikumbi Zambia 37 15.14S 28.21E
Chikwawa Malaŵi 37 16.00S 34.54E
Chīl r. Iran 31 25.12N 61.30E
Chilapa Mexico 56 17.38N 99.11W
Chilcoot U.S.A. 54 39.49N 120.08W
Childers Australia 44 25.14S 152.17E
Chile S. America 62 32.30S 71.00W
Chile Chico Chile 63 46.33S 71.44W
Chilko L. Canada 50 51.20N 124.05W
Chillagoe Australia 44 17.09S 144.32E
Chillán Chile 63 36.36S 72.07W
Chillicothe Ohio U.S.A. 55 39.20N 82.59W
Chilliwack Canada 54 49.10N 122.00W
Chiloé, Isla de i. Chile 63 43.00S 73.00W
Chilonga Zambia 37 12.02S 31.17E
Chilpancingo Mexico 56 17.33N 99.30W
Chiltern Australia 47 36.11S 146.36E
Chiltern Hills U.K. 5 51.40N 0.53W
Chilumba Malaŵi 37 10.25S 34.18E
Chilwa, L. Malaŵi 37 15.15S 35.45E
Chimanimani Zimbabwe 39 19.48S 32.52E
Chimay Belgium 8 50.03N 4.20E
Chimbas Argentina 62 31.28S 68.30W
Chimbay Uzbekistan 20 42.56N 59.46E
Chimborazo mtn. Ecuador 60 1.29S 78.52W
Chimbote Peru 60 9.04S 78.34W
Chimishliya Moldova 15 46.30N 28.50E
Chimoio Mozambique 39 19.04S 33.29E
China Asia 24 33.00N 103.00E
China Lake town U.S.A. 54 35.46N 117.39W
Chinandega Nicaragua 57 12.35N 87.10W
Chinati Peak U.S.A. 52 29.57N 104.29W
Chincha Alta Peru 60 13.25S 76.07W
Chinchilla Australia 45 26.44S 150.39E
Chinchón Spain 10 40.09N 3.26W
Chindio Mozambique 37 17.46S 35.23E
Chindwin r. Myanmar 24 21.30N 95.12E
Chinga Mozambique 37 15.14S 38.40E
Chingleput India 29 12.42N 79.59E
Chingola Zambia 37 12.29S 27.53E
Chingombe Zambia 37 14.25S 29.56E
Chin Hills Myanmar 29 22.40N 93.30E
Chinhoyi Zimbabwe 39 17.22S 30.10E
Chinkapook Australia 46 35.11S 142.57E
Chinle U.S.A. 54 36.09N 109.33W
Chinon France 11 47.10N 0.15E
Chinook U.S.A. 54 48.35N 109.14W
Chino Valley town U.S.A. 54 34.45N 112.27W
Chinsali Zambia 37 10.33S 32.05E
Chintheche Malaŵi 37 11.50S 34.13E
Chiny Belgium 8 49.45N 5.20E
Chiôco Mozambique 37 16.27S 32.49E
Chioggia Italy 9 45.13N 12.17E
Chipata Zambia 37 13.37S 32.40E
Chipera Mozambique 37 15.20S 32.35E
Chipie r. Canada 55 51.30N 83.16W
Chipinge Zimbabwe 39 20.12S 32.38E
Chippenham U.K. 5 51.27N 2.07W
Chipping Norton U.K. 5 51.56N 1.32W
Chiquian Peru 60 10.10S 77.00W
Chiquinquirá Colombia 60 5.37N 73.50W
Chir r. Russian Fed. 19 48.34N 42.53E
Chirchik Uzbekistan 24 41.28N 69.31E
Chiredzi Zimbabwe 39 21.03S 31.39E
Chiredzi r. Zimbabwe 39 21.10S 31.50E
Chiriquí mtn. Panama 57 8.49N 82.38W
Chiriquí, Laguna de b. Panama 57 9.00N 82.00W
Chiromo Malaŵi 37 16.28S 35.10E
Chirripó mtn. Costa Rica 57 9.31N 83.30W
Chirundu Zimbabwe 37 16.04S 28.51E
Chisamba Zambia 37 14.58S 28.23E
Chisasibi Canada 51 53.50N 79.01W
Chişinău see Kishinev Moldova 15
Chisone r. Italy 9 44.49N 7.25E
Chistopol Russian Fed. 18 55.25N 50.38E
Chita Russian Fed. 25 52.03N 113.35E
Chitipa Malaŵi 37 9.41S 33.19E
Chitorgarh India 28 24.53N 74.38E
Chitrāl Pakistan 28 35.52N 71.58E
Chittagong Bangla. 29 22.20N 91.48E
Chittoor India 29 13.13N 79.06E
Chiuta, L. Malaŵi/Mozambique 37 14.45S 35.50E
Chivasso Italy 9 45.11N 7.53E
Chivhu Zimbabwe 39 19.01S 30.53E
Chivilcoy Argentina 63 34.52S 60.02W
Chiwanda Tanzania 37 11.21S 34.55E
Chobe d. Botswana 39 18.30S 25.15E
Chobe r. Namibia/Botswana 39 17.48S 25.12E
Chobe Swamp f. Namibia 39 18.20S 23.40E
Chocolate Mts. U.S.A. 54 33.20N 115.15W
Chocope Peru 60 7.47S 79.12W
Choele-Choel Argentina 63 39.15S 65.30W
Chōfu Japan 23 35.39N 139.33E
Choix Mexico 56 26.43N 108.17W
Chojnice Poland 15 53.42N 17.32E
Cholet France 11 47.04N 0.53W
Cholon Vietnam 26 10.45N 106.39E
Choluteca Honduras 57 13.16N 87.11W
Choma Zambia 36 16.51S 27.04E
Chomutov Czech Republic 14 50.28N 13.25E
Chon Buri Thailand 29 13.21N 101.01E
Chone Ecuador 60 0.44S 80.04W
Ch'ŏngjin N. Korea 25 41.55N 129.50E
Ch'ŏngju S. Korea 25 36.39N 127.31E
Chongqing China 29 29.31N 106.35E
Chŏnju S. Korea 25 35.50N 127.05E
Chonos, Archipelago de los is. Chile 63 45.00S 74.00W
Chorley U.K. 4 53.39N 2.39W
Chorokh r. Georgia 19 41.36N 41.35E
Chortkov Ukraine 15 49.01N 25.42E
Chorzów Poland 15 50.19N 18.56E
Chosica Peru 60 11.55S 76.38W
Chos Malal Argentina 63 37.20S 70.15W
Choszczno Poland 14 53.10N 15.26E
Choteau U.S.A. 54 47.49N 112.11W
Chott Djerid f. Tunisia 34 33.30N 8.30E
Chott ech Chergui f. Algeria 34 34.00N 0.30E
Chott Melrhir f. Algeria 34 34.15N 7.00E
Choum Mauritania 34 21.10N 13.00W
Chowchilla U.S.A. 54 37.07N 120.16W
Christchurch New Zealand 48 43.33S 172.40E
Christchurch U.K. 5 50.44N 1.47W
Christianshåb Greenland 51 68.50N 51.00W
Christmas Creek town Australia 42 18.55S 125.56E
Christmas I. Indian Oc. 26 10.30S 105.40E
Chrudim Czech Republic 14 49.57N 15.48E
Chu r. Kazakhstan 24 42.30N 76.10E
Chubbuck U.S.A. 54 34.22N 115.20W
Chūbu d. Japan 23 35.25N 137.40E
Chubut d. Argentina 63 44.00S 68.00W
Chubut r. Argentina 63 43.18S 65.06W
Chudleigh U.K. 5 50.35N 3.36W
Chudnov Ukraine 15 50.05N 28.01E
Chudovo Russian Fed. 18 59.10N 31.41E
Chuiquimula Guatemala 57 15.52N 89.50W
Chukai Malaysia 26 4.16N 103.24E
Chukotskiy Poluostrov pen. Russian Fed. 21 66.00N 174.30W
Chukudukraal Botswana 39 22.30S 23.22E
Chula Vista U.S.A. 54 32.39N 117.05W
Chulman Russian Fed. 21 56.54N 124.55E
Chulucanas Peru 60 5.08S 80.00W
Chulym Russian Fed. 20 55.09N 80.59E
Chum Russian Fed. 18 67.05N 63.15E
Chumbicha Argentina 62 28.50S 66.18W
Chumikan Russian Fed. 21 54.40N 135.15E
Chumphon Thailand 29 10.35N 99.14E
Chuna r. Russian Fed. 21 58.00N 94.00E
Ch'unch'ŏn S. Korea 25 37.53N 127.45E
Chungking see Chongqing China 29
Chunya Tanzania 37 8.31S 33.28E
Chuquicamata Chile 62 22.20S 68.56W
Chuquisaca d. Bolivia 62 21.00S 64.00W
Chur Switz. 11 46.52N 9.32E
Churchill Canada 51 58.45N 94.00W
Churchill r. Man. Canada 51 58.20N 94.15W
Churchill r. Nfld. Canada 51 53.20N 60.00W
Churchill, C. Canada 51 58.50N 93.00W
Churchill L. Canada 50 56.00N 108.00W
Churchill Peak mtn. Canada 50 58.10N 125.00W
Church Stretton U.K. 5 52.32N 2.49W
Chusovoy Russian Fed. 18 58.18N 57.50E
Chuxiong China 29 25.03N 101.33E
Ciechanów Poland 15 52.53N 20.38E
Ciego de Avila Cuba 57 21.51N 78.47W
Ciénaga Colombia 60 11.11N 74.15W
Cienfuegos Cuba 57 22.10N 80.27W
Cieszyn Poland 15 49.45N 18.38E
Cieza Spain 10 38.14N 1.25W
Cifuentes Spain 10 40.47N 2.37W
Cigüela r. Spain 10 39.47N 3.00W
Cijara, Embalse de resr. Spain 10 39.20N 4.50W
Cilacap Indonesia 26 7.44S 109.00E
Cimarron r. U.S.A. 53 36.15N 96.55W
Cimone, Monte mtn. Italy 9 44.12N 10.42E
Cîmpina Romania 13 45.08N 25.44E
Cîmpulung Romania 13 45.16N 25.03E
Cinca r. Spain 10 41.22N 0.20E
Cincinnati U.S.A. 55 39.10N 84.30W
Ciney Belgium 8 50.17N 5.06E
Cinto, Monte mtn. France 11 42.23N 8.57E
Cipolletti Argentina 63 38.56S 67.59W
Circle U.S.A. 54 47.25N 105.35W
Circleville Ohio U.S.A. 55 39.36N 82.57W
Circleville Utah U.S.A. 54 38.10N 112.16W
Cirebon Indonesia 26 6.46S 108.33E
Cirencester U.K. 5 51.43N 1.59W
Ciriè Italy 9 45.14N 7.36E
Cirò Marina Italy 13 39.22N 17.08E
Cittadella Italy 9 45.39N 11.47E
Cittanova Italy 12 38.21N 16.05E
Ciudad Bolívar Venezuela 60 8.06N 63.36W
Ciudad Camargo Mexico 56 27.40N 105.10W
Ciudad de México Mexico 56 19.25N 99.10W
Ciudadela Spain 10 40.00N 3.50E
Ciudad Guayana Venezuela 60 8.22N 62.40W
Ciudad Guerrero Mexico 56 28.33N 107.28W
Ciudad Guzmán Mexico 56 19.41N 103.29W
Ciudad Ixtepec Mexico 56 16.32N 95.10W
Ciudad Jiménez Mexico 56 27.08N 104.55W
Ciudad Juárez Mexico 56 31.44N 106.29W
Ciudad Madero Mexico 56 22.19N 97.50W
Ciudad Mante Mexico 56 22.44N 98.57W
Ciudad Obregón Mexico 56 27.29N 109.56W
Ciudad Ojeda Venezuela 60 10.05N 71.17W
Ciudad Piar Venezuela 60 7.27N 63.19W
Ciudad Real Spain 10 38.59N 3.55W
Ciudad Rodrigo Spain 10 40.36N 6.33W
Ciudad Victoria Mexico 56 23.43N 99.10W
Civitanova Italy 12 43.19N 13.40E
Civitavecchia Italy 12 42.06N 11.48E
Civray France 11 46.09N 0.18E
Çivril Turkey 30 38.18N 29.43E
Cizre Turkey 30 37.21N 42.11E
Clackline Australia 43 31.43S 116.31E
Clacton on Sea U.K. 5 51.47N 1.10E
Claire, L. Canada 50 58.30N 112.00W
Clamecy France 9 47.27N 3.31E
Clara Rep. of Ire. 7 53.21N 7.37W
Clare N.S.W. Australia 46 33.27S 143.55E
Clare S.A. Australia 46 33.50S 138.38E
Clare d. Rep. of Ire. 7 52.52N 8.55W
Clare r. Rep. of Ire. 7 53.17N 9.04W
Clare U.S.A. 55 43.49N 84.47W
Clare I. Rep. of Ire. 7 53.48N 10.00W
Claremorris Rep. of Ire. 7 53.44N 9.00W
Clarence r. Australia 47 29.25S 153.02E
Clarence r. New Zealand 48 42.10S 173.55E
Clarence I. Antarctica 64 61.30S 53.50W
Clarence Str. Australia 42 12.00S 131.00E
Clarie Coast f. Antarctica 64 67.00S 133.00E
Clarke I. Australia 45 40.30S 148.10E
Clark Fork r. U.S.A. 54 48.09N 116.15W
Clark, L. U.S.A. 50 60.15N 154.15W
Clarksburg U.S.A. 55 39.16N 80.22W
Clarksdale U.S.A. 53 34.12N 90.33W
Clarkston U.S.A. 54 46.26N 117.02W
Clarksville Tenn. U.S.A. 53 36.31N 87.21W
Clary France 8 50.05N 3.21E
Clayton r. Australia 46 29.06S 137.59E
Clayton Idaho U.S.A. 54 44.16N 114.25W
Clayton N.Mex. U.S.A. 52 36.27N 103.12W
Clear, C. Rep. of Ire. 3 51.25N 9.32W
Clearfield Utah U.S.A. 54 41.07N 112.01W
Clear I. Rep. of Ire. 7 51.26N 9.30W
Clear L. U.S.A. 54 39.02N 122.50W
Clearwater U.S.A. 53 27.57N 82.48W
Clearwater Mts. U.S.A. 54 46.00N 115.30W
Cle Elum U.S.A. 54 47.12N 120.56W
Cleethorpes U.K. 4 53.33N 0.02W
Clermont Australia 44 22.49S 147.39E
Clermont France 9 49.23N 2.24E
Clermont-en-Argonne France 9 49.05N 5.05E
Clermont-Ferrand France 11 45.47N 3.05E
Clervaux Lux. 8 50.04N 6.01E
Cles Italy 9 46.22N 11.02E
Cleve Australia 46 33.37S 136.32E
Clevedon U.K. 5 51.26N 2.52W
Cleveland d. U.K. 4 54.37N 1.08W
Cleveland Miss. U.S.A. 53 33.43N 90.46W
Cleveland Ohio U.S.A. 55 41.30N 81.41W
Cleveland Tenn. U.S.A. 53 35.10N 84.51W
Cleveland, C. Australia 44 19.11S 147.01E
Cleveland Heights town U.S.A. 55 41.30N 81.34W
Cleveland Hills U.K. 4 54.25N 1.10W
Cleveleys U.K. 4 53.52N 3.01W
Clew B. Rep. of Ire. 7 53.50N 9.47W
Clifden Rep. of Ire. 7 53.29N 10.02W
Cliffy Head Australia 43 34.58S 116.24E
Clifton Ariz. U.S.A. 54 33.03N 109.18W
Clinton B.C. Canada 50 51.05N 121.35W
Clinton New Zealand 48 46.13S 169.23E
Clinton Iowa U.S.A. 53 41.51N 90.12W
Clinton Okla. U.S.A. 52 35.32N 98.59W
Clisham mtn. U.K. 6 57.58N 6.50W
Cliza Bolivia 62 17.36S 65.56W
Cloghan Offaly Rep. of Ire. 7 53.13N 7.54W
Clogher Head Kerry Rep. of Ire. 7 52.09N 10.28W
Clonakilty Rep. of Ire. 7 51.37N 8.54W
Cloncurry Australia 44 20.42S 140.30E
Clones Rep. of Ire. 7 54.11N 7.16W
Clonmel Rep. of Ire. 7 52.21N 7.44W
Clonroche Rep. of Ire. 7 52.27N 6.45W
Cloppenburg Germany 8 52.52N 8.02E
Clorinda Argentina 62 25.20S 57.40W
Cloud Peak mtn. U.S.A. 54 44.25N 107.10W
Cloughton U.K. 4 54.20N 0.27W
Cloverdale U.S.A. 54 38.48N 123.01W
Clovis Calif. U.S.A. 54 36.49N 119.42W
Clovis N.Mex. U.S.A. 52 34.14N 103.13W
Clowne U.K. 4 53.18N 1.16W
Cluj-Napoca Romania 15 46.47N 23.37E

Clunes Australia 46 37.16S 143.47E
Cluny France 11 46.26N 4.39E
Clusone Italy 9 45.53N 9.57E
Clutha r. New Zealand 48 46.18S 169.05E
Clwyd d. U.K. 4 53.07N 3.20W
Clwyd r. U.K. 4 53.19N 3.30W
Clyde Canada 51 70.30N 68.30W
Clyde New Zealand 48 45.11S 169.19E
Clyde r. U.K. 6 55.58N 4.53W
Clydebank U.K. 6 55.53N 4.23W
Coachella U.S.A. 54 33.41N 116.10W
Coahuila d. Mexico 56 27.00N 103.00W
Coalinga U.S.A. 54 36.09N 120.21W
Coalville U.K. 5 52.43N 1.21W
Coast d. Kenya 37 3.00S 39.30E
Coast Mts. Canada 50 55.30N 128.00W
Coast Range mts. U.S.A. 54 42.40N 123.30W
Coatbridge U.K. 6 55.52N 4.02W
Coats I. Canada 51 62.30N 83.00W
Coats Land f. Antarctica 64 77.00S 25.00W
Coatzacoalcos Mexico 56 18.10N 94.25W
Cobalt Canada 55 47.24N 79.41W
Cobán Guatemala 56 15.28N 90.20W
Cobar Australia 47 31.32S 145.51E
Cobargo Australia 47 36.24S 149.52E
Cobden Australia 46 38.21S 143.07E
Cobden Canada 55 45.38N 76.53W
Cobh Rep. of Ire. 7 51.50N 8.18W
Cobham L. Australia 46 30.09S 142.05E
Cobija Bolivia 62 11.02S 68.44W
Cobourg Canada 55 43.58N 78.11W
Cobourg Pen. Australia 44 11.20S 132.15E
Cobram Australia 47 35.56S 145.40E
Cobre U.S.A. 54 41.07N 114.25W
Cobue Mozambique 37 12.10S 34.50E
Coburg Germany 14 50.15N 10.58E
Coburg I. Canada 51 76.00N 79.25W
Cochabamba Bolivia 62 17.24S 66.09W
Cochabamba d. Bolivia 62 17.30S 65.40W
Cochem Germany 8 50.08N 7.10E
Cochrane Ont. Canada 55 49.04N 81.02W
Cochrane Chile 63 47.20S 72.30W
Cockaleechie Australia 46 34.07S 135.53E
Cockburn Australia 46 32.05S 141.00E
Cockburnspath U.K. 6 55.56N 2.22W
Cocklebiddy Australia 43 32.02S 126.05E
Coco r. Honduras 57 14.58N 83.15W
Cocoparra Range mts. Australia 47 34.00S 146.00E
Codăeşti Romania 15 46.52N 27.46E
Codajás Brazil 60 3.55S 62.00W
Cod, C. U.S.A. 55 41.42N 70.15W
Codigoro Italy 9 44.49N 12.08E
Codó Brazil 61 4.28S 43.51W
Codogno Italy 9 45.09N 9.42E
Codroipo Italy 9 45.58N 12.59E
Cody U.S.A. 54 44.32N 109.03W
Coen Australia 44 13.56S 143.12E
Coesfeld Germany 8 51.55N 7.13E
Coeur d'Alene U.S.A. 52 47.40N 116.46W
Coevorden Neth. 8 52.39N 6.45E
Coffin B. Australia 46 34.27S 135.19E
Coffin Bay Pen. Australia 46 34.30S 135.14E
Coff's Harbour Australia 47 30.19S 153.05E
Cofre de Perote mtn. Mexico 56 19.30N 97.10W
Coghinas r. Italy 12 40.57N 8.50E
Cognac France 11 45.42N 0.19W
Cohoes U.S.A. 55 42.46N 73.42W
Cohuna Australia 46 35.47S 144.15E
Coiba, Isla de i. Panama 57 7.23N 81.45W
Coihaique Chile 63 45.35S 72.08W
Coimbatore India 28 11.00N 76.57E
Coimbra Brazil 59 19.55S 57.47W
Coimbra Portugal 10 40.12N 8.25W
Coín Spain 10 36.40N 4.45W
Cojimies Ecuador 60 0.20N 80.00W
Cokeville U.S.A. 54 42.05N 110.57W
Colac Australia 46 38.22S 143.38E
Colatina Brazil 59 19.35S 40.37W
Colbeck, C. Antarctica 64 77.20S 159.00W
Colchester U.K. 5 51.54N 0.55E
Coldstream U.K. 6 55.39N 2.15W
Coldwater U.S.A. 55 41.57N 85.01W
Coldwell Canada 55 48.46N 86.31W
Coleambally Australia 47 34.48S 145.53E
Coleman r. Australia 44 15.06S 141.38E
Colenso R.S.A. 39 28.43S 29.49E
Coleraine Australia 46 37.36S 141.42E
Coleraine U.K. 7 55.08N 6.40W
Colesberg R.S.A. 39 30.43S 25.05E
Colico Italy 9 46.08N 9.22E
Colima Mexico 56 19.14N 103.41W
Colima d. Mexico 56 19.05N 104.00W
Colinas Brazil 61 6.02S 44.14W
Coll i. U.K. 6 56.38N 6.34W
Collarenebri Australia 47 29.33S 148.36E
College U.S.A. 50 64.54N 147.55W
College Park town Md. U.S.A. 55 39.00N 76.55W
Collerina Australia 47 29.22S 146.32E
Collie N.S.W. Australia 47 31.41S 148.22E
Collie W.A. Australia 43 33.21S 116.09E
Collie Cardiff Australia 43 33.27S 116.09E
Collier B. Australia 42 16.10S 124.15E
Collingwood Canada 55 44.29N 80.13W
Collingwood New Zealand 48 40.41S 172.41E
Collingwood B. P.N.G. 44 9.20S 149.30E
Collinsville Australia 44 20.34S 147.51E
Collin Top mtn. U.K. 7 54.58N 6.08W
Collon Rep. of Ire. 7 53.47N 6.30W
Collooney Rep. of Ire. 7 54.11N 8.29W
Colmar France 11 48.05N 7.21E
Colmenar Viejo Spain 10 40.39N 3.46W
Colne r. Essex U.K. 5 51.50N 0.59E
Colnett, C. Mexico 56 31.00N 116.20W
Colnett, Cabo c. Mexico 54 31.00N 116.20W
Colo r. Australia 47 33.26S 150.53E
Cologne see Köln Germany 8
Colombia S. America 60 4.00N 72.30W
Colombo Sri Lanka 29 6.55N 79.52E
Colón Argentina 63 32.15S 58.10W
Colón Panama 60 9.21N 79.54W
Colona Australia 45 31.38S 132.05E
Colonia del Sacramento Uruguay 63 34.28S 57.51W
Colonia Las Heras Argentina 63 46.33S 68.57W
Colonia Lavelleja Uruguay 63 31.06S 57.01W
Colonsay i. U.K. 6 56.04N 6.13W
Colorado r. Argentina 63 39.50S 62.02W
Colorado d. U.S.A. 52 39.07N 105.27W
Colorado r. Ariz. U.S.A. 54 31.45N 114.40W
Colorado r. Tex. U.S.A. 53 28.30N 96.00W
Colorado Plateau f. U.S.A. 54 36.30N 108.00W
Colorado Springs town U.S.A. 52 38.50N 104.49W
Columbia Mo. U.S.A. 53 38.58N 92.20W
Columbia r. U.S.A. 54 46.15N 124.05W
Columbia S.C. U.S.A. 53 34.00N 81.00W
Columbia Tenn. U.S.A. 53 35.37N 87.02W
Columbia Basin f. U.S.A. 54 46.55N 117.36W
Columbia Falls town U.S.A. 54 48.23N 114.11W
Columbia Plateau f. U.S.A. 54 44.00N 117.30W
Columbretes, Islas is. Spain 10 39.50N 0.40E
Columbus Ga. U.S.A. 53 32.28N 84.59W
Columbus Ind. U.S.A. 55 39.12N 85.57W
Columbus Miss. U.S.A. 53 33.30N 88.27W
Columbus Mont. U.S.A. 54 45.38N 109.15W
Columbus Ohio U.S.A. 55 39.59N 83.03W
Colville r. U.S.A. 50 70.06N 151.30W
Colwyn Bay town U.K. 4 53.18N 3.43W
Comacchio Italy 9 44.42N 12.11E
Comacchio, Valli di b. Italy 9 44.38N 12.06E
Comayagua Honduras 57 14.30N 87.39W
Comblain-au-Pont Belgium 8 50.29N 5.32E
Combles France 8 50.01N 2.52E
Combourg France 9 48.25N 1.45W
Comboyne Australia 47 31.35S 152.27E
Comeragh Mts. Rep. of Ire. 7 52.17N 7.34W
Comilla Bangla. 29 23.28N 91.10E
Comitán Mexico 56 16.15N 92.08W
Commentry France 11 46.17N 2.44E
Commonwealth Territory d. Australia 47 35.00S 151.00E
Como Italy 9 45.48N 9.04E
Comodoro Rivadavia Argentina 63 45.50S 67.30W
Como, Lago di l. Italy 9 46.05N 9.17E
Comorin, C. India 28 8.04N 77.35E
Comoros Africa 37 12.15S 44.00E
Compiègne France 9 49.24N 2.50E
Conakry Guinea 34 9.30N 13.43W
Concarneau France 11 47.53N 3.55W
Conceição do Araguaia Brazil 61 8.15S 49.17W
Concepción Argentina 62 27.20S 65.36W
Concepción Chile 63 36.50S 73.03W
Concepción Paraguay 62 23.22S 57.26W
Concepción del Oro Mexico 56 24.38N 101.25W
Concepción del Uruguay Argentina 63 32.30S 58.14W
Conception B. Namibia 39 23.53S 14.28E
Conception, Pt. U.S.A. 54 34.27N 120.27W
Conches France 9 48.58N 0.58E
Conchillas Uruguay 63 34.15S 58.04W
Conchos r. Mexico 56 29.32N 104.25W
Concord N.H. U.S.A. 55 43.12N 71.32W
Concordia Argentina 63 31.24S 58.02W
Concórdia Brazil 60 4.35S 66.35W
Concordia U.S.A. 52 39.35N 97.39W
Condé France 9 48.51N 0.33W
Condé-sur-l'Escaut France 8 50.28N 3.35E
Condobolin Australia 47 33.03S 147.11E
Condom France 11 43.58N 0.22E
Conegliano Italy 9 45.53N 12.18E
Confolens France 11 46.01N 0.40E
Congleton U.K. 4 53.10N 2.12W
Congo Africa 36 1.00S 16.00E
Congonhas Brazil 59 20.30S 43.53W
Coningsby U.K. 4 53.07N 0.09W
Coniston U.K. 4 54.22N 3.06W
Connah's Quay town U.K. 4 53.13N 3.03W
Conneaut U.S.A. 55 41.58N 80.34W
Connecticut d. U.S.A. 55 41.45N 72.45W
Connecticut r. U.S.A. 55 41.17N 72.21W
Connellsville U.S.A. 55 40.01N 79.35W
Connemara f. Rep. of Ire. 7 53.32N 9.56W
Conner, Mt. Australia 44 25.35S 131.49E
Conn, Lough Rep. of Ire. 7 54.01N 9.15W
Conon r. U.K. 6 57.33N 4.33W
Conrad U.S.A. 54 48.10N 111.57W
Conselheiro Lafaiete Brazil 59 20.40S 43.48W
Consett U.K. 4 54.52N 1.50W
Con Son is. Vietnam 26 8.30N 106.30E
Constance, L. see Bodensee Europe 14
Constanţa Romania 13 44.10N 28.31E
Constantina Spain 10 37.54N 5.36W
Constantine Algeria 34 36.22N 6.38E
Constitución Chile 63 35.20S 72.25W
Constitución Uruguay 63 31.05S 57.50W
Consuegra Spain 10 39.28N 3.43W
Contact U.S.A. 54 41.48N 114.46W
Contamana Peru 60 7.19S 75.00W
Contas r. Brazil 61 14.15S 39.00W
Contreras, Embalse de resr. Spain 10 39.32N 1.30W
Contres France 9 47.25N 1.26E
Contwoyto L. Canada 50 65.42N 110.50W
Conty France 9 49.44N 2.09E
Conway N.H. U.S.A. 55 43.59N 71.07W
Conway, L. Australia 46 28.17S 135.35E
Coober Pedy Australia 46 29.01S 134.43E
Cook, C. Canada 50 50.08N 127.55W
Cooke, Mt. Australia 43 32.26S 116.18E
Cookhouse R.S.A. 39 32.44S 25.47E
Cook Inlet U.S.A. 50 60.30N 152.00W
Cook Is. Pacific Oc. 40 15.00S 160.00W
Cook, Mt. New Zealand 48 43.45S 170.12E
Cookstown U.K. 7 54.39N 6.46W
Cook Str. New Zealand 48 41.15S 174.30E
Cooktown Australia 44 15.29S 145.15E
Coolabah Australia 47 31.02S 146.45E
Coolah Australia 47 31.48S 149.45E
Coolamara Australia 46 31.59S 143.42E
Coolamon Australia 47 34.48S 147.12E
Coolangatta Australia 47 28.10S 153.26E
Coolgardie Australia 43 31.01S 121.12E
Coolidge U.S.A. 54 32.59N 111.31W
Cooma Australia 47 36.15S 149.07E
Coombah Australia 46 32.58S 141.39E
Coomberdale Australia 43 30.29S 116.03E
Coonabarabran Australia 47 31.16S 149.18E
Coonalpyn Australia 46 35.41S 139.52E
Coonamble Australia 47 30.55S 148.26E
Coonana Australia 43 31.01S 123.05E
Coonawarra Australia 46 37.16S 140.50E
Coondambo Australia 46 31.07S 135.20E
Cooper Creek r. Australia 46 28.33S 137.46E
Coorow Australia 43 29.53S 116.01E
Coos Bay town U.S.A. 54 43.22N 124.13W
Cootamundra Australia 47 34.41S 148.03E
Cootehill Rep. of Ire. 7 54.05N 7.05W
Copainalá Mexico 56 17.05N 93.12W
Copán ruins Honduras 57 14.52N 89.10W
Copenhagen see København Denmark 17
Copiapó Chile 62 27.22S 70.20W
Copparo Italy 9 44.54N 11.49E
Copperbelt d. Zambia 37 13.00S 28.00E
Copper Belt f. Zambia 37 12.40S 28.00E
Copper Center U.S.A. 50 61.58N 145.19W
Copper Cliff town Canada 55 46.28N 81.04W
Copper Harbor U.S.A. 55 47.28N 87.54W
Coppermine r. Canada 50 67.54N 115.10W
Coppermine see Qurlurtuuq town Canada 50
Copper Queen Zimbabwe 39 17.31S 29.20E
Copperton R.S.A. 39 30.00S 22.15E
Coqên China 29 31.20N 85.25E
Coquet r. U.K. 4 55.21N 1.35W
Coquille U.S.A. 54 43.11N 124.11W
Coquimbo Chile 62 29.58S 71.21W
Corabia Romania 13 43.45N 24.29E
Coracora Peru 60 15.02S 73.48W
Coraki Australia 47 23.00S 153.17E
Coral Bay town Australia 42 23.02S 113.48E
Coral Harbour town Canada 51 64.10N 83.15W
Coral Sea Pacific Oc. 44 14.30S 149.30E
Corangamite, L. Australia 46 38.10S 143.25E
Corbeil France 9 48.37N 2.29E
Corbeny France 9 49.28N 3.49E
Corbigny France 9 47.15N 3.40E
Corby U.K. 5 52.29N 0.41W
Corcubión Spain 10 42.56N 9.12W
Córdoba Argentina 62 31.25S 64.10W
Córdoba d. Argentina 62 30.30S 64.30W
Córdoba Mexico 56 18.55N 96.55W
Córdoba Spain 10 37.53N 4.46W
Córdoba, Sierras de mts. Argentina 62 30.30S 64.40W
Cordova U.S.A. 50 60.33N 139.44W
Corentyne r. Guyana 61 5.10N 57.20W
Corfield Australia 44 21.43S 143.22E
Corfu i. see Kérkira i. Greece 13
Coricudgy, Mt. Australia 47 32.51S 150.25E
Corigliano Italy 13 39.36N 16.31E
Corindi Australia 47 30.00S 153.21E
Corinth Miss. U.S.A. 53 34.58N 88.30W
Corinto Nicaragua 57 12.29N 87.14W
Cork Rep. of Ire. 7 51.54N 8.28W
Cork d. Rep. of Ire. 7 52.00N 8.40W
Cork Harbour est. Rep. of Ire. 7 51.50N 8.17W
Cormeilles France 9 49.15N 0.23E
Corner Brook town Canada 51 48.58N 57.58W
Corner Inlet b. Australia 47 38.43S 146.20E
Corning N.Y. U.S.A. 55 42.09N 77.04W
Corno, Monte mtn. Italy 12 42.29N 13.33E
Cornwall Canada 55 45.02N 74.45W
Cornwall d. U.K. 5 50.26N 4.40W
Cornwallis I. Canada 51 75.00N 95.00W
Coro Venezuela 60 11.27N 69.41W
Coroatá Brazil 61 4.08S 44.08W
Coroico Bolivia 62 16.10S 67.44W
Coromandel New Zealand 48 36.46S 175.30E
Coromandel Pen. New Zealand 48 36.45S 175.30E
Coronation G. Canada 50 68.00N 112.00W
Coronda Argentina 63 31.55S 60.55W
Coronel Chile 63 37.01S 73.08W
Coronel Brandsen Argentina 63 35.10S 58.15W
Coronel Pringles Argentina 63 37.56S 61.25W
Coronel Suárez Argentina 63 37.30S 61.52W
Coropuna mtn. Peru 60 15.31S 72.45W
Corowa Australia 47 36.00S 146.20E
Corozal Belize 57 18.23N 88.23W
Corpus Christi U.S.A. 53 27.47N 97.26W
Correggio Italy 9 44.46N 10.47E
Correntes, Cabo das c. Mozambique 39 24.11S 35.35E
Corrib, Lough Rep. of Ire. 7 53.26N 9.14W
Corrientes Argentina 62 27.30S 58.48W
Corrientes d. Argentina 62 28.00S 57.00W
Corrientes, Cabo c. Colombia 60 5.30N 77.34W
Corrigin Australia 43 32.21S 117.52E
Corry U.S.A. 55 41.56N 79.39W
Corryong Australia 47 36.11S 147.58E
Corse d. France 11 42.00N 9.10E
Corse i. France 11 42.00N 9.10E
Corse, Cap c. France 11 43.00N 9.21E
Corsham U.K. 5 51.25N 2.11W
Corsica i. see Corse i. France 11
Corsicana U.S.A. 53 32.05N 96.27W
Corte France 11 42.18N 9.08E
Cortegana Spain 10 37.55N 6.49W
Cortez Colo. U.S.A. 54 37.21N 108.35W
Cortez Nev. U.S.A. 54 40.09N 116.38W
Cortina Italy 12 46.32N 12.08E
Cortland N.Y. U.S.A. 55 42.36N 76.11W
Cortona Italy 12 43.16N 11.59E
Coruche Portugal 10 38.58N 8.31W
Çoruh Nehri r. Turkey see Chorokh r. Georgia 30
Çorum Turkey 30 40.31N 34.57E
Corumbá Brazil 62 19.00S 57.27W
Corumbá r. Brazil 59 18.15S 48.55W
Corvallis U.S.A. 54 44.34N 123.16W
Corwen U.K. 4 52.59N 3.23W
Cosenza Italy 12 39.17N 16.14E
Cosne France 9 47.25N 2.55E
Coso Junction U.S.A. 54 36.03N 117.58W
Cosson r. France 9 47.30N 1.15E
Costa Brava f. Spain 10 41.30N 3.00E
Costa del Sol f. Spain 10 36.30N 4.00W
Costa Mesa U.S.A. 54 33.39N 117.55W
Costa Rica C. America 57 10.00N 84.00W
Costeşti Romania 13 44.40N 24.53E
Cotabato Phil. 27 7.14N 124.15E
Cotagaita Bolivia 62 20.50S 65.41W
Côte d'Azur f. France 11 43.20N 6.45E
Côte d'Ivoire Africa 34 8.00N 5.30W
Côte-d'Or d. France 9 47.30N 4.50E
Côte d'Or f. France 9 47.10N 4.50E
Cotonou Benin 38 6.24N 2.31E
Cotopaxi mtn. Ecuador 60 0.40S 78.28W
Cotswold Hills U.K. 5 51.50N 2.00W
Cottage Grove U.S.A. 54 43.48N 123.03W
Cottbus Germany 14 51.43N 14.21E
Cottonvale Australia 47 28.32S 151.57E
Cottonwood U.S.A. 54 34.45N 112.01W
Coucy France 9 49.31N 3.19E
Couer d'Alene U.S.A. 54 47.41N 117.00W
Couesnon r. France 9 48.37N 1.31W
Coulagh B. Rep. of Ire. 7 51.42N 10.00W
Coulee City U.S.A. 54 47.37N 119.17W
Coulommiers France 9 48.49N 3.05E
Coulonge r. Canada 55 45.51N 76.45W
Council U.S.A. 50 64.55N 163.44W
Council Bluffs U.S.A. 53 41.14N 95.54W
Coupar Angus U.K. 6 56.33N 3.17W
Courland Lagoon Russian Fed./Lithuania 17 55.00N 21.00E
Courson-les-Carrières France 9 47.36N 3.30E
Courtalain France 9 48.05N 1.09E
Courtenay Canada 50 49.41N 125.00W
Courtrai see Kortrijk Belgium 8
Coutances France 9 49.03N 1.29W
Coutras France 11 45.02N 0.07W
Couvin Belgium 8 50.03N 4.30E
Cové Benin 38 7.16N 2.20E
Coventry U.K. 5 52.25N 1.31W
Covilhã Portugal 10 40.17N 7.30W
Covington Ky. U.S.A. 55 39.04N 84.30W
Cowal, L. Australia 47 33.36S 147.22E
Cowangie Australia 46 35.14S 141.28E
Cowan, L. Australia 43 32.00S 122.00E
Cowansville Canada 55 45.13N 72.44W
Cowcowing Lakes Australia 43 31.01S 117.18E
Cowdenbeath U.K. 6 56.07N 3.21W
Cowell Australia 46 33.41S 136.55E
Cowes Australia 47 38.27S 145.15E
Cowes U.K. 5 50.45N 1.18W
Cowra Australia 47 33.50S 148.45E
Cox r. Australia 44 15.19S 135.25E
Coxim Brazil 62 18.28S 54.37W
Cox's Bāzār Bangla. 29 21.25N 91.59E
Coyuca de Catalán Mexico 56 18.20N 100.39W
Cozes France 11 45.35N 0.50W
Cozumel, Isla de i. Mexico 57 20.30N 87.00W
Cradock Australia 46 31.59S 138.34E
Cradock R.S.A. 39 32.10S 25.35E
Craig Colo. U.S.A. 54 40.31N 107.33W
Craigavon U.K. 7 54.28N 6.25W
Craignure U.K. 6 56.28N 5.42W
Craigsville U.S.A. 55 38.04N 79.23W
Crail U.K. 6 56.16N 2.38W
Crailsheim Germany 14 49.09N 10.06E
Craiova Romania 13 44.18N 23.46E
Cranbourne Australia 47 38.07S 145.19E
Cranbrook Australia 43 34.15S 117.32E
Cranbrook Canada 50 49.29N 115.48W
Crane U.S.A. 54 43.25N 118.34W
Cranston U.S.A. 55 41.47N 71.26W
Craon France 9 47.50N 0.58W
Craonne France 9 49.27N 3.46E
Crater L. U.S.A. 54 42.56N 122.06W
Crateús Brazil 61 5.10S 40.39W
Crati r. Italy 13 39.43N 16.29E
Crato Amazonas Brazil 60 7.25S 63.00W
Crato Ceará Brazil 61 7.10S 39.25W
Craughwell Rep. of Ire. 7 53.14N 8.44W
Crawfordsville U.S.A. 55 40.03N 86.54W
Crawley U.K. 5 51.07N 0.10W
Crazy Mts. U.S.A. 54 46.08N 110.20W
Crécy France 11 50.15N 1.53E
Crécy-sur-Serre France 9 49.42N 3.37E
Cree r. Canada 50 59.00N 105.47W
Creede U.S.A. 54 37.51N 106.56W
Cree L. Canada 50 57.20N 108.30W
Creil France 9 49.16N 2.29E
Crema Italy 9 45.22N 9.41E
Cremona Italy 9 45.08N 10.03E
Crépy France 9 49.36N 3.31E
Crépy-en-Valois France 9 49.14N 2.54E
Cres i. Croatia 12 44.50N 14.20E
Cres town Croatia 12 44.58N 14.25E
Crescent U.S.A. 54 43.29N 121.41W
Crescent City U.S.A. 54 41.45N 124.12W
Crescent Head town Australia 47 31.10S 152.59E
Crespo Argentina 63 32.02S 60.20W
Cressy Australia 46 38.02S 143.38E
Crest France 11 44.44N 5.02E
Creston Iowa U.S.A. 53 41.04N 94.20W
Creswick Australia 46 37.25S 143.54E
Crete i. see Kriti i. Greece 13
Crete, Sea of see Kritikón Pélagos sea Greece 13
Creus, Cabo de c. Spain 10 42.20N 3.19E
Creuse r. France 11 47.00N 0.35E
Crewe U.K. 4 53.06N 2.28W
Crianlarich U.K. 6 56.23N 4.37W
Criccieth U.K. 4 52.55N 4.15W
Criciúma Brazil 59 28.40S 49.23W
Crieff U.K. 6 56.23N 3.52W
Crimea pen. see Krym pen. Ukraine 19
Crinan U.K. 6 56.06N 5.34W
Cristóbal Colón mtn. Colombia 60 10.53N 73.48W
Crişu Alb r. Romania 15 46.42N 21.17E
Crna r. Macedonia 13 41.33N 21.58E
Crna Gora d. Yugo. 13 43.00N 19.30E
Croaghnameal mtn. Rep. of Ire. 7 54.40N 7.57W
Croatia Europe 13 45.10N 15.30E
Crocodile r. R.S.A. 39 24.11S 26.48E
Croker I. Australia 44 11.12S 132.32E
Cromarty U.K. 6 57.40N 4.02W
Cromarty Firth est. U.K. 6 57.41N 4.10W
Cromer U.K. 4 52.56N 1.18E
Cromwell New Zealand 48 45.03S 169.14E
Crooked I. Bahamas 57 22.45N 74.00W
Crookhaven Rep. of Ire. 7 51.29N 9.45W
Crookwell Australia 47 34.27S 149.28E
Croom Rep. of Ire. 7 52.31N 8.43W
Croppa Creek town Australia 47 29.08S 150.28E
Crosby I.o.M Europe 4 54.11N 4.34W
Cross Fell mtn. U.K. 4 54.43N 2.28W
Cross River d. Nigeria 38 5.45N 8.25E
Cross Sd. U.S.A. 50 58.10N 136.30W
Crotone Italy 13 39.05N 17.06E
Crow Agency U.S.A. 54 45.36N 107.27W
Crowl Creek r. Australia 47 31.58S 144.53E
Crowsnest Pass Canada 50 49.40N 114.41W
Croyde U.K. 5 51.07N 4.13W
Croyden Australia 41 18.12S 142.14E
Croydon Australia 44 18.12S 142.14E
Croydon U.K. 5 51.23N 0.06W
Crucero U.S.A. 54 35.03N 116.10W
Cruz Alta Brazil 59 28.38S 53.38W
Cruz, Cabo c. Cuba 57 19.52N 77.44W
Cruz del Eje Argentina 62 30.44S 64.49W
Cruzeiro Brazil 59 22.33S 44.59W
Cruzeiro do Sul Brazil 60 7.40S 72.39W
Crystal Brook town Australia 46 33.21S 138.13E
Csorna Hungary 15 47.37N 17.16E
Csurgó Hungary 15 46.16N 17.06E
Cuamba Mozambique 37 14.48S 36.32E
Cuando r. Angola 36 18.30S 23.32E
Cuangar Angola 39 17.34S 18.39E
Cuango r. see Kwango r. Angola 36
Cuanza r. Angola 36 9.22S 13.09E
Cuaró Uruguay 63 30.37S 56.54W
Cuaró r. Uruguay 63 30.15S 57.01W
Cuba C. America 57 22.00N 79.00W
Cuballing Australia 43 32.50S 117.07E
Cubango r. see Okavango r. Angola 36
Cubo Mozambique 39 23.48S 33.55E
Cuckfield U.K. 5 51.00N 0.08W
Cucuí Brazil 60 1.12N 66.50W
Cúcuta Colombia 60 7.55N 72.31W
Cuddalore India 29 11.43N 79.46E
Cue Australia 42 27.25S 117.54E
Cuenca Ecuador 60 2.54S 79.00W
Cuenca Spain 10 40.04N 2.07W
Cuenca, Serranía de mts. Spain 10 40.25N 2.00W
Cuernavaca Mexico 56 18.57N 99.15W
Cuero U.S.A. 53 29.06N 97.19W
Cuiabá Brazil 61 15.32S 56.05W
Cuiabá r. Brazil 62 18.00S 57.25W
Cuillin Hills U.K. 6 57.12N 6.13W
Cuito r. Angola 39 18.01S 20.50E
Culcairn Australia 47 35.40S 147.03E
Culemborg Neth. 8 51.57N 5.14E
Culgoa r. Australia 47 29.56S 146.20E
Culiacán Mexico 56 24.48N 107.24W
Cullen U.K. 6 57.41N 2.50W
Cullera Spain 10 39.10N 0.15W
Cullin Sd. U.K. 6 57.03N 6.13W
Culloden Moor U.K. 6 57.29N 3.55W
Culpeper U.S.A. 55 38.28N 77.53W
Culuene r. Brazil 61 12.56S 52.51W
Culver, Pt. Australia 43 32.52S 124.41E
Cumaná Venezuela 60 10.29N 64.12W
Cumberland Md. U.S.A. 55 39.39N 78.46W
Cumberland r. U.S.A. 53 37.16N 88.25W
Cumberland, L. U.S.A. 53 37.00N 85.00W
Cumberland Pen. Canada 51 66.50N 64.00W
Cumberland Sd. Canada 51 65.00N 65.30W
Cumbernauld U.K. 6 55.57N 4.00W
Cumbria d. U.K. 4 54.30N 3.00W
Cumbrian Mts. U.K. 4 54.32N 3.05W
Cuminá r. Brazil 61 1.30S 56.00W
Cummins Australia 46 34.16S 135.44E
Cumnock Australia 47 32.56S 148.46E
Cumnock U.K. 6 55.27N 4.15W
Cunderdin Australia 43 31.39S 117.15E
Cunene d. Angola 39 16.00S 16.00E
Cunene r. Angola 39 17.15S 11.50E
Cuneo Italy 9 44.22N 7.32E
Cungena Australia 46 32.33S 134.40E
Cunnamulla Australia 47 28.04S 145.40E
Cuokkaraš'ša mtn. Norway 16 69.57N 24.32E
Cuorgnè Italy 9 45.23N 7.39E
Cupar U.K. 6 56.19N 3.01W
Cupica, Golfo de g. Colombia 60 6.35N 77.25W
Curaçao i. Neth. Antilles 60 12.15N 69.00W
Curacautín Chile 63 38.26S 71.53W
Curaco r. Argentina 63 38.49S 65.01W
Curanilahue Chile 63 37.28S 73.21W
Curaray r. Peru 60 2.20S 74.05W
Curban Australia 47 31.33S 148.36E
Curdlawidny L. Australia 46 30.16S 136.20E
Cure r. France 9 47.40N 3.41E
Curiapo Venezuela 60 8.33N 61.05W
Curicó Chile 63 34.59S 71.14W
Curitiba Brazil 59 25.24S 49.16W
Curlewis Australia 47 31.08S 150.16E
Curnamona Australia 46 31.40S 139.35E
Currane, Lough Rep. of Ire. 7 51.50N 10.07W
Currant U.S.A. 54 38.44N 115.30W
Curranyalpa Australia 47 30.57S 144.33E
Currie Australia 45 39.56S 143.52E

rie U.S.A. 54 40.17N 114.44W
tin Australia 43 30.50S 122.05E
tis I. Australia 44 23.38S 151.09E
uá r. Brazil 61 5.23S 54.22W
urupu Brazil 61 1.50S 44.52W
uzú Cuatiá Argentina 63 29.50S 58.05W
velo Brazil 59 18.45S 44.27W
shendall U.K. 7 55.06N 6.05W
sna, Monte mtn. Italy 9 44.17N 10.23E
Bank U.S.A. 54 48.38N 112.20W
ttaburra Creek r. Australia 47 29.18S 145.00E
ttack India 29 20.26N 85.56E
khaven Germany 14 53.52N 8.42E
yuni r. Guyana 60 6.24N 58.38W
zco Peru 60 13.32S 71.57W
mbran U.K. 5 51.39N 3.01W
lades is. see Kikládhes is. Greece 13
nthiana U.S.A. 55 38.22N 84.18W
prus Asia 32 35.00N 33.00E
renaica f. see Barqah f. Libya 35
ech Republic Europe 14 49.30N 15.00E
eremcha Poland 15 52.32N 23.15E
ersk Poland 15 53.48N 18.00E
ęstochowa Poland 15 50.49N 19.07E
an China 25 45.30N 124.18E
'ah Jordan 32 31.36N 36.04E
bakala Côte d'Ivoire 38 8.19N 4.24W
bāgh, Jabal mtn. Saudi Arabia 32 27.51N .43E
cca see Dhākā Bangla. 29
chau Germany 14 48.15N 11.26E
danawa Guyana 60 2.30N 59.30W
du Pakistan 28 26.44N 67.47E
du He r. China 29 28.47N 104.40E
et Phil. 27 14.07N 122.58E
gali Norway 17 60.25N 8.27E
gana Senegal 34 16.28N 15.35W
gua P.N.G. 27 3.25S 143.20E
guan China 24 27.44N 103.53E
gupan Phil. 27 16.02N 120.21E
guragu Australia 42 17.33S 130.30E
Hinggan Ling mts. China 25 50.00N 122.10E
hlak Archipelago is. Eritrea 35 15.45N 40.30E
hlem Germany 14 50.23N 6.33E
hūk Iraq 30 36.52N 43.00E
miel Spain 10 39.05N 3.35W
tō Japan 23 34.42N 135.38E
arra Australia 44 21.42S 139.31E
ing China 25 28.24N 121.08E
kar Senegal 34 14.38N 17.27W
khal, Wādī ad r. Egypt 32 28.49N 32.45E
khilah, Al Wāḥāt ad oasis Egypt 30 25.30N .10E
khla W. Sahara 34 23.43N 15.57W
kingari Nigeria 38 11.40N 4.06E
kovica Yugo. 13 42.23N 20.25E
kwa Zaïre 36 4.00N 26.26E
r. Sweden 17 60.38N 17.27E
andzadgad Mongolia 24 43.34N 104.20E
Lat Vietnam 26 11.56N 108.25E
beattie U.K. 6 54.55N 3.49W
by Australia 45 27.11S 151.12E
by Sweden 17 55.40N 13.20E
e Hordaland Norway 17 60.35N 5.49E
e Sogn og Fj. Norway 17 61.22N 5.24E
en Norway 17 59.27N 8.00E
housie Canada 55 48.03N 66.22W
i China 24 25.33N 100.09E
i China 24 25.42N 100.11E
ian China 25 38.53N 121.37E
keith U.K. 6 55.54N 3.04W
las Oreg. U.S.A. 54 44.55N 123.19W
las Tex. U.S.A. 53 32.47N 96.48W
mally U.K. 6 56.25N 4.58W
mellington U.K. 6 55.19N 4.24W
nerechensk Russian Fed. 25 45.55N 133.45E
oa Côte d'Ivoire 34 6.56N 6.28W
ou Shan mts. China 24 28.00N 106.40E
rymple, Mt. Australia 44 21.02S 148.38E
ton Canada 55 48.10N 84.04W
tonganj India 29 24.02N 84.07E
vik Iceland 16 65.58N 18.28W
whinnie U.K. 6 56.56N 4.15W
y r. Australia 42 13.20S 130.19E
y City U.S.A. 54 37.42N 122.29W
y Waters town Australia 44 16.15S 133.22E
mān India 28 20.25N 72.58E
manhūr Egypt 32 31.03N 30.28E
mar i. Indonesia 27 7.10S 128.30E
mascus see Dimashq Syria 32
maturu Nigeria 38 11.49N 11.50E
māvand, Qolleh-ye mtn. Iran 31 35.47N .04E
mā, Wādī r. Saudi Arabia 30 27.04N 35.48E
mba Angola 36 6.44S 15.17E
mghān Iran 31 36.09N 54.22E
mmartin-en-Goële France 9 49.03N 2.41E
mongo Ghana 38 9.06N 1.48W
mpier Australia 42 20.40S 116.42E
mpier Land Australia 42 17.20S 123.00E
mpier, Selat str. Pacific Oc. 27 0.30S 130.50E
mqawt Yemen 28 16.34N 52.54E
Nang Vietnam 26 16.04N 108.14E
nba China 24 30.57N 101.55E
nbury Conn. U.S.A. 55 41.24N 73.26W
ndaragan Australia 43 30.40S 115.42E
ndenong Australia 47 37.59S 145.14E
ndong China 25 40.06N 124.25E
ngriga Belize 57 16.58N 88.13W
niel U.S.A. 54 42.52N 110.04W
nilov Russian Fed. 18 58.10N 40.12E
ning China 25 36.32N 110.47E
nisa Hills Kenya 37 3.10N 39.37E
nja Nigeria 38 11.29N 7.30E
nlí Honduras 57 14.02N 86.30W
nnenberg Germany 14 53.06N 11.05E
Dannevirke New Zealand 48 40.12S 176.08E
Dannhauser R.S.A. 39 28.00S 30.03E
Dansville U.S.A. 55 42.34N 77.41W
Danube r. Europe 15 45.26N 29.38E
Danube, Mouths of the see Dunării, Delta f. Romania 15
Danville Va. U.S.A. 53 36.34N 79.25W
Dan Xian China 25 19.31N 109.33E
Daoukro Côte d'Ivoire 38 7.10N 3.58W
Dapango Togo 38 10.51N 0.15E
Da Qaidam China 24 37.44N 95.08E
Daqq-e Patargān f. Iran 31 33.30N 60.40E
Dar'ā Syria 32 32.37N 36.06E
Dārāb Iran 31 28.45N 54.34E
Darabani Romania 15 48.11N 26.35E
Dārān Iran 31 33.00N 50.27E
Darband, Kūh-e mtn. Iran 31 31.33N 57.08E
Darbhanga India 29 26.10N 85.54E
Darby Mont. U.S.A. 54 46.01N 114.11W
Dardanelles see Çanakkale Boğazi str. Turkey 13
Dar es Salaam Tanzania 37 6.51S 39.18E
Dar es Salaam d. Tanzania 37 34.04S 142.40E
Dareton Australia 46 34.04S 142.04E
Darfield New Zealand 48 43.29S 172.07E
Dargan Ata Turkmenistan 20 40.30N 62.10E
Dargaville New Zealand 48 35.57S 173.53E
Dargo Australia 47 37.30S 147.16E
Darhan Mongolia 24 49.34N 106.23E
Darién, Golfo del g. Colombia 60 9.20N 77.30W
Darjeeling India 29 27.02N 88.20E
Darkan Australia 43 33.19S 116.42E
Darke Peak mtn. Australia 46 33.28S 136.12E
Darling r. Australia 46 34.05S 141.57E
Darling Downs f. Australia 45 28.00S 149.45E
Darling Range mts. Australia 43 32.00S 116.30E
Darlington U.K. 4 54.33N 1.33W
Darlington Point town Australia 47 34.36S 146.01E
Darłowo Poland 14 54.26N 16.23E
Darmstadt Germany 14 49.52N 8.30E
Darnah Libya 35 32.45N 22.39E
Darnétal France 9 49.27N 1.09E
Darnick Australia 46 32.55S 143.39E
Darnley, C. Antarctica 64 68.00S 69.00E
Daroca Spain 10 41.09N 1.25W
Darreh Gaz Iran 31 37.22N 59.08E
Dartmoor Australia 46 37.58S 141.19E
Dartmoor Forest hills U.K. 5 50.33N 3.55W
Dartmouth Canada 51 44.40N 63.34W
Dartmouth U.K. 5 50.21N 3.35W
Dartmouth Resr. Australia 47 36.36S 147.38E
Dartry Mts. Rep. of Ire. 7 54.23N 8.25W
Daru P.N.G. 44 9.04S 143.12E
Darvaza Turkmenistan 20 40.12N 58.24E
Darvel, Teluk b. Malaysia 26 4.40N 118.30E
Darwen U.K. 4 53.42N 2.29W
Darwin Australia 44 12.23S 130.44E
Daryācheh-ye Bakhtegān l. Iran 31 29.20N 54.05E
Daryācheh-ye Namak l. Iran 31 34.45N 51.36E
Daryācheh-ye Orūmīyeh l. Iran 31 37.40N 45.28E
Daryācheh-ye Sīstān f. Iran 31 31.00N 61.15E
Dasht r. Pakistan 28 25.07N 61.45E
Dashte-e Mārgow des. Afghan. 31 30.45N 63.00E
Dasht-e Kavīr des. Iran 31 34.40N 55.00E
Dasht-e Lūt des. Iran 31 31.30N 58.00E
Dassa-Zoumé Benin 38 7.50N 2.13E
Dastgardān Iran 31 34.19N 56.51E
Dastjerd Iran 31 34.33N 50.15E
Datong China 25 40.12N 113.12E
Datteln Germany 8 51.40N 7.20E
Datu Piang Phil. 27 7.02N 124.30E
Datu, Tanjung c. Malaysia 26 2.00N 109.30E
Daugavpils Latvia 18 55.52N 26.31E
Daun Germany 8 50.11N 6.50E
Dauphin Canada 51 51.09N 100.05W
Dauphiné, Alpes du mts. France 11 44.35N 5.45E
Daura Nigeria 38 13.05N 8.18E
Dāvangere India 28 14.30N 75.52E
Davao Phil. 27 7.05N 125.38E
Davao G. Phil. 27 6.30N 126.00E
Davenport U.S.A. 53 41.40N 90.36W
Daventry U.K. 5 52.16N 1.10W
David Panama 57 8.26N 82.26W
David-Gorodok Belarus 15 52.04N 27.10E
Davis U.S.A. 54 38.33N 121.44W
Davis Creek town U.S.A. 54 41.44N 120.24W
Davis Sea Antarctica 64 66.00S 90.00E
Davis Str. N. America 51 66.00N 58.00W
Davlekanovo Russian Fed. 18 54.12N 55.00E
Davos Switz. 14 46.47N 9.50E
Dawei see Tavoy Myanmar 29
Dawlish U.K. 5 50.34N 3.28W
Dawna Range mts. Myanmar 29 16.10N 98.30E
Dawson Canada 50 64.04N 139.24W
Dawson Creek town Canada 50 55.44N 120.15W
Dawson Range f. Canada 50 62.40N 139.00W
Dawu China 24 31.00N 101.09E
Dax France 11 43.43N 1.03W
Daxian China 29 31.10N 107.28E
Daylesford Australia 46 37.22S 144.12E
Dayman r. Uruguay 63 31.25S 58.00W
Dayr az Zawr Syria 30 35.20N 40.08E
Dayton Ohio U.S.A. 55 39.45N 84.10W
Dayton Wash. U.S.A. 54 46.19N 117.59W
Daytona Beach town U.S.A. 53 29.11N 81.01W
De Aar R.S.A. 39 30.39S 24.01E
Dead Sea Jordan 32 31.25N 35.30E
Deal U.K. 5 51.13N 1.25E
Deán Funes Argentina 62 30.25S 64.20W
Dearborn U.S.A. 55 42.18N 83.14W
Dease Arm b. Canada 50 66.52N 119.37W
Death Valley f. U.S.A. 54 36.30N 117.00W
Death Valley town U.S.A. 54 36.18N 116.25W
Death Valley Nat. Monument U.S.A. 54 36.30N 117.00W
Deauville France 9 49.21N 0.04E
Debar Macedonia 13 41.31N 20.31E
Debica Poland 15 50.04N 21.24E
Deblin Poland 15 51.35N 21.50E
Deborah, L. Australia 43 30.45S 119.07E
Debrecen Hungary 15 47.30N 21.37E
Debre Tabor Ethiopia 35 11.50N 38.05E
Decatur Ill. U.S.A. 53 39.44N 88.57W
Decatur Ind. U.S.A. 55 40.50N 84.57W
Deccan f. India 28 18.30N 77.30E
Decelles, Lac l. Canada 55 47.40N 78.08W
Děčín Czech Republic 14 50.48N 14.15E
Decize France 14 46.50N 3.27E
De Cocksdorp Neth. 8 53.12N 4.52E
Deda Romania 15 46.57N 24.53E
Dédi Côte d'Ivoire 38 8.34N 3.33W
Dedza Malaŵi 37 14.20S 34.24E
Dee r. D. and G. U.K. 6 54.50N 4.05W
Dee r. Grampian U.K. 6 57.07N 2.04W
Dee r. Wales U.K. 4 53.13N 3.05W
Deep River town Canada 55 46.06N 77.30W
Deepwater Australia 47 29.26S 151.51E
Deep Well Australia 44 24.25S 134.05E
Deer Lodge U.S.A. 54 46.24N 112.44W
Deesa India 28 24.15N 72.10E
Deeth U.S.A. 54 41.04N 115.18W
Defiance U.S.A. 55 41.17N 84.21W
Deggendorf Germany 14 48.51N 12.59E
De Grey r. Australia 42 20.12S 119.11E
Deh Bīd Iran 31 30.38N 53.12E
Dehra Dūn India 29 30.19N 78.00E
Deinze Belgium 8 50.59N 3.32E
Dej Romania 15 47.08N 23.55E
Deje Sweden 17 59.36N 13.28E
Dekina Nigeria 38 7.43N 7.04E
Delano U.S.A. 54 35.41N 119.15W
Delaware d. U.S.A. 55 39.10N 75.30W
Delaware r. U.S.A. 55 39.20N 75.25W
Delaware town U.S.A. 55 40.18N 83.06W
Delaware B. U.S.A. 55 39.05N 75.15W
Delegate Australia 47 37.03S 148.58E
Delfinópolis Brazil 59 20.21S 46.51W
Delft Neth. 8 52.01N 4.23E
Delfzijl Neth. 8 53.20N 6.56E
Delgado, C. Mozambique 37 10.45S 40.38E
Delhi India 28 28.40N 77.14E
Delicias Mexico 56 28.13N 105.28W
Delingha China 24 37.16N 97.12E
Delmenhorst Germany 14 53.03N 8.37E
De Long Mts. U.S.A. 50 68.20N 162.00W
Delphos U.S.A. 55 40.50N 84.21W
Del Rio U.S.A. 52 29.23N 100.56W
Delta d. Nigeria 38 5.30N 6.00E
Delta Colo. U.S.A. 54 38.44N 108.04W
Delta Utah U.S.A. 54 39.21N 112.35W
Delungra Australia 47 29.38S 150.50E
Demer r. Belgium 8 50.59N 4.42E
Deming U.S.A. 52 32.16N 107.45W
Demmin Germany 14 53.54N 13.02E
Demonte Italy 9 44.19N 7.17E
Demotte U.S.A. 55 41.07N 87.14W
Denain France 8 50.20N 3.24E
Denakil f. Ethiopia 35 13.00N 41.00E
Denbigh U.K. 4 53.11N 3.25W
Den Burg Neth. 8 53.03N 4.47E
Dendermonde Belgium 8 51.01N 4.07E
Dendre r. Belgium 8 51.01N 4.07E
Denham Australia 42 25.54S 113.35E
Denham Range mts. Australia 44 21.55S 147.46E
Den Helder Neth. 8 52.58N 4.46E
Denia Spain 10 38.51N 0.07E
Deniliquin Australia 47 35.33S 144.58E
Denizli Turkey 30 37.46N 29.05E
Denman Australia 47 32.23S 150.42E
Denmark Australia 43 34.54S 117.25E
Denmark Europe 17 55.50N 10.00E
Den Oever Neth. 8 52.56N 5.01E
Denpasar Indonesia 26 8.40S 115.14E
Denton Mont. U.S.A. 54 47.19N 109.57W
D'Entrecasteaux Is. P.N.G. 44 9.30S 150.40E
D'Entrecasteaux, Pt. Australia 43 34.50S 116.00E
Denver U.S.A. 52 39.43N 105.01W
Deo r. Cameroon 38 8.33N 12.45E
Deogarh Orissa India 29 21.22N 84.45E
De Peel f. Belgium 8 51.30N 5.50E
Depew U.S.A. 55 42.54N 78.41W
Dêqên China 24 28.45N 98.58E
Dera Ghāzi Khān Pakistan 28 30.05N 70.44E
Dera Ismāīl Khān Pakistan 28 31.51N 70.56E
Derazhnya Ukraine 15 49.18N 27.28E
Derbent Russian Fed. 31 42.03N 48.18E
Derby Tas. Australia 45 41.08S 147.47E
Derby W.A. Australia 42 17.19S 123.38E
Derby U.K. 4 52.55N 1.28W
Derbyshire d. U.K. 4 52.55N 1.28W
Derg, Lough Donegal Rep. of Ire. 7 54.37N 7.55W
Derg, Lough Tipperary Rep. of Ire. 7 52.57N 8.18W
Déroute, Passage de la str. France/U.K. 5 49.10N 1.45W
Derrynasaggart Mts. Rep. of Ire. 7 51.58N 9.15W
Derryveagh Mts. Rep. of Ire. 7 55.00N 8.07W
Derval France 9 47.40N 1.40W
Derwent r. Cumbria U.K. 4 54.38N 3.34W
Derwent r. N. Yorks. U.K. 4 53.44N 0.57W
Desaguadero r. Bolivia 62 18.24S 67.05W
Deschutes r. U.S.A. 54 45.38N 120.54W
Desē Ethiopia 35 11.05N 39.40E
Deseado Argentina 63 47.39S 65.20W
Deseado r. Argentina 63 47.45S 65.50W
Desenzano del Garda Italy 9 45.28N 10.32E
Desert Center U.S.A. 54 33.44N 115.25W
Des Moines Iowa U.S.A. 53 41.35N 93.35W
Desna r. Ukraine 15 50.32N 30.37E
Dessau Germany 14 51.51N 12.15E
Dete Zimbabwe 39 18.39S 26.49E
Detroit U.S.A. 55 42.23N 83.05W
Deurne Belgium 8 51.13N 4.26E
Deurne Neth. 8 51.29N 5.44E
Deutsche Bucht b. Germany 14 54.00N 8.15E
Deva Romania 15 45.54N 22.55E
Deventer Neth. 8 52.15N 6.10E
Deveron r. U.K. 6 57.40N 2.30W
Devil's Bridge U.K. 5 52.23N 3.50W
Devils Lake town U.S.A. 52 48.08N 98.50W
Devin Bulgaria 13 41.44N 24.24E
Devizes U.K. 5 51.21N 2.00W
Devon d. U.K. 5 50.50N 3.40W
Devon I. Canada 51 75.00N 86.00W
Devonport Australia 45 41.09S 146.16E
Devrez r. Turkey 30 41.07N 34.25E
Dewsbury U.K. 4 53.42N 1.38W
Dey-Dey L. Australia 45 29.12S 131.02E
Dez r. Iran 31 31.38N 48.54E
Dezfūl Iran 31 32.24N 48.27E
Dezhou China 25 37.29N 116.11E
Dezh Shāhpūr Iran 31 35.31N 46.10E
Dhahab Egypt 32 28.30N 34.31E
Dhahran see Aẓ Ẓahrān Saudi Arabia 31
Dhākā Bangla. 29 23.43N 90.25E
Dhānbād India 29 23.47N 86.32E
Dhaulāgiri mtn. Nepal 29 28.39N 83.28E
Dhodhekánisos is. Greece 13 37.00N 27.00E
Dholpur India 28 26.43N 77.54E
Dhule India 28 20.52N 74.50E
Diamante Argentina 63 32.05S 60.35W
Diamantina r. Australia 44 26.45S 139.10E
Diamantina Brazil 59 18.17S 43.37W
Diamantina, Chapada hills Brazil 61 13.00S 42.30W
Diamantino Brazil 59 14.25S 56.29W
Diane Bank is. Australia 44 15.50S 149.48E
Diapaga Burkina 38 12.04N 1.48E
Dibi Cameroon 38 7.09N 13.43E
Dibrugarh India 29 27.29N 94.56E
Dickinson U.S.A. 52 46.53N 102.47W
Dicle r. Turkey see Dijlah r. Asia 30
Didcot U.K. 5 51.36N 1.14W
Die France 11 44.45N 5.23E
Diekirch Lux. 8 49.52N 6.10E
Diélette France 9 49.33N 1.52W
Diemen Neth. 8 52.22N 4.58E
Diemuchuoke Jammu & Kashmir 29 32.42N 79.29E
Dien Bien Phu Vietnam 26 21.23N 103.02E
Diepholz Germany 14 52.35N 8.21E
Dieppe France 9 49.55N 1.05E
Dierdorf Germany 8 50.33N 7.38E
Dieren Neth. 8 52.03N 6.06E
Diesdorf Germany 14 52.45N 10.52E
Diest Belgium 8 50.59N 5.03E
Dieuze France 11 48.49N 6.43E
Dif Kenya 37 1.04N 40.57E
Diffa Niger 38 13.19N 12.35E
Diffa d. Niger 38 16.00N 13.00E
Digne France 11 44.05N 6.14E
Digoin France 11 46.29N 3.59E
Digul r. Indonesia 27 7.10S 139.08E
Dijlah r. Asia 31 31.00N 47.27E
Dijle r. Belgium 8 51.02N 4.25E
Dijon France 11 47.20N 5.02E
Dikhil Djibouti 35 11.06N 42.22E
Dikili Turkey 13 39.05N 26.52E
Dikirnis Egypt 32 31.05N 31.35E
Dikodougou Côte d'Ivoire 38 9.00N 5.45W
Diksmuide Belgium 8 51.01N 2.52E
Dikwa Nigeria 38 12.01N 13.55E
Dili Indonesia 27 8.35S 125.35E
Dilling Sudan 35 12.03N 29.39E
Dillingham U.S.A. 50 59.02N 158.29W
Dillon U.S.A. 54 45.13N 112.38W
Dimashq Syria 32 33.30N 36.19E
Dimbokro Côte d'Ivoire 38 6.43N 4.46W
Dimboola Australia 46 36.27S 142.02E
Dîmbovița r. Romania 15 44.13N 26.22E
Dimitrovgrad Bulgaria 13 42.01N 25.34E
Dimona Israel 32 31.04N 35.01E
Dinagat i. Phil. 27 10.15N 125.30E
Dinan France 11 48.27N 2.02W
Dinant Belgium 8 50.16N 4.55E
Dinar Turkey 30 38.05N 30.09E
Dinara Planina mts. Europe 14 44.00N 16.30E
Dīnār, Kūh-e mtn. Iran 31 30.45N 51.39E
Dindigul India 28 10.23N 78.00E
Dingle Rep. of Ire. 7 52.09N 10.17W
Dingle B. Rep. of Ire. 7 52.05N 10.12W
Dingolfing Germany 14 48.38N 12.31E
Dingwall U.K. 6 57.35N 4.26W
Dinokwe Botswana 39 23.24S 26.40E
Dinuba U.S.A. 54 36.32N 119.23W
Diö Sweden 17 56.38N 14.13E
Diourbel Senegal 34 14.30N 16.10W
Dipolog Phil. 27 8.34N 123.28E
Dirdal Norway 17 58.47N 6.14E
Diré Mali 38 16.16N 3.24W
Direction, C. Australia 44 12.51S 143.32E
Dirē Dawa Ethiopia 35 9.35N 41.50E
Dirico Angola 39 17.58S 20.40E
Dirk Hartog I. Australia 42 25.50S 113.00E
Dirranbandi Australia 47 28.35S 148.10E
Disappointment, L. Australia 42 23.30S 122.55E
Disaster B. Australia 47 37.20S 149.58E
Discovery Canada 50 63.10N 113.58W
Discovery B. Australia 46 38.12S 141.07E
Disko i. Greenland 51 69.45N 53.00W
Disneyland Paris France 9 48.50N 2.50E
Diss U.K. 5 52.23N 1.06E
Distrito Federal d. Brazil 61 15.45S 47.50W
Distrito Federal d. Mexico 56 19.20N 99.10W
Disūq Egypt 32 31.09N 30.39E
Diu India 28 20.41N 70.59E
Diver Canada 55 46.43N 79.30W
Dives r. France 9 49.19N 0.05W
Divinópolis Brazil 59 20.08S 44.55W
Divnoye Russian Fed. 19 45.55N 43.21E
Divo Côte d'Ivoire 38 5.48N 5.15W
Divriği Turkey 30 39.23N 38.06E
Dixcove Ghana 38 4.49N 1.57W
Dixie U.S.A. 54 45.34N 115.28W
Dixon Entrance str. Canada/U.S.A. 50 54.10N 133.30W
Diyālā r. Iraq 31 33.13N 44.33E
Diyarbakir Turkey 30 37.55N 40.14E
Djado Niger 34 21.00N 12.20E
Djado, Plateau du f. Niger 34 22.00N 12.30E
Djambala Congo 36 2.33S 14.38E
Djanet Algeria 34 24.34N 9.29E
Djelfa Algeria 34 34.43N 3.14E
Djénne Mali 38 13.55N 4.31W
Djibo Burkina 38 14.09N 1.38W
Djibouti Africa 35 12.00N 42.50E
Djibouti town Djibouti 35 11.35N 43.11E
Djougou Benin 38 9.40N 1.47E
Djugu Zaïre 37 1.55N 30.31E
Djúpivogur Iceland 16 64.41N 14.16W
Dmitriya Lapteva, Proliv str. Russian Fed. 21 73.00N 142.00E
Dnepr r. Ukraine 15 50.00N 31.00E
Dneprodzerzhinsk Ukraine 19 48.30N 34.37E
Dnepropetrovsk Ukraine 19 48.29N 35.00E
Dneprovskaya Nizmennost f. Belarus 15 52.30N 29.45E
Dneprovsko-Bugskiy Kanal Belarus 15 52.03N 25.35E
Dnestr r. Ukraine 15 46.21N 30.20E
Dnieper see Dnepr r. Belarus 15
Dniester see Dnestr r. Ukraine 15
Dno Russian Fed. 18 57.50N 30.00E
Doba Chad 34 8.40N 16.50E
Dobele Latvia 17 56.37N 23.16E
Dobo Indonesia 27 5.46S 134.13E
Doboj Bosnia-Herzegovina 15 44.44N 18.02E
Dobrich Bulgaria 13 43.34N 27.52E
Dobrodzień Poland 15 50.44N 18.27E
Dobruja f. Romania 15 44.30N 28.15E
Dobrush Belarus 15 52.24N 31.19E
Dobryanka Russian Fed. 18 58.30N 56.26E
Doce r. Brazil 59 19.32S 39.57W
Docking U.K. 4 52.55N 0.39E
Doda, Lac l. Canada 55 49.24N 75.13W
Dodecanese is. see Dhodhekánisos is. Greece 13
Dodge City U.S.A. 52 37.45N 100.02W
Dodman Pt. U.K. 5 50.13N 4.48W
Dodoma Tanzania 37 6.10S 35.40E
Dodoma d. Tanzania 37 6.00S 36.00E
Dodson U.S.A. 54 48.24N 108.15W
Doetinchem Neth. 8 51.57N 6.17E
Dogai Coring l. China 29 34.30N 89.00E
Doğubayazit Turkey 31 39.32N 44.08E
Doha see Ad Dawḥah Qatar 31
Dokkum Neth. 8 53.20N 6.00E
Dolbeau Canada 55 48.52N 72.15W
Dol-de-Bretagne France 9 48.33N 1.45W
Dole France 11 47.05N 5.30E
Dolgellau U.K. 5 52.44N 3.53W
Dolina Ukraine 15 49.00N 23.59E
Dolinskaya Ukraine 19 48.06N 32.46E
Dollard b. Germany 8 53.20N 7.10E
Dolny Kubín Slovakia 15 49.12N 19.17E
Dolomiti mts. Italy 9 46.25N 11.50E
Dolores Argentina 63 36.19S 57.40W
Dolores Uruguay 63 33.33S 58.13W
Dolores U.S.A. 54 37.28N 108.30W
Dolphin and Union Str. Canada 50 69.20N 118.00W
Doma Nigeria 38 8.23N 8.21E
Domadare Somali Rep. 37 1.48N 41.13E
Domažlice Czech Republic 14 49.27N 12.56E
Dombås Norway 17 62.05N 9.08E
Dombey, C. Australia 46 37.12S 139.43E
Dombóvár Hungary 15 46.23N 18.08E
Domburg Neth. 8 51.35N 3.31E
Domfront France 9 48.36N 0.39W
Dominica Windward Is. 57 15.30N 61.30W
Dominican Republic C. America 57 18.00N 70.00W
Dommel r. Neth. 8 51.44N 5.17E
Domo Ethiopia 35 7.54N 46.52E
Domodossola Italy 9 46.07N 8.17E
Domuyo mtn. Argentina 63 36.37S 70.28W
Don r. Russian Fed. 19 47.06N 39.16E
Don r. England U.K. 4 53.41N 0.50W
Don r. Scotland U.K. 6 57.10N 2.05W
Donaghadee U.K. 7 54.39N 5.33W
Donald Australia 46 36.25S 143.04E
Donau r. Germany see Danube r. Europe 14
Donaueschingen Germany 14 47.57N 8.29E
Donauwörth Germany 14 48.44N 10.48E
Don Benito Spain 10 38.57N 5.52W
Doncaster U.K. 4 53.31N 1.09W
Dondo Mozambique 39 19.39S 34.39E
Donegal Rep. of Ire. 7 54.39N 8.06W
Donegal d. Rep. of Ire. 7 54.52N 8.00W
Donegal B. Rep. of Ire. 7 54.32N 8.18W
Donegal Pt. Rep. of Ire. 7 52.43N 9.38W
Donetsk Ukraine 19 48.00N 37.50E
Donga Nigeria 38 7.45N 10.05E
Donga r. Nigeria 38 8.20N 10.00E
Dongara Australia 43 29.15S 114.56E
Dongbei Pingyuan f. China 25 42.30N 123.00E
Dongchuan China 24 26.10N 103.02E
Dongfang China 25 19.04N 108.39E
Donggala Indonesia 26 0.48S 119.45E
Dong Hoi Vietnam 26 17.32N 106.35E
Dongkalang Indonesia 27 0.12N 120.07E
Dongou Congo 36 2.05N 18.00E
Dongsheng China 25 39.49N 109.59E
Dongtai China 25 32.51N 120.18E
Dongting Hu l. China 25 29.40N 113.00E
Donington U.K. 4 52.55N 0.12W
Donja Stubica Croatia 14 45.59N 15.58E
Dönna i. Norway 16 66.05N 12.30E
Donnacona Canada 55 46.41N 71.45W

83

a Mozambique 39 26.11S 32.08E
abis Namibia 39 22.28S 18.58E
des. Asia 24 43.30N 103.30E
n Germany 8 51.41N 6.09E
nas Namibia 39 24.50S 18.48E
alming U.K. 5 51.11N 0.37W
āvari r. India 29 16.40N 82.15E
bout Canada 55 49.20N 67.38W
erich Canada 55 43.45N 81.43W
erville France 9 49.39N 0.22E
navn Greenland 51 69.20N 53.30W
nra India 28 22.49N 73.40E
oy Cruz Argentina 63 32.55S 68.50W
s L. Canada 51 54.40N 94.20W
thåb Greenland 51 64.10N 51.40W
land, Lac au l. Canada 55 49.47N 76.41W
s Neth. 8 51.30N 3.54E
ama Canada 55 47.35N 81.35W
onou Benin 38 10.50N 2.50E
ra r. see Ghāghra India 29
ana Brazil 61 7.30S 35.00W
nia Brazil 61 16.43S 49.18W
s Brazil 61 15.57S 50.07W
s d. Brazil 61 15.00S 48.00W
o Italy 9 45.15N 10.40E
Japan 23 34.21N 135.42E
çeada i. Turkey 13 40.10N 25.51E
sun Turkey 30 38.03N 36.30E
teik Myanmar 29 22.26N 97.00E
we Zimbabwe 39 18.14S 28.54E
Norway 17 60.42N 8.57E
n Heights mts. Syria 32 32.55N 35.42E
conda U.S.A. 54 40.57N 117.30W
dap Poland 15 54.19N 22.19E
d Beach town U.S.A. 54 42.25N 124.25W
den Rep. of Ire. 7 52.30N 7.59W
den B. New Zealand 48 40.45S 172.50E
dendale U.S.A. 54 45.49N 120.50W
den Ridge town Australia 43 30.51S 121.42E
den Vale f. Rep. of Ire. 7 52.30N 8.07W
dfield U.S.A. 54 37.42N 117.14W
dsworthy Australia 42 20.20S 119.30E
eniów Poland 14 53.36N 14.50E
ets Skalisty mtn. Russian Fed. 21 56.00N
).40E
ito Costa Rica 57 8.42N 83.10W
o degli Aranci town Italy 12 41.00N 9.38E
ing Austria 14 47.36N 13.10E
nud China 24 36.22N 94.55E
ovanevsk Ukraine 15 48.25N 30.30E
bāyegān Iran 31 33.23N 50.18E
spie U.K. 6 57.58N 3.58W
na Zaïre 37 1.37S 29.10E
nbe Nigeria 38 10.17N 11.20E
nbe r. Tanzania 37 4.43S 31.30E
nel Belarus 15 52.25N 31.00E
nez Palacio Mexico 56 25.39N 103.30W
nīshān Iran 31 37.04N 54.06E
aïves Haiti 57 19.29N 72.42W
âve, Golfe de la g. Haiti 57 19.20N 73.00W
âve, Île de la i. Haiti 57 18.50N 73.00W
bad-e Kāvūs Iran 31 37.15N 55.11E
da India 29 27.08N 81.58E
der Ethiopia 35 12.39N 37.29E
dia India 29 21.27N 80.12E
gbo'gyamda China 29 29.56N 93.23E
gga Shan mtn. China 24 29.30N 101.30E
gola r. Nigeria 38 9.30N 12.06E
golgon Australia 47 30.22S 146.56E
i Uruguay 63 33.31S 56.24W
iri Nigeria 38 11.30N 12.15E
zaga Italy 9 44.57N 10.49E
d Hope, C. of R.S.A. 39 34.21S 18.28E
ding U.S.A. 54 42.56N 114.43W
dooga Australia 47 29.08S 147.30E
dsprings U.S.A. 54 35.50N 115.26W
le U.K. 4 53.42N 0.52W
lgowi Australia 47 33.59S 145.42E
lma Australia 47 32.21S 149.20E
loogong Australia 47 33.36S 148.27E
lwa Australia 46 35.31S 138.45E
malling Australia 43 31.19S 116.49E
mbalie Australia 47 29.59S 145.24E
ndiwindi Australia 47 28.30S 150.17E
ngarrie Australia 43 30.03S 121.09E
r Neth. 8 52.16N 6.33E
se L. U.S.A. 54 41.57N 120.25W
pingen Germany 14 48.43N 9.39E
akhpur India 29 26.45N 83.23E
don r. Australia 43 34.12S 117.00E
don Downs town Australia 42 18.43S
8.33E
donvale Australia 44 17.05S 145.47E
é Chad 34 7.57N 16.31E
ē Ethiopia 35 8.08N 35.33E
e New Zealand 48 46.06S 168.58E
gān Iran 31 36.50N 54.29E
gān r. Iran 31 37.00N 54.00E
Georgia 31 41.59N 44.05E
inchem Neth. 8 51.50N 4.59E
izia Italy 12 45.58N 13.37E
ki see Nizhniy Novgorod Russian Fed 18
kovskoye Vodokhranilishche resr. Russian
d. 18 56.49N 43.00E
litz Germany 14 51.09N 15.00E
ovka Ukraine 19 48.17N 38.05E
na Oryakhovitsa Bulgaria 13 43.07N 25.40E
no Altaysk Russian Fed. 20 51.59N 85.56E
no Filinskoye Russian Fed. 20 60.06N
.58E
nyatskiy Russian Fed. 18 67.30N 64.03E
odenka Ukraine 15 48.40N 25.30E
odishche Belarus 15 53.18N 26.00E
odishche Belarus 15 53.45N 29.45E
odnitsa Ukraine 15 50.50N 27.19E
odnya Ukraine 15 51.54N 31.37E
odok Ukraine 15 49.48N 23.39E
oka P.N.G. 27 6.02S 145.22E
oke Australia 46 36.43S 141.30E
Gorokhov Ukraine 15 50.30N 24.46E
Gorongosa r. Mozambique 39 20.29S 34.36E
Gorontalo Indonesia 27 0.33N 123.05E
Gort Rep. of Ire. 7 53.04N 8.49W
Goryn r. Ukraine 15 52.08N 27.17E
Gorzów Wielkopolski Poland 14 52.42N 15.12E
Gosford Australia 47 33.25S 151.18E
Goslar Germany 14 51.54N 10.25E
Gospić Croatia 14 44.34N 15.23E
Gosport U.K. 5 50.48N 1.08W
Gossi Mali 38 15.49N 1.17W
Gostivar Macedonia 13 41.47N 20.24E
Gostynin Poland 15 52.26N 19.29E
Göta r. Sweden 17 57.42N 11.52E
Göta Kanal Sweden 17 58.50N 13.58E
Göteborg Sweden 17 57.43N 11.58E
Göteborg och Bohus d. Sweden 17 58.30N
11.30E
Gotemba Japan 23 35.18N 138.56E
Götene Sweden 17 58.32N 13.29E
Gotha Germany 14 50.57N 10.43E
Gothenburg see Göteborg Sweden 17
Gothèye Niger 38 13.51N 1.31E
Gotland d. Sweden 17 57.30N 18.30E
Gotland i. Sweden 17 57.30N 18.33E
Göttingen Germany 14 51.32N 9.57E
Gouda Neth. 8 52.01N 4.43E
Gouin, Résr. Canada 55 48.38N 74.50W
Goulburn Australia 47 34.47S 149.43E
Goulburn r. Australia 47 36.08S 144.30E
Goulburn Is. Australia 44 11.33S 133.26E
Goundam Mali 38 17.27N 3.39W
Gourdon France 11 44.45N 1.22E
Gouré Niger 38 13.59N 10.15E
Gourma-Rharous Mali 38 16.58N 1.50W
Gournay France 9 49.29N 1.44E
Governador Valadares Brazil 59 18.51S 42.00W
Gowanda U.S.A. 55 42.28N 78.57W
Gowd-e Zereh des. Afghan. 31 30.00N 62.00E
Gower pen. U.K. 5 51.37N 4.10W
Goya Argentina 62 29.10S 59.20W
Goyder r. Australia 44 12.38S 135.11E
Gozo i. Malta 12 36.03N 14.16E
Graaff Reinet R.S.A. 39 32.15S 24.31E
Gračac Croatia 14 44.18N 15.51E
Grace, L. Australia 43 33.18S 118.15E
Gracias á Dios, Cabo c. Honduras/Nicaragua 57
15.00N 83.10W
Grado Italy 9 45.40N 13.23E
Grado Spain 10 43.23N 6.04W
Grafton Australia 47 29.40S 152.56E
Grafton N.Dak. U.S.A. 53 48.28N 97.25W
Grafton W.Va. U.S.A. 55 39.21N 80.03W
Graham Land f. Antarctica 64 67.00S 60.00W
Graham, Mt. U.S.A. 54 32.42N 109.52W
Grahamstown R.S.A. 39 33.18S 26.30E
Graiguenamanagh Rep. of Ire. 7 52.33N 6.57W
Grajaú r. Brazil 61 3.41S 44.48W
Grampian d. U.K. 6 57.22N 2.35W
Grampian Mts. U.K. 6 56.55N 4.00W
Grampians mts. Australia 46 37.12S 142.34E
Granada Nicaragua 57 11.58N 85.59W
Granada Spain 10 37.10N 3.35W
Granby Canada 55 45.23N 72.44W
Gran Canaria i. Canary Is. 34 28.00N 15.30W
Gran Chaco f. S. America 62 22.00S 60.00W
Grand r. S.Dak. U.S.A. 52 45.40N 100.32W
Grand Bahama I. Bahamas 57 26.35N 78.00W
Grand Bassam Côte d'Ivoire 38 5.14N 3.45W
Grand Canyon f. U.S.A. 54 36.10N 112.45W
Grand Canyon town U.S.A. 54 36.03N 112.09W
Grand Canyon Nat. Park U.S.A. 54 36.15N
112.58W
Grand Cayman i. Cayman Is. 57 19.20N 81.30W
Grand Couronne France 9 49.21N 1.00E
Grande r. Bolivia 62 15.10S 64.55W
Grande r. Bahia Brazil 61 11.05S 43.09W
Grande r. Minas Gerais Brazil 62 20.00S 51.00W
Grande, Bahía b. Argentina 63 51.30S 67.30W
Grande Cascapédia Canada 55 48.21N 65.52W
Grande Comore i. Comoros 37 11.35S 43.20E
Grande do Gurupá, Ilha i. Brazil 61 1.00S
51.30W
Grande, Ilha i. Brazil 59 23.07S 44.16W
Grande Prairie town Canada 50 55.10N 118.52W
Grand Erg de Bilma des. Niger 38 18.30N
14.00E
Grandes Bergeronnes Canada 55 48.16N
69.35W
Grandes, Salinas f. Argentina 62 29.37S 64.56W
Grand Falls town Nfld. Canada 51 48.57N
55.40W
Grand Falls town N.B. Canada 55 46.55N
67.45W
Grand Forks U.S.A. 53 47.57N 97.05W
Grand Fougeray France 9 47.44N 1.44W
Grand Island town U.S.A. 52 40.56N 98.21W
Grand Junction U.S.A. 54 39.05N 108.33W
Grand L. N.B. Canada 55 45.38N 67.38W
Grand L. U.S.A. 55 45.15N 67.50W
Grand Lahou Côte d'Ivoire 38 5.09N 5.01W
Grand Manan I. Canada 55 44.38N 66.50W
Grand Marais U.S.A. 53 47.55N 90.15W
Grand' Mère Canada 55 46.37N 72.41W
Grândola Portugal 10 38.10N 8.34W
Grand Rapids town Canada 51 53.08N 99.20W
Grand Rapids town Mich. U.S.A. 55 42.57N
85.40W
Grand St. Bernard, Col du pass Italy/Switz. 9
45.52N 7.11E
Grand Teton mtn. U.S.A. 54 43.44N 110.48W
Grand Teton Nat. Park U.S.A. 54 43.30N
110.37W
Grand Traverse B. U.S.A. 55 45.02N 85.30W
Grand Valley town U.S.A. 54 39.27N 108.03W
Grandville U.S.A. 55 42.54N 85.48W
Grangemouth U.K. 6 56.01N 3.44W
Granger U.S.A. 54 41.35N 109.58W
Grängesberg Sweden 17 60.05N 14.59E
Grangeville U.S.A. 54 45.56N 116.07W
Granite Peak town Australia 42 25.38S 121.21E
Granite Peak mtn. U.S.A. 52 45.10N 109.50W
Granity New Zealand 48 41.38S 171.51E
Granja Brazil 61 3.06S 40.50W
Gränna Sweden 17 58.01N 14.28E
Granollers Spain 10 41.37N 2.18E
Granön Sweden 16 64.15N 19.19E
Gran Paradiso mtn. Italy 9 45.31N 7.15E
Grant Mich. U.S.A. 55 43.20N 85.49W
Grantham U.K. 4 52.55N 0.39W
Grantown-on-Spey U.K. 6 57.20N 3.38W
Grant Range mts. U.S.A. 54 38.25N 115.30W
Grants U.S.A. 54 35.09N 107.52W
Grants Pass town U.S.A. 54 42.26N 123.19W
Grantsville U.S.A. 55 38.55N 81.07W
Granville France 9 48.50N 1.35W
Graskop R.S.A. 39 24.55S 30.50E
Gras, Lac de l. Canada 50 64.30N 110.30W
Grasse France 11 43.40N 6.56E
Grasset, L. Canada 55 49.53N 78.07W
Grass Valley town Calif. U.S.A. 54 39.13N
121.04W
Grass Valley town Oreg. U.S.A. 54 45.22N
120.47W
Grave Neth. 8 51.45N 5.45E
Gravenhurst Canada 55 44.55N 79.22W
Grave, Pointe de c. France 11 45.35N 1.04W
Gravesend Australia 47 29.35S 150.20E
Gravesend U.K. 5 51.27N 0.24E
Gray France 11 47.27N 5.35E
Grayling U.S.A. 55 44.40N 84.43W
Grays U.K. 5 51.29N 0.20E
Graz Austria 14 47.05N 15.22E
Grdelica Yugo. 13 42.54N 22.04E
Great Abaco I. Bahamas 57 26.30N 77.00W
Great Artesian Basin f. Australia 44 26.30S
143.02E
Great Australian Bight Australia 43 33.10S
129.30E
Great Barrier I. New Zealand 48 36.15S 175.30E
Great Barrier Reef f. Australia 44 16.30S
146.30E
Great Basin f. U.S.A. 54 40.35N 116.00W
Great Bear L. Canada 50 66.00N 120.00W
Great Bend town U.S.A. 52 38.22N 98.46W
Great Bitter L. see Murrah al Kubrá, Al Buḩayrah
al Egypt 32
Great Blasket I. Rep. of Ire. 7 52.05N 10.32W
Great Coco i. Myanmar 29 14.10N 93.25E
Great Divide Basin f. U.S.A. 54 42.00N 108.10W
Great Dividing Range mts. Australia 47 29.00S
152.00E
Great Driffield U.K. 4 54.01N 0.26W
Greater Antilles is. C. America 57 17.00N
70.00W
Greater London d. U.K. 5 51.31N 0.06W
Greater Manchester d. U.K. 4 53.30N 2.18W
Great Exuma i. Bahamas 57 23.00N 76.00W
Great Falls town U.S.A. 54 47.30N 111.17W
Great Inagua I. Bahamas 57 21.00N 73.20W
Great Indian Desert see Thar Desert
India/Pakistan 28
Great Karoo f. R.S.A. 39 32.40S 22.20E
Great Kei r. R.S.A. 39 32.39S 28.23E
Great L. Australia 45 41.50S 146.43E
Great Malvern U.K. 5 52.07N 2.19W
Great Namaland f. Namibia 39 25.30S 17.20E
Great Nicobar i. India 29 7.00N 93.50E
Great Ouse r. U.K. 4 52.47N 0.23E
Great Ruaha r. Tanzania 37 7.55S 37.52E
Great Salt L. U.S.A. 54 41.10N 112.30W
Great Salt Lake Desert U.S.A. 54 40.40N
113.30W
Great Sandy Desert Australia 42 20.30S 123.35E
Great Sandy Desert see An Nafūd des. Saudi
Arabia 30
Great Slave L. Canada 50 61.30N 114.20W
Great Victoria Desert Australia 43 29.00S
127.30E
Great Whernside mtn. U.K. 4 54.09N 1.59W
Great Yarmouth U.K. 5 52.40N 1.45E
Great Zimbabwe ruins Zimbabwe 39 20.30S
30.30E
Gréboun, Mont mtn. Niger 38 20.01N 8.35E
Gredos, Sierra de mts. Spain 10 40.18N 5.20W
Greece Europe 13 39.00N 22.00E
Greeley U.S.A. 52 40.25N 104.42W
Green r. U.S.A. 54 38.11N 109.53W
Green Bay town U.S.A. 53 44.32N 88.00W
Greenbushes Australia 43 33.50S 116.00E
Greencastle Ind. U.S.A. 55 39.39N 86.51W
Greene U.S.A. 55 42.20N 75.46W
Greenhills Australia 43 31.58S 117.01E
Greening Canada 55 48.07N 74.55W
Greenland N. America 51 68.00N 45.00W
Greenlaw U.K. 6 55.43N 2.28W
Greenock U.K. 6 55.57N 4.45W
Greenore Pt. Rep. of Ire. 7 52.14N 6.19W
Greenough r. Australia 43 29.22S 114.34E
Green River town Utah U.S.A. 54 38.59N
110.10W
Green River town Wyo. U.S.A. 54 41.32N
109.28W
Greensboro N.C. U.S.A. 53 36.03N 79.50W
Greensburg Ind. U.S.A. 55 39.20N 85.29W
Greenvale Australia 44 18.57S 144.53E
Greenville Liberia 34 5.01N 9.03W
Greenville Ala. U.S.A. 53 31.50N 86.40W
Greenville Mich. U.S.A. 55 43.11N 85.13W
Greenville Miss. U.S.A. 53 33.23N 91.03W
Greenville S.C. U.S.A. 53 34.52N 82.25W
Greenville Tex. U.S.A. 53 33.09N 96.07W
Greenwood Miss. U.S.A. 53 33.31N 90.10W
Gregory r. Australia 44 17.53S 139.17E
Gregory, L. S.A. Australia 46 28.55S 139.00E
Gregory L. W.A. Australia 42 20.10S 127.20E
Gregory Range mts. Australia 44 19.00S 143.05E
Greifswald Germany 14 54.06N 13.24E
Gremikha Russian Fed. 18 68.03N 39.38E
Grenå Denmark 17 56.25N 10.53E
Grenada C. America 57 12.07N 61.40W
Grenade France 11 43.47N 1.10E
Grenfell Australia 47 33.53S 148.11E
Grenoble France 11 45.11N 5.43E
Grenville, C. Australia 44 12.00S 143.13E
Gretna U.K. 6 55.00N 3.04W
Greven Germany 8 52.07N 7.38E
Grevenbroich Germany 8 51.07N 6.33E
Grevesmühlen Germany 14 53.51N 11.10E
Grey r. New Zealand 48 42.28S 171.13E
Greybull U.S.A. 54 44.30N 108.03W
Grey, C. Australia 44 13.00S 136.40E
Greymouth New Zealand 48 42.28S 171.12E
Grey Range mts. Australia 45 27.30S 143.59E
Greystones Rep. of Ire. 7 53.09N 6.04W
Greytown R.S.A. 39 29.04S 30.36E
Griffin U.S.A. 53 33.15N 84.17W
Griffith Australia 47 34.18S 146.04E
Grignan France 11 44.25N 4.54E
Grigoriopol Moldova 15 47.08N 29.18E
Grim, C. Australia 45 40.45S 144.45E
Grimsby U.K. 4 53.35N 0.05W
Grimstad Norway 17 58.20N 8.36E
Grimsvötn mtn. Iceland 16 64.30N 17.10W
Grindavik Iceland 16 63.50N 22.27W
Grindsted Denmark 17 55.45N 8.56E
Griqualand East f. R.S.A. 39 30.40S 29.10E
Griqualand West f. R.S.A. 39 28.50S 23.30E
Griva Russian Fed. 18 60.35N 50.58E
Grobina Latvia 17 56.33N 21.10E
Groblershoop R.S.A. 39 28.55S 20.59E
Grodno Belarus 15 53.40N 23.50E
Grodzisk Poland 14 52.14N 16.22E
Grodzyanka Belarus 15 53.30N 28.41E
Groenlo Neth. 8 52.02N 6.36E
Groix, Île de i. France 11 47.38N 3.26W
Gronau Germany 8 52.14N 7.02E
Grong Norway 16 64.27N 12.19E
Groningen Neth. 8 53.13N 6.35E
Groningen d. Neth. 8 53.15N 6.45E
Groot r. R.S.A. 39 33.58S 25.03E
Groote Eylandt i. Australia 44 14.00S 136.40E
Grootfontein Namibia 39 19.32S 18.07E
Groot Karasberge mts. Namibia 39 27.20S
18.50E
Grootlaagte r. Botswana 39 20.58S 21.42E
Groot Swartberge mts. R.S.A. 39 33.20S 22.00E
Grossenbrode Germany 14 54.23N 11.07E
Grossenhain Germany 14 51.17N 13.31E
Grosseto Italy 12 42.46N 11.08E
Gross Glockner mtn. Austria 14 47.05N 12.50E
Grote Nete r. Belgium 8 51.07N 4.20E
Groundhog r. Canada 55 49.43N 81.58W
Grouse Creek town U.S.A. 54 41.22N 113.53W
Grover City U.S.A. 54 35.07N 120.37W
Groznyy Russian Fed. 19 43.21N 45.42E
Grudziądz Poland 15 53.29N 18.45E
Grumeti r. Tanzania 37 2.05S 33.45E
Grünau Namibia 39 27.44S 18.18E
Grundarfjördhur town Iceland 16 64.55N 23.20W
Grungedal Norway 17 59.44N 7.43E
Gryazovets Russian Fed. 18 58.52N 40.12E
Gryfice Poland 14 53.56N 15.12E
Guachipas Argentina 62 25.31S 65.31W
Guacuí Brazil 59 20.44S 41.40W
Guadalajara Mexico 56 20.30N 103.20W
Guadalajara Spain 10 40.37N 3.10W
Guadalcanal i. Solomon Is. 40 9.32S 160.12E
Guadalete r. Spain 10 36.37N 6.15W
Guadalmena r. Spain 10 38.00N 3.50W
Guadalquivir r. Spain 10 36.50N 6.20W
Guadalupe Mexico 56 25.41N 100.15W
Guadalupe, Isla de i. Mexico 52 29.00N 118.16W
Guadalupe, Sierra de mts. Spain 10 39.30N
5.25W
Guadarrama r. Spain 10 39.55N 4.10W
Guadarrama, Sierra de mts. Spain 10 41.00N
3.50W
Guadeloupe i. Leeward Is. 57 16.20N 61.40W
Guadiana r. Portugal 10 37.10N 7.36W
Guadix Spain 10 37.19N 3.08W
Guafo, Golfo de g. Chile 63 43.35S 74.15W
Guainía r. Colombia 60 2.01N 67.07W
Guaíra Brazil 62 24.04S 54.15W
Guajará Mirim Brazil 60 10.48S 65.22W
Guajira, Península de la pen. Colombia 60
12.00N 72.00W
Gualeguay Argentina 63 33.10S 59.20W
Gualeguay r. Argentina 63 33.18S 59.38W
Gualeguaychu Argentina 63 33.00S 58.30W
Guam i. Mariana Is. 40 13.30N 144.40E
Guamal Colombia 60 9.10N 74.15W
Guanajuato Mexico 56 21.00N 101.16W
Guanajuato d. Mexico 56 21.00N 101.00W
Guanare Venezuela 60 9.04N 69.45W
Guanarito Venezuela 60 8.43N 69.12W
Guane Cuba 57 22.13N 84.07W
Guangdong d. China 25 23.00N 113.00E
Guanghua see Laohekou China 25
Guangxi Zhuangzu d. China 25 23.50N 109.00E
Guangyuan China 29 32.26N 105.52E
Guangzhou China 25 23.20N 113.30E
Guanling China 29 25.57N 105.38E
Guantánamo Cuba 57 20.09N 75.14W
Guan Xian Sichuan China 29 30.59N 103.40E
Guaporé r. Bolivia/Brazil 62 12.00S 65.15W
Guaqui Bolivia 62 16.35S 68.51W
Guarabira Brazil 61 6.46S 35.25W
Guarapuava Brazil 59 25.22S 51.28W
Guaratinguetá Brazil 59 22.49S 45.09W
Guarda Portugal 10 40.32N 7.17W
Guardavalle Italy 13 38.30N 16.30E
Guardo Spain 10 42.47N 4.50W
Guareim r. Uruguay see Quaraí r. Brazil 63
Guasipati Venezuela 60 7.28N 61.54W
Guastalla Italy 9 44.55N 10.39E
Guatemala C. America 57 15.40N 90.00W
Guatemala town Guatemala 56 14.38N 90.22W
Guatire Venezuela 60 10.28N 66.32W
Guaviare r. Colombia 60 4.00N 67.35W
Guaxupé Brazil 59 21.17S 46.44W
Guayaquil Ecuador 60 2.13S 79.54W
Guayaquil, Golfo de g. Ecuador 60 3.00S
80.35W
Guaymallén Argentina 63 32.54S 68.47W
Guaymas Mexico 56 27.56N 110.54W
Guayquiraró r. Argentina 63 30.25S 59.36W
Gubakha Russian Fed. 18 58.55N 57.30E
Gubeikou China 25 40.41N 117.09E
Gubin Poland 14 51.59N 14.42E
Gubio Nigeria 38 12.31N 12.44E
Guchab Namibia 39 19.40S 17.47E
Gúdar, Sierra de mts. Spain 10 40.27N 0.42W
Gudbrandsdalen f. Norway 17 61.30N 10.00E
Gudvangen Norway 17 60.52N 6.50E
Guecho Spain 10 43.21N 3.01W
Guelph Canada 55 43.33N 80.15W
Guéméné-sur-Scorff France 11 48.04N 3.13W
Guéret France 11 46.10N 1.52E
Guernica Spain 10 43.19N 2.40W
Guernsey i. U.K. 5 49.27N 2.35W
Guerra Mozambique 37 13.05S 35.12E
Guerrero d. Mexico 56 18.00N 100.00W
Guiana S. America 61 3.40N 53.00W
Guiana Highlands S. America 60 4.00N 59.00W
Guichón Uruguay 63 32.21S 57.12W
Guildford Australia 43 31.55S 115.55E
Guildford U.K. 5 51.14N 0.35W
Guilin China 25 25.21N 110.11E
Guimarães Brazil 61 2.08S 44.36W
Guimarães Portugal 10 41.27N 8.18W
Guinan China 24 35.20N 100.50E
Guinea Africa 34 10.30N 11.30W
Guinea Bissau Africa 34 11.30N 15.00W
Guinea, G. of Africa 38 3.00N 3.00E
Güines Cuba 57 22.50N 82.02W
Guingamp France 11 48.34N 3.09W
Guiping China 25 23.20N 110.04E
Guiscard France 8 49.39N 3.01E
Guiscard France 9 49.39N 3.03E
Guise France 9 49.54N 3.38E
Guiuan Phil. 27 11.02N 125.44E
Guiyang China 24 26.35N 106.40E
Guizhou d. China 24 27.00N 106.30E
Gujarat d. India 28 22.45N 71.30E
Gujrānwāla Pakistan 28 32.06N 74.11E
Gujrāt Pakistan 28 32.35N 74.06E
Gulargambone Australia 47 31.21S 148.32E
Gulbarga India 28 17.22N 76.47E
Gulfport U.S.A. 53 30.21N 89.08W
Gulgong Australia 47 32.20S 149.49E
Gulma Nigeria 38 12.41N 4.24E
Gulshad Kazakhstan 24 46.37N 74.22E
Gulu Uganda 37 2.46N 32.21E
Gulwe Tanzania 37 6.27S 36.27E
Gumel Nigeria 38 12.39N 9.23E
Gummersbach Germany 8 51.03N 7.32E
Gümüşhane Turkey 30 40.26N 39.26E
Guna India 28 24.39N 77.18E
Gunbar Australia 47 34.04S 145.25E
Gundagai Australia 47 35.07S 148.05E
Gundlupet India 28 11.48N 76.41E
Gungu Zaïre 36 5.43S 19.20E
Gunnedah Australia 47 30.59S 150.15E
Gunning Australia 47 34.46S 149.17E
Gunnison r. U.S.A. 54 39.03N 108.35W
Gunnison Utah U.S.A. 54 39.09N 111.49W
Guntersville L. U.S.A. 53 34.35N 86.00W
Guntūr India 29 16.20N 80.27E
Gunungsitoli Indonesia 26 1.17N 97.37E
Günzburg Germany 14 48.27N 10.16E
Gura Portiței f. Romania 15 44.40N 29.00E
Gurgueia r. Brazil 61 6.45S 43.35W
Gursköy i. Norway 16 62.16N 5.42E
Gurué Mozambique 37 15.30S 36.58E
Gürün Turkey 30 38.44N 37.15E
Gurupá Brazil 61 1.25S 51.39W
Gurupi r. Brazil 61 1.13S 46.06W
Guruve Zimbabwe 37 16.42S 30.40E
Gusau Nigeria 38 12.12N 6.40E
Gusev Russian Fed. 15 54.32N 22.12E
Guspini Italy 12 39.32N 8.38E
Gustav Holm, Kap c. Greenland 51 67.00N
34.00W
Güstrow Germany 14 53.48N 12.11E
Gütersloh Germany 14 51.54N 8.22E
Guyana S. America 60 4.40N 59.00W
Guyra Australia 47 30.14S 151.40E
Guzhen Anhui China 25 33.19N 117.19E
Gwa Myanmar 29 17.36N 94.35E
Gwabegar Australia 47 30.34S 149.00E
Gwadabawa Nigeria 38 13.23N 5.15E
Gwādar Pakistan 28 25.09N 62.21E
Gwagwada Nigeria 38 10.15N 7.15E
Gwai Zimbabwe 39 19.15S 27.42E
Gwai r. Zimbabwe 39 17.59S 26.55E
Gwalior India 29 26.12N 78.09E
Gwanda Zimbabwe 39 20.59S 29.00E
Gwasero Nigeria 38 9.30N 8.30E
Gweebarra B. Rep. of Ire. 7 54.52N 8.28W
Gwent d. U.K. 5 51.44N 3.00W
Gweru Zimbabwe 39 19.25S 29.50E
Gwydir r. Australia 47 29.35S 148.45E
Gwynedd d. U.K. 4 53.00N 4.00W
Gyandzha Azerbaijan 31 40.39N 46.20E
Gyangzê China 29 29.00N 89.40E
Gydanskiy Poluostrov pen. Russian Fed. 20
70.00N 78.30E
Gympie Australia 44 26.11S 152.40E
Gyöngyös Hungary 15 47.47N 19.56E
Györ Hungary 15 47.41N 17.40E
Gypsumville Canada 51 51.45N 98.35W

H

Haan Germany 8 51.10N 7.02E

Haapajärvi Finland 16 63.45N 25.20E
Haapamäki Finland 16 62.15N 24.28E
Haapavesi Finland 16 64.08N 25.22E
Haapsalu Estonia 17 58.56N 23.33E
Hä Arava r. Israel/Jordan 32 30.30N 35.10E
Haarlem Neth. 8 52.22N 4.38E
Haarlem R.S.A. 39 33.46S 23.28E
Habahe China 24 47.53N 86.12E
Ḩabarūt Yemen 28 17.18N 52.44E
Habaswein Kenya 37 1.06N 39.26E
Habay-la-Neuve Belgium 8 49.45N 5.38E
Habikino Japan 23 34.33N 135.37E
Habo Sweden 17 57.55N 14.04E
Hachinohe Japan 25 40.30N 141.30E
Hachiōji Japan 23 35.39N 139.20E
Hack, Mt. Australia 46 30.44S 138.45E
Hadano Japan 23 35.22N 139.14E
Haddington U.K. 6 55.57N 2.47W
Ḩadd, Ra's al c. Oman 31 22.32N 59.49E
Hadejia Nigeria 38 12.30N 10.03E
Hadejia r. Nigeria 38 12.47N 10.44E
Hadera Israel 32 32.26N 34.55E
Haderslev Denmark 17 55.15N 9.30E
Ḩaḑramawt f. Yemen 35 16.30N 49.30E
Hadsten Denmark 17 56.20N 10.03E
Hadsund Denmark 17 56.43N 10.07E
Haedo, Cuchilla de mts. Uruguay 63 31.50S 56.10W
Haegeland Norway 17 58.15N 7.50E
Haeju N. Korea 25 38.04N 125.40E
Ḩafar al Bāţin Saudi Arabia 31 28.28N 46.00E
Hafnarfjördhur town Iceland 16 64.04N 21.58W
Haft Gel Iran 31 31.28N 49.35E
Hagen Germany 8 51.22N 7.27E
Hagerstown U.S.A. 55 39.39N 77.43W
Hagfors Sweden 17 60.02N 13.42E
Ha Giang Vietnam 26 22.50N 105.01E
Hags Head Rep. of Ire. 7 52.56N 9.29W
Hague, Cap de la c. France 9 49.44N 1.56W
Haguenau France 11 48.49N 7.47E
Hai Duong Vietnam 26 20.56N 106.21E
Haifa see Hefa Israel 32
Haikou China 25 20.05N 110.25E
Ḩā'il Saudi Arabia 30 27.31N 41.45E
Hailar China 25 49.15N 119.41E
Hailsham U.K. 5 50.52N 0.17E
Hailun China 25 47.29N 126.58E
Hailuoto i. Finland 16 65.02N 24.42E
Hainan d. China 25 18.30N 109.40E
Hainaut d. Belgium 8 50.30N 3.45E
Haines Alas. U.S.A. 50 59.11N 135.23W
Haines Oreg. U.S.A. 54 44.55N 117.56W
Haiphong Vietnam 26 20.48N 106.40E
Haiti C. America 57 19.00N 73.00W
Hajdúböszörmény Hungary 15 47.41N 21.30E
Hajdúszoboszló Hungary 15 47.27N 21.24E
Hakkâri Turkey 31 37.36N 43.45E
Hakodate Japan 25 41.46N 140.44E
Ḩalab Syria 30 36.14N 37.10E
Ḩalabjah Iraq 31 35.10N 45.59E
Ḩalbā Lebanon 32 34.34N 36.05E
Halberstadt Germany 14 51.54N 11.04E
Halden Norway 17 59.09N 11.23E
Half Assini Ghana 38 5.04N 2.53W
Halfmoon Bay town New Zealand 48 46.45S 168.08E
Haliburton Canada 55 45.03N 78.03W
Haliburton Highlands Canada 55 45.03N 78.03W
Halifax Canada 51 44.38N 63.35W
Halifax U.K. 4 53.43N 1.51W
Halīl r. Iran 28 27.35N 58.44E
Halkett, C. U.S.A. 50 71.00N 152.00W
Halkirk U.K. 6 58.30N 3.30W
Halladale r. U.K. 6 58.34N 3.54W
Halland d. Sweden 17 56.45N 13.00E
Halle Belgium 8 50.45N 4.14E
Halle Germany 14 51.28N 11.58E
Hällefors Sweden 17 59.47N 14.30E
Hallingdal f. Norway 17 60.30N 9.00E
Hall Lake town Canada 51 68.40N 81.30W
Hällnäs Sweden 16 64.19N 19.38E
Hall Pen. Canada 51 63.30N 66.00W
Hallsberg Sweden 17 59.04N 15.07E
Hall's Creek town Australia 42 18.13S 127.39E
Hallstavik Sweden 17 60.03N 18.36E
Hallstead U.S.A. 55 41.58N 75.45W
Halmahera i. Indonesia 27 0.45N 128.00E
Halmstad Sweden 17 56.39N 12.50E
Halsa Norway 16 63.03N 8.14E
Hälsingborg Sweden 17 56.03N 12.42E
Haltern Germany 8 51.45N 7.10E
Haltia Tunturi mtn. Finland 16 69.17N 21.21E
Haltwhistle U.K. 4 54.58N 2.27W
Ham France 9 49.45N 3.04E
Hamadān Iran 31 34.47N 48.33E
Ḩamad, Wādī al r. Saudi Arabia 30 25.49N 36.37E
Ḩamāh Syria 32 35.09N 36.44E
Hamakita Japan 23 34.48N 137.47E
Hamamatsu Japan 23 34.42N 137.44E
Hamar Norway 17 60.48N 11.06E
Hamarøy Norway 16 68.05N 15.40E
Ḩamāţah, Jabal mtn. Egypt 30 24.11N 35.01E
Hamborn Germany 8 51.29N 6.46E
Hamburg Germany 14 53.33N 10.00E
Hamburg R.S.A. 39 33.17S 27.27E
Häme d. Finland 17 61.20N 24.30E
Hämeenlinna Finland 17 61.00N 24.27E
Hamelin B. Australia 43 34.10S 115.00E
Hameln Germany 14 52.06N 9.21E
Hamersley Range mts. Australia 42 22.00S 118.00E
Hamhŭng N. Korea 25 39.54N 127.35E
Hami China 24 42.40N 93.30E
Hamilton Australia 46 37.45S 142.04E
Hamilton r. Australia 45 27.12S 135.28E
Hamilton Canada 55 43.15N 79.51W
Hamilton New Zealand 48 37.46S 175.18E
Hamilton U.K. 6 55.46N 4.10W
Hamilton Mont. U.S.A. 54 46.15N 114.09W
Hamilton Ohio U.S.A. 55 39.23N 84.33W
Hamley Bridge town Australia 46 34.21S 138.41E
Hamm Germany 8 51.40N 7.49E
Ḩammār, Hawr al l. Iraq 31 30.50N 47.00E
Hammerdal Sweden 16 63.35N 15.20E
Hammerfest Norway 16 70.40N 23.42E
Hammond Australia 46 32.33S 138.20E
Hammond N.Y. U.S.A. 55 44.27N 75.42W
Hamoir Belgium 8 50.25N 5.32E
Hampshire d. U.K. 5 51.03N 1.20W
Ḩamrīn, Jabal mts. Iraq 31 34.40N 44.10E
Hāmūn-e Jaz Mūrīān l. Iran 28 27.20N 58.55E
Hanang mtn. Tanzania 37 4.30S 35.21E
Hancheng China 25 35.28N 110.29E
Hancock Mich. U.S.A. 55 47.08N 88.34W
Handa Japan 23 34.53N 136.56E
Handa Somali Rep. 35 10.39N 51.08E
Handan China 25 36.35N 114.29E
Handeni Tanzania 37 5.25S 38.04E
HaNegev des. Israel 32 30.42N 34.55E
Hanford U.S.A. 54 36.20N 119.39W
Hanggin Houqi China 24 40.52N 107.04E
Hangö Finland 17 59.50N 22.57E
Hangzhou China 25 30.10N 120.07E
Hankey R.S.A. 39 33.50S 24.52E
Hanksville U.S.A. 54 38.21N 110.44W
Hänle Jammu & Kashmir 29 32.48N 79.00E
Hanmer Springs town New Zealand 48 42.31S 172.50E
Hanna Canada 50 51.38N 111.54W
Hannah B. Canada 55 51.05N 79.45W
Hannibal Mo. U.S.A. 53 39.41N 91.25W
Hann, Mt. Australia 42 15.55S 125.57E
Hannover Germany 14 52.23N 9.44E
Hannut Belgium 8 50.40N 5.05E
Hanöbukten b. Sweden 17 55.45N 14.30E
Ha Noi Vietnam 26 21.01N 105.53E
Hanover Canada 55 44.09N 81.02W
Hanover R.S.A. 39 31.04S 24.25E
Hanover Penn. U.S.A. 55 39.48N 76.59W
Hanover, Isla i. Chile 63 50.57S 74.40W
Han Pijesak Bosnia-Herzegovina 13 44.04N 18.59E
Han Shui r. China 25 30.45N 114.24E
Hanson, L. Australia 46 31.02S 136.13E
Hantengri Feng mtn. China 24 42.09N 80.12E
Hanzhong China 29 33.10N 107.02E
Haparanda Sweden 16 65.50N 24.10E
Hapsu N. Korea 25 41.12N 128.48E
Ḩaql Saudi Arabia 32 29.14N 34.56E
Ḩaraḑ Saudi Arabia 31 24.12N 49.08E
Harare Zimbabwe 39 17.49S 31.04E
Har-Ayrag Mongolia 25 45.42N 109.14E
Harbin China 25 45.45N 126.41E
Harbour Grace town Canada 51 47.42N 53.13W
Harburg Germany 14 53.27N 9.58E
Hardangerfjorden est. Norway 17 60.10N 6.00E
Hardangerjökulen mtn. Norway 17 60.33N 7.26E
Hardanger Vidda f. Norway 17 60.20N 7.30E
Hardenberg Neth. 8 52.36N 6.40E
Harderwijk Neth. 8 52.21N 5.37E
Harding R.S.A. 39 30.34S 29.52E
Hardman U.S.A. 54 45.10N 119.40W
Hardwār India 29 29.58N 78.10E
Hardwicke B. Australia 46 34.52S 137.10E
Haren Germany 8 52.48N 7.15E
Härer Ethiopia 35 9.20N 42.10E
Harfleur France 9 49.30N 0.12E
Hargeysa Somali Rep. 35 9.31N 44.02E
Har Hu l. China 24 38.20N 97.40E
Hari r. Indonesia 26 1.00S 104.15E
Harīrūd r. Afghan. 28 35.42N 61.12E
Harlech U.K. 4 52.52N 4.08W
Harlem U.S.A. 54 48.32N 108.47W
Harlingen Neth. 8 53.10N 5.25E
Harlow U.K. 5 51.47N 0.08E
Harlowton U.S.A. 54 46.26N 109.50W
Harney Basin f. U.S.A. 54 43.15N 120.40W
Harney L. U.S.A. 54 43.14N 119.07W
Härnösand Sweden 16 62.37N 17.55E
Har Nuur l. Mongolia 24 48.00N 93.25E
Harricana r. Canada 55 51.10N 79.45W
Harrington Australia 47 31.50S 152.43E
Harris i. U.K. 6 57.50N 6.55W
Harrisburg Oreg. U.S.A. 54 44.16N 123.10W
Harrisburg Penn. U.S.A. 55 40.16N 76.52W
Harris, L. Australia 46 31.08S 135.14E
Harrismith Australia 43 32.55S 117.50E
Harrismith R.S.A. 39 28.15S 29.07E
Harrison, C. Canada 51 55.00N 58.00W
Harris, Sd. of U.K. 6 57.43N 7.05W
Harrogate U.K. 4 53.59N 1.32W
Harrow U.K. 5 51.35N 0.21W
Harstad Norway 16 68.48N 16.30E
Hartford U.S.A. 55 41.45N 72.42W
Hart, L. Australia 46 31.08S 136.24E
Hartland Canada 55 46.18N 67.31W
Hartland U.K. 5 50.59N 4.29W
Hartland Pt. U.K. 5 51.01N 4.32W
Hartlepool U.K. 4 54.42N 1.11W
Hartola Finland 17 61.35N 26.01E
Harts Range town Australia 44 23.06S 134.55E
Har Us Nuur l. Mongolia 24 48.10N 92.10E
Hārūt r. Afghan. 31 31.36N 61.12E
Harvey Australia 43 33.06S 115.50E
Harwich U.K. 5 51.56N 1.18E
Haryana d. India 28 29.15N 76.00E
Hasa Oasis see Aḩsā', Wāḩat al oasis Saudi Arabia 31
Ḩasā, Wādī al r. Jordan 32 31.01N 35.29E
Hase r. Germany 8 52.42N 7.17E
Haselünne Germany 8 52.40N 7.30E
Hasenkamp Argentina 63 31.30S 59.50W
Ḩasharūd Iran 31 37.29N 47.05E
Hashimoto Japan 23 34.19N 135.37E
Haslemere U.K. 5 51.05N 0.41W
Hasselt Belgium 8 50.56N 5.20E
Hassi Messaoud Algeria 34 31.43N 6.03E
Hässleholm Sweden 17 56.09N 13.46E
Hastings Australia 47 38.18S 145.12E
Hastings New Zealand 48 39.39S 176.52E
Hastings U.K. 5 50.51N 0.36E
Hastings Nebr. U.S.A. 52 40.37N 98.22W
Hatches Creek town Australia 44 20.56S 135.12E
Hatfield Australia 46 33.53S 143.47E
Hatfield U.K. 5 51.46N 0.13W
Ha Tinh Vietnam 26 18.21N 105.55E
Hattah Australia 46 34.52S 142.23E
Hattem Neth. 8 52.29N 6.06E
Hatteras, C. U.S.A. 53 35.14N 75.31W
Hattiesburg U.S.A. 53 31.25N 89.19W
Hattingen Germany 8 51.24N 7.09E
Hatton U.S.A. 54 46.46N 118.49W
Hatvan Hungary 15 47.40N 19.41E
Hauge Norway 17 58.18N 6.15E
Haugesund Norway 17 59.25N 5.18E
Haugsdorf Austria 14 48.42N 16.05E
Hauraki G. New Zealand 48 36.30S 175.00E
Haut Atlas mts. Morocco 34 32.00N 5.50W
Haute Maurice Prov. Park Canada 55 48.35N 74.21W
Haute-Normandie d. France 9 49.30N 1.00E
Hauterive Canada 55 49.11N 68.16W
Hautmont France 8 50.16N 3.52E
Hauts Bassins d. Burkina 38 10.45N 3.45W
Haut Zaïre d. Zaïre 37 2.00N 27.00E
Havana see La Habana Cuba 57
Havant U.K. 5 50.51N 0.59W
Havel r. Germany 14 52.51N 11.57E
Havelange Belgium 8 50.23N 5.14E
Havelberg Germany 14 52.50N 12.04E
Havelock New Zealand 48 41.17S 173.46E
Haverfordwest U.K. 5 51.48N 4.59W
Haverhill U.K. 5 52.06N 0.27E
Havlíčkuv Brod Czech Republic 14 49.38N 15.35E
Havre U.S.A. 54 48.33N 109.41W
Hawaii d. U.S.A. 52 21.00N 156.00W
Hawaii i. U.S.A. 52 19.30N 155.30W
Hawaiian Is. U.S.A. 52 21.00N 157.00W
Hawdon North, L. Australia 46 37.09S 139.54E
Hawea, L. New Zealand 48 44.30S 169.15E
Hawera New Zealand 48 39.35S 174.19E
Hawick U.K. 6 55.25N 2.47W
Hawke B. New Zealand 48 39.18S 177.15E
Hawker Australia 46 31.53S 138.25E
Hawker Gate Australia 46 29.46S 141.00E
Hawke's Bay d. New Zealand 48 39.00S 176.35E
Ḩawrān, Wādī r. Iraq 30 33.57N 42.35E
Ḩawsh 'Īsá Egypt 32 30.55N 30.17E
Hawthorne U.S.A. 54 38.32N 118.38W
Hay Australia 47 34.31S 144.31E
Hay r. Australia 44 25.00S 138.00E
Haya r. Japan 23 35.30N 138.26E
Hayange France 11 49.20N 6.02E
Hayden U.S.A. 54 33.00N 110.47W
Hayes r. Canada 51 57.00N 92.30W
Hayes Creek town Australia 42 13.27S 131.25E
Hay-on-Wye U.K. 5 52.04N 3.09W
Hay River town Canada 50 60.51N 115.42W
Haywards Heath f. U.K. 5 51.00N 0.05E
Hazārān, Kūh-e mtn. Iran 31 29.30N 57.18E
Hazelton Canada 50 55.16N 127.18W
Hazen U.S.A. 54 39.34N 119.03W
Hazleton U.S.A. 55 40.58N 75.59W
Healdsburg U.S.A. 54 38.37N 122.52W
Healesville Australia 47 37.40S 145.31E
Healy U.S.A. 50 63.52N 148.58W
Heanor U.K. 4 53.01N 1.20W
Hearst Canada 55 49.42N 83.40W
Heathcote Australia 47 36.54S 144.42E
Hebei d. China 25 39.20N 117.15E
Hebel Australia 47 28.55S 147.49E
Hebi China 25 35.57N 114.08E
Hebron Canada 51 58.05N 62.30W
Hebron see Al Khalīl Jordan 32
Heby Sweden 17 59.56N 16.53E
Hecate Str. Canada 50 53.00N 131.00W
Hechtel Belgium 8 51.07N 5.22E
Hechuan China 29 30.00N 106.15E
Hede Sweden 17 62.25N 13.30E
Hedemora Sweden 17 60.17N 15.59E
Hedmark d. Norway 17 61.20N 11.30E
Heemstede Neth. 8 52.21N 4.38E
Heerde Neth. 8 52.23N 6.02E
Heerenveen Neth. 8 52.57N 5.55E
Heerlen Neth. 8 50.53N 5.59E
Hefa Israel 32 32.49N 34.59E
Hefei China 25 31.55N 117.18E
Hegang China 25 47.36N 130.30E
Heide Germany 14 54.12N 9.06E
Heidelberg Germany 14 49.25N 8.42E
Heidelberg C.P. R.S.A. 39 34.05S 20.58E
Heilbron R.S.A. 39 27.16S 27.57E
Heilbronn Germany 14 49.08N 9.14E
Heilongjiang d. China 25 47.15N 128.50E
Heiloo Neth. 8 52.37N 4.43E
Heinola Finland 17 61.13N 26.02E
Heinsberg Germany 8 51.04N 6.06E
Heishui China 25 42.06N 119.22E
Hejaz f. see Al Ḩijāz f. Saudi Arabia 30
Hekinan Japan 23 34.51N 136.58E
Hekla, Mt. Iceland 16 64.00N 19.45W
Hekou China 29 22.39N 103.57E
Helagsfjället mtn. Sweden 16 62.58N 12.25E
Helena U.S.A. 54 46.36N 112.01W
Helen Reef i. Pacific Ocean 27 2.43N 131.46E
Helensburgh U.K. 6 56.01N 4.44W
Helensville New Zealand 48 36.40S 174.27E
Hellendoorn Neth. 8 52.24N 6.29E
Hellenthal Germany 8 50.28N 6.25E
Hellesylt Norway 17 62.05N 6.54E
Hellevoetsluis Neth. 8 51.49N 4.08E
Hellín Spain 10 38.31N 1.43W
Helmand r. Asia 28 31.10N 61.20E
Helmond Neth. 8 51.28N 5.40E
Helmsdale U.K. 6 58.07N 3.40W
Helmsdale r. U.K. 6 58.05N 3.39W
Helsingfors see Helsinki Finland 17
Helsingör Denmark 17 56.02N 12.37E
Helsinki Finland 17 60.08N 25.00E
Helston U.K. 5 50.07N 5.17W
Helvecia Argentina 63 31.06S 60.05W
Hemel Hempstead U.K. 5 51.46N 0.28W
Hemse Sweden 17 57.14N 18.22E
Hemsedal Norway 17 60.52N 8.34E
Henan d. China 25 33.45N 113.00E
Henares r. Spain 10 40.26N 3.35W
Henbury Australia 44 24.35S 133.15E
Hendaye France 11 43.22N 1.46W
Henderson Ky. U.S.A. 55 37.50N 87.35W
Henderson Nev. U.S.A. 54 36.02N 114.59W
Hendrik Verwoerd Dam R.S.A. 39 30.37S 25.29E
Hendrina R.S.A. 39 26.09S 29.42E
Hengelo Neth. 8 52.16N 6.46E
Hengyang China 25 26.58N 112.31E
Hénin-Beaumont France 8 50.25N 2.55E
Hennebont France 11 47.48N 3.16W
Henrietta Maria, C. Canada 51 55.00N 82.15W
Hentiesbaai Namibia 39 22.10S 14.19E
Henty Australia 47 35.30S 147.03E
Henzada Myanmar 29 17.38N 95.35E
Heppner U.S.A. 54 45.21N 119.33W
Heqing China 29 26.34N 100.12E
Herāt Afghan. 31 34.21N 62.10E
Herceg-Novi Yugo. 13 42.27N 18.32E
Hereford U.K. 5 52.04N 2.43W
Hereford and Worcester d. U.K. 5 52.08N 2.30W
Herentals Belgium 8 51.12N 4.42E
Herford Germany 14 52.07N 8.40E
Hermannsburg Australia 44 23.56S 132.46E
Hermanus R.S.A. 39 34.24S 19.16E
Hermidale Australia 47 31.33S 146.44E
Hermiston U.S.A. 54 45.51N 119.17W
Hermosillo Mexico 56 29.04N 110.58W
Herne Germany 8 51.32N 7.12E
Herne Bay town U.K. 5 51.23N 1.10E
Herning Denmark 17 56.08N 8.59E
Heron Bay town Canada 55 48.41N 86.28W
Herrera del Duque Spain 10 39.10N 5.03W
Herstal Belgium 8 50.14N 5.38E
Herten Germany 8 51.36N 7.08E
Hertford U.K. 5 51.48N 0.05W
Hertfordshire d. U.K. 5 51.51N 0.05W
Hervey B. Australia 44 25.00S 153.00E
Herzliyya Israel 32 32.10N 34.50E
Hesbaye f. Belgium 8 50.32N 5.07E
Hesel Germany 8 53.19N 7.35E
Hessen d. Germany 14 50.30N 9.15E
Hesso Australia 46 32.08S 137.58E
Hetzerath Germany 8 49.54N 6.50E
Hewett, C. Canada 51 70.20N 68.00W
Hexham U.K. 4 54.58N 2.06W
Hexigten Qi China 25 43.17N 117.24E
Heysham U.K. 4 54.03N 2.53W
Heyuan China 25 23.44N 114.41E
Heywood Australia 46 38.08S 141.38E
Heywood U.K. 4 53.36N 2.13W
Hiawatha Utah U.S.A. 54 39.29N 111.01W
Hibbing U.S.A. 53 47.25N 92.55W
Hicks Bay town New Zealand 48 37.35S 178.18E
Hidalgo d. Mexico 56 20.50N 98.30W
Hidalgo Tamaulipas Mexico 56 24.15N 99.26W
Hidalgo del Parral Mexico 56 26.56N 105.40W
Hieradhsvotn r. Iceland 16 65.45N 18.50W
Higashimatsuyama Japan 23 36.02N 139.24E
Higashimurayama Japan 23 35.46N 139.29E
Higashiōsaka Japan 23 34.39N 135.35E
Higginsville Australia 43 31.46S 121.43E
Highland d. U.K. 6 57.42N 5.00W
High Peak mtn. U.K. 4 53.22N 1.48W
High Willhays mtn. U.K. 5 50.41N 4.00W
High Wycombe U.K. 5 51.38N 0.46W
Hiiumaa i. Estonia 17 58.52N 22.40E
Híjar Spain 10 41.10N 0.27W
Hikone Japan 23 35.15N 136.15E
Hikurangi New Zealand 48 35.36S 174.17E
Hikurangi mtn. New Zealand 48 37.50S 178.10E
Hilden Germany 8 51.10N 6.56E
Hildesheim Germany 14 52.09N 9.58E
Hillegom Neth. 8 52.19N 4.35E
Hill End Australia 47 33.01S 149.26E
Hillsboro Oreg. U.S.A. 54 45.31N 122.59W
Hillsdale U.S.A. 55 41.56N 84.37W
Hillsport Canada 55 49.27N 85.34W
Hillston Australia 47 33.30S 145.33E
Hilo Hawaii U.S.A. 52 19.42N 155.04W
Hiltrup Germany 8 51.55N 7.36E
Hilversum Neth. 8 52.14N 5.12E
Himachal Pradesh d. India 28 31.45N 77.30E
Himalaya mts. Asia 29 29.00N 84.00E
Himanka Finland 16 64.04N 23.39E
Himarë Albania 13 40.07N 19.44E
Ḩimş Syria 32 34.44N 36.43E
Hinchinbrook I. Australia 44 18.23S 146.17E
Hinckley U.K. 5 52.33N 1.21W
Hindmarsh, L. Australia 46 36.03S 141.53E
Hindu Kush mts. Asia 28 36.40N 70.00E
Hindupur India 28 13.49N 77.29E
Hines Creek town Canada 50 56.15N 118.36W
Hingol r. Pakistan 28 25.25N 65.32E
Hinnöy i. Norway 16 68.35N 15.50E
Hinojosa Spain 10 38.30N 5.17W
Hinsdale Mont. U.S.A. 54 48.24N 107.05W
Hippolytushoef Neth. 8 52.57N 4.58E
Hirakata Japan 23 34.48N 135.38E
Hīrākud resr. India 29 21.32N 83.55E
Hiratsuka Japan 23 35.19N 139.21E
Hiroshima Japan 25 34.23N 132.27E
Hirson France 8 49.56N 4.05E
Hîrşova Romania 15 44.41N 27.57E
Hirtshals Denmark 17 57.35N 9.58E
Hisai Japan 23 34.40N 136.28E
Hisār India 28 29.10N 75.43E
Ḩismá f. Saudi Arabia 32 28.45N 35.56E
Hispaniola i. C. America 57 19.00N 71.00W
Ḩisyah Syria 32 34.24N 36.45E
Hīt Iraq 30 33.38N 42.50E
Hitchin U.K. 5 51.57N 0.16W
Hitra i. Norway 16 63.37N 8.46E
Hjälmaren l. Sweden 17 59.15N 15.45E
Hjörring Denmark 17 57.28N 9.59E
Hlotse Lesotho 39 28.52S 28.02E
Ho Ghana 38 6.38N 0.38E
Hoare B. Canada 51 65.20N 62.30W
Hobart Australia 45 42.54S 147.18E
Hobart Ind. U.S.A. 55 41.32N 87.14W
Hoboken Belgium 8 51.11N 4.21E
Hobro Denmark 17 56.38N 9.48E
Hobyo Somali Rep. 35 5.20N 48.30E
Ho Chi Minh Vietnam 26 10.46N 106.43E
Hodgson Canada 51 51.13N 97.34W
Hod HaSharon Israel 32 32.15N 34.55E
Hódmezövásárhely Hungary 13 46.26N 20.21E
Hoek van Holland Neth. 8 51.59N 4.08E
Hoeryŏng N.Korea 23 42.27N 129.44E
Hof Germany 14 50.19N 11.56E
Höfn Iceland 16 64.16N 15.10W
Hofors Sweden 17 60.33N 16.17E
Hofsjökull mtn. Iceland 16 64.50N 19.00W
Hofsos Iceland 16 65.53N 19.26W
Höganäs Sweden 17 56.12N 12.33E
Hohhot China 25 40.49N 111.37E
Hoi An Vietnam 26 15.54N 108.19E
Hoima Uganda 37 1.25N 31.22E
Hokitika New Zealand 48 42.42S 170.59E
Hokkaidō i. Japan 25 43.30N 143.20E
Hokksund Norway 17 59.47N 9.59E
Hola Kenya 37 1.29S 40.02E
Holbaek Denmark 17 55.43N 11.43E
Holbrook Australia 47 35.46S 147.20E
Holbrook U.S.A. 54 34.54N 110.10W
Holguín Cuba 57 20.54N 76.15W
Höljes Sweden 17 60.54N 12.36E
Hollabrunn Austria 14 48.34N 16.05E
Holland Mich. U.S.A. 55 42.46N 86.06W
Holman Island town Canada 50 70.43N 117.43W
Holmavik Iceland 16 65.43N 21.39W
Holmestrand Norway 17 59.29N 10.18E
Holmön i. Sweden 16 63.47N 20.53E
Holmsund Sweden 16 63.41N 20.20E
Holon Israel 32 32.01N 34.46E
Holroyd r. Australia 44 14.10S 141.36E
Holstebro Denmark 17 56.21N 8.38E
Holstein Canada 55 44.03N 80.45W
Holsteinsborg Greenland 51 66.55N 53.30W
Holsworthy U.K. 5 50.48N 4.21W
Holt U.K. 4 52.55N 1.04E
Holten Neth. 8 52.18N 6.26E
Holwerd Neth. 8 53.22N 5.54E
Holy Cross U.S.A. 50 62.12N 159.47W
Holyhead U.K. 4 53.18N 4.38W
Holyhead B. U.K. 4 53.22N 4.40W
Holy I. England U.K. 4 55.41N 1.47W
Holy I. Wales U.K. 4 53.15N 4.38W
Holywood U.K. 7 54.38N 5.50W
Hombori Mali 38 15.20N 1.38W
Home B. Canada 51 69.00N 66.00W
Home Hill town Australia 44 19.40S 147.25E
Homer Alas. U.S.A. 50 59.40N 151.37W
Homer Tunnel New Zealand 48 44.40S 168.15E
Homoine Mozambique 39 23.45S 35.09E
Homoljske Planina f. Yugo. 15 44.20N 21.45E
Honda Colombia 60 5.15N 74.50W
Hondeklipbaai R.S.A. 39 30.19S 17.12E
Hondo r. Mexico 57 18.33N 88.22W
Honduras C. America 57 14.30N 87.00W
Honduras, G. of Carib. Sea 57 16.20N 87.30W
Honfleur France 9 49.25N 0.14E
Hong Hà r. Vietnam 26 20.15N 106.36E
Hong Kong Asia 25 22.30N 114.10E
Hongshui He r. China 25 23.20N 110.04E
Honiton U.K. 5 50.48N 3.13W
Honkajoki Finland 17 62.00N 22.15E
Honolulu Hawaii U.S.A. 52 21.19N 157.50W
Honshū i. Japan 25 36.00N 138.00E
Hood Pt. Australia 43 34.23S 119.34E
Hood Range mts. Australia 47 28.35S 144.30E
Hoogeveen Neth. 8 52.44N 6.29E
Hoogezand Neth. 8 53.10N 6.47E
Hoogstade Belgium 8 50.59N 2.42E
Hook Head Rep. of Ire. 7 52.07N 6.55W
Hoopa U.S.A. 54 41.03N 123.40W
Hoopstad R.S.A. 39 27.48S 25.52E
Hoorn Neth. 8 52.38N 5.03E
Hoover Dam U.S.A. 54 36.00N 114.27W
Hope W.A. U.S.A. 53 33.40N 93.36W
Hopedale Canada 51 55.30N 60.10W
Hopefield R.S.A. 39 33.04S 18.19E
Hope, L. S.A. Australia 43 32.31S 120.25E
Hope, L. S.A. Australia 46 28.23S 139.19E
Hopetoun Vic. Australia 46 35.43S 142.20E
Hopetoun W.A. Australia 43 33.57S 120.05E
Hopetown R.S.A. 39 29.37S 24.04E
Hopkins r. Australia 46 38.25S 142.00E
Hopkins, L. Australia 42 24.15S 128.50E
Hopland U.S.A. 54 38.58N 123.07W
Hoquiam U.S.A. 54 46.59N 123.53W
Hordaland d. Norway 17 60.30N 6.30E
Horde Germany 8 51.29N 7.30E
Horlick Mts. Antarctica 64 86.00S 102.00W
Hormuz, Str. of Asia 31 26.35N 56.20E
Horn Austria 14 48.40N 15.40E
Hornavan l. Sweden 16 66.10N 17.30E
Horn, C. see Hornos, Cabo de c. S. America 63
Horncastle U.K. 4 53.13N 0.08W
Horndal Sweden 17 60.18N 16.25E
Hornell U.S.A. 55 42.19N 77.39W
Hornepayne Canada 55 49.14N 84.48W
Hornindal Norway 17 61.58N 6.31E
Horn Mts. Canada 50 62.15N 119.15W
Hornos, Cabo de c. S. America 63 55.47S 67.00W

'nsby Australia **47** 33.11S 151.06E
'nsea U.K. **4** 53.55N 0.10W
'ovice Czech Republic **14** 49.50N 13.54E
'rsens Denmark **17** 55.52N 9.52E
'rsham Australia **46** 36.45S 142.15E
'rsham U.K. **5** 51.04N 0.20W
'rten Norway **17** 59.25N 10.30E
'ton *r.* Canada **50** 70.00N 127.00W
'ton L. Canada **50** 67.30N 122.28W
se, Pegunungan *mts.* Malaysia **26** 1.30N 14.10E
shiārpur India **28** 31.30N 75.59E
sh 'Isa Egypt **32** 30.55N 30.17E
skins P.N.G. **41** 5.30S 150.27E
spitalet de Llobregat Spain **10** 41.20N 2.06E
ste, Isla *i.* Chile **63** 55.10S 69.00W
tan China **24** 37.07N 79.57E
tazel R.S.A. **39** 27.16S 22.57E
tham *r.* Australia **43** 32.58S 116.22E
tham, Mt. Australia **47** 36.58S 147.11E
ting Sweden **16** 64.07N 16.10E
t Springs *town* Ark. U.S.A. **53** 34.30N 93.02W
t Springs *town* S.Dak. U.S.A. **52** 43.26N 03.29W
ttah L. Canada **50** 65.04N 118.29W
udan France **9** 48.47N 1.36E
uffalize Belgium **8** 50.08N 5.50E
ughton L. U.S.A. **55** 44.16N 84.48W
ughton-le-Spring U.K. **4** 54.51N 1.28W
ulton U.S.A. **55** 46.08N 67.51W
uma U.S.A. **53** 29.35N 90.44W
undé Burkina **38** 11.34N 3.31W
urn, Loch U.K. **6** 57.06N 5.33W
uston Tex. U.S.A. **53** 29.45N 95.25W
vd Mongolia **24** 46.40N 90.45E
ve U.K. **5** 50.50N 0.10W
vsgöl Nuur *l.* Mongolia **24** 51.00N 100.30E
we, C. Australia **47** 37.30S 149.59E
witt, Mt. Australia **47** 37.15S 146.40E
wrah India **29** 22.35N 88.20E
wth Head Rep. of Ire. **7** 53.22N 6.03W
y *i.* U.K. **6** 58.51N 3.17W
yanger Norway **17** 61.13N 6.05E
yos Spain **10** 40.09N 6.45W
adec Králové Czech Republic **14** 50.13N 5.50E
on *r.* Slovakia **15** 47.49N 18.45E
ubieszów Poland **15** 50.49N 23.55E
ab *r.* Namibia **39** 20.55S 13.28E
abei Pingyuan *f.* China **25** 34.30N 117.00E
acho Peru **60** 11.05S 77.36W
ade China **25** 41.57N 114.04E
ai He *r.* China **25** 32.58N 118.18E
ainan China **25** 32.41N 117.06E
ajuápan Mexico **56** 17.50N 97.48W
alian Taiwan **25** 24.00N 121.39E
allaga *r.* Peru **60** 5.02S 75.30W
amanrazo *mtn.* Peru **60** 12.54S 75.04W
ambo Angola **36** 12.47S 15.44E
anan China **25** 46.13N 130.31E
ancané Peru **60** 15.10S 69.44W
ancapi Peru **60** 13.35S 74.05W
ancavelica Peru **60** 12.45S 75.03W
ancayo Peru **60** 12.05S 75.12W
anggang China **25** 30.40N 114.50E
ang Hai *b.* N. Korea **25** 39.00N 124.00E
ang He *r.* China **25** 37.55N 118.46E
anghua China **25** 38.22N 117.20E
angshi China **25** 30.13N 115.05E
anta Peru **60** 12.54S 74.13W
ánuco Peru **60** 9.55S 76.11W
araz Peru **60** 9.33S 77.31W
armey Peru **60** 10.05S 78.05W
ascaran *mtn.* Peru **60** 9.08S 77.36W
asco Chile **62** 28.28S 71.14W
ubei *d.* China **25** 31.15N 112.15E
ubli India **28** 15.20N 75.14E
ückelhoven Germany **8** 51.04N 6.10E
ucknall U.K. **4** 53.03N 1.12W
uddersfield U.K. **4** 53.38N 1.49W
uddinge Sweden **17** 59.14N 17.59E
udiksvall Sweden **17** 61.44N 17.07E
udson N.Y. U.S.A. **55** 42.15N 73.47W
udson *r.* U.S.A. **55** 40.42N 74.02W
udson Wyo. U.S.A. **54** 42.54N 108.35W
udson B. Canada **51** 58.00N 86.00W
udson Hope Canada **50** 56.02N 121.55W
udson Mts. Antarctica **64** 76.00S 99.00W
udson Str. Canada **51** 62.00N 70.00W
ue Vietnam **26** 16.28N 107.35E
uedin Romania **15** 46.52N 23.02E
uehuetenango Guatemala **56** 15.19N 91.26W
uelva Spain **10** 37.15N 6.56W
uelva *r.* Spain **10** 37.25N 6.00W
uércal-Overa Spain **10** 37.23N 1.56W
uesca Spain **10** 42.02N 0.25W
ugh *r.* Australia **44** 25.01S 134.01E
ughenden Australia **44** 20.51S 144.12E
ughes Australia **45** 30.40S 129.32E
ughes U.S.A. **50** 66.03N 154.16W
uiarau Range *mts.* New Zealand **48** 38.20S 177.15E
uimin China **25** 37.29N 117.29E
uisne *r.* France **9** 47.59N 0.11E
uixtla Mexico **56** 15.09N 92.30W
uizen Neth. **8** 52.18N 5.12E
ukuntsi Botswana **39** 24.02S 21.48E
'ulayfā' Saudi Arabia **30** 26.00N 40.47E
ulín Czech Republic **15** 49.19N 17.28E
ull Canada **55** 45.26N 75.45W
üls Germany **8** 51.23N 6.30E
ulst Neth. **8** 51.18N 4.01E
ultsfred Sweden **17** 57.29N 15.50E
ulun Nur *l.* China **25** 49.00N 117.27E
ulwān Egypt **32** 29.51N 31.20E
umaitá Brazil **60** 7.31S 63.02W
umansdorp R.S.A. **39** 34.02S 24.45E
umber *r.* U.K. **4** 53.40N 0.12W
umberside *d.* U.K. **4** 53.48N 0.35W
Humboldt *r.* U.S.A. **54** 40.02N 118.31W
Hūmedān Iran **31** 25.24N 59.39E
Hume, L. Australia **47** 36.06S 147.05E
Humenné Slovakia **15** 48.56N 21.55E
Humphreys Peak *mtn.* U.S.A. **54** 35.20N 111.40W
Hūn Libya **34** 29.06N 15.57E
Húnaflói *b.* Iceland **16** 65.45N 20.50W
Hunan *d.* China **25** 27.30N 111.30E
Hunedoara Romania **15** 45.45N 22.54E
Hungary Europe **15** 47.30N 19.00E
Hungerford Australia **46** 29.00S 144.26E
Hungerford U.K. **5** 51.25N 1.30W
Hŭngnam N. Korea **25** 39.49N 127.40E
Hunsberge *mts.* Namibia **39** 27.40S 17.12E
Hunse *r.* Neth. **8** 53.20N 6.18E
Hunsrück *mts.* Germany **8** 49.44N 7.05E
Hunstanton U.K. **4** 52.57N 0.30E
Hunte *r.* Germany **14** 52.30N 8.19E
Hunter *r.* Australia **47** 32.50S 151.42E
Hunter I. Australia **45** 40.30S 144.46E
Huntingdon U.K. **5** 52.20N 0.11W
Huntingdon Penn. U.S.A. **55** 40.29N 78.01W
Huntington Ind. U.S.A. **55** 40.54N 85.30W
Huntington Oreg. U.S.A. **54** 44.21N 117.16W
Huntington Utah U.S.A. **54** 39.20N 110.58W
Huntington W.Va. U.S.A. **55** 38.24N 82.26W
Huntington Beach *town* U.S.A. **54** 33.39N 118.01W
Huntly New Zealand **48** 37.35S 175.10E
Huntly U.K. **6** 57.27N 2.47W
Huntsville Canada **55** 45.20N 79.13W
Huntsville Ala. U.S.A. **53** 34.44N 86.35W
Huntsville Tex. U.S.A. **53** 34.44N 86.35W
Hunyani *r.* Mozambique **39** 15.41S 30.38E
Huon Pen. P.N.G. **27** 6.00S 147.00E
Huonville Australia **45** 43.01S 147.01E
Huron S.Dak. U.S.A. **52** 44.22N 98.12W
Huron, L. Canada/U.S.A. **55** 44.30N 82.15W
Húsavík Iceland **16** 66.03N 17.21W
Huşi Romania **15** 46.40N 28.04E
Huskvarna Sweden **17** 57.48N 14.16E
Husum Germany **14** 54.29N 9.04E
Hutchinson R.S.A. **39** 31.30S 23.10E
Hutchinson U.S.A. **52** 38.03N 97.56W
Huy Belgium **8** 50.31N 5.14E
Hvar *i.* Croatia **13** 43.10N 16.45E
Hvita *r.* Iceland **16** 64.33N 21.45W
Hwange Zimbabwe **39** 18.20S 26.29E
Hwange Nat. Park Zimbabwe **39** 19.00S 26.30E
Hyargas Nuur *l.* Mongolia **24** 49.30N 93.35E
Hyde U.K. **4** 53.26N 2.06W
Hyden Australia **43** 32.27S 118.53E
Hyderābād India **29** 17.22N 78.26E
Hyderābād Pakistan **28** 25.23N 68.24E
Hydesville U.S.A. **54** 40.31N 124.00W
Hyères France **11** 43.07N 6.08E
Hyères, Îles d' *is.* France **11** 43.01N 6.25E
Hyland, Mt. Australia **47** 30.09S 152.25E
Hyllestad Norway **17** 61.10N 5.18E
Hyndman Peak U.S.A. **54** 43.50N 114.10W
Hysham U.S.A. **54** 46.18N 107.14W
Hythe Kent U.K. **5** 51.04N 1.05E
Hyvinkää Finland **17** 60.38N 24.52E

I

Ialomiţa *r.* Romania **15** 44.41N 27.52E
Iar Connacht *f.* Rep. of Ire. **7** 53.21N 9.22W
Iaşi Romania **15** 47.09N 27.38E
Iauaretê Brazil **60** 0.36N 69.12W
Iaupolo P.N.G. **44** 9.34S 150.30E
Ibadan Nigeria **38** 7.23N 3.56E
Ibagué Colombia **60** 4.25N 75.20W
Ibar *r.* Yugo. **13** 43.44N 20.44E
Ibaraki Japan **23** 34.49N 135.34E
Ibarra Ecuador **60** 0.23N 78.05W
Ibbenbüren Germany **8** 52.17N 7.44E
Ibi *r.* Japan **23** 35.03N 136.42E
Ibi Nigeria **38** 8.11N 9.44E
Ibiapaba, Serra da *mts.* Brazil **61** 5.30S 41.00W
Ibicaraí Brazil **61** 14.52S 39.37W
Ibicuy Argentina **63** 33.45S 59.13W
Ibina *r.* Zaïre **37** 1.00N 28.40E
Ibitinga Brazil **59** 21.43S 48.47W
Ibiza *i.* Spain **10** 39.00N 1.23E
Ibiza *town* Spain **10** 38.55N 1.30E
Ibotirama Brazil **61** 12.13S 43.12W
Ibshawāy Egypt **32** 29.21N 30.40E
Içá *r.* Brazil **60** 3.07S 67.58W
Ica Peru **60** 14.02S 75.48W
Içana Brazil **60** 0.21N 67.19W
Içana *r.* Brazil **60** 0.00 67.10W
Iceland Europe **16** 64.45N 18.00W
Ichihara Japan **23** 35.31N 140.05E
Ichikawa Japan **23** 35.44N 139.55E
Ichinomiya Japan **23** 35.18N 136.48E
Icoraci Brazil **61** 1.16S 48.28W
Idah Nigeria **38** 7.05N 6.45E
Idaho *d.* U.S.A. **54** 44.58N 115.56W
Idaho Falls *town* U.S.A. **54** 43.30N 112.02W
Idar-Oberstein Germany **8** 49.43N 7.19E
Ideles Algeria **34** 23.58N 5.53E
Idfū Egypt **30** 24.58N 32.50E
Ídhi Óros *mtn.* Greece **13** 35.13N 24.45E
Ídhra *i.* Greece **13** 37.20N 23.32E
Idmū Egypt **32** 28.09N 30.41E
Idre Sweden **17** 61.52N 12.43E
Ieper Belgium **8** 50.51N 2.53E
Ierápetra Greece **13** 35.00N 25.45E
Iesi Italy **12** 43.32N 13.15E
Iesolo Italy **9** 45.32N 12.38E
Ifakara Tanzania **37** 8.09S 36.41E
Ifalik *is.* Federated States of Micronesia **27** 7.15N 144.27E
Ife Oyo Nigeria **38** 7.33N 4.34E
Iferouâne Niger **38** 19.04N 8.24E
Iga *r.* Japan **23** 34.45N 136.01E
Iggesund Sweden **17** 61.38N 17.04E
Iglesias Italy **12** 39.18N 8.32E
Igli Algeria **34** 30.25N 2.12W
Igloolik Island *town* Canada **51** 69.05N 81.25W
Ignace Canada **51** 49.26N 91.40W
Iğneada Burnu *c.* Turkey **13** 41.50N 28.05E
Igoumenítsa Greece **13** 39.32N 20.14E
Igra Russian Fed. **18** 57.31N 53.09E
Iguaçu *r.* Brazil **59** 25.33S 54.35W
Iguaçu, Saltos do *f.* Brazil/Argentina **59** 25.35S 54.22W
Iguala Mexico **56** 18.21N 99.31W
Igualada Spain **10** 41.35N 1.37E
Iguassu Falls *see* Iguaçu, Saltos do *f.* Brazil/Argentina **59**
Iguatu Brazil **61** 6.22S 39.20W
Ihiala Nigeria **38** 5.51N 6.52E
Ihosy Madagascar **36** 22.24S 46.08E
Ii *r.* Finland **16** 65.19N 25.20E
Iida Japan **23** 35.31N 137.50E
Iisalmi Finland **16** 63.34N 27.11E
Ijebu Ode Nigeria **38** 6.47N 3.54E
IJmuiden Neth. **8** 52.28N 4.37E
IJssel *r.* Zuid Holland Neth. **8** 51.54N 4.32E
IJssel *r.* Overijssel Neth. **8** 52.34N 5.50E
IJsselmeer *l.* Neth. **8** 52.45N 5.20E
Ijuí Brazil **59** 28.23S 53.55W
Ijzendijke Neth. **8** 51.19N 3.37E
Ijzer *r.* Belgium **8** 51.09N 2.44E
Ikaría *i.* Greece **13** 37.35N 26.10E
Ikdū Egypt **32** 31.18N 30.18E
Ikela Zaïre **36** 1.06S 23.04E
Ikerre Nigeria **38** 7.30N 5.14E
Ila Nigeria **38** 8.01N 4.55E
Ilagan Phil. **27** 17.07N 121.53E
Īlām Iran **31** 33.27N 46.27E
Ilangali Tanzania **37** 6.50S 35.06E
Ilaro Nigeria **38** 6.53N 3.03E
Iława Poland **15** 53.37N 19.33E
Ilebo Zaïre **36** 4.20S 20.35E
Ilek *r.* Russian Fed. **19** 51.30N 54.00E
Ileret Kenya **37** 4.22N 36.13E
Ilesha Oyo Nigeria **38** 7.39N 4.45E
Ilfracombe Australia **44** 23.30S 144.30E
Ilfracombe U.K. **5** 51.13N 4.08W
Ilhabela Brazil **59** 23.47S 45.20W
Ilha Grande, Baía da *b.* Brazil **59** 23.09S 44.30W
Ilha Grande, Reprêsa *resr.* Brazil **59** 23.10S 53.40W
Ilhéus Brazil **61** 14.50S 39.06W
Ili *r.* Kazakhstan **24** 45.00N 74.20E
Ilia Romania **15** 45.56N 22.39E
Iliamna L. U.S.A. **50** 59.30N 155.00W
Ilich Russian Fed. **24** 40.50N 68.29E
Iligan Phil. **27** 8.12N 124.13E
Ilintsy Ukraine **15** 49.08N 29.11E
Ilion U.S.A. **55** 43.01N 75.02W
Ilkley U.K. **4** 53.56N 1.49W
Illapel Chile **62** 31.38S 71.10W
Ille-et-Vilaine *d.* France **9** 48.10N 1.30W
Illéla Niger **38** 14.30N 5.09E
Iller *r.* Germany **14** 48.23N 9.58E
Illiers France **9** 48.18N 1.15E
Illinois *d.* U.S.A. **53** 40.00N 89.00W
Illizi Algeria **34** 26.20N 8.20E
Ilmajoki Finland **16** 62.44N 22.34E
Ilminster U.K. **5** 50.55N 2.56W
Ilo Peru **62** 17.38S 71.20W
Iloilo Phil. **27** 10.45N 122.33E
Ilorin Nigeria **38** 8.32N 4.34E
Ilovlya Russian Fed. **19** 49.19N 44.01E
Imala Mozambique **37** 14.39S 39.34E
Imandra Russian Fed. **18** 67.53N 33.30E
Imandra, Ozero *l.* Russian Fed. **18** 67.30N 32.45E
Imbābah Egypt **32** 30.05N 31.12E
Īmī Ethiopia **35** 6.28N 42.18E
Immingham U.K. **4** 53.37N 0.12W
Imo *d.* Nigeria **38** 5.30N 7.20E
Imola Italy **9** 44.21N 11.42E
Imperatriz Brazil **61** 5.32S 47.28W
Imperia Italy **9** 43.53N 8.01E
Imperial Calif. U.S.A. **54** 32.51N 115.34W
Imperial Dam U.S.A. **54** 32.55N 114.30W
Imperial Valley *f.* U.S.A. **54** 32.50N 115.30W
Impfondo Congo **36** 1.36N 17.58E
Imphāl India **29** 24.47N 93.55E
Imroz *i. see* Gökçeada *i.* Turkey **13**
Ina Japan **23** 35.50N 137.57E
Ina *r.* Japan **23** 34.43N 135.28E
In Abbangarit *well* Niger **38** 17.49N 6.15E
Inangahua Junction New Zealand **48** 41.53S 171.58E
Inanwatan Indonesia **27** 2.08S 132.10E
Inari *l.* Finland **16** 69.00N 28.00E
Inari *town* Finland **16** 68.54N 27.01E
Inazawa Japan **23** 35.15N 136.47E
Inca Spain **10** 39.43N 2.54E
Incesu Turkey **30** 38.39N 35.12E
Inch'on S. Korea **25** 37.30N 126.38E
Indals *r.* Sweden **16** 62.30N 17.20E
Indaw Myanmar **24** 24.14N 96.07E
Independence Calif. U.S.A. **54** 36.48N 118.12W
Inderborskiy Kazakhstan **19** 48.32N 51.44E
India Asia **29** 23.00N 78.30E
Indiana *d.* U.S.A. **55** 40.00N 86.15W
Indiana *town* U.S.A. **55** 40.37N 79.09W
Indianapolis U.S.A. **55** 39.45N 86.10W
Indian Harbour Canada **51** 54.25N 57.20W
Indiga Russian Fed. **18** 67.40N 49.00E
Indigirka *r.* Russian Fed. **21** 71.00N 148.45E
Indija Yugo. **15** 45.03N 20.05E
Indio U.S.A. **54** 33.43N 116.13W
Indonesia Asia **26** 6.00S 118.00E
Indore India **28** 22.42N 75.54E
Indragiri *r.* Indonesia **26** 0.30S 103.08E
Indrāvati *r.* India **29** 18.45N 80.16E
Indre *r.* France **11** 47.16N 0.19W
Indus *r.* Pakistan **28** 24.00N 67.33E
Inebolu Turkey **30** 41.57N 33.45E
Inegöl Turkey **30** 40.06N 29.31E
Infiesto Spain **10** 43.21N 5.21W
I-n-Gall Niger **38** 16.47N 6.56E
Ingatestone U.K. **5** 51.41N 0.22E
Ingersoll Canada **55** 43.02N 80.53W
Ingham Australia **44** 18.35S 146.12E
Ingleborough Qld. U.K. **4** 54.10N 2.23W
Inglewood Qld. Australia **47** 28.25S 151.02E
Inglewood Vic. Australia **46** 36.33S 143.53E
Inglewood New Zealand **48** 39.09S 174.12E
Inglewood U.S.A. **54** 33.58N 118.21W
Ingolstadt Germany **14** 48.46N 11.27E
Ingomar Australia **46** 29.38S 134.48E
Ingulets Ukraine **19** 47.43N 33.16E
Ingwiller France **11** 48.52N 7.29E
Inhambane Mozambique **39** 23.51S 35.29E
Inhambane *d.* Mozambique **39** 22.20S 34.00E
Inhaminga Mozambique **39** 18.24S 35.00E
Inharrime Mozambique **39** 24.29S 35.01E
Inhassoro Mozambique **39** 21.32S 35.10E
Inirida *r.* Colombia **60** 3.59N 67.45W
Inishbofin *i.* Galway Rep. of Ire. **7** 53.38N 10.14W
Inisheer *i.* Rep. of Ire. **7** 53.04N 9.32W
Inishmaan *i.* Rep. of Ire. **7** 53.06N 9.36W
Inishmore *i.* Rep. of Ire. **7** 53.08N 9.43W
Inishowen Pen. Rep. of Ire. **7** 55.08N 7.20W
Inishturk *i.* Rep. of Ire. **7** 53.43N 10.08W
Injune Australia **44** 25.51S 148.34E
Inn *r.* Europe **14** 48.33N 13.26E
Innaminka Australia **45** 27.43S 140.46E
Inner Hebrides *is.* U.K. **6** 56.50N 6.45W
Inner Mongolia *d. see* Nei Monggol Zizhiqu *d.* China **25**
Inner Sd. U.K. **6** 57.30N 5.55W
Innisfail Australia **44** 17.32S 146.02E
Innsbruck Austria **14** 47.17N 11.25E
Innset Norway **16** 68.41N 18.50E
Inongo Zaïre **36** 1.55S 18.20E
Inowrocław Poland **15** 52.49N 18.12E
I-n-Salah Algeria **34** 27.12N 2.29E
Insein Myanmar **26** 16.54N 96.08E
In Tasik *well* Mali **38** 18.03N 2.00E
Interlaken Switz. **14** 46.42N 7.52E
Intute Mozambique **37** 14.08S 39.55E
Inukjuak Canada **51** 58.25N 78.18W
Inuvik Canada **50** 68.16N 133.40W
Inuvik *d.* Canada **50** 68.00N 130.00W
Inuyama Japan **23** 35.23N 136.56E
Inveraray U.K. **6** 56.24N 5.05W
Inverbervie U.K. **6** 56.51N 2.17W
Invercargill New Zealand **48** 46.26S 168.21E
Inverell Australia **47** 29.46S 151.10E
Invergordon U.K. **6** 57.42N 4.10W
Inverness U.K. **6** 57.27N 4.15W
Inverurie U.K. **6** 57.17N 2.23W
Inverway Australia **42** 17.49S 129.40E
Investigator Group *is.* Australia **46** 33.45S 134.30E
Investigator Str. Australia **46** 35.25S 137.10E
Invinheima *r.* Brazil **62** 22.52S 53.20W
Inya Russian Fed. **20** 50.24N 86.47E
Inyangani *mtn.* Zimbabwe **39** 18.18S 32.50E
Inyonga Tanzania **37** 6.43S 32.02E
Ioánnina Greece **13** 39.39N 20.49E
Iona *i.* U.K. **6** 56.20N 6.25W
Ionia U.S.A. **55** 42.58N 85.06W
Ionian Is. *see* Iónioi Nísoi *is.* Greece **13**
Ionian Sea Med. Sea **13** 38.30N 18.45E
Iónioi Nísoi *is.* Greece **13** 38.45N 20.00E
Íos *i.* Greece **13** 36.42N 25.20E
Iowa *d.* U.S.A. **53** 42.00N 93.00W
Iowa City U.S.A. **53** 41.39N 91.30W
Ipatovo Russian Fed. **19** 45.44N 42.56E
Ipiales Colombia **60** 0.52N 77.38W
Ipiaú Brazil **61** 14.07S 39.43W
Ipixuna Brazil **60** 7.00S 71.30W
Ipoh Malaysia **26** 4.36N 101.02E
Ippa *r.* Belarus **15** 52.13N 29.08E
Ipswich Australia **47** 27.38S 152.40E
Ipswich U.K. **5** 52.04N 1.09E
Ipu Brazil **61** 4.23S 40.44W
Ipuh Indonesia **26** 2.58S 101.28E
Iquique Chile **62** 20.13S 70.10W
Iquitos Peru **60** 3.51S 73.13W
Irago-suidō *str.* Japan **23** 34.35N 137.00E
Iráklion Greece **13** 35.20N 25.08E
Iran Asia **31** 32.00N 54.30E
Iran, Pegunungan *mts.* Indonesia/Malaysia **26** 3.20N 115.00E
Īrānshahr Iran **31** 27.14N 60.42E
Irapuato Mexico **56** 20.40N 101.40W
Iraq Asia **30** 33.00N 44.00E
Irayel Russian Fed. **18** 64.23N 55.25E
Irazú *mtn.* Costa Rica **57** 9.59N 83.52W
Irbid Jordan **32** 32.33N 35.51E
Irbīl Iraq **31** 36.12N 44.01E
Irian Jaya *d.* Indonesia **27** 4.00S 138.00E
Iringa Tanzania **37** 7.49S 35.39E
Iringa *d.* Tanzania **37** 8.30S 35.00E
Iriomote jima *i.* Japan **25** 24.30N 124.00E
Iriri *r.* Brazil **61** 3.50S 52.40W
Irish Sea U.K./Rep. of Ire. **7** 53.30N 5.40W
Irkutsk Russian Fed. **24** 52.18N 104.15E
Iron Baron Australia **46** 32.59S 137.09E
Iron Gate *f.* Romania/Yugo. **15** 44.40N 22.30E
Iron Knob Australia **46** 32.44S 137.08E
Iron Mountain *town* U.S.A. **55** 45.51N 88.03W
Iron Mts. Rep. of Ire. **7** 54.10N 7.56W
Iron River *town* U.S.A. **53** 46.05N 88.38W
Irons U.S.A. **55** 44.08N 85.55W
Ironton U.S.A. **55** 38.32N 82.40W
Ironwood U.S.A. **55** 46.25N 90.08W
Iroquois Falls *town* Canada **55** 48.47N 80.41W
Irosin Phil. **27** 12.45N 124.02E
Irō-zaki *c.* Japan **23** 34.36N 138.51E
Irpen Ukraine **15** 50.31N 30.29E
Irrapatana Australia **46** 29.03S 136.28E
Irrawaddy *r.* Myanmar **29** 17.45N 95.25E
Irrawaddy Delta Myanmar **29** 16.30N 95.20E
Irsha *r.* Ukraine **15** 50.45N 29.30E
Irtysh *r.* Russian Fed. **20** 61.00N 68.40E
Iruma *r.* Japan **23** 35.57N 139.30E
Irumu Zaïre **37** 1.29N 29.48E
Irún Spain **10** 43.20N 1.48W
Irvine U.K. **6** 55.37N 4.40W
Irvinestown U.K. **7** 54.29N 7.40W
Irwin, Pt. Australia **43** 35.03S 116.20E
Isa Nigeria **38** 13.14N 6.24E
Isaac *r.* Australia **44** 22.52S 149.20E
Isabelia, Cordillera *mts.* Nicaragua **57** 13.30N 85.00W
Ísafjördhur *town* Iceland **16** 66.05N 23.06W
Isaka Tanzania **37** 3.52S 32.54E
Isakogorka Russian Fed. **18** 64.23N 40.31E
Isar *r.* Germany **14** 48.48N 12.57E
Isbergues France **8** 50.38N 2.24E
Ischia *i.* Italy **12** 40.43N 13.54E
Ise Japan **23** 34.29N 136.42E
Iseo, Lago d' *l.* Italy **9** 45.43N 10.04E
Isère *r.* France **11** 45.02N 4.54E
Iserlohn Germany **8** 51.23N 7.42E
Isernia Italy **12** 41.36N 14.14E
Ise-wan *b.* Japan **23** 34.45N 136.40E
Iseyin Nigeria **38** 7.59N 3.36E
Isfahan *see* Eşfahān Iran **28**
Ishim Russian Fed. **20** 56.10N 69.30E
Ishim *r.* Russian Fed. **20** 57.50N 71.00E
Ishinomaki Japan **25** 38.25N 141.18E
Ishpeming U.S.A. **55** 46.29N 87.40W
Isigny France **9** 49.18N 1.06W
Isiolo Kenya **37** 0.20N 37.36E
Isipingo Beach *town* R.S.A. **39** 30.00S 30.57E
Isiro Zaïre **37** 2.50N 27.40E
Iskenderun Turkey **30** 36.37N 36.08E
Iskenderun Körfezi *g.* Turkey **30** 36.40N 35.50E
Iskilip Turkey **30** 40.45N 34.28E
Iskŭr *r.* Bulgaria **13** 43.42N 24.27E
Isla *r.* U.K. **6** 56.32N 3.22W
Islāmābād Pakistan **28** 33.40N 73.08E
Island L. Australia **46** 31.30S 136.40E
Island L. Canada **51** 53.58N 94.47W
Island Magee *pen.* U.K. **7** 54.48N 5.44W
Islands, B. of New Zealand **48** 35.15S 174.15E
Islay *i.* U.K. **6** 55.45N 6.20W
Isle *r.* France **11** 45.02N 0.08W
Isle of Portland *f.* U.K. **5** 50.32N 2.25W
Isle of Wight *d.* U.K. **5** 50.40N 1.17W
Ismael Cortinas Uruguay **63** 33.58S 57.06W
Isnā Egypt **30** 25.16N 32.30E
Isoka Zambia **37** 10.06S 32.39E
Isola della Scala Italy **9** 45.16N 11.00E
Isparta Turkey **30** 37.46N 30.32E
Ispica Italy **12** 36.46N 14.55E
Israel Asia **32** 32.00N 34.50E
Israelite B. Australia **43** 33.40S 123.55E
Israelite Bay *town* Australia **43** 33.37S 123.48E
Issoire France **11** 45.33N 3.15E
Is-sur-Tille France **11** 47.30N 5.10E
Issyk Kul *l.* Kyrgyzstan **24** 43.30N 77.20E
Istanbul Turkey **13** 41.02N 28.58E
Istanbul Boğazi *str.* Turkey **13** 41.07N 29.04E
Isthmus of Kra Thailand **29** 10.10N 99.00E
Istiaía Greece **13** 38.57N 23.09E
Istok Yugo. **13** 42.47N 20.29E
Istra *pen.* Croatia **14** 45.12N 13.55E
Itabaiana Brazil **61** 7.20S 35.20W
Itabira Brazil **59** 19.39S 43.14W
Itabirito Brazil **59** 20.21S 43.45W
Itabuna Brazil **61** 14.48S 39.18W
Itacajuna *r.* Brazil **61** 5.20S 49.08W
Itacoatiara Brazil **60** 3.06S 58.22W
Itagüí Colombia **60** 6.10N 75.36W
Itaí Brazil **59** 23.23S 49.05W
Itaim *r.* Brazil **61** 6.43S 42.48W
Itaipu, Reprêsa *resr.* Brazil/Paraguay **59** 24.30S 54.20W
Itaituba Brazil **61** 4.17S 55.59W
Itajaí Brazil **59** 26.50S 48.39W
Itajubá Brazil **59** 22.24S 45.25W
Itaka Tanzania **37** 8.51S 32.48E
Italy Europe **12** 43.00N 12.00E
Itami Japan **23** 34.46N 135.25E
Itapecerica Brazil **59** 20.28S 45.09W
Itapecuru Mirim Brazil **61** 3.24S 44.20W
Itaperuna Brazil **59** 21.14S 41.51W
Itapetinga Brazil **61** 15.17S 40.16W
Itapetininga Brazil **59** 23.36S 48.07W
Itapeva Brazil **59** 23.59S 48.59W
Itapicuru *r.* Brazil **61** 11.50S 37.30W
Itapira Brazil **59** 22.24S 46.56W
Itaqui Brazil **59** 29.07S 56.33W
Itatiba Brazil **59** 22.59S 46.51W
Itatinga Brazil **59** 23.06S 48.36W
Itatuba Brazil **60** 5.40S 63.20W
Itaúna Brazil **59** 20.04S 44.14W
Ithaca U.S.A. **55** 42.26N 76.30W
Itháki Greece **13** 38.23N 20.42E
Itmurinkol, Ozero *l.* Kazakhstan **19** 49.30N 52.17E
Itō Japan **23** 34.58N 139.05E
Iton *r.* France **9** 49.09N 1.12E
Iţsa Egypt **32** 29.14N 30.47E
Itu Brazil **59** 23.17S 47.18W
Ituí *r.* Brazil **60** 4.38S 70.19W
Ituiutaba Brazil **59** 19.00S 49.25W
Ituri *r.* Zaïre **37** 1.45N 27.06E
Iturup *i.* Russian Fed. **25** 44.00N 147.30E
Ituverava Brazil **59** 20.22S 47.48W
Ituxi *r.* Brazil **60** 7.20S 64.50W
Ityāy al Bārūd Egypt **32** 30.53N 30.40E
Itzehoe Germany **14** 53.56N 9.32E
Ivaí *r.* Brazil **59** 23.20S 53.23W
Ivalo Finland **16** 68.42N 27.30E
Ivalo *r.* Finland **16** 68.43N 27.36E
Ivanhoe Australia **46** 32.56S 144.22E
Ivano-Frankovsk Ukraine **15** 48.55N 24.42E
Ivanovo Belarus **15** 52.10N 25.13E

Ivanovo Russian Fed. 18 57.00N 41.00E
Ivdel Russian Fed. 18 60.45N 60.30E
Ivenets Belarus 15 53.50N 26.40E
Ivigtût Greenland 51 61.10N 48.00W
Ivittuut see Ivigtût Greenland 51
Iviza i. see Ibiza i. Spain 10
Ivory Coast see Côte d'Ivoire Africa 34
Ivrea Italy 9 45.28N 7.52E
Ivujivik Canada 51 62.24N 77.55W
Ivybridge U.K. 5 50.24N 3.56W
Iwata Japan 23 34.42N 137.48E
Iwo Nigeria 38 7.38N 4.11E
Ixiamas Bolivia 62 13.45S 68.09W
Izabal, Lago de l. Guatemala 57 15.30N 89.00W
Izberbash Russian Fed. 19 42.31N 47.52E
Izhevsk Russian Fed. 18 56.49N 53.11E
Izhma Russian Fed. 18 65.03N 53.48E
Izhma r. Russian Fed. 18 65.16N 53.18E
Izmail Ukraine 15 45.20N 28.50E
Izmir Turkey 13 38.24N 27.09E
Izmir Körfezi g. Turkey 13 38.30N 26.45E
Izmit Turkey 30 40.48N 29.55E
Izozog, Bañados de f. Bolivia 62 18.30S 62.05W
Izozog Marshes f. see Izozog, Bañados de f. Bolivia 62
Izu-hantō pen. Japan 23 34.53N 138.55E
Izumi Japan 23 34.29N 135.26E
Izumi-ōtsu Japan 23 34.30N 135.24E
Izumi-sano Japan 23 34.25N 135.19E
Izumo r. Japan 23 34.38N 136.33E
Izyaslav Ukraine 15 50.10N 26.46E
Izyum Ukraine 19 49.12N 37.19E

J

Jabal, Baḩr al r. Sudan 35 9.30N 30.20E
Jabalón r. Spain 10 38.55N 4.07W
Jabalpur India 29 23.10N 79.59E
Jabālyah Egypt 32 31.32N 34.29E
Jabbān, Arḑ al f. Jordan 32 32.08N 36.35E
Jabiru Australia 44 12.39S 132.55E
Jablah Syria 32 35.22N 35.56E
Jablonec nad Nisou Czech Republic 14 50.44N 15.10E
Jaboticabal Brazil 59 21.15S 48.17W
Jaca Spain 10 42.34N 0.33W
Jacareí Brazil 59 23.17S 45.57W
Jackman U.S.A. 55 45.38N 70.16W
Jackson Mich. U.S.A. 55 42.15N 84.24W
Jackson Miss. U.S.A. 53 32.20N 90.11W
Jackson Ohio U.S.A. 55 39.03N 82.40W
Jackson Tenn. U.S.A. 53 35.37N 88.50W
Jackson Wyo. U.S.A. 54 43.29N 110.38W
Jacksonville Fla. U.S.A. 53 30.20N 81.40W
Jacobābād Pakistan 28 28.16N 68.30E
Jacobina Brazil 61 11.13S 40.30W
Jacob Lake town U.S.A. 54 36.41N 112.14W
Jacques Cartier, Mt. Canada 55 49.00N 65.55W
Jacuí r. Brazil 59 29.56S 51.13W
Jacundá r. Brazil 61 1.57S 50.26W
Jade Germany 8 53.21N 8.11E
Jadebusen b. Germany 8 53.30N 8.12E
Jaén Peru 60 5.21S 78.28W
Jaén Spain 10 37.46N 3.48W
Jaffa see Tel Aviv-Yafo Israel 32
Jaffa, C. Australia 46 36.58S 139.39E
Jaffna Sri Lanka 29 9.38N 80.02E
Jagdalpur India 29 19.04N 82.05E
Jagodina Yugo. 13 43.58N 21.16E
Jaguarão Brazil 59 32.30S 53.25W
Jahrom Iran 31 28.30N 53.30E
Jailolo Indonesia 27 1.05N 127.29E
Jaipur India 28 26.53N 75.50E
Jajawijaya Mts. Asia 27 4.20S 139.10E
Jājpur India 29 20.50N 86.20E
Jakarta Indonesia 26 6.08S 106.45E
Jäkkvik Sweden 16 66.23N 17.00E
Jakobstad see Pietarsaari Finland 16
Jalālah al Baḩrīyah, Jabal mts. Egypt 32 29.20N 32.12E
Jalālat al Qiblīyah, Jabal al mts. Egypt 32 28.42N 32.23E
Jalapa Mexico 56 19.45N 96.48W
Jālgaon India 28 21.01N 75.39E
Jalingo Nigeria 38 8.54N 11.21E
Jalisco d. Mexico 56 21.00N 103.00W
Jālna India 28 19.50N 75.58E
Jalón r. Spain 10 41.47N 1.02W
Jālor India 28 25.21N 72.37E
Jalpaiguri India 29 26.30N 88.50E
Jālū Libya 35 29.00N 21.30E
Jalūlā Iraq 31 34.16N 45.10E
Jamaame Somali Rep. 37 0.04N 42.46E
Jamaari Nigeria 38 11.44N 9.53E
Jamaica C. America 57 18.00N 77.00W
Jamālpur Bangla. 29 24.54N 89.57E
Jamanxim r. Brazil 61 4.43S 56.18W
Jambes Belgium 8 50.28N 4.52E
Jambi Indonesia 26 1.36S 103.39E
Jambi d. Indonesia 26 2.00S 102.30E
James r. S.Dak. U.S.A. 53 42.50N 97.15W
James B. Canada 51 53.00N 80.00W
James Bay Prov. Park Canada 55 51.24N 79.00W
Jamestown Australia 46 33.12S 138.38E
Jamestown N.Dak. U.S.A. 52 46.54N 98.42W
Jamestown N.Y. U.S.A. 55 42.06N 79.14W
Jammerbugt b. Denmark 17 57.20N 9.30E
Jammu Jammu & Kashmir 28 32.44N 74.52E
Jammu & Kashmir Asia 28 33.30N 76.00E
Jāmnagar India 28 22.28N 70.06E
Jamsah Egypt 32 27.39N 33.35E
Jämsänkoski Finland 17 61.55N 25.11E
Jamshedpur India 29 22.47N 86.12E
Jämtland d. Sweden 16 63.00N 14.30E
Janda, Laguna de la l. Spain 10 36.15N 5.50W
Jándula r. Spain 10 38.08N 4.08W
Janesville U.S.A. 53 42.42N 89.02W
Jangamo Mozambique 39 24.06S 35.21E
Janīn Jordan 32 32.28N 35.18E
Jan Kempdorp R.S.A. 39 27.55S 24.48E
Jan Mayen i. Arctic Oc. 64 71.00N 9.00W
Januária Brazil 59 15.28S 44.23W
Janzé France 9 47.58N 1.30W
Japan Asia 25 36.00N 136.00E
Japan, Sea of Asia 25 40.00N 135.00E
Japurá r. Brazil 60 3.00S 64.50W
Jarama r. Spain 10 40.27N 3.32W
Jarash Jordan 32 32.17N 35.54E
Jardee Australia 43 34.18S 116.04E
Jardine r. Australia 44 11.07S 142.30E
Jardines de la Reina is. Cuba 57 20.30N 79.00W
Jardinópolis Brazil 59 20.59S 47.48W
Jargeau France 9 47.52N 2.07E
Jarocin Poland 15 51.59N 17.31E
Jarosław Poland 15 50.02N 22.42E
Jarrāḩī r. Iran 31 30.40N 48.23E
Järvenpää Finland 17 60.28N 25.06E
Jāsk Iran 31 25.40N 57.45E
Jasło Poland 15 49.45N 21.29E
Jasper Canada 50 52.55N 118.05W
Jastrebarsko Croatia 14 45.40N 15.39E
Jastrowie Poland 14 53.26N 16.49E
Jászberény Hungary 15 47.30N 19.55E
Jataí Brazil 59 17.58S 51.45W
Játiva Spain 10 39.00N 0.32W
Jaú Brazil 59 22.11S 48.35W
Jauja Peru 60 11.50S 75.15W
Jaunjelgava Latvia 18 56.34N 25.02E
Jaunpur India 29 25.44N 82.41E
Java i. see Jawa i. Indonesia 26
Javari r. Peru 60 4.30S 71.20W
Java Sea see Jawa, Laut sea Indonesia 26
Java Trench f. Indonesia 26 10.00S 110.00E
Jawa i. Indonesia 26 7.30S 110.00E
Jawa Barat d. Indonesia 26 7.15S 107.00E
Jawa, Laut sea Indonesia 26 5.00S 111.00E
Jawa Tengah d. Indonesia 26 7.40S 109.40E
Jawa Timur d. Indonesia 26 7.00S 112.00E
Jayah, Wādī al see Hā 'Arava Jordan/Israel 32
Jayapura Indonesia 27 2.28S 140.38E
Jazirah Doberai f. Indonesia 27 1.10S 132.30E
Jazzīn Lebanon 32 33.32N 35.34E
Jean U.S.A. 54 35.46N 115.20W
Jean Marie River town Canada 50 61.32N 120.40W
Jebāl Bārez, Kūh-e mts. Iran 31 28.40N 58.10E
Jebba Nigeria 38 9.11N 4.49E
Jedburgh U.K. 6 55.29N 2.33W
Jedda see Jiddah Saudi Arabia 35
Jedrzejów Poland 15 50.39N 20.18E
Jefferson City U.S.A. 53 38.33N 92.10W
Jefferson, Mt. Nev. U.S.A. 54 38.46N 116.55W
Jefferson, Mt. Oreg. U.S.A. 54 44.40N 121.47W
Jeffersonville U.S.A. 55 38.16N 85.45W
Jega Nigeria 38 12.12N 4.23E
Jēkabpils Latvia 18 56.28N 25.58E
Jelenia Góra Poland 14 50.55N 15.45E
Jelgava Latvia 17 56.39N 23.42E
Jember Indonesia 26 8.07S 113.45E
Jena Germany 14 50.56N 11.35E
Jenbach Austria 14 47.24N 11.47E
Jenolan Caves town Australia 47 33.53S 150.03E
Jeparit Australia 46 36.09S 141.59E
Jeppo Finland 16 63.24N 22.37E
Jequié Brazil 61 13.52S 40.06W
Jequitinhonha r. Brazil 59 16.46S 39.45W
Jerantut Malaysia 26 3.56N 102.22E
Jérémie Haiti 57 18.40N 74.09W
Jerez Spain 10 38.20N 6.45W
Jerez de la Frontera Spain 10 36.41N 6.08W
Jericho see Arīḩā Jordan 32
Jerilderie Australia 47 35.23S 145.41E
Jerome U.S.A. 54 42.43N 114.31W
Jerramungup Australia 43 33.57S 118.53E
Jersey i. U.K. 5 49.13N 2.08W
Jersey City U.S.A. 55 40.44N 74.04W
Jerusalem see Yerushalayim Israel/Jordan 32
Jervis B. Australia 47 35.05S 150.44E
Jesenice Slovenia 12 46.27N 14.04E
Jessore Bangla. 29 23.10N 89.12E
Jesús Carranza Mexico 56 17.26N 95.02W
Jever Germany 8 53.34N 7.54E
Jevnaker Norway 17 60.15N 10.28E
Jeypore India 29 18.51N 82.41E
Jeziorak, Jezioro l. Poland 15 53.40N 19.04E
Jhang Sadar Pakistan 28 31.16N 72.19E
Jhānsi India 29 25.27N 78.34E
Jhelum r. Pakistan 28 31.04N 72.10E
Jialing Jiang r. China 29 29.33N 106.30E
Jiamusi China 25 46.50N 130.21E
Ji'an China 25 27.08N 115.00E
Jiange China 29 32.04N 105.26E
Jiangling China 25 30.20N 112.20E
Jiangsu d. China 25 34.00N 119.00E
Jiangxi d. China 25 27.25N 115.20E
Jianyang Fujian China 25 27.20N 117.50E
Jiaohe China 25 43.42N 127.19E
Jiashan China 25 32.47N 117.59E
Jiaxian China 25 38.02N 110.29E
Jiaxing China 25 30.40N 120.50E
Jiayi Taiwan 25 23.38N 120.27E
Jiddah Saudi Arabia 35 21.30N 39.10E
Jigawa d. Nigeria 38 12.30N 9.30E
Jihlava Czech Republic 14 49.24N 15.35E
Jilib Somali Rep. 37 0.28N 42.50E
Jilin China 25 43.53N 126.35E
Jilin d. China 25 44.50N 125.00E
Jilong Taiwan 25 25.10N 121.43E
Jīma Ethiopia 35 7.39N 36.47E
Jiménez Mexico 56 27.08N 104.55W
Jimeta Nigeria 38 9.19N 12.25E
Jinan China 25 36.50N 117.00E
Jindabyne Australia 47 36.24S 148.37E
Jingdezhen China 25 29.16N 117.11E
Jingellic Australia 47 35.54S 147.44E
Jinggu Yunnan China 29 23.29N 100.19E
Jinghong China 24 21.59N 100.49E
Jing Xian China 25 26.35N 109.41E
Jinhua China 25 29.06N 119.40E
Jining Nei Monggol China 25 40.56N 113.00E
Jining Shantung China 25 35.25N 116.40E
Jinja Uganda 37 0.27N 33.10E
Jinotepe Nicaragua 57 11.50N 86.10W
Jinsha Jiang r. China 29 26.30N 101.40E
Jinxi Liaoning China 25 40.54N 120.36E
Jin Xian Liaoning China 25 39.04N 121.45E
Jinzhou China 25 41.07N 121.06E
Jipijapa Ecuador 60 1.23S 80.35W
Jirjā Egypt 30 26.20N 31.53E
Jitarning Australia 43 32.48S 117.57E
Jiu r. Romania 13 43.44N 23.52E
Jiujiang China 25 29.41N 116.03E
Jixi China 25 45.17N 131.00E
Jīzān Saudi Arabia 35 16.56N 42.33E
Jizl, Wādī al r. Saudi Arabia 30 25.37N 38.20E
João Pessoa Brazil 61 7.06S 34.53W
Jódar Spain 10 37.50N 3.21W
Jodhpur India 28 26.18N 73.08E
Jodoigne Belgium 8 50.45N 4.52E
Joensuu Finland 18 62.35N 29.46E
Joetsu Japan 23 37.07N 138.15E
Johannesburg R.S.A. 39 26.11S 28.04E
John Day U.S.A. 54 44.25N 118.57W
John Day r. U.S.A. 54 45.44N 120.39W
John O'Groats U.K. 6 58.39N 3.02W
Johnson City Tenn. U.S.A. 53 36.20N 82.23W
Johnston, L. Australia 43 32.25S 120.30E
Johnstown Penn. U.S.A. 55 40.20N 78.55W
Johor Baharu Malaysia 26 1.29N 103.40E
Joigny France 9 48.00N 3.20E
Joinville Brazil 59 26.20S 48.49W
Joinville France 11 48.27N 5.08E
Jokkmokk Sweden 16 66.37N 19.50E
Jökulsá á Brú r. Iceland 16 65.33N 14.23W
Jökulsá á Fjöllum r. Iceland 16 66.05N 16.32W
Jolfa Iran 31 32.40N 51.39E
Joliette Canada 55 46.02N 73.27W
Jolo i. Phil. 27 5.55N 121.20E
Jolo town Phil. 27 6.03N 121.00E
Jombang Indonesia 26 7.30S 112.21E
Jomda China 29 31.30N 98.16E
Jonava Lithuania 17 55.05N 24.17E
Jonesboro Ark. U.S.A. 53 35.50N 90.41W
Jones Sd. Canada 51 76.00N 85.00W
Jönköping Sweden 17 57.47N 14.11E
Jönköping d. Sweden 17 57.30N 14.30E
Joplin U.S.A. 53 37.04N 94.31W
Jordan Asia 30 31.00N 36.00E
Jordan r. see Al Urdunn r. Asia 32
Jordan Mont. U.S.A. 54 47.19N 106.55W
Jordan Valley town U.S.A. 54 42.58N 117.03W
Jorhāt India 29 26.45N 94.13E
Jörn Sweden 16 65.04N 20.02E
Jos Nigeria 38 9.54N 8.53E
José de San Martin Argentina 63 44.04S 70.26W
José Enrique Rodó Uruguay 63 33.41S 57.34W
Joseph Bonaparte G. Australia 42 14.00S 128.30E
Joseph City U.S.A. 54 34.57N 110.20W
Jos Plateau f. Nigeria 38 10.00N 9.00E
Jotunheimen mts. Norway 17 61.38N 8.18E
Joué-lès-Tours France 9 47.21N 0.40E
Joure Neth. 8 52.59N 5.49E
Joverega Botswana 39 19.08S 24.15E
Juan Aldama Mexico 56 24.19N 103.21W
Juan B. Arruabarrena Argentina 63 30.25S 58.15W
Juan de Fuca, Str. of Canada/U.S.A. 54 48.15N 124.00W
Juan de Nova i. Madagascar 37 17.03S 42.45E
Juárez Argentina 63 37.40S 59.48W
Juàzeiro Brazil 61 9.25S 40.30W
Juàzeiro do Norte Brazil 61 7.10S 39.18W
Jūbā Sudan 35 4.50N 31.35E
Jūbāl, Maḑīq str. Egypt 32 27.40N 33.55E
Jubal, Str. of see Jūbāl, Maḑīq str. Egypt 32
Jubba r. Somali Rep. 37 0.20S 42.40E
Jubilee Downs town Australia 42 18.22S 125.17E
Júcar r. Spain 10 39.10N 0.15W
Juchitán Mexico 56 16.27N 95.05W
Judenburg Austria 14 47.10N 14.40E
Judith Basin f. U.S.A. 54 47.10N 109.58W
Juist Germany 8 53.41N 7.01E
Juist i. Germany 8 53.43N 7.00E
Juiz de Fora Brazil 59 21.47S 43.23W
Jujuy d. Argentina 62 23.00S 66.00W
Juklegga mtn. Norway 17 61.03N 8.13E
Juliaca Peru 60 15.29S 70.09W
Julia Creek town Australia 44 20.39S 141.45E
Juliana Kanaal canal Neth. 8 51.00N 5.48E
Julianehåb Greenland 51 60.45N 46.00W
Jülich Germany 8 50.55N 6.21E
Jullundur India 28 31.18N 75.40E
Jumboo Somali Rep. 37 0.12S 42.38E
Jumet Belgium 8 50.27N 4.27E
Jumilla Spain 10 38.28N 1.19W
Jumla Nepal 29 29.17N 82.10E
Jumna r. see Yamuna India 28
Junāgadh India 28 21.32N 70.32E
Junan China 25 35.11N 118.50E
Junction B. Australia 44 11.50S 134.15E
Junction City Kans. U.S.A. 53 39.02N 96.51W
Junction City Oreg. U.S.A. 54 44.13N 123.12W
Jundah Australia 44 24.50S 143.02E
Jundiaí Brazil 59 23.10S 46.54W
Juneau U.S.A. 50 58.20N 134.20W
Junee Australia 47 34.51S 147.40E
Jungfrau mtn. Switz. 11 46.30N 8.00E
Junggar Pendi f. Asia 24 44.20N 86.30E
Junglinster Lux. 8 49.41N 6.13E
Junín Argentina 63 34.35S 60.58W
Junín de los Andes Argentina 63 39.57S 71.05W
Juniville France 9 49.24N 4.23E
Jūnīyah Lebanon 32 33.59N 35.38E
Junnah, Jabal mts. Egypt 32 28.52N 34.15E
Junsele Sweden 16 63.40N 16.55E
Juntura U.S.A. 54 43.46N 118.05W
Jura mts. Europe 11 46.55N 6.45E
Jura i. U.K. 6 55.58N 5.55W
Jurado Colombia 60 7.07N 77.46W
Jura Krakowska mts. Poland 15 50.30N 19.30E
Jura, Sd. of U.K. 6 56.00N 5.45W
Jurhen Ul Shan mts. China 29 34.00N 91.00E
Jūrmala Latvia 17 56.58N 23.42E
Juruá r. Brazil 60 2.33S 65.50W
Juruena Brazil 62 12.50S 58.58W
Juruena r. Brazil 61 7.20S 57.30W
Juruti Brazil 61 2.09S 56.04W
Jussey France 11 47.49N 5.54E
Jutaí r. Brazil 60 2.35S 67.00W
Juticalpa Honduras 57 14.45N 86.12W
Jutland pen. see Jylland pen. Denmark 17
Jūyom Iran 31 28.10N 53.52E
Juzur al Halaniyat is. Oman 28 17.30N 56.00E
Jwayyā Lebanon 32 33.14N 35.20E
Jylland pen. Denmark 17 56.00N 9.15E
Jyväskylä Finland 16 62.14N 25.44E

K

K2 mtn. Asia 24 35.53N 76.32E
Ka r. Nigeria 38 11.35N 4.10E
Kaabong Uganda 37 3.28N 34.08E
Kaapstad see Cape Town R.S.A. 39
Kabaena i. Indonesia 27 5.25S 122.00E
Kabala Sierra Leone 34 9.40N 11.36W
Kabale Uganda 37 1.13S 30.00E
Kabalega Falls f. Uganda 37 2.17N 31.46E
Kabalega Falls Nat. Park Uganda 37 2.15N 31.45E
Kabalo Zaïre 36 6.02S 27.00E
Kabambare Zaïre 37 4.40S 27.41E
Kabanga Zambia 39 17.36S 26.45E
Kabba Nigeria 38 7.50N 6.07E
Kabinakagami r. Canada 55 50.20N 84.20W
Kabīr Kūh mts. Iran 31 33.00N 47.00E
Kābol Afghan. 28 34.30N 69.10E
Kabongo Zaïre 36 7.22S 25.34E
Kabonzo Zaïre 37 6.41S 27.49E
Kabūd Gonbad Iran 31 37.02N 59.46E
Kabul see Kābol Afghan. 28
Kabunda Zaïre 37 12.27S 29.15E
Kabwe Zambia 37 14.27S 28.25E
Kāchā Kūh mts. Iran 31 29.30N 61.20E
Kachchh, G. of India 28 22.30N 69.30E
Kachiry Kazakhstan 20 53.07N 76.08E
Kade Ghana 38 6.08N 0.51W
Kadina Australia 46 33.58S 137.14E
Kadioli Mali 38 10.38N 5.45W
Kadoma Zimbabwe 39 18.23S 29.52E
Kaduna Nigeria 38 10.28N 7.25E
Kaduna d. Nigeria 38 11.00N 7.35E
Kaduna r. Nigeria 38 8.45N 5.45E
Kāduqlī Sudan 35 11.01N 29.43E
Kadusam mtn. China 29 28.30N 96.45E
Kadzherom Russian Fed. 18 64.42N 55.59E
Kaédi Mauritania 34 16.12N 13.32W
Kaélé Cameroon 38 10.05N 14.28E
Kaesŏng N. Korea 25 37.59N 126.30E
Kafanchan Nigeria 38 9.38N 8.20E
Kafirévs, Ákra c. Greece 13 38.11N 24.30E
Kafr ad Dawwār Egypt 32 31.08N 30.08E
Kafr al Baţţīkh Egypt 32 31.24N 31.44E
Kafr ash Shaykh Egypt 32 31.07N 30.56E
Kafr az Zayyāt Egypt 32 30.50N 30.49E
Kafr Salīm Egypt 32 31.09N 30.07E
Kafu r. Uganda 37 1.40N 32.07E
Kafue Zambia 37 15.40S 28.13E
Kafue r. Zambia 36 15.53S 28.55E
Kafue Dam Zambia 37 15.40S 27.10E
Kafunzo Uganda 37 1.05S 30.26E
Kaga Bandoro C.A.R. 36 7.00N 19.10E
Kagan Uzbekistan 20 39.45N 64.32E
Kagarlyk Ukraine 15 49.50N 30.50E
Kagera d. Tanzania 37 2.00S 31.20E
Kağizman Turkey 30 40.08N 43.07E
Kagoshima Japan 25 31.37N 130.32E
Kagul Moldova 15 45.54N 28.11E
Kahama Tanzania 37 3.48S 32.38E
Kahayan r. Indonesia 26 3.20S 114.04E
Kahnūj Iran 31 27.55N 57.45E
Kahraman Maraş Turkey 30 37.34N 36.54E
Kaiama Nigeria 38 9.37N 4.03E
Kaiapoi New Zealand 48 43.23S 172.39E
Kaifeng China 25 34.47N 114.20E
Kai, Kepulauan is. Indonesia 27 5.45S 132.55E
Kaikohe New Zealand 48 35.25S 173.49E
Kaikoura New Zealand 48 42.24S 173.41E
Kaikoura Range mts. New Zealand 48 42.00S 173.40E
Kaimana Indonesia 27 3.39S 133.44E
Kaimanawa Mts. New Zealand 48 39.10S 176.15E
Kainantu P.N.G. 27 6.16S 145.50E
Kainji Resr. Nigeria 38 10.00N 4.35E
Kaipara Harbour New Zealand 48 36.30S 174.00E
Kaiserslautern Germany 8 49.27N 7.47E
Kaitaia New Zealand 48 35.08S 173.18E
Kaitum r. Sweden 16 67.30N 21.05E
Kaizuka Japan 23 34.27N 135.21E
Kajaani Finland 16 64.14N 27.41E
Kajabbi Australia 44 20.02S 140.02E
Kajiado Kenya 37 1.50S 36.48E
Kajuru Nigeria 38 10.19N 7.40E
Kakamas R.S.A. 39 28.44S 20.35E
Kakamega Kenya 37 0.21N 34.47E
Kakamigahara Japan 23 35.28N 136.48E
Kakegawa Japan 23 34.46N 138.01E
Kakhovskoye Vodokhranilishche resr. Ukraine 19 47.33N 34.40E
Kākī Iran 31 28.19N 51.34E
Kākināda India 29 16.59N 82.20E
Kakonko Tanzania 37 3.19S 30.54E
Kakuma Kenya 37 3.38N 34.48E
Kakuto Uganda 37 0.54S 31.26E
Kala r. Finland 16 64.17N 23.55E
Kalaallit Nunaat see Greenland N.America 51
Kalabahi Indonesia 27 8.13S 124.31E
Kalabáka Greece 13 39.42N 21.43E
Kalabity Australia 46 31.53S 140.18E
Kalach-na-Donu Russian Fed. 19 48.43N 43.
Kalahari Desert Botswana 39 23.30S 22.00E
Kalahari Gemsbok Nat. Park R.S.A. 39 25.4 20.25E
Kalajoki Finland 16 64.15N 23.57E
Kalakan Russian Fed. 21 55.10N 116.45E
Kalámai Greece 13 37.02N 22.05E
Kalamazoo U.S.A. 55 42.17N 85.36W
Kalamera Tanzania 37 2.07S 33.43E
Kalamurra, L. Australia 46 28.00S 138.00E
Kalannie Australia 43 30.21S 117.04E
Kalarash Moldova 15 47.18N 28.16E
Kalāt Pakistan 28 29.01N 66.38E
Kalbarri Australia 43 27.40S 114.12E
Kalecik Turkey 30 40.06N 33.22E
Kalehe Zaïre 37 2.05S 28.53E
Kalemie Zaïre 37 5.57S 29.10E
Kalgan r. Australia 43 34.55S 117.58E
Kalgoorlie Australia 43 30.49S 121.29E
Kaliakra, Nos c. Bulgaria 13 43.23N 28.29E
Kalianda Indonesia 26 5.50S 105.45E
Kalimantan d. Indonesia 26 1.00S 113.00E
Kalimantan f. Indonesia 26 0.05N 112.30E
Kalimantan Barat d. Indonesia 26 0.30N 110.
Kalimantan Selatan d. Indonesia 26 2.30S 115.30E
Kalimantan Tengah d. Indonesia 26 2.00S 113.30E
Kalimantan Timur d. Indonesia 26 2.20N 116.30E
Kálimnos i. Greece 13 37.00N 27.00E
Kaliningrad Russian Fed. 17 54.43N 20.30E
Kalinkovichi Belarus 15 52.10N 29.13E
Kalinovka Ukraine 15 49.29N 28.30E
Kalispell U.S.A. 54 48.12N 114.19W
Kalisz Poland 15 51.46N 18.02E
Kaliua Tanzania 37 5.08S 31.50E
Kalix r. Sweden 16 65.50N 23.11E
Kalkar Germany 8 51.45N 6.17E
Kalkfontein Botswana 39 22.08S 20.54E
Kalkrand Namibia 39 24.05S 17.34E
Kallsjön l. Sweden 16 63.35N 13.00E
Kalmar Sweden 17 56.40N 16.22E
Kalmar d. Sweden 17 57.20N 16.00E
Kalmarsund str. Sweden 17 56.40N 16.25E
Kalmthout Belgium 8 51.23N 4.28E
Kalmykovo Kazakhstan 19 49.02N 51.55E
Kalo P.N.G. 44 10.05S 147.45E
Kalocsa Hungary 15 46.32N 18.59E
Kalole Zaïre 37 3.40S 27.22E
Kalomo Zambia 36 17.03S 26.29E
Kalonje Zambia 37 12.21S 31.06E
Kaltag U.S.A. 50 64.20N 158.44W
Kaluga Russian Fed. 18 54.31N 36.16E
Kalumburu Australia 42 14.14S 126.38E
Kalundborg Denmark 17 55.41N 11.06E
Kalush Ukraine 15 49.02N 24.20E
Kalutara Sri Lanka 29 6.35N 79.58E
Kama r. Russian Fed. 18 55.30N 52.00E
Kamakura Japan 23 35.19N 139.33E
Kamanashi r. Japan 23 35.33N 138.28E
Kamanjab Namibia 39 19.39S 14.50E
Kamba Nigeria 38 11.52N 3.42E
Kambalda Australia 43 31.12S 121.40E
Kambarka Russian Fed. 18 56.18N 54.13E
Kamchatka, Poluostrov pen. Russian Fed. 21 56.00N 160.00E
Kamen mtn. Russian Fed. 21 68.40N 94.20E
Kamenets Podolskiy Ukraine 15 48.40N 26.3
Kamenka Russian Fed. 18 65.55N 44.02E
Kamenka Russian Fed. 18 53.10N 44.05E
Kamenka Bugskaya Ukraine 15 50.07N 24.30
Kamen Kashirskiy Ukraine 15 51.32N 24.59E
Kamen-na-Obi Russian Fed. 20 53.46N 81.18
Kamenskoye Russian Fed. 21 62.31N 165.15
Kamensk-Shakhtinskiy Russian Fed. 19 48.2 40.16E
Kamensk-Ural'skiy Russian Fed. 20 56.29N 61.49E
Kāmet mtn. China 29 31.03N 79.25E
Kameyama Japan 23 34.51N 136.27E
Kamiah U.S.A. 54 46.14N 116.02W
Kamieskroon R.S.A. 39 30.12S 17.53E
Kamina Zaïre 36 8.46S 25.00E
Kamloops Canada 50 50.39N 120.24W
Kamo r. Japan 23 35.00N 139.52E
Kamp Germany 8 50.14N 7.37E
Kampa Indonesia 26 1.46S 105.26E
Kampala Uganda 37 0.19N 32.35E
Kampar r. Indonesia 26 0.20N 102.55E
Kampen Neth. 8 52.33N 5.55E
Kamp-Lintfort Germany 8 51.34N 6.38E
Kâmpóng Cham Cambodia 26 11.59N 105.26E
Kâmpóng Chhnăng Cambodia 26 12.16N 104.39E
Kâmpóng Saôm Cambodia 26 10.38N 103.30E
Kâmpôt Cambodia 26 10.37N 104.11E
Kampti Burkina 38 10.07N 3.22W
Kamsack Canada 51 51.34N 101.54W
Kamskoye Vodokhranilishche resr. Russian Fed. 18 58.55N 56.20E
Kamyshin Russian Fed. 19 50.05N 45.24E
Kana r. Zimbabwe 39 18.30S 26.50E
Kanagawa d. Japan 23 35.25N 139.10E
Kananga Zaïre 36 5.53S 22.26E
Kanash Russian Fed. 18 55.30N 47.27E
Kanawha r. U.S.A. 55 38.50N 82.08W
Kanazawa Japan 25 36.35N 136.38E
Kanchanaburi Thailand 29 14.08N 99.31E
Kānchenjunga mtn. Asia 29 27.44N 88.11E
Kānchipuram India 29 12.50N 79.44E
Kandalaksha Russian Fed. 18 67.09N 32.31E

ndalakshskaya Guba g. Russian Fed. 18 6.30N 34.00E
ndangan Indonesia 26 2.50S 115.15E
ndi Benin 38 11.05N 2.59E
ndira Turkey 30 41.05N 30.08E
ndos Australia 47 32.53S 149.59E
ndrāch Pakistan 28 25.29N 65.29E
ndreho Madagascar 37 17.29S 46.06E
ndy Sri Lanka 29 7.18N 80.43E
ne U.S.A. 55 41.40N 78.49W
nem d. Chad 38 15.10N 15.30E
nevka Russian Fed. 18 67.08N 39.50E
ng Botswana 39 23.43S 22.51E
ngaarsussuaq see Parry, Kap Greenland 51
ngān Iran 31 27.50N 52.07E
ngar Malaysia 26 6.28N 100.10E
ngaroo I. Australia 46 35.50S 137.06E
ngding China 24 30.05N 102.04E
ngean, Kepulauan is. Indonesia 26 7.00S 115.45E
ngerlussuaq see Söndreströmfjord Greenland
ngiqsualujjuaq Canada 51 58.35N 65.59W
ngiqsujuaq Canada 51 61.30N 72.00W
ngirsuk Canada 51 60.01N 70.01W
ningo Kenya 37 0.52S 38.31E
nin Nos, Mys c. Russian Fed. 18 68.38N 3.20E
nin, Poluostrov pen. Russian Fed. 18 68.00N 5.00E
niva Australia 46 36.33S 141.17E
njiža Yugo. 15 46.04N 20.04E
nkakee U.S.A. 53 41.08N 87.52W
nkan Guinea 34 10.22N 9.11W
nker India 29 20.17N 81.30E
no r. Japan 23 35.05N 138.52E
no Nigeria 38 12.00N 8.31E
no d. Nigeria 38 11.45N 8.30E
nona Zambia 37 13.03S 30.37E
nowna Australia 43 30.36S 121.36E
npur India 29 26.27N 80.14E
nsas d. U.S.A. 52 38.00N 99.00W
nsas r. U.S.A. 53 39.07N 94.36W
nsas City Mo. U.S.A. 53 39.02N 94.33W
nsk Russian Fed. 21 56.11N 95.20E
nsŏng S. Korea 25 38.20N 128.28E
ntché Niger 38 13.31N 8.30E
ntemirovka Russian Fed. 19 49.40N 39.52E
ntō d. Japan 23 35.35N 139.30E
ntōheiya f. Japan 23 36.02N 140.10E
ntō-sanchi mts. Japan 23 36.00N 138.35E
nye Botswana 39 24.58S 25.17E
nyu Botswana 39 20.05S 24.39E
olack Senegal 34 14.09N 16.08W
pchagay Kazakhstan 24 43.51N 77.14E
penguria Kenya 37 1.13N 35.07E
pfenberg Austria 14 47.27N 15.18E
piri Mposhi Zambia 37 13.59S 28.40E
pit Malaysia 26 2.01N 112.56E
piti I. New Zealand 48 40.50S 174.50E
pongolo Zaïre 37 7.51S 28.12E
posvár Hungary 13 46.22N 17.47E
ps Namibia 39 22.22S 17.52E
psabet Kenya 37 0.12N 35.05E
puas r. Indonesia 26 0.13S 109.12E
punda Australia 46 34.21S 138.54E
puskasing Canada 55 49.25N 82.26W
putar, Mt. Australia 47 30.20S 150.10E
puvár Hungary 15 47.36N 17.02E
ra Russian Fed. 20 69.12N 65.00E
ra-Bogaz Gol, Zaliv b. Turkmenistan 31 1.20N 53.40E
rabük Turkey 30 41.12N 32.36E
rabutak Kazakhstan 20 49.55N 60.05E
rāchi Pakistan 28 24.51N 67.02E
rād India 28 17.17N 74.12E
raganda Kazakhstan 20 49.53N 73.07E
raginskiy, Ostrov i. Russian Fed. 21 59.00N 65.00E
rakas Kazakhstan 24 48.20N 83.30E
rakelong i. Indonesia 27 4.20N 126.50E
rakoram Pass Asia 29 35.33N 77.51E
rakoram Range mts. Jammu & Kashmir 28 5.30N 76.30E
raköse see Ağri Turkey 19
rakumskiy Kanal canal Turkmenistan 31 7.30N 65.48E
rakumy, Peski f. Turkmenistan 31 37.45N 0.00E
rakuwisa Namibia 39 18.56S 19.43E
raman Turkey 30 37.11N 33.13E
ramay China 24 45.48N 84.30E
ramea New Zealand 48 41.15S 172.07E
ramea Bight b. New Zealand 48 41.15S 71.30E
ramürsel Turkey 30 40.42N 29.37E
rand Iran 31 34.16N 46.15E
rasburg Namibia 39 28.00S 18.46E
rasjok Norway 16 69.27N 25.30E
rasuk Russian Fed. 20 53.45N 78.01E
ratau, Khrebet mts. Kazakhstan 19 44.15N 2.10E
ratobe Kazakhstan 19 49.44N 53.30E
raton Kazakhstan 19 46.26N 53.32E
razhal Kazakhstan 20 48.00N 70.55E
rbalā' Iraq 31 32.37N 44.03E
rcag Hungary 15 47.19N 20.56E
rdhitsa Greece 13 39.22N 21.59E
rdla Estonia 17 59.00N 22.42E
rema Tanzania 37 6.50S 30.25E
ren India 29 12.50N 92.55E
repino Russian Fed. 18 61.05N 58.02E
resuando Finland 16 68.25N 22.30E
rgasok Russian Fed. 20 59.07N 80.58E
rgi Kenya 37 2.31N 37.34E
rgil Jammu & Kashmir 28 34.32N 76.12E
rgopol Russian Fed. 18 61.32N 38.59E
ri Nigeria 38 11.17N 10.35E
riba Zimbabwe 37 16.32S 28.50E
Kariba Dam Zimbabwe/Zambia 37 16.15S 28.55E
Kariba, L. Zimbabwe/Zambia 37 16.50S 28.00E
Karibib Namibia 39 21.56S 15.52E
Kārikāl India 29 10.58N 79.50E
Karimama Benin 38 12.02N 3.15E
Karis Finland 17 60.05N 23.40E
Karisimbi, Mt. Zaïre/Rwanda 37 1.31S 29.25E
Kariya Japan 23 34.59N 136.59E
Kariyangwe Zimbabwe 39 17.57S 27.30E
Karkaralinsk Kazakhstan 20 49.21N 75.27E
Karkar I. P.N.G. 27 4.40S 146.00E
Karkas, Kūh-e mtn. Iran 31 33.25N 51.40E
Karkheh r. Iran 31 31.45N 47.52E
Karkinitskiy Zaliv g. Ukraine 19 45.50N 32.45E
Karkoo Australia 46 34.02S 135.44E
Karlino Poland 14 54.03N 15.51E
Karl-Marx-Stadt see Chemnitz Germany 14
Karlovac Croatia 12 45.30N 15.34E
Karlovy Vary Czech Republic 14 50.14N 12.53E
Karlsborg Sweden 17 58.32N 14.31E
Karlshamn Sweden 17 56.10N 14.51E
Karlskoga Sweden 17 59.20N 14.31E
Karlskrona Sweden 17 56.10N 15.35E
Karlsruhe Germany 14 49.00N 8.24E
Karlstad Sweden 17 59.22N 13.30E
Karmöy i. Norway 17 59.15N 5.15E
Karnafuli Resr. Bangla. 29 22.40N 92.05E
Karnataka d. India 28 14.45N 76.00E
Karnobat Bulgaria 13 42.40N 27.00E
Kärnten d. Austria 14 46.50N 13.50E
Karonga Malaŵi 37 9.54S 33.55E
Karonie Australia 43 30.58S 122.32E
Karoonda Australia 46 35.09S 139.54E
Karos Dam R.S.A. 39 28.27S 21.39E
Karpach Moldova 15 48.00N 27.10E
Kárpathos Greece 13 35.30N 27.14E
Kárpathos i. Greece 13 35.35N 27.08E
Karpineny Moldova 15 46.46N 28.18E
Karpinsk Russian Fed. 18 59.48N 59.59E
Karpogory Russian Fed. 18 64.01N 44.30E
Karragullen Australia 43 32.05S 116.03E
Karratha Australia 42 20.44S 116.50E
Karridale Australia 43 34.12S 115.04E
Kars Turkey 30 40.35N 43.05E
Karsakpay Kazakhstan 20 47.47N 66.43E
Kärsämäki Finland 16 63.58N 25.46E
Kārsava Russian Fed. 18 56.45N 27.40E
Karskoye More sea Russian Fed. 20 73.00N 65.00E
Kartaly Russian Fed. 20 53.06N 60.37E
Karufa Indonesia 27 3.50S 133.27E
Karumba Australia 44 17.28S 140.50E
Kārūn r. Iran 31 30.25N 48.12E
Karungi Sweden 16 66.03N 23.55E
Karungu Kenya 37 0.50S 34.09E
Karviná Czech Republic 15 49.50N 18.30E
Kasai r. Zaïre 36 3.10S 16.13E
Kasama Zambia 37 10.10S 31.11E
Kasane Botswana 39 17.48S 25.09E
Kasanga Tanzania 37 8.27S 31.10E
Kāsaragod India 28 12.30N 75.00E
Kasba L. Canada 51 60.18N 102.07W
Kasese Uganda 37 0.07N 30.06E
Kāshān Iran 31 33.59N 51.31E
Kashi China 24 39.29N 76.02E
Kashin Russian Fed. 18 57.22N 37.39E
Kashiwa Japan 23 35.52N 139.59E
Kāshmar Iran 31 35.12N 58.26E
Kasimov Russian Fed. 18 54.55N 41.25E
Kaskinen Finland 16 62.23N 21.13E
Kaskö see Kaskinen Finland 16
Kásos i. Greece 13 35.22N 26.56E
Kassalā Sudan 35 15.24N 36.30E
Kassel Germany 14 51.18N 9.30E
Kastamonu Turkey 30 41.22N 33.47E
Kastoría Greece 13 40.32N 21.15E
Kasugai Japan 23 35.14N 136.58E
Kasukabe Japan 23 35.58N 139.45E
Kasulu Tanzania 37 4.34S 30.06E
Kasungu Malaŵi 37 13.04S 33.29E
Kasūr Pakistan 28 31.07N 74.30E
Katanning Australia 43 33.42S 117.33E
Katarniān Ghāt India 29 28.20N 81.09E
Katchall i. India 29 7.57N 93.22E
Katete Zambia 37 14.08S 31.50E
Katha Myanmar 29 24.11N 96.20E
Katherine Australia 44 14.29S 132.20E
Kathmandu Nepal 29 27.42N 85.19E
Kati Mali 34 12.41N 8.04W
Katima Rapids f. Zambia 39 17.27S 24.13E
Katiola Côte d'Ivoire 38 8.10N 5.10W
Katonga r. Uganda 37 0.03N 30.15E
Katoomba Australia 47 33.42S 150.23E
Katowice Poland 15 50.15N 18.59E
Kātrīnā, Jabal mtn. Egypt 32 28.30N 33.57E
Katrineholm Sweden 17 59.00N 16.12E
Katrine, Loch U.K. 6 56.15N 4.30W
Katsina Nigeria 38 13.00N 7.32E
Katsina d. Nigeria 38 12.25N 7.55E
Katsina Ala Nigeria 38 7.10N 9.30E
Katsina Ala r. Nigeria 38 7.50N 8.58E
Katsura r. Japan 23 34.53N 135.42E
Katsuura Japan 23 35.08N 140.18E
Kattegat str. Denmark/Sweden 17 57.00N 11.20E
Katwijk aan Zee Neth. 8 52.13N 4.27E
Kauai i. Hawaii U.S.A. 52 22.05N 159.30W
Kaub Germany 8 50.07N 7.50E
Kaufbeuren Germany 14 47.53N 10.37E
Kauhajoki Finland 16 62.26N 22.11E
Kauhava Finland 16 63.06N 23.05E
Kaukauveld mts. Namibia 39 20.00S 20.15E
Kauliranta Finland 16 66.26N 23.40E
Kaunas Lithuania 17 54.54N 23.54E
Kaura Namoda Nigeria 38 12.39N 6.38E
Kautokeino Norway 16 69.00N 23.02E
Kavála Greece 13 40.56N 24.24E
Kāvali India 29 14.55N 80.01E
Kavarna Bulgaria 13 43.26N 28.22E
Kavimba Botswana 39 18.05S 24.34E
Kavkaz Russian Fed. 19 45.20N 36.39E
Kaw Guiana 61 4.29N 52.02W
Kawachi-nagano Japan 23 34.25N 135.32E
Kawagoe Japan 23 35.55N 139.29E
Kawaguchi Japan 23 35.48N 139.43E
Kawambwa Zambia 37 9.47S 29.10E
Kawasaki Japan 23 35.32N 139.43E
Kawerau New Zealand 48 38.05S 176.42E
Kawhia New Zealand 48 38.04S 174.49E
Kaya Burkina 38 13.04N 1.04W
Kayambi Zambia 37 9.26S 32.01E
Kayan r. Indonesia 26 2.47N 117.46E
Kaycee U.S.A. 54 43.43N 106.38W
Kayenta U.S.A. 54 36.44N 110.17W
Kayes Mali 34 14.26N 11.28W
Kayseri Turkey 30 38.42N 35.28E
Kaysville U.S.A. 54 41.02N 111.56W
Kazachye Russian Fed. 21 70.46N 136.15E
Kazakhskiy Zaliv b. Kazakhstan 19 42.43N 52.30E
Kazakhstan Asia 19 48.00N 52.30E
Kazan Russian Fed. 18 55.45N 49.10E
Kazanlŭk Bulgaria 13 42.38N 25.26E
Kazatin Ukraine 15 49.41N 28.49E
Kazaure Nigeria 38 12.40N 8.25E
Kazbek mtn. Russian Fed. 19 42.42N 44.30E
Kāzerūn Iran 31 29.35N 51.39E
Kazhim Russian Fed. 18 60.18N 51.34E
Kazincbarcika Hungary 15 48.16N 20.37E
Kazo Japan 23 36.07N 139.36E
Kéa i. Greece 13 37.36N 24.20E
Kearney U.S.A. 52 40.42N 99.04W
Keban Turkey 30 38.48N 38.45E
Kebbi d. Nigeria 38 11.30N 3.45E
Kebnekaise mtn. Sweden 16 67.53N 18.33E
K'ebrī Dehar Ethiopia 35 6.47N 44.17E
Kecskemét Hungary 15 46.54N 19.42E
Kedainiai Lithuania 17 55.17N 24.00E
Kedgwick Canada 55 47.38N 67.21W
Kediri Indonesia 26 7.55S 112.01E
Kédougou Senegal 34 12.35N 12.09W
Keele Peak mtn. Canada 50 63.15N 129.50W
Keene U.S.A. 55 42.56N 72.17W
Keepit, L. Australia 47 30.52S 150.30E
Keer-Weer, C. Australia 44 13.58S 141.30E
Keetmanshoop Namibia 39 26.34S 18.07E
Keewatin d. Canada 51 65.00N 90.00W
Kefallinía i. Greece 13 38.15N 20.33E
Kefar Sava Israel 32 32.11N 34.54E
Keffi Nigeria 38 8.52N 7.53E
Keflavík Iceland 16 64.01N 22.35W
Keighley U.K. 4 53.52N 1.54W
Keila Estonia 17 59.18N 24.29E
Keimoes R.S.A. 39 28.41S 20.58E
Keitele l. Finland 16 62.55N 26.00E
Keith Australia 46 36.06S 140.22E
Keith U.K. 6 57.32N 2.57W
Keith Arm b. Canada 50 65.20N 122.15W
Kelang Malaysia 26 2.57N 101.24E
Kelberg Germany 8 50.17N 6.56E
Kelkit r. Turkey 30 40.46N 36.32E
Keller U.S.A. 54 48.03N 118.40W
Kellerberrin Australia 43 31.38S 117.43E
Kellet, C. Canada 50 71.59N 125.34W
Kelloselkä Finland 16 66.55N 28.50E
Kells Meath Rep. of Ire. 7 53.44N 6.53W
Kelme Lithuania 17 55.38N 22.56E
Kelowna Canada 50 49.50N 119.29W
Kelso U.K. 6 55.36N 2.26W
Kelso Calif. U.S.A. 54 35.01N 115.39W
Kelso Wash. U.S.A. 54 46.09N 122.54W
Keluang Malaysia 26 2.01N 103.18E
Kelvedon U.K. 5 51.50N 0.43E
Kem Russian Fed. 18 64.58N 34.39E
Kema Indonesia 27 1.22N 125.08E
Ke Macina Mali 38 14.05N 5.20W
Kemah Turkey 30 39.35N 39.02E
Kemaliye Turkey 30 39.16N 38.29E
Kemerovo Russian Fed. 20 55.25N 86.10E
Kemi Finland 16 65.49N 24.32E
Kemi r. Finland 16 65.47N 24.30E
Kemijärvi Finland 16 66.36N 27.24E
Kemmerer U.S.A. 54 41.48N 110.32W
Kempen f. Belgium 8 51.05N 5.00E
Kemp Land f. Antarctica 64 69.00S 57.00E
Kempsey Australia 47 31.05S 152.50E
Kempten Germany 14 47.44N 10.19E
Kempt, Lac l. Canada 55 47.26N 74.30W
Kenai U.S.A. 50 60.33N 151.15W
Kendal U.K. 4 54.19N 2.44W
Kendall Australia 47 31.28S 152.40E
Kendari Indonesia 27 3.57S 122.36E
Kendenup Australia 43 34.28S 117.35E
Kendrick U.S.A. 54 46.37N 116.39W
Kenebri Australia 47 30.45S 149.02E
Kenema Sierra Leone 34 7.57N 11.11W
Kengeja Tanzania 37 5.24S 39.45E
Keng Tung Myanmar 29 21.16N 99.39E
Kenhardt R.S.A. 39 29.21S 21.08E
Kenilworth U.K. 5 52.22N 1.35W
Kenitra Morocco 34 34.20N 6.34W
Kenmare Rep. of Ire. 7 51.53N 9.36W
Kennebec r. U.S.A. 55 44.00N 69.50W
Kennet r. U.K. 5 51.28N 0.57W
Kennewick U.S.A. 54 46.12N 119.07W
Kenogami r. Canada 55 50.24N 84.20W
Keno Hill town Canada 50 63.58N 135.22W
Kenora Canada 51 49.47N 94.26W
Kenosha U.S.A. 53 42.34N 87.50W
Kenozero, Ozero l. Russian Fed. 18 62.20N 37.00E
Kent d. U.K. 5 51.12N 0.40E
Kent Ohio U.S.A. 55 41.10N 81.20W
Kent Wash. U.S.A. 54 47.23N 122.14W
Kentau Kazakhstan 24 43.28N 68.36E
Kentland U.S.A. 55 40.46N 87.26W
Kenton U.S.A. 55 40.38N 83.38W
Kent Pen. Canada 50 68.30N 107.00W
Kentucky d. U.S.A. 53 38.00N 85.00W
Kentucky L. U.S.A. 53 36.15N 88.00W
Kenya Africa 37 1.00N 38.00E
Kenya, Mt. see Kirinyaga Kenya 37
Keokuk U.S.A. 53 40.23N 91.25W
Kepi Indonesia 27 6.32S 139.19E
Kepno Poland 15 51.17N 17.59E
Keppel B. Australia 44 23.21S 150.55E
Kerala d. India 28 10.30N 76.30E
Kerang Australia 46 35.42S 143.59E
Kerch Ukraine 19 45.22N 36.27E
Kerchenskiy Proliv str. Ukraine/Russian Fed. 19 45.15N 36.35E
Kerema P.N.G. 27 7.59S 145.46E
Kericho Kenya 37 0.22S 35.19E
Kerinci, Gunung mtn. Indonesia 26 1.45S 101.20E
Kerio r. Kenya 37 3.00N 36.14E
Kerkebet Eritrea 35 16.13N 37.30E
Kerki Russian Fed 18 63.40N 54.00E
Kerki Turkmenistan 20 37.53N 65.10E
Kérkira Greece 13 39.37N 19.50E
Kérkira i. Greece 13 39.35N 19.50E
Kerkrade Neth. 8 50.52N 6.02E
Kermān Iran 31 30.18N 57.05E
Kermānshāh Iran 31 34.19N 47.04E
Kerme Körfezi g. Turkey 13 36.52N 27.53E
Kerpen Germany 8 50.52N 6.42E
Kerry d. Rep. of Ire. 7 52.07N 9.35W
Kerry Head Rep. of Ire. 7 52.24N 9.56W
Kerulen r. Mongolia 25 48.45N 117.00E
Kesagami L. Canada 55 50.23N 80.15W
Keşan Turkey 13 40.50N 26.39E
Keshod India 28 21.18N 70.15E
Keskal India 29 20.05N 81.35E
Keski-Suomi d. Finland 16 62.30N 25.30E
Keswick U.K. 4 54.35N 3.09W
Keszthely Hungary 15 46.46N 17.15E
Ketapang Kalimantan Indonesia 26 1.50S 110.02E
Ketchikan U.S.A. 50 55.25N 131.40W
Ketchum U.S.A. 54 43.41N 114.22W
Kete Krachi Ghana 38 7.50N 0.03W
Ketrzyn Poland 15 54.06N 21.23E
Kettering U.K. 5 52.24N 0.44W
Kettering U.S.A. 55 39.41N 84.10W
Kettle Falls town U.S.A. 54 48.36N 118.03W
Keweenaw B. U.S.A. 55 46.46N 88.26W
Keweenaw Pen. U.S.A. 55 47.10N 88.30W
Key Harbour Canada 55 45.52N 80.48W
Key, Lough Rep. of Ire. 7 54.00N 8.15W
Keynsham U.K. 5 51.25N 2.30W
Kezhma Russian Fed. 21 58.58N 101.08E
Kežmarok Slovakia 15 49.08N 20.25E
Kgalagadi d. Botswana 39 25.00S 21.30E
Kgatleng d. Botswana 39 24.20S 26.20E
Khabarovsk Russian Fed. 25 48.32N 135.08E
Khairpur Sind Pakistan 28 27.30N 68.50E
Khalkhāl Iran 31 37.36N 48.36E
Khalkís Greece 13 38.27N 23.36E
Khalmer Yu Russian Fed. 18 67.58N 64.48E
Khalūf Oman 28 20.31N 58.04E
Khambhāt, G. of India 28 20.30N 72.00E
Khamkeut Laos 29 18.14N 104.44E
Khānaqīn Iraq 31 34.22N 45.22E
Khandwa India 28 21.49N 76.23E
Khāneh Khvodī Iran 31 36.05N 56.04E
Khaniá Greece 13 35.30N 24.02E
Khanka, Ozero l. Russian Fed. 25 45.00N 132.30E
Khankendy see Stepanakert Armenia 31
Khanty-Mansiysk Russian Fed. 20 61.00N 69.00E
Khān Yūnus Egypt 32 31.21N 34.18E
Khapcheranga Russian Fed. 25 49.46N 112.20E
Kharagpur India 29 22.23N 87.22E
Khārān r. Iran 31 27.37N 58.48E
Khārijah, Al Wāḥāt al oasis Egypt 30 24.55N 30.35E
Kharkov Ukraine 19 50.00N 36.15E
Khār Kūh mtn. Iran 31 31.37N 53.47E
Kharovsk Russian Fed. 18 59.67N 40.07E
Khartoum see Al Kharṭūm Sudan 35
Kharutayuvam Russian Fed. 18 66.51N 59.31E
Khasavyurt Russian Fed. 19 43.16N 46.36E
Khāsh r. Afghan. 31 31.12N 62.00E
Khāsh Iran 31 28.14N 61.15E
Khashgort Russian Fed. 18 65.25N 65.40E
Khaskovo Bulgaria 13 41.57N 25.33E
Khatanga Russian Fed. 21 71.50N 102.31E
Khatangskiy Zaliv g. Russian Fed. 21 75.00N 112.10E
Khemmarat Thailand 29 16.04N 105.10E
Khenifra Morocco 34 33.00N 5.40W
Khersān r. Iran 31 31.29N 48.53E
Kherson Ukraine 19 46.39N 32.38E
Khíos Greece 13 38.23N 26.07E
Khíos i. Greece 13 38.23N 26.04E
Khiva Uzbekistan 31 41.25N 60.49E
Khmelnik Ukraine 15 49.36N 27.59E
Khmelnitskiy Ukraine 15 49.25N 26.49E
Khodorov Ukraine 15 49.20N 24.19E
Kholm Russian Fed. 18 57.10N 31.11E
Kholmogory Russian Fed. 18 63.51N 41.46E
Khomas-Hochland mts. Namibia 39 22.50S 16.25E
Khonu Russian Fed. 21 66.29N 143.12E
Khoper r. Russian Fed. 19 49.35N 42.17E
Khorixas Namibia 39 20.24S 14.58E
Khorog Tajikistan 24 37.32N 71.32E
Khorramābād Iran 31 33.29N 48.21E
Khorramshahr Iran 31 30.26N 48.09E
Khotimsk Belarus 15 53.24N 32.36E
Khotin Ukraine 15 48.30N 26.31E
Khowrnag, Kūh-e mtn. Iran 31 32.10N 54.38E
Khoyniki Belarus 15 51.54N 30.00E
Khudzhand Tajikistan 24 40.14N 69.40E
Khuis Botswana 39 26.37S 21.45E
Khulga r. Russian Fed. 18 63.33N 61.53E
Khulna Bangla. 29 22.49N 89.34E
Khurra Bārīk r. Iraq 30 32.00N 44.15E
Khust Ukraine 15 48.11N 23.19E
Khvor Iran 31 33.47N 55.06E
Khvormuj Iran 31 28.40N 51.20E
Khvoy Iran 31 38.32N 45.02E
Khyber Pass Asia 28 34.06N 71.05E
Kiama Australia 47 34.41S 150.49E
Kibali r. Zaïre 37 3.37N 28.38E
Kibombo Zaïre 36 3.58S 25.57E
Kibondo Tanzania 37 3.35S 30.41E
Kibre Mengist Ethiopia 35 5.52N 39.00E
Kibungu Rwanda 37 2.10S 30.31E
Kibwesa Tanzania 37 6.30S 29.57E
Kibwezi Kenya 37 2.28S 37.57E
Kichiga Russian Fed. 21 59.50N 163.27E
Kicking Horse Pass Canada 50 51.28N 116.23W
Kidal Mali 38 18.27N 1.25E
Kidderminster U.K. 5 52.24N 2.13W
Kidete Morogoro Tanzania 37 6.39S 36.42E
Kidsgrove U.K. 4 53.06N 2.15W
Kiel Germany 14 54.20N 10.08E
Kielce Poland 15 50.52N 20.37E
Kielder resr. U.K. 4 55.12N 2.30W
Kieler Bucht b. Germany 14 54.30N 10.30E
Kiev see Kiyev Ukraine 15
Kiffa Mauritania 34 16.38N 11.28W
Kigali Rwanda 37 1.59S 30.05E
Kigoma Tanzania 37 4.52S 29.36E
Kigoma d. Tanzania 37 4.45S 30.00E
Kigosi r. Tanzania 37 4.37S 31.29E
Kiiminkin r. Finland 16 65.12N 25.18E
Kikinda Yugo. 15 45.51N 20.30E
Kikládhes is. Greece 13 37.00N 25.00E
Kikori P.N.G. 27 7.25S 144.13E
Kikori r. P.N.G. 27 7.10S 144.05E
Kikwit Zaïre 36 5.02S 18.51E
Kil Sweden 17 59.30N 13.19E
Kilafors Sweden 17 61.14N 16.34E
Kila Kila P.N.G. 27 9.31S 147.10E
Kilchu N. Korea 25 40.55N 129.21E
Kilcoy Australia 45 26.57S 152.33E
Kilcullen Rep. of Ire. 7 53.08N 6.46W
Kildare Rep. of Ire. 7 53.10N 6.55W
Kildare d. Rep. of Ire. 7 53.10N 6.50W
Kildonan Zimbabwe 39 17.22S 30.33E
Kilfinan U.K. 6 55.58N 5.18W
Kilifi Kenya 37 3.30S 39.50E
Kilimanjaro d. Tanzania 37 3.45S 37.40E
Kilimanjaro mtn. Tanzania 37 3.02S 37.20E
Kilindoni Tanzania 37 7.55S 39.39E
Kilingi-Nõmme Estonia 17 58.09N 24.58E
Kilis Turkey 30 36.43N 37.07E
Kiliya Ukraine 15 45.30N 29.16E
Kilkee Rep. of Ire. 7 52.41N 9.40W
Kilkenny Rep. of Ire. 7 52.39N 7.16W
Kilkenny d. Rep. of Ire. 7 52.35N 7.15W
Kilkieran B. Rep. of Ire. 7 53.20N 9.42W
Kilkís Greece 13 40.59N 22.51E
Killala B. Rep. of Ire. 7 54.15N 9.10W
Killard Pt. U.K. 7 54.19N 5.31W
Killarney Australia 47 28.18S 152.15E
Killarney Rep. of Ire. 7 52.04N 9.32W
Killary Harbour est. Rep. of Ire. 7 53.38N 9.56W
Killin U.K. 6 56.29N 4.19W
Killíni mtn. Greece 13 37.56N 22.22E
Killorglin Rep. of Ire. 7 52.07N 9.45W
Killybegs Rep. of Ire. 7 54.38N 8.27W
Killyleagh U.K. 7 54.24N 5.39W
Kilmarnock U.K. 6 55.37N 4.30W
Kilmichael Pt. Rep. of Ire. 7 52.44N 6.09W
Kilmore Australia 47 37.18S 144.58E
Kilninver U.K. 6 56.21N 5.30W
Kilombero r. Tanzania 37 8.30S 37.28E
Kilosa Tanzania 37 6.49S 37.00E
Kilronan Rep. of Ire. 7 53.08N 9.41W
Kilrush Rep. of Ire. 7 52.39N 9.30W
Kilsyth U.K. 6 55.59N 4.04W
Kilvo Sweden 16 66.50N 21.04E
Kilwa Kivinje Tanzania 37 8.45S 39.21E
Kilwa Masoko Tanzania 37 8.55S 39.31E
Kimaan Indonesia 27 7.54S 138.51E
Kimba Australia 46 33.09S 136.25E
Kimberley R.S.A. 39 28.44S 24.44E
Kimberley Plateau Australia 42 17.20S 127.20E
Kimito i. Finland 17 60.10N 22.30E
Kimparana Mali 38 12.52N 4.59W
Kimry Russian Fed. 18 56.51N 37.20E
Kinabalu mtn. Malaysia 26 6.10N 116.40E
Kincardine Canada 55 44.11N 81.38W
Kindia Guinea 34 10.03N 12.49W
Kindu Zaïre 36 3.00S 25.56E
Kinel Russian Fed. 18 53.17N 50.42E
Kineshma Russian Fed. 18 57.28N 42.08E
Kingaroy Australia 44 26.33S 151.50E
King City U.S.A. 54 36.13N 121.08W
King Edward r. Australia 42 14.12S 126.34E
King George Is. Canada 51 57.20N 78.25W
King George Sd. Australia 43 35.03S 117.57E
King I. Australia 45 39.50S 144.00E
King Leopold Range mts. Australia 42 17.00S 125.30E
Kingman Ariz. U.S.A. 54 35.12N 114.04W
Kingoonya Australia 46 30.54S 135.18E
Kings r. U.S.A. 54 36.03N 119.49W
Kingsbridge U.K. 5 50.17N 3.46W
Kings Canyon Australia 44 24.15S 131.33E
Kings Canyon Nat. Park U.S.A. 54 36.48N 118.30W
Kingsclere U.K. 5 51.20N 1.14W
Kingscote Australia 46 35.40S 137.38E
King Sd. Australia 42 17.00S 123.30E
Kingsdown Kent U.K. 5 51.21N 0.17E
Kingsley Dam U.S.A. 52 41.15N 101.30W
King's Lynn U.K. 4 52.45N 0.25E
Kings Peaks mts. U.S.A. 54 40.46N 110.23W
Kingston Canada 55 44.14N 76.30W
Kingston Jamaica 57 17.58N 76.48W
Kingston New Zealand 48 45.20S 168.43E
Kingston N.Y. U.S.A. 55 41.55N 74.00W

shida *r.* Japan **23** 34.36N 136.34E
shiro Japan **25** 42.58N 144.24E
shka Turkmenistan **31** 35.14N 62.15E
skokwim B. U.S.A. **50** 59.45N 162.25W
skokwim Mts. U.S.A. **50** 62.50N 156.00W
stanay Kazakhstan **20** 53.15N 63.40E
stenkanal Germany **8** 53.05N 7.46E
sti Sudan **35** 13.11N 32.38E
ahya Turkey **30** 39.25N 29.56E
aisi Georgia **19** 42.15N 42.44E
ná Hora Czech Republic **14** 49.57N 15.16E
no Poland **15** 52.15N 19.23E
u Zaïre **36** 2.42S 18.09E
ujjuaq Canada **51** 58.10N 68.15W
ujjuarapik Canada **51** 55.25N 77.45W
usamo Finland **18** 65.57N 29.15E
vango Angola **36** 14.28S 16.25E
wait Asia **31** 29.20N 47.40E
wait *town see* Al Kuwayt Kuwait **31**
wana Japan **23** 35.04N 136.42E
ybyshev *see* Samara Russian Fed. **18**
ybyshevskoye Vodokhranilishche *resr.* Russian Fed. **18** 55.00N 49.00E
yeda Russian Fed. **18** 56.25N 55.33E
zey Anadolu Dağlari *mts.* Turkey **30** 40.32N 38.00E
znetsk Russian Fed. **18** 53.08N 46.36E
zomen Russian Fed. **18** 66.15N 36.51E
zreka Russian Fed. **18** 66.35N 34.48E
aenangen *est.* Norway **16** 69.50N 21.30E
vale Kenya **37** 4.20S 39.25E
angju S. Korea **25** 35.07N 126.52E
ango *r.* Zaïre **36** 3.20S 17.23E
ara *d.* Nigeria **38** 8.20N 5.35E
atisore Indonesia **27** 3.18S 134.50E
a Zulu *f.* R.S.A. **39** 27.30S 32.00E
ekwe Zimbabwe **39** 18.59S 29.46E
eneng *d.* Botswana **39** 24.30S 25.40E
ethluk U.S.A. **50** 60.49N 161.27W
idzyn Poland **15** 53.45N 18.56E
igillingok U.S.A. **50** 59.51N 163.08W
iguk U.S.A. **50** 62.45N 164.28W
inana Australia **43** 32.15S 115.48E
oka *mtn.* Indonesia **27** 1.30S 132.30E
abé Chad **34** 9.28N 18.54E
abram Australia **47** 36.18S 145.05E
aka Tanzania **37** 1.16S 31.27E
akhta Russian Fed. **24** 50.22N 106.30E
alite Australia **46** 34.57S 143.31E
ancutta Australia **46** 33.08S 135.34E
aukpyu Myanmar **29** 19.28N 93.30E
ybolite Australia **46** 36.54S 140.58E
chema Russian Fed. **18** 65.32N 42.42E
le of Lochalsh *town* U.K. **6** 57.17N 5.43W
ll *r.* Germany **8** 49.48N 6.42E
llburg Germany **8** 50.03N 6.36E
luchevskaya *mtn.* Russian Fed. **21** 56.00N 160.30E
neton Australia **46** 37.14S 144.28E
nuna Australia **44** 21.35S 141.55E
oga, L. Uganda **37** 1.30N 33.00E
ogle Australia **47** 28.36S 152.59E
otera Uganda **37** 0.40S 31.31E
ōto Japan **23** 35.00N 135.45E
ōto *d.* Japan **23** 34.55N 135.35E
rgyzstan Asia **24** 41.30N 75.00E
rön *r.* Finland **16** 63.14N 21.45E
rta Russian Fed. **18** 64.02N 57.40E
ūshū *i.* Japan **25** 32.50N 130.50E
ustendil Bulgaria **13** 42.18N 22.39E
wong Australia **47** 35.01S 146.45E
yjärvi Finland **16** 63.02N 24.34E
yzyl Russian Fed. **24** 51.42N 94.28E
yzyl Kum, Peski *f.* Uzbekistan **20** 42.00N 64.30E
zyl Orda Kazakhstan **20** 44.52N 65.28E

aas Caanood Somali Rep. **35** 8.26N 47.24E
a Asunción Venezuela **60** 11.06N 63.53W
aâyoune *see* El Aaiún W. Sahara **34**
a Baleine *r.* Canada **51** 58.00N 57.50W
a Banda Argentina **62** 27.44S 64.15W
a Bañeza Spain **10** 42.17N 5.55W
abao Indonesia **27** 8.12S 122.49E
a Barca Mexico **56** 20.20N 102.33W
a Barge U.S.A. **54** 42.16N 110.12W
a Bassée France **8** 50.32N 2.49E
a Baule France **11** 47.18N 2.23W
abbezanga Mali **38** 14.57N 0.42E
abe *r.* Czech. *see* Elbe *r.* Germany **14**
abé Guinea **34** 11.17N 12.11W
abinsk Russian Fed. **19** 44.39N 40.44E
a Blanquilla *i.* Venezuela **57** 11.53N 64.38W
abouheyre France **11** 44.13N 0.55W
aboulaye Argentina **63** 34.05S 63.25W
abrador *f.* Canada **51** 54.00N 61.30W
abrador City Canada **51** 52.54N 66.50W
abrador Sea Canada/Greenland **51** 57.00N 53.00W
ábrea Brazil **60** 7.16S 64.47W
abrit France **11** 44.07N 0.33W
abuan *i.* Malaysia **26** 5.20N 115.15E
abuha Indonesia **27** 0.37S 127.29E
abyrinth, L. Australia **46** 30.43S 135.07E
ac *d.* Chad **38** 13.30N 14.35E
a Calera Chile **63** 32.47S 71.12W
a Capelle France **8** 49.59N 3.57E
a Carlota Argentina **63** 33.25S 63.18W
a Carolina Spain **10** 38.16N 3.36W
acaune France **11** 43.42N 2.41E
a Ceiba Honduras **57** 15.45N 86.45W
acepede B. Australia **46** 36.47S 139.45E
ac Giao Vietnam **26** 12.41N 108.02E
acha, Ozero *l.* Russian Fed. **18** 61.25N 39.00E
a Charité France **11** 47.11N 3.01E
a Chartre France **9** 47.44N 0.35E
a Chaux-de-Fonds Switz. **14** 47.07N 6.51E

Lach Dera *r.* Somali Rep. **37** 0.01S 42.45E
Lachlan *r.* Australia **46** 34.21S 143.58E
Lackan Resr. Rep. of Ire. **7** 53.09N 6.31W
Lackawanna U.S.A. **55** 42.49N 78.49W
Lac la Biche *town* Canada **50** 54.46N 111.58W
La Cocha Argentina **62** 27.45S 65.35W
Lacombe Canada **50** 52.28N 113.44W
La Concepción Venezuela **60** 10.25N 71.41W
La Concordia Mexico **56** 16.05N 92.38W
La Coruña Spain **10** 43.22N 8.24W
La Crosse Wisc. U.S.A. **53** 43.48N 91.15W
La Cruz Uruguay **63** 33.56S 56.15W
La Demanda, Sierra de *mts.* Spain **10** 42.10N 3.20W
Ladismith R.S.A. **39** 33.29S 21.15E
Ladispoli Italy **12** 41.56N 12.05E
Lādīz Iran **31** 28.57N 61.18E
Ladoga *l. see* Ladozhskoye Ozero *l.* Russian Fed. **18**
La Dorada Colombia **60** 5.27N 74.40W
Ladozhskoye Ozero *l.* Russian Fed. **18** 61.00N 32.00E
Ladushkin Russian Fed. **15** 54.30N 20.05E
Ladva Vetka Russian Fed. **18** 61.16N 34.23E
Ladybrand R.S.A. **39** 29.11S 27.26E
Ladysmith Canada **50** 48.58N 123.49W
Ladysmith R.S.A. **39** 28.32S 29.47E
Lae P.N.G. **27** 6.45S 146.30E
Laesö *i.* Denmark **17** 57.16N 11.01E
La Estrada Spain **10** 42.40N 8.30W
Lafayette Ind. U.S.A. **55** 40.25N 86.54W
Lafayette La. U.S.A. **53** 30.12N 92.18W
La Fère France **9** 49.40N 3.22E
La Ferté-Bernard France **9** 48.11N 0.40E
La Ferté-Gaucher France **9** 48.47N 3.18E
La Ferté-Macé France **9** 48.36N 0.22W
La Ferté-St. Aubin France **9** 47.43N 1.56E
Lafia Nigeria **38** 8.35N 8.34E
Lafiagi Nigeria **38** 8.50N 5.23E
La Flèche France **9** 47.42N 0.05W
Laforest Canada **55** 47.02N 81.13W
La Fregeneda Spain **10** 40.58N 6.54W
La Fuente de San Esteban Spain **10** 40.48N 6.15W
Lagan *r.* U.K. **7** 54.37N 5.44W
Lågen *r.* Akershus Norway **17** 60.10N 11.28E
Lågen *r.* Vestfold Norway **17** 59.03N 10.05E
Laghouat Algeria **34** 33.50N 2.59E
Lagos Mexico **56** 21.21N 101.55W
Lagos Nigeria **38** 6.27N 3.28E
Lagos *d.* Nigeria **38** 6.32N 3.30E
Lagos Portugal **10** 37.05N 8.40W
La Grande U.S.A. **54** 45.20N 118.05W
La Grande Résr. 2 Canada **51** 53.35N 77.10W
La Grande Résr. 3 Canada **51** 53.35N 74.55W
Lagrange Australia **42** 18.46S 121.49E
La Grange U.S.A. **53** 33.02N 85.02W
La Guaira Venezuela **60** 10.38N 66.55W
La Guerche-de-Bretagne France **9** 47.56N 1.14W
Laguna Brazil **62** 28.29S 48.47W
Laguna Dam U.S.A. **54** 32.55N 114.25W
Lagunas Chile **62** 20.59S 69.37W
Lagunas Peru **60** 5.10S 73.35W
La Habana Cuba **57** 23.07N 82.25W
Lahad Datu Malaysia **26** 5.05N 118.20E
Lahat Indonesia **26** 3.46S 103.32E
La Haye-du-Puits France **9** 49.18N 1.33W
Lāhījān Iran **31** 37.12N 50.00E
Lahn *r.* Germany **8** 50.18N 7.36E
Lahnstein Germany **8** 50.17N 7.38E
Laholm Sweden **17** 56.31N 13.02E
Lahore Pakistan **28** 31.34N 74.22E
Lahti Finland **17** 60.58N 25.40E
Laï Chad **34** 9.22N 16.14E
Laiagam P.N.G. **27** 5.31S 143.39E
L'Aigle France **9** 48.45N 0.38E
Laignes France **9** 47.50N 4.22E
Laihia Finland **16** 62.58N 22.01E
Laingsburg R.S.A. **39** 33.11S 20.49E
Lainio *r.* Sweden **16** 67.28N 22.50E
Lairg U.K. **6** 58.01N 4.25W
Laisamis Kenya **37** 1.38N 37.47E
Laissac France **11** 44.23N 2.49E
Laitila Finland **17** 60.53N 21.41E
Laizhou Wan *b.* China **25** 37.30N 119.30E
Lajes Brazil **59** 27.48S 50.20W
La Junta U.S.A. **52** 37.59N 103.33W
Lak Bor *r.* Somali Rep. **37** 0.32N 42.05E
Lake Biddy *town* Australia **43** 33.01S 118.51E
Lake Boga *town* Australia **46** 35.27S 143.39E
Lake Bolac *town* Australia **46** 37.42S 142.50E
Lake Brown *town* Australia **43** 30.57S 118.19E
Lake Cargelligo *town* Australia **47** 33.19S 146.23E
Lake Charles *town* U.S.A. **53** 30.13N 93.13W
Lake City U.S.A. **53** 30.05N 82.40W
Lake District *f.* U.K. **4** 54.30N 3.10W
Lake Grace *town* Australia **43** 33.06S 118.28E
Lake Harbour *town* Canada **51** 62.50N 69.50W
Lake King *town* Australia **43** 33.05S 119.40E
Lakeland *town* U.S.A. **53** 28.02N 81.59W
Lake Mead Nat. Recreation Area U.S.A. **54** 36.00N 114.30W
Lake Nash *town* Australia **44** 21.00S 137.55E
Lake Placid *town* U.S.A. **55** 44.17N 73.59W
Lakes Entrance *town* Australia **47** 37.53S 147.59E
Lakeshore U.S.A. **54** 37.15N 119.12W
Lakeside Utah U.S.A. **54** 41.13N 112.54W
Lake Superior Prov. Park Canada **55** 47.43N 84.53W
Lakeview U.S.A. **54** 42.11N 120.21W
Lakewood N.J. U.S.A. **55** 40.06N 74.12W
Lakewood Ohio U.S.A. **55** 41.29N 81.50W
Lakhpat India **28** 23.49N 68.47E
Lakonikós Kólpos *g.* Greece **13** 36.35N 22.42E
Lakota Côte d'Ivoire **38** 5.50N 5.30W
Laksefjorden *est.* Norway **16** 70.58N 27.00E

Lakselv Norway **16** 70.03N 24.55E
Lakshadweep Is. Indian Oc. **28** 11.00N 72.00E
Lalaua Mozambique **37** 14.20S 38.30E
Lālehzār, Kūh-e *mtn.* Iran **31** 29.26N 56.48E
La Libertad El Salvador **57** 13.28N 89.20W
Lalín Spain **10** 42.40N 8.05W
La Línea Spain **10** 36.10N 5.21W
Lalitpur India **29** 24.42N 78.24E
La Loupe France **9** 48.28N 1.01E
La Louvière Belgium **8** 50.29N 4.11E
Lamar U.S.A. **52** 38.04N 102.37W
Lambaréné Gabon **36** 0.41S 10.13E
Lambayeque Peru **60** 6.36S 79.50W
Lambay I. Rep. of Ire. **7** 53.29N 6.01W
Lambert's Bay *town* R.S.A. **39** 32.06S 18.16E
Lamé Chad **38** 9.14N 14.33E
Lame Nigeria **38** 10.27N 9.12E
Lamego Portugal **10** 41.05N 7.49W
Lameroo Australia **46** 35.20S 140.33E
La Mesa Calif. U.S.A. **54** 32.46N 117.01W
Lamía Greece **13** 38.53N 22.25E
Lammermuir Hills U.K. **6** 55.51N 2.40W
Lammhult Sweden **17** 57.09N 14.35E
Lamont U.S.A. **54** 42.12N 107.28W
Lamotrek *i.* Federated States of Micronesia **27** 7.28N 146.23E
Lamotte-Beuvron France **9** 47.37N 2.01E
Lampa Peru **60** 15.10S 70.30W
Lampazos Mexico **56** 27.01N 100.31W
Lampedusa *i.* Italy **12** 35.30N 12.35E
Lampeter U.K. **5** 52.06N 4.06W
Lampione *i.* Italy **12** 35.33N 12.18E
Lamu Kenya **37** 2.20S 40.54E
La Mure France **11** 44.54N 5.47E
La Nao, Cabo de Spain **10** 38.42N 0.15E
Lanark U.K. **6** 55.41N 3.47W
Lancang Jiang *r.* China *see* Mekong *r.* Asia **24**
Lancashire *d.* U.K. **4** 53.53N 2.30W
Lancaster U.K. **4** 54.03N 2.48W
Lancaster Calif. U.S.A. **54** 34.42N 118.08W
Lancaster Ohio U.S.A. **55** 39.43N 82.37W
Lancaster Penn. U.S.A. **55** 40.02N 76.19W
Lancaster Sd. Canada **51** 74.00N 85.00W
Lancelin Australia **43** 31.01S 115.19E
Lanchow *see* Lanzhou China **24**
Landau Bayern Germany **14** 48.40N 12.43E
Landeck Austria **14** 47.09N 10.35E
Landen Belgium **8** 50.46N 5.04E
Lander *r.* Australia **44** 20.25S 132.00E
Lander U.S.A. **54** 42.50N 108.44W
Landerneau France **11** 48.27N 4.16W
Landor Australia **42** 25.06S 116.50E
Landrecies France **8** 50.08N 3.40E
Land's End *c.* U.K. **5** 50.03N 5.45W
Landshut Germany **14** 48.31N 12.10E
Landskrona Sweden **17** 55.52N 12.50E
Langå Denmark **17** 56.23N 9.55E
Langadhás Greece **13** 40.45N 23.04E
Langanes *c.* Iceland **16** 66.30N 14.30W
Langao China **25** 32.22N 109.04E
Langeais France **9** 47.20N 0.24E
Langeland *i.* Denmark **17** 55.00N 10.50E
Längelmävesi *l.* Finland **17** 61.32N 24.22E
Langeoog *i.* Germany **8** 53.46N 7.30E
Langesund Norway **17** 59.00N 9.45E
Langholm U.K. **6** 55.09N 3.00W
Langjökull *ice cap* Iceland **16** 63.43N 20.03W
Langkawi *i.* Malaysia **26** 6.20N 99.30E
Langlade Canada **55** 48.14N 75.59W
Langon France **11** 44.33N 0.14W
Langöy *i.* Norway **16** 68.45N 15.00E
Langres France **11** 47.53N 5.20E
Langsa Indonesia **26** 4.28N 97.59E
Lang Son Vietnam **26** 21.50N 106.55E
Languedoc-Roussillon *d.* France **11** 43.50N 3.30E
Lannion France **11** 48.44N 3.27W
Lansing U.S.A. **55** 42.44N 84.34W
Lanslebourg France **9** 45.17N 6.52E
Lantewa Nigeria **38** 12.15N 11.45E
Lanzarote *i.* Canary Is. **34** 29.00N 13.55W
Lanzhou China **24** 36.01N 103.45E
Lanzo Torinese Italy **9** 45.16N 7.28E
Laoag Phil. **27** 18.14N 120.36E
Lào Cai Vietnam **26** 22.30N 104.00E
Laohekou China **25** 32.26N 111.41E
Laois *d.* Rep. of Ire. **7** 53.00N 7.20W
Laon France **9** 49.34N 3.37E
La Oroya Peru **60** 11.36S 75.54W
Laos Asia **26** 19.00N 104.00E
La Palma *i.* Canary Is. **34** 28.50N 18.00W
La Palma Spain **10** 37.23N 6.33W
La Pampa *d.* Argentina **63** 37.00S 66.00W
La Paragua Venezuela **60** 6.53N 63.22W
La Paz Entre Ríos Argentina **63** 30.45S 59.38W
La Paz Mendoza Argentina **63** 33.28S 67.34W
La Paz Bolivia **62** 16.30S 68.09W
La Paz *d.* Bolivia **62** 16.00S 68.10W
La Paz Mexico **56** 24.10N 110.18W
La Pedrera Colombia **60** 1.18S 69.43W
Lapeer U.S.A. **55** 43.03N 83.09W
La Peña, Sierra de *mts.* Spain **10** 42.30N 0.50W
La Perouse Str. Russian Fed. **21** 45.50N 142.30E
La Pine U.S.A. **54** 43.40N 121.30W
Lapinjärvi Finland **17** 60.38N 26.13E
Lapland *f.* Sweden/Finland **16** 68.10N 24.10E
La Plata Argentina **63** 34.55S 57.57W
La Plata, Río de *est.* Argentina/Uruguay **63** 35.15S 56.45W
Lappajärvi *l.* Finland **16** 63.08N 23.40E
Lappeenranta Finland **18** 61.04N 28.05E
Lappi *d.* Finland **16** 67.20N 26.00E
Laptevykh, More *sea* Russian Fed. **21** 74.30N 125.00E
Lapua Finland **16** 62.57N 23.00E
La Push U.S.A. **54** 47.55N 124.38W
La Quiaca Argentina **62** 22.05S 65.36W
L'Aquila Italy **12** 42.22N 13.25E
Lār Iran **31** 27.37N 54.16E

Lara Australia **46** 38.01S 144.26E
Larache Morocco **34** 35.12N 6.10W
Laramie U.S.A. **52** 41.19N 105.35W
Lärbro Sweden **17** 57.47N 18.47E
Larche, Col de France/Italy **9** 44.25N 6.53E
Laredo U.S.A. **52** 27.32N 99.22W
Largeau Chad **34** 17.55N 19.07E
Largs U.K. **6** 55.48N 4.52W
Lariang Indonesia **26** 1.35S 119.25E
La Rioja Argentina **62** 29.25S 66.50W
La Rioja *d.* Argentina **62** 29.00S 66.00W
La Rioja *d.* Spain **10** 42.15N 2.25W
Lárisa Greece **13** 39.36N 22.24E
Lark *r.* U.K. **5** 52.26N 0.20E
Lärkāna Pakistan **28** 27.32N 68.18E
Larnaca *see* Lárnax Cyprus **32**
Lárnax Cyprus **32** 34.54N 33.39E
Larne U.K. **7** 54.51N 5.49W
La Robla Spain **10** 42.50N 5.41W
La Roche Belgium **8** 50.11N 5.35E
La Rochelle France **11** 46.10N 1.10W
La Roche-sur-Yon France **11** 46.40N 1.25W
La Roda Spain **10** 39.13N 2.10W
La Romana Dom. Rep. **57** 18.27N 68.57W
La Ronge Canada **50** 55.07N 105.18W
La Ronge, Lac *l.* Canada **50** 55.07N 105.15W
Laroquebrou France **11** 44.58N 2.11E
Larrimah Australia **44** 15.35S 133.12E
Larvik Norway **17** 59.04N 10.00E
La Sagra *mtn.* Spain **10** 37.58N 2.35W
La Sarre Canada **55** 48.49N 79.12W
Las Cruces U.S.A. **52** 32.23N 106.29W
La Seine, Baie de France **11** 49.40N 0.30W
La Serena Chile **62** 29.54S 71.16W
La Seyne France **11** 43.06N 5.53E
Las Flores Argentina **63** 36.02S 59.07W
Lāsh-e Joveyn Afghan. **31** 31.43N 61.39E
Las Heras Argentina **63** 32.50S 68.50W
Lashio Myanmar **29** 22.58N 97.48E
Las Lomitas Argentina **62** 24.43S 60.35W
Las Marismas *f.* Spain **10** 37.00N 6.15W
Las Palmas Canary Is. **34** 28.08N 15.27W
Las Perlas, Archipelago de Panama **57** 8.45N 79.30W
La Spezia Italy **9** 44.07N 9.49E
Las Piedras Uruguay **63** 34.44S 56.13W
Las Plumas Argentina **63** 43.40S 67.15W
Lassay France **9** 48.26N 0.30W
Lassen Peak *mtn.* U.S.A. **54** 40.29N 121.31W
Lastoursville Gabon **36** 0.50S 12.47E
Lastovo *i.* Croatia **13** 42.45N 16.52E
Lastrup Germany **8** 52.48N 7.55E
La Suze France **9** 47.54N 0.02E
Las Vegas Nev. U.S.A. **54** 36.11N 115.08W
Las Vegas N.Mex. U.S.A. **52** 35.36N 105.13W
Latacunga Ecuador **60** 0.58S 78.36W
La Tagua Colombia **60** 0.03S 74.40W
Latakia *see* Al Lādhiqīyah Syria **32**
La Teste-de-Buch France **11** 44.38N 1.09W
Lathen Germany **8** 52.54N 7.20E
Latina Italy **12** 41.28N 12.52E
Latisana Italy **9** 45.47N 13.00E
La Tortuga *i.* Venezuela **60** 11.00N 65.20W
La Trobe, Mt. Australia **47** 39.03S 146.25E
La Tuque Canada **55** 47.26N 72.47W
Latvia Europe **18** 56.45N 25.00E
Lau Nigeria **38** 9.14N 11.15E
Lauchhammer Germany **14** 51.30N 13.48E
Lauenburg Germany **14** 53.22N 10.33E
Laughlen, Mt. Australia **44** 23.23S 134.23E
Launceston Australia **45** 41.25S 147.07E
Launceston U.K. **5** 50.38N 4.21W
La Unión Chile **63** 40.15S 73.02W
La Unión Spain **10** 37.38N 0.53W
Laura Australia **46** 33.08S 138.19E
La Urbana Venezuela **60** 7.08N 66.56W
Laurel Miss. U.S.A. **53** 31.41N 89.09W
Laurel Mont. U.S.A. **54** 45.40N 108.46W
Laurencekirk U.K. **6** 56.50N 2.29W
Laurentides Prov. Park Canada **55** 47.46N 71.40W
Laurieton Australia **47** 31.38S 152.46E
Lausanne Switz. **14** 46.32N 6.39E
Laut *i.* Indonesia **26** 3.45S 116.20E
Lautaro Chile **63** 38.31S 72.27W
Lauterecken Germany **8** 49.39N 7.36E
Lavagh More *mtn.* Rep. of Ire. **7** 54.45N 8.07W
Lava Hot Springs *town* U.S.A. **54** 42.37N 112.01W
Laval France **9** 48.04N 0.45W
La Vega Dom. Rep. **57** 19.15N 70.33W
La Vela Venezuela **60** 11.27N 69.34W
La Vérendrye Prov. Park Canada **55** 47.29N 77.06W
Laverton Australia **43** 28.49S 122.25E
Lavia Finland **17** 61.36N 22.36E
Lavik Norway **17** 61.06N 5.30E
Lavras Brazil **59** 21.15S 44.59W
Lávrion Greece **13** 37.44N 24.04E
Lawra Ghana **38** 10.40N 2.49W
Lawrence New Zealand **48** 45.55S 169.42E
Lawrence Kans. U.S.A. **53** 38.58N 95.15W
Lawrence Mass. U.S.A. **55** 42.42N 71.09W
Lawton Okla. U.S.A. **52** 34.36N 98.25W
Lawz, Jabal al *mtn.* Saudi Arabia **32** 28.40N 35.20E
Laxå Sweden **17** 58.59N 14.37E
Laytonville U.S.A. **54** 39.41N 123.29W
Lazio *d.* Italy **12** 42.20N 12.00E
Leadhills U.K. **6** 55.25N 3.46W
Leamington U.S.A. **54** 39.31N 112.17W
Learmonth Australia **42** 22.13S 114.04E
Leavenworth U.S.A. **53** 39.19N 94.55W
Lebak Phil. **27** 6.32N 124.03E
Lebanon Asia **32** 34.00N 36.00E
Lebanon Ind. U.S.A. **55** 40.02N 87.28W
Lebanon Oreg. U.S.A. **54** 44.32N 122.54W
Lebanon Penn. U.S.A. **55** 40.20N 76.25W
Lebanon Tenn. U.S.A. **53** 36.11N 86.19W

Lebec U.S.A. **54** 34.50N 118.52W
Lebesby Norway **16** 70.34N 27.00E
Le Blanc France **11** 46.37N 1.03E
Lebork Poland **15** 54.33N 17.44E
Lebrija Spain **10** 36.55N 6.10W
Lebu Chile **63** 37.37S 73.39W
Le Bugue France **11** 44.55N 0.56E
Le Cateau France **8** 50.07N 3.33E
Le Catelet France **8** 50.00N 3.12E
Lecce Italy **13** 40.21N 18.11E
Lecco Italy **9** 45.51N 9.23E
Lech *r.* Germany **14** 48.45N 10.51E
Le Chesne France **8** 49.31N 4.46E
Lechiguanas, Islas de las *is.* Argentina **63** 33.26S 59.42W
Le Creusot France **11** 46.48N 4.27E
Lectoure France **11** 43.56N 0.38E
Ledbury U.K. **5** 52.03N 2.25W
Ledesma Spain **10** 41.05N 6.00W
Le Dorat France **11** 46.14N 1.05E
Leduc Canada **50** 53.16N 113.33W
Lee *r.* Rep. of Ire. **7** 51.53N 8.25W
Leech L. U.S.A. **53** 47.10N 94.30W
Leeds U.K. **4** 53.48N 1.34W
Leek U.K. **4** 53.07N 2.02W
Leer Germany **8** 53.14N 7.27E
Leeston New Zealand **48** 43.46S 172.18E
Leeton Australia **47** 34.33S 146.24E
Leeuwarden Neth. **8** 53.12N 5.48E
Leeuwin, C. Australia **43** 34.22S 115.08E
Leeward Is. C. America **57** 18.00N 61.00W
Lefroy, L. Australia **43** 31.15S 121.40E
Legazpi Phil. **27** 13.10N 123.45E
Legges Tor *mtn.* Australia **45** 41.32S 147.40E
Legget U.S.A. **54** 39.52N 123.34W
Leghorn *see* Livorno Italy **12**
Legion Mine Zimbabwe **39** 21.23S 28.33E
Legionowo Poland **15** 52.25N 20.56E
Legnago Italy **9** 45.11N 11.18E
Legnano Italy **9** 45.36N 8.54E
Legnica Poland **14** 51.12N 16.10E
Le Grand-Lucé France **9** 47.52N 0.28E
Le Grand-Quevilly France **9** 49.25N 1.02E
Leh Jammu & Kashmir **28** 34.09N 77.35E
Le Havre France **9** 49.30N 0.06E
Lehrte Germany **14** 52.22N 9.59E
Lehututu Botswana **39** 23.54S 21.52E
Leibnitz Austria **14** 46.48N 15.32E
Leicester U.K. **5** 52.39N 1.09W
Leicestershire *d.* U.K. **5** 52.29N 1.10W
Leichardt *r.* Australia **44** 17.35S 139.48E
Leiden Neth. **8** 52.10N 4.30E
Leie *r.* Belgium **8** 51.03N 3.44E
Leigh Creek *r.* Australia **46** 29.49S 138.10E
Leigh Creek *town* Australia **46** 30.31S 138.25E
Leighton Buzzard U.K. **5** 51.55N 0.39W
Leikanger Norway **17** 61.10N 6.52E
Leinster Australia **43** 27.59S 120.30E
Leipzig Germany **14** 51.20N 12.20E
Leiria Portugal **10** 39.45N 8.48W
Leitrim *d.* Rep. of Ire. **7** 54.08N 8.00W
Leizhou Bandao *pen.* China **25** 20.40N 109.30E
Lek *r.* Neth. **8** 51.55N 4.29E
Leksvik Norway **16** 63.40N 10.40E
Lelchitsy Belarus **15** 51.48N 28.20E
Leleque Argentina **63** 42.24S 71.04W
Le Lion-d'Angers France **9** 47.38N 0.43W
Le Lude France **9** 47.39N 0.09E
Lelystad Neth. **8** 52.32N 5.29E
Léman, Lac *l.* Switz. **14** 46.30N 6.30E
Le Mans France **9** 48.01N 0.10E
Leme Brazil **59** 22.10S 47.23W
Le Merlerault France **9** 48.42N 0.18E
Lemesós Cyprus **32** 34.40N 33.03E
Lemgo Germany **14** 52.02N 8.54E
Lemhi Range *mts.* U.S.A. **54** 44.30N 113.25W
Lemmer Neth. **8** 52.50N 5.43E
Lemmon U.S.A. **52** 45.56N 102.10W
Lemvig Denmark **17** 56.32N 8.18E
Lena *r.* Russian Fed. **21** 72.00N 127.10E
Lendery Russian Fed. **18** 63.24N 31.04E
Lendinara Italy **9** 45.05N 11.36E
Lengerich Germany **8** 52.12N 7.52E
Lenina, Kanal *canal* Russian Fed. **19** 43.46N 45.00E
Lenina, Pik *mtn.* Tajikistan **24** 40.14N 69.40E
Leningrad *see* Sankt-Peterburg Russian Fed. **18**
Leninogorsk Kazakhstan **20** 50.23N 83.32E
Leninsk Russian Fed. **19** 48.42N 45.14E
Leninsk Kuznetskiy Russian Fed. **20** 54.44N 86.13E
Lenkoran Azerbaijan **31** 38.45N 48.50E
Lenmalu Indonesia **27** 1.58S 130.00E
Lenne *r.* Germany **8** 51.24N 7.30E
Lens France **8** 50.26N 2.50E
Lentini Italy **12** 37.17N 15.00E
Lenvik Norway **16** 69.22N 18.10E
Léo Burkina **38** 11.05N 2.06W
Leoben Austria **14** 47.23N 15.06E
Leominster U.K. **5** 52.15N 2.43W
Leominster U.S.A. **55** 42.32N 71.45W
León Mexico **56** 21.10N 101.42W
León Nicaragua **57** 12.24N 86.52W
León Spain **10** 42.35N 5.34W
Leonardville Namibia **39** 23.21S 18.47E
Leonárison Cyprus **32** 35.28N 34.08E
Leongatha Australia **47** 38.29S 145.57E
Leonora Australia **43** 28.54S 121.20E
Leopoldina Brazil **59** 21.30S 42.38W
Leopoldsburg Belgium **8** 51.08N 5.13E
Leovo Moldova **15** 46.29N 28.12E
Lepel Russian Fed. **18** 54.48N 28.40E
Le Puy France **11** 45.03N 3.54E
Le Quesnoy France **8** 50.15N 3.39E
Lerbäck Sweden **17** 58.56N 15.02E
Léré Chad **38** 9.41N 14.17E
Lerici Italy **9** 44.04N 9.55E
Lérida Spain **10** 41.37N 0.38E
Lerma Spain **10** 42.02N 3.46W

Le Roy Mich. U.S.A. **55** 44.03N 85.29W
Lerwick U.K. **6** 60.09N 1.09W
Les Andelys France **9** 49.15N 1.25E
Les Cayes Haiti **57** 18.15N 73.46W
Leschenault, C. Australia **43** 31.50S 115.23E
Les Ecrins *mtn.* France **11** 44.50N 6.20E
Leshan China **29** 29.34N 103.42E
Leshukonskoye Russian Fed. **18** 64.55N 45.50E
Lesjaskog Norway **17** 62.15N 8.22E
Leskovac Yugo. **13** 43.00N 21.56E
Lesotho Africa **39** 29.00S 28.00E
Lesozavodsk Russian Fed. **25** 45.30N 133.29E
Les Pieux France **9** 49.35N 1.50W
Les Riceys France **9** 47.59N 4.22E
Les Sables d'Olonne France **11** 46.30N 1.47W
Lessay France **9** 49.14N 1.30W
Lesser Antilles *is.* C. America **57** 13.00N 65.00W
Lesser Slave L. Canada **50** 55.30N 115.00W
Lesser Sunda Is. *see* Nusa Tenggara *is.* Indonesia **26**
Lessines Belgium **8** 50.43N 3.50E
Lesti *r.* Finland **16** 64.04N 23.38E
Lésvos *i.* Greece **13** 39.10N 26.16E
Leszno Poland **14** 51.51N 16.35E
Letchworth U.K. **5** 51.58N 0.13W
Lethbridge Canada **50** 49.43N 112.48W
Lethem Guyana **60** 3.18N 59.46W
Letiahau *r.* Botswana **39** 21.16S 24.00E
Leticia Colombia **60** 4.09S 69.57W
Leti, Kepulauan *is.* Indonesia **27** 8.20S 128.00E
Le Tréport France **11** 50.04N 1.22E
Letterkenny Rep. of Ire. **7** 54.56N 7.45W
Leuk Switz. **9** 46.19N 7.38E
Leuser *mtn.* Indonesia **26** 3.50N 97.10E
Leuven Belgium **8** 50.53N 4.45E
Leuze Hainaut Belgium **8** 50.36N 3.37E
Leuze Namur Belgium **8** 50.34N 4.53E
Levanger Norway **16** 63.45N 11.19E
Levanto Italy **9** 44.10N 9.38E
Levelland U.S.A. **52** 33.35N 102.23W
Lévêque, C. Australia **42** 16.25S 123.00E
Le Verdon France **11** 45.33N 1.04W
Leverkusen Germany **8** 51.02N 6.59E
Levice Slovakia **15** 48.13N 18.37E
Levin New Zealand **48** 40.37S 175.18E
Lévis Canada **55** 46.49N 71.12W
Lévka Cyprus **32** 35.06N 32.51E
Levkás Greece **13** 38.50N 20.41E
Levkás *i.* Greece **13** 38.44N 20.37E
Levkosía Cyprus **32** 35.11N 33.23E
Lewes U.K. **5** 50.53N 0.02E
Lewis *i.* U.K. **6** 58.10N 6.40W
Lewis Pass *f.* New Zealand **48** 42.30S 172.15E
Lewis Range *mts.* U.S.A. **54** 48.30N 113.15W
Lewiston Idaho U.S.A. **54** 46.25N 117.01W
Lewiston Maine U.S.A. **55** 44.06N 70.13W
Lewistown Mont. U.S.A. **54** 47.04N 109.26W
Lewistown Penn. U.S.A. **55** 40.36N 77.31W
Lexington Ky. U.S.A. **55** 38.02N 84.30W
Lexington Oreg. U.S.A. **54** 45.27N 119.41W
Leyburn U.K. **4** 54.19N 1.50W
Leydsdorp R.S.A. **39** 23.59S 30.32E
Leyte *i.* Phil. **27** 10.40N 124.50E
Lezignan France **11** 43.12N 2.46E
Lhasa China **29** 29.41N 91.10E
Lhazê China **29** 29.10N 87.45E
Lhokseumawe Indonesia **26** 5.09N 97.09E
Liangdang China **24** 33.56N 106.12E
Lianyungang China **25** 34.37N 119.10E
Liaocheng China **25** 36.29N 115.55E
Liaodong Bandao *pen.* China **25** 40.00N 122.50E
Liaodong Wan *b.* China **25** 40.20N 121.00E
Liaoning *d.* China **25** 41.30N 123.00E
Liaoyang China **25** 41.16N 123.12E
Liaoyuan China **25** 42.53N 125.10E
Liard *r.* Canada **50** 61.56N 120.35W
Liart France **9** 49.46N 4.20E
Libby U.S.A. **54** 48.23N 115.33W
Libenge Zaïre **34** 3.39N 18.39E
Liberal U.S.A. **52** 37.03N 100.56W
Liberdade Brazil **59** 22.01S 44.22W
Liberec Czech Republic **14** 50.48N 15.05E
Liberia Africa **34** 6.30N 9.30W
Liberia Costa Rica **57** 10.39N 85.28W
Lībīyah, Aş Şaḥrā' al *des.* Africa **30** 24.00N 25.30E
Libourne France **11** 44.55N 0.14W
Libramont Belgium **8** 49.56N 5.22E
Libreville Gabon **36** 0.30N 9.25E
Libyan Desert *see* Lībīyah, Aş Şaḥrā' al Africa **30**
Libyan Plateau *see* Aḑ Ḑiffah *f.* Africa **30**
Licantén Chile **63** 34.59S 72.00W
Licata Italy **12** 37.07N 13.58E
Lichfield U.K. **5** 52.40N 1.50W
Lichinga Mozambique **37** 13.09S 35.17E
Lichtenburg R.S.A. **39** 26.08S 26.09E
Lichtenvoorde Neth. **8** 51.59N 6.32E
Lida Belarus **15** 53.50N 25.19E
Lida U.S.A. **54** 37.29N 117.29W
Lidköping Sweden **17** 58.30N 13.10E
Liechtenstein Europe **14** 47.08N 9.35E
Liège Belgium **8** 50.38N 5.35E
Liège *d.* Belgium **8** 50.32N 5.35E
Lienz Austria **14** 46.50N 12.47E
Liepāja Latvia **17** 56.31N 21.01E
Lier Belgium **8** 51.08N 4.35E
Lierneux Belgium **8** 50.18N 5.50E
Liești Romania **15** 45.38N 27.32E
Liévin France **8** 50.27N 2.49E
Lièvre, Rivière du *r.* Canada **55** 45.31N 75.26W
Liffey *r.* Rep. of Ire. **7** 53.21N 6.14W
Liffré France **9** 48.13N 1.30W
Lightning Ridge *town* Australia **47** 29.27S 148.00E
Liguria *d.* Italy **9** 42.25N 8.40E
Ligurian Sea Med. Sea **12** 43.30N 9.00E
Lihou Reef and Cays Australia **44** 17.25S 151.40E
Lihue Hawaii U.S.A. **52** 21.59N 159.23W
Lihula Estonia **17** 58.41N 23.50E
Lijiang China **29** 26.50N 100.15E
Likasi Zaïre **36** 10.58S 26.47E
Lille France **8** 50.39N 3.05E
Lille Baelt *str.* Denmark **17** 55.20N 9.45E
Lillebonne France **9** 49.31N 0.33E
Lillehammer Norway **17** 61.08N 10.30E
Lillers France **8** 50.34N 2.29E
Lillesand Norway **17** 58.15N 8.24E
Lilleström Norway **17** 59.57N 11.05E
Lillhärdal Sweden **17** 61.51N 14.04E
Lillooet Canada **50** 50.42N 121.56W
Lilongwe Malaŵi **37** 13.58S 33.49E
Liloy Phil. **27** 8.08N 122.40E
Lilydale Australia **46** 32.58S 139.59E
Lim *r.* Bosnia-Herzegovina **13** 43.45N 19.13E
Lima Peru **60** 12.06S 77.03W
Lima *r.* Portugal **10** 41.40N 8.50W
Lima Sweden **17** 60.56N 13.26E
Lima Mont. U.S.A. **54** 44.38N 112.36W
Lima Ohio U.S.A. **55** 40.43N 84.06W
Limassol *see* Lemesós Cyprus **32**
Limavady U.K. **7** 55.03N 6.57W
Limay *r.* Argentina **63** 39.02S 68.07W
Limbang Malaysia **26** 4.50N 115.00E
Limbe Cameroon **38** 4.01N 9.12E
Limbourg Belgium **8** 50.36N 5.57E
Limburg *d.* Belgium **8** 50.36N 5.57E
Limburg *d.* Neth. **8** 51.15N 5.45E
Limeira Brazil **59** 22.34S 47.25W
Limerick Rep. of Ire. **7** 52.40N 8.37W
Limerick *d.* Rep. of Ire. **7** 52.40N 8.37W
Limfjorden *str.* Denmark **17** 56.55N 9.10E
Liminka Finland **16** 64.49N 25.24E
Limmen Bight Australia **44** 14.45S 135.40E
Límnos *i.* Greece **13** 39.55N 25.14E
Limoges France **11** 45.50N 1.15E
Limogne France **11** 44.24N 1.46E
Limón Costa Rica **57** 10.00N 83.01W
Limone Piemonte Italy **9** 44.12N 7.34E
Limousin *d.* France **11** 45.45N 1.30E
Limpopo *r.* Mozambique **39** 25.14S 33.33E
Līnah Saudi Arabia **31** 28.48N 43.45E
Linakhamari Russian Fed. **18** 69.39N 31.21E
Linares Chile **63** 35.51S 71.36W
Linares Mexico **56** 24.54N 99.38W
Linares Spain **10** 38.05N 3.38W
Lincang China **24** 24.00N 100.10E
Lincoln Argentina **63** 34.55S 61.30W
Lincoln New Zealand **48** 43.38S 172.29E
Lincoln U.K. **4** 53.14N 0.32W
Lincoln Nebr. U.S.A. **53** 40.49N 96.41W
Lincoln N.H. U.S.A. **55** 44.03N 71.40W
Lincoln City U.S.A. **54** 44.59N 124.00W
Lincoln Sea Greenland **64** 82.00N 55.00W
Lincolnshire *d.* U.K. **4** 53.14N 0.32W
Lincoln Wolds *hills* U.K. **4** 53.22N 0.08W
Lindeman Group *is.* Australia **44** 20.28S 149.05E
Lindesnes *c.* Norway **17** 58.00N 7.02E
Lindhos Greece **13** 36.05N 28.02E
Lindi Tanzania **37** 10.00S 39.41E
Lindsay Canada **55** 44.21N 78.44W
Lindsay U.S.A. **54** 36.12N 119.05W
Linfen China **25** 36.05N 111.32E
Lingayen Phil. **27** 16.02N 120.14E
Lingbo Sweden **17** 61.03N 16.41E
Lingen Germany **8** 52.32N 7.19E
Lingga *i.* Indonesia **26** 0.20S 104.30E
Linguère Senegal **34** 15.22N 15.11W
Linköping Sweden **17** 58.25N 15.37E
Linnhe, Loch U.K. **6** 56.35N 5.25W
Linosa *i.* Italy **12** 35.52N 12.50E
Lins Brazil **59** 21.40S 49.44W
Lintan China **24** 34.39N 103.40E
Linton Ind. U.S.A. **55** 39.01N 87.10W
Lintorf Germany **8** 51.19N 6.50E
Linxe France **11** 43.56N 1.10W
Linxia China **24** 35.31N 103.08E
Linz Austria **14** 48.19N 14.18E
Linz Germany **8** 50.34N 7.19E
Lion, Golfe du *g.* France **11** 43.12N 4.15E
Lions, G. of *see* Lion, Golfe du *g.* France **11**
Lipetsk Russian Fed. **18** 52.37N 39.36E
Liphook U.K. **5** 51.05N 0.49W
Lipkany Moldova **15** 48.18N 26.48E
Lipova Romania **15** 46.05N 21.40E
Lipovets Ukraine **15** 49.11N 29.01E
Lippe *r.* Germany **8** 51.38N 6.37E
Lippstadt Germany **14** 51.41N 8.20E
Liptovský Mikuláš Slovakia **15** 49.06N 19.37E
Liptrap, C. Australia **47** 38.53S 145.55E
Lira Uganda **37** 2.15N 32.55E
Liri *r.* Italy **12** 41.12N 13.45E
Liria Spain **10** 39.37N 0.35W
Lisala Zaïre **35** 2.08N 21.37E
Lisboa Portugal **10** 38.44N 9.08W
Lisbon *see* Lisboa Portugal **10**
Lisburn U.K. **7** 54.30N 6.03W
Lisburne, C. U.S.A. **50** 69.00N 165.50W
Liscannor B. Rep. of Ire. **7** 52.55N 9.24W
Lishui China **25** 28.30N 119.59E
Lisichansk Ukraine **19** 48.53N 38.25E
Lisieux France **9** 49.09N 0.14E
Liskeard U.K. **5** 50.27N 4.29W
Liski Russian Fed. **19** 51.00N 39.30E
Lismore N.S.W. Australia **47** 28.48S 153.17E
Lismore Vic. Australia **46** 37.58S 143.22E
Lismore Rep. of Ire. **7** 52.08N 7.57W
Liss U.K. **5** 51.03N 0.53W
Lisse Neth. **8** 52.18N 4.33E
Listowel Rep. of Ire. **7** 52.27N 9.30W
Litang Qu *r.* China **29** 28.09N 101.30E
Lithgow Australia **47** 33.30S 150.09E
Lithuania Europe **18** 55.30N 24.00E
Little Andaman *i.* India **29** 10.50N 92.38E
Little Belt Mts. U.S.A. **54** 46.45N 110.35W
Little Cayman *i.* Cayman Is. **57** 19.40N 80.00W
Little Coco *i.* Myanmar **26** 13.50N 93.10E
Little Colorado *r.* U.S.A. **54** 36.11N 111.48W
Little Current *r.* Canada **55** 50.57N 84.36W
Little Current *town* Canada **55** 45.58N 81.56W
Little Falls *town* N.Y. U.S.A. **55** 43.03N 74.52W
Littlehampton U.K. **5** 50.48N 0.32W
Little Inagua *i.* Bahamas **57** 21.30N 73.00W
Little Karoo *f.* R.S.A. **39** 33.40S 21.40E
Little Lake *town* U.S.A. **54** 35.58N 117.53W
Little Missouri *r.* U.S.A. **52** 47.30N 102.25W
Little Nicobar *i.* India **29** 7.20N 93.40E
Little Ouse *r.* U.K. **5** 52.34N 0.20E
Little Rock *town* U.S.A. **53** 34.42N 92.17W
Little Topar Australia **46** 31.44S 142.14E
Liuli Tanzania **37** 11.07S 34.34E
Liuzhou China **25** 24.17N 109.15E
Livarot France **9** 49.01N 0.09E
Livermore, Mt. U.S.A. **52** 30.39N 104.11W
Liverpool Australia **47** 33.57S 150.52E
Liverpool Canada **51** 44.03N 64.43W
Liverpool U.K. **4** 53.25N 3.00W
Liverpool B. U.K. **4** 53.30N 3.10W
Liverpool, C. Canada **51** 73.38N 78.06W
Liverpool Range *mts.* Australia **47** 31.45S 150.45E
Livingston U.K. **6** 55.54N 3.31W
Livingston Mont. U.S.A. **54** 45.40N 110.34W
Livingstone *see* Maramba Zambia **39**
Livingstonia Malaŵi **37** 10.35S 34.10E
Livo *r.* Finland **16** 65.24N 26.48E
Livorno Italy **12** 43.33N 10.18E
Liwale Tanzania **37** 9.47S 38.00E
Lizard U.K. **5** 49.58N 5.12W
Lizard I. Australia **44** 14.39S 145.28E
Lizard Pt. U.K. **5** 49.57N 5.15W
Ljubljana Slovenia **12** 46.04N 14.28E
Ljugarn Sweden **17** 57.19N 18.42E
Ljungan *r.* Sweden **17** 62.19N 17.23E
Ljungby Sweden **17** 56.50N 13.56E
Ljungdalen Sweden **16** 62.54N 12.45E
Ljusdal Sweden **17** 61.50N 16.05E
Ljusnan *r.* Sweden **17** 61.12N 17.08E
Ljusne Sweden **17** 61.13N 17.08E
Llandeilo U.K. **5** 51.54N 4.00W
Llandovery U.K. **5** 51.59N 3.49W
Llandrindod Wells U.K. **5** 52.15N 3.23W
Llandudno U.K. **4** 53.19N 3.49W
Llanelli U.K. **5** 51.41N 4.11W
Llanes Spain **10** 43.25N 4.45W
Llangadfan U.K. **5** 52.41N 3.28W
Llangollen U.K. **4** 52.58N 3.10W
Llanidloes U.K. **5** 52.28N 3.31W
Llanos *f.* S. America **60** 7.30N 70.00W
Llanwrtyd Wells U.K. **5** 52.06N 3.39W
Lleida *see* Lérida Spain **10**
Llerena Spain **10** 38.14N 6.00W
Lloret de Mar Spain **10** 41.41N 2.53E
Lloydminster Canada **50** 53.18N 110.00W
Lobatse Botswana **39** 25.12S 25.39E
Löbau Germany **14** 51.05N 14.40E
Lobería Argentina **63** 38.08S 58.48W
Lobito Angola **36** 12.20S 13.34E
Lobonäs Sweden **17** 61.33N 15.20E
Lobos Argentina **63** 35.10S 59.05W
Locarno Switz. **14** 46.10N 8.48E
Lochboisdale *town* U.K. **6** 57.09N 7.19W
Lochem Neth. **8** 52.10N 6.25E
Loches France **11** 47.08N 1.00E
Lochgilphead U.K. **6** 56.02N 5.26W
Lochinver U.K. **6** 58.09N 5.15W
Lochmaddy *town* U.K. **6** 57.36N 7.10W
Lochnagar *mtn.* U.K. **6** 56.57N 3.15W
Lochranza U.K. **6** 55.42N 5.18W
Lochy, Loch U.K. **6** 56.58N 4.55W
Lock Australia **46** 33.34S 135.46E
Lockerbie U.K. **6** 55.07N 3.21W
Lockhart Australia **47** 35.16S 146.42E
Lockhart, L. Australia **43** 33.27S 119.00E
Lockhart River *town* Australia **44** 12.58S 143.29E
Lock Haven U.S.A. **55** 41.08N 77.27W
Lockport U.S.A. **55** 43.11N 78.39W
Loc Ninh Vietnam **26** 11.55N 106.35E
Lodalskåpa *mtn.* Norway **17** 61.47N 7.13E
Loddon *r.* Australia **46** 35.40S 143.59E
Lodeynoye Pole Russian Fed. **18** 60.43N 33.30E
Lodge Grass U.S.A. **54** 45.19N 107.22W
Lodhrān Pakistan **28** 29.32N 71.38E
Lodi Italy **9** 45.19N 9.30E
Lodi Calif. U.S.A. **54** 38.08N 121.16W
Lodja Zaïre **36** 3.29S 23.33E
Lodwar Kenya **37** 3.06N 35.38E
Łódź Poland **15** 51.49N 19.28E
Lofoten Vesterålen *is.* Norway **16** 68.15N 13.50E
Log Russian Fed. **19** 49.28N 43.51E
Loga Niger **38** 13.40N 3.15E
Logan Utah U.S.A. **54** 41.44N 111.50W
Logan, Mt. Canada **50** 60.45N 140.00W
Logansport U.S.A. **55** 40.45N 86.25W
Logone *r.* Cameroon/Chad **34** 12.10N 15.00E
Logoysk Belarus **15** 54.08N 27.42E
Logroño Spain **10** 42.28N 2.26W
Løgstør Denmark **17** 56.58N 9.15E
Lohja Finland **17** 60.15N 24.05E
Lohjanjärvi *l.* Finland **17** 60.15N 23.55E
Loimaa Finland **17** 60.51N 23.03E
Loir *r.* France **9** 47.29N 0.32W
Loire *r.* France **9** 47.18N 2.00W
Loiret *d.* France **9** 47.55N 2.20E
Loir-et-Cher *d.* France **9** 47.30N 1.30E
Loja Ecuador **60** 3.59S 79.16W
Loja Spain **10** 37.10N 4.09W
Löken Norway **17** 59.48N 11.29E
Loken tekojärvi *resr.* Finland **16** 67.55N 27.40E
Lokeren Belgium **8** 51.06N 3.59E
Lokichar Kenya **37** 2.23N 35.39E
Lokitaung Kenya **37** 4.15N 35.45E
Lokka Finland **16** 67.49N 27.44E
Løkken Denmark **17** 57.22N 9.43E
Lökken Norway **16** 63.06N 9.43E
Loknya Russian Fed. **18** 56.49N 30.00E
Lokoja Nigeria **38** 7.49N 6.44E
Lolland *i.* Denmark **17** 54.46N 11.30E
Lom Bulgaria **15** 43.49N 23.13E
Lom Norway **17** 61.50N 8.33E
Loma U.S.A. **54** 47.57N 110.30W
Lomas de Zamora Argentina **63** 34.46S 58.24W
Lombardia *d.* Italy **9** 45.25N 10.00E
Lombok *i.* Indonesia **26** 8.30S 116.20E
Lomé Togo **38** 6.10N 1.21E
Lomela Zaïre **36** 2.15S 23.15E
Lomié Cameroon **38** 3.09N 13.35E
Lomme France **8** 50.38N 2.59E
Lommel Belgium **8** 51.15N 5.18E
Lomond, Loch U.K. **6** 56.07N 4.36W
Lompoc U.S.A. **54** 34.38N 120.27W
Łomża Poland **15** 53.11N 22.04E
Londinières France **9** 49.50N 1.24E
London Canada **55** 42.59N 81.14W
London U.K. **5** 51.32N 0.06W
Londonderry U.K. **7** 55.00N 7.21W
Londonderry *d.* U.K. **7** 55.00N 7.00W
Londonderry, C. Australia **42** 13.58S 126.55E
Londonderry, Isla *i.* Chile **63** 55.03S 70.40W
Londrina Brazil **62** 23.30S 51.13W
Lone Pine U.S.A. **54** 36.36N 118.04W
Longa, Proliv *str.* Russian Fed. **21** 70.00N 178.00E
Longarone Italy **9** 46.16N 12.18E
Long Beach *town* Calif. U.S.A. **54** 33.46N 118.11W
Longchamps Belgium **8** 50.05N 5.42E
Long Creek *town* U.S.A. **54** 44.43N 119.06W
Long Eaton U.K. **4** 52.54N 1.16W
Longford Rep. of Ire. **7** 53.44N 7.48W
Longford *d.* Rep. of Ire. **7** 53.42N 7.45W
Long I. Bahamas **57** 23.00N 75.00W
Long I. U.S.A. **55** 40.46N 73.00W
Longido Tanzania **37** 2.43S 36.41E
Longiram Indonesia **26** 0.05S 115.45E
Long L. Canada **55** 49.29N 86.44W
Longlac *town* Canada **55** 49.47N 86.24W
Longnawan Indonesia **26** 1.54N 114.53E
Longniddry U.K. **6** 55.58N 2.53W
Longquan China **25** 28.05N 119.07E
Longreach Australia **44** 23.26S 144.15E
Longs Peak U.S.A. **52** 40.15N 105.37W
Longtown U.K. **4** 55.01N 2.58W
Longué France **9** 47.23N 0.06W
Longuyon France **8** 49.27N 5.35E
Longview Tex. U.S.A. **53** 32.30N 94.45W
Longview Wash. U.S.A. **54** 46.08N 122.57W
Longwy France **8** 49.32N 5.46E
Longxi China **24** 35.00N 105.00E
Long Xuyen Vietnam **26** 10.23N 105.25E
Lonigo Italy **9** 45.23N 11.23E
Löningen Germany **8** 52.44N 7.46E
Lönsdal Norway **16** 66.46N 15.26E
Lonsdale, L. Australia **46** 37.05S 142.15E
Lons-le-Saunier France **11** 46.40N 5.33E
Looc Phil. **27** 12.20N 122.05E
Looe U.K. **5** 50.51N 4.26W
Lookout, C. U.S.A. **53** 34.34N 76.34W
Loolmalassin *mtn.* Tanzania **37** 3.00S 35.45E
Loop Head Rep. of Ire. **7** 52.33N 9.56W
Lop Buri Thailand **26** 14.49N 100.37E
Lopez, C. Gabon **36** 0.36S 8.45E
Lop Nur *l.* China **24** 40.30N 90.30E
Lopphavet *est.* Norway **16** 70.30N 20.00E
Lopydino Russian Fed. **18** 61.10N 52.02E
Lora Creek *r.* Australia **46** 28.10S 135.22E
Lorain U.S.A. **55** 41.28N 82.11W
Loralai Pakistan **28** 30.20N 68.41E
Lorca Spain **10** 37.40N 1.41W
Lordsburg U.S.A. **52** 32.21N 108.43W
Lorena Brazil **59** 22.44S 45.07W
Lorengau P.N.G. **27** 2.01S 147.15E
Lorenzo Geyres Uruguay **63** 32.05S 57.55W
Loreto Brazil **61** 7.05S 45.09W
Loreto Italy **12** 43.26N 13.36E
Lorian Swamp Kenya **37** 0.35N 39.40E
Lorient France **11** 47.45N 3.21W
Lormes France **9** 47.17N 3.49E
Lorne Australia **46** 38.34S 144.01E
Lorraine *d.* France **11** 49.00N 6.20E
Lorris France **9** 47.53N 2.31E
Lorup Germany **8** 52.58N 7.39E
Los Andes Chile **63** 32.50S 70.37W
Los Angeles Chile **63** 37.28S 72.21W
Los Angeles U.S.A. **52** 34.00N 118.17W
Los Banos U.S.A. **54** 37.04N 120.51W
Los Blancos Argentina **62** 23.40S 62.35W
Los Blancos Spain **10** 37.37N 0.48W
Los Canarreos, Archipiélago de Cuba **57** 21.40N 82.30W
Lošinj *i.* Croatia **12** 44.36N 14.20E
Losinovka Ukraine **15** 50.50N 31.57E
Los Mochis Mexico **56** 25.45N 108.57W
Los Olivos U.S.A. **54** 34.40N 120.06W
Los Roques *is.* Venezuela **60** 12.00N 67.00W
Lossiemouth U.K. **6** 57.43N 3.18W
Lost Cabin U.S.A. **54** 43.19N 107.36W
Los Teques Venezuela **60** 10.25N 67.01W
Los Vilos Chile **62** 31.55S 71.31W
Lot *r.* France **11** 44.17N 0.22E
Lota Chile **63** 37.05S 73.10W
Lotagipi Swamp Sudan **36** 4.36N 34.55E
Lothian *d.* U.K. **6** 55.50N 3.00W
Lotsani *r.* Botswana **39** 22.42S 28.11E
Lötschberg Tunnel Switz. **11** 46.25N 7.53E
Louang Namtha Laos **29** 20.57N 101.25E
Louangphrabang Laos **29** 19.53N 102.10E
Loubomo Congo **36** 4.09S 12.40E
Loudéac France **11** 48.11N 2.45W
Loué France **9** 48.00N 0.09W
Loughborough U.K. **4** 52.47N 1.11W
Loughrea Rep. of Ire. **7** 53.12N 8.35W
Loughros More B. Rep. of Ire. **7** 54.48N 8.32W
Louisburgh Rep. of Ire. **7** 53.46N 9.49W
Louisiade Archipelago *is.* P.N.G. **44** 11.00S 153.00E
Louisiana *d.* U.S.A. **53** 31.00N 92.30W
Louis Trichardt R.S.A. **39** 23.03S 29.54E
Louisville Ky. U.S.A. **55** 38.13N 85.48W
Loukhi Russian Fed. **18** 66.05N 33.04E
Loulé Portugal **10** 37.08N 8.02W
Loum Cameroon **38** 4.46N 9.45E
Lourches France **8** 50.19N 3.20E
Lourdes France **11** 43.06N 0.02W
Louth Australia **47** 30.34S 145.09E
Louth *d.* Rep. of Ire. **7** 53.55N 6.30W
Louth U.K. **4** 53.23N 0.00
Louviers France **9** 49.13N 1.10E
Louvigné-du-Désert France **9** 48.29N 1.08W
Lövånger Sweden **16** 64.22N 21.18E
Lovat *r.* Russian Fed. **18** 58.06N 31.37E
Lovech Bulgaria **13** 43.08N 24.44E
Lovell U.S.A. **54** 44.50N 108.24W
Lovelock U.S.A. **54** 40.11N 118.28W
Lovere Italy **9** 45.49N 10.04E
Lovoi *r.* Zaïre **37** 8.14S 26.40E
Lovozero Russian Fed. **18** 68.01N 35.08E
Lovrin Romania **15** 45.58N 20.48E
Lowell U.S.A. **55** 42.39N 71.18W
Lower California *pen. see* Baja California *pen.* Mexico **56**
Lower Egypt *see* Mişr Baḩrī *f.* Egypt **32**
Lower Hutt New Zealand **48** 41.13S 174.55E
Lower Lough Erne U.K. **7** 54.28N 7.48W
Lowestoft U.K. **5** 52.29N 1.44E
Łowicz Poland **15** 52.06N 19.55E
Loxton Australia **46** 34.38S 140.38E
Loyauté, Îles *is.* N. Cal. **40** 21.00S 167.00E
Loyoro Uganda **37** 3.22N 34.16E
Loznica Yugo. **13** 44.32N 19.13E
Luachimo Angola **36** 7.25S 20.43E
Lualaba *r.* Zaïre **36** 0.18N 25.30E
Luama *r.* Zaïre **37** 4.45S 26.55E
Luanda Angola **36** 8.50S 13.20E
Luangwa *r.* Zambia **37** 15.32S 30.28E
Luanshya Zambia **37** 13.09S 28.24E
Luan Xian China **25** 39.45N 118.44E
Luapula *r.* Zambia **37** 9.25S 28.36E
Luarca Spain **10** 43.33N 6.31W
Luau Angola **36** 10.41S 22.09E
Lubango Angola **36** 14.55S 13.30E
Lubbock U.S.A. **52** 33.35N 101.53W
Lubeck Australia **46** 36.47S 142.38E
Lübeck Germany **14** 53.52N 10.40E
Lubenka Kazakhstan **19** 50.22N 54.13E
Lubersac France **11** 45.27N 1.24E
Lubika Zaïre **37** 7.50S 29.12E
Lubin Poland **14** 51.24N 16.13E
Lublin Poland **15** 51.18N 22.31E
Lubliniec Poland **15** 50.40N 18.41E
Lubny Ukraine **19** 50.01N 33.00E
Lubumbashi Zaïre **37** 11.44S 27.29E
Lucas González Argentina **63** 32.25S 59.33W
Lucca Italy **9** 43.50N 10.29E
Luce B. U.K. **6** 54.45N 4.47W
Lucena Phil. **27** 13.56N 121.37E
Lucena Spain **10** 37.25N 4.29W
Lucena del Cid Spain **10** 40.09N 0.17W
Lučenec Slovakia **15** 48.20N 19.40E
Lucera Italy **12** 41.30N 15.20E
Lucerne U.S.A. **54** 48.12N 120.36W
Lucero Mexico **56** 30.49N 106.30W
Lucin U.S.A. **54** 41.22N 113.55W
Lucindale Australia **46** 36.59S 140.25E
Luckenwalde Germany **14** 52.05N 13.11E
Lucknow India **29** 26.50N 80.54E
Lucy Creek *town* Australia **44** 22.25S 136.20E
Lüda *see* Dalian China **25**
Lüdenscheid Germany **8** 51.13N 7.36E
Lüderitz Namibia **39** 26.37S 15.09E
Ludhiāna India **28** 30.56N 75.52E
Lüdinghausen Germany **8** 51.46N 7.27E
Ludington U.S.A. **55** 43.58N 86.27W
Ludlow U.K. **5** 52.23N 2.42W
Ludogorie *mts.* Bulgaria **15** 43.45N 27.00E
Luduș Romania **15** 46.29N 24.05E
Ludvika Sweden **17** 60.09N 15.11E
Ludwigsburg Germany **14** 48.53N 9.11E
Ludwigshafen Germany **14** 49.29N 8.27E
Luena Angola **36** 11.46S 19.55E
Luena Zambia **37** 10.40S 30.21E
Lufeng China **25** 22.57N 115.38E
Lufkin U.S.A. **53** 31.21N 94.47W
Luga Russian Fed. **18** 58.42N 29.49E
Lugano Switz. **9** 46.01N 8.58E
Lugano, Lago di *l.* Switz./Italy **9** 46.00N 9.00E
Lugansk Ukraine **19** 48.35N 39.20E
Lugela Mozambique **37** 16.25S 36.42E
Lugenda *r.* Mozambique **37** 11.23S 38.30E
Luginy Ukraine **15** 51.05N 28.21E
Lugnaquilla Mtn. Rep. of Ire. **7** 52.58N 6.28W
Lugo Italy **9** 44.25N 11.54E
Lugo Spain **10** 43.00N 7.33W
Lugoj Romania **15** 45.42N 21.56E
Luiana Angola **39** 17.08S 22.59E
Luiana *r.* Angola **39** 17.28S 23.02E
Luino Italy **9** 46.00N 8.44E
Luiro *r.* Finland **16** 67.18N 27.28E
Łuków Poland **15** 51.56N 22.23E
Lukoyanov Russian Fed. **18** 55.03N 44.29E
Lukuga *r.* Zaïre **37** 5.37S 26.58E
Lukumbule Tanzania **37** 11.34S 37.24E
Lule *r.* Sweden **16** 65.35N 22.03E
Luleå Sweden **16** 65.34N 22.10E
Lüleburgaz Turkey **13** 41.25N 27.23E
Lulua *r.* Zaïre **36** 5.03S 21.07E
Lumberton N.Mex. U.S.A. **54** 36.55N 106.56W
Lumsden New Zealand **48** 45.44S 168.26E
Lund Sweden **17** 55.42N 13.11E
Lund Nev. U.S.A. **54** 38.52N 115.00W
Lund Utah U.S.A. **54** 38.01N 113.28W
Lundazi Zambia **37** 12.19S 33.11E
Lundy *i.* U.K. **5** 51.10N 4.41W

93

94

95

Mount Isa *town* Australia **44** 20.50S 139.29E
Mount Lofty Range *mts.* Australia **46** 34.40S 139.03E
Mount Magnet *town* Australia **43** 28.06S 117.50E
Mount Manara *town* Australia **46** 32.28S 143.59E
Mountmellick Rep. of Ire. **7** 53.08N 7.21W
Mount Morgan *town* Australia **44** 23.39S 150.23E
Mount Murchison *town* Australia **46** 31.23S 143.42E
Mount Pleasant *town* Mich. U.S.A. **55** 43.36N 84.46W
Mount's B. U.K. **5** 50.05N 5.25W
Mount Vernon *town* Australia **42** 24.09S 118.10E
Mount Vernon *town* Wash. U.S.A. **54** 48.25N 122.20W
Mount Walker *town* Australia **43** 27.47S 152.32E
Mount Willoughby Australia **46** 27.58S 134.08E
Moura Australia **44** 24.33S 149.58E
Moura Brazil **60** 1.27S 61.38W
Mourdi, Dépression de *f.* Chad **35** 18.10N 23.00E
Mourne Mts. U.K. **7** 54.10N 6.02W
Mouscron Belgium **8** 50.46N 3.10E
Moussoro Chad **34** 13.41N 16.31E
Moy *r.* Rep. of Ire. **7** 54.10N 9.09W
Moyale Kenya **37** 3.31N 39.04E
Moyeni Lesotho **39** 30.24S 27.41E
Moyobamba Peru **60** 6.04S 76.56W
Moyowosi *r.* Tanzania **37** 4.59S 30.58E
Mozambique Africa **36** 17.30S 35.45E
Mozambique Channel Indian Oc. **36** 16.00S 42.30E
Mozdok Russian Fed. **19** 43.45N 44.43E
Mozyr Belarus **15** 52.02N 29.10E
Mpala Zaïre **37** 6.45S 29.31E
Mpanda Tanzania **37** 6.21S 31.01E
Mpésoba Mali **38** 12.31N 5.39W
Mphoengs Zimbabwe **39** 21.10S 27.51E
Mpika Zambia **37** 11.52S 31.30E
Mponela Malaŵi **37** 13.32S 33.43E
Mporokoso Zambia **37** 9.22S 30.06E
Mpunde *mtn.* Tanzania **37** 6.12S 33.48E
Mpwapwa Tanzania **37** 6.23S 36.38E
Msaken Tunisia **34** 35.44N 10.35E
Mseleni R.S.A. **39** 27.21S 32.33E
Msingu Tanzania **37** 4.52S 39.08E
Msta *r.* Russian Fed. **18** 58.28N 31.20E
Mtakuja Tanzania **37** 7.21S 30.37E
Mtama Tanzania **37** 10.20S 39.19E
Mtito Andei Kenya **37** 2.32S 38.10E
Mtsensk Russian Fed. **18** 53.18N 36.35E
Mtwara Tanzania **37** 10.17S 40.11E
Mtwara *d.* Tanzania **37** 10.00S 38.30E
Muaná Brazil **61** 1.32S 49.13W
Muang Chiang Rai Thailand **29** 19.56N 99.51E
Muang Khammouan Laos **29** 17.25N 104.45E
Muang Khon Kaen Thailand **29** 16.25N 102.50E
Muang Lampang Thailand **29** 18.16N 99.30E
Muang Nakhon Phanom Thailand **26** 17.22N 104.45E
Muang Nakhon Sawan Thailand **29** 15.35N 100.10E
Muang Nan Thailand **29** 18.52N 100.42E
Muang Ngoy Laos **29** 20.43N 102.41E
Muang Pak Lay Laos **29** 18.12N 101.25E
Muang Phichit Thailand **29** 16.29N 100.21E
Muang Phitsanulok Thailand **29** 16.50N 100.15E
Muang Phrae Thailand **29** 18.07N 100.09E
Muang Ubon Thailand **29** 15.15N 104.50E
Muar Malaysia **26** 2.01N 102.35E
Muara Brunei **26** 5.01N 115.01E
Muara Indonesia **26** 0.32S 101.20E
Muarakaman Indonesia **26** 0.02S 116.45E
Muaratewe Indonesia **26** 0.57S 114.53E
Mubende Uganda **37** 0.30N 31.24E
Mubi Nigeria **38** 10.16N 13.17E
Muchea Australia **43** 31.36S 115.57E
Muchinga Mts. Zambia **37** 12.15S 31.00E
Muck *i.* U.K. **6** 56.50N 6.14W
Mucojo Mozambique **37** 12.05S 40.26E
Mudanjiang China **25** 44.36N 129.42E
Mudgee Australia **47** 32.37S 149.36E
Mudyuga Russian Fed. **18** 63.45N 39.29E
Muèda Mozambique **37** 11.40S 39.31E
Mufulira Zambia **37** 12.30S 28.12E
Muganskaya Ravnina *f.* Azerbaijan **31** 39.40N 48.30E
Mugia Spain **10** 43.06N 9.14W
Muğla Turkey **13** 37.12N 28.22E
Muḥammad, Ra's *c.* Egypt **32** 27.42N 34.13E
Mühldorf Germany **14** 48.15N 12.32E
Mühlhausen Germany **14** 51.12N 10.27E
Mühlig Hofmann fjella *mts.* Antarctica **64** 72.30S 5.00E
Muhola Finland **16** 63.20N 25.05E
Muhos Finland **16** 64.48N 25.59E
Muhu *i.* Estonia **17** 58.32N 23.20E
Muhu Väin *str.* Estonia **17** 58.45N 23.30E
Mui Ca Mau *c.* Vietnam **26** 8.30N 104.35E
Muine Bheag *town* Rep. of Ire. **7** 52.42N 6.58W
Muir, L. Australia **43** 34.30S 116.30E
Mukachevo Ukraine **15** 48.26N 22.45E
Mukah Malaysia **26** 2.56N 112.02E
Mukawa P.N.G. **44** 9.48S 150.00E
Mukinbudin Australia **43** 30.52S 118.08E
Muko *r.* Japan **23** 34.41N 135.23E
Mukwela Zambia **39** 17.02S 26.39E
Mulanje Mts. Malaŵi **37** 15.57S 35.33E
Mulchén Chile **63** 37.43S 72.14W
Mulde *r.* Germany **14** 51.10N 12.48E
Mulgathing Australia **46** 30.15S 134.00E
Mulgrave Canada **51** 45.37N 61.23W
Mulhacén *mtn.* Spain **10** 37.04N 3.22W
Mülheim N.-Westfalen Germany **8** 51.25N 6.50E
Mülheim N.-Westfalen Germany **8** 50.58N 7.00E
Mulhouse France **11** 47.45N 7.21E
Mull *i.* U.K. **6** 56.28N 5.56W
Mullaghanattin *mtn.* Rep. of Ire. **7** 51.56N 9.51W
Mullaghareirk Mts. Rep. of Ire. **7** 52.19N 9.06W
Mullaghmore *mtn.* U.K. **7** 54.51N 6.51W
Mullaley Australia **47** 31.06S 149.55E
Mullengudgery Australia **47** 31.40S 147.23E
Mullet Pen. Rep. of Ire. **7** 54.12N 10.04W
Mullewa Australia **43** 28.33S 115.31E
Mullingar Rep. of Ire. **7** 53.31N 7.21W
Mull of Galloway *c.* U.K. **6** 54.39N 4.52W
Mull of Kintyre *c.* U.K. **6** 55.17N 5.45W
Mullovka Russian Fed. **18** 54.12N 49.26E
Mull, Sd. of *str.* U.K. **6** 56.32N 5.55W
Mullumbimby Australia **47** 28.32S 153.30E
Mulobezi Zambia **39** 16.49S 25.09E
Muloorina Australia **46** 29.10S 137.51E
Multān Pakistan **28** 30.10N 71.36E
Multyfarnham Rep. of Ire. **7** 53.37N 7.25W
Mulyungarie Australia **46** 31.30S 140.45E
Mumbai *see* Bombay India **28**
Muna *i.* Indonesia **27** 5.00S 122.30E
Munābāo India **28** 25.45N 70.17E
Münchberg Germany **14** 50.11N 11.47E
München Germany **14** 48.08N 11.35E
Muncie U.S.A. **55** 40.11N 85.23W
Mundaring Weir Australia **43** 31.59S 116.13E
Münden Germany **14** 51.25N 9.39E
Mundiwindi Australia **42** 23.50S 120.07E
Mundo *r.* Spain **10** 38.20N 1.50W
Mungari Mozambique **39** 17.12S 33.31E
Mungbere Zaïre **37** 2.40N 28.25E
Mungeranie Australia **46** 28.00S 138.36E
Mungindi Australia **47** 28.58S 148.56E
Munich *see* München Germany **14**
Muniz Freire Brazil **59** 20.25S 41.23W
Munkfors Sweden **17** 59.50N 13.32E
Munning *r.* Australia **47** 31.50S 152.30E
Münster N.-Westfalen Germany **8** 51.58N 7.37E
Muntadgin Australia **43** 31.41S 118.32E
Munyati *r.* Zimbabwe **39** 17.32S 29.23E
Muonio Finland **16** 67.57N 23.42E
Muonio *r.* Finland/Sweden **16** 67.10N 23.40E
Mupa *r.* Mozambique **39** 19.07S 35.50E
Muqdisho Somali Rep. **37** 2.02N 45.21E
Mur *r.* Austria *see* Mura *r.* Croatia **14**
Mura *r.* Croatia **14** 46.18N 16.53E
Murallón *mtn.* Argentina/Chile **63** 49.48S 73.25W
Muranga Kenya **37** 0.43S 37.10E
Murashi Russian Fed. **18** 59.20N 48.59E
Murchison Australia **47** 36.36S 145.14E
Murchison *r.* Australia **42** 27.30S 114.10E
Murchison *Ld* New Zealand **48** 41.48S 172.20E
Murcia Spain **10** 37.59N 1.08W
Murcia Spain **10** 38.15N 1.50W
Mureş *r.* Romania **15** 46.16N 20.10E
Muret France **11** 43.28N 1.19E
Murewa Zimbabwe **39** 17.40S 31.47E
Murgon Australia **44** 26.15S 151.57E
Murguia Spain **10** 42.57N 2.49W
Muriaé Brazil **59** 21.08S 42.33W
Müritzsee *l.* Germany **14** 52.25N 12.45E
Murjek Sweden **16** 66.29N 20.50E
Murmansk Russian Fed. **18** 68.59N 33.08E
Murom Russian Fed. **18** 55.04N 42.04E
Muroran Japan **25** 42.21N 140.59E
Murrah al Kubrá, Al Buḥayrah al *l.* Egypt **32** 30.20N 32.20E
Murra Murra Australia **47** 28.18S 146.48E
Murray *r.*S.A. Australia **46** 35.23S 139.20E
Murray *r.*W.A. Australia **43** 32.35S 115.46E
Murray Utah U.S.A. **54** 40.40N 111.53W
Murray Bridge *town* Australia **46** 35.10S 139.17E
Murray, L. P.N.G. **27** 7.00S 141.30E
Murrayville Australia **46** 35.16S 141.14E
Murringo Australia **47** 34.19S 148.36E
Murrumbidgee *r.* Australia **46** 34.38S 143.10E
Murrumburrah Australia **47** 34.33S 148.21E
Murrurundi Australia **47** 31.47S 150.51E
Murtoa Australia **46** 36.40S 142.31E
Murud *mtn.* Malaysia **26** 3.45N 115.30E
Murwāra India **29** 23.49N 80.28E
Murwillumbah Australia **47** 28.20S 153.24E
Muş Turkey **30** 38.45N 41.30E
Mûsá, Jabal *mtn.* Egypt **32** 28.31N 33.59E
Musala *mtn.* Bulgaria **13** 42.11N 23.35E
Musay'īd Qatar **31** 24.47N 51.36E
Muscat *see* Masqaṭ Oman **31**
Musgrave Australia **44** 14.47S 143.30E
Musgrave Ranges *mts.* Australia **42** 26.10S 131.50E
Mushin Nigeria **38** 6.33N 3.22E
Musi *r.* Indonesia **26** 2.20S 104.57E
Muskegon U.S.A. **55** 43.13N 86.15W
Muskegon *r.* U.S.A. **55** 43.13N 86.16W
Muskegon Heights *town* U.S.A. **55** 43.03N 86.16W
Muskogee U.S.A. **53** 35.45N 95.21W
Muskoka, L. Canada **55** 45.00N 79.25W
Musoma Tanzania **37** 1.31S 33.48E
Musselburgh U.K. **6** 55.57N 3.04W
Musselkanaal Neth. **8** 52.57N 7.01E
Musselshell *r.* U.S.A. **54** 47.21N 107.58W
Mustang Nepal **29** 29.10N 83.55E
Mustjala Estonia **17** 58.28N 22.14E
Muswellbrook Australia **47** 32.17S 150.55E
Mut Turkey **30** 36.38N 33.27E
Mutala Mozambique **37** 15.54S 37.51E
Mutare Zimbabwe **39** 18.59S 32.40E
Mutoko Zimbabwe **39** 17.23S 32.13E
Mutooroo Australia **46** 32.30S 140.58E
Mutoray Russian Fed. **21** 61.20N 100.32E
Muwale Tanzania **37** 6.22S 33.46E
Muya Russian Fed. **21** 56.28N 115.50E
Muyinga Burundi **37** 2.48S 30.21E
Muzaffarnagar India **28** 29.28N 77.42E
Muzaffarpur India **29** 26.07N 85.23E
Muzhi Russian Fed. **18** 65.25N 64.40E
Muztag *mtn.* China **24** 36.25N 87.25E
Mvomero Tanzania **37** 6.18S 37.26E
Mvuma Zimbabwe **39** 19.16S 30.30E
Mwali *see* Mohéli *i.* Comoros **37**
Mwanza Tanzania **37** 2.30S 32.54E
Mwanza *d.* Tanzania **37** 3.00S 32.30E
Mwaya Mbeya Tanzania **37** 9.33S 33.56E
Mweka Zaïre **36** 4.51S 21.34E
Mwene Ditu Zaïre **36** 7.01S 23.27E
Mwenezi *r.* Mozambique **39** 22.42S 31.45E
Mwenezi Zimbabwe **39** 21.22S 30.45E
Mweru, L. Zaïre/Zambia **37** 9.00S 28.40E
Mwingi Kenya **37** 1.00S 38.04E
Mwinilunga Zambia **36** 11.44S 24.24E
Myanaung Myanmar **29** 18.25N 95.10E
Myanmar Asia **29** 21.00N 96.30E
Myingyan Myanmar **29** 21.25N 95.20E
Myitkyinā Myanmar **29** 25.24N 97.25E
Mymensingh Bangla. **29** 24.45N 90.23E
Myrdal Norway **17** 60.44N 7.08E
Myrdalsjökull *ice cap* Iceland **16** 63.40N 19.06W
Myrtle Creek *town* U.S.A. **54** 43.01N 123.17W
Myrtleford Australia **47** 36.35S 146.44E
Myrtle Point *town* U.S.A. **54** 43.04N 124.08W
Myślenice Poland **15** 49.51N 19.56E
Mysore India **28** 12.18N 76.37E
My Tho Vietnam **26** 10.21N 106.21E
Mytishchi Russian Fed. **18** 55.54N 37.47E
Mziha Tanzania **37** 5.53S 37.48E
Mzimba Malaŵi **37** 12.00S 33.39E

N

Naab *r.* Germany **14** 49.01N 12.02E
Naantali Finland **17** 60.27N 22.02E
Naas Rep. of Ire. **7** 53.13N 6.41W
Näätamö *r.* Norway **16** 69.40N 29.30E
Nababeep R.S.A. **39** 29.36S 17.44E
Nabadwīp India **29** 23.25N 88.22E
Nabari *r.* Japan **23** 34.45N 136.01E
Naberezhnyye Chelny Russian Fed. **18** 55.42N 52.20E
Nabingora Uganda **37** 0.31N 31.11E
Naboomspruit R.S.A. **39** 24.31S 28.24E
Nabq Egypt **32** 28.04N 34.26E
Nābulus Jordan **32** 32.13N 35.16E
Nacala Mozambique **37** 14.34S 40.41E
Nachingwea Tanzania **37** 10.21S 38.46E
Nadiād India **28** 22.42N 72.55E
Nadūshan Iran **31** 32.03N 53.33E
Nadvoitsy Russian Fed. **18** 63.56N 34.20E
Nadvornaya Ukraine **15** 48.37N 24.30E
Nadym Russian Fed. **20** 65.25N 72.40E
Naeröy Norway **16** 64.48N 11.17E
Naestved Denmark **17** 55.14N 11.46E
Nafada Nigeria **38** 11.08N 11.20E
Nafishah Egypt **32** 30.34N 32.15E
Naft-e Safid Iran **31** 31.38N 49.20E
Naga Phil. **27** 13.36N 123.12E
Nāgāland *d.* India **29** 26.10N 94.30E
Nagambie Australia **47** 36.48S 145.12E
Nagano Japan **25** 36.39N 138.10E
Nagano *d.* Japan **23** 35.33N 137.50E
Nagaoka Japan **25** 37.30N 138.50E
Nāgappattinam India **29** 10.45N 79.50E
Nagara *r.* Japan **23** 35.01N 136.43E
Nagasaki Japan **25** 32.45N 129.52E
Nāgaur India **28** 27.12N 73.44E
Nagele Neth. **8** 52.39N 5.43E
Nāgercoil India **28** 8.11N 77.30E
Nagles Mts. Rep. of Ire. **7** 52.06N 8.26W
Nagorskoye Russian Fed. **18** 58.18N 50.50E
Nagoya Japan **23** 35.10N 136.55E
Nāgpur India **29** 21.10N 79.12E
Nagqên China **29** 32.15N 96.13E
Nagykanizsa Hungary **15** 46.27N 17.01E
Naha Japan **25** 26.10N 127.40E
Nahanni Butte *town* Canada **50** 61.03N 123.31W
Nahariyya Israel **32** 33.01N 35.05E
Nahāvand Iran **31** 34.13N 48.23E
Nahe *r.* Germany **8** 49.58N 7.54E
Nahr al Furāt *r.* Asia **31** 31.00N 47.27E
Nain Canada **51** 56.30N 61.45W
Nā'īn Iran **31** 32.52N 53.05E
Nairn U.K. **6** 57.35N 3.52W
Nairobi Kenya **37** 1.17S 36.50E
Naivasha Kenya **37** 0.44S 36.26E
Najd *f.* Saudi Arabia **30** 25.00N 45.00E
Naj 'Hammādī Egypt **30** 26.04N 32.13E
Nakambe *r.* Burkina *see* White Volta *r.* Ghana **38**
Nakatsugawa Japan **23** 35.29N 137.30E
Nakhichevan Azerbaijan **31** 39.12N 45.24E
Nakhodka Russian Fed. **25** 42.53N 132.54E
Nakhon Pathom Thailand **29** 13.50N 100.01E
Nakhon Ratchasima Thailand **29** 14.59N 102.12E
Nakhon Si Thammarat Thailand **29** 8.29N 100.00E
Nakina Canada **55** 50.11N 86.43W
Nakło Poland **15** 53.08N 17.35E
Naknek U.S.A. **50** 58.45N 157.00W
Nakop Namibia **39** 28.05S 19.57E
Nakskov Denmark **17** 54.50N 11.09E
Näkten *l.* Sweden **16** 65.50N 14.35E
Nakuru Kenya **37** 0.16S 36.04E
Nalchik Russian Fed. **19** 43.31N 43.38E
Nalón *r.* Spain **10** 43.35N 6.06W
Nālūt Libya **34** 31.53N 10.59E
Namacurra Mozambique **37** 17.35S 37.00E
Namakī *r.* Iran **31** 31.02N 55.20E
Namanga Kenya **37** 2.33S 36.48E
Namangan Uzbekistan **24** 40.59N 71.41E
Namanyere Tanzania **37** 7.34S 31.00E
Namapa Mozambique **37** 13.48S 39.44E
Namaponda Mozambique **37** 15.51S 39.52E
Namarroi Mozambique **37** 15.58S 36.55E
Namatele Tanzania **37** 10.01S 38.26E
Nambour Australia **45** 26.36S 152.59E
Nambucca Heads *town* Australia **47** 30.38S 152.59E
Nam Co *l.* China **24** 30.40N 90.30E
Nam Dinh Vietnam **26** 20.25N 106.12E
Namecala Mozambique **37** 12.50S 39.38E
Nametil Mozambique **37** 15.41S 39.30E
Namib Desert Namibia **39** 23.00S 15.20E
Namibe Angola **36** 15.10S 12.10E
Namibia Africa **36** 21.30S 16.45E
Namīn Iran **31** 38.25N 48.30E
Namlea Indonesia **27** 3.15S 127.07E
Namoi *r.* Australia **47** 30.14S 148.28E
Nampa U.S.A. **54** 43.44N 116.34W
Nam Phong Thailand **29** 16.45N 102.52E
Namp'o N. Korea **25** 38.40N 125.30E
Nampula Mozambique **37** 15.09S 39.14E
Nampula *d.* Mozambique **37** 15.00S 39.00E
Namsen *r.* Norway **16** 64.27N 12.19E
Namsos Norway **16** 64.28N 11.30E
Namuchabawashan *mtn.* China **29** 29.30N 95.10E
Namungua Mozambique **37** 13.11S 40.30E
Namur Belgium **8** 50.28N 4.52E
Namur *d.* Belgium **8** 50.20N 4.45E
Namutoni Namibia **39** 18.48S 16.58E
Nanaimo Canada **50** 49.08N 123.58W
Nanango Australia **45** 26.42S 151.58E
Nanchang China **25** 28.38N 115.56E
Nanchong China **24** 30.54N 106.06E
Nancy France **11** 48.42N 6.12E
Nanda Devi *mtn.* India **29** 30.21N 79.50E
Nānded India **28** 19.11N 77.21E
Nandewar Range *mts.* Australia **47** 30.20S 150.45E
Nandyāl India **29** 15.29N 78.29E
Nanga Eboko Cameroon **38** 4.41N 12.21E
Nānga Parbat *mtn.* Jammu & Kashmir **28** 35.10N 74.35E
Nangapinoh Indonesia **26** 0.20S 111.44E
Nangqên China **24** 32.15N 96.13E
Nanjing China **25** 32.00N 118.40E
Nan Ling *mts.* China **25** 25.20N 110.30E
Nannine Australia **42** 26.53S 118.20E
Nanning China **25** 22.50N 108.19E
Nannup Australia **43** 33.57S 115.42E
Nanortalik Greenland **51** 60.09N 45.15W
Nanping Fujian China **25** 26.40N 118.07E
Nansei shotō *is.* Japan **25** 26.30N 125.00E
Nanshan *is.* S. China Sea **26** 10.30N 116.00E
Nantes France **9** 47.14N 1.35W
Nanteuil-le-Haudouin France **9** 49.08N 2.48E
Nanticoke U.S.A. **55** 41.12N 76.00W
Nantong China **25** 32.05N 120.59E
Nantua France **14** 46.09N 5.37E
Nantucket I. U.S.A. **55** 41.16N 70.03W
Nantucket Sd. U.S.A. **55** 41.30N 70.15W
Nantwich U.K. **4** 53.05N 2.31W
Nanyang China **25** 33.06N 112.31E
Nanyuki Kenya **37** 0.01N 37.03E
Naococane, Lac *l.* Canada **51** 52.52N 70.40W
Napa U.S.A. **54** 38.18N 122.17W
Napadogan Canada **55** 46.25N 67.01W
Napier New Zealand **48** 39.29S 176.58E
Naples *see* Napoli Italy **12**
Napo *r.* Peru **60** 3.30S 73.10W
Napoleon U.S.A. **55** 41.24N 84.09W
Napoli Italy **12** 40.50N 14.14E
Napoli, Golfo di *g.* Italy **12** 40.42N 14.15E
Naqb Ishtar Jordan **32** 30.00N 35.30E
Nara Japan **23** 34.41N 135.50E
Nara *d.* Japan **23** 34.27N 135.55E
Nara Mali **34** 15.13N 7.20W
Naracoorte Australia **46** 36.58S 140.46E
Naradhan Australia **47** 33.39S 146.20E
Naran Mongolia **25** 45.20N 113.41E
Narathiwat Thailand **29** 6.25N 101.48E
Nārāyanganj Bangla. **29** 23.36N 90.28E
Narbada *r. see* Narmada *r.* India **28**
Narbonne France **11** 43.11N 3.00E
Nardò Italy **13** 40.11N 18.02E
Narembeen Australia **43** 32.04S 118.23E
Nares Str. Canada **51** 78.30N 75.00W
Naretha Australia **43** 31.01S 124.50E
Narita Japan **23** 35.47N 140.19E
Narmada *r.* India **28** 21.40N 73.00E
Narodichi Ukraine **15** 51.11N 29.01E
Narodnaya *mtn.* Russian Fed. **18** 65.00N 61.00E
Narok Kenya **37** 1.04S 35.54E
Narooma Australia **47** 36.15S 150.06E
Narrabri Australia **47** 30.20S 149.49E
Narrabri West Australia **47** 30.22S 149.47E
Narran *r.* Australia **47** 29.45S 147.20E
Narrandera Australia **47** 34.36S 146.34E
Narran L. Australia **47** 29.40S 147.25E
Narrogin Australia **43** 32.58S 117.10E
Narromine Australia **47** 32.17S 148.20E
Narsimhapur India **29** 22.58N 79.15E
Narubis Namibia **39** 26.56S 18.36E
Narva Russian Fed. **18** 59.22N 28.17E
Narvik Norway **16** 68.26N 17.25E
Naryan Mar Russian Fed. **18** 67.37N 53.02E
Naryilco Australia **46** 28.41S 141.50E
Naryn Kyrgyzstan **20** 41.24N 76.00E
Nasa *mtn.* Norway **16** 66.29N 15.23E
Nasarawa Nigeria **38** 8.35N 7.44E
Naseby New Zealand **48** 45.01S 170.09E
Nashua Mont. U.S.A. **54** 48.08N 106.22W
Nashua N.H. U.S.A. **55** 42.46N 71.27W
Nashville U.S.A. **53** 36.10N 86.50W
Našice Croatia **15** 45.29N 18.06E
Näsijärvi *l.* Finland **17** 61.37N 23.42E
Nāsik India **28** 20.00N 73.52E
Nāşir, Buḥayrat *l.* Egypt **30** 22.40N 32.00E
Naşr Egypt **32** 30.36N 30.23E
Nassau Bahamas **57** 25.03N 77.20W
Nasser, L. *see* Nāşir, Buḥayrat *l.* Egypt **30**
Nassian Côte d'Ivoire **38** 8.33N 3.18W
Nässjö Sweden **17** 57.39N 14.41E
Nata Botswana **39** 20.12S 26.12E
Natal Brazil **61** 5.46S 35.15W
Natal Indonesia **26** 0.35N 99.07E
Natanes Plateau *f.* U.S.A. **54** 33.35N 110.15W
Naṭanz Iran **31** 33.30N 51.57E
Natashquan Canada **51** 50.12N 61.49W
Natchez U.S.A. **53** 31.22N 91.24W
Nathalia Australia **47** 36.02S 145.14E
National City U.S.A. **54** 32.40N 117.06W
Natitingou Benin **38** 10.17N 1.19E
Natron, L. Tanzania **37** 2.18S 36.05E
Naṭrūn, Wādī an *f.* Egypt **32** 30.25N 30.18E
Natuna Besar *i.* Indonesia **26** 4.00N 108.20E
Natuna Selatan, Kepulauan *is.* Indonesia **26** 3.00N 108.50E
Naturaliste, C. Australia **43** 33.32S 115.01E
Naubinway U.S.A. **55** 46.05N 85.27W
Naumburg Germany **14** 51.09N 11.48E
Nā'ūr Jordan **32** 31.53N 35.50E
Nauru Pacific Oc. **40** 0.32S 166.55E
Naustdal Norway **17** 61.31N 5.43E
Nauta Peru **60** 4.30S 73.40W
Nautla Mexico **56** 20.13N 96.47W
Navalmoral de la Mata Spain **10** 39.54N 5.33W
Navan Rep. of Ire. **7** 53.39N 6.42W
Navarra *d.* Spain **10** 42.40N 1.45W
Navarre Australia **46** 36.54S 143.09E
Navarro Argentina **63** 35.00S 59.10W
Naver *r.* U.K. **6** 58.32N 4.14W
Navlya Russian Fed. **18** 52.51N 34.30E
Navoi Uzbekistan **20** 40.04N 65.20E
Navojoa Mexico **56** 27.06N 109.26W
Návpaktos Greece **13** 38.24N 21.49E
Návplion Greece **13** 37.33N 22.47E
Navrongo Ghana **38** 10.51N 1.03W
Nawá Syria **32** 32.53N 36.03E
Nawābshāh Pakistan **28** 26.15N 68.26E
Náxos Greece **13** 37.06N 25.23E
Náxos *i.* Greece **13** 37.03N 25.30E
Nayarit *d.* Mexico **56** 21.30N 104.00W
Nāy Band Iran **31** 27.23N 52.38E
Nāy Band Iran **31** 32.20N 57.34E
Nāy Band, Kūh-e *mtn.* Iran **31** 32.25N 57.30E
Nazaré Brazil **61** 13.00S 39.00W
Nazarovka Russian Fed. **18** 54.19N 41.20E
Nazas *r.* Mexico **56** 25.34N 103.25W
Nazca Peru **60** 14.53S 74.54W
Nazerat Israel **32** 32.41N 35.16E
Nazilli Turkey **30** 37.55N 28.20E
Nazinon *r.* Burkina *see* Red Volta *r.* Ghana **38**
Nchanga Zambia **37** 12.30S 27.55E
Ncheu Malaŵi **37** 14.50S 34.45E
Ndali Benin **38** 9.53N 2.45E
Ndasegera *mtn.* Tanzania **37** 1.58S 35.41E
Ndélé C.A.R. **35** 8.24N 20.39E
Ndélélé Cameroon **38** 4.03N 14.55E
N'Dendé Gabon **36** 2.23S 11.23E
Ndikiniméki Cameroon **38** 4.46N 10.49E
N'Djamena Chad **38** 12.10N 14.59E
Ndola Zambia **37** 12.58S 28.39E
Ndungu Tanzania **37** 4.25S 38.04E
Nea *r.* Norway **16** 63.15N 11.00E
Neagh, Lough U.K. **7** 54.36N 6.25W
Neale, L. Australia **44** 24.21S 130.04E
Néa Páfos Cyprus **32** 34.45N 32.25E
Neápolis Greece **13** 36.30N 23.04E
Neath U.K. **5** 51.39N 3.49W
Nebit-Dag Turkmenistan **31** 39.31N 54.24E
Nebraska *d.* U.S.A. **52** 41.30N 100.00W
Nebraska City U.S.A. **53** 40.41N 95.50W
Nebrodi, Monti *mts.* Italy **12** 37.53N 14.32E
Neches *r.* U.S.A. **53** 29.55N 93.50W
Neckar *r.* Germany **14** 49.32N 8.26E
Necochea Argentina **63** 38.31S 58.46W
Necuto Angola **36** 4.55S 12.38E
Needles U.S.A. **54** 34.51N 114.37W
Neerpelt Belgium **8** 51.13N 5.28E
Neftegorsk Russian Fed. **19** 44.21N 39.44E
Nefyn U.K. **4** 52.55N 4.31W
Negaunee U.S.A. **55** 46.31N 87.37W
Negele Ethiopia **35** 5.20N 39.36E
Negev *des. see* HaNegev *des.* Israel **32**
Negoiu *mtn.* Romania **15** 45.36N 24.32E
Negomano Mozambique **37** 11.26S 38.30E
Negombo Sri Lanka **29** 7.13N 79.50E
Negotin Yugo. **15** 44.14N 22.33E
Negrais, C. Myanmar **29** 16.00N 94.30E
Negritos Peru **60** 4.42S 81.18W
Negro *r.* Argentina **63** 40.50S 63.00W
Negro *r.* Brazil **60** 3.00S 59.55W
Negro *r.* Uruguay **63** 33.27S 58.20W
Negros *i.* Phil. **27** 10.00N 123.00E
Negru-Vodă Romania **15** 43.50N 28.12E
Neijiang China **24** 29.32N 105.03E
Nei Monggol Zizhiqu *d.* China **25** 41.60N 109.60E
Neisse *r.* Poland Germany **14** 52.05N 14.42E
Neiva Colombia **60** 2.58N 75.15W
Neksö Denmark **17** 55.04N 15.09E
Nelidovo Russian Fed. **18** 56.13N 32.46E
Nelkan Russian Fed. **21** 57.40N 136.04E
Nelligen Australia **47** 35.39S 150.06E
Nellore India **29** 14.29N 80.00E
Nelson Australia **46** 38.04S 141.05E
Nelson Canada **50** 49.29N 117.17W
Nelson *r.* Canada **51** 57.00N 93.20W
Nelson New Zealand **48** 41.18S 173.17E
Nelson U.K. **4** 53.50N 2.14W
Nelson U.S.A. **54** 35.30N 113.16W
Nelson Bay *town* Australia **47** 32.43S 152.08E
Nelson, C. Australia **46** 38.27S 141.35E
Nelson, Estrecho *str.* Chile **63** 51.33S 74.40W
Nelson-Marlborough *d.* New Zealand **48** 41.40S 173.40E
Nelspoort R.S.A. **39** 32.07S 23.00E
Nelspruit R.S.A. **39** 25.27S 30.58E
Néma Mauritania **34** 16.32N 7.12W
Nembe Nigeria **38** 4.32N 6.25E
Nemours France **9** 48.16N 2.41E
Nemunas *r.* Lithuania **17** 55.18N 21.23E
Nenagh Rep. of Ire. **7** 52.52N 8.13W
Nenana U.S.A. **50** 64.35N 149.20W
Nene *r.* U.K. **4** 52.49N 0.12E
Nenjiang China **25** 49.10N 125.15E
Nepal Asia **29** 28.00N 84.30E
Nephi U.S.A. **54** 39.43N 111.50W

in Beg *mtn.* Rep. of Ire. **7** 54.02N 9.38W
in Beg Range *mts.* Rep. of Ire. **7** 54.00N
W
r. Italy **12** 42.33N 12.43E
France **11** 44.08N 0.20E
khta Russian Fed. **18** 57.30N 40.40E
tva *r.* Bosnia-Herzegovina **13** 43.02N 17.28E
uinha Angola **36** 15.50S 21.40E
Deep Pacific Oc. **27** 12.40N 145.50E
nde France **11** 45.50N 4.14E
a Spain **10** 37.42N 6.30W
Neth. **8** 53.27N 5.46E
yen Norway **17** 60.34N 9.09E
France **9** 49.46N 2.51E
a Norway **16** 66.13N 13.04E
y *i.* Norway **16** 66.35N 12.40E
, Loch U.K. **6** 57.16N 4.30W
aocano *r.* Canada **55** 48.40N 73.25W
erov Ukraine **15** 50.04N 24.00E
os *r.* Greece **13** 40.51N 24.48E
un Norway **17** 60.19N 5.20E
izh Belarus **15** 53.16N 26.40E
nya Israel **32** 32.20N 34.51E
erlands Europe **8** 52.00N 5.30E
erlands Antilles S. America **57** 12.30N
00W
r. Italy **13** 39.12N 17.08E
lling L. Canada **51** 66.30N 70.40W
randenburg Germany **14** 53.33N 13.16E
hâtel Switz. **14** 47.00N 6.56E
hâtel, Lac de *l.* Switz. **14** 46.55N 6.55E
enhaus Germany **8** 52.30N 6.58E
château Belgium **8** 49.51N 5.26E
châtel France **9** 49.44N 1.26E
llé-Pont-Pierre France **9** 47.33N 0.33E
markt Germany **14** 49.16N 11.28E
münster Germany **14** 54.06N 9.59E
quén Argentina **63** 39.00S 68.05W
quén *d.* Argentina **63** 38.30S 70.00W
quén *r.* Argentina **63** 39.02S 68.07W
uppin Germany **14** 52.55N 12.48E
se *r.* U.S.A. **53** 35.04N 77.04W
siedler See *l.* Austria **14** 47.52N 16.45E
ss Germany **8** 51.12N 6.42E
stadt Bayern Germany **14** 49.44N 12.11E
strelitz Germany **14** 53.22N 13.05E
vic France **11** 45.23N 2.16E
wied Germany **8** 50.26N 7.28E
ada *d.* U.S.A. **54** 39.50N 116.10W
ada, Sierra *mts.* Spain **10** 37.04N 3.20W
ada, Sierra *mts.* U.S.A. **52** 37.30N 119.00W
anka Russian Fed. **21** 56.31N 98.57E
el Russian Fed. **18** 56.00N 29.59E
ers France **11** 47.00N 3.09E
ertire Australia **47** 31.52S 147.47E
nnomyssk Russian Fed. **19** 44.38N 41.59E
şehir Turkey **30** 38.38N 34.43E
ala Tanzania **37** 10.56S 39.15E
Albany Ind. U.S.A. **55** 38.17N 85.50W
Amsterdam Guyana **61** 6.18N 57.30W
Angledool Australia **47** 29.06S 147.57E
ark N.J. U.S.A. **55** 40.44N 74.11W
ark N.Y. U.S.A. **55** 43.03N 77.06W
ark Ohio U.S.A. **55** 40.03N 82.25W
ark-on-Trent U.K. **4** 53.06N 0.48E
Bedford U.S.A. **55** 41.38N 70.56W
berg U.S.A. **54** 45.18N 122.58W
Bern U.S.A. **53** 35.05N 77.04W
berry Mich. U.S.A. **55** 46.22N 85.30W
biggin-by-the-Sea U.K. **4** 55.11N 1.30W
Braunfels U.S.A. **52** 29.43N 98.09W
Britain *i.* P.N.G. **41** 6.00S 150.00E
Brunswick *d.* Canada **55** 46.30N 66.15W
Brunswick U.S.A. **55** 40.29N 74.27W
burgh U.S.A. **55** 41.30N 74.00W
bury U.K. **5** 51.24N 1.19W
Bussa Nigeria **38** 9.53N 4.29E
castle Australia **47** 32.55S 151.46E
castle N.B. Canada **55** 47.01N 65.36W
castle Ont. Canada **55** 43.55N 78.35W
castle R.S.A. **39** 27.44S 29.55E
castle U.K. **7** 54.13N 5.53W
Castle Penn. U.S.A. **55** 41.00N 80.22W
castle Wyo. U.S.A. **52** 43.50N 104.11W
castle B. Australia **44** 10.50S 142.37E
castle Emlyn U.K. **5** 52.02N 4.29W
castle-under-Lyme U.K. **4** 53.02N 2.15W
castle upon Tyne U.K. **4** 54.58N 1.36W
castle Waters *town* Australia **44** 17.24S
3.24E
castle West Rep. of Ire. **7** 52.26N 9.04W
degate Australia **43** 33.06S 119.01E
Delhi India **28** 28.37N 77.13E
England Range *mts.* Australia **47** 30.30S
1.50E
enham, C. U.S.A. **50** 58.37N 162.12W
ent U.K. **5** 51.56N 2.24W
Forest *f.* U.K. **5** 50.50N 1.35W
foundland *d.* Canada **51** 55.00N 60.00W
foundland *i.* Canada **51** 48.30N 56.00W
Galloway U.K. **6** 55.05N 4.09W
Guinea *i.* Austa. **27** 5.00S 140.00E
Hampshire *d.* U.S.A. **55** 43.35N 71.40W
Hanover *i.* Pacific Oc. **41** 2.00S 150.00E
haven U.K. **5** 50.47N 0.04E
Haven U.S.A. **55** 41.18N 72.55W
Ireland *i.* P.N.G. **41** 2.30S 151.30E
Jersey *d.* U.S.A. **55** 40.15N 74.30W
Liskeard Canada **55** 47.30N 79.40W
London Conn. U.S.A. **55** 41.21N 72.06W
man Australia **42** 23.22S 119.43E
man, Mt. Australia **42** 23.15S 119.33E
market Rep. of Ire. **7** 52.13N 9.00W
market U.K. **5** 52.15N 0.23E
market on Fergus Rep. of Ire. **7** 52.46N
55W
Martinsville U.S.A. **55** 39.39N 80.52W
Meadows U.S.A. **54** 44.58N 116.32W
Mexico *d.* U.S.A. **52** 33.30N 106.00W

New Norcia Australia **43** 30.58S 116.15E
New Norfolk Australia **45** 42.46S 147.02E
New Orleans U.S.A. **53** 30.00N 90.03W
New Philadelphia U.S.A. **55** 40.31N 81.28W
New Plymouth New Zealand **48** 39.03S 174.04E
Newport Mayo Rep. of Ire. **7** 53.53N 9.34W
Newport Tipperary Rep. of Ire. **7** 52.42N 8.25W
Newport Dyfed U.K. **5** 52.01N 4.51W
Newport Essex U.K. **5** 51.58N 0.13E
Newport Gwent U.K. **5** 51.34N 2.59W
Newport Hants. U.K. **5** 50.43N 1.18W
Newport Ark. U.S.A. **53** 35.35N 91.16W
Newport Maine U.S.A. **55** 44.50N 69.17W
Newport N.H. U.S.A. **55** 43.21N 72.09W
Newport Oreg. U.S.A. **54** 44.38N 124.03W
Newport R.I. U.S.A. **55** 41.13N 71.18W
Newport News U.S.A. **53** 36.59N 76.26W
New Providence *i.* Bahamas **57** 25.03N 77.25W
Newquay U.K. **5** 50.24N 5.06W
New Quay U.K. **5** 52.13N 4.22W
New Radnor U.K. **5** 52.15N 3.10W
New Romney U.K. **5** 50.59N 0.58E
New Ross Rep. of Ire. **7** 52.24N 6.57W
Newry U.K. **7** 54.11N 6.21W
New Scone U.K. **6** 56.25N 3.25W
New South Wales *d.* Australia **47** 32.40S 147.40E
Newton Kans. U.S.A. **53** 38.02N 97.22W
Newton Abbot U.K. **5** 50.32N 3.37W
Newton Aycliffe U.K. **4** 54.36N 1.34W
Newtonmore U.K. **6** 57.04N 4.08W
Newton Stewart U.K. **6** 54.57N 4.29W
Newtown U.K. **5** 52.31N 3.19W
Newtownabbey U.K. **7** 54.39N 5.57W
Newtownards U.K. **7** 54.35N 5.41W
Newtown Butler U.K. **7** 54.12N 7.22W
Newtown St. Boswells U.K. **6** 55.35N 2.40W
Newtownstewart U.K. **7** 54.43N 7.25W
New Westminster Canada **50** 49.12N 122.55W
New York U.S.A. **55** 40.40N 73.50W
New York *d.* U.S.A. **55** 43.00N 75.00W
New Zealand Austa. **48** 41.00S 175.00E
Neya Russian Fed. **18** 58.18N 43.40E
Neyagawa Japan **23** 34.46N 135.38E
Neyrīz Iran **31** 29.12N 54.17E
Neyshābūr Iran **31** 36.13N 58.49E
Nezhin Ukraine **15** 51.03N 31.54E
Ngala Nigeria **38** 12.21N 14.10E
Ngami, L. Botswana **39** 20.32S 22.38E
Ngamiland *d.* Botswana **39** 19.40S 22.00E
Ngamiland *f.* Botswana **39** 20.00S 22.30E
Ngangla Ringco *l.* China **29** 31.40N 83.00E
Nganglong Kangri *mtn.* China **24** 32.45N 81.12E
N'Gao Congo **36** 2.28S 15.40E
Ngaoundéré Cameroon **38** 7.20N 13.35E
Ngaruawahia New Zealand **48** 37.40S 175.09E
Ngaruroro *r.* New Zealand **48** 39.34S 176.54E
Ngauruhoe *mtn.* New Zealand **48** 39.10S 175.35E
Ng'iro, Mt. Kenya **37** 2.06N 36.44E
N'Giva Angola **39** 17.03S 15.47E
Ngomba Tanzania **37** 8.16S 32.51E
Ngomeni Kenya **37** 3.00S 40.11E
Ngong Kenya **37** 1.22S 36.40E
Ngorongoro Crater *f.* Tanzania **37** 3.13S 35.32E
Ngozi Burundi **37** 2.52S 29.50E
Nguigmi Niger **38** 14.00N 13.11E
Nguru Nigeria **38** 12.53N 10.30E
Nguruka Tanzania **37** 5.08S 30.58E
Ngwaketse *d.* Botswana **39** 25.10S 25.00E
Ngwerere Zambia **37** 15.18S 28.20E
Nhaccongo Mozambique **39** 24.18S 35.14E
Nhachengue Mozambique **39** 22.52S 35.10E
Nhandugue *r.* Mozambique **39** 18.47S 34.30E
Nha Trang Vietnam **26** 12.15N 109.10E
Nhill Australia **46** 36.20S 141.40E
Nhulunbuy Australia **44** 12.11S 136.46E
Niafounké Mali **38** 15.56N 4.00W
Niagara Falls *town* U.S.A. **55** 43.06N 79.02W
Niah Malaysia **26** 3.52N 113.44E
Niamey Niger **38** 13.32N 2.05E
Niamey *d.* Niger **38** 14.00N 1.40E
Nia-Nia Zaïre **37** 1.30N 27.41E
Niapa, Gunung *mtn.* Indonesia **26** 1.45N 117.30E
Nias *i.* Indonesia **26** 1.05N 97.30E
Niassa *d.* Mozambique **37** 13.00S 36.30E
Nicaragua C. America **57** 13.00N 85.00W
Nicaragua, Lago de *l.* Nicaragua **57** 11.30N 85.30W
Nicastro Italy **12** 38.58N 16.16E
Nice France **11** 43.42N 7.16E
Nichelino Italy **9** 44.59N 7.38E
Nicholson Australia **42** 18.02S 128.54E
Nicholson *r.* Australia **44** 17.31S 139.36E
Nicobar Is. India **29** 8.00N 94.00E
Nicolls Town Bahamas **57** 25.08N 78.00W
Nicosia *see* Levkosía Cyprus **32**
Nicoya, Golfo de *g.* Costa Rica **57** 9.30N 85.00W
Nicoya, Península de *pen.* Costa Rica **57** 10.30N 85.30W
Nid *r.* Norway **17** 58.24N 8.48E
Nida *r.* Poland **15** 50.18N 20.52E
Nidzica Poland **15** 53.22N 20.26E
Niederösterreich *d.* Austria **14** 48.20N 15.50E
Niedersachsen *d.* Germany **8** 52.55N 7.40E
Niekerkshoop R.S.A. **39** 29.19S 22.48E
Niéllé Côte d'Ivoire **38** 10.05N 5.28W
Nienburg Germany **14** 52.38N 9.13E
Niers *r.* Neth. **8** 51.43N 5.56E
Nieuw Nickerie Surinam **61** 5.57N 56.59W
Nieuwpoort Belgium **8** 51.08N 2.45E
Niğde Turkey **30** 37.58N 34.42E
Niger Africa **34** 17.00N 9.30E
Niger *d.* Nigeria **38** 9.50N 6.00E
Niger *r.* Nigeria **38** 4.15N 6.05E
Niger Delta Nigeria **38** 4.00N 6.10E
Nigeria Africa **38** 9.00N 9.00E
Nightcaps New Zealand **48** 45.58S 168.02E
Niigata Japan **25** 37.58N 139.02E

Niiza Japan **23** 35.48N 139.34E
Nijmegen Neth. **8** 51.50N 5.52E
Nikel Russian Fed. **16** 69.20N 30.00E
Nikiniki Indonesia **42** 9.49S 124.29E
Nikki Benin **38** 9.55N 3.18E
Nikolayev Ukraine **19** 46.57N 32.00E
Nikolayevskiy Russian Fed. **19** 50.05N 45.32E
Nikolayevsk-na-Amure Russian Fed. **21** 53.20N 140.44E
Nikolsk Russian Fed. **18** 59.33N 45.30E
Nikopol Ukraine **19** 47.34N 34.25E
Niksar Turkey **30** 40.35N 36.59E
Nīkshahr Iran **31** 26.14N 60.15E
Nikšić Yugo. **13** 42.48N 18.56E
Nila *i.* Indonesia **27** 6.45S 129.30E
Nīl, An *r.* Egypt **32** 31.30N 30.25E
Nile *r. see* Nīl, An *r.* Egypt **32**
Nile Delta Egypt **32** 31.00N 31.00E
Niles Mich. U.S.A. **55** 41.51N 86.15W
Nilgiri Hills India **28** 11.30N 77.30E
Nimbin Australia **47** 28.35S 153.12E
Nîmes France **11** 43.50N 4.21E
Nindigully Australia **47** 28.20S 148.47E
Ninety Mile Beach *f.* Australia **47** 38.07S 147.30E
Ninety Mile Beach *f.* New Zealand **48** 34.45S 173.00E
Nineveh *ruins* Iraq **30** 36.24N 43.08E
Ningbo China **25** 29.54N 121.33E
Ningde China **25** 26.41N 119.32E
Ningnan China **24** 27.03N 102.46E
Ningwu China **25** 39.00N 112.19E
Ningxia Huizu *d.* China **24** 37.00N 106.00E
Ninh Binh Vietnam **26** 20.14N 106.00E
Ninove Belgium **8** 50.50N 4.02E
Niobrara *r.* U.S.A. **52** 42.45N 98.10W
Nioro Mali **34** 15.12N 9.35W
Niort France **11** 46.19N 0.27W
Nipāni India **28** 16.24N 74.23E
Nipigon Canada **55** 49.00N 88.17W
Nipigon B. Canada **55** 48.53N 87.50W
Nipigon, L. Canada **55** 49.50N 88.30W
Nipissing, L. Canada **55** 46.17N 80.00W
Niquelândia Brazil **59** 14.27S 48.27W
Nirasaki Japan **23** 35.42N 138.27E
Niš Yugo. **13** 43.20N 21.54E
Nisa Portugal **10** 39.31N 7.39W
Nishinomiya Japan **23** 34.43N 135.20E
Nisko Poland **15** 50.35N 22.07E
Nissedal Norway **17** 59.10N 8.30E
Nisser *l.* Norway **17** 59.10N 8.30E
Niţā' Saudi Arabia **31** 27.13N 48.25E
Niterói Brazil **59** 22.54S 43.06W
Nith *r.* U.K. **6** 55.00N 3.35W
Nitra Slovakia **15** 48.20N 18.05E
Niue *i.* Cook Is. **40** 19.02S 169.52W
Niut, Gunung *mtn.* Indonesia **26** 1.00N 110.00E
Nivala Finland **16** 63.55N 24.58E
Nivelles Belgium **8** 50.36N 4.20E
Nizāmābād India **29** 18.40N 78.05E
Nizhneangarsk Russian Fed. **21** 55.48N 109.35E
Nizhnekamskoye Vodokhranilishche Russian Fed. **18** 55.45N 53.50E
Nizhne Kolymsk Russian Fed. **21** 68.34N 160.58E
Nizhneudinsk Russian Fed. **21** 54.55N 99.00E
Nizhnevartovsk Russian Fed. **20** 60.57N 76.40E
Nizhniy Novgorod Russian Fed **18** 56.20N 44.00E
Nizhniy Tagil Russian Fed. **18** 58.00N 60.00E
Nizhnyaya Tunguska *r.* Russian Fed. **21** 65.50N 88.00E
Nizhnyaya Tura Russian Fed. **18** 58.40N 59.48E
Nizke Tatry *mts.* Slovakia **15** 48.54N 19.40E
Nizza Monferrato Italy **9** 44.46N 8.21E
Njazídja *see* Grande Comore *i.* Comoros **37**
Njombe Tanzania **37** 9.20S 34.47E
Njombe *r.* Tanzania **37** 7.02S 35.55E
Njoro Tanzania **37** 5.16S 36.30E
Nkalagu Nigeria **38** 6.28N 7.46E
Nkawkaw Ghana **38** 6.35N 0.47W
Nkayi Zimbabwe **39** 19.00S 28.54E
Nkhata Bay *town* Malaŵi **37** 11.37S 34.20E
Nkhotakota Malaŵi **37** 12.55S 34.19E
Nkongsamba Cameroon **38** 4.59N 9.53E
Nkungwe Mt. Tanzania **37** 6.15S 29.54E
Noatak U.S.A. **50** 67.34N 162.59W
Noce *r.* Italy **9** 46.09N 11.04E
Nogales Mexico **56** 31.20N 110.56W
Nogara Italy **9** 45.11N 11.04E
Nogayskiye Step *f.* Russian Fed. **19** 44.25N 45.30E
Nogent-le-Rotrou France **9** 48.19N 0.50E
Nogent-sur-Seine France **9** 48.29N 3.30E
Nogoyá Argentina **63** 32.22S 59.49W
Noguera Ribagorçana *r.* Spain **10** 41.27N 0.25E
Noirmoutier, Île de *i.* France **11** 47.00N 2.15W
Nojima-zaki *c.* Japan **23** 34.56N 139.53E
Nokia Finland **17** 61.28N 23.30E
Nok Kundi Pakistan **28** 28.48N 62.46E
Nokomis Canada **50** 51.30N 105.00W
Nokou Chad **38** 14.35N 14.47E
Nolinsk Russian Fed. **18** 57.38N 49.52E
Noma Omuramba *r.* Botswana **39** 19.14S 22.15E
Nome U.S.A. **50** 64.30N 165.30W
Nomgon Mongolia **24** 42.50N 105.13E
Nonancourt France **9** 48.47N 1.11E
Nonburg Russian Fed. **18** 65.32N 50.37E
Nong Khai Thailand **29** 17.50N 102.46E
Nongoma R.S.A. **39** 27.58S 31.35E
Nonning Australia **46** 32.30S 136.30E
Nonthaburi Thailand **26** 13.48N 100.31E
Noojee Australia **47** 37.57S 146.00E
Noonamah Australia **42** 12.35S 131.03E
Noongaar Australia **43** 31.21S 118.55E
Noonkanbah Australia **42** 18.30S 124.50E
Noonthorangee Range *mts.* Australia **46** 31.00S 142.20E
Noorama Creek *r.* Australia **47** 28.05S 145.55E
Noord Beveland *f.* Neth. **8** 51.35N 3.45E

Noord Brabant *d.* Neth. **8** 51.37N 5.00E
Noord Holland *d.* Neth. **8** 52.37N 4.50E
Noordoost-Polder *f.* Neth. **8** 52.45N 5.45E
Noordwijk Neth. **8** 52.16N 4.29E
Noorvik U.S.A. **50** 66.50N 161.14W
Noosa Heads *town* Australia **44** 26.23S 153.07E
Nora Sweden **17** 59.31N 15.02E
Noranda Canada **55** 48.18N 79.01W
Nord *d.* Burkina **38** 13.50N 2.20W
Nord *d.* France **8** 50.17N 3.14E
Nordaustlandet *i.* Arctic Oc. **64** 79.55N 23.00E
Norddeich Germany **8** 53.35N 7.10E
Norden Germany **8** 53.34N 7.13E
Nordenham Germany **14** 53.30N 8.29E
Norderney Germany **8** 53.43N 7.09E
Norderney *i.* Germany **8** 53.45N 7.15E
Nordfjord *est.* Norway **17** 61.54N 5.12E
Nordfjordeid Norway **17** 61.54N 6.00E
Nordfold Norway **16** 67.48N 15.20E
Nordfriesische Inseln *is.* Germany **14** 54.30N 8.00E
Nordhausen Germany **14** 51.31N 10.48E
Nordhorn Germany **8** 52.27N 7.05E
Nordkapp *c.* Norway **16** 71.11N 25.48E
Nordkinnhalvöya *pen.* Norway **16** 70.55N 27.45E
Nordland *d.* Norway **16** 66.50N 14.50E
Nord-Ostsee-Kanal Germany **14** 53.54N 9.12E
Nordreisa Norway **16** 69.46N 21.00E
Nordrhein-Westfalen *d.* Germany **8** 51.18N 6.32E
Nord Tröndelag *d.* Norway **16** 64.20N 12.00E
Nordvik Russian Fed. **21** 73.40N 110.50E
Nore Norway **17** 60.10N 9.01E
Nore *r.* Rep. of Ire. **7** 52.25N 6.58W
Norfolk *d.* U.K. **5** 52.39N 1.00E
Norfolk Va. U.S.A. **53** 36.54N 76.18W
Norfolk Broads *f.* U.K. **4** 52.43N 1.35E
Norheimsund Norway **17** 60.22N 6.08E
Norilsk Russian Fed. **21** 69.21N 88.02E
Norman *r.* Australia **44** 17.28S 140.49E
Normanby *r.* Australia **44** 14.25S 144.08E
Normanby New Zealand **48** 39.32S 174.16E
Normanby I. P.N.G. **44** 10.05S 151.05E
Normandie, Collines de *hills* France **9** 48.50N 0.40W
Normanton Australia **44** 17.40S 141.05E
Norman Wells Canada **50** 65.19N 126.46W
Nornalup Australia **43** 34.58S 116.49E
Ñorquinco Argentina **63** 41.50S 70.55W
Norrahammar Sweden **17** 57.42N 14.06E
Norra Kvarken *str.* Sweden/Finland **16** 63.36N 20.43E
Norra Storfjället *mtn.* Sweden **16** 65.52N 15.18E
Norrbotten *d.* Sweden **16** 67.00N 19.50E
Nörresundby Denmark **17** 57.04N 9.56E
Norris L. U.S.A. **53** 36.20N 83.55W
Norristown U.S.A. **55** 40.07N 75.20W
Norrköping Sweden **17** 58.36N 16.11E
Norrsundet Sweden **17** 60.56N 17.08E
Norrtälje Sweden **17** 59.46N 18.42E
Norseman Australia **43** 32.15S 121.47E
Norsk Russian Fed. **21** 52.22N 129.57E
Norte, C. Brazil **61** 1.40N 49.55W
Norte, Punta *c.* Argentina **63** 36.17S 56.46W
Northallerton U.K. **4** 54.20N 1.26W
Northam Australia **43** 31.41S 116.40E
Northampton Australia **43** 28.21S 114.37E
Northampton U.K. **5** 52.14N 0.54W
Northamptonshire *d.* U.K. **5** 52.18N 0.55W
North Battleford Canada **50** 52.47N 108.19W
North Bay *town* Canada **55** 46.19N 79.28W
North Bend Oreg. U.S.A. **54** 43.24N 124.14W
North Berwick U.K. **6** 56.04N 2.43W
North Bourke Australia **47** 30.01S 145.59E
North C. Antarctica **64** 71.00S 166.00E
North C. New Zealand **48** 34.28S 173.00E
North Canadian *r.* U.S.A. **53** 35.30N 95.45W
North Carolina *d.* U.S.A. **53** 35.30N 79.00W
North Channel *str.* Canada **55** 46.02N 82.50W
North Channel U.K. **7** 55.15N 5.52W
North China Plain *f. see* Huabei Pingyuan *f.* China **25**
Northcliffe Australia **43** 34.36S 116.04E
North Dakota *d.* U.S.A. **52** 47.00N 100.00W
North Dorset Downs *hills* U.K. **5** 50.46N 2.25W
North Downs *hills* U.K. **5** 51.18N 0.40E
North East *d.* Botswana **39** 20.45S 27.05E
North Eastern *d.* Kenya **37** 1.00N 40.00E
Northern *d.* Ghana **38** 9.00N 1.30W
Northern Ireland *d.* U.K. **7** 54.40N 6.45W
Northern Mariana Islands Pacific Oc. **40** 15.00N 145.00E
Northern Territory *d.* Australia **44** 20.00S 133.00E
North Esk *r.* U.K. **6** 56.45N 2.25W
North Foreland *c.* U.K. **5** 51.23N 1.26E
North French *r.* Canada **55** 51.03N 80.52W
North Frisian Is. *see* Nordfriesische Inseln *is.* Germany **14**
North Horr Kenya **37** 3.19N 37.00E
North I. New Zealand **48** 39.00S 175.00E
Northiam U.K. **5** 50.59N 0.39E
North Korea Asia **25** 40.00N 128.00E
Northland *d.* New Zealand **48** 35.25S 174.00E
North Las Vegas U.S.A. **54** 36.12N 115.07W
North Ogden U.S.A. **54** 41.18N 112.00W
North Platte U.S.A. **52** 41.09N 100.45W
North Platte *r.* U.S.A. **52** 41.09N 100.55W
North Powder U.S.A. **54** 45.13N 117.55W
North Ronaldsay *i.* U.K. **6** 59.23N 2.26W
North Sea Europe **3** 56.00N 5.00E
North Sporades *see* Voríai Sporádhes *is.* Greece **13**
North Taranaki Bight *b.* New Zealand **48** 38.45S 174.15E
North Tawton U.K. **5** 50.48N 3.55W
North Tonawanda U.S.A. **55** 43.02N 78.54W
North Uist *i.* U.K. **6** 57.35N 7.20W
Northumberland *d.* U.K. **4** 55.12N 2.00W

Northumberland, C. Australia **46** 38.04S 140.40E
Northumberland Is. Australia **44** 21.40S 150.00E
North Walsham U.K. **4** 52.49N 1.22E
Northway U.S.A. **50** 62.58N 142.00W
North West C. Australia **42** 21.48S 114.10E
North West Highlands U.K. **6** 57.30N 5.15W
North West River *town* Canada **51** 53.30N 60.10W
Northwest Territories *d.* Canada **51** 66.00N 95.00W
Northwich U.K. **4** 53.16N 2.30W
North York Moors *hills* U.K. **4** 54.21N 0.50W
North Yorkshire *d.* U.K. **4** 54.14N 1.14W
Norton Sound *b.* U.S.A. **50** 63.50N 164.00W
Nort-sur-Erdre France **9** 47.26N 1.30W
Norwalk Conn. U.S.A. **55** 41.07N 73.25W
Norwalk Ohio U.S.A. **55** 41.14N 82.37W
Norway Europe **16** 65.00N 13.00E
Norway House *town* Canada **51** 53.59N 97.50W
Norwegian Dependency Antarctica **64** 77.00S 10.00E
Norwegian Sea Europe **64** 65.00N 5.00E
Norwich U.K. **5** 52.38N 1.17E
Norwood Ohio U.S.A. **55** 39.12N 84.21W
Noshul Russian Fed. **18** 60.04N 49.30E
Nosovka Ukraine **15** 50.55N 31.37E
Noşratābād Iran **31** 29.54N 59.58E
Noss Head U.K. **6** 58.28N 3.03W
Nossob *r.* R.S.A./Botswana **36** 26.54S 20.39E
Noteć *r.* Poland **14** 52.44N 15.26E
Noto Italy **12** 36.53N 15.05E
Notodden Norway **17** 59.34N 9.17E
Notre Dame, Monts *mts.* Canada **55** 48.00N 69.00W
Nottawasaga B. Canada **55** 44.40N 80.30W
Nottaway *r.* Canada **55** 51.25N 78.50W
Nottingham U.K. **4** 52.57N 1.10W
Nottinghamshire *d.* U.K. **4** 53.10N 1.00W
Notwani *r.* Botswana **39** 23.46S 26.57E
Nouadhibou Mauritania **34** 20.54N 17.01W
Nouakchott Mauritania **34** 18.09N 15.58W
Nouméa New Caledonia **40** 22.16S 166.27E
Nouna Burkina **38** 12.44N 3.54W
Noupoort R.S.A. **39** 31.11S 24.56E
Nouvelle Calédonia *is.* Pacific Oc. **40** 21.30S 165.30E
Nouzonville France **9** 49.49N 4.45E
Novafeltria Bagnodi Romagna Italy **9** 43.53N 12.17E
Nova Friburgo Brazil **59** 22.16S 42.32W
Nova Iguaçu Brazil **59** 22.45S 43.27W
Nova Lima Brazil **59** 19.59S 43.51W
Novara Italy **9** 45.27N 8.37E
Nova Scotia *d.* Canada **51** 45.00N 64.00W
Nova Sofala Mozambique **39** 20.09S 34.24E
Novato U.S.A. **54** 38.06N 122.34W
Novaya Ladoga Russian Fed. **18** 60.09N 32.15E
Novaya Lyalya Russian Fed. **20** 59.02N 60.38E
Novaya Sibir, Ostrov *i.* Russian Fed. **21** 75.20N 148.00E
Novaya Ushitsa Ukraine **15** 48.50N 27.12E
Novaya Zemlya *i.* Russian Fed. **20** 74.00N 56.00E
Novelda Spain **10** 38.24N 0.45W
Nové Zámky Slovakia **15** 47.59N 18.11E
Novgorod Russian Fed. **18** 58.30N 31.20E
Novgorod Severskiy Belarus **18** 52.00N 33.15E
Novi di Modena Italy **9** 44.54N 10.54E
Novigrad Croatia **14** 45.19N 13.34E
Novi Ligure Italy **9** 44.46N 8.47E
Novi Pazar Yugo. **13** 43.08N 20.28E
Novi Sad Yugo. **15** 45.16N 19.52E
Novoalekseyevka Ukraine **19** 46.14N 34.36E
Novoanninskiy Russian Fed. **19** 50.32N 42.42E
Novo Arkhangel'sk Ukraine **15** 48.34N 30.50E
Novocherkassk Russian Fed. **19** 47.25N 40.05E
Novofedorovka Ukraine **19** 47.04N 35.18E
Novograd Volynskiy Ukraine **15** 50.34N 27.32E
Novogrudok Belarus **15** 53.35N 25.50E
Novo Hamburgo Brazil **59** 29.37S 51.07W
Novokazalinsk Kazakhstan **20** 45.48N 62.06E
Novokuznetsk Russian Fed. **20** 53.45N 87.12E
Novomoskovsk Russian Fed. **18** 54.06N 38.15E
Novomoskovsk Ukraine **19** 48.38N 35.15E
Novorossiysk Russian Fed. **19** 44.44N 37.46E
Novoshakhtinsk Russian Fed. **19** 47.46N 39.55E
Novosibirsk Russian Fed. **20** 55.04N 82.55E
Novosibirskiye Ostrova *is.* Russian Fed. **21** 76.00N 144.00E
Novouzensk Russian Fed. **19** 50.29N 48.08E
Novo-Vyatsk Russian Fed. **18** 58.30N 49.40E
Novozybkov Russian Fed. **15** 52.31N 31.58E
Novska Croatia **14** 45.21N 16.59E
Nový Jičín Czech Republic **15** 49.36N 18.00E
Novyy Bykhov Belarus **15** 53.20N 30.21E
Novyy Port Russian Fed. **20** 67.38N 72.33E
Nowa Ruda Poland **14** 50.34N 16.30E
Nowa Sól Poland **14** 51.49N 15.41E
Nowendoc Australia **47** 31.35S 151.45E
Nowgong Assam India **29** 26.20N 92.41E
Nowingi Australia **46** 34.36S 142.15E
Nowra Australia **47** 35.54S 150.36E
Nowy Dwór Mazowiecki Poland **15** 52.26N 20.43E
Nowy Korczyn Poland **15** 50.19N 20.48E
Nowy Săcz Poland **15** 49.39N 20.40E
Nowy Targ Poland **15** 49.29N 20.02E
Nowy Tomśyl Poland **14** 52.20N 16.07E
Noxon U.S.A. **54** 48.01N 115.47W
Noyant France **9** 47.31N 0.08E
Noyon France **9** 49.35N 3.00E
Nozay France **9** 47.34N 1.38W
Nsanje Malaŵi **37** 16.55S 35.12E
Nsawam Ghana **38** 5.49N 0.20W
Nsombo Zambia **37** 10.50S 29.56E
Nsukka Nigeria **38** 6.51N 7.29E
Nuatja Togo **38** 6.59N 1.11E
Nubian Desert Sudan **35** 21.00N 34.00E
Nueces *r.* U.S.A. **53** 27.55N 97.30W

Petauke Zambia **37** 14.16S 31.21E
Petawawa Canada **55** 45.54N 77.17W
Peterborough S.A. Australia **46** 33.00S 138.51E
Peterborough Vic. Australia **46** 38.36S 142.55E
Peterborough Canada **55** 44.18N 78.19W
Peterborough U.K. **5** 52.35N 0.14W
Peterhead U.K. **6** 57.30N 1.46W
Peterlee U.K. **4** 54.45N 1.18W
Petermann Ranges *mts.* Australia **42** 25.00S 129.46E
Petersburg W.Va. U.S.A. **55** 39.00N 79.07W
Petersfield U.K. **5** 51.00N 0.56W
Petitot *r.* Canada **50** 60.14N 123.29W
Petit St. Bernard, Col du *pass* France/Italy **9** 45.40N 6.53E
Petoskey U.S.A. **55** 45.22N 84.59W
Petra *ruins* Jordan **32** 30.19N 35.26E
Petrich Bulgaria **13** 41.25N 23.13E
Petrikov Belarus **15** 52.09N 28.30E
Petrodvorets Russian Fed. **18** 59.50N 29.57E
Petrolina Brazil **61** 9.22S 40.30W
Petropavlovsk Kazakhstan **20** 54.53N 69.13E
Petropavlovsk Kamchatskiy Russian Fed. **21** 53.03N 158.43E
Petrópolis Brazil **59** 22.30S 43.06W
Petroşani Romania **15** 45.25N 23.22E
Petrovaradin Yugo. **15** 45.16N 19.55E
Petrovsk Russian Fed. **18** 52.20N 45.24E
Petrovsk Zabaykal'skiy Russian Fed. **21** 51.20N 108.55E
Petrozavodsk Russian Fed. **18** 61.46N 34.19E
Petrus Steyn R.S.A. **39** 27.38S 28.08E
Peureulak Indonesia **26** 4.48N 97.45E
Pevek Russian Fed. **21** 69.41N 170.19E
Pézenas France **11** 43.28N 3.25E
Pezinok Slovakia **15** 48.18N 17.17E
Pezmog Russian Fed. **18** 61.50N 51.45E
Pfaffenhofen Germany **14** 48.31N 11.30E
Pfälzel Germany **8** 49.47N 6.41E
Pforzheim Germany **14** 48.53N 8.41E
Phangan, Ko *i.* Thailand **26** 9.50N 100.00E
Phangnga Thailand **29** 8.29N 98.31E
Phan Rang Vietnam **26** 11.35N 109.00E
Pharenda India **29** 27.06N 83.17E
Phenix City U.S.A. **53** 32.28N 85.01W
Phet Buri Thailand **29** 13.01N 99.55E
Philadelphia Penn. U.S.A. **55** 39.57N 75.07W
Philippeville Belgium **8** 50.12N 4.32E
Philippines Asia **27** 13.00N 123.00E
Philippine Sea Pacific Oc. **40** 18.00N 135.00E
Philippine Trench Pacific Oc. **27** 8.45N 127.20E
Philipstown R.S.A. **39** 30.25S 24.26E
Phillip I. Australia **47** 38.29S 145.14E
Phillips *r.* Australia **43** 33.55S 120.01E
Phillips Maine U.S.A. **55** 44.49N 70.21W
Phillipson, L. Australia **46** 29.28S 134.28E
Phnom Penh Cambodia **26** 11.35N 104.55E
Phoenix Ariz. U.S.A. **54** 33.27N 112.05W
Phoenix I. Kiribati **40** 4.00S 172.00W
Phôngsali Laos **29** 21.40N 102.06E
Phukao Miang *mtn.* Thailand **29** 16.50N 101.00E
Phuket Thailand **29** 8.00N 98.28E
Phuket, Ko *i.* Thailand **29** 8.10N 98.20E
Phumĭ Sâmraông Cambodia **26** 14.12N 103.31E
Phu Quoc *i.* Cambodia **26** 10.10N 104.00E
Phu Tho Vietnam **26** 21.23N 105.13E
Piacá Brazil **61** 7.42S 47.18W
Piacenza Italy **9** 45.03N 9.42E
Pialba Australia **44** 25.13S 152.55E
Pian *r.* Australia **47** 30.03S 148.18E
Piana France **11** 42.14N 8.38E
Piangil Australia **45** 35.04S 143.20E
Pianoro Italy **9** 44.22N 11.20E
Pianosa *i.* Italy **12** 42.35N 10.05E
Piatra-Neamţ Romania **15** 46.56N 26.22E
Piauí *d.* Brazil **61** 7.45S 42.30W
Piauí *r.* Brazil **61** 6.14S 42.51W
Piave *r.* Italy **9** 45.33N 12.45E
Piawaning Australia **43** 30.51S 116.22E
Pic *r.* Canada **55** 48.36N 86.28W
Picardie *d.* France **8** 49.47N 3.12E
Pickering U.K. **4** 54.15N 0.46W
Pickle Crow Canada **51** 51.30N 90.04W
Pickwick L. *resr.* U.S.A. **53** 35.00N 88.10W
Picos Brazil **61** 7.05S 41.28W
Picquigny France **9** 49.57N 2.09E
Picton Australia **47** 34.12S 150.35E
Picton Canada **55** 44.01N 77.09W
Picton New Zealand **48** 41.17S 174.02E
Picún Leufú Argentina **63** 39.30S 69.15W
Pidálion, Akrotírion *c.* Cyprus **32** 34.56N 34.05E
Piedecuesta Colombia **60** 6.59N 73.03W
Piedras *r.* Peru **60** 12.30S 69.10W
Piedras Negras Mexico **56** 28.40N 100.32W
Piedra Sola Uruguay **63** 32.04S 56.21W
Piedras, Punta *c.* Argentina **63** 35.25S 57.07W
Pielavesi Finland **16** 63.14N 26.45E
Pielinen *l.* Finland **18** 63.20N 29.50E
Piemonte *d.* Italy **9** 44.45N 8.00E
Pierce U.S.A. **54** 46.29N 115.48W
Pierre U.S.A. **52** 44.23N 100.20W
Piesseville Australia **43** 33.11S 117.12E
Piešt'any Slovakia **15** 48.36N 17.50E
Pietarsaari Finland **16** 63.40N 22.42E
Pietermaritzburg R.S.A. **39** 29.36S 30.23E
Pietersburg R.S.A. **39** 23.54S 29.27E
Pietrasanta Italy **9** 43.57N 10.14E
Piet Retief R.S.A. **39** 27.00S 30.49E
Pietrosu *mtn.* Romania **15** 47.36N 24.38E
Pietrosul *mtn.* Romania **15** 47.08N 25.11E
Pieve di Cadore Italy **9** 46.26N 12.22E
Pigailoe *i.* Federated States of Micronesia **27** 8.08N 146.40E
Pigna Italy **9** 43.56N 7.40E
Pihtipudas Finland **16** 63.23N 25.34E
Pikalevo Russian Fed. **18** 59.35N 34.07E
Pikes Peak *mtn.* U.S.A. **52** 38.51N 105.03W
Piketberg R.S.A. **39** 32.54S 18.43E
Piketon U.S.A. **55** 39.03N 83.01W
Pila Argentina **63** 36.00S 58.10W
Piła Poland **14** 53.09N 16.44E
Pilar Paraguay **59** 26.52S 58.23W
Pilar do Sul Brazil **59** 23.48S 47.45W
Pilcomayo *r.* Argentina/Paraguay **62** 25.15S 57.43W
Pilica *r.* Poland **15** 51.52N 21.17E
Pilliga Australia **47** 30.23S 148.55E
Pílos Greece **13** 36.55N 21.40E
Pilsum Germany **8** 53.29N 7.06E
Pimba Australia **46** 31.18S 136.47E
Pimenta Bueno Brazil **60** 11.40S 61.14W
Pinang, Pulau *i.* Malaysia **26** 5.30N 100.10E
Pinarbaşi Turkey **30** 38.43N 36.23E
Pinar del Río Cuba **57** 22.24N 83.42W
Píndhos Óros *mts.* Albania/Greece **13** 39.40N 21.00E
Pindiga Nigeria **38** 9.58N 10.53E
Pine Bluff *town* U.S.A. **53** 34.13N 92.00W
Pine Creek *town* Australia **42** 13.51S 131.50E
Pinega Russian Fed. **18** 64.42N 43.28E
Pinega *r.* Russian Fed. **18** 63.51N 41.48E
Pinerolo Italy **9** 44.53N 7.21E
Pinetown R.S.A. **39** 29.49S 30.52E
Piney France **9** 48.22N 4.20E
Ping *r.* Thailand **29** 15.45N 100.10E
Pingaring Australia **43** 34.45S 118.34E
Pingdingshan Liaoning China **25** 41.26N 124.46E
Pingdong Taiwan **25** 22.40N 120.30E
Pingelly Australia **43** 32.34S 117.04E
Pingliang China **24** 35.25N 107.14E
Pingrup Australia **43** 33.33S 118.30E
Pingxiang Guang. Zhuang. China **24** 22.05N 106.46E
Pinhal Brazil **59** 22.10S 46.46W
Pinhel Portugal **10** 40.46N 7.04W
Pini *i.* Indonesia **26** 0.10N 98.30E
Piniós *r.* Greece **13** 39.51N 22.37E
Pinjarra Australia **43** 32.37S 115.53E
Pinnaroo Australia **46** 35.18S 140.54E
Pinos, Isla de *i.* Cuba **57** 21.40N 82.40W
Pinrang Indonesia **26** 3.48S 119.41E
Pinsk Belarus **15** 52.08N 26.01E
Pinto Argentina **62** 29.09S 62.38W
Pinyug Russian Fed. **18** 60.10N 47.43E
Piombino Italy **12** 42.56N 10.30E
Piorini, L. Brazil **60** 3.34S 63.15W
Piotrków Trybunalski Poland **15** 51.25N 19.42E
Piove di Sacco Italy **9** 45.18N 12.02E
Pipinas Argentina **63** 35.30S 57.19W
Pipmouacane, Résr. Canada **55** 49.35N 70.30W
Piqua U.S.A. **55** 40.08N 84.14W
Piracicaba Brazil **59** 22.45S 47.40W
Piracicaba *r.* Brazil **59** 22.35S 48.14W
Piracuruca Brazil **61** 3.56S 41.42W
Piraeus *see* Piraiévs Greece **13**
Piraiévs Greece **13** 37.56N 23.38E
Pirassununga Brazil **59** 21.59S 47.25W
Pírgos Greece **13** 37.42N 21.27E
Pirna Germany **14** 50.58N 13.58E
Pirot Yugo. **13** 43.10N 22.32E
Piryatin Ukraine **19** 50.14N 32.31E
Pisa Italy **12** 43.43N 10.24E
Pisciotta Italy **12** 40.08N 15.12E
Pisco Peru **60** 13.46S 76.12W
Písek Czech Republic **14** 49.19N 14.10E
Pishan China **24** 37.30N 78.20E
Pistoia Italy **9** 43.55N 10.54E
Pisuerga *r.* Spain **10** 41.35N 5.40W
Pisz Poland **15** 53.38N 21.49E
Pita Guinea **34** 11.05N 12.15W
Pitalito Colombia **60** 1.51N 76.01W
Pitarpunga, L. Australia **46** 34.23S 143.32E
Pite *r.* Sweden **16** 65.14N 21.32E
Piteå Sweden **16** 65.20N 21.30E
Piteşti Romania **15** 44.52N 24.51E
Pithāpuram India **29** 17.07N 82.16E
Pithiviers France **9** 48.10N 2.15E
Pitlochry U.K. **6** 56.43N 3.45W
Pittsburg N.H. U.S.A. **55** 45.03N 71.26W
Pittsburgh U.S.A. **55** 40.26N 80.00W
Pittsfield U.S.A. **55** 42.27N 73.15W
Pittston U.S.A. **55** 41.19N 75.47W
Pittville U.S.A. **54** 41.03N 121.20W
Piũí Brazil **59** 20.28S 45.58W
Piura Peru **60** 5.15S 80.38W
Placentia Canada **51** 47.14N 53.58W
Plains U.S.A. **54** 47.27N 114.53W
Plainview U.S.A. **52** 34.12N 101.43W
Plampang Indonesia **26** 8.48S 117.48E
Planá Czech Republic **14** 49.52N 12.44E
Plana Cays *is.* Bahamas **57** 21.31N 72.14W
Plasencia Spain **10** 40.02N 6.05W
Plassen Norway **17** 61.08N 12.31E
Plaster Rock *town* Canada **55** 46.55N 67.24W
Platani *r.* Italy **12** 37.24N 13.15E
Plateau *d.* Nigeria **38** 8.50N 9.00E
Plate, R. *est. see* La Plata, Río de Argentina/Uruguay **63**
Platí, Ákra *c.* Greece **13** 40.26N 23.59E
Platinum U.S.A. **50** 59.00N 161.50W
Plato Colombia **60** 9.54N 74.46W
Platte *r.* U.S.A. **53** 41.05N 96.50W
Plattling Germany **14** 48.47N 12.53E
Plattsburgh U.S.A. **55** 44.42N 73.28W
Plauen Germany **14** 50.29N 12.08E
Plavsk Russian Fed. **18** 53.40N 37.20E
Pleasantville U.S.A. **55** 39.23N 74.32W
Pleiku Vietnam **26** 13.57N 108.01E
Plenty, B. of New Zealand **48** 37.40S 176.50E
Plesetsk Russian Fed. **18** 62.42N 40.21E
Pleshchenitsy Belarus **15** 54.24N 27.52E
Pleszew Poland **15** 51.54N 17.48E
Pleven Bulgaria **13** 43.25N 24.39E
Pljevlja Yugo. **13** 43.22N 19.22E
Płock Poland **15** 52.33N 19.43E
Ploieşti Romania **15** 44.57N 26.02E
Plomb du Cantal *mtn.* France **11** 45.04N 2.45E
Plombières France **11** 47.58N 6.28E
Plön Germany **14** 54.09N 10.25E
Płońsk Poland **15** 52.38N 20.23E
Ploudalmézeau France **11** 48.33N 4.39W
Plovdiv Bulgaria **13** 42.09N 24.45E
Plumtree Zimbabwe **39** 20.30S 27.50E
Plymouth U.K. **5** 50.23N 4.09W
Plymouth Ind. U.S.A. **55** 41.20N 86.19W
Plzeň Czech Republic **14** 49.45N 13.22E
Pô Burkina **38** 11.11N 1.10W
Po *r.* Italy **9** 44.51N 12.30E
Pobé Benin **38** 7.00N 2.56E
Pobeda, Gora *mtn.* Russian Fed. **21** 65.20N 145.50E
Pobla de Segur Spain **10** 42.15N 0.58E
Pocatello U.S.A. **54** 42.52N 112.27W
Pocklington U.K. **4** 53.56N 0.48W
Poços de Caldas Brazil **59** 21.48S 46.33W
Poděbrady Czech Republic **14** 50.08N 15.07E
Podgaytsy Ukraine **15** 49.19N 25.10E
Podgorica Yugo. **13** 42.30N 19.16E
Podkamennaya Tunguska Russian Fed. **21** 61.45N 90.13E
Podkamennaya Tunguska *r.* Russian Fed. **21** 61.40N 90.00E
Podolsk Russian Fed. **18** 55.23N 37.32E
Podor Senegal **34** 16.35N 15.02W
Podporozhye Russian Fed. **18** 60.55N 34.02E
Pofadder R.S.A. **39** 29.08S 19.22E
Pogrebishche Ukraine **15** 49.30N 29.15E
Poh Indonesia **27** 1.00S 122.50E
P'ohang S. Korea **25** 36.00N 129.26E
Poinsett, C. Antarctica **64** 65.35S 113.00E
Point Arena *f.* U.S.A. **54** 38.55N 123.41W
Pointe-à-Pitre Guadeloupe **57** 16.14N 61.32W
Pointe aux Anglais *town* Canada **55** 49.38N 67.11W
Pointe-aux-Trembles *town* Canada **55** 45.40N 73.30W
Pointe Noire *town* Congo **36** 4.46S 11.53E
Point Hope *town* U.S.A. **50** 68.21N 166.41W
Point Lookout *town* Australia **47** 30.33S 152.20E
Point Pleasant *town* W.Va. U.S.A. **55** 38.53N 82.07W
Point Samson *town* Australia **42** 20.46S 117.10E
Poissy France **9** 48.56N 2.03E
Poitiers France **11** 46.35N 0.20E
Poitou-Charentes *d.* France **11** 46.00N 0.00
Poix France **9** 49.47N 2.00E
Poix-Terron France **9** 49.39N 4.39E
Pokhara Nepal **29** 28.14N 83.58E
Pokrovsk Russian Fed. **19** 51.30N 46.07E
Polacca U.S.A. **54** 35.50N 110.23W
Pola de Lena Spain **10** 43.10N 5.49W
Polān Iran **31** 25.29N 61.15E
Poland Europe **15** 52.30N 19.00E
Polatli Turkey **30** 39.34N 32.08E
Polch Germany **8** 50.18N 7.19E
Polda Australia **46** 33.30S 135.10E
Polesye *f.* Belarus **15** 52.15N 28.00E
Poli Cameroon **38** 8.30N 13.15E
Policastro, Golfo di *g.* Italy **12** 40.00N 15.35E
Poligny France **11** 46.50N 5.42E
Pólis Cyprus **32** 35.02N 32.26E
Políyiros Greece **13** 40.23N 23.27E
Pollino *mtn.* Italy **12** 39.53N 16.11E
Pollock Reef Australia **43** 34.28S 123.40E
Polnovat Russian Fed. **20** 63.47N 65.54E
Polonnoye Ukraine **15** 50.10N 27.30E
Polotsk Russian Fed. **18** 55.30N 28.43E
Polperro U.K. **5** 50.19N 4.31W
Polson U.S.A. **54** 47.41N 114.09W
Poltava Ukraine **19** 49.35N 34.35E
Polunochnoye Russian Fed. **18** 60.52N 60.28E
Polyarnyy Russian Fed. **18** 69.14N 33.30E
Polynesia *is.* Pacific Oc. **40** 4.00S 165.00W
Pomarkku Finland **17** 61.42N 22.00E
Pombal Brazil **61** 6.45S 37.45W
Pombal Portugal **10** 39.55N 8.38W
Pomene Mozambique **39** 22.53S 35.33E
Pomeroy Wash. U.S.A. **54** 46.28N 117.36W
Pomona Namibia **39** 27.09S 15.18E
Pomona U.S.A. **54** 34.04N 117.45W
Pompey's Pillar *town* U.S.A. **54** 45.59N 107.56W
Ponca City U.S.A. **53** 36.41N 97.04W
Ponce Puerto Rico **57** 18.00N 66.40W
Pondicherry India **29** 11.59N 79.50E
Pond Inlet *str.* Canada **51** 72.30N 75.00W
Ponferrada Spain **10** 42.32N 6.31W
Pongani P.N.G. **44** 9.05S 148.35E
Pongola *r.* Mozambique **39** 26.13S 32.38E
Ponnāni India **28** 10.46N 75.54E
Ponoy Russian Fed. **18** 67.02N 41.03E
Ponoy *r.* Russian Fed. **18** 67.00N 41.10E
Ponta Grossa Brazil **59** 25.00S 50.09W
Pont-à-Mousson France **11** 48.55N 6.03E
Ponta Porã Brazil **59** 22.27S 55.39W
Pont-Audemer France **9** 49.21N 0.31E
Pont Canavese Italy **9** 45.25N 7.36E
Pontchartrain, L. U.S.A. **53** 30.50N 90.00W
Pont-d'Ain France **11** 46.03N 5.20E
Pontedera Italy **12** 43.40N 10.38E
Pontefract U.K. **4** 53.42N 1.19W
Ponte Nova Brazil **59** 20.25S 42.54W
Pontevedra Spain **10** 42.25N 8.39W
Pontiac Mich. U.S.A. **55** 42.39N 83.18W
Pontianak Indonesia **26** 0.05N 109.16E
Pontivy France **11** 48.05N 3.00W
Pont l'Évêque France **9** 49.18N 0.11E
Pontoise France **9** 49.03N 2.05E
Pontorson France **9** 48.33N 1.31W
Pontremoli Italy **9** 44.22N 9.53E
Pontresina Switz. **9** 46.28N 9.53E
Pontrilas U.K. **5** 51.56N 2.53W
Pont-sur-Yonne France **9** 48.17N 3.12E
Pontypool U.K. **5** 51.42N 3.01W
Pontypridd U.K. **5** 51.36N 3.21W
Ponziane, Isole *is.* Italy **12** 40.56N 12.58E
Poochera Australia **46** 32.42S 134.52E
Poole U.K. **5** 50.42N 2.02W
Pooncarie Australia **46** 33.23S 142.34E
Poopelloe L. Australia **46** 31.39S 144.00E
Poopó, Lago de *l.* Bolivia **62** 19.00S 67.00W
Popayán Colombia **60** 2.27N 76.32W
Poperinge Belgium **8** 50.51N 2.44E
Popilta L. Australia **46** 33.09S 141.45E
Poplar Bluff *town* U.S.A. **53** 36.40N 90.25W
Popocatépetl *mtn.* Mexico **56** 19.02N 98.38W
Popondetta P.N.G. **44** 8.45S 148.15E
Poprad Slovakia **15** 49.03N 20.18E
Popricani Romania **15** 47.18N 27.31E
Porbandar India **28** 21.40N 69.40E
Porcupine *r.* U.S.A. **50** 66.25N 145.20W
Pordenone Italy **9** 45.57N 12.39E
Pori Finland **17** 61.29N 21.47E
Porirua New Zealand **48** 41.08S 174.50E
Porjus Sweden **16** 66.57N 19.50E
Porkhov Russian Fed. **18** 57.43N 29.31E
Porkkala Finland **17** 59.59N 24.26E
Porlamar Venezuela **60** 11.01N 63.54W
Pornic France **11** 47.07N 2.05W
Porog Russian Fed. **18** 63.50N 38.32E
Poronaysk Russian Fed. **21** 49.13N 142.55E
Porosozero Russian Fed. **18** 62.45N 32.48E
Porretta Terme Italy **9** 44.09N 10.59E
Porsangen *est.* Norway **16** 70.58N 25.30E
Porsangerhalvöya *pen.* Norway **16** 70.50N 25.00E
Porsgrunn Norway **17** 59.09N 9.40E
Porsuk *r.* Turkey **30** 39.41N 31.56E
Portachuela Bolivia **62** 17.21S 63.24W
Portadown U.K. **7** 54.25N 6.27W
Portaferry U.K. **7** 54.23N 5.33W
Portage la Prairie *town* Canada **51** 49.58N 98.20W
Port Albert Australia **47** 38.09S 146.40E
Portalegre Portugal **10** 39.17N 7.25W
Port Alfred R.S.A. **39** 33.36S 26.52E
Port Alice Canada **50** 50.23N 127.27W
Port Angeles U.S.A. **54** 48.07N 123.27W
Port Antonio Jamaica **57** 18.10N 76.27W
Port Arthur Australia **45** 43.08S 147.50E
Port Arthur U.S.A. **53** 29.55N 93.56W
Port Augusta Australia **46** 32.30S 137.46E
Port-au-Prince Haiti **57** 18.33N 72.20W
Port Austin U.S.A. **55** 44.04N 82.59W
Port Blair India **29** 11.40N 92.30E
Portbou Spain **10** 42.25N 3.09E
Port Bouet Côte d'Ivoire **38** 5.14N 3.58W
Port Bradshaw *b.* Australia **44** 12.30S 136.42E
Port Broughton Australia **46** 33.36S 137.56E
Port Campbell Australia **46** 38.37S 143.04E
Port Cartier Canada **55** 50.01N 66.53W
Port Chalmers New Zealand **48** 45.49S 170.37E
Port Curtis Australia **44** 23.50S 151.13E
Port-de-Paix Haiti **57** 19.57N 72.50W
Port Edward R.S.A. **39** 31.03S 30.13E
Portela Brazil **59** 21.38S 41.59W
Port Elizabeth R.S.A. **39** 33.57S 25.34E
Port Ellen U.K. **6** 55.38N 6.12W
Port-en-Bessin France **9** 49.21N 0.45W
Port Erin I.o.M Europe **4** 54.05N 4.45W
Porterville R.S.A. **39** 33.01S 19.00E
Porterville U.S.A. **54** 36.04N 119.01W
Port Fairy Australia **46** 38.23S 142.17E
Port Germein Australia **46** 33.01S 138.00E
Portglenone U.K. **7** 54.52N 6.30W
Port Harcourt Nigeria **38** 4.43N 7.05E
Port Harrison *see* Inukjuak Canada **51**
Port Hawkesbury Canada **51** 45.37N 61.21W
Porthcawl U.K. **5** 51.28N 3.42W
Port Hedland Australia **42** 20.24S 118.36E
Port Henry U.S.A. **55** 44.03N 73.28W
Porthmadog U.K. **4** 52.55N 4.08W
Port Huron U.S.A. **55** 42.59N 82.28W
Portimão Portugal **10** 37.08N 8.32W
Port Isaac B. U.K. **5** 50.36N 4.50W
Portiţei, Gura *f.* Romania **13** 44.40N 29.00E
Port Jervis U.S.A. **55** 41.22N 74.40W
Port Keats Australia **42** 14.15S 129.35E
Port Kembla Australia **47** 34.28S 150.54E
Port Kenny Australia **46** 33.09S 134.42E
Portland N.S.W. Australia **47** 33.20S 150.00E
Portland Vic. Australia **46** 38.21S 141.38E
Portland Maine U.S.A. **55** 43.39N 70.17W
Portland Oreg. U.S.A. **54** 45.33N 122.36W
Port-la-Nouvelle France **11** 43.01N 3.03E
Port Laoise Rep. of Ire. **7** 53.03N 7.20W
Port Lavaca U.S.A. **53** 28.36N 96.39W
Port Lincoln Australia **46** 34.43S 135.49E
Port MacDonnell Australia **46** 38.03S 140.46E
Port Macquarie Australia **47** 31.28S 152.25E
Port Maitland N.S. Canada **55** 43.59N 66.04W
Portmarnock Rep. of Ire. **7** 53.25N 6.09W
Port Moresby P.N.G. **44** 9.30S 147.07E
Port Musgrave *b.* Australia **44** 11.59S 142.00E
Portnaguiran U.K. **6** 58.15N 6.10W
Port Neill Australia **46** 34.07S 136.20E
Port Nelson Canada **51** 57.10N 92.35W
Port Nolloth R.S.A. **39** 29.16S 16.54E
Porto Portugal **10** 41.09N 8.37W
Pôrto Alegre Brazil **59** 30.03S 51.10W
Porto Amboim Angola **36** 10.45S 13.43E
Pôrto de Moz Brazil **61** 1.45S 52.13W
Pôrto Esperança Brazil **59** 19.36S 57.24W
Pôrto Feliz Brazil **59** 23.11S 47.32W
Portoferraio Italy **12** 42.49N 10.19E
Port of Ness U.K. **6** 58.30N 6.13W
Pôrto Franco Brazil **61** 6.21S 47.25W
Port of Spain Trinidad **57** 10.38N 61.31W
Porto Grande Brazil **61** 0.42N 51.24W
Portogruaro Italy **9** 45.47N 12.50E
Pörtom Finland **16** 62.42N 21.37E
Portomaggiore Italy **9** 44.42N 11.48E
Pôrto Murtinho Brazil **59** 21.42S 57.52W
Porton U.K. **5** 51.08N 1.44W
Pôrto Nacional Brazil **61** 10.42S 48.25W
Porto-Novo Benin **38** 6.30N 2.47E
Pôrto Primavera, Reprêsa *resr.* Brazil **59** 21.50S 52.00W
Porto San Giorgio Italy **12** 43.11N 13.48E
Porto Tolle Italy **9** 44.56N 12.22E
Porto Torres Italy **12** 40.49N 8.24E
Pôrto Valter Brazil **60** 8.15S 72.45W
Porto Vecchio France **11** 41.35N 9.16E
Pôrto Velho Brazil **60** 8.45S 63.54W
Portoviejo Ecuador **60** 1.07S 80.28W
Portpatrick U.K. **6** 54.51N 5.07W
Port Phillip B. Australia **47** 38.05S 144.50E
Port Pirie Australia **46** 33.11S 138.01E
Port Radium Canada **50** 66.05N 118.02W
Portree U.K. **6** 57.24N 6.12W
Port Renfrew Canada **54** 48.30N 124.20W
Portrush U.K. **7** 55.12N 6.40W
Port Said *see* Būr Sa'īd Egypt **32**
Portsea Australia **47** 38.19S 144.43E
Port Shepstone R.S.A. **39** 30.44S 30.27E
Portsmouth U.K. **5** 50.48N 1.06W
Portsmouth N.H. U.S.A. **55** 43.04N 70.46W
Portsmouth Ohio U.S.A. **55** 38.45N 82.59W
Portsoy U.K. **6** 57.41N 2.41W
Port Stanley Canada **55** 42.40N 81.13W
Portstewart U.K. **7** 55.11N 6.43W
Port St. Louis France **11** 43.25N 4.40E
Port Sudan *see* Būr Sūdān Sudan **35**
Port Talbot U.K. **5** 51.35N 3.48W
Porttipahdan tekojärvi *resr.* Finland **16** 68.08N 26.40E
Port Townsend U.S.A. **54** 48.07N 122.46W
Portugal Europe **10** 39.30N 8.05W
Port Vendres France **11** 42.31N 3.06E
Port Victoria Australia **46** 34.30S 137.30E
Port Wakefield Australia **46** 34.12S 138.11E
Port Warrender Australia **42** 14.30S 125.50E
Porvenir Chile **63** 53.18S 70.22W
Porz Germany **8** 50.53N 7.05E
Posada Italy **12** 40.38N 9.43E
Posadas Argentina **62** 27.25S 55.48W
Poschiavo Switz. **9** 46.18N 10.04E
Posht *r.* Iran **31** 29.09N 58.09E
Poso Indonesia **27** 1.23S 120.45E
Posse Brazil **59** 14.05S 46.22W
Postavy Lithuania **18** 55.07N 26.50E
Poste Maurice Cortier Algeria **34** 22.18N 1.05E
Postmasburg R.S.A. **39** 28.19S 23.03E
Postojna Slovenia **14** 45.47N 14.13E
Postoli Belarus **15** 52.30N 28.00E
Potchefstroom R.S.A. **39** 26.42S 27.05E
Potenza Italy **12** 40.40N 15.47E
Potgietersrus R.S.A. **39** 24.11S 29.00E
Poti *r.* Brazil **61** 5.01S 42.48W
Poti Georgia **19** 42.11N 41.41E
Potiskum Nigeria **38** 11.40N 11.03E
Potosí Bolivia **62** 19.35S 65.45W
Potosí *d.* Bolivia **62** 21.00S 67.00W
Pototan Phil. **27** 10.54N 122.38E
Potsdam Germany **14** 52.24N 13.04E
Potsdam U.S.A. **55** 44.40N 74.59W
Pottstown U.S.A. **55** 40.15N 75.38W
Pouancé France **9** 47.47N 1.11W
Poughkeepsie U.S.A. **55** 41.43N 73.56W
Pouso Alegre Brazil **59** 22.13S 45.49W
Poŭthĭsăt Cambodia **26** 12.33N 103.55E
Povenets Russian Fed. **18** 62.52N 34.05E
Póvoa de Varzim Portugal **10** 41.22N 8.46W
Povorino Russian Fed. **19** 51.12N 42.15E
Powder *r.* U.S.A. **54** 46.44N 105.26W
Powder River *town* U.S.A. **54** 43.03N 106.58W
Powell U.S.A. **54** 44.45N 108.46W
Powell, L. U.S.A. **54** 37.25N 110.45W
Powers U.S.A. **55** 45.42N 87.31W
Powys *d.* U.K. **5** 52.26N 3.26W
Poyang Hu *l.* China **25** 29.05N 116.20E
Požarevac Yugo. **15** 44.38N 21.12E
Poza Rica de Hidalgo Mexico **56** 20.34N 97.26W
Poznań Poland **14** 52.25N 16.53E
Pozoblanco Spain **10** 38.23N 4.51W
Prachuap Khiri Khan Thailand **29** 11.50N 99.49E
Pradera Colombia **60** 3.23N 76.11W
Prades France **11** 42.38N 2.25E
Praestö Denmark **17** 55.07N 12.03E
Prague *see* Praha Czech Republic **14**
Praha Czech Republic **14** 50.05N 14.25E
Prainha Amazonas Brazil **60** 7.16S 60.23W
Prainha Para Brazil **61** 1.48S 53.29W
Prairie City U.S.A. **54** 44.28N 118.43W
Prang Ghana **38** 8.02N 0.58W
Prato Italy **9** 43.52N 11.06E
Pravia Spain **10** 43.30N 6.12W
Predazzo Italy **9** 46.19N 11.36E
Pré-en-Pail France **9** 48.27N 0.12W
Preesall U.K. **4** 53.55N 2.58W
Pregel *r.* Russian Fed. **15** 54.41N 20.22E
Premer Australia **47** 31.26S 149.54E
Prenzlau Germany **14** 53.19N 13.52E
Preparis *i.* Myanmar **29** 14.40N 93.40E
Přerov Czech Republic **15** 49.27N 17.27E
Prescott Ariz. U.S.A. **54** 34.33N 112.28W
Presidencia Roque Sáenz Peña Argentina **62** 26.50S 60.30W
Presidente Epitácio Brazil **59** 21.56S 52.07W
Presidente Hermes Brazil **62** 11.17S 61.55W
Presidente Prudente Brazil **59** 22.09S 51.24W
Presidio U.S.A. **52** 29.34N 104.23W
Prešov Slovakia **15** 49.00N 21.15E
Prespa, L. Albania/Greece/Macedonia **13** 40.53N 21.02E
Presque Isle *town* Maine U.S.A. **55** 46.41N 68.01W
Prestea Ghana **38** 5.26N 2.07W
Presteigne U.K. **5** 52.17N 3.00W
Preston U.K. **4** 53.46N 2.42W
Preston Idaho U.S.A. **54** 42.06N 111.53W
Prestonpans U.K. **6** 55.57N 3.00W
Prestwick U.K. **6** 55.30N 4.36W
Prêto *r.* Brazil **59** 22.00S 43.21W
Pretoria R.S.A. **39** 25.43S 28.11E

Ré, Île de *i.* France **11** 46.10N 1.26W
Reims France **9** 49.15N 4.02E
Reindeer L. Canada **50** 57.00N 102.20W
Reinosa Spain **10** 43.01N 4.09W
Remanso Brazil **61** 9.41S 42.04W
Remarkable, Mt. Australia **46** 32.48S 138.10E
Rembang Indonesia **26** 6.45S 111.22E
Remeshk Iran **31** 26.52N 58.46E
Remich Lux. **8** 49.34N 6.23E
Remiremont France **11** 48.01N 6.35E
Remscheid Germany **8** 51.10N 7.11E
Rena Norway **17** 61.08N 11.22E
Rendsburg Germany **14** 54.19N 9.39E
Renfrew Canada **55** 45.28N 76.41W
Rengat Indonesia **26** 0.26S 102.35E
Rengo Chile **63** 34.25S 70.52W
Renheji China **25** 31.56N 115.07E
Reni Ukraine **15** 45.28N 28.17E
Renkum Neth. **8** 51.59N 5.46E
Renmark Australia **46** 34.10S 140.45E
Renner Springs *town* Australia **44** 18.20S 133.48E
Rennes France **9** 48.06N 1.40W
Reno *r.* Italy **9** 44.36N 12.17E
Reno U.S.A. **54** 39.31N 119.48W
Renton U.S.A. **54** 47.30N 122.11W
Réo Burkina **38** 12.20N 2.27W
Repki Ukraine **15** 51.47N 31.06E
Republic Wash. U.S.A. **54** 48.39N 118.44W
Republican *r.* U.S.A. **53** 39.05N 94.50W
Republic of Ireland Europe **7** 53.00N 8.00W
Republic of South Africa Africa **39** 28.30S 24.50E
Repulse B. Australia **44** 20.36S 148.43E
Repulse Bay *town* Canada **51** 66.35N 86.20W
Requa U.S.A. **54** 41.34N 124.05W
Requena Peru **60** 5.05S 73.52W
Requena Spain **10** 39.29N 1.08W
Resistencia Argentina **62** 27.28S 59.00W
Reşiţa Romania **15** 45.17N 21.53E
Resolute Canada **51** 74.40N 95.00W
Resolution I. Canada **51** 61.30N 65.00W
Resolution I. New Zealand **48** 45.40S 166.30E
Restigouche *r.* Canada **55** 48.02N 66.22W
Rethel France **9** 49.31N 4.22E
Réthimnon Greece **13** 35.22N 24.29E
Reus Spain **10** 41.10N 1.06E
Reusel Neth. **8** 51.21N 5.09E
Reutlingen Germany **14** 48.30N 9.13E
Reutte Austria **14** 47.29N 10.43E
Revda Russian Fed. **18** 56.49N 59.58E
Revelstoke Canada **50** 51.02N 118.12W
Revilla Gigedo, Islas de *is.* Mexico **56** 19.00N 111.00W
Revin France **8** 49.58N 4.40E
Revue *r.* Mozambique **39** 19.58S 34.40E
Rexburg U.S.A. **54** 43.49N 111.47W
Rexford U.S.A. **54** 48.53N 115.13W
Rey Iran **31** 35.35N 51.27E
Reykjavík Iceland **16** 64.09N 21.58W
Reynosa Mexico **56** 26.09N 97.10W
Rezé France **11** 47.12N 1.34W
Rēzekne Latvia **18** 56.30N 27.22E
Rhayader U.K. **5** 52.19N 3.30W
Rheden Neth. **8** 52.01N 6.02E
Rhein *r.* Europe **8** 51.53N 6.03E
Rheinbach Germany **8** 50.39N 6.59E
Rheine Germany **8** 52.17N 7.26E
Rheinland-Pfalz *d.* Germany **8** 50.05N 7.09E
Rhenen Neth. **8** 51.58N 5.34E
Rheydt Germany **8** 51.10N 6.25E
Rhine *see* Rhein *r.* Europe **8**
Rhinelander U.S.A. **53** 45.39N 89.23W
Rhino Camp *town* Uganda **37** 2.58N 31.20E
Rho Italy **9** 45.32N 9.02E
Rhode Island *d.* U.S.A. **55** 41.40N 71.30W
Rhodes *i. see* Ródhos *i.* Greece **13**
Rhodopi Planina *mts.* Bulgaria **13** 41.35N 24.35E
Rhondda U.K. **5** 51.39N 3.30W
Rhône *r.* France **11** 43.25N 4.45E
Rhône-Alpes *d.* France **11** 45.20N 5.45E
Rhosneigr U.K. **4** 53.14N 4.31W
Rhyl U.K. **4** 53.19N 3.29W
Riachão Brazil **61** 7.22S 46.37W
Riau *d.* Indonesia **26** 0.00 102.35E
Riau, Kepulauan *is.* Indonesia **26** 0.50N 104.00E
Ribadeo Spain **10** 43.32N 7.04W
Ribarroja, Embalse de *resr.* Spain **10** 41.12N 0.20E
Ribauè Mozambique **37** 14.57S 38.27E
Ribble *r.* U.K. **4** 53.45N 2.44W
Ribe Denmark **17** 55.21N 8.46E
Ribeauvillé France **11** 48.12N 7.19E
Ribécourt France **8** 49.31N 2.52E
Ribécourt France **9** 49.31N 2.55E
Ribeirão Prêto Brazil **59** 21.09S 47.48W
Ribérac France **11** 45.14N 0.22E
Riberalta Bolivia **62** 10.59S 66.06W
Ribnitz-Damgarten Germany **14** 54.15N 12.28E
Riccione Italy **9** 43.59N 12.39E
Rice U.S.A. **54** 34.06N 114.50W
Richard's Bay *town* R.S.A. **39** 28.47S 32.06E
Richfield Idaho U.S.A. **54** 43.03N 114.09W
Richfield Utah U.S.A. **54** 38.46N 112.05W
Richland U.S.A. **54** 46.17N 119.18W
Richmond Qld. Australia **44** 20.44S 143.08E
Richmond New Zealand **48** 41.20S 173.10E
Richmond C.P. R.S.A. **39** 31.24S 23.56E
Richmond U.K. **4** 54.24N 1.43W
Richmond Ind. U.S.A. **55** 39.50N 84.51W
Richmond Utah U.S.A. **54** 41.55N 111.48W
Richmond Va. U.S.A. **53** 37.34N 77.27W
Richmond Hill *town* Canada **55** 43.53N 79.26W
Richmond Range *mts.* Australia **47** 29.00S 152.48E
Ricobayo, Embalse de *resr.* Spain **10** 41.40N 5.50W
Ridderkerk Neth. **8** 51.53N 4.39E
Rideau Lakes Canada **55** 44.45N 76.14W
Ridgway U.S.A. **55** 41.26N 78.44W
Ried Austria **14** 48.13N 13.30E
Riemst Belgium **8** 50.49N 5.38E
Riesa Germany **14** 51.18N 13.18E
Rieti Italy **12** 42.24N 12.53E
Rifle U.S.A. **54** 39.32N 107.47W
Rift Valley *d.* Kenya **37** 1.00N 36.00E
Riga Latvia **17** 56.53N 24.08E
Riga, G of Latvia/Estonia **17** 57.30N 23.35E
Rīgān Iran **31** 28.40N 58.58E
Rīgas Jūras Līcis *see* Riga, G. of *g.* Latvia **17**
Rīgestān *f.* Afghan. **28** 31.00N 65.00E
Riggins U.S.A. **54** 45.25N 116.19W
Rīg Matī Iran **31** 27.40N 58.11E
Rigo P.N.G. **44** 9.50S 147.35E
Rigolet Canada **51** 54.10N 58.30W
Riia Laht *see* Riga, G of Estonia **17**
Riihimäki Finland **17** 60.45N 24.46E
Riiser-Larsenhalvöya *pen.* Antarctica **64** 68.00S 35.00E
Rijeka Croatia **12** 45.20N 14.25E
Rijssen Neth. **8** 52.19N 6.31E
Rijswijk Neth. **8** 52.03N 4.22E
Riley U.S.A. **54** 43.31N 119.28W
Rimah, Wādī ar *r.* Saudi Arabia **30** 26.10N 44.00E
Rimavská Sobota Slovakia **15** 48.23N 20.02E
Rimbo Sweden **17** 59.45N 18.22E
Rimini Italy **9** 44.01N 12.34E
Rîmnicu-Sărat Romania **15** 45.24N 27.06E
Rîmnicu-Vîlcea Romania **15** 45.06N 24.22E
Rimouski Canada **55** 48.27N 68.32W
Rinconada Argentina **62** 22.26S 66.10W
Rindal Norway **16** 63.04N 9.13E
Ringebu Norway **17** 61.31N 10.10E
Ringerike Norway **17** 60.10N 10.12E
Ringim Nigeria **38** 12.09N 9.08E
Ringköbing Denmark **17** 56.05N 8.15E
Ringling U.S.A. **54** 46.16N 110.49W
Ringsted Denmark **17** 55.27N 11.49E
Ringvassöy *i.* Norway **16** 69.55N 19.10E
Ringwood U.K. **5** 50.50N 1.48W
Riobamba Ecuador **60** 1.44S 78.40W
Rio Branco Brazil **60** 9.59S 67.49W
Rio Bueno Chile **63** 40.20S 72.55W
Rio Casca Brazil **59** 20.13S 42.38W
Rio Claro Brazil **59** 22.19S 47.35W
Río Cuarto Argentina **63** 33.08S 64.20W
Rio de Janeiro Brazil **59** 22.53S 43.17W
Rio de Janeiro *d.* Brazil **59** 22.00S 42.30W
Río Gallegos Argentina **63** 51.37S 69.10W
Rio Grande *town* Argentina **63** 53.50S 67.40W
Rio Grande *town* Brazil **59** 32.03S 52.08W
Rio Grande *r.* Mexico/U.S.A. **56** 25.55N 97.08W
Río Grande *r.* Nicaragua **57** 12.48N 83.30W
Rio Grande do Norte *d.* Brazil **61** 6.00S 36.30W
Rio Grande do Sul *d.* Brazil **59** 30.15S 53.30W
Ríohacha Colombia **60** 11.34N 72.58W
Rio Largo Brazil **61** 9.28S 35.50W
Río Negro *d.* Argentina **63** 40.00S 67.00W
Rio Negro Brazil **59** 26.06S 49.48W
Río Negro, Embalse del *resr.* Uruguay **63** 32.45S 56.00W
Rio Novo Brazil **59** 21.15S 43.09W
Rio Piracicaba Brazil **59** 19.54S 43.10W
Rio Pomba Brazil **59** 21.15S 43.12W
Rio Prêto Brazil **59** 22.06S 43.52W
Ríosucio Colombia **60** 7.27N 77.07W
Río Tercero Argentina **62** 32.10S 64.05W
Rio Verde *town* Brazil **62** 17.50S 50.55W
Ripley N.Y. U.S.A. **55** 42.16N 79.43W
Ripon U.K. **4** 54.08N 1.31W
Rirapora Brazil **59** 17.20S 45.02W
Risbäck Sweden **16** 64.42N 15.32E
Riscle France **11** 43.40N 0.05W
Rishā, Wādī ar *r.* Saudi Arabia **31** 25.40N 44.08E
Rishon LeZiyyon Israel **32** 31.57N 34.48E
Risle *r.* France **9** 49.26N 0.23E
Risör Norway **17** 58.43N 9.14E
Riti Nigeria **38** 7.57N 9.41E
Ritzville U.S.A. **54** 47.08N 118.23W
Rivadavia Argentina **62** 24.11S 62.53W
Rivarolo Canavese Italy **9** 45.25N 7.36E
Rivas Nicaragua **57** 11.26N 85.50W
Rivera Uruguay **63** 30.54S 55.31W
River Cess *town* Liberia **34** 5.28N 9.32W
Rivergaro Italy **9** 44.55N 9.36E
Riverhead U.S.A. **55** 40.55N 72.40W
Riverina *f.* Australia **47** 34.30S 145.20E
Rivers *d.* Nigeria **38** 4.45N 6.35E
Riversdale R.S.A. **39** 34.05S 21.15E
Riverside U.S.A. **54** 33.59N 117.22W
Riverton Australia **46** 34.08S 138.24E
Riverton Canada **51** 50.59N 96.59W
Riverton New Zealand **48** 46.21S 168.01E
Riverton U.S.A. **54** 43.02N 108.23W
Riviera di Levante *f.* Italy **9** 44.00N 9.40E
Riviera di Ponente *f.* Italy **9** 43.40N 8.00E
Rivière-du-Loup *town* Canada **55** 47.49N 69.32W
Rivière Pentecôte *town* Canada **55** 49.46N 67.12W
Rivoli Italy **9** 45.04N 7.31E
Riyadh *see* Ar Riyāḍ Saudi Arabia **31**
Rize Turkey **30** 41.03N 40.31E
Rizokárpason Cyprus **32** 35.35N 34.24E
Rizzuto, Capo *c.* Italy **13** 38.54N 17.06E
Rjukan Norway **17** 59.52N 8.34E
Roa Norway **17** 60.17N 10.37E
Roag, Loch U.K. **6** 58.14N 6.50W
Roanne France **11** 46.02N 4.05E
Roanoke *r.* U.S.A. **53** 36.00N 76.35W
Roanoke Va. U.S.A. **53** 37.15N 79.58W
Robāţ Iran **31** 30.04N 54.49E
Robe Australia **46** 37.11S 139.45E
Robe, Mt. Australia **46** 31.39S 141.16E
Robertson R.S.A. **39** 33.48S 19.52E
Robertsport Liberia **34** 6.45N 11.22W
Robertstown Australia **46** 33.59S 139.03E
Roberval Canada **55** 48.31N 72.16W
Robin Hood's Bay *town* U.K. **4** 54.26N 0.31W
Robinson *r.* Australia **44** 16.03S 137.16E
Robinson Range *mts.* Australia **42** 25.45S 119.00E
Robinvale Australia **46** 34.37S 142.50E
Robledo Spain **10** 38.46N 2.26W
Roboré Bolivia **62** 18.20S 59.45W
Robson, Mt. Canada **50** 53.00N 119.09W
Roccella Italy **13** 38.19N 16.24E
Rocciamelone *mtn.* Italy **9** 45.12N 7.05E
Rocha Uruguay **59** 34.30S 54.22W
Rocha da Gale, Barragem *resr.* Portugal **10** 38.20N 7.35W
Rochdale U.K. **4** 53.36N 2.10W
Rochechouart France **11** 45.49N 0.50E
Rochefort Belgium **8** 50.10N 5.13E
Rochefort France **11** 45.57N 0.58W
Rochester Australia **47** 36.22S 144.42E
Rochester Kent U.K. **5** 51.22N 0.30E
Rochester Minn. U.S.A. **53** 44.01N 92.27W
Rochester N.Y. U.S.A. **55** 43.12N 77.37W
Rochfort Bridge Rep. of Ire. **7** 53.25N 7.19W
Rock U.S.A. **55** 46.03N 87.10W
Rockefeller Plateau Antarctica **64** 80.00S 140.00W
Rockford U.S.A. **53** 42.16N 89.06W
Rockhampton Australia **44** 23.22S 150.32E
Rockingham Australia **43** 32.16S 115.21E
Rock Island *town* U.S.A. **53** 41.30N 90.34W
Rockland Idaho U.S.A. **54** 42.34N 112.53W
Rockland Maine U.S.A. **55** 44.06N 69.06W
Rockland Mich. U.S.A. **55** 46.44N 89.12W
Rocklands Resr. Australia **46** 37.13S 141.52E
Rockport U.S.A. **54** 39.45N 123.47W
Rock Sound *town* Bahamas **57** 24.54N 76.11W
Rock Springs Wyo. U.S.A. **54** 41.35N 109.13W
Rockville U.S.A. **55** 39.05N 77.09W
Rocky Ford U.S.A. **52** 38.03N 103.44W
Rocky Gully *town* Australia **43** 34.31S 117.01E
Rocky Island L. Canada **55** 46.56N 82.55W
Rocky Mts. N. America **52** 43.21N 109.50W
Rocroi France **8** 49.56N 4.31E
Rod Pakistan **28** 28.10N 63.05E
Rödby Denmark **17** 54.42N 11.24E
Rodel U.K. **6** 57.44N 6.58W
Rodez France **11** 44.21N 2.34E
Ródhos *i.* Greece **13** 36.12N 28.00E
Ródhos *town* Greece **13** 36.24N 28.15E
Rodonit, Kep-i- *c.* Albania **13** 41.34N 19.25E
Roebourne Australia **42** 20.45S 117.08E
Roebuck B. Australia **42** 19.04S 122.17E
Roe, L. Australia **43** 30.40S 122.10E
Roermond Neth. **8** 51.12N 6.00E
Roeselare Belgium **8** 50.57N 3.06E
Rogachev Belarus **15** 53.05N 30.02E
Rogaland *d.* Norway **17** 59.00N 6.15E
Rogerson U.S.A. **54** 42.14N 114.47W
Rogliano France **11** 42.57N 9.25E
Rogue *r.* U.S.A. **54** 42.26N 124.25W
Rohtak India **28** 28.54N 76.35E
Rojas Argentina **63** 34.15S 60.44W
Rokan *r.* Indonesia **26** 2.00N 101.00E
Rola Co *l.* China **29** 35.26N 88.24E
Röldal Norway **17** 59.49N 6.48E
Rolla Mo. U.S.A. **53** 37.56N 91.55W
Rolleston Australia **44** 24.25S 148.35E
Rolleville Bahamas **57** 23.41N 76.00W
Rolvsöya *i.* Norway **16** 70.58N 24.00E
Roma Australia **44** 26.35S 148.47E
Roma Italy **12** 41.54N 12.29E
Roma Sweden **17** 57.32N 18.28E
Romain, C. U.S.A. **53** 33.01N 79.23W
Romaine *r.* Canada **51** 50.20N 63.45W
Roman Romania **15** 46.55N 26.56E
Romang *i.* Indonesia **27** 7.45S 127.20E
Romania Europe **15** 46.30N 24.00E
Romano, C. U.S.A. **53** 25.50N 81.42W
Romans France **11** 45.03N 5.03E
Rome *see* Roma Italy **12**
Rome Ga. U.S.A. **53** 34.01N 85.02W
Rome N.Y. U.S.A. **55** 43.13N 75.27W
Romeo U.S.A. **55** 42.47N 83.01W
Romilly France **9** 48.31N 3.44E
Romney Marsh *f.* U.K. **5** 51.03N 0.55E
Romorantin France **9** 47.22N 1.44E
Rona *i.* U.K. **6** 57.33N 5.58W
Ronan U.S.A. **54** 47.32N 114.06W
Roncesvalles Spain **10** 43.01N 1.19W
Ronda Spain **10** 36.45N 5.10W
Rondane *mtn.* Norway **17** 61.55N 9.45E
Rondônia *d.* Brazil **60** 12.10S 62.30W
Rondonópolis Brazil **61** 16.29S 54.37W
Rongcheng China **25** 37.09N 122.23E
Rönne Denmark **17** 55.06N 14.42E
Ronneby Sweden **17** 56.12N 15.18E
Ronse Belgium **8** 50.45N 3.36E
Ronuro *r.* Brazil **61** 11.56S 53.33W
Roof Butte *mtn.* U.S.A. **54** 36.28N 109.05W
Roosendaal Neth. **8** 51.32N 4.28E
Roosevelt *r.* Brazil **60** 7.35S 60.20W
Roosevelt U.S.A. **54** 40.18N 109.59W
Roosevelt I. Antarctica **64** 79.00S 161.00W
Ropcha Russian Fed. **18** 62.50N 51.55E
Roper *r.* Australia **44** 14.40S 135.30E
Roque Pérez Argentina **63** 35.23S 59.22W
Roraima *d.* Brazil **60** 2.00N 62.00W
Roraima, Mt. Guyana **60** 5.14N 60.44W
Röros Norway **16** 62.35N 11.23E
Rosamond U.S.A. **54** 34.52N 118.10W
Rosa, Monte *mtn.* Italy/Switz. **9** 45.56N 7.51E
Rosario Argentina **63** 32.57S 60.40W
Rosário Brazil **61** 3.00S 44.15W
Rosario Uruguay **63** 34.19S 57.21W
Rosario de la Frontera Argentina **62** 25.50S 64.55W
Rosario del Tala Argentina **63** 32.20S 59.10W
Rosário do Sul Brazil **59** 30.15S 54.55W
Roscoff France **11** 48.44N 4.00W
Roscommon Rep. of Ire. **7** 53.38N 8.13W
Roscommon *d.* Rep. of Ire. **7** 53.38N 8.11W
Roscrea Rep. of Ire. **7** 52.57N 7.49W
Roseau Dominica **57** 15.18N 61.23W
Rosebud Australia **47** 38.21S 144.54E
Roseburg U.S.A. **54** 43.13N 123.20W
Rosenheim Germany **14** 47.51N 12.09E
Roses Spain **10** 42.19N 3.10E
Rosetown Canada **50** 51.34N 107.59W
Rosetta R.S.A. **39** 29.18S 29.58E
Roseville Calif. U.S.A. **54** 38.45N 121.17W
Rosières France **9** 49.49N 2.43E
Rosignano Marittimo Italy **12** 43.24N 10.28E
Roşiori-de-Vede Romania **15** 44.07N 25.00E
Rositsa Bulgaria **15** 43.57N 27.57E
Roska *r.* Ukraine **15** 49.27N 29.45E
Roskilde Denmark **17** 55.39N 12.05E
Roslags-Näsby Sweden **17** 59.26N 18.04E
Roslavl Russian Fed. **18** 53.55N 32.53E
Ross New Zealand **48** 42.54S 170.49E
Rossano Italy **13** 39.35N 16.39E
Ross Dependency Antarctica **64** 75.00S 170.00W
Rossing Namibia **39** 22.31S 14.52E
Rosslare Rep. of Ire. **7** 52.17N 6.23W
Ross-on-Wye U.K. **5** 51.55N 2.36W
Rossosh Russian Fed. **19** 50.12N 39.35E
Rössvatnet *l.* Norway **16** 65.45N 14.00E
Rosta Norway **16** 68.59N 19.40E
Rosthern Canada **50** 52.40N 106.17W
Rostock Germany **14** 54.06N 12.09E
Rostov Russian Fed **18** 57.11N 39.23E
Rostov Russian Fed. **19** 47.15N 39.45E
Rotem Belgium **8** 51.04N 5.44E
Rothbury U.K. **4** 55.19N 1.54W
Rotherham U.K. **4** 53.26N 1.21W
Rothes U.K. **6** 57.31N 3.13W
Rothesay Canada **55** 45.23N 66.00W
Rothesay U.K. **6** 55.50N 5.03W
Roti *i.* Indonesia **42** 10.30S 123.10E
Roto Australia **47** 33.04S 145.27E
Rotondella Italy **13** 40.10N 16.32E
Rotorua New Zealand **48** 38.07S 176.17E
Rotorua, L. New Zealand **48** 38.00S 176.00E
Rotterdam Neth. **8** 51.55N 4.29E
Rottnest I. Australia **43** 32.01S 115.28E
Rottweil Germany **14** 48.10N 8.37E
Roubaix France **8** 50.42N 3.10E
Rouen France **9** 49.26N 1.05E
Rougé France **9** 47.47N 1.26W
Rouku P.N.G. **44** 8.40S 141.35E
Round Mt. Australia **47** 30.26S 152.15E
Roundup U.S.A. **54** 46.27N 108.33W
Rousay *i.* U.K. **6** 59.10N 3.02W
Rouyn Canada **55** 48.20N 79.00W
Rovaniemi Finland **16** 66.30N 25.40E
Rovato Italy **9** 45.34N 10.00E
Rovereto Italy **9** 45.53N 11.02E
Rovigo Italy **9** 45.04N 11.47E
Rovinj Croatia **14** 45.06N 13.39E
Rovno Ukraine **15** 50.39N 26.10E
Rowena Australia **47** 29.49S 148.54E
Rowley Shoals *f.* Australia **42** 17.30S 119.00E
Roxburgh New Zealand **48** 45.33S 169.19E
Roxby Downs *town* Australia **46** 30.42S 136.46E
Roxen *l.* Sweden **17** 58.30N 15.41E
Royale, Isle *i.* U.S.A. **55** 48.00N 89.00W
Royal Leamington Spa U.K. **5** 52.18N 1.32W
Royal Tunbridge Wells U.K. **5** 51.07N 0.16E
Royan France **11** 45.37N 1.02W
Roye France **9** 49.42N 2.48E
Royston U.K. **5** 52.03N 0.01W
Rozhishche Ukraine **15** 50.58N 25.15E
Rožňava Slovakia **15** 48.40N 20.32E
Rtishchevo Russian Fed. **18** 52.16N 43.45E
Ruahine Range *mts.* New Zealand **48** 40.00S 176.00E
Ruapehu *mtn.* New Zealand **48** 39.20S 175.30E
Ruapuke I. New Zealand **48** 46.45S 168.30E
Rub 'al Khali *des. see* Ar Rub 'al Khālī *des.* Saudi Arabia **28**
Rubino Côte d'Ivoire **38** 6.04N 4.18W
Rubio Colombia **60** 7.42N 72.23W
Rubryn Belarus **15** 51.52N 27.30E
Rubtsovsk Russian Fed. **20** 51.29N 81.10E
Ruby Mts. U.S.A. **54** 40.25N 115.35W
Rūdān *r.* Iran **31** 27.02N 56.53E
Rūdbār Afghan. **31** 30.10N 62.38E
Rudewa Tanzania **37** 6.40S 37.08E
Rudki Ukraine **15** 49.40N 23.28E
Rudnaya Pristan Russian Fed. **25** 44.18N 135.51E
Rudnichnyy Russian Fed. **18** 59.10N 52.28E
Rudnik Poland **15** 50.28N 22.15E
Rudnyy Kazakhstan **20** 53.00N 63.05E
Rudolstadt Germany **14** 50.44N 11.20E
Rue France **11** 50.15N 1.40E
Ruffec France **11** 46.02N 0.12E
Rufiji *r.* Tanzania **37** 8.02S 39.19E
Rufino Argentina **63** 34.16S 62.45W
Rufunsa Zambia **37** 15.02S 29.35E
Rugao China **25** 32.27N 120.35E
Rugby U.K. **5** 52.23N 1.16W
Rugby U.S.A. **52** 48.24N 99.59W
Rügen *i.* Germany **14** 54.30N 13.30E
Ruhr *f.* Germany **8** 51.22N 7.26E
Ruhr *r.* Germany **8** 51.27N 6.41E
Ruinen Neth. **8** 52.47N 6.21E
Rukwa *d.* Tanzania **37** 7.05S 31.25E
Rukwa, L. Tanzania **37** 8.00S 32.20E
Rum *i.* U.K. **6** 57.00N 6.20W
Ruma Yugo. **15** 44.59N 19.51E
Rum Cay *i.* Bahamas **57** 23.41N 74.53W
Rumford U.S.A. **55** 44.33N 70.33W
Rummānah Egypt **32** 31.01N 32.40E
Runcorn U.K. **4** 53.20N 2.44W
Runde *r.* Zimbabwe **39** 21.20S 32.23E
Rundvik Sweden **16** 63.30N 19.24E
Rungwa *r.* Tanzania **37** 7.38S 31.55E
Rungwa Singida Tanzania **37** 6.57S 33.35E
Rungwe Mt. Tanzania **37** 9.10S 33.40E
Runka Nigeria **38** 12.28N 7.20E
Ruoqiang China **24** 39.00N 88.00E
Ruo Shui *r.* China **24** 42.15N 101.03E
Rupert *r.* Canada **55** 51.30N 78.45W
Rupununi *r.* Guyana **60** 4.00N 58.30W
Rur *r.* Neth. **8** 51.12N 5.58E
Rusape Zimbabwe **39** 18.30S 32.08E
Ruse Bulgaria **13** 43.50N 25.59E
Rushden U.K. **5** 52.17N 0.37W
Rushworth Australia **47** 36.38S 145.02E
Russell Pt. Canada **50** 73.30N 115.00W
Russell Range *mts.* Australia **43** 33.15S 123.30E
Russian Federation Europe/Asia **20** 62.00N 80.00E
Russkaya Polyana Russian Fed. **20** 53.48N 73.54E
Rustavi Georgia **19** 41.34N 45.03E
Rustenburg R.S.A. **39** 25.39S 27.13E
Rutana Burundi **37** 3.58S 30.00E
Rutanzige, L. *see* Edward, L. Uganda/Zaïre **37**
Rütenbrock Germany **8** 52.51N 7.06E
Ruteng Indonesia **27** 8.35S 120.28E
Rutenga Zimbabwe **39** 21.15S 30.46E
Ruth U.S.A. **54** 39.17N 114.59W
Ruthin U.K. **4** 53.07N 3.18W
Rutland U.S.A. **55** 43.36N 72.59W
Rutog China **29** 33.30N 79.40E
Rutshuru Zaïre **37** 1.10S 29.26E
Ruvu Coast Tanzania **37** 6.50S 38.42E
Ruvuma *r.* Mozambique/Tanzania **37** 10.30S 40.30E
Ruvuma *d.* Tanzania **37** 10.45S 36.15E
Ruwenzori Range *mts.* Uganda/Zaïre **37** 0.30N 30.00E
Ruyigi Burundi **37** 3.26S 30.14E
Ruzayevka Russian Fed. **18** 54.04N 44.55E
Ruzitgort Russian Fed. **18** 62.51N 64.52E
Ružomberok Slovakia **15** 49.06N 19.18E
Rwanda Africa **37** 2.00S 30.00E
Ryan, Loch U.K. **6** 54.56N 5.02W
Ryasna Belarus **15** 54.00N 31.14E
Ryazan Russian Fed. **18** 54.37N 39.43E
Ryazhsk Russian Fed. **18** 53.40N 40.07E
Rybachiy, Poluostrov *pen.* Russian Fed. **18** 69.45N 32.30E
Rybachye Kazakhstan **24** 46.27N 81.30E
Rybinsk Russian Fed. **18** 58.01N 38.52E
Rybinskoye Vodokhranilishche *resr.* Russian Fed. **18** 58.30N 38.25E
Rybnik Poland **15** 50.06N 18.32E
Rybnitsa Moldova **15** 47.42N 29.00E
Ryd Sweden **17** 56.28N 14.41E
Rye U.K. **5** 50.57N 0.46E
Rye *r.* U.K. **4** 54.10N 0.44W
Ryki Poland **15** 51.39N 21.56E
Rylstone Australia **47** 32.48S 149.58E
Ryūgasaki Japan **23** 35.54N 140.11E
Ryukyu Is. *see* Nansei shotō *is.* Japan **25**
Rzeszów Poland **15** 50.04N 22.00E
Rzhev Russian Fed. **18** 56.15N 34.18E

S

Saa Cameroon **38** 4.24N 11.25E
Saale *r.* Germany **14** 51.58N 11.53E
Saanich Canada **54** 48.28N 123.22W
Saar *r.* Germany **8** 49.43N 6.34E
Saarbrücken Germany **14** 49.15N 6.58E
Saarburg Germany **8** 49.36N 6.33E
Saaremaa *i.* Estonia **17** 58.25N 22.30E
Saarijärvi Finland **16** 62.43N 25.16E
Saariselkä *mts.* Finland **16** 68.15N 28.30E
Saarland *d.* Germany **8** 49.30N 6.50E
Saba *i.* Leeward Is. **57** 17.42N 63.26W
Šabac Yugo. **15** 44.45N 19.41E
Sabadell Spain **10** 41.33N 2.07E
Sabah *d.* Malaysia **26** 5.30N 117.00E
Sabalān, Kūhhā-ye *mts.* Iran **31** 38.15N 47.50E
Sabana, Archipiélago de Cuba **57** 23.30N 80.00W
Sabanalarga Colombia **60** 10.38N 75.00W
Sab'atayn, Ramlat as *f.* Yemen **35** 15.30N 46.10E
Sabaudia Italy **12** 41.18N 13.01E
Sabbioneta Italy **9** 45.00N 10.39E
Sabhā Libya **34** 27.04N 14.25E
Sabinas Mexico **56** 26.33N 101.10W
Sabinas Hidalgo Mexico **56** 26.33N 100.10W
Sabine *r.* U.S.A. **53** 29.40N 93.50W
Sabkhat al Bardawīl *l.* Egypt **32** 31.10N 33.15E
Sablayan Phil. **27** 12.50N 120.50E
Sable, C. Canada **51** 43.30N 65.50W
Sable I. Canada **51** 44.00N 60.00W
Sablé-sur-Sarthe France **9** 47.50N 0.20W
Sabon Birni Nigeria **38** 13.37N 6.15E
Sabongidda Nigeria **38** 6.54N 5.56E
Sabrina Coast *f.* Antarctica **64** 67.00S 120.00E
Sabzevār Iran **31** 36.13N 57.38E
Sacaca Bolivia **62** 18.05S 66.25W
Sacajawea *mtn.* U.S.A. **54** 45.15N 117.17W
Sacedón Spain **10** 40.29N 2.44W
Sachigo *r.* Canada **51** 55.06N 88.58W
Sachsen *d.* Germany **14** 51.10N 13.15E
Sachsen-Anhalt *d.* Germany **14** 52.05N 11.30E
Saco U.S.A. **55** 43.29N 70.28W
Sacramento Brazil **59** 19.51S 26.47W
Sacramento U.S.A. **54** 38.35N 121.30W
Sacramento *r.* U.S.A. **54** 38.03N 121.56W
Sacramento Valley *f.* U.S.A. **54** 39.15N 122.00W
Sádaba Spain **10** 42.19N 1.10W
Sadani Tanzania **37** 6.00S 38.40E
Sadiya India **29** 27.49N 95.38E
Şafājah *des.* Saudi Arabia **30** 26.30N 39.30E
Şafāniyah Egypt **32** 28.49N 30.48E
Şafarābād Iran **31** 38.59N 47.25E
Säffle Sweden **17** 59.08N 12.56E

ron Walden U.K. 5 52.02N 0.15E
Morocco 34 32.20N 9.17W
d r. Iran 31 37.23N 50.11E
novo Russian Fed. 18 55.08N 33.16E
novo Russian Fed. 18 65.40N 48.10E
aing Myanmar 29 22.00N 96.00E
ala Mali 38 14.09N 6.38W
ami r. Japan 23 35.14N 139.23E
amihara Japan 23 35.32N 139.23E
ami-nada b. Japan 23 34.55N 139.30E
ar India 29 23.50N 78.44E
ara Japan 23 34.41N 138.12E
e U.S.A. 54 41.49N 110.59W
inaw U.S.A. 55 43.25N 83.54W
inaw B. U.S.A. 55 43.56N 83.40W
iz Kazakhstan 19 47.31N 54.55E
res Portugal 10 37.00N 8.56W
ua la Grande Cuba 57 22.55N 80.05W
uenay r. Canada 55 48.10N 69.45W
unto Spain 10 39.40N 0.17W
agún Spain 10 42.23N 5.02W
and, Kūh-e mtn. Iran 31 37.37N 46.27E
ara des. Africa 34 18.00N 12.00E
āranpur India 28 29.58N 77.33E
bā, Wādī as r. Saudi Arabia 31 23.48N .50E
el d. Burkina 38 14.00N 0.50W
īwāl Punjab Pakistan 28 31.57N 72.22E
bai i. Australia 44 9.24S 142.40E
dābād Iran 31 29.28N 55.43E
dpur Bangla. 29 25.48N 89.00E
gon see Ho Chi Minh Vietnam 26
maa l. Finland 18 61.20N 28.00E
mbeyli Turkey 30 38.07N 36.08E
Abb's Head U.K. 6 55.54N 2.07W
Agapit Canada 55 46.34N 71.26W
Albans U.K. 5 51.46N 0.21W
Albans Vt. U.S.A. 55 44.49N 73.05W
Amand France 8 50.27N 3.26E
Amand-Mont-Rond town France 11 46.43N 29E
Andrews U.K. 6 56.20N 2.48W
Andries Belgium 8 51.12N 3.10E
Ann's Bay town Jamaica 57 18.26N 77.12W
Anthony Canada 51 51.24N 55.37W
Anthony U.S.A. 52 43.59N 111.40W
Arnaud Australia 46 36.40S 143.20E
Augustine U.S.A. 53 29.54N 81.19W
Augustin Saguenay Canada 51 51.14N .39W
Austell U.K. 5 50.20N 4.48W
Barthélemy i. Leeward Is. 57 17.55N 62.50W
Bees Head U.K. 4 54.31N 3.39W
Boniface Canada 51 49.54N 97.07W
Brides B. U.K. 5 51.48N 5.03W
Brieuc France 11 48.31N 2.45W
Calais France 9 47.55N 0.45E
Catharines Canada 55 43.10N 79.15W
Catherine's Pt. U.K. 5 50.34N 1.18W
Céré France 11 44.52N 1.53E
Cloud U.S.A. 53 45.34N 94.10W
Croix i. U.S.V.Is. 57 17.45N 64.35W
David's U.K. 5 51.54N 5.16W
David's Head U.K. 5 51.55N 5.19W
Denis France 9 48.56N 2.21E
Dié France 11 48.17N 6.57E
Dizier France 9 48.38N 4.58E
inte-Agathe-des-Monts Canada 55 46.03N 4.19W
inte Anne de Beaupré Canada 55 47.02N 0.58W
Elias, Mt. U.S.A. 50 60.20N 139.00W
Éloi Canada 55 48.03N 69.14W
inte Menehould France 9 49.05N 4.54E
inte Menehould France 14 49.05N 4.54E
inte Mère-Église France 9 49.24N 1.19W
intes France 11 45.44N 0.38W
inte-Thérèse-de-Blainville Canada 55 45.38N 3.50W
Étienne France 11 45.26N 4.26E
Fargeau France 9 47.38N 3.04E
intfield U.K. 7 54.28N 5.50W
Florent France 11 42.41N 9.18E
Florentin France 9 48.00N 3.44E
Flour France 11 45.02N 3.05E
Gallen Switz. 14 47.25N 9.23E
Gaudens France 11 43.07N 0.44E
George Australia 45 28.03S 148.30E
George N.B. Canada 55 45.08N 66.56W
George U.S.A. 54 37.06N 113.35W
Georges Belgium 8 50.37N 5.20E
George's Grenada 57 12.04N 61.44W
Georges Guiana 61 3.54N 51.48W
. George's Channel Rep. of Ire./U.K. 7 51.30N .20W
. Germain France 9 48.53N 2.04E
. Gheorghe's Mouth est. Romania 13 44.51N 29.37E
. Gilles-Croix-de-Vie France 11 46.42N 1.56W
. Girons France 11 42.59N 1.08E
. Gotthard Pass Switz. 11 46.30N 8.55E
. Govan's Head U.K. 5 51.36N 4.55W
. Helena B. R.S.A. 39 32.35S 18.05E
. Helens U.K. 4 53.28N 2.43W
. Helens U.S.A. 54 45.52N 122.48W
. Helier U.K. 5 49.12N 2.07W
. Hilaire-du-Harcouët France 9 48.35N 1.06W
. Hubert Belgium 8 50.02N 5.22E
. Hyacinthe Canada 55 45.38N 72.57W
. Ignace U.S.A. 55 45.53N 84.44W
. Ives U.K. 5 50.13N 5.29W
. Jean Canada 55 45.18N 73.16W
. Jean France 11 45.17N 6.21E
. Jean de Matha Canada 55 46.14N 73.33W
. Jean, Lac l. Canada 55 48.35N 72.00W
. Jean Pied-de-Port France 11 43.10N 1.14W
. Jérôme Canada 55 45.47N 74.01W
. John Canada 55 45.16N 66.03W
. John r. Canada 55 45.15N 66.04W
St. John's Antigua 57 17.07N 61.51W
St. John's Canada 51 47.34N 52.41W
St. Johns U.S.A. 54 34.30N 109.22W
St. Johnsbury U.S.A. 55 44.25N 72.01W
St. John's Pt. U.K. 7 54.14N 5.39W
St. Jordi, Golf de g. Spain 10 40.50N 1.10E
St. Joseph Mich. U.S.A. 55 42.05N 86.30W
St. Joseph Mo. U.S.A. 53 39.45N 94.51W
St. Joseph, L. Canada 51 51.05N 90.35W
St. Junien France 11 45.53N 0.55E
St. Just-en-Chaussée France 9 49.30N 2.26E
St. Kitts-Nevis Leeward Is. 57 17.20N 62.45W
St. Laurent Que. Canada 55 45.31N 73.42W
St. Laurent du Maroni Guiana 61 5.30N 54.02W
St. Lawrence r. Canada 55 48.45N 68.30W
St. Lawrence, G. of Canada 51 48.00N 62.00W
St. Lawrence I. U.S.A. 50 63.00N 170.00W
St. Lô France 9 49.07N 1.05W
St. Louis Senegal 34 16.01N 16.30W
St. Louis U.S.A. 53 38.40N 90.15W
St. Lucia Windward Is. 57 14.05N 61.00W
St. Lucia, L. R.S.A. 39 28.05S 32.26E
St. Maixent France 11 46.25N 0.12W
St. Malo France 9 48.39N 2.00W
St. Malo, Golfe de g. France 11 49.20N 2.00W
St.-Marc Haiti 57 19.08N 72.41W
St. Margaret's Hope U.K. 6 58.49N 2.57W
St. Maries U.S.A. 54 47.19N 116.35W
St. Martin i. Leeward Is. 57 18.05N 63.05W
St. Martin U.K. 5 49.27N 2.34W
St. Martin's i. U.K. 5 49.57N 6.16W
St. Mary U.K. 5 49.14N 2.10W
St.Mary Peak Australia 46 31.30S 138.35E
St. Marys Australia 45 41.33S 148.12E
St. Mary's i. U.K. 5 49.55N 6.16W
St. Matthew I. U.S.A. 50 60.30N 172.45W
St. Maur France 9 48.48N 2.30E
St. Maurice r. Canada 55 46.21N 72.31W
St. Moritz Switz. 14 46.30N 9.51E
St. Nazaire France 11 47.17N 2.12W
St. Neots U.K. 5 52.14N 0.16W
St. Niklaas Belgium 8 51.10N 4.09E
St. Omer France 11 50.45N 2.15E
St. Pacôme Canada 55 47.24N 69.58W
St. Pascal Canada 55 47.32N 69.48W
St. Paul Pyr. Or. France 11 42.49N 2.29E
St. Paul Minn. U.S.A. 53 45.00N 93.10W
St. Paul du Nord Canada 55 48.27N 69.16W
St. Peter Port U.K. 5 49.27N 2.32W
St. Petersburg U.S.A. 53 27.45N 82.40W
St. Pierre Char. Mar. France 11 45.57N 1.19W
St. Pierre S. Mar. France 9 49.48N 0.29E
St. Pierre and Miquelon is. N. America 51 47.00N 56.15W
St. Pierre-Église France 9 49.40N 1.24W
St. Pölten Austria 14 48.13N 15.37E
St. Quentin France 9 49.51N 3.17E
St. Seine-l'Abbaye France 9 47.26N 4.47E
St. Siméon Canada 55 47.56N 69.58W
St. Stephen Canada 55 45.12N 67.18W
St. Thomas Canada 55 42.47N 81.12W
St. Thomas i. U.S.V.Is. 57 18.22N 64.57W
St. Tropez France 11 43.16N 6.39E
St. Truiden Belgium 8 50.49N 5.11E
St. Valéry France 9 49.52N 0.43E
St. Vallier France 11 45.11N 4.49E
St. Vincent and the Grenadines Windward Is. 57 13.00N 61.15W
St. Vincent, G. Australia 46 35.00S 138.05E
St. Vith Belgium 8 50.15N 6.08E
St. Wendel Germany 8 49.27N 7.10E
St. Yrieix France 11 45.31N 1.12E
Saitama d. Japan 23 35.55N 139.00E
Sajama mtn. Bolivia 62 18.06S 69.00W
Saka Kenya 37 0.09S 39.18E
Sakai Japan 23 34.35N 135.28E
Sakākah Saudi Arabia 30 29.59N 40.12E
Sakania Zaïre 37 12.44S 28.34E
Sakarya r. Turkey 30 41.08N 30.36E
Sakété Benin 38 6.45N 2.45E
Sakhalin i. Russian Fed. 25 50.00N 143.00E
Sakht-Sar Iran 31 36.54N 50.41E
Sakivier R.S.A. 36 30.50S 20.26E
Sakrivier R.S.A. 39 30.53S 20.24E
Sakuma Japan 23 35.05N 137.48E
Sal r. Russian Fed. 19 47.33N 40.40E
Sala Sweden 17 59.55N 16.36E
Salaca r. Latvia 17 57.45N 24.21E
Salacgriva Latvia 17 57.45N 24.21E
Salado r. Buenos Aires Argentina 63 35.44S 57.22W
Salado r. Santa Fé Argentina 63 31.40S 60.41W
Salado r. La Pampa Argentina 63 36.15S 66.55W
Salado r. Mexico 56 26.46N 98.55W
Salaga Ghana 38 8.36N 0.32W
Salālah Oman 28 17.00N 54.04E
Salamanca Spain 10 40.58N 5.40W
Salamina Colombia 60 5.24N 75.31W
Salatiga Indonesia 26 7.15S 110.34E
Salbris France 9 47.26N 2.03E
Salcombe U.K. 5 50.14N 3.47W
Saldaña Spain 10 42.32N 4.48W
Saldanha R.S.A. 39 33.00S 17.56E
Saldanha B. R.S.A. 39 33.05S 17.50E
Saldus Latvia 17 56.40N 22.30E
Sale Australia 47 38.06S 147.06E
Salekhard Russian Fed. 18 66.33N 66.35E
Salem India 29 11.38N 78.08E
Salem Ind. U.S.A. 55 38.38N 86.06W
Salem Oreg. U.S.A. 54 44.57N 123.01W
Sälen Sweden 17 61.10N 13.16E
Salerno Italy 12 40.41N 14.45E
Salerno, Golfo di g. Italy 12 40.30N 14.45E
Salford U.K. 4 53.30N 2.17W
Salgótarján Hungary 15 48.07N 19.48E
Salgueiro Brazil 61 8.04S 39.05W
Salima Malaŵi 37 13.45S 34.29E
Salim's Tanzania 37 10.37S 36.33E
Salina Cruz Mexico 56 16.11N 95.12W
Salinas Ecuador 60 2.13S 80.58W
Salinas U.S.A. 54 36.40N 121.38W
Salinas r. U.S.A. 52 36.45N 121.48W
Salinópolis Brazil 61 0.37S 47.20W
Salins France 11 46.56N 5.53E
Salisbury U.K. 5 51.04N 1.48W
Salisbury Md. U.S.A. 55 38.22N 75.36W
Salisbury Plain f. U.K. 5 51.15N 1.55W
Şalkhad Syria 32 32.29N 36.42E
Salluit Canada 51 62.10N 75.40W
Salmās Iran 31 38.13N 44.50E
Salmi Russian Fed. 18 61.19N 31.46E
Salmon U.S.A. 54 45.11N 113.55W
Salmon r. U.S.A. 54 45.51N 116.46W
Salmon Gums Australia 43 32.59S 121.39E
Salmon River Mts. U.S.A. 54 44.45N 115.30W
Salo Finland 17 60.23N 23.08E
Salò Italy 9 45.36N 10.31E
Salobreña Spain 10 36.45N 3.35W
Salome U.S.A. 54 33.47N 113.37W
Salon France 11 43.38N 5.06E
Salonta Romania 15 46.48N 21.40E
Salsk Russian Fed. 19 46.30N 41.33E
Salso r. Italy 12 37.07N 13.57E
Salsomaggiore Terme Italy 9 44.49N 9.59E
Salt r. U.S.A. 54 33.23N 112.18W
Salta Argentina 62 24.47S 65.24W
Salta d. Argentina 62 25.00S 65.00W
Saltdal Norway 16 67.06N 15.25E
Saltee Is. Rep. of Ire. 7 52.08N 6.36W
Saltfjorden est. Norway 16 67.15N 14.10E
Saltfleet U.K. 4 53.25N 0.11E
Salt Fork r. U.S.A. 53 36.41N 97.05W
Saltillo Mexico 56 25.30N 101.00W
Salt Lake City U.S.A. 54 40.46N 111.53W
Salto Argentina 63 34.17S 60.15W
Salto Brazil 59 23.10S 47.16W
Salto r. Italy 12 42.23N 12.54E
Salto Uruguay 63 31.23S 57.58W
Salto da Divisa Brazil 61 16.04S 40.00W
Salto Grande, Embalse de resr. Argentina/Uruguay 63 31.00S 57.50W
Salton Sea l. U.S.A. 54 33.19N 115.50W
Saluzzo Italy 9 44.39N 7.29E
Salvador Brazil 61 12.58S 38.29W
Salween r. Myanmar 29 16.30N 97.33E
Salyany Azerbaijan 31 39.36N 48.59E
Salzbrunn Namibia 39 24.23S 18.00E
Salzburg Austria 14 47.54N 13.03E
Salzburg d. Austria 14 47.25N 13.15E
Salzgitter Germany 14 52.02N 10.22E
Salzwedel Germany 14 52.51N 11.09E
Samālūt Egypt 32 28.18N 30.43E
Samaná Dom. Rep. 57 19.14N 69.20W
Samana Cay i. Bahamas 57 23.05N 73.45W
Samanga Tanzania 37 8.24S 39.18E
Samannūd Egypt 32 30.58N 31.14E
Samar i. Phil. 27 11.45N 125.15E
Samara Russian Fed. 18 53.10N 50.15E
Samara r. Russian Fed. 18 53.17N 50.42E
Samarai P.N.G. 44 10.37S 150.40E
Samarinda Indonesia 26 0.30S 117.09E
Samarkand Uzbekistan 20 39.40N 66.57E
Sāmarrā Iraq 31 34.13N 43.52E
Sambalpur India 29 21.28N 84.04E
Sambor Ukraine 15 49.31N 23.10E
Samborombón, Bahía b. Argentina 63 36.00S 57.00W
Sambre r. Belgium 8 50.29N 4.52E
Samburu Kenya 37 3.46S 39.17E
Samch'ŏk S. Korea 25 37.30N 129.10E
Same Tanzania 37 4.10S 37.43E
Samobor Slovenia 14 45.48N 15.43E
Samorogouan Burkina 38 11.21N 4.57W
Sámos i. Greece 13 37.44N 26.45E
Samothráki i. Greece 13 40.26N 25.35E
Sampit Indonesia 26 2.34S 112.59E
Samsang China 29 30.22N 82.50E
Samsun Turkey 30 41.17N 36.22E
Samtredia Georgia 19 42.10N 42.22E
Samui, Ko i. Thailand 29 9.30N 100.00E
Samur r. Russian Fed. 19 42.00N 48.20E
Samut Sakhon Thailand 29 13.32N 100.17E
San Mali 38 13.21N 4.57W
San r. Poland 15 50.25N 22.20E
Şan'ā' Yemen 35 15.23N 44.14E
Sanaba Burkina 38 12.25N 3.47W
Sanaga r. Cameroon 38 3.35N 9.40E
Sanandaj Iran 31 35.18N 47.01E
San Andreas U.S.A. 54 38.12N 120.41W
San Andrés, Isla de i. Colombia 57 12.33N 81.42W
San Andrés Tuxtla Mexico 56 18.27N 95.13W
San Angelo U.S.A. 52 31.28N 100.28W
San Antonio Chile 63 33.35S 71.38W
San Antonio Tex. U.S.A. 52 29.25N 98.30W
San Antonio Abad Spain 10 38.58N 1.18E
San Antonio, C. Cuba 57 21.50N 84.57W
San Antonio, Cabo c. Argentina 63 36.40S 56.42W
San Antonio de Areco Argentina 63 34.16S 59.30W
San Antonio Oeste Argentina 63 40.44S 64.57W
San Antonio, Punta c. Mexico 56 29.45N 115.41W
San Benedetto Italy 12 42.57N 13.53E
San Benedetto Po Italy 9 45.02N 10.55E
San Benito Guatemala 57 16.55N 89.54W
San Bernardino U.S.A. 54 34.06N 117.17W
San Bernardo Chile 63 33.36S 70.43W
San Blas, C. U.S.A. 53 29.40N 85.25W
San Bonifacio Italy 9 45.24N 11.16E
San Carlos Chile 63 36.25S 71.58W
San Carlos Mexico 56 29.01N 100.51W
San Carlos Nicaragua 57 11.07N 84.47W
San Carlos Phil. 27 15.59N 120.22E
San Carlos Venezuela 60 9.39N 68.35W
San Carlos Venezuela 60 1.55N 67.04W
San Carlos de Bariloche Argentina 63 41.08S 71.15W
San Carlos del Zulia Venezuela 60 9.01N 71.55W
Sancerre France 9 47.20N 2.51E
Sancerrois, Collines du hills France 9 47.25N 2.45E
San Clemente U.S.A. 54 33.26N 117.37W
San Clemente i. U.S.A. 54 32.54N 118.29W
San Cristóbal Argentina 62 30.20S 61.41W
San Cristóbal Dom. Rep. 57 18.27N 70.07W
San Cristóbal Venezuela 60 7.46N 72.15W
Sancti Spíritus Cuba 57 21.55N 79.28W
Sand Norway 17 59.29N 6.15E
Sanda i. U.K. 6 55.17N 5.34W
Sandakan Malaysia 26 5.52N 118.04E
Sanday i. U.K. 6 59.15N 2.33W
Sandbach U.K. 4 53.09N 2.23W
Sandefjord Norway 17 59.08N 10.14E
Sanders U.S.A. 54 35.13N 109.20W
Sandgate Australia 47 27.18S 153.00E
Sandhornöy i. Norway 16 67.05N 14.10E
Sandia Peru 60 14.14S 69.25W
San Diego U.S.A. 54 32.43N 117.09W
San Diego, C. Argentina 63 54.38S 65.05W
Sand Lake town Canada 55 47.46N 84.31W
Sandnes Norway 17 58.51N 5.44E
Sandness U.K. 6 60.18N 1.38W
Sandö i. Faroe Is. 16 61.50N 6.45W
Sandoa Zaïre 36 9.41S 22.56E
Sandomierz Poland 15 50.41N 21.45E
San Donà di Piave Italy 9 45.38N 12.34E
Sandover r. Australia 44 21.43S 136.32E
Sandoway Myanmar 29 18.28N 94.20E
Sandown U.K. 5 50.39N 1.09W
Sandpoint town U.S.A. 54 48.17N 116.34W
Sandringham U.K. 4 52.50N 0.30E
Sandstone Australia 43 27.59S 119.17E
Sandusky Ohio U.S.A. 55 41.27N 82.42W
Sandveld f. Namibia 39 21.25S 20.00E
Sandviken Sweden 17 60.37N 16.46E
Sandy U.S.A. 54 40.35N 111.53W
Sandy Bight b. Australia 43 33.53S 123.25E
Sandy C. Australia 44 24.42S 153.17E
Sandy Creek town U.S.A. 55 43.39N 76.05W
Sandy L. Ont. Canada 51 53.00N 93.07W
San Enrique Argentina 63 35.47S 60.22W
San Felipe Chile 63 32.45S 70.44W
San Felipe Colombia 60 1.55N 67.06W
San Felipe Mexico 56 31.00N 114.52W
San Felipe Venezuela 60 10.25N 68.40W
San Fernando Argentina 63 34.26S 58.34W
San Fernando Chile 63 34.35S 71.00W
San Fernando Phil. 27 16.39N 120.19E
San Fernando Spain 10 36.28N 6.12W
San Fernando Trinidad 60 10.16N 61.28W
San Fernando de Apure Venezuela 60 7.35N 67.15W
San Fernando de Atabapo Venezuela 60 4.03N 67.45W
Sanford r. Australia 42 27.22S 115.53E
Sanford Fla. U.S.A. 53 28.49N 81.17W
San Francisco Argentina 62 31.29S 62.06W
San Francisco U.S.A. 54 37.48N 122.24W
San Francisco r. U.S.A. 54 32.59N 109.22W
San Francisco, C. Ecuador 60 0.50N 80.05W
San Francisco de Macorís Dom. Rep. 57 19.19N 70.15W
Sanga-Tolon Russian Fed. 21 61.44N 149.30E
Sanggan He r. China 25 40.23N 115.18E
Sangha r. Congo 36 1.10S 16.47E
Sangihe i. Indonesia 27 3.30N 125.30E
Sangihe, Kepulauan is. Indonesia 27 2.45N 125.20E
San Gil Colombia 60 6.35N 73.08W
San Giovanni in Persiceto Italy 9 44.38N 11.11E
Sangkulirang Indonesia 26 1.00N 117.58E
Sāngli India 28 16.55N 74.37E
Sangmélima Cameroon 38 2.55N 12.01E
Sangonera r. Spain 10 37.58N 1.04W
San Gottardo, Passo del pass Switz. 14 46.30N 8.55E
San Gregorio Uruguay 63 32.37S 55.40W
Sangri China 24 29.18N 92.05E
San Ignacio Bolivia 62 16.23S 60.59W
San Ignacio Paraguay 62 26.52S 57.03W
San Isidro Argentina 63 34.29S 58.31W
Sanīyah, Hawr as l. Iraq 31 31.52N 46.50E
San Javier Argentina 63 30.40S 59.55W
San Javier Bolivia 62 16.22S 62.38W
San Javier Chile 63 35.35S 71.45W
San Joaquin r. U.S.A. 54 38.03N 121.50W
San Jorge, Golfo g. Argentina 63 46.00S 66.00W
San José Costa Rica 57 9.59N 84.04W
San José Guatemala 56 13.58N 90.50W
San Jose U.S.A. 54 37.20N 121.53W
San José de Chiquitos Bolivia 62 17.53S 60.45W
San José de Feliciano Argentina 63 30.25S 58.45W
San José de Guanipa Venezuela 60 8.54N 64.09W
San José del Guaviare Colombia 60 2.35N 72.38W
San José de Mayo Uruguay 63 34.20S 56.42W
San José de Ocuné Colombia 60 4.15N 70.20W
San Juan Argentina 62 31.30S 68.30W
San Juan d. Argentina 62 31.00S 68.30W
San Juan r. Costa Rica 57 10.50N 83.40W
San Juan Dom. Rep. 57 18.40N 71.05W
San Juan Peru 62 15.20S 75.09W
San Juan Phil. 27 8.25N 126.22E
San Juan Puerto Rico 57 18.29N 66.08W
San Juan r. U.S.A. 54 37.18N 110.28W
San Juan Bautista Spain 10 39.05N 1.30E
San Juan, C. Argentina 63 54.45S 63.50W
San Juan del Norte Nicaragua 57 10.58N 83.40W
San Juan de los Morros Venezuela 60 9.53N 67.23W
San Juan del Río Querétaro Mexico 56 20.23N 100.00W
San Juan Mts. U.S.A. 54 37.35N 107.10W
San Julián Argentina 63 49.19S 67.40W
San Justo Argentina 63 30.47S 60.35W
Sankt Niklaus Switz. 9 46.11N 7.48E
Sankt-Peterburg Russian Fed. 18 59.55N 30.25E
San Lázaro, Cabo c. Mexico 56 24.50N 112.18W
San Leonardo Spain 10 41.49N 3.04W
Şanlıurfa Turkey 30 37.08N 38.45E
San Lorenzo Argentina 63 32.45S 60.44W
San Lorenzo mtn. Chile 63 47.37S 72.19W
San Lorenzo Ecuador 60 1.17N 78.50W
San Lorenzo de El Escorial Spain 10 40.34N 4.08W
Sanlúcar de Barrameda Spain 10 36.46N 6.21W
Sanlúcar la Mayor Spain 10 37.26N 6.18W
San Lucas Bolivia 62 20.06S 65.07W
San Lucas, Cabo c. Mexico 56 22.50N 109.55W
San Luis Argentina 63 33.20S 66.20W
San Luis d. Argentina 63 34.00S 66.00W
San Luis Cuba 57 20.13N 75.50W
San Luis Obispo U.S.A. 54 35.17N 120.40W
San Luis Potosí Mexico 56 22.10N 101.00W
San Luis Potosí d. Mexico 56 23.00N 100.00W
San Marcos U.S.A. 52 29.54N 97.57W
San Marino Europe 9 43.55N 12.27E
San Marino town San Marino 9 43.55N 12.27E
San Martín r. Bolivia 62 12.25S 64.25W
San Mateo U.S.A. 54 37.35N 122.19W
San Matías Bolivia 60 16.22S 58.24W
San Matías, Golfo g. Argentina 63 41.30S 64.00W
Sanmenxia China 25 34.46N 111.17E
San Miguel r. Bolivia 60 13.52S 63.56W
San Miguel r. Bolivia 62 12.25S 64.25W
San Miguel El Salvador 57 13.28N 88.10W
San Miguel del Monte Argentina 63 35.25S 58.49W
San Miguel de Tucumán Argentina 62 26.49S 65.13W
San Miguelito Panama 57 9.02N 79.30W
Sannār Sudan 35 13.31N 33.38E
Sannicandro Italy 12 41.50N 15.34E
San Nicolas Argentina 63 33.20S 60.13W
Sanok Poland 15 49.35N 22.10E
San Pablo Phil. 27 13.58N 121.10E
San Pedro Buenos Aires Argentina 63 33.40S 59.41W
San Pedro Jujuy Argentina 62 24.14S 64.50W
San Pedro Dom. Rep. 57 18.30N 69.18W
San Pedro Paraguay 59 24.08S 57.08W
San Pedro de las Colonias Mexico 56 25.50N 102.59W
San Pedro, Punta c. Costa Rica 57 8.38N 83.45W
San Pedro, Sierra de mts. Spain 10 39.20N 6.20W
San Pedro Sula Honduras 57 15.26N 88.01W
San Pellegrino Terme Italy 9 45.50N 9.40E
San Pietro i. Italy 12 39.09N 8.16E
Sanquhar U.K. 6 55.22N 3.56W
San Quintín Mexico 56 30.28N 115.58W
San Rafael U.S.A. 54 37.59N 122.31W
San Raphael Argentina 63 34.40S 68.21W
San Remo Italy 9 43.48N 7.46E
San Salvador Argentina 63 31.37S 58.30W
San Salvador i. Bahamas 57 24.00N 74.32W
San Salvador El Salvador 57 13.40N 89.10W
San Salvador de Jujuy Argentina 62 24.10S 65.20W
San Sebastián Argentina 63 53.15S 68.30W
San Sebastián Spain 10 43.19N 1.59W
San Severo Italy 12 41.40N 15.24E
Santa r. Peru 60 9.00S 78.35W
Santa Ana Argentina 62 27.20S 65.35W
Santa Ana Bolivia 62 13.45S 65.35W
Santa Ana El Salvador 57 14.00N 89.31W
Santa Ana U.S.A. 54 33.44N 117.54W
Santa Bárbara Mexico 56 26.48N 105.49W
Santa Barbara U.S.A. 54 34.25N 119.42W
Santa Catarina d. Brazil 59 27.00S 52.00W
Santa Clara Cuba 57 22.25N 79.58W
Santa Clara Calif. U.S.A. 54 37.21N 121.57W
Santa Clara Utah U.S.A. 54 37.08N 113.39W
Santa Clotilde Peru 60 2.25S 73.35W
Santa Comba Dão Portugal 10 40.24N 8.08W
Santa Cruz d. Argentina 63 48.00S 69.30W
Santa Cruz r. Argentina 63 50.03S 68.35W
Santa Cruz Bolivia 62 17.45S 63.14W
Santa Cruz d. Bolivia 62 17.45S 62.00W
Santa Cruz Canary Is. 34 28.27N 16.14W
Santa Cruz U.S.A. 54 36.58N 122.08W
Santa Cruz i. U.S.A. 54 34.01N 119.45W
Santa Cruz Is. Solomon Is. 40 10.30S 166.00E
Santa Domingo Mexico 54 25.32N 112.02W
Santa Elena Argentina 63 31.00S 59.50W
Santa Elena, C. Costa Rica 57 10.54N 85.56W
Santa Fé Argentina 63 31.40S 60.40W
Santa Fé d. Argentina 62 30.00S 61.00W
Santa Fe U.S.A. 52 35.42N 106.57W
Santa Filomena Brazil 61 9.07S 45.56W
Santa Inés, Isla i. Chile 63 53.40S 73.00W
Santa Isabel Argentina 63 36.15S 66.55W
Santa Isabel do Morro Brazil 61 11.36S 50.37W
Santa Lucía Uruguay 63 34.27S 56.24W
Santa Lucía r. Uruguay 63 34.48S 56.22W
Santa Lucia Range mts. U.S.A. 54 36.00N 121.20W
Santa Margherita Ligure Italy 9 44.20N 9.12E
Santa María Brazil 59 29.40S 53.47W
Santa Maria U.S.A. 54 34.57N 120.26W
Santa Maria di Leuca, Capo c. Italy 13 39.47N 18.24E
Santa Maria Madalena Brazil 59 21.58S 42.02W
Santa Marta Colombia 60 11.18N 74.10W

Southend-on-Sea U.K. 5 51.32N 0.43E
Southern Alps *mts.* New Zealand 48 43.20S 170.45E
Southern Cross Australia 43 31.14S 119.16E
Southern Indian L. Canada 51 57.10N 98.40W
Southern Ocean Pacific Oc. 40 50.00S 135.00E
Southern Uplands *hills* U.K. 6 55.30N 3.30W
South Esk *r.* U.K. 6 56.43N 2.32W
South Esk Tablelands *f.* Australia 42 20.50S 126.40E
South Glamorgan *d.* U.K. 5 51.27N 3.22W
South-haa U.K. 6 60.34N 1.17W
South Haven U.S.A. 55 42.25N 86.16W
South Horr Kenya 37 2.10N 36.45E
South I. Kenya 37 2.36N 36.38E
South I. New Zealand 48 43.00S 171.00E
South Korea Asia 25 36.00N 128.00E
South Lake Tahoe *town* U.S.A. 54 38.57N 119.57W
Southland *d.* New Zealand 48 45.40S 168.00E
South Molton U.K. 5 51.01N 3.50W
South Nahanni *r.* Canada 50 61.00N 123.20W
Southport Qld. Australia 47 27.58S 153.20E
Southport Tas. Australia 45 43.25S 146.59E
Southport U.K. 4 53.38N 3.01W
South Ronaldsay *i.* U.K. 6 58.47N 2.56W
South Shields U.K. 4 55.00N 1.24W
South Tyne *r.* U.K. 6 54.59N 2.08W
South Uist *i.* U.K. 6 57.15N 7.20W
Southwest C. New Zealand 48 47.15S 167.30E
South Windham U.S.A. 55 43.44N 70.26W
Southwold U.K. 5 52.19N 1.41E
South Yorkshire *d.* U.K. 4 53.28N 1.25W
Soutpansberg *mts.* R.S.A. 39 22.58S 29.50E
Sovetsk Lithuania 17 55.05N 21.53E
Sovetsk Russian Fed. 18 57.39N 48.59E
Sovetskaya Gavan Russian Fed. 21 48.57N 140.16E
Soweto R.S.A. 39 26.16S 27.51E
Soyo Angola 36 6.12S 12.25E
Sozh *r.* Belarus 15 51.57N 30.48E
Spa Belgium 8 50.29N 5.52E
Spain Europe 10 40.00N 4.00W
Spalding Australia 46 33.29S 138.40E
Spalding U.K. 4 52.47N 0.09W
Spandau Germany 14 52.32N 13.13E
Spanish Fork U.S.A. 54 40.07N 111.39W
Sparks U.S.A. 54 39.32N 119.45W
Spartanburg U.S.A. 53 34.56N 81.57W
Spárti Greece 13 37.04N 22.28E
Spartivento, Capo *c.* Calabria Italy 12 37.55N 16.04E
Spartivento, Capo *c.* Sardegna Italy 12 38.53N 8.50E
Spátha, Ákra *c.* Greece 13 35.42N 23.43E
Speculator U.S.A. 55 43.30N 74.17W
Speke G. Tanzania 37 2.20S 33.30E
Spence Bay *town* Canada 51 69.30N 93.20W
Spencer Idaho U.S.A. 54 44.21N 112.11W
Spencer Iowa U.S.A. 53 43.08N 95.08W
Spencer, C. Australia 46 35.18S 136.53E
Spencer G. Australia 46 34.00S 137.00E
Sperrin Mts. U.K. 7 54.49N 7.06W
Spétsai *i.* Greece 13 37.15N 23.10E
Spey *r.* U.K. 6 57.40N 3.06W
Speyer Germany 14 49.18N 8.26E
Spiekeroog *i.* Germany 8 53.48N 7.45E
Spilimbergo Italy 9 46.07N 12.54E
Spilsby U.K. 4 53.10N 0.06E
Spina *ruins* Italy 9 44.42N 12.08E
Spinazzola Italy 12 40.58N 16.06E
Spišská Nova Ves Slovakia 15 48.57N 20.34E
Spithead *str.* U.K. 5 50.45N 1.05W
Spitsbergen *is.* Arctic Oc. 64 78.00N 17.00E
Spittal an der Drau Austria 14 46.48N 13.30E
Split Croatia 13 43.32N 16.27E
Spokane U.S.A. 54 47.40N 117.23W
Spokane *r.* U.S.A. 54 47.44N 118.20W
Spratly *i.* S. China Sea 26 8.45N 111.54E
Spray U.S.A. 54 44.50N 119.48W
Spree *r.* Germany 14 52.32N 13.15E
Springbok R.S.A. 39 29.40S 17.50E
Springerville U.S.A. 54 34.08N 109.17W
Springfield New Zealand 48 43.20S 171.56E
Springfield Ill. U.S.A. 53 39.49N 89.39W
Springfield Mass. U.S.A. 55 42.07N 72.35W
Springfield Miss. U.S.A. 53 37.11N 93.19W
Springfield Ohio U.S.A. 55 39.55N 83.48W
Springfield Oreg. U.S.A. 54 44.03N 123.01W
Springfield Vt. U.S.A. 55 43.18N 72.29W
Springfontein R.S.A. 39 30.15S 25.41E
Springs *town* R.S.A. 39 26.16S 28.27E
Springsure Australia 44 24.07S 148.05E
Springville Utah U.S.A. 54 40.10N 111.37W
Spry U.S.A. 54 37.55N 112.28W
Spurn Head U.K. 4 53.35N 0.08E
Squamish Canada 50 49.42N 123.09W
Squillace Italy 13 38.46N 16.31E
Srbija *d.* Yugo. 13 44.30N 20.30E
Srednekolymsk Russian Fed. 21 67.27N 153.35E
Sredne Russkaya Vozvyshennost *f.* Russian Fed. 18 53.00N 37.00E
Sredne Sibirskoye Ploskogor'ye *f.* Russian Fed. 21 66.00N 108.00E
Sretensk Russian Fed. 25 52.15N 117.52E
Srīkākulam India 29 18.18N 83.54E
Sri Lanka Asia 29 7.30N 80.50E
Srīnagar Jammu & Kashmir 28 34.08N 74.50E
Srnetica Bosnia-Herzegovina 13 44.26N 16.40E
Staaten *r.* Australia 44 16.24S 141.17E
Stadskanaal Neth. 8 53.02N 6.55E
Stadtkyll Germany 8 50.21N 6.32E
Stadtlohn Germany 8 52.00N 6.58E
Staffa *i.* U.K. 6 56.26N 6.21W
Stafford U.K. 4 52.49N 2.09W
Staffordshire *d.* U.K. 4 52.40N 1.57W
Staines U.K. 5 51.26N 0.31W
Stainforth U.K. 4 53.37N 1.01W
Stakhanov Ukraine 19 48.34N 38.40E
Stalina Kanal *canal* Russian Fed. 18 64.33N 34.48E
Stamford U.K. 5 52.39N 0.28W
Stamford Conn. U.S.A. 55 41.03N 73.32W
Stamford N.Y. U.S.A. 55 42.25N 74.37W
Standerton R.S.A. 39 26.57S 29.14E
Stanger R.S.A. 39 29.20S 31.17E
Stanley Canada 50 55.45N 104.55W
Stanley Falkland Is. 63 51.42S 57.51W
Stanley U.K. 4 54.53N 1.42W
Stanley Idaho U.S.A. 54 44.13N 114.35W
Stanovoy Khrebet *mts.* Russian Fed. 21 56.00N 125.40E
Stanthorpe Australia 47 28.37S 151.52E
Starachowice Poland 15 51.03N 21.04E
Stara Dorogi Belarus 15 53.02N 28.18E
Stara Planina *mts.* Bulgaria 13 42.50N 24.30E
Staraya Russa Russian Fed. 18 58.00N 31.22E
Staraya Sinyava Ukraine 15 49.38N 27.39E
Stara Zagora Bulgaria 13 42.26N 25.37E
Stargard Szczeciński Poland 14 53.21N 15.01E
Staritsa Russian Fed. 18 56.29N 34.59E
Starnberg Germany 14 48.00N 11.20E
Starobin Belarus 15 52.40N 27.29E
Starogard Gdański Poland 15 53.59N 18.33E
Starokonstantinov Ukraine 15 49.48N 27.10E
Start Pt. U.K. 5 50.13N 3.38W
Staryy Oskol Russian Fed. 19 51.20N 37.50E
State College U.S.A. 55 40.48N 77.52W
Staten I. *see* Estados, Isla de los *i.* Argentina 63
Staunton U.S.A. 53 38.10N 79.05W
Stavanger Norway 17 58.58N 5.45E
Stavelot Belgium 8 50.23N 5.54E
Staveren Neth. 8 52.53N 5.21E
Stavropol' Russian Fed. 19 45.03N 41.59E
Stavropolskaya Vozvyshennost *mts.* Russian Fed. 19 45.00N 42.30E
Stawell Australia 46 37.06S 142.52E
Stawiski Poland 15 53.23N 22.09E
Steamboat Springs *town* U.S.A. 54 40.29N 106.50W
Steelpoort R.S.A. 39 24.44S 30.13E
Steelton U.S.A. 55 40.14N 76.49W
Steenbergen Neth. 8 51.36N 4.19E
Steenvoorde France 8 50.49N 2.35E
Steenwijk Neth. 8 52.47N 6.07E
Steep Rock Lake *town* Canada 51 48.50N 91.38W
Steiermark *d.* Austria 14 47.10N 15.10E
Steilloopbrug R.S.A. 39 23.26S 28.37E
Steinkjer Norway 16 64.00N 11.30E
Steinkopf R.S.A. 39 29.16S 17.41E
Stella R.S.A. 39 26.32S 24.51E
Stellenbosch R.S.A. 39 33.56S 18.51E
Stenay France 9 49.29N 5.11E
Stendal Germany 14 52.36N 11.52E
Stensträsk Sweden 16 66.20N 19.50E
Stepan Ukraine 15 51.09N 26.18E
Stepanakert Azerbaijan 31 39.48N 46.45E
Stepnyak Kazakhstan 20 52.52N 70.49E
Sterkstroom R.S.A. 39 31.32S 26.31E
Sterling Colo. U.S.A. 52 40.37N 103.13W
Sterling Mich. U.S.A. 55 44.02N 84.02W
Sterlitamak Russian Fed. 18 53.40N 55.59E
Šternberk Czech Republic 15 49.44N 17.18E
Stettler Canada 50 52.21N 112.40W
Steuben U.S.A. 55 46.12N 86.27W
Steubenville U.S.A. 55 40.22N 80.39W
Stevenage U.K. 5 51.54N 0.11W
Stevenston U.K. 6 55.39N 4.45W
Stewart Canada 50 55.56N 130.01W
Stewart I. New Zealand 48 47.00S 168.00E
Stewart River *town* Canada 50 63.19N 139.26W
Steynsburg R.S.A. 39 31.17S 25.48E
Steyr Austria 14 48.04N 14.25E
Stikine *r.* Canada 50 56.45N 132.30W
Stikine Mts. Canada 50 59.00N 129.00W
Stiklestad Norway 16 63.48N 11.22E
Stilbaai R.S.A. 39 34.22S 21.22E
Stillwater Range *mts.* U.S.A. 54 39.50N 118.15W
Stilton U.K. 5 52.29N 0.17W
Stimson Canada 55 48.58N 80.37W
Stinchar *r.* U.K. 6 55.06N 5.00W
Stinisoara, Munţii *mts.* Romania 15 47.10N 26.00E
Štip Macedonia 13 41.44N 22.12E
Stirling U.K. 6 56.07N 3.57W
Stirling Range *mts.* Australia 43 34.23S 117.50E
Stjørdalshalsen Norway 16 63.29N 10.51E
Stockaryd Sweden 17 57.18N 14.35E
Stockbridge U.K. 5 51.07N 1.30W
Stockerau Austria 14 48.23N 16.13E
Stockett U.S.A. 54 47.21N 111.10W
Stockholm Sweden 17 59.20N 18.03E
Stockholm *d.* Sweden 17 59.40N 18.10E
Stockinbingal Australia 47 34.03S 147.53E
Stockport U.K. 4 53.25N 2.11W
Stocksbridge U.K. 4 53.30N 1.36W
Stockton Calif. U.S.A. 54 37.57N 121.17W
Stockton-on-Tees U.K. 4 54.34N 1.20W
Stoeng Tréng Cambodia 26 13.31N 105.58E
Stoffberg R.S.A. 39 25.25S 29.49E
Stoke-on-Trent U.K. 4 53.01N 2.11W
Stokes Bay *town* Canada 55 44.55N 81.21W
Stokhod *r.* Ukraine 15 51.52N 25.38E
Stokksund Norway 16 64.03N 10.05E
Stolac Bosnia-Herzegovina 13 43.05N 17.58E
Stolberg Germany 8 50.47N 6.12E
Stolbtsy Belarus 15 53.30N 26.44E
Stolin Belarus 15 51.52N 26.51E
Stone U.K. 4 52.55N 2.10W
Stonehaven U.K. 6 56.58N 2.13W
Stooping *r.* Canada 55 52.08N 82.00W
Stora Lulevatten *l.* Sweden 16 67.10N 19.16E
Stora Sjöfallets Nat. Park Sweden 16 67.44N 18.16E
Storavan *l.* Sweden 16 65.40N 18.15E
Storby Finland 17 60.13N 19.34E
Stord *i.* Norway 17 59.53N 5.25E
Store Baelt *str.* Denmark 17 55.30N 11.00E
Stor Elvdal Norway 17 61.32N 11.02E
Stören Norway 16 63.03N 10.18E
Storlien Sweden 16 63.20N 12.05E
Stornoway U.K. 6 58.12N 6.23W
Storozhevsk Russian Fed. 18 62.00N 52.20E
Storozhinets Ukraine 15 48.11N 25.40E
Storsjön *l.* Sweden 16 63.10N 14.20E
Storuman Sweden 16 65.06N 17.06E
Storuman *l.* Sweden 16 65.10N 16.40E
Stour *r.* Dorset U.K. 5 50.43N 1.47W
Stour *r.* Kent U.K. 5 51.19N 1.22E
Stour *r.* Suffolk U.K. 5 51.56N 1.03E
Stourport-on-Severn U.K. 5 52.21N 2.16W
Stowmarket U.K. 5 52.11N 1.00E
Stow on the Wold U.K. 5 51.55N 1.42W
Strabane U.K. 7 54.50N 7.30W
Stradbally Laois Rep. of Ire. 7 53.01N 7.09W
Stradbroke I. Australia 45 27.38S 153.45E
Stradella Italy 9 45.05N 9.18E
Straelen Germany 8 51.27N 6.14E
Strahan Australia 45 42.08S 145.21E
Strakonice Czech Republic 14 49.16N 13.55E
Stralsund Germany 14 54.18N 13.06E
Strand R.S.A. 39 34.07S 18.50E
Stranda Norway 16 62.19N 6.58E
Strangford Lough U.K. 7 54.28N 5.35W
Strangways Australia 46 29.08S 136.35E
Stranraer U.K. 6 54.54N 5.02W
Strasbourg France 11 48.35N 7.45E
Stratford Australia 47 37.57S 147.05E
Stratford Canada 55 43.22N 80.57W
Stratford New Zealand 48 39.20S 174.18E
Stratford-upon-Avon U.K. 5 52.12N 1.42W
Strathalbyn Australia 46 35.16S 138.54E
Strathclyde *d.* U.K. 6 55.45N 4.45W
Strathmore *f.* Tayside U.K. 6 56.44N 2.45W
Strathspey *f.* U.K. 6 57.25N 3.25W
Straubing Germany 14 48.53N 12.35E
Straumnes *c.* Iceland 16 66.30N 23.05W
Streaky B. Australia 46 32.36S 134.08E
Streaky Bay *town* Australia 46 32.48S 134.13E
Street U.K. 5 51.07N 2.43W
Stresa Italy 9 45.53N 8.32E
Stretton Australia 43 32.30S 117.42E
Strimon *r.* Greece 13 40.47N 23.51E
Stromboli *i.* Italy 12 38.48N 15.14E
Stromeferry U.K. 6 57.21N 5.34W
Stromness U.K. 6 58.57N 3.18W
Strömö *i.* Faroe Is. 16 62.08N 7.00W
Strömsbruk Sweden 17 61.53N 17.19E
Strömstad Sweden 17 58.56N 11.10E
Strömsund Sweden 16 63.51N 15.35E
Strömsvattudal *f.* Sweden 16 64.15N 15.00E
Stronsay *i.* U.K. 6 59.07N 2.36W
Stroud Australia 47 32.25S 151.58E
Stroud U.K. 5 51.44N 2.12W
Struan Australia 46 37.08S 140.49E
Struer Denmark 17 56.29N 8.37E
Struga Macedonia 13 41.10N 20.41E
Struma *r.* Bulgaria *see* Strimon *r.* Greece 13
Strumica Macedonia 13 41.26N 22.39E
Strydenburg R.S.A. 39 29.56S 23.39E
Stryker U.S.A. 54 48.40N 114.44W
Stryy Ukraine 15 49.16N 23.51E
Strzelecki Creek *r.* Australia 46 29.37S 139.59E
Strzelno Poland 15 52.38N 18.11E
Stuart Creek *town* Australia 46 29.43S 137.01E
Stuart L. Canada 50 54.32N 124.35W
Stuart Range *mts.* Australia 46 29.10S 134.56E
Stuart Town Australia 47 32.51S 149.08E
Sturgeon Falls *town* Canada 55 46.22N 79.55W
Sturgeon L. Ont. Canada 55 49.47N 90.40W
Sturminster Newton U.K. 5 50.56N 2.18W
Sturt B. Australia 46 35.24S 137.32E
Sturt Creek *r.* Australia 42 20.08S 127.24E
Sturt Desert Australia 46 28.30S 141.12E
Sturt Plain *f.* Australia 44 17.00S 132.48E
Stutterheim R.S.A. 39 32.32S 27.25E
Stuttgart Germany 14 48.47N 9.12E
Stviga *r.* Belarus 15 52.04N 27.54E
Stykkishólmur Iceland 16 65.06N 22.48W
Styr *r.* Belarus 15 52.07N 26.35E
Subotica Yugo. 13 46.04N 19.41E
Suceava Romania 15 47.39N 26.19E
Suck *r.* Rep. of Ire. 7 53.16N 8.04W
Suckling, Mt. P.N.G. 44 9.45S 148.55E
Sucre Bolivia 62 19.05S 65.17W
Sucuriu *r.* Brazil 59 20.44S 51.40W
Sudan Africa 35 14.00N 30.00E
Sudbury Canada 55 46.30N 81.00W
Sudbury U.K. 5 52.03N 0.45E
Sudety *mts.* Czech Republic/Poland 14 50.30N 16.30E
Sudirman, Pegunungan *mts.* Indonesia 27 3.50S 136.30E
Sud Ouest *d.* Burkina 38 10.45N 3.10W
Sueca Spain 10 39.12N 0.21W
Suez *see* As Suways Egypt **32**
Suez Canal *see* Suways, Qanāt as *canal* Egypt **32**
Suez, G. of *see* Suways, Khalīj as *g.* Egypt **32**
Şufaynah Saudi Arabia 30 23.09N 40.32E
Suffolk *d.* U.K. 5 52.16N 1.00E
Şuḩār Oman 31 24.23N 56.43E
Suhl Germany 14 50.37N 10.43E
Suibin China 25 47.19N 131.49E
Suide China 25 37.32N 110.12E
Suihua China 25 46.39N 126.59E
Suileng China 25 47.15N 127.05E
Suipacha Argentina 63 34.47S 59.40W
Suiping China 25 33.09N 113.59E
Suippes France 9 49.08N 4.32E
Suir *r.* Rep. of Ire. 7 52.17N 7.00W
Suita Japan 23 34.45N 135.32E
Sui Xian Hubei China 25 31.43N 113.22E
Sukabumi Indonesia 26 6.55S 106.50E
Sukadana Indonesia 26 1.15S 110.00E
Sukaraja Indonesia 26 2.23S 110.35E
Sukhinichi Russian Fed. 18 54.07N 35.21E
Sukhona *r.* Russian Fed. 18 61.30N 46.28E
Sukhumi Georgia 19 43.01N 41.01E
Sukkertoppen Greenland 51 65.40N 53.00W
Sukkur Pakistan 28 27.42N 68.54E
Sula *i.* Norway 17 61.08N 4.55E
Sulaimān Range *mts.* Pakistan 28 30.50N 70.20E
Sulak *r.* Russian Fed. 19 43.18N 47.35E
Sula, Kepulauan *is.* Indonesia 27 1.50S 125.10E
Sulawesi *i.* Indonesia 27 2.00S 120.30E
Sulawesi Selatan *d.* Indonesia 27 3.45S 120.30E
Sulawesi Utara *d.* Indonesia 27 1.45S 120.30E
Sulechów Poland 14 52.06N 15.37E
Sulejów Poland 15 51.22N 19.53E
Sulina Romania 13 45.08N 29.40E
Sulitjelma Norway 16 67.10N 16.05E
Sullana Peru 60 4.52S 80.39W
Sully France 9 47.46N 2.22E
Sulmona Italy 12 42.04N 13.57E
Sultan Canada 55 47.36N 82.47W
Sultan Hamud Kenya 37 2.02S 37.20E
Sulu Archipelago Phil. 27 5.30N 121.00E
Sulu Sea Pacific Oc. 27 8.00N 120.00E
Sumatera *i.* Indonesia 26 2.00S 102.00E
Sumatera Barat *d.* Indonesia 26 1.00S 100.00E
Sumatera Selatan *d.* Indonesia 26 3.00S 104.00E
Sumatera Utara *d.* Indonesia 26 2.00N 99.00E
Sumatra *see* Sumatera *i.* Indonesia **26**
Sumatra U.S.A. 54 46.38N 107.31W
Sumba *i.* Indonesia 26 9.30S 119.55E
Sumbar *r.* Turkmenistan 31 38.00N 55.20E
Sumbawa *i.* Indonesia 26 8.45S 117.50E
Sumbawanga Tanzania 37 7.58S 31.36E
Sumbe Angola 36 11.11S 13.52E
Sumburgh Head U.K. 6 59.51N 1.16W
Šumen Bulgaria 13 43.15N 26.55E
Sumgait Azerbaijan 31 40.35N 49.38E
Šumperk Czech Republic 14 49.58N 16.58E
Sumusţā al Waqf Egypt 32 28.55N 30.51E
Sumy Ukraine 19 50.55N 34.49E
Sunart, Loch U.K. 6 56.43N 5.45W
Sunbury Australia 47 37.36S 144.45E
Sundarbans *f.* India/Bangla. 29 22.00N 89.00E
Sunda, Selat *str.* Indonesia 26 6.00S 105.50E
Sundays *r.* R.S.A. 39 33.43S 25.50E
Sunderland U.K. 4 54.55N 1.22W
Sundsvall Sweden 17 62.23N 17.18E
Sungaipakning Indonesia 26 1.19N 102.00E
Sungaipenuh Indonesia 26 2.00S 101.28E
Sungguminasa Indonesia 26 5.14S 119.27E
Sungurlu Turkey 30 40.10N 34.23E
Sunne Sweden 17 59.50N 13.09E
Sunnyside U.S.A. 54 46.20N 120.00W
Suntar Russian Fed. 21 62.10N 117.35E
Sun Valley *town* U.S.A. 52 43.42N 114.21W
Sunwu China 25 49.40N 127.10E
Sunyani Ghana 38 7.22N 2.18W
Suoyarvi Russian Fed. 18 62.02N 32.20E
Superior Mont. U.S.A. 54 47.12N 114.53W
Superior Wisc. U.S.A. 53 46.42N 92.05W
Superior Wyo. U.S.A. 54 41.46N 108.58W
Superior, L. Canada/U.S.A. 55 48.00N 88.00W
Süphan Dagi *mtn.* Turkey 19 38.55N 42.55E
Süphan Dağlari *mtn.* Turkey 30 38.55N 42.55E
Suquţrā *i.* Indian Oc. 35 12.30N 54.00E
Şūr Lebanon 32 33.16N 35.12E
Şūr Oman 31 22.23N 59.32E
Sura Russian Fed. 18 53.52N 45.45E
Surabaya Indonesia 26 7.14S 112.45E
Surakarta Indonesia 26 7.32S 110.50E
Şūrān Syria 32 35.18N 36.44E
Surany Slovakia 15 48.06N 18.14E
Surat Australia 45 27.09S 149.05E
Surat India 28 21.10N 72.54E
Sūratgarh India 28 29.19N 73.54E
Surat Thani Thailand 29 9.03N 99.28E
Surazh Russian Fed. 15 53.00N 32.22E
Sûre *r.* Lux. 8 49.43N 6.31E
Surfer's Paradise Australia 47 27.58S 153.26E
Surgut Russian Fed. 20 61.13N 73.20E
Surigao Phil. 27 9.47N 125.29E
Surin Thailand 29 14.50N 103.34E
Surinam S. America 61 4.00N 56.00W
Suriname *r.* Surinam 61 5.52N 55.14W
Sur, Punta *c.* Argentina 63 36.53S 56.41W
Surrey *d.* U.K. 5 51.16N 0.30W
Surt Libya 34 31.10N 16.39E
Surt, Khalīj *g.* Libya 34 31.45N 17.50E
Surtsey *i.* Iceland 16 63.18N 20.30W
Surud Ad *mtn.* Somali Rep. 35 10.41N 47.18E
Suruga-wan *b.* Japan 23 34.45N 138.30E
Susa Italy 9 45.08N 7.03E
Susanino Russian Fed. 21 52.46N 140.09E
Susanville U.S.A. 54 40.25N 120.39W
Susquehanna *r.* U.S.A. 55 39.33N 76.05W
Sussex Wyo. U.S.A. 54 43.42N 106.19W
Sutherland Australia 47 34.02S 151.04E
Sutherland R.S.A. 39 32.23S 20.38E
Sutherlin U.S.A. 54 43.25N 123.19W
Sutlej *r.* Pakistan 28 29.26N 71.09E
Sutton England U.K. 5 51.22N 0.12W
Sutton W. Va. U.S.A. 55 38.41N 80.43W
Sutton in Ashfield U.K. 4 53.08N 1.16W
Suva Fiji 40 18.08S 178.25E
Suwałki Poland 15 54.07N 22.56E
Suwanee *r.* U.S.A. 53 29.15N 82.50W
Suways, Khalīj as *g.* Egypt 32 28.48N 33.00E
Suways, Qanāt as *canal* Egypt 32 30.40N 32.20E
Suwon S. Korea 25 37.16N 126.59E
Suzhou China 25 31.21N 120.40E
Suzuka Japan 23 34.51N 136.35E
Suzuka *r.* Japan 23 34.54N 136.39E
Suzuka-sammyaku *mts.* Japan 23 35.00N 136.20E
Suzzara Italy 9 45.00N 10.45E
Svalyava Ukraine 15 48.33N 23.00E
Svanvik Norway 16 69.25N 30.00E
Svappavaara Sweden 16 67.39N 21.04E
Svarhofthalvöya Norway 16 70.35N 26.00E
Svartenhuk Halvo *c.* Greenland 51 71.55N 55.00W
Svartisen *mtn.* Norway 16 66.40N 13.56E
Svatovo Ukraine 19 49.24N 38.11E
Svedala Sweden 17 55.30N 13.14E
Sveg Sweden 17 62.02N 14.21E
Svelgen Norway 17 61.47N 5.15E
Svendborg Denmark 17 55.03N 10.37E
Svenstrup Denmark 17 56.59N 9.52E
Sverdlovsk *see* Yekaterinburg Russian Fed. **18**
Svetlograd Russian Fed. 19 45.25N 42.58E
Svetogorsk Russian Fed. 18 61.07N 28.50E
Svinö *i.* Faroe Is. 16 62.17N 6.18W
Svir *r.* Russian Fed. 18 60.09N 32.15E
Svishtov Bulgaria 13 43.36N 25.23E
Svisloch Belarus 15 53.28N 29.00E
Svitavy Czech Republic 14 49.45N 16.27E
Svobodnyy Russian Fed. 25 51.24N 128.05E
Svolvaer Norway 16 68.15N 14.40E
Swaffham U.K. 5 52.38N 0.42E
Swain Reefs Australia 44 21.40S 152.15E
Swakop *r.* Namibia 39 22.38S 14.32E
Swakopmund Namibia 39 22.40S 14.34E
Swale *r.* U.K. 4 54.05N 1.20W
Swan *r.* Australia 43 32.03S 115.45E
Swanage U.K. 5 50.36N 1.59W
Swan Hill *town* Australia 46 35.23S 143.37E
Swansea Australia 45 42.08S 148.00E
Swansea U.K. 5 51.37N 3.57W
Swastika Canada 55 48.07N 80.06W
Swatow *see* Shantou China **25**
Swaziland Africa 39 26.30S 32.00E
Sweden Europe 16 63.00N 16.00E
Swedru Ghana 38 5.31N 0.42W
Sweetwater U.S.A. 52 32.37N 100.25W
Swidnica Poland 14 50.51N 16.29E
Świebodzin Poland 14 52.15N 15.32E
Świetokrzyskie, Góry *mts.* Poland 15 51.00N 20.30E
Swift Current *town* Canada 50 50.17N 107.49W
Swilly, Lough Rep. of Ire. 7 55.10N 7.32W
Swindon U.K. 5 51.33N 1.47W
Świnoujście Poland 14 53.55N 14.18E
Switzerland Europe 11 47.00N 8.00E
Syderö *i.* Faroe Is. 16 61.30N 6.50W
Sydney Australia 47 33.55S 151.10E
Sydney Canada 51 46.10N 60.10W
Sydpröven Greenland 51 60.30N 45.35W
Syktyvkar Russian Fed. 18 61.42N 50.45E
Sylhet Bangla. 29 24.53N 91.51E
Sylt *i.* Germany 14 54.50N 8.20E
Sylte Norway 16 62.31N 7.07E
Syracuse N.Y. U.S.A. 55 43.03N 76.09W
Syr Darya *r.* Kazakhstan 20 46.00N 61.12E
Syria Asia 30 35.00N 38.00E
Syriam Myanmar 26 16.45N 96.17E
Syrian Desert *see* Bādiyat ash Shām *des.* Asia **30**
Syzran Russian Fed. 18 53.10N 48.29E
Szarvas Hungary 15 46.52N 20.34E
Szczecin Poland 14 53.25N 14.32E
Szczecinek Poland 14 53.42N 16.41E
Szczytno Poland 15 53.34N 21.00E
Szécsény Hungary 15 48.06N 19.31E
Szeged Hungary 13 46.16N 20.08E
Székesfehérvár Hungary 15 47.12N 18.25E
Szekszárd Hungary 13 46.22N 18.44E
Szentes Hungary 15 46.39N 20.16E
Szolnok Hungary 15 47.10N 20.12E
Szombathely Hungary 14 47.12N 16.38E
Sztutowo Poland 15 54.20N 19.15E

T

Tabagne Côte d'Ivoire 38 7.59N 3.04W
Ţabāh Saudi Arabia 30 27.02N 42.10E
Ţabas Khorāsān Iran 31 33.36N 56.55E
Ţabas Khorāsān Iran 31 32.48N 60.14E
Tabasco *d.* Mexico 56 18.30N 93.00W
Tābask, Kūh-e *mtn.* Iran 31 29.51N 51.52E
Tabili Zaïre 37 0.04N 28.01E
Table B. R.S.A. 39 33.52S 18.26E
Tábor Czech Republic 14 49.25N 14.41E
Tabora Tanzania 37 5.02S 32.50E
Tabora *d.* Tanzania 37 5.30S 32.50E
Tabou Côte d'Ivoire 34 4.28N 7.20W
Tabrīz Iran 31 38.05N 46.18E
Tabūk Saudi Arabia 32 28.23N 36.36E
Tabulam Australia 47 28.50S 152.35E
Tachikawa Japan 23 35.42N 139.25E
Tacloban Phil. 27 11.15N 124.59E
Tacna Peru 62 18.01S 70.15W
Tacoma U.S.A. 54 47.15N 122.27W
Tacora *mtn.* Chile 62 17.40S 69.45W
Tacuarembó Uruguay 63 31.44S 55.59W
Tademaït, Plateau du *f.* Algeria 34 28.45N 2.10E
Tadmor New Zealand 48 41.26S 172.47E
Tadmur Syria 30 34.36N 38.15E
Tadoussac Canada 55 48.09N 69.43W
Taegu S. Korea 25 35.52N 128.36E
Taejŏn S. Korea 25 36.20N 127.26E
Tafalla Spain 10 42.31N 1.40W
Tafí Viejo Argentina 62 26.45S 65.15W
Taftān, Kūh-e *mtn.* Iran 31 28.38N 61.08E
Taganrog Russian Fed. 19 47.14N 38.55E
Taganrogskiy Zaliv *g.* Ukraine/Russian Fed. 19 47.00N 38.30E
Tagaytay City Phil. 27 14.07N 120.58E
Tagbilaran Phil. 27 9.38N 123.53E
Tagish Canada 50 60.18N 134.16W
Tagliamento *r.* Italy 9 45.38N 13.06E
Taglio di Po Italy 9 45.00N 12.12E
Tagula I. P.N.G. 44 11.30S 153.30E
Tagum Phil. 27 7.33N 125.53E
Tagus *r.* Portugal/Spain *see* Tejo *r.* Portugal **10**
Tahara Japan 23 34.40N 137.16E
Tahat *mtn.* Algeria 34 23.20N 5.40E

Tichit Mauritania 34 18.28N 9.30W
Ticino r. Italy 9 45.09N 9.12E
Ticonderoga U.S.A. 55 43.51N 73.26W
Tidaholm Sweden 17 58.11N 13.57E
Tidjikdja Mauritania 34 18.29N 11.31W
Tiel Neth. 8 51.53N 5.26E
Tieling China 25 42.18N 123.49E
Tielt Belgium 8 51.00N 3.20E
Tienen Belgium 8 50.49N 4.56E
Tiénigbé Côte d'Ivoire 38 8.11N 5.43W
Tientsin see Tianjin China 25
Tierp Sweden 17 60.20N 17.30E
Tierra Blanca Mexico 56 18.28N 96.12W
Tierra del Fuego d. Argentina 63 54.30S 67.00W
Tierra del Fuego i. Argentina/Chile 63 54.00S 69.00W
Tietar r. Spain 10 39.50N 6.00W
Tietê Brazil 59 23.04S 47.41W
Tiger U.S.A. 54 48.42N 117.24W
Tigil Russian Fed. 21 57.49N 158.40E
Tignère Cameroon 38 7.23N 12.37E
Tigre r. Venezuela 60 9.20N 62.30W
Tigris r. see Dijlah r. Asia 31
Tihāmah f. Saudi Arabia 35 20.30N 40.30E
Tīh, Jabal at f. Egypt 32 28.50N 34.00E
Tijuana Mexico 56 32.32N 117.01W
Tikaré Burkina 38 13.16N 1.44W
Tikhoretsk Russian Fed. 19 45.52N 40.07E
Tikhvin Russian Fed. 18 59.35N 33.29E
Tikitiki New Zealand 48 37.47S 178.25E
Tiksha Russian Fed. 18 64.04N 32.35E
Tiksi Russian Fed. 21 71.40N 128.45E
Tilburg Neth. 8 51.34N 5.05E
Tilbury U.K. 5 51.28N 0.23E
Tilemsi, Vallée du f. Mali 38 16.15N 0.02E
Till r. Northum. U.K. 4 55.41N 2.12W
Tillabéri Niger 38 14.28N 1.27E
Tillamook U.S.A. 54 45.27N 123.51W
Tílos i. Greece 13 36.25N 27.25E
Tilpa Australia 46 30.57S 144.24E
Timanskiy Kryazh mts. Russian Fed. 18 66.00N 49.00E
Timaru New Zealand 48 44.23S 171.41E
Timashevsk Russian Fed. 19 45.38N 38.56E
Timbákion Greece 13 35.04N 24.46E
Timber Creek town Australia 42 15.38S 130.28E
Timboon Australia 46 38.32S 143.02E
Timbuktu see Tombouctou Mali 38
Timimoun Algeria 34 29.14N 0.16E
Timiş r. Yugo./Romania 15 44.49N 20.28E
Timişoara Romania 15 45.47N 21.15E
Timişul r. Yugo. 13 44.49N 20.28E
Timmins Canada 55 48.30N 81.20W
Timok r. Yugo. 13 44.13N 22.40E
Timor i. Indonesia 42 9.30S 125.00E
Timor Sea Austa. 42 11.00S 127.00E
Timor Timur d. Indonesia 27 9.00S 125.00E
Timpahute Range mts. U.S.A. 54 37.38N 115.34W
Tinahely Rep. of Ire. 7 52.48N 6.19W
Tindouf Algeria 34 27.50N 8.04W
Tingha Australia 47 29.58S 151.16E
Tingo María Peru 60 9.09S 75.56W
Tingréla Côte d'Ivoire 38 10.26N 6.20W
Tingsryd Sweden 17 56.32N 14.59E
Tinguipaya Bolivia 62 19.11S 65.51W
Tinne r. Norway 3 59.05N 9.43E
Tinnenburra Australia 47 28.40S 145.30E
Tinnoset Norway 17 59.43N 9.02E
Tínos i. Greece 13 37.36N 25.08E
Tinsukia India 29 27.30N 95.22E
Tintinara Australia 46 35.52S 140.04E
Tioman, Pulau i. Malaysia 26 2.45N 104.10E
Tionaga Canada 55 48.05N 82.06W
Tione di Trento Italy 9 46.02N 10.43E
Tipperary Rep. of Ire. 7 52.29N 8.10W
Tipperary d. Rep. of Ire. 7 52.37N 7.55W
Tiranë Albania 13 41.20N 19.48E
Tirān, Jazīrat Saudi Arabia 32 27.56N 34.34E
Tirano Italy 9 46.12N 10.10E
Tiraspol Moldova 15 46.50N 29.38E
Tirat Karmel Israel 32 32.46N 34.58E
Tirebolu Turkey 30 41.02N 38.49E
Tiree i. U.K. 6 56.30N 6.50W
Tirgovişte Romania 15 44.56N 25.27E
Tirgu-Jiu Romania 15 45.03N 23.17E
Tirgu-Lăpuş Romania 15 47.27N 23.52E
Tirgu Mureş Romania 15 46.33N 24.34E
Tirgu-Neamţ Romania 15 47.12N 26.22E
Tirgu-Ocna Romania 15 46.15N 26.37E
Tirgu-Secuiesc Romania 15 46.00N 26.08E
Tírnavos Greece 13 39.45N 22.17E
Tirol d. Austria 14 47.15N 11.20E
Tir Pol Afghan. 31 34.38N 61.19E
Tirso r. Italy 12 39.52N 8.33E
Tiruchchirāppalli India 29 10.50N 78.43E
Tirunelveli India 28 8.45N 77.43E
Tirupati India 29 13.39N 79.25E
Tiruppur India 28 11.05N 77.20E
Tisa r. Yugo. 15 45.09N 20.16E
Tis'ah Egypt 32 30.02N 32.35E
Tisdale Canada 50 52.51N 104.01W
Tisza r. Hungary see Tisa r. Yugo. 15
Titicaca, L. Bolivia/Peru 62 16.00S 69.00W
Titiwa Nigeria 38 12.14N 12.53E
Titov Veles Macedonia 13 41.43N 21.49E
Titran Norway 16 63.42N 8.22E
Ti Tree Australia 44 22.06S 133.17E
Titusville Penn. U.S.A. 55 41.38N 79.41W
Tiverton U.K. 5 50.54N 3.30W
Tivoli Italy 12 41.58N 12.48E
Tizimín Mexico 57 21.10N 88.09W
Tizi Ouzou Algeria 34 36.44N 4.05E
Tiznit Morocco 34 29.43N 9.44W
Tjeuke Meer l. Neth. 8 52.55N 5.51E
Tjörn i. Sweden 17 58.00N 11.38E
Tlaxcala d. Mexico 56 19.45N 98.20W
Tlemcen Algeria 34 34.53N 1.21W
Tmassah Libya 34 26.22N 15.47E
Toab U.K. 6 59.53N 1.16W
Toamasina Madagascar 36 18.10S 49.23E
Toano Italy 9 44.23N 10.34E
Toba Japan 23 34.29N 136.51E
Toba, Danau l. Indonesia 26 2.45N 98.50E
Toba Kākar Range mts. Pakistan 28 31.15N 68.00E
Tobar U.S.A. 54 40.53N 114.54W
Tobelo Indonesia 27 1.45N 127.59E
Tobermory Canada 55 45.15N 81.39W
Tobermory U.K. 6 56.37N 6.04W
Tobi i. Pacific Ocean 27 3.01N 131.10E
Toboali Indonesia 26 3.00S 106.30E
Tobol r. Russian Fed. 20 58.15N 68.12E
Tobolsk Russian Fed. 20 58.15N 68.12E
Tobseda Russian Fed. 18 68.34N 52.16E
Tocantinópolis Brazil 61 6.20S 47.25W
Tocantins d. Brazil 61 10.15S 48.30W
Tocantins r. Brazil 61 1.50S 49.15W
Töcksfors Sweden 17 59.30N 11.50E
Tocopilla Chile 62 22.05S 70.12W
Tocorpuri mtn. Bolivia/Chile 62 22.26S 67.53W
Tocumwal Australia 47 35.51S 145.34E
Tocuyo r. Venezuela 60 11.03N 68.23W
Todenyang Kenya 37 4.34N 35.52E
Togian, Kepulauan is. Indonesia 27 0.20S 122.00E
Togo Africa 38 8.00N 1.00E
Toijala Finland 17 61.10N 23.52E
Toili Indonesia 27 1.25S 122.23E
Tokaj Hungary 15 48.08N 21.27E
Tokala mtn. Indonesia 27 1.36S 121.41E
Tokat Turkey 30 40.20N 36.35E
Tokelau Is. Pacific Oc. 40 9.00S 171.45W
Toki Japan 23 35.21N 137.11E
Toki r. Japan 23 35.12N 136.52E
Tokmak Kyrgyzstan 24 42.49N 75.15E
Tokoname Japan 23 34.53N 136.51E
Tokoroa New Zealand 48 38.13S 175.53E
Tokuno shima i. Japan 25 27.40N 129.00E
Tōkyō Japan 23 35.42N 139.46E
Tōkyō-wan b. Japan 23 35.25N 139.45E
Tolaga Bay town New Zealand 48 38.22S 178.18E
Toledo Spain 10 39.52N 4.02W
Toledo U.S.A. 55 41.40N 83.35W
Toledo, Montes de mts. Spain 10 39.35N 4.30W
Toliara Madagascar 36 23.21S 43.40E
Tolmezzo Italy 9 46.24N 13.01E
Tolosa Spain 10 43.09N 2.04W
Tolo, Teluk g. Indonesia 27 2.00S 122.30E
Tolstyy-Les Ukraine 15 51.24N 29.48E
Toluca Mexico 56 19.20N 99.40W
Toluca mtn. Mexico 56 19.10N 99.40W
Tol'yatti Russian Fed. 18 53.32N 49.24E
Tomar Portugal 10 39.36N 8.25W
Tomás Gomensoro Uruguay 63 30.26S 57.26W
Tomaszów Lubelski Poland 15 50.28N 23.25E
Tomaszów Mazowiecki Poland 15 51.32N 20.01E
Tombigbee r. U.S.A. 53 31.05N 87.55W
Tombos Brazil 59 20.53S 42.03W
Tombouctou Mali 38 16.49N 2.59W
Tombouctou d. Mali 38 18.30N 3.40W
Tombua Angola 36 15.55S 11.51E
Tomé Chile 63 36.37S 72.57W
Tomelilla Sweden 17 55.33N 13.57E
Tomelloso Spain 10 39.09N 3.01W
Tomingley Australia 47 32.06S 148.15E
Tomini Indonesia 27 0.31N 120.30E
Tominian Mali 38 13.17N 4.35W
Tomini, Teluk g. Indonesia 27 0.30S 120.45E
Tomintoul U.K. 6 57.15N 3.24W
Tomislavgrad Yugo. 15 43.43N 17.14E
Tomkinson Ranges mts. Australia 42 26.11S 129.05E
Tom Price Australia 42 22.49S 117.51E
Tomra Norway 16 62.34N 6.55E
Tomsk Russian Fed. 20 56.30N 85.05E
Toms River town U.S.A. 55 39.57N 74.12W
Tonalá Mexico 56 16.08N 93.41W
Tonalea U.S.A. 54 36.20N 110.58W
Tonasket U.S.A. 54 48.42N 119.26W
Tonbridge U.K. 5 51.12N 0.16E
Tondano Indonesia 27 1.19N 124.56E
Tönder Denmark 17 54.56N 8.54E
Tondibi Mali 38 16.39N 0.14W
Tondoro Namibia 39 17.45S 18.50E
Tone r. Japan 23 35.44N 140.51E
Tonga Pacific Oc. 40 20.00S 175.00W
Tongaat R.S.A. 39 29.34S 31.07E
Tongeren Belgium 8 50.47N 5.28E
Tongguan Shaanxi China 25 34.36N 110.21E
Tonghai China 29 24.07N 102.45E
Tonghua China 25 41.40N 126.52E
Tongking, G. of Asia 26 20.00N 107.50E
Tongling China 25 30.57N 117.40E
Tongo Australia 46 30.30S 143.47E
Tongoy Chile 62 30.15S 71.30W
Tongue U.K. 6 58.28N 4.25W
Tongue r. U.S.A. 54 46.24N 105.25W
Tongyu China 25 44.48N 123.06E
Tonk India 28 26.10N 75.50E
Tonkābon Iran 31 36.49N 50.54E
Tônlé Sap l. Cambodia 26 12.50N 104.00E
Tonnerre France 9 47.51N 3.59E
Tonopah U.S.A. 54 38.04N 117.14W
Tonota Botswana 39 21.28S 27.24E
Tönsberg Norway 17 59.17N 10.25E
Tonstad Norway 17 58.40N 6.43E
Tonto Basin town U.S.A. 54 33.55N 111.18W
Toobeah Australia 47 28.22S 149.50E
Toodyay Australia 43 31.35S 116.26E
Tooele U.S.A. 54 40.32N 112.18W
Toolondo Australia 46 36.55S 142.00E
Toowoomba Australia 45 27.35S 151.54E
Topeka U.S.A. 53 39.03N 95.41W
Topko mtn. Russian Fed. 21 57.20N 138.10E
Toplița Romania 15 46.55N 25.21E
Topock U.S.A. 54 34.44N 114.27W
Topolovgrad Bulgaria 13 42.05N 26.20E
Topozero, Ozero l. Russian Fed. 18 65.45N 32.00E
Toppenish U.S.A. 54 46.23N 120.19W
Tora-Khem Russian Fed. 21 52.31N 96.13E
Torbat-e Ḩeydarīyeh Iran 31 35.16N 59.13E
Torbat-e Jām Iran 31 35.15N 60.37E
Tördal Norway 17 59.10N 8.45E
Tordesillas Spain 10 41.30N 5.00W
Töre Sweden 16 65.54N 22.39E
Töreboda Sweden 17 58.43N 14.08E
Torgau Germany 14 51.34N 13.00E
Torhout Belgium 8 51.04N 3.06E
Toride Japan 23 35.53N 140.04E
Torino Italy 9 45.04N 7.40E
Tormes r. Spain 10 41.18N 6.29W
Torne r. Sweden see Tornio r. Finland 16
Torneträsk Sweden 16 68.15N 19.30E
Torneträsk l. Sweden 16 68.20N 19.10E
Tornio Finland 16 65.52N 24.10E
Tornio r. Finland 16 65.53N 24.07E
Tornquist Argentina 63 38.06S 62.14W
Toro Spain 10 41.31N 5.24W
Toronaíos Kólpos g. Greece 13 40.05N 23.38E
Toronto Canada 55 43.39N 79.23W
Toropets Russian Fed. 18 56.30N 31.40E
Tororo Uganda 37 0.42N 34.13E
Toros Dağlari mts. Turkey 30 37.15N 34.15E
Torquay Australia 46 38.20S 144.20E
Torquay U.K. 5 50.27N 3.31W
Torrance U.S.A. 54 33.50N 118.19W
Torreblanca Spain 10 40.14N 0.12E
Torre de Moncorvo Portugal 10 41.10N 7.03W
Torrelavega Spain 10 43.21N 4.00W
Torremolinos Spain 10 36.38N 4.30W
Torrens Creek r. Australia 44 22.22S 145.09E
Torrens Creek town Australia 44 20.50S 145.00E
Torrens, L. Australia 46 31.00S 137.50E
Torreón Mexico 56 25.34N 103.25W
Torre Pellice Italy 9 44.49N 9.13E
Torres Str. Australia 44 10.00S 142.20E
Torres Vedras Portugal 10 39.05N 9.15W
Torrevieja Spain 10 37.59N 0.40W
Torrey U.S.A. 54 38.18N 111.25W
Torridge r. U.K. 5 51.01N 4.12W
Torridon U.K. 6 57.23N 5.31W
Torridon, Loch U.K. 6 57.35N 5.45W
Torriglia Italy 9 44.31N 9.10E
Torsby Sweden 17 60.08N 13.00E
Tortola i. B.V.Is. 57 18.28N 64.40W
Tortona Italy 9 44.54N 8.52E
Tortosa Spain 10 40.49N 0.31E
Tortue, Île de la i. Cuba 57 20.05N 72.57W
Toruń Poland 15 53.01N 18.35E
Tory I. Rep. of Ire. 7 55.16N 8.13W
Tory Sd. Rep. of Ire. 7 55.14N 8.15W
Torzhok Russian Fed. 18 57.02N 34.51E
Toscana d. Italy 12 43.35N 11.10E
Tosen Norway 16 65.16N 12.50E
Toshkent see Tashkent Uzbekistan 24
Tosno Russian Fed. 18 59.38N 30.46E
Tostado Argentina 62 29.15S 61.45W
Totana Spain 10 37.46N 1.30W
Tôtes France 9 49.41N 1.03E
Totma Russian Fed. 18 59.59N 42.44E
Totora Bolivia 62 17.42S 65.09W
Tottenham Australia 47 32.14S 147.24E
Tottori Japan 25 35.32N 134.12E
Toubkal mtn. Morocco 34 31.03N 7.57W
Toucy France 9 47.44N 3.18E
Tougan Burkina 38 13.05N 3.04W
Touggourt Algeria 34 33.08N 6.04E
Toul France 11 48.41N 5.54E
Toulnustouc r. Canada 55 49.35N 68.25W
Toulon France 11 43.07N 5.53E
Toulouse France 11 43.33N 1.24E
Toummo Niger 34 22.45N 14.08E
Toungoo Myanmar 29 19.00N 96.30E
Touques r. France 9 49.22N 0.06E
Tourcoing France 8 50.44N 3.09E
Tournai Belgium 8 50.36N 3.23E
Tournon France 11 45.04N 4.50E
Tournus France 11 46.33N 4.55E
Tours France 9 47.23N 0.42E
Toury France 9 48.11N 1.56E
Touwsrivier town R.S.A. 39 33.20S 20.02E
Towcester U.K. 5 52.07N 0.56W
Townsend, Mt. Australia 47 36.24S 148.15E
Townshend I. Australia 44 22.15S 150.30E
Townsville Australia 44 19.13S 146.48E
Towson U.S.A. 55 39.24N 76.36W
Towyn U.K. 5 52.37N 4.08W
Toyama Japan 25 36.42N 137.14E
Toyo r. Japan 23 34.47N 137.20E
Toyohashi Japan 23 34.46N 137.23E
Toyokawa Japan 23 34.49N 137.24E
Toyota Japan 23 35.05N 137.09E
Tozeur Tunisia 34 33.55N 8.08E
Traben-Trarbach Germany 8 49.57N 7.07E
Trabzon Turkey 30 41.00N 39.43E
Trafalgar, Cabo c. Spain 10 36.11N 6.02W
Traiguén Chile 63 38.15S 72.41W
Trail Canada 50 49.04N 117.39W
Trajanova Vrata pass Bulgaria 13 42.13N 23.58E
Trakt Russian Fed. 18 62.40N 51.26E
Tralee Rep. of Ire. 7 52.16N 9.42W
Tralee B. Rep. of Ire. 7 52.18N 9.55W
Tranås Sweden 17 58.03N 14.59E
Trang Thailand 29 7.35N 99.35E
Trangan i. Indonesia 27 6.30S 134.15E
Trangie Australia 47 32.03S 148.01E
Trani Italy 12 41.17N 16.26E
Tranqueras Uruguay 63 31.12S 55.45W
Transkei f. R.S.A. 39 32.12S 28.20E
Transylvanian Alps see Carpații Meridionali mts. Romania 13
Trapani Italy 12 38.02N 12.30E
Traralgon Australia 47 38.12S 146.32E
Traryd Sweden 17 56.35N 13.45E
Trasimeno, Lago l. Italy 12 43.09N 12.07E
Traunstein Germany 14 47.52N 12.38E
Travellers L. Australia 46 33.18S 142.00E
Traverse City U.S.A. 55 44.46N 85.38W
Travers, Mt. New Zealand 48 42.05S 172.45E
Travnik Bosnia-Herzegovina 13 44.14N 17.40E
Trayning Australia 43 31.09S 117.46E
Trbovlje Slovenia 14 46.10N 15.03E
Trebbia r. Italy 9 45.04N 9.41E
Třebíč Czech Republic 14 49.13N 15.55E
Trebinje Bosnia-Herzegovina 13 42.43N 18.20E
Trebišov Slovakia 15 48.40N 21.47E
Třeboň Czech Republic 14 49.01N 14.50E
Trecate Italy 9 45.26N 8.44E
Tredegar U.K. 5 51.47N 3.16W
Tregaron U.K. 5 52.14N 3.56W
Tregosse Islets and Reefs Australia 44 17.41S 150.43E
Tréguier France 11 48.47N 3.16W
Treinta-y-Tres Uruguay 59 33.16S 54.17W
Treis Germany 8 50.10N 7.20E
Trélazé France 9 47.27N 0.28W
Trelew Argentina 63 43.15S 65.20W
Trelleborg Sweden 17 55.22N 13.10E
Trélon France 8 50.04N 4.05E
Tremadog B. U.K. 4 52.52N 4.14W
Tremp Spain 10 42.10N 0.52E
Trenčín Slovakia 15 48.54N 18.04E
Trenque Lauquen Argentina 63 35.56S 62.43W
Trent r. U.K. 4 53.41N 0.41W
Trentino-Alto Adige d. Italy 9 46.30N 11.20E
Trento Italy 9 46.04N 11.08E
Trenton Canada 55 44.06N 77.35W
Trenton N.J. U.S.A. 55 40.15N 74.43W
Trepassey Canada 51 46.44N 53.22W
Tres Árboles Uruguay 63 32.24S 56.43W
Tres Arroyos Argentina 63 38.26S 60.17W
Três Corações Brazil 59 21.44S 45.15W
Três Lagoas Brazil 59 20.46S 51.43W
Três Marias, Represa resr. Brazil 59 18.15S 45.15W
Três Pontas Brazil 59 21.23S 45.29W
Três Rios Brazil 59 22.07S 43.12W
Treuchtlingen Germany 14 48.57N 10.55E
Treviglio Italy 9 45.31N 9.35E
Treviso Italy 9 45.40N 12.14E
Tribulation, C. Australia 44 16.03S 145.30E
Trida Australia 47 33.00S 145.01E
Trier Germany 8 49.45N 6.39E
Trieste Italy 12 45.40N 13.47E
Triglav mtn. Slovenia 12 46.21N 13.50E
Tríkala Greece 13 39.34N 21.46E
Tríkomon Cyprus 32 35.17N 33.53E
Trincomalee Sri Lanka 29 8.34N 81.13E
Trinidad Bolivia 62 14.47S 64.47W
Trinidad Colombia 60 5.25N 71.40W
Trinidad Cuba 57 21.48N 80.00W
Trinidad Uruguay 63 33.32S 56.54W
Trinidad U.S.A. 52 37.10N 104.31W
Trinidad & Tobago S. America 57 10.30N 61.20W
Trinity r. U.S.A. 53 29.55N 94.45W
Trinity B. Australia 44 16.26S 145.26E
Trinity Range mts. U.S.A. 54 40.13N 119.12W
Trino Italy 9 45.12N 8.18E
Tripoli see Țarābulus Lebanon 32
Tripoli see Țarābulus Libya 34
Trípolis Greece 13 37.31N 22.21E
Tripolitania f. see Țarābulus f. Libya 34
Tripura d. India 29 23.45N 91.45E
Trivandrum see Thiruvananthapuram India 28
Trnava Slovakia 15 48.23N 17.35E
Troarn France 9 49.11N 0.11W
Trobriand Is. P.N.G. 44 8.35S 151.05E
Troglav mtn. Croatia 13 43.57N 16.36E
Troisdorf Germany 8 50.50N 7.07E
Trois-Rivières town Canada 55 46.21N 72.33W
Troitsk Russian Fed. 20 54.08N 61.33E
Troitsko-Pechorsk Russian Fed. 18 62.40N 56.08E
Troitskoye Russian Fed. 18 52.18N 56.26E
Troitskoye Ukraine 15 47.38N 30.19E
Trölladyngja mtn. Iceland 16 64.54N 17.16W
Trollhättan Sweden 17 58.16N 12.18E
Trollheimen mts. Norway 16 62.50N 9.15E
Troms d. Norway 16 69.20N 19.30E
Tromsö Norway 16 69.42N 19.00E
Trondheim Norway 16 63.36N 10.23E
Trondheimsfjorden est. Norway 16 63.40N 10.30E
Troödos mts. Cyprus 32 34.57N 32.50E
Troon U.K. 6 55.33N 4.40W
Tropic U.S.A. 54 37.37N 112.05W
Trosh Russian Fed. 18 66.24N 56.08E
Trostan mtn. U.K 7 55.03N 6.10W
Trostyanets Ukraine 15 48.35N 29.10E
Trout Creek town Canada 55 45.59N 79.22W
Trouville France 9 49.22N 0.55E
Trowbridge U.K. 5 51.18N 2.12W
Troy Mont. U.S.A. 54 48.28N 115.53W
Troy N.Y. U.S.A. 55 42.43N 73.40W
Troy Ohio U.S.A. 55 40.02N 84.12W
Troyes France 9 48.18N 4.05E
Troy Peak mtn. U.S.A. 54 38.19N 115.30W
Trpanj Croatia 13 43.00N 17.17E
Truchas Peak mtn. U.S.A. 52 35.58N 105.39W
Truckee U.S.A. 54 39.20N 120.11W
Trujillo Honduras 57 15.55N 86.00W
Trujillo Peru 60 8.06S 79.00W
Trujillo Spain 10 39.28N 5.53W
Trujillo Venezuela 60 9.20N 70.37W
Trundle Australia 47 32.54S 147.35E
Truro Australia 46 34.23S 139.09E
Truro Canada 51 45.24N 63.18W
Truro U.K. 5 50.17N 5.02W
Trustrup Denmark 17 56.21N 10.47E
Trysil Norway 17 61.19N 12.16E
Trysil r. Norway 17 61.03N 12.30E
Trzemeszno Poland 15 52.35N 17.50E
Tsaratanana, Massif de mts. Madagascar 36 14.00S 49.00E
Tsarevo Bulgaria 13 42.09N 27.51E
Tsau Botswana 39 20.10S 22.29E
Tsavo Nat. Park Kenya 37 2.45S 38.45E
Tses Namibia 39 25.58S 18.08E
Tsévié Togo 38 6.28N 1.15E
Tshabong Botswana 39 26.03S 22.25E
Tshane Botswana 39 24.02S 21.54E
Tshesebe Botswana 39 20.45S 27.31E
Tsimlyansk Russian Fed. 19 47.40N 42.06E
Tsimlyanskoye Vodokhranilishche resr. Russian Fed. 19 48.00N 43.00E
Tsingtao see Qingdao China 25
Tsiribihina Madagascar 39 19.42S 44.31E
Tsivilsk Russian Fed. 18 55.50N 47.28E
Tskhinvali Georgia 19 42.14N 43.58E
Tsna r. Belarus 15 52.10N 27.03E
Tsna r. Russian Fed. 18 54.45N 41.54E
Tsobis Namibia 39 19.27S 17.30E
Tsu Japan 23 34.43N 136.31E
Tsuchiura Japan 23 36.05N 140.12E
Tsudakhar Russian Fed. 19 42.20N 47.11E
Tsumeb Namibia 39 19.12S 17.43E
Tsuru Japan 23 35.30N 138.56E
Tsushima Japan 23 35.10N 136.43E
Tsushima i. Japan 25 34.30N 129.20E
Tuam Rep. of Ire. 7 53.32N 8.52W
Tuamotu, Îles is. Pacific Oc. 40 17.00S 142.00W
Tuapse Russian Fed. 19 44.06N 39.05E
Tuatapere New Zealand 48 46.08S 167.41E
Tuba City U.S.A. 54 36.08N 111.14W
Tubarão Brazil 59 28.30S 49.01W
Țubayq, Jabal aț mts. Saudi Arabia 32 29.30N 37.15E
Tubbercurry Rep. of Ire. 7 54.03N 8.45W
Tübingen Germany 14 48.32N 9.04E
Țubjah, Wādī r. Saudi Arabia 30 25.35N 38.22E
Țubruq Libya 35 32.06N 23.58E
Tucacas Venezuela 60 10.48N 68.19W
Tuchola Poland 15 53.35N 17.50E
Tucson U.S.A. 52 32.13N 110.58W
Tucumán d. Argentina 62 26.30S 65.20W
Tucumcari U.S.A. 52 35.10N 103.44W
Tucupita Venezuela 60 9.02N 62.04W
Tucuruí Brazil 61 3.42S 49.44W
Tucuruí, Represa de resr. Brazil 61 4.35S 49.33W
Tudela Spain 10 42.04N 1.37W
Tufi P.N.G. 44 9.05S 149.20E
Tugela R.S.A. 39 29.10S 31.25E
Tuguegarao Phil. 27 17.36N 121.44E
Tugur Russian Fed. 21 53.44N 136.45E
Tukangbesi, Kepulauan is. Indonesia 27 5.30S 124.00E
Tukayyid well Iraq 31 29.47N 45.36E
Țūkh Egypt 32 30.21N 31.12E
Tuktoyaktuk Canada 50 69.27N 133.00W
Tukums Latvia 17 57.00N 23.10E
Tukuyu Tanzania 37 9.20S 33.37E
Tula Mexico 56 23.00N 99.43W
Tula Russian Fed. 18 54.11N 37.38E
Tulare U.S.A. 54 36.13N 119.21W
Tulare L. resr. U.S.A. 54 36.03N 119.49W
Tulcan Ecuador 60 0.50N 77.48W
Tulcea Romania 13 45.10N 28.50E
Tulchin Ukraine 15 48.40N 28.49E
Tuli Zimbabwe 39 21.50S 29.15E
Tuli r. Zimbabwe 39 21.49S 29.00E
Țūlkarm Jordan 32 32.19N 35.02E
Tullamore Australia 47 32.39S 147.39E
Tullamore Rep. of Ire. 7 53.17N 7.31W
Tulle France 11 45.16N 1.46E
Tullins France 11 45.18N 5.29E
Tullow Rep. of Ire. 7 52.49N 6.45W
Tully Australia 44 17.55S 145.59E
Tully U.S.A. 55 42.47N 76.06W
Tuloma r. Russian Fed. 18 68.56N 33.00E
Tulsa U.S.A. 53 36.07N 95.58W
Tuluá Colombia 60 4.05N 76.12W
Tulumbasy Russian Fed. 18 57.27N 57.40E
Tulun Russian Fed. 21 54.32N 100.35E
Tulungagung Indonesia 26 8.03S 111.54E
Tum Indonesia 27 3.28S 130.21E
Tumaco Colombia 60 1.51N 78.46W
Tumba Sweden 17 59.12N 17.49E
Tumbarumba Australia 47 35.49S 148.01E
Tumbes Peru 60 3.37S 80.27W
Tumby Bay town Australia 46 34.20S 136.05E
Tumeremo Venezuela 60 7.18N 61.30W
Tummel, Loch U.K. 6 56.43N 3.55W
Tump Pakistan 28 26.06N 62.24E
Tumuc Humac Mts. S. America 61 2.20N 54.50W
Tumut Australia 47 35.20S 148.14E
Tunari mtn. Bolivia 62 17.18S 66.22W
Tūnat al Jabal Egypt 32 27.46N 30.44E
Tunceli Turkey 30 39.07N 39.34E
Tuncurry Australia 47 32.17S 152.29E
Tunduma Tanzania 37 9.19S 32.47E
Tunduru Tanzania 37 11.08S 37.21E
Tundzha r. Bulgaria 13 41.40N 26.34E
Tungabhadra r. India 28 16.00N 78.15E
Tungsten U.S.A. 54 40.48N 118.08W
Tunis Tunisia 34 36.47N 10.10E
Tunisia Africa 34 34.00N 9.00E
Tunja Colombia 60 5.33N 73.23W
Tunnsjöen l. Norway 16 64.45N 13.25E
Tunuyán r. Argentina 63 33.33S 67.30W
Tuoy-Khaya Russian Fed. 21 62.33N 111.25E
Tupă Brazil 59 21.57S 50.28W
Tupelo U.S.A. 53 34.15N 88.43W
Tupinambaranas, Ilha f. Brazil 61 3.00S 58.00W
Tupiza Bolivia 62 21.27S 65.43W
Tuquan China 25 45.22N 121.41E
Túquerres Colombia 60 1.06N 77.37W
Tura Russian Fed. 21 64.05N 100.00E
Tura Tanzania 37 5.30S 33.50E
Turangi New Zealand 48 38.59S 175.48E

aco Colombia 60 10.20N 75.25W
anovo Russian Fed. 18 60.05N 50.46E
o Colombia 60 8.06N 76.44W
a Romania 15 46.34N 23.47E
k Poland 15 52.02N 18.30E
eon r. Canada 55 50.00N 78.54W
ovishte Bulgaria 13 43.14N 26.37E
utlu Turkey 13 38.30N 27.43E
al Turkey 30 40.23N 36.05E
Estonia 17 58.48N 25.26E
r. Spain 10 39.27N 0.19W
açu Brazil 61 1.41S 45.21W
açu r. Brazil 61 1.36S 45.19W
n see Torino Italy 9
a Ukraine 15 49.10N 23.02E
ana, L. Kenya 37 4.00N 36.00E
estan Kazakhstan 24 43.17N 68.16E
ey Asia 30 39.00N 35.00E
ey Creek town Australia 42 17.04S 128.15E
menistan Asia 20 40.00N 60.00E
s Is. Turks & Caicos Is. 57 21.30N 71.10W
u Finland 17 60.27N 22.17E
u-Pori d. Finland 17 61.00N 22.35E
wel r. Kenya 37 3.08N 35.39E
effe Is. Belize 57 17.30N 87.45W
hout Belgium 8 51.19N 4.57E
u Măgurele Romania 13 43.43N 24.53E
u Roşu, Pasul pass Romania 13 45.37N 17E
u-Severin Romania 13 44.37N 22.39E
n r. Australia 47 33.03S 149.33E
v Belarus 15 52.04N 27.40E
an China 24 42.55N 89.06E
an Pendi f. China 24 43.40N 89.00E
uino mtn. Cuba 57 20.05N 76.50W
iff U.K. 6 57.32N 2.28W
kul Uzbekistan 31 41.30N 61.00E
khansk Russian Fed. 21 65.21N 88.05E
a r. Ukraine 15 51.48N 24.52E
caloosa U.S.A. 53 33.12N 87.33W
carora U.S.A. 54 41.19N 116.14W
ra see Tudela Spain 10
corin India 29 8.48N 78.10E
ia Brazil 61 2.45S 42.16W
akan Bulgaria 13 44.02N 26.40E
lingen Germany 14 47.59N 8.49E
ala Indonesia 27 8.24S 127.15E
bu Tanzania 37 5.28S 32.43E
n Egypt 32 29.09N 30.46E
Gol r. Mongolia 24 48.53N 104.35E
alu Pacific Oc. 40 8.00S 178.00E
pan Mexico 56 21.00N 97.23W
tla Gutiérrez Mexico 56 16.45N 93.09W
Spain 10 42.03N 8.39W
Gölü l. Turkey 30 38.45N 33.24E
Khurmātū Iraq 31 34.53N 44.38E
a Bosnia-Herzegovina 13 44.33N 18.41E
destrand Norway 17 58.37N 8.55E
tsund Norway 17 59.01N 8.32E
' Russian Fed. 18 56.47N 35.57E
ed r. U.K. 6 55.46N 2.00W
ed Heads town Australia 47 28.13S 153.33E
ntynine Palms U.S.A. 54 34.08N 116.03W
n Bridges town U.S.A. 54 45.33N 112.20W
n Falls town U.S.A. 54 42.34N 114.28W
ns Creek r. Australia 46 29.10S 139.27E
zel New Zealand 48 44.15S 170.06E
fold B. Australia 47 37.06S 149.55E
ford U.K. 5 51.01N 1.19W
er Tex. U.S.A. 53 32.22N 95.18W
dinskiy Russian Fed. 21 55.11N 124.34E
e r. U.K. 4 55.00N 1.25W
e and Wear d. U.K. 4 54.57N 1.35W
emouth U.K. 4 55.01N 1.24W
set Norway 17 62.17N 10.47E
e see Şūr Lebanon 32
ifjorden l. Norway 17 60.02N 10.08E
one d. U.K. 7 54.35N 7.15W
one U.S.A. 55 40.40N 78.14W
rell r. Australia 46 35.28S 142.55E
rell, L. Australia 46 35.22S 142.50E
rhenian Sea Med. Sea 12 40.00N 12.00E
nesöy i. Norway 17 60.00N 5.35E
men Russian Fed. 20 57.11N 65.29E
vi r. U.K. 5 51.46N 4.22W
neen R.S.A. 39 23.49S 30.10E

umã r. Brazil 61 2.30S 57.40W
upés Brazil 60 0.07S 67.05W
upés r. Brazil 60 0.00S 67.10W
á Brazil 59 21.08S 42.59W
angi r. Congo/Zaïre 36 0.25S 17.50E
atuba Brazil 59 23.26S 45.05W
ayyiḑ, Wādī al r. Iraq 30 32.04N 42.17E
eda Spain 10 38.01N 3.22W
eraba Brazil 59 19.47S 47.57W
erlândia Brazil 59 18.57S 48.17W
ombo R.S.A. 39 27.35S 32.05E
ort r. Belarus 15 52.06N 28.28E
undu Zaïre 35 0.24S 25.28E
ayali r. Peru 60 4.40S 73.20W
aipur India 28 24.36N 73.47E
aquiola Argentina 63 36.35S 58.30W
devalla Sweden 17 58.21N 11.55E
djaur l. Sweden 16 65.55N 17.49E
ne Italy 9 46.03N 13.15E
pi India 28 13.21N 74.45E
on Thani Thailand 29 17.29N 102.46E
e r. Zaïre 36 4.08N 22.25E
zen Germany 14 52.58N 10.34E
no Japan 23 34.45N 136.08E
Russian Fed. 18 54.45N 55.58E
r. Russian Fed. 18 54.45N 56.00E
culme U.K. 5 50.45N 3.19W
ab r. Namibia 39 21.12S 13.37E
alla r. Tanzania 37 5.43S 31.10E
anda Africa 37 2.00N 33.00E
Ugep Nigeria 38 5.48N 8.05E
Ughelli Nigeria 38 5.33N 6.00E
Uglegorsk Russian Fed. 21 49.01N 142.04E
Uglovka Russian Fed. 18 58.13N 33.30E
Ugoma mtn. Zaïre 37 4.00S 28.45E
Ugra r. Russian Fed. 18 54.30N 36.10E
Uherske Hradiště Czech Republic 15 49.05N 17.28E
Uig U.K. 6 57.35N 6.22W
Uíge Angola 36 7.40S 15.09E
Uil Kazakhstan 19 49.08N 54.43E
Uil r. Kazakhstan 19 48.33N 52.25E
Uinta Mts. U.S.A. 54 40.45N 110.05W
Uitenhage R.S.A. 39 33.46S 25.23E
Uithuizen Neth. 8 53.24N 6.41E
Uivlleq see Nanortalik Greenland 51
Uji r. Japan 23 34.53N 135.48E
Ujiji Tanzania 37 4.55S 29.39E
Ujjain India 28 23.11N 75.50E
Ujpest Hungary 15 47.33N 19.05E
Ujście Poland 14 53.04N 16.43E
Ujung Pandang Indonesia 26 5.09S 119.28E
Uka Russian Fed. 21 57.50N 162.02E
Ukerewe I. Tanzania 37 2.00S 33.00E
Ukhta Russian Fed. 18 63.33N 53.44E
Ukiah U.S.A. 54 39.09N 123.13W
Ukmerge Lithuania 18 55.14N 24.49E
Ukraine Europe 15 49.45N 27.00E
Ukwi Botswana 39 23.22S 20.30E
Ulaanbaatar Mongolia 24 47.54N 106.52E
Ulaangom Mongolia 24 49.59N 92.00E
Ulan Bator see Ulaanbaatar Mongolia 24
Ulan-Ude Russian Fed. 24 51.55N 107.40E
Ulan Ul Hu l. China 29 34.45N 90.25E
Ulcinj Yugo. 13 41.55N 19.11E
Ulenia, L. Australia 46 29.57S 142.24E
Ulhāsnagar India 28 19.13N 73.07E
Uliastay Mongolia 24 47.42N 96.52E
Ulla r. Spain 10 42.38N 8.45W
Ulladulla Australia 47 35.21S 150.25E
Ullånger Sweden 16 62.58N 18.16E
Ullapool U.K. 6 57.54N 5.10W
Ullswater l. U.K. 4 54.34N 2.52W
Ulm Germany 14 48.24N 10.00E
Ulongwé Mozambique 37 14.34S 34.21E
Ulricehamn Sweden 17 57.47N 13.25E
Ulsan S. Korea 25 35.32N 129.21E
Ulsberg Norway 16 62.45N 9.59E
Ultima Australia 46 35.30S 143.20E
Ulúa r. Honduras 57 15.50N 87.38W
Uluguru Mts. Tanzania 37 7.05S 37.40E
Uluru mtn. Australia 44 25.20S 131.01E
Ulverston U.K. 4 54.13N 3.07W
Ulverstone Australia 45 41.09S 146.10E
Umaisha Nigeria 38 8.01N 7.12E
Umala Bolivia 62 17.21S 68.00W
Uman Ukraine 15 48.45N 30.10E
Umbria d. Italy 12 42.55N 12.10E
Ume r. Sweden 16 63.47N 20.16E
Ume r. Zimbabwe 39 17.00S 28.22E
Umeå Sweden 16 63.45N 20.20E
Umfors Sweden 16 65.56N 15.00E
Umfuli r. Zimbabwe 39 17.32S 29.23E
Umiat U.S.A. 50 69.25N 152.20W
Umm-al-Qaywayn U.A.E. 31 25.32N 55.34E
Umm Durmān Sudan 35 15.37N 32.59E
Umm el Faḩm Israel 32 32.31N 35.09E
Umm Lajj Saudi Arabia 30 25.03N 37.17E
Umniati Zimbabwe 39 18.41S 29.45E
Umtata R.S.A. 39 31.35S 28.47E
Umuahia Nigeria 38 5.31N 7.26E
Umzimkulu R.S.A. 39 30.15S 29.56E
Umzimvubu R.S.A. 39 31.37S 29.32E
Una r. Bosnia-Herzegovina 13 45.16N 16.55E
Unalakleet U.S.A. 50 63.53N 160.47W
'Unayzah Jordan 32 30.29N 35.48E
'Unayzah Saudi Arabia 31 26.05N 43.57E
'Unayzah, Jabal mtn. Iraq 30 32.15N 39.19E
Uncia Bolivia 62 18.27S 66.37W
Uncompahgre Peak U.S.A. 54 38.04N 107.28W
Uncompahgre Plateau f. U.S.A. 54 38.30N 108.25W
Underberg R.S.A. 39 29.46S 29.26E
Underbool Australia 46 35.10S 141.50E
Unecha Russian Fed. 15 52.52N 32.42E
Ungarie Australia 47 33.38S 147.00E
Ungava B. Canada 51 59.00N 67.30W
Ungava, Péninsule d' pen. Canada 51 60.00N 74.00W
União Brazil 61 4.35S 42.52W
União da Vitória Brazil 59 26.13S 51.05W
Unimak I. U.S.A. 50 54.50N 164.00W
Unini Peru 60 10.41S 73.59W
Uniondale R.S.A. 39 33.39S 23.07E
Union Gap U.S.A. 54 46.34N 120.34W
Uniontown U.S.A. 55 39.54N 79.44W
United Arab Emirates Asia 31 24.00N 54.00E
United Kingdom Europe 3 54.00N 2.00W
United States of America N. America 52 39.00N 100.00W
Unna Germany 8 51.32N 7.41E
Unst i. U.K. 6 60.45N 0.55W
Ünye Turkey 30 41.09N 37.15E
Upata Venezuela 60 8.02N 62.25W
Upernavik Greenland 51 72.50N 56.00W
Upington R.S.A. 39 28.26S 21.12E
Upper East d. Ghana 38 10.40N 0.20W
Upper Egypt see Aş Şa'īd f. Egypt 30
Upper Hutt New Zealand 48 41.07S 175.04E
Upper Klamath L. U.S.A. 54 42.23N 122.55W
Upper Lough Erne U.K 7 54.13N 7.32W
Upper Tean U.K. 4 52.57N 1.59W
Upper Volta see Burkina Africa 38
Upper West d. Ghana 38 10.25N 2.00W
Upper Yarra Resr. Australia 47 37.43S 145.56E
Uppsala Sweden 17 59.52N 17.38E
Uppsala d. Sweden 17 60.10N 17.50E
Uqlat aş Şuqūr Saudi Arabia 30 25.50N 42.12E
Ur ruins Iraq 31 30.55N 46.07E
Uracoa Venezuela 60 9.03N 62.27W
Uraga-suido str. Japan 23 35.10N 139.42E
Ural r. Kazakhstan 19 47.00N 52.00E
Uralla Australia 47 30.40S 151.31E
Ural Mts. see Ural'skiye Gory mts. Russian Fed. 18
Ural'sk Kazakhstan 19 51.19N 51.20E
Ural'skiye Gory mts. Russian Fed. 18 60.00N 59.00E
Urana Australia 47 35.21S 146.19E
Urana, L. Australia 47 35.21S 146.19E
Urandangi Australia 44 21.36S 138.18E
Uranium City Canada 50 59.32N 108.43W
Urapunga Australia 44 14.41S 134.34E
Uraricoera r. Brazil 60 3.10N 60.30W
Urawa Japan 23 35.51N 139.39E
Uray Russian Fed. 20 60.11N 65.00E
Urbino Italy 12 43.43N 12.38E
Urcos Peru 60 13.40S 71.38W
Urda Kazakhstan 19 48.44N 47.30E
Urdzhar Kazakhstan 20 47.06N 81.33E
Ure r. U.K. 4 54.05N 1.20W
Urechye Belarus 15 52.59N 27.50E
Uren Russian Fed. 18 57.30N 45.50E
Urengoy Russian Fed. 20 65.59N 78.30E
Ures Mexico 56 29.26N 110.24W
Ürgüp Turkey 30 38.39N 34.55E
Uribia Colombia 60 11.43N 72.16W
Urisino Australia 46 29.44S 143.49E
Urjala Finland 17 61.05N 23.32E
Urk Neth. 8 52.40N 5.36E
Urlingford Rep. of Ire. 7 52.44N 7.35W
Urmia, L. see Daryācheh-ye Orūmīyeh l. Iran 31
Ursus Poland 15 52.12N 20.53E
Uruaçu Brazil 61 14.30S 49.10W
Uruapan Mexico 56 19.26N 102.04W
Urubamba Peru 60 13.20S 72.07W
Urubamba r. Peru 60 10.43S 73.55W
Urucará Brazil 61 2.32S 57.45W
Uruçui Brazil 61 7.14S 44.33W
Uruguaiana Brazil 63 29.45S 57.05W
Uruguay r. Argentina/Uruguay 63 34.00S 58.30W
Uruguay S. America 59 33.15S 56.00W
Ürümqi China 24 43.43N 87.38E
Urun P.N.G. 44 8.36S 147.15E
Urunga Australia 47 30.30S 152.28E
Urup r. Russian Fed. 19 44.59N 41.12E
Urzhum Russian Fed. 18 57.08N 50.00E
Urziceni Romania 13 44.43N 26.38E
Usa r. Russian Fed. 18 65.58N 56.35E
Uşak Turkey 30 38.42N 29.25E
Usakos Namibia 39 22.02S 15.35E
Usambara Mts. Tanzania 37 4.45S 38.25E
Ushant i. see Ouessant, Île d' i. France 11
Ush-Tobe Kazakhstan 24 45.15N 77.59E
Ushuaia Argentina 63 54.47S 68.20W
Ushumun Russian Fed. 21 52.48N 126.27E
Usisya Malaŵi 37 11.10S 34.12E
Usk r. U.K. 5 51.34N 2.59W
Uskedal Norway 17 59.56N 5.52E
Üsküdar Turkey 13 41.00N 29.03E
Usman Russian Fed. 19 52.02N 39.43E
Usovo Ukraine 15 51.20N 28.01E
Uspenskiy Kazakhstan 20 48.41N 72.43E
Ussuriysk Russian Fed. 25 43.48N 131.59E
Ustaoset Norway 17 60.30N 8.04E
Ustica i. Italy 12 38.42N 13.11E
Ust'-Ilga Russian Fed. 21 54.59N 105.00E
Ústí nad Labem Czech Republic 14 50.41N 14.00E
Ust Ishim Russian Fed. 20 57.45N 71.05E
Ustka Poland 14 54.35N 16.50E
Ust'kamchatsk Russian Fed. 21 56.14N 162.28E
Ust-Kamenogorsk Kazakhstan 20 50.00N 82.40E
Ust Kulom Russian Fed. 18 61.34N 53.40E
Ust Kut Russian Fed. 21 56.40N 105.50E
Ust Lyzha Russian Fed. 18 65.45N 56.38E
Ust'Maya Russian Fed. 21 60.25N 134.28E
Ust Nem Russian Fed. 18 61.38N 54.50E
Ust Olenëk Russian Fed. 21 72.59N 120.00E
Ust-Omchug Russian Fed. 21 61.08N 149.38E
Ust Port Russian Fed. 20 69.44N 84.23E
Ust Tapsuy Russian Fed. 18 62.25N 61.42E
Ust'Tsilma Russian Fed. 18 65.28N 53.09E
Ust-Tungir Russian Fed. 21 55.25N 120.15E
Ust Ura Russian Fed. 18 63.06N 44.41E
Ust Vaga Russian Fed. 18 62.42N 42.45E
Ust Vym Russian Fed. 18 62.15N 50.25E
Ustyurt, Plato f. Kazakhstan 19 43.30N 55.00E
Usu China 24 44.27N 84.37E
Usumacinta r. Mexico 56 18.22N 92.40W
U.S. Virgin Is. C. America 57 18.30N 65.00W
Ut Belarus 15 52.18N 31.10E
Utah d. U.S.A. 54 39.37N 112.28W
Utah L. U.S.A. 54 40.13N 111.49W
'Utaybah, Buḩayrat al l. Syria 32 33.31N 36.37E
Utengule Tanzania 37 8.55S 35.43E
Utete Tanzania 37 8.00S 38.49E
Utiariti Brazil 60 13.02S 58.17W
Utica N.Y. U.S.A. 55 43.05N 75.14W
Utiel Spain 10 39.33N 1.13W
Utopia Australia 44 22.14S 134.33E
Utrecht Neth. 8 52.04N 5.07E
Utrecht d. Neth. 8 52.04N 5.10E
Utrecht R.S.A. 39 27.38S 30.19E
Utrera Spain 10 37.10N 5.47W
Utsjoki Finland 16 69.53N 27.00E
Utsunomiya Japan 25 36.33N 139.52E
Utta Russian Fed. 19 46.24N 46.01E
Uttaradit Thailand 29 17.38N 100.05E
Uttar Pradesh d. India 29 27.40N 80.00E
Uummanarsuaq see Farvel, Kap c. Greenland 51
Uusikaupunki Finland 17 60.48N 21.25E
Uusimaa d. Finland 17 60.30N 25.00E
Uvalde U.S.A. 52 29.14N 99.49W
Uvarovichi Belarus 15 52.35N 30.44E
Uvat Russian Fed. 20 59.10N 68.49E
Uvinza Tanzania 37 5.08S 30.23E
Uvira Zaïre 37 3.22S 29.06E
Uvs Nuur l. Mongolia 24 50.30N 92.30E
Uwajima Japan 25 33.13N 132.32E
Uwayl Sudan 35 8.46N 27.24E
Uyo Nigeria 38 5.01N 7.56E
Uyuni Bolivia 62 20.28S 66.50W
Uyuni, Salar de f. Bolivia 62 20.20S 67.42W
Uzbekistan Asia 20 42.00N 63.00E
Uzda Belarus 15 53.28N 27.11E
Uzh r. Ukraine 15 51.15N 30.12E
Uzhgorod Ukraine 15 48.38N 22.15E
Užice Yugo. 15 43.52N 19.51E
Užice Yugo. 15 43.52N 19.51E

V

Vaagö i. Faroe Is. 16 62.03N 7.14W
Vaal r. R.S.A. 39 29.04S 23.37E
Vaala Finland 16 64.26N 26.48E
Vaal Dam R.S.A. 39 26.51S 28.08E
Vaasa Finland 16 63.06N 21.36E
Vaasa d. Finland 16 62.50N 22.50E
Vác Hungary 15 47.49N 19.10E
Vadodara India 28 22.19N 73.14E
Vado Ligure Italy 9 44.17N 8.27E
Vadsö Norway 16 70.05N 29.46E
Vaduz Liech. 14 47.08N 9.32E
Vaeröy i. Norway 16 67.40N 12.40E
Vaga r. Russian Fed. 18 62.45N 42.48E
Vågåmo Norway 17 61.53N 9.06E
Vaggeryd Sweden 17 57.30N 14.07E
Váh r. Slovakia 15 47.40N 17.50E
Vahsel B. Antarctica 64 77.00S 38.00W
Vailly-sur-Aisne France 9 49.25N 3.31E
Vakarai Sri Lanka 29 8.08N 81.26E
Vålådalen Sweden 16 63.09N 13.00E
Valavsk Belarus 15 51.40N 28.38E
Valcheta Argentina 63 40.40S 66.10W
Valdagno Italy 9 45.39N 11.18E
Valday Russian Fed. 18 57.59N 33.10E
Valdayskaya Vozvyshennost mts. Russian Fed. 18 57.10N 33.00E
Valdemārpils Latvia 17 57.22N 22.35E
Valdemarsvik Sweden 17 58.12N 16.36E
Valdepeñas Spain 10 38.46N 3.24W
Valdés, Pen. Argentina 63 42.30S 64.00W
Valdez U.S.A. 50 61.07N 146.17W
Val d'Isère France 9 45.27N 6.59E
Valdivia Chile 63 39.46S 73.15W
Val d'Oise d. France 9 49.10N 2.10E
Val d'Or town Canada 55 48.07N 77.47W
Valença Bahia Brazil 61 13.22S 39.06W
Valença R. de Janeiro Brazil 59 22.14S 43.45W
Valença Portugal 10 42.02N 8.38W
Valence France 11 44.56N 4.54E
Valencia Spain 10 39.29N 0.24W
Valencia d. Spain 10 39.30N 0.40W
Valencia Venezuela 60 10.14N 67.59W
Valencia de Alcántara Spain 10 39.25N 7.14W
Valencia, Golfo de g. Spain 10 39.38N 0.20W
Valenciennes France 8 50.22N 3.32E
Vale of Evesham f. U.K. 5 52.05N 1.55W
Vale of Pewsey f. U.K. 5 51.21N 1.45W
Vale of York f. U.K. 4 54.12N 1.25W
Valera Venezuela 60 9.21N 70.38W
Valga Estonia 18 57.44N 26.00E
Valinco, Golfe de g. France 11 41.40N 8.50E
Valjevo Yugo. 15 44.16N 19.56E
Valkeakoski Finland 17 61.16N 24.02E
Valkenswaard Neth. 8 51.21N 5.27E
Valladolid Mexico 57 20.41N 88.12W
Valladolid Spain 10 41.39N 4.45W
Vall de Uxó town Spain 10 39.49N 0.15W
Valle Norway 17 59.12N 7.32E
Valle d'Aosta d. Italy 9 45.45N 7.25E
Valle de la Pascua Venezuela 60 9.15N 66.00W
Valledupar Colombia 60 10.31N 73.16W
Valle Edén Uruguay 63 31.50S 56.09W
Vallegrande Bolivia 62 18.29S 64.06W
Vallenar Chile 62 28.35S 70.46W
Valletta Malta 12 35.53N 14.31E
Valley City U.S.A. 52 46.57N 97.58W
Valley Falls town U.S.A. 54 42.29N 120.16W
Valleyfield Canada 55 45.15N 74.08W
Vallgrund i. Finland 16 63.12N 21.14E
Valls Spain 10 41.18N 1.15E
Valmiera Latvia 18 57.32N 25.29E
Valnera mtn. Spain 10 43.10N 3.40W
Valognes France 9 49.31N 1.28W
Valparaíso Chile 63 33.02S 71.38W
Valparaíso Mexico 56 22.46N 103.34W
Vals, Tanjung c. Indonesia 27 8.30S 137.30E
Valverde Dom. Rep. 57 19.37N 71.04W
Valverde del Camino Spain 10 37.35N 6.45W
Vammala Finland 17 61.20N 22.54E
Van Turkey 30 38.28N 43.20E
Van Blommestein Meer, W.J. resr. Surinam 61 4.45N 55.05W
Vancouver Canada 50 49.13N 123.06W
Vancouver U.S.A. 54 45.39N 122.40W
Vancouver I. Canada 50 50.00N 126.00W
Vanderbilt U.S.A. 55 45.09N 84.39W
Vanderlin I. Australia 44 15.44S 137.02E
Van Diemen, C. Australia 44 16.31S 139.41E
Van Diemen G. Australia 44 11.50S 132.00E
Vandry Canada 55 47.50N 73.34W
Vänern l. Sweden 17 59.00N 13.15E
Vänersborg Sweden 17 58.22N 12.19E
Vang Norway 17 61.10N 8.40E
Vanga Kenya 37 4.37S 39.13E
Van Gölü l. Turkey 30 38.35N 42.52E
Vanimo P.N.G. 27 2.40S 141.17E
Vankarem Russian Fed. 21 67.50N 175.51E
Vanna i. Norway 16 70.10N 19.40E
Vännäs Sweden 16 63.58N 19.48E
Vannes France 11 47.40N 2.44W
Vanrhynsdorp R.S.A. 39 31.37S 18.42E
Vansbro Sweden 17 60.31N 14.13E
Vantaa Finland 17 60.13N 25.01E
Vanua Levu i. Fiji 40 16.33S 179.15E
Vanuatu Pacific Oc. 40 16.00S 167.00E
Van Wert U.S.A. 55 40.53N 84.36W
Vanzylsrus R.S.A. 39 26.51S 22.03E
Vapnyarka Ukraine 15 48.31N 28.44E
Var r. France 14 43.39N 7.11E
Varades France 9 47.23N 1.02W
Varallo Italy 9 45.49N 8.15E
Varāmīn Iran 31 35.20N 51.39E
Vārānasi India 29 25.20N 83.00E
Varangerfjorden est. Norway 16 70.00N 30.00E
Varangerhalvöya pen. Norway 16 70.25N 29.30E
Varaždin Croatia 12 46.18N 16.20E
Varazze Italy 9 44.22N 8.34E
Varberg Sweden 17 57.06N 12.15E
Vardar r. Macedonia see Axiós r. Greece 13
Varde Denmark 17 55.38N 8.29E
Varel Germany 8 53.24N 8.08E
Varennes France 11 46.19N 3.24E
Varese Italy 9 45.48N 8.48E
Varese Ligure Italy 9 44.22N 9.37E
Varginha Brazil 59 21.33S 45.25W
Varley Australia 43 32.48S 119.31E
Värmland d. Sweden 17 59.55N 13.00E
Varna Bulgaria 15 43.13N 27.57E
Värnamo Sweden 17 57.11N 14.02E
Várpalota Hungary 15 47.12N 18.09E
Vartofta Sweden 17 58.06N 13.40E
Varzo Italy 9 46.12N 8.15E
Varzy France 9 47.21N 3.23E
Vasa see Vaasa Finland 16
Vashka r. Russian Fed. 18 64.55N 45.50E
Vasilkov Ukraine 15 50.12N 30.15E
Vaslui Romania 15 46.38N 27.44E
Västerås Sweden 17 59.37N 16.33E
Västerbotten d. Sweden 16 64.50N 18.10E
Västerdal r. Sweden 17 60.33N 15.08E
Västernorrland d. Sweden 16 63.20N 17.30E
Västervik Sweden 17 57.45N 16.38E
Västmanland d. Sweden 17 59.50N 16.15E
Vasto Italy 12 42.07N 14.42E
Vatan France 11 47.05N 1.48E
Vatican City Italy 12 41.54N 12.27E
Vatiua Mozambique 37 14.15S 37.22E
Vatnajökull mts. Iceland 16 64.20N 17.00W
Vatneyri Iceland 16 65.36N 23.59W
Vatra Dornei Romania 15 47.21N 25.21E
Vättern l. Sweden 17 58.30N 14.30E
Vaughn Mont. U.S.A. 54 47.35N 111.34W
Vaughn N.Mex. U.S.A. 52 34.36N 105.13W
Vaupés r. Colombia 60 0.20N 69.00W
Vavuniya Sri Lanka 29 8.45N 80.30E
Växjö Sweden 17 56.52N 14.49E
Vaygach Russian Fed. 20 70.28N 58.59E
Vaygach, Ostrov i. Russian Fed. 18 70.00N 59.00E
Vecht r. Neth. 8 52.39N 6.01E
Vecsés Hungary 15 47.26N 19.19E
Veddige Sweden 17 57.16N 12.19E
Veendam Neth. 8 53.08N 6.52E
Veenendaal Neth. 8 52.03N 5.32E
Vega i. Norway 16 65.39N 11.50E
Veghel Neth. 8 51.37N 5.35E
Vegreville Canada 50 53.30N 112.02W
Veinticinco de Mayo Argentina 63 35.25S 60.11W
Vejen Denmark 17 55.29N 9.09E
Vejer Spain 10 36.15N 5.59W
Vejle Denmark 17 55.42N 9.32E
Velddrif R.S.A. 39 32.47S 18.09E
Vélez Málaga Spain 10 36.48N 4.05W
Vélez Rubio Spain 10 37.41N 2.05W
Velhas r. Brazil 59 17.20S 44.55W
Velikiye-Luki Russian Fed. 18 56.19N 30.31E
Velikiy Ustyug Russian Fed. 18 60.48N 45.15E
Veliko Tŭrnovo Bulgaria 13 43.04N 25.39E
Velizh Russian Fed. 18 55.36N 31.13E
Velletri Italy 12 41.41N 12.47E
Vellore India 29 12.56N 79.09E
Velsen Neth. 8 52.28N 4.39E
Velsk Russian Fed. 18 61.05N 42.06E
Veluwe f. Neth. 8 52.17N 5.45E
Vemdalen Sweden 16 62.29N 13.55E
Venado Tuerto Argentina 63 33.45S 61.56W
Venaria Italy 9 45.08N 7.38E
Vence France 9 43.43N 7.07E
Vendas Novas Portugal 10 38.41N 8.27W
Vendeuvre-sur-Barse France 9 48.14N 4.28E
Vendôme France 9 47.48N 1.04E
Veneto d. Italy 9 45.25N 11.50E
Venev Russian Fed. 18 54.22N 38.15E
Venezia Italy 9 45.26N 12.20E
Venezuela S. America 60 7.00N 65.20W
Venezuela, Golfo de g. Venezuela 60 11.30N 71.00W
Vengurla India 28 15.52N 73.38E
Veniaminof Mtn. U.S.A. 50 56.05N 159.20W
Venice see Venezia Italy 9
Venice, G. of Med. Sea 14 45.20N 13.00E
Venlo Neth. 8 51.22N 6.10E
Venraij Neth. 8 51.32N 5.58E
Venta r. Latvia 17 57.24N 21.33E
Ventersdorp R.S.A. 39 26.19S 26.48E
Ventimiglia Italy 9 43.47N 7.36E
Ventnor U.K. 5 50.35N 1.12W
Ventspils Latvia 17 57.24N 21.36E
Ventuari r. Venezuela 60 4.00N 67.35W
Venus B. Australia 47 38.40S 145.43E
Vera Argentina 59 29.31S 60.30W
Vera Spain 10 37.15N 1.51W
Veracruz Mexico 56 19.11N 96.10W
Veracruz d. Mexico 56 18.00N 95.00W
Verāval India 28 20.53N 70.28E
Verbania Italy 9 45.56N 8.33E
Vercelli Italy 9 45.19N 8.26E
Verde r. Argentina 63 42.10S 65.03W
Verde r. Brazil 62 19.11S 50.44W
Verden Germany 14 52.55N 9.13E
Verdon r. France 11 43.42N 5.39E

Verdun Canada **55** 45.28N 73.35W
Verdun Meuse France **11** 49.10N 5.24E
Vereeniging R.S.A. **39** 26.40S 27.55E
Vergelee R.S.A. **39** 25.46S 24.09E
Verín Spain **10** 41.55N 7.26W
Verkhniy Baskunchak Russian Fed. **19** 48.14N 46.44E
Verkhniy Lyulyukary Russian Fed. **18** 65.45N 64.28E
Verkhniy Shar Russian Fed. **18** 68.21N 50.45E
Verkhniy Ufaley Russian Fed. **18** 56.05N 60.14E
Verkhnyaya Taymyra *r.* Russian Fed. **21** 74.10N 99.50E
Verkhnyaya Tura Russian Fed. **18** 58.22N 59.50E
Verkhovye Russian Fed. **18** 52.49N 37.14E
Verkhoyansk Russian Fed. **21** 67.25N 133.25E
Verkhoyanskiy Khrebet *mts.* Russian Fed. **21** 66.00N 130.00E
Vermenton France **9** 47.40N 3.42E
Vermilion Canada **50** 53.21N 110.52W
Vermilion U.S.A. **55** 41.24N 82.21W
Vermont *d.* U.S.A. **55** 43.50N 72.45W
Vernal U.S.A. **54** 40.27N 109.32W
Verneuil France **9** 48.44N 0.56E
Vernon Canada **50** 50.16N 119.16W
Vernon France **9** 49.05N 1.29E
Véroia Greece **13** 40.31N 22.12E
Verona Italy **9** 45.27N 10.59E
Verónica Argentina **63** 35.24S 57.22W
Verrès Italy **9** 45.40N 7.42E
Versailles France **9** 48.48N 2.08E
Vert, Cap *c.* Senegal **34** 14.45N 17.25W
Vertou France **11** 47.10N 1.28W
Vertus France **9** 48.54N 4.00E
Verviers Belgium **8** 50.36N 5.52E
Vervins France **9** 49.50N 3.54E
Vesanto Finland **16** 62.56N 26.25E
Veselí nad Lužnicí Czech Republic **14** 49.11N 14.43E
Vesle *r.* France **9** 49.23N 3.38E
Vesoul France **14** 47.38N 6.09E
Vest-Agder *d.* Norway **17** 58.30N 7.10E
Vestfjorden *est.* Norway **16** 68.10N 15.00E
Vestfold *d.* Norway **17** 59.20N 10.10E
Vestmanhavn Faroe Is. **16** 62.09N 7.11W
Vestmannaeyjar *is.* Iceland **16** 63.30N 20.20W
Vestvågöy *i.* Norway **16** 68.10N 13.50E
Vesuvio *mtn.* Italy **12** 40.48N 14.25E
Vesyegonsk Russian Fed. **18** 58.38N 37.19E
Veszprém Hungary **15** 47.06N 17.55E
Vésztö Hungary **15** 46.55N 21.16E
Vetka Belarus **15** 52.35N 31.13E
Vetlanda Sweden **17** 57.26N 15.04E
Vetluga Russian Fed. **18** 57.50N 45.42E
Vetluga *r.* Russian Fed. **18** 56.18N 46.19E
Vettore, Monte *mtn.* Italy **12** 42.50N 13.18E
Veurne Belgium **8** 51.04N 2.40E
Vevelstad Norway **16** 65.43N 12.30E
Vézelise France **11** 48.29N 6.05E
Vézère *r.* France **11** 44.53N 0.55E
Vezhen *mtn.* Bulgaria **13** 42.45N 24.22E
Viacha Bolivia **60** 16.40S 68.17W
Viadana Italy **9** 44.56N 10.31E
Viana Brazil **61** 3.13S 45.00W
Viana Portugal **10** 38.20N 8.00W
Viana do Castelo Portugal **10** 41.41N 8.50W
Viangchan *see* Vientiane Laos **29**
Viar *r.* Spain **10** 37.45N 5.54W
Viareggio Italy **9** 43.52N 10.14E
Viborg Denmark **17** 56.26N 9.24E
Vibo Valentia Italy **12** 38.40N 16.06E
Vibraye France **9** 48.03N 0.44E
Vic *see* Vich Spain **10**
Vicente López Argentina **63** 34.32S 58.29W
Vicenza Italy **9** 45.33N 11.32E
Vich Spain **10** 41.56N 2.16E
Vichada *r.* Colombia **60** 4.58N 67.35W
Vichuga Russian Fed. **18** 57.12N 41.50E
Vichy France **11** 46.07N 3.25E
Vicksburg U.S.A. **53** 32.21N 90.51W
Viçosa Alagoas Brazil **61** 9.22S 36.10W
Viçosa Minas Gerais Brazil **59** 20.45S 42.53W
Victor Harbor Australia **46** 35.36S 138.35E
Victoria Argentina **63** 32.40S 60.10W
Victoria *d.* Australia **47** 37.20S 145.00E
Victoria *r.* Australia **42** 15.12S 129.43E
Victoria Canada **50** 48.26N 123.20W
Victoria Chile **63** 38.13S 72.20W
Victoria U.S.A. **53** 28.49N 97.01W
Victoria Beach *town* Canada **51** 50.43N 96.33W
Victoria Falls *f.* Zimbabwe/Zambia **39** 17.58S 25.45E
Victoria I. Canada **50** 71.00N 110.00W
Victoria, L. Africa **37** 1.00S 33.00E
Victoria, L. Australia **46** 34.00S 141.15E
Victoria L. Australia **46** 32.29S 143.22E
Victoria, Mt. P.N.G. **44** 8.55S 147.35E
Victoria Nile *r.* Uganda **37** 2.14N 31.20E
Victoria River *town* Australia **42** 15.36S 131.06E
Victoria River Downs *town* Australia **44** 16.24S 131.00E
Victoriaville Canada **55** 46.04N 71.57W
Victoria West R.S.A. **39** 31.24S 23.07E
Victorica Argentina **63** 36.15S 65.25W
Videle Romania **15** 44.16N 25.31E
Viderö *i.* Faroe Is. **16** 62.20N 6.30W
Vidin Bulgaria **15** 43.58N 22.51E
Viedma Argentina **63** 40.50S 63.00W
Viedma, L. Argentina **63** 49.40S 72.30W
Vienna *see* Wien Austria **14**
Vienne France **11** 45.32N 4.54E
Vienne *r.* France **11** 47.13N 0.05W
Vientiane Laos **29** 18.01N 102.48E
Vieques *i.* Puerto Rico **57** 18.08N 65.30W
Viersen Germany **8** 51.16N 6.22E
Vierwaldstätter See *l.* Switz. **14** 47.10N 8.50E
Vierzon France **9** 47.14N 2.03E
Vietnam Asia **26** 15.00N 108.00E
Vieux-Condé France **8** 50.29N 3.31E
Vigan Phil. **27** 17.35N 120.23E
Vigevano Italy **9** 45.19N 8.51E
Vignemale, Pic de *mtn.* France **11** 42.46N 0.08W
Vigo Spain **10** 42.15N 8.44W
Vigrestad Norway **17** 58.34N 5.42E
Vijayawāda India **29** 16.34N 80.40E
Vik Norway **16** 65.19N 12.10E
Vikajärvi Finland **16** 66.37N 26.12E
Vikeke Indonesia **27** 8.42S 126.30E
Vikersund Norway **17** 59.59N 10.02E
Vikna *i.* Norway **16** 64.52N 10.57E
Vikulovo Russian Fed. **20** 56.51N 70.30E
Vila Vanuatu **40** 17.44S 168.19E
Vila da Maganja Mozambique **37** 17.25S 37.32E
Vila Franca Portugal **10** 38.57N 8.59W
Vilaine *r.* France **11** 47.30N 2.25W
Vilanculos Mozambique **39** 21.59S 35.16E
Vilanova i la Geltrú *see* Villanueva y Geltrú Spain **10**
Vila Real Portugal **10** 41.17N 7.45W
Vila Real de Santo António Portugal **10** 37.12N 7.25W
Vila Velha Brazil **59** 20.20S 40.17W
Vileyka Belarus **15** 54.30N 26.50E
Vilhelmina Sweden **16** 64.37N 16.39E
Vilhena Brazil **60** 12.40S 60.08W
Viliga Kushka Russian Fed. **21** 61.35N 156.55E
Viljandi Estonia **18** 58.22N 25.30E
Vilkavišhkis Lithuania **15** 54.39N 23.02E
Vil'kitskogo, Proliv *str.* Russian Fed. **21** 77.57N 102.30E
Vilkovo Ukraine **15** 45.28N 29.32E
Villa Angela Argentina **62** 27.34S 60.45W
Villa Bella Bolivia **62** 10.23S 65.24W
Villablino Spain **10** 42.57N 6.19W
Villacañas Spain **10** 39.38N 3.20W
Villach Austria **14** 46.37N 13.51E
Villa Clara Argentina **63** 31.46S 58.50W
Villa Constitución Argentina **63** 33.14S 60.21W
Villa Dolores Argentina **62** 31.58S 65.12W
Villafranca di Verona Italy **9** 45.21N 10.50E
Villagarcía Spain **10** 42.35N 8.45W
Villaguay Argentina **63** 31.55S 59.00W
Villahermosa Mexico **56** 18.00N 92.53W
Villa Hernandarias Argentina **63** 31.15S 59.58W
Villa Huidobro Argentina **63** 34.50S 64.34W
Villaines-la-Juhel France **9** 48.21N 0.17W
Villajoyosa Spain **10** 38.31N 0.14W
Villalba Spain **10** 43.18N 7.41W
Villa María Argentina **62** 32.25S 63.15W
Villa Montes Bolivia **62** 21.15S 63.30W
Villanueva de la Serena Spain **10** 38.58N 5.48W
Villaputzu Italy **12** 39.28N 9.35E
Villarrica Chile **63** 39.15S 72.15W
Villarrica Paraguay **59** 25.45S 56.28W
Villarrobledo Spain **10** 39.16N 2.36W
Villa San José Argentina **63** 32.12S 58.15W
Villasayas Spain **10** 41.24N 2.39W
Villavicencio Colombia **60** 4.09N 73.38W
Villaviciosa Spain **10** 43.29N 5.26W
Villazón Bolivia **62** 22.06S 65.36W
Villedieu France **9** 48.50N 1.13W
Villefranche France **11** 46.00N 4.43E
Villena Spain **10** 38.39N 0.52W
Villenauxe-la-Grande France **9** 48.35N 3.33E
Villeneuve France **11** 44.25N 0.43E
Villeneuve d'Ascq France **8** 50.37N 3.10E
Villeneuve-St. Georges France **9** 48.44N 2.27E
Villeneuve-sur-Yonne France **9** 48.05N 3.18E
Villers-Bocage France **9** 49.05N 0.39W
Villers-Cotterêts France **9** 49.15N 3.04E
Villers-sur-Mer France **9** 49.21N 0.02W
Villeurbanne France **14** 45.46N 4.54E
Vilnius Lithuania **15** 54.40N 25.19E
Vilvoorde Belgium **8** 50.56N 4.25E
Vilyuy *r.* Russian Fed. **21** 64.20N 126.55E
Vilyuysk Russian Fed. **21** 63.46N 121.35E
Vimianzo Spain **10** 43.07N 9.02W
Vimmerby Sweden **17** 57.40N 15.51E
Vimoutiers France **9** 48.55N 0.12E
Vina *r.* Chad **38** 7.43N 15.30E
Viña del Mar Chile **63** 33.02S 71.34W
Vinaroz Spain **10** 40.30N 0.27E
Vincennes France **9** 48.51N 2.26E
Vincennes U.S.A. **55** 38.42N 87.30W
Vindel *r.* Sweden **16** 63.54N 19.52E
Vindeln Sweden **16** 64.12N 19.44E
Vinderup Denmark **17** 56.29N 8.47E
Vindhya Range *mts.* India **28** 22.55N 76.00E
Vineland U.S.A. **55** 39.29N 75.02W
Vingåker Sweden **17** 59.02N 15.52E
Vinh Vietnam **26** 18.42N 105.41E
Vînju Mare Romania **15** 44.26N 22.52E
Vinkovci Croatia **13** 45.17N 18.38E
Vinnitsa Ukraine **15** 49.11N 28.30E
Vinson Massif Antarctica **64** 78.00S 85.00W
Vioolsdrif R.S.A. **39** 28.45S 17.33E
Vipava Slovenia **14** 45.51N 13.58E
Virac Phil. **27** 13.35N 124.15E
Viranşehir Turkey **30** 37.13N 39.45E
Vire France **11** 48.50N 0.53W
Vire *r.* France **9** 49.20N 0.53W
Vírgenes, C. Argentina **63** 52.00S 68.50W
Virgin Gorda *i.* B.V.Is. **57** 18.30N 64.26W
Virginia U.S.A. **53** 47.30N 92.28W
Virginia *d.* U.S.A. **53** 37.30N 79.00W
Virginia City Mont. U.S.A. **54** 45.18N 111.56W
Virginia City Nev. U.S.A. **54** 39.19N 119.39W
Virovitica Croatia **15** 45.51N 17.23E
Virrat Finland **16** 62.14N 23.47E
Virserum Sweden **17** 57.19N 15.35E
Virton Belgium **8** 49.35N 5.32E
Virtsu Estonia **17** 58.34N 23.31E
Virunga Nat. Park Zaïre **37** 0.30S 29.15E
Vis Croatia **12** 43.03N 16.21E
Vis *i.* Croatia **12** 43.03N 16.10E
Visalia U.S.A. **54** 36.20N 119.18W
Visayan Sea Phil. **27** 11.35N 123.51E
Visby Sweden **17** 57.38N 18.18E
Visconde do Rio Branco Brazil **59** 21.00S 42.51W
Viscount Melville Sd. Canada **50** 74.30N 104.00W
Visé Belgium **8** 50.44N 5.42E
Višegrad Bosnia-Herzegovina **13** 43.47N 19.20E
Viseu Brazil **61** 1.12S 46.07W
Viseu Portugal **10** 40.40N 7.55W
Viseu de Sus Romania **15** 47.44N 24.22E
Vishākhapatnam India **29** 17.42N 83.24E
Viso, Monte *mtn.* Italy **9** 44.38N 7.05E
Visp Switz. **9** 46.18N 7.53E
Vista U.S.A. **54** 33.12N 117.15W
Vistula *r. see* Wisła *r.* Poland **15**
Vitarte Peru **60** 12.03S 76.51W
Vitebsk Belarus **18** 55.10N 30.14E
Viterbo Italy **12** 42.26N 12.07E
Vitim Russian Fed. **21** 59.28N 112.35E
Vitim *r.* Russian Fed. **21** 59.30N 112.36E
Vitoria Spain **10** 42.51N 2.40W
Vitória da Conquista Brazil **61** 14.53S 40.52W
Vitória Espírito Santo Brazil **59** 20.19S 40.21W
Vitré France **9** 48.07N 1.12W
Vitry-le-François France **9** 48.44N 4.35E
Vitteaux France **9** 47.24N 4.30E
Vittoria Italy **12** 36.57N 14.21E
Vittorio Veneto Italy **9** 45.59N 12.18E
Viveiro *see* Vivero Spain **10**
Vivero Spain **10** 43.40N 7.24W
Vivonne Bay *town* Australia **46** 35.58S 137.10E
Vizcaíno, Desierto de *des.* Mexico **56** 27.40N 114.40W
Vizianagaram India **29** 18.07N 83.30E
Vizinga Russian Fed. **18** 61.06N 50.05E
Vjosë *r.* Albania **13** 40.39N 19.20E
Vlaardingen Neth. **8** 51.55N 4.20E
Vladikavkaz Russian Fed. **19** 43.02N 44.43E
Vladimir Russian Fed. **18** 56.08N 40.25E
Vladimirets Ukraine **15** 51.28N 26.03E
Vladimir Volynskiy Ukraine **15** 50.51N 24.19E
Vladivostok Russian Fed. **25** 43.09N 131.53E
Vlasenica Bosnia-Herzegovina **15** 44.11N 18.56E
Vlieland *i.* Neth. **8** 53.15N 5.00E
Vlissingen Neth. **8** 51.27N 3.35E
Vlorë Albania **13** 40.28N 19.27E
Vltava *r.* Czech Republic **14** 50.22N 14.28E
Voerde Germany **8** 51.37N 6.39E
Vogelkop *f. see* Jazirah Doberai *f.* Indonesia **27**
Voghera Italy **9** 44.59N 9.01E
Voi Kenya **37** 3.23S 38.35E
Voiron France **11** 45.22N 5.35E
Volborg U.S.A. **54** 45.50N 105.40W
Volda Norway **17** 62.09N 6.06E
Volga *r.* Russian Fed. **19** 45.45N 47.50E
Volgograd Russian Fed. **19** 48.45N 44.30E
Volgogradskoye Vodokhranilishche *resr.* Russian Fed. **19** 51.00N 46.05E
Volkhov Russian Fed. **18** 59.54N 32.47E
Volkhov *r.* Russian Fed. **18** 60.15N 32.15E
Völklingen Germany **14** 49.15N 6.50E
Volkovysk Belarus **15** 53.10N 24.28E
Vollenhove Neth. **8** 52.41N 5.59E
Volnovakha Ukraine **19** 47.36N 37.32E
Volochanka Russian Fed. **21** 70.59N 94.18E
Volochisk Ukraine **15** 49.34N 26.10E
Volodarsk Russian Fed. **18** 56.14N 43.10E
Vologda Russian Fed. **18** 59.10N 39.55E
Volokolamsk Russian Fed. **18** 56.02N 35.56E
Vólos Greece **13** 39.22N 22.57E
Volovets Ukraine **15** 48.44N 23.14E
Volsk Russian Fed. **18** 52.04N 47.22E
Volta *d.* Ghana **38** 7.30N 0.25E
Volta *r.* Ghana **38** 5.50N 0.41E
Volta, L. Ghana **38** 7.00N 0.00
Volta-Noire *d.* Burkina **38** 12.30N 3.25W
Volta Redonda Brazil **59** 22.31S 44.05W
Volterra Italy **12** 43.24N 10.51E
Voltri Italy **9** 44.26N 8.45E
Volturno *r.* Italy **12** 41.02N 13.56E
Volzhskiy Russian Fed. **19** 48.48N 44.45E
Voorburg Neth. **8** 52.05N 4.22E
Vopnafjördhur *est.* Iceland **16** 65.50N 14.30W
Vopnafjördhur *town* Iceland **16** 65.46N 14.50W
Vorarlberg *d.* Austria **14** 47.15N 9.55E
Vordingborg Denmark **17** 55.01N 11.55E
Voríai Sporádhes *is.* Greece **13** 39.00N 24.00E
Vorkuta Russian Fed. **18** 67.27N 64.00E
Vormsi *i.* Estonia **17** 59.00N 23.20E
Voronezh Russian Fed. **19** 51.40N 39.13E
Voronovo Belarus **15** 54.09N 25.19E
Vosges *mts.* France **14** 48.10N 7.00E
Voss Norway **17** 60.39N 6.26E
Vostochno Sibirskoye More *sea* Russian Fed. **21** 73.00N 160.00E
Vostochnyy Sayan *mts.* Russian Fed. **24** 51.30N 102.00E
Votkinsk Russian Fed. **18** 57.02N 53.59E
Votkinskoye Vodokhranilishche *resr.* Russian Fed. **18** 57.00N 55.00E
Votuporanga Brazil **62** 20.26S 49.53W
Vouga *r.* Portugal **10** 40.41N 8.38W
Vouillé France **11** 46.38N 0.10E
Vouziers France **9** 49.24N 4.42E
Voves France **9** 48.16N 1.37E
Voxna Sweden **17** 61.20N 15.30E
Voxna *r.* Sweden **17** 61.17N 16.26E
Voyvozh Russian Fed. **18** 64.19N 55.12E
Vozhega Russian Fed. **18** 60.25N 40.11E
Voznesensk Ukraine **19** 47.34N 31.21E
Vrangelya, Ostrov *i.* Russian Fed. **21** 71.00N 180.00
Vranje Yugo. **13** 42.34N 21.52E
Vratsa Bulgaria **13** 43.12N 23.33E
Vrbas *r.* Bosnia-Herzegovina **13** 45.06N 17.29E
Vrede R.S.A. **39** 27.24S 29.09E
Vredendal R.S.A. **39** 31.40S 18.28E
Vresse Belgium **8** 49.53N 4.57E
Vries Neth. **8** 53.06N 6.35E
Vrnograč Bosnia-Herzegovina **12** 45.10N 15.56E
Vršac Yugo. **15** 45.08N 21.18E
Vryburg R.S.A. **39** 26.57S 24.42E
Vught Neth. **8** 51.39N 5.18E
Vukovar Croatia **15** 45.21N 19.00E
Vung Tau Vietnam **26** 10.21N 107.04E
Vyatka Russian Fed. **18** 58.38N 49.38E
Vyatka *r.* Russian Fed. **20** 55.40N 51.40E
Vyatskiye Polyany Russian Fed. **18** 56.14N 51.08E
Vyazma Russian Fed. **18** 55.12N 34.17E
Vyazniki Russian Fed. **18** 56.14N 42.08E
Vyborg Russian Fed. **18** 60.45N 28.41E
Vychegda *r.* Russian Fed. **18** 61.15N 46.28E
Vychodné Beskydy *mts.* Europe **15** 49.30N 22.00E
Vygozero, Ozero *l.* Russian Fed. **18** 63.30N 34.30E
Vyrnwy, L. U.K. **4** 52.46N 3.30W
Vyshka Turkmenistan **31** 39.19N 54.10E
Vyshniy-Volochek Russian Fed. **18** 57.34N 34.23E
Vytegra Russian Fed. **18** 61.04N 36.27E

W

Wa Ghana **38** 10.07N 2.28W
Waal *r.* Neth. **8** 51.45N 4.40E
Waalwijk Neth. **8** 51.42N 5.04E
Wabag P.N.G. **27** 5.28S 143.40E
Wabash U.S.A. **55** 40.47N 85.48W
Wabash *r.* U.S.A. **53** 38.25N 87.45W
Wabrzeźno Poland **15** 53.17N 18.57E
Wabush City Canada **51** 53.00N 66.50W
Waco U.S.A. **53** 31.33N 97.10W
Wad Pakistan **28** 27.21N 66.30E
Waddeneilanden *is.* Neth. **8** 53.20N 5.00E
Waddenzee *b.* Neth. **8** 53.15N 5.05E
Waddikee Australia **46** 33.18S 136.12E
Waddington, Mt. Canada **50** 51.30N 125.00W
Wadhurst U.K. **5** 51.03N 0.21E
Wādī Ḩalfā' Sudan **30** 21.56N 31.20E
Wādī Mūsá *town* Jordan **32** 30.19N 35.29E
Wad Madanī Sudan **35** 14.24N 33.30E
Wafrah Kuwait **31** 28.39N 47.56E
Wageningen Neth. **8** 51.58N 5.39E
Wager B. Canada **51** 65.26N 88.40W
Wager Bay *town* Canada **51** 65.55N 90.40W
Wagga Wagga Australia **47** 35.07S 147.24E
Wagin Australia **43** 33.18S 117.21E
Wāh Pakistan **28** 33.50N 72.44E
Wahai Indonesia **27** 2.48S 129.30E
Wahiba Sands *des.* Oman **28** 21.56N 58.55E
Wahpeton U.S.A. **53** 46.16N 96.36W
Waiau New Zealand **48** 42.39S 173.03E
Waidhofen Austria **14** 47.58N 14.47E
Waigeo *i.* Indonesia **27** 0.05S 130.30E
Waihi New Zealand **48** 37.24S 175.50E
Waikato *d.* New Zealand **48** 38.15S 175.10E
Waikato *r.* New Zealand **48** 37.19S 174.50E
Waikerie Australia **46** 34.11S 139.59E
Waikokopu New Zealand **48** 39.05S 177.50E
Waikouaiti New Zealand **48** 45.36S 170.41E
Waimakariri *r.* New Zealand **48** 43.23S 172.40E
Waimate New Zealand **48** 44.45S 171.03E
Waingapu Indonesia **27** 9.30S 120.10E
Wainwright U.S.A. **50** 70.39N 160.00W
Waiouru New Zealand **48** 39.39S 175.40E
Waipara New Zealand **48** 43.03S 172.45E
Waipawa New Zealand **48** 39.56S 176.35E
Waipiro New Zealand **48** 38.02S 178.21E
Waipu New Zealand **48** 35.59S 174.26E
Waipukurau New Zealand **48** 40.00S 176.33E
Wairau *r.* New Zealand **48** 41.32S 174.08E
Wairoa New Zealand **48** 39.03S 177.25E
Waitaki *r.* New Zealand **48** 44.56S 171.10E
Waitara New Zealand **48** 38.59S 174.13E
Waiuku New Zealand **48** 37.15S 174.44E
Wajir Kenya **37** 1.46N 40.05E
Wakatipu, L. New Zealand **48** 45.10S 168.30E
Wakayama Japan **23** 34.13N 135.11E
Wakefield U.K. **4** 53.41N 1.31W
Wakkanai Japan **25** 45.26N 141.43E
Wakre Indonesia **27** 0.30S 131.05E
Walamba Zambia **37** 13.27S 28.44E
Wałbrzych Poland **14** 50.48N 16.19E
Walcha Australia **47** 31.00S 151.36E
Walcheren *f.* Neth. **8** 51.32N 3.35E
Wałcz Poland **14** 53.17N 16.28E
Waldbröl Germany **8** 50.52N 7.34E
Waldeck Germany **14** 51.12N 9.04E
Walden U.S.A. **54** 40.34N 106.11W
Waldorf U.S.A. **55** 38.37N 76.54W
Waldport U.S.A. **54** 44.26N 124.04W
Wales *d.* U.K. **5** 52.30N 3.45W
Walgett Australia **47** 30.03S 148.10E
Walikale Zaïre **37** 1.29S 28.05E
Walker L. U.S.A. **54** 38.44N 118.43W
Wallace Idaho U.S.A. **54** 47.28N 115.55W
Wallaceburg Canada **55** 42.36N 82.23W
Wallachia *f.* Romania **15** 44.35N 25.00E
Wallambin, L. Australia **43** 30.58S 117.30E
Wallangarra Australia **47** 28.51S 151.52E
Wallaroo Australia **46** 33.57S 137.36E
Walla Walla Australia **47** 35.48S 146.52E
Walla Walla U.S.A. **54** 46.08N 118.20W
Wallis, Îles *is.* Pacific Oc. **40** 13.16S 176.15W
Wallowa U.S.A. **54** 45.34N 117.32W
Wallowa Mts. U.S.A. **54** 45.10N 117.30W
Wallsend Australia **47** 32.55S 151.40E
Walpole Australia **43** 34.57S 116.44E
Walsall U.K. **5** 52.36N 1.59W
Walsenburg U.S.A. **52** 37.37N 104.47W
Walton on the Naze U.K. **5** 51.52N 1.17E
Walton on the Wolds U.K. **4** 52.49N 0.49W
Walvis B. R.S.A. **39** 22.55S 14.30E
Walvisbaai R.S.A. **39** 22.57S 14.30E
Walvis Bay *town see* Walvisbaai R.S.A. **39**
Walvis Bay *d.* R.S.A. **39** 22.56S 14.35E
Walvis Bay *town* R.S.A. **36** 22.50S 14.31E
Wamanfo Ghana **38** 7.16N 2.44W
Wamba Kenya **37** 0.58N 37.19E
Wamba Nigeria **38** 8.57N 8.42E
Wamba Zaïre **37** 2.10N 27.59E
Wami *r.* Tanzania **37** 6.10S 38.50E
Wamsasi Indonesia **27** 3.27S 126.07E
Wan Indonesia **44** 8.23S 137.55E
Wāna Pakistan **28** 32.20N 69.32E
Wanaaring Australia **46** 29.42S 144.14E
Wanaka New Zealand **48** 44.42S 169.08E
Wanaka, L. New Zealand **48** 44.30S 169.10E
Wan'an China **25** 26.27N 114.46E
Wanapiri Indonesia **27** 4.30S 135.50E
Wanapitei *r.* Canada **55** 46.02N 80.51W
Wanapitei L. Canada **55** 46.45N 80.45W
Wanbi Australia **46** 34.46S 140.19E
Wandana Australia **46** 32.04S 133.45E
Wandoan Australia **44** 26.09S 149.51E
Wanganella Australia **47** 35.13S 144.53E
Wanganui New Zealand **48** 39.56S 175.00E
Wangaratta Australia **47** 36.22S 146.20E
Wangary Australia **46** 34.30S 135.26E
Wangerooge *i.* Germany **8** 53.50N 7.50E
Wangianna Australia **46** 29.42S 137.32E
Wantage U.K. **5** 51.35N 1.25W
Wanxian China **29** 30.52N 108.20E
Wanyuan China **29** 32.04N 108.02E
Warangal India **29** 18.00N 79.35E
Waranga Resr. Australia **47** 36.32S 145.04E
Waratah B. Australia **45** 38.55S 146.04E
Warburton *r.* Australia **45** 27.55S 137.15E
Warburton Range *mts.* S.A. Australia **46** 30.30S 134.32E
Warburton Range *mts.* W.A. Australia **42** 26.09S 126.38E
Ward Rep. of Ire. **7** 53.26N 6.20W
Warden R.S.A. **39** 27.49S 28.57E
Wardenburg Germany **8** 53.04N 8.11E
Wardha India **29** 20.41N 78.40E
Waren Germany **14** 53.31N 12.40E
Warendorf Germany **8** 51.57N 8.00E
Warialda Australia **47** 29.33S 150.36E
Wark Forest *hills* U.K. **4** 55.06N 2.24W
Warkopi Indonesia **27** 1.12S 134.09E
Warkworth New Zealand **48** 36.24S 174.40E
Warley U.K. **5** 52.29N 2.02W
Warmbad Namibia **39** 28.26S 18.41E
Warminster U.K. **5** 51.12N 2.11W
Warm Springs *town* U.S.A. **54** 39.39N 114.49W
Waroona Australia **43** 32.51S 115.50E
Warracknabeal Australia **46** 36.15S 142.28E
Warragul Australia **47** 38.11S 145.55E
Warrakalanna, L. Australia **46** 28.13S 139.23E
Warrambool *r.* Australia **47** 30.04S 147.38E
Warrego *r.* Australia **47** 30.25S 145.18E
Warrego Range *mts.* Australia **44** 24.55S 146.20E
Warren Australia **47** 31.44S 147.53E
Warren Mich. U.S.A. **55** 42.28N 83.01W
Warren Ohio U.S.A. **55** 41.15N 80.49W
Warren Penn. U.S.A. **55** 41.51N 79.08W
Warrenpoint U.K. **7** 54.06N 6.15W
Warrenton R.S.A. **39** 28.07S 24.49E
Warri Nigeria **38** 5.36N 5.46E
Warrina Australia **46** 28.10S 135.49E
Warriner Creek *r.* Australia **46** 29.15S 137.03E
Warrington U.K. **4** 53.25N 2.38W
Warrnambool Australia **46** 38.23S 142.03E
Warrumbungle Range *mts.* Australia **47** 31.20S 149.00E
Warsaw *see* Warszawa Poland **15**
Warsaw Ind. U.S.A. **55** 41.13N 85.52W
Warszawa Poland **15** 52.15N 21.00E
Warta *r.* Poland **14** 52.45N 15.09E
Warwick Australia **47** 28.12S 152.00E
Warwick U.K. **5** 52.17N 1.36W
Warwickshire *d.* U.K. **5** 52.13N 1.30W
Wasatch Plateau *f.* U.S.A. **54** 39.20N 111.30W
Wasco Calif. U.S.A. **54** 35.36N 119.20W
Wasco Oreg. U.S.A. **54** 45.35N 120.42W
Washburn L. Canada **50** 70.03N 106.50W
Washington U.K. **4** 54.55N 1.30W
Washington *d.* U.S.A. **54** 47.43N 120.00W
Washington D.C. U.S.A. **55** 38.55N 77.00W
Washington Ind. U.S.A. **55** 38.40N 87.10W
Washington N.C. U.S.A. **53** 35.33N 77.04W
Washington Utah U.S.A. **54** 37.08N 113.30W
Washington Va. U.S.A. **55** 38.43N 78.10W
Wasian Indonesia **27** 1.51S 133.21E
Wasior Indonesia **27** 2.38S 134.27E
Wasiri Indonesia **27** 7.30S 126.30E
Waskaganish Canada **55** 51.29N 78.45W
Wassenaar Neth. **8** 52.10N 4.26E
Wassy France **9** 48.30N 4.59E
Waswanipi Lac *l.* Canada **55** 49.36N 76.39W
Watampone Indonesia **27** 4.33S 120.20E
Watchet U.K. **5** 51.10N 3.20W
Waterbury U.S.A. **55** 41.33N 73.03W
Waterford Rep. of Ire. **7** 52.16N 7.08W
Waterford *d.* Rep. of Ire. **7** 52.10N 7.40W
Waterford Harbour *est.* Rep. of Ire. **7** 52.12N 6.56W
Waterloo Belgium **8** 50.44N 4.24E
Waterloo Canada **55** 43.28N 80.31W
Waterloo Iowa U.S.A. **53** 42.30N 92.20W
Watertown N.Y. U.S.A. **55** 43.59N 75.55W
Watertown S.Dak. U.S.A. **53** 44.54N 97.08W
Watervale Australia **46** 33.58S 138.39E
Waterville Rep. of Ire. **7** 51.50N 10.11W
Waterville Maine U.S.A. **55** 44.33N 69.38W
Waterville Wash. U.S.A. **54** 47.39N 120.04W
Watford U.K. **5** 51.40N 0.25W
Watrous Canada **50** 51.40N 105.29W
Watsa Zaïre **37** 3.03N 29.29E
Watson Lake *town* Canada **50** 60.07N 128.49W
Watsonville U.S.A. **54** 36.55N 121.45W
Wattiwarriganna Creek *r.* Australia **46** 28.57S 136.10E

P.N.G. 27 7.22S 146.40E
chope N.S.W. Australia 47 31.27S 152.43E
chope N.T. Australia 44 20.39S 134.13E
karinga Australia 46 32.18S 139.27E
sau U.S.A. 53 44.58N 89.40W
e Hill *town* Australia 42 17.29S 130.57E
eney *r.* U.K. 5 52.29N 1.46E
re Belgium 8 50.43N 4.37E
Sudan 35 7.40N 28.04E
weiler Germany 8 50.08N 6.20E
cross U.S.A. 53 31.08N 82.22W
, L. Australia 42 26.47S 120.21E
nesboro Penn. U.S.A. 55 39.45N 77.35W
ciers France 8 50.24N 3.05E
ar *r.* U.K. 4 54.55N 1.21W
da Indonesia 27 0.30N 127.52E
ddell Sea Antarctica 64 70.00S 40.00W
dderburn Australia 46 36.26S 143.39E
dgeport Canada 55 43.44N 66.00W
dmore U.K. 5 51.14N 2.50W
dza Zimbabwe 39 18.37S 31.33E
elde Belgium 8 51.25N 5.00E
emelah Australia 47 29.02S 149.15E
ert Neth. 8 51.14N 5.40E
e Waa Australia 47 30.34S 149.27E
gorzyno Poland 14 53.32N 15.33E
grów Poland 15 52.25N 22.01E
chang China 25 41.56N 117.34E
den in der Oberpfalz Germany 14 49.40N
.10E
fang China 25 36.44N 119.10E
hai China 25 37.30N 122.04E
lmoringle Australia 47 29.16S 146.55E
mar Germany 14 50.59N 11.20E
pa Australia 44 12.41S 141.52E
r *r.* Australia 47 29.10S 149.06E
ser U.S.A. 54 44.37N 116.58W
ssenfels Germany 14 51.12N 11.58E
ya China 24 41.50N 94.24E
herowo Poland 15 54.37N 18.15E
don U.S.A. 54 35.40N 118.20W
kom R.S.A. 39 27.59S 26.42E
land Canada 55 42.59N 79.14W
land *r.* U.K. 4 52.53N 0.00
lesley Is. Australia 44 16.42S 139.30E
lin Belgium 8 50.05N 5.07E
lingborough U.K. 5 52.18N 0.41W
lington N.S.W. Australia 47 32.33S 148.59E
lington S.A. Australia 46 35.21S 139.23E
lington New Zealand 48 41.17S 174.47E
llington *d.* New Zealand 48 40.00S 175.30E
llington Shrops. U.K. 5 52.42N 2.31W
llington Somerset U.K. 5 50.58N 3.13W
llington Nev. U.S.A. 54 38.45N 119.22W
llington, Isla *i.* Chile 63 49.30S 75.00W
lls U.K. 5 51.12N 2.39W
lls Nev. U.S.A. 54 41.07N 114.58W
llsboro U.S.A. 55 41.45N 77.18W
lls-next-the-Sea U.K. 4 52.57N 0.51E
llton U.S.A. 54 32.40N 114.08W
's Austria 14 48.10N 14.02E
shpool U.K. 5 52.40N 3.09W
lwyn Garden City U.K. 5 51.48N 0.13W
m U.K. 4 52.52N 2.45W
mbere *r.* Tanzania 37 4.07S 34.15E
mindji Canada 51 53.00N 78.42W
natchee U.S.A. 54 47.25N 120.19W
nchi Ghana 38 7.40N 2.06W
ndel U.S.A. 54 40.20N 120.14W
ndover U.S.A. 54 40.44N 114.02W
nebegon L. Canada 55 47.24N 83.08W
nlock *r.* Australia 44 12.02S 141.55E
nquan China 29 33.13N 91.50E
nshan China 29 23.25N 104.15E
nsleydale *f.* U.K. 4 54.19N 2.04W
ntworth Australia 46 34.06S 141.56E
nzhou China 25 28.02N 120.40E
ott U.S.A. 54 40.19N 123.54W
epener R.S.A. 39 29.43S 27.01E
erda Botswana 39 25.15S 23.16E
erdohl Germany 8 51.16N 7.47E
eri Indonesia 27 3.10S 132.30E
erne Germany 8 51.39N 7.36E
erra *r.* Germany 14 51.26N 9.39E
erribee Australia 47 37.54S 144.40E
erris Creek *town* Australia 47 31.20S 150.41E
esel Germany 8 51.39N 6.37E
eser *r.* Germany 14 53.15N 8.30E
essel, C. Australia 44 10.59S 136.46E
essel Is. Australia 44 11.30S 136.25E
est Bank Jordan 32 32.00N 35.25E
est Bengal *d.* India 29 23.00N 87.40E
est Bromwich U.K. 5 52.32N 2.01W
estbrook U.S.A. 55 43.41N 70.21W
est Coast *d.* New Zealand 48 43.15S 170.10E
estende Belgium 8 51.10N 2.46E
estern *d.* Ghana 38 6.00N 2.40W
estern *d.* Kenya 37 0.30N 34.30E
estern Australia *d.* Australia 42 24.20S
22.30E
estern Ghāts *mts.* India 28 15.30N 74.30E
estern Isles *d.* U.K. 6 57.40N 7.10W
estern Sahara Africa 34 25.00N 13.30W
estern Samoa Pacific Oc. 40 13.55S 172.00W
esterschelde *est.* Neth. 8 51.25N 3.40E
esterstede Germany 8 53.15N 7.56E
esterwald *f.* Germany 8 50.40N 8.00E
est Falkland *i.* Falkland Is. 63 51.40S 60.00W
est Felton U.K. 4 52.49N 2.58W
estfield Mass. U.S.A. 55 42.07N 72.45W
estfield Penn. U.S.A. 55 41.55N 77.32W
est Frisian Is. *see* Waddeneilanden Neth. 14
est Glamorgan *d.* U.K. 5 51.42N 3.47W
est Lafayette U.S.A. 55 40.26N 86.56W
est Linton U.K. 6 55.45N 3.21W
estmeath *d.* Rep. of Ire. 7 53.30N 7.30W
est Midlands *d.* U.K. 5 52.28N 1.50W
estmoreland Australia 44 17.18S 138.12E
est Nicholson Zimbabwe 39 21.06S 29.25E
Weston Malaysia 26 5.14N 115.35E
Weston-Super-Mare U.K. 5 51.20N 2.59W
West Palm Beach *town* U.S.A. 53 26.42N 80.05W
Westport New Zealand 48 41.46S 171.38E
Westport Rep. of Ire. 7 53.48N 9.32W
Westport Wash. U.S.A. 54 46.53N 124.06W
Westray *i.* U.K. 6 59.18N 2.58W
West Siberian Plain *f. see* Zapadno-Sibirskaya *Ravnina* Russian Fed. 20
West Sussex *d.* U.K. 5 50.58N 0.30W
West Terschelling Neth. 8 53.22N 5.13E
West Virginia *d.* U.S.A. 53 38.45N 80.30W
West Vlaanderen *d.* Belgium 8 51.00N 3.00E
West Wyalong Australia 47 33.54S 147.12E
West Yellowstone U.S.A. 54 44.30N 111.05W
West Yorkshire *d.* U.K. 4 53.45N 1.40W
Wetar *i.* Indonesia 27 7.45S 126.00E
Wetaskiwin Canada 50 52.57N 113.20W
Wetteren Belgium 8 51.00N 3.51E
Wetzlar Germany 14 50.33N 8.30E
Wewak P.N.G. 27 3.35S 143.35E
Wexford Rep. of Ire. 7 52.20N 6.28W
Wexford *d.* Rep. of Ire. 7 52.20N 6.25W
Wexford B. Rep. of Ire. 7 52.27N 6.18W
Weyburn Canada 50 49.41N 103.52W
Weymouth U.K. 5 50.36N 2.28W
Weymouth, C. Australia 44 12.32S 143.36E
Whakatane New Zealand 48 37.56S 177.00E
Whalan *r.* Australia 47 29.10S 148.42E
Whale Cove *town* Canada 51 62.30N 93.00W
Whalsay *i.* U.K. 6 60.22N 0.59W
Whangarei New Zealand 48 35.43S 174.20E
Wharfe *r.* U.K. 4 53.50N 1.07W
Wharfedale *f.* U.K. 4 54.00N 1.55W
Whataroa New Zealand 48 43.16S 170.22E
Wheeler Peak *mtn.* Nev. U.S.A. 54 38.59N 114.19W
Wheeler Peak *mtn.* N.Mex. U.S.A. 52 36.34N 105.25W
Wheeler Ridge *town* U.S.A. 54 35.06N 119.01W
Wheeler Springs *town* U.S.A. 54 34.30N 119.18W
Wheeling U.S.A. 55 40.05N 80.43W
Whernside *mtn.* U.K. 4 54.14N 2.25W
Whidbey Is. Australia 46 34.50S 135.00E
Whitburn U.K. 6 55.52N 3.41W
Whitby Canada 55 43.52N 78.56W
Whitby U.K. 4 54.29N 0.37W
Whitchurch Shrops. U.K. 4 52.58N 2.42W
White *r.* Ark. U.S.A. 53 33.53N 91.10W
White *r.* Ind. U.S.A. 55 38.29N 87.45W
White *r.* S.Dak. U.S.A. 52 43.40N 99.30W
White *r.* Utah U.S.A. 52 40.04N 109.41W
White Cliffs *town* Australia 46 30.51S 143.05E
Whitefish U.S.A. 54 48.25N 114.20W
Whitefish B. U.S.A. 55 46.32N 84.45W
Whitehall Mont. U.S.A. 54 45.52N 112.06W
Whitehaven U.K. 4 54.33N 3.35W
Whitehorse Canada 50 60.41N 135.08W
White, L. Australia 42 21.05S 129.00E
Whitemark Australia 45 40.07S 148.00E
White Mountain Peak U.S.A. 54 37.38N 118.15W
White Mts. Calif. U.S.A. 54 37.30N 118.15W
White Plains *town* U.S.A. 55 41.02N 73.46W
White Sea *see* Beloye More *sea* Russian Fed. 18
White Volta *r.* Ghana 38 9.13N 1.15W
Whitewater Baldy *mtn.* U.S.A. 54 33.20N 108.39W
Whitfield Australia 47 36.49S 146.22E
Whithorn U.K. 6 54.44N 4.25W
Whitianga New Zealand 48 36.50S 175.42E
Whitley Bay *town* U.K. 4 55.03N 1.25W
Whitney Canada 55 45.30N 78.14W
Whitney, Mt. U.S.A. 54 36.35N 118.18W
Whitstable U.K. 5 51.21N 1.02E
Whitsunday I. Australia 44 20.17S 148.59E
Whittier U.S.A. 50 60.46N 148.41W
Whittlesea Australia 47 37.31S 145.08E
Whitton U.K. 4 53.42N 0.39W
Wholdaia L. Canada 50 60.43N 104.10W
Whyalla Australia 46 33.02S 137.35E
Wichita U.S.A. 53 37.43N 97.20W
Wichita Falls *town* U.S.A. 52 33.55N 98.30W
Wick U.K. 6 58.26N 3.06W
Wickenburg U.S.A. 54 33.58N 112.44W
Wickepin Australia 43 32.45S 117.31E
Wicklow Rep. of Ire. 7 52.59N 6.03W
Wicklow *d.* Rep. of Ire. 7 52.59N 6.25W
Wicklow Head Rep. of Ire. 7 52.58N 6.00W
Wicklow Mts. Rep. of Ire. 7 53.06N 6.20W
Widgiemooltha Australia 43 31.30S 121.34E
Widnes U.K. 4 53.22N 2.44W
Wiehl Germany 8 50.57N 7.32E
Wieluń Poland 15 51.14N 18.34E
Wien Austria 14 48.13N 16.22E
Wiener Neustadt Austria 14 47.49N 16.15E
Wieprz *r.* Poland 15 51.34N 21.49E
Wiesbaden Germany 14 50.05N 8.15E
Wigan U.K. 4 53.33N 2.38W
Wight, Isle of U.K. 3 50.40N 1.17W
Wigton U.K. 4 54.50N 3.09W
Wigtown U.K. 6 54.47N 4.26W
Wigtown B. U.K. 6 54.47N 4.15W
Wilcannia Australia 46 31.33S 143.24E
Wildhorn *mtn.* Switz. 11 46.22N 7.22E
Wildon Austria 14 46.53N 15.31E
Wildspitze *mtn.* Austria 14 46.55N 10.55E
Wildwood U.S.A. 55 38.59N 74.49W
Wilgena Australia 46 30.46S 134.44E
Wilhelm II Land Antarctica 64 68.00S 89.00E
Wilhelm, Mt. P.N.G. 27 6.00S 144.55E
Wilhelmshaven Germany 8 53.32N 8.07E
Wilkes-Barre U.S.A. 55 41.15N 75.50W
Wilkes Land *f.* Antarctica 64 69.00S 120.00E
Wilkie Canada 50 52.27N 108.42W
Wilkinsburg U.S.A. 55 40.27N 79.53W
Wilkinson Lakes Australia 45 29.40S 132.39E
Willandra Billabong *r.* Australia 46 33.08S 144.06E
Willemstad Neth. Antilles 60 12.12N 68.56W
Willeroo Australia 42 15.17S 131.35E
William Creek *town* Australia 46 28.52S 136.18E
William, Mt. Australia 46 37.20S 142.41E
Williams Australia 43 33.01S 116.45E
Williams *r.* Australia 43 32.59S 116.24E
Williams Lake *town* Canada 50 52.08N 122.09W
Williamsport Penn. U.S.A. 55 41.14N 77.00W
Willis Group *is.* Australia 44 16.18S 150.00E
Williston R.S.A. 39 31.21S 20.53E
Williston U.S.A. 52 48.09N 103.37W
Williston L. Canada 50 55.00N 126.00W
Willits U.S.A. 54 39.25N 123.21W
Willmar U.S.A. 53 45.06N 95.00W
Willochra Australia 46 32.12S 138.10E
Willochra *r.* Australia 46 31.57S 137.52E
Willow U.S.A. 50 61.42N 150.08W
Willowmore R.S.A. 39 33.18S 23.28E
Willow Ranch U.S.A. 54 41.55N 120.21W
Willunga Australia 46 35.18S 138.33E
Wilmington Del. U.S.A. 55 39.44N 75.33W
Wilmington N.C. U.S.A. 53 34.14N 77.55W
Wilmslow U.K. 4 53.19N 2.14W
Wilpena *r.* Australia 46 31.13S 139.25E
Wilson's Promontory *c.* Australia 47 39.06S 146.23E
Wilton *r.* Australia 44 14.45S 134.33E
Wilton U.K. 5 51.05N 1.52W
Wiltshire *d.* U.K. 5 51.20N 0.34W
Wiltz Lux. 8 49.59N 5.53E
Wiluna Australia 42 26.36S 120.13E
Wimmera *r.* Australia 46 36.05S 141.56E
Winam *b.* Kenya 37 0.15S 34.30E
Winburg R.S.A. 39 28.30S 27.01E
Wincanton U.K. 5 51.03N 2.24W
Winchester U.K. 5 51.04N 1.19W
Winchester Va. U.S.A. 55 39.11N 78.10W
Winchester Wyo. U.S.A. 54 43.51N 108.10W
Windermere *l.* U.K. 4 54.20N 2.56W
Windhoek Namibia 39 22.34S 17.06E
Windorah Australia 44 25.26S 142.39E
Wind River Range *mts.* U.S.A. 54 43.05N 109.25W
Windsor Australia 47 33.38S 150.47E
Windsor Ont. Canada 55 42.18N 83.01W
Windsor Que. Canada 55 45.35N 72.01W
Windsor U.K. 5 51.29N 0.38W
Windward Is. C. America 57 13.00N 60.00W
Windward Passage *str.* Carib. Sea 57 20.00N 74.00W
Wingen Australia 47 31.43S 150.54E
Wingham Australia 47 31.50S 152.20E
Wingham Canada 55 43.53N 81.19W
Winifred U.S.A. 54 47.34N 109.23W
Winisk Canada 51 55.15N 85.12W
Winisk *r.* Canada 51 55.20N 85.20W
Winisk L. Canada 51 52.55N 87.22W
Winneba Ghana 38 5.22N 0.38W
Winnebago, L. U.S.A. 53 44.00N 88.25W
Winnemucca U.S.A. 52 40.58N 117.45W
Winnemucca L. U.S.A. 54 40.09N 119.20W
Winnipeg Canada 51 49.53N 97.10W
Winnipeg, L. Canada 51 52.45N 98.00W
Winnipegosis, L. Canada 51 52.00N 100.00W
Winona Minn. U.S.A. 53 44.02N 91.37W
Winooski U.S.A. 55 44.29N 73.11W
Winschoten Neth. 8 53.07N 7.02E
Winsford U.K. 4 53.12N 2.31W
Winslow Ariz. U.S.A. 54 35.01N 110.42W
Winslow Maine U.S.A. 55 44.32N 69.38W
Winston U.S.A. 54 46.28N 111.38W
Winston-Salem U.S.A. 53 36.05N 80.05W
Winsum Neth. 8 53.20N 6.31E
Winterswijk Neth. 8 51.58N 6.44E
Winterthur Switz. 14 47.30N 8.45E
Winthrop Wash. U.S.A. 54 48.29N 120.11W
Winton Australia 44 22.22S 143.00E
Winton New Zealand 48 46.10S 168.20E
Winton U.S.A. 54 41.45N 109.10W
Wirrabara Australia 46 33.03S 138.18E
Wirraminna Australia 46 31.11S 136.04E
Wirrappa Australia 46 31.28S 137.00E
Wirrega Australia 46 36.11S 140.37E
Wirrida, L. Australia 46 29.45S 134.39E
Wirulla Australia 46 32.24S 134.33E
Wisbech U.K. 5 52.39N 0.10E
Wisconsin *d.* U.S.A. 53 45.00N 90.00W
Wisconsin Rapids *town* U.S.A. 53 44.24N 89.55W
Wisdom U.S.A. 54 45.37N 113.27W
Wisła *r.* Poland 15 54.23N 18.52E
Wismar Germany 14 53.54N 11.28E
Wisznice Poland 15 51.48N 23.12E
Witham *r.* U.K. 4 52.56N 0.04E
Withernsea U.K. 4 53.43N 0.02E
Witkowo Poland 15 52.27N 17.47E
Witney U.K. 5 51.47N 1.29W
Witsand R.S.A. 39 34.23S 20.49E
Witten Germany 8 51.26N 7.19E
Wittenberg Germany 14 51.53N 12.39E
Wittenberge Germany 14 52.59N 11.45E
Wittenoom Australia 42 22.19S 118.21E
Wittlich Germany 8 49.59N 6.54E
Witu Kenya 37 2.22S 40.20E
Witvlei Namibia 39 22.25S 18.29E
Wiveliscombe U.K. 5 51.02N 3.20W
Wkra *r.* Poland 15 52.27N 20.44E
Władysławowo Poland 15 54.49N 18.25E
Włocławek Poland 15 52.39N 19.01E
Włodawa Poland 15 51.33N 23.31E
Wodonga Australia 47 36.08S 146.09E
Woerden Neth. 8 52.07N 4.55E
Wokam *i.* Indonesia 27 5.45S 134.30E
Woking U.K. 5 51.20N 0.34W
Wolf Creek *town* U.S.A. 54 46.50N 112.20W
Wolfenbüttel Germany 14 52.10N 10.33E
Wolf Point *town* U.S.A. 54 48.05N 105.39W
Wolfsberg Austria 14 46.51N 14.51E
Wolfsburg Germany 14 52.27N 10.49E
Wolin Poland 14 53.51N 14.38E
Wollaston L. Canada 50 58.15N 103.30W
Wollaston Pen. Canada 50 70.00N 115.00W
Wollongong Australia 47 34.25S 150.52E
Wolmaransstad R.S.A. 39 27.11S 25.58E
Wołomin Poland 15 52.21N 21.14E
Wolseley Australia 46 36.21S 140.55E
Wolvega Neth. 8 52.53N 6.00E
Wolverhampton U.K. 5 52.35N 2.06W
Wondai Australia 44 26.19S 151.52E
Wongan Hills *town* Australia 43 30.55S 116.41E
Wŏnsan N. Korea 25 39.07N 127.26E
Wonthaggi Australia 47 38.38S 145.37E
Woocalla Australia 46 31.44S 137.10E
Woodbridge U.K. 5 52.06N 1.19E
Woodbridge U.S.A. 55 38.39N 77.15W
Woodburn Australia 47 29.04S 153.21E
Wooded Bluff *f.* Australia 47 29.22S 153.22E
Woodenbong Australia 47 28.28S 152.35E
Woodland U.S.A. 54 38.41N 121.46W
Woodlark I. P.N.G. 44 9.05S 152.50E
Woodroffe, Mt. Australia 44 26.20S 131.45E
Woodside Australia 47 38.31S 146.52E
Woods, L. Australia 44 17.50S 133.30E
Woods, L. of the Canada/U.S.A. 51 49.15N 94.45W
Woodstock Canada 55 43.08N 80.45W
Woodstock U.K. 5 51.51N 1.20W
Woodville New Zealand 48 40.20S 175.52E
Wooler U.K. 4 55.33N 2.01W
Woolgoolga Australia 47 30.07S 153.12E
Wooltana Australia 46 30.28S 139.26E
Woomera Australia 46 31.11S 136.54E
Woonsocket U.S.A. 55 42.00N 71.31W
Wooramel Australia 42 25.42S 114.20E
Wooramel *r.* Australia 42 25.47S 114.10E
Woorong, L. Australia 46 29.24S 134.06E
Worcester R.S.A. 39 33.39S 19.25E
Worcester U.K. 5 52.12N 2.12W
Worcester U.S.A. 55 42.16N 71.48W
Workington U.K. 4 54.39N 3.34W
Worksop U.K. 4 53.19N 1.09W
Workum Neth. 8 53.00N 5.26E
Worland U.S.A. 54 44.01N 107.57W
Worms Germany 14 49.38N 8.23E
Worthing U.K. 5 50.49N 0.21W
Worthington Minn. U.S.A. 53 43.37N 95.36W
Worthington Ohio U.S.A. 55 40.03N 83.03W
Worthville U.S.A. 55 38.38N 85.05W
Wosi Indonesia 27 0.15S 128.00E
Woutchaba Cameroon 38 5.13N 13.05E
Wowoni *i.* Indonesia 27 4.10S 123.10E
Wragby U.K. 4 53.17N 0.18E
Wrangel I. *see* Vrangelya, Ostrov *i.* Russian Fed. 21
Wrangell U.S.A. 50 56.28N 132.23W
Wrangell Mts. U.S.A. 50 62.00N 143.00W
Wrangle U.K. 4 53.03N 0.09E
Wrath, C. U.K. 6 58.37N 5.01W
Wrexham U.K. 4 53.05N 3.00W
Wrigley Canada 50 63.16N 123.39W
Wrocław Poland 15 51.05N 17.00E
Wronki Poland 14 52.43N 16.23E
Września Poland 15 52.20N 17.34E
Wubin Australia 43 30.06S 116.38E
Wuchang China 25 30.32N 114.18E
Wudham 'Alwā' Oman 31 23.48N 57.33E
Wudinna Australia 46 33.03S 135.28E
Wuhan China 25 30.35N 114.19E
Wuhu China 25 31.23N 118.25E
Wu Jiang *r.* China 24 30.10N 107.26E
Wukari Nigeria 38 7.57N 9.42E
Wuliang Shan *mts.* China 24 24.27N 100.43E
Wum Cameroon 38 6.25N 10.03E
Wumbulgal Australia 47 34.25S 146.16E
Wuppertal Germany 8 51.15N 7.10E
Wuppertal R.S.A. 39 32.16S 19.12E
Wurno Nigeria 38 13.20N 5.28E
Würzburg Germany 14 49.48N 9.57E
Wutongqiao China 24 29.21N 103.48E
Wuwei China 24 38.00N 102.54E
Wuxi Jiangsu China 25 31.35N 120.19E
Wuzhan China 25 50.14N 125.18E
Wuzhou China 25 23.30N 111.21E
Wyalkatchem Australia 43 31.21S 117.22E
Wyalong Australia 47 33.55S 147.17E
Wyandotte U.S.A. 55 42.11N 83.10W
Wyandra Australia 45 27.15S 146.00E
Wyangala Resr. Australia 47 33.58S 148.55E
Wyara, L. Australia 46 28.42S 144.16E
Wycheproof Australia 46 36.04S 143.14E
Wye U.K. 5 51.11N 0.56E
Wye *r.* U.K. 5 51.37N 2.40W
Wymondham U.K. 5 52.34N 1.07E
Wynbring Australia 45 30.33S 133.32E
Wyndham Australia 42 15.29S 128.05E
Wyoming *d.* U.S.A. 52 43.10N 107.36W
Wyong Australia 47 33.17S 151.25E
Wyszków Poland 15 52.36N 21.28E

X

Xainza China 24 30.56N 88.38E
Xai-Xai Mozambique 39 25.05S 33.38E
Xam Nua Laos 29 20.25N 104.04E
Xangongo Angola 36 16.43S 15.01E
Xanten Germany 8 51.40N 6.29E
Xánthi Greece 13 41.07N 24.55E
Xau, L. Botswana 39 21.15S 24.50E
Xenia U.S.A. 55 39.41N 83.56W
Xhora R.S.A. 39 31.58S 28.40E
Xiaguan *see* Dali China 24
Xiamen China 25 24.26N 118.07E
Xi'an China 25 34.16N 108.54E
Xiangfan China 25 32.20N 112.05E
Xiangkhoang Laos 29 19.11N 103.23E
Xiangtan China 25 27.55N 112.47E
Xiangyin China 25 28.40N 112.53E
Xianyang China 25 34.23N 108.40E
Xiao Hinggan Ling *mts.* China 25 48.40N 128.30E
Xichang China 24 27.53N 102.18E
Xigazê China 24 29.18N 88.50E
Xi Jiang *r.* China 25 22.23N 113.20E
Xilin China 29 24.30N 105.03E
Ximeng China 29 22.45N 99.29E
Xinfeng Jiangxi China 25 25.27N 114.58E
Xing'an China 25 25.37N 110.40E
Xingkai Hu *l. see* Khanka, Ozero China/Russian Fed. 25
Xingtai China 25 37.08N 114.29E
Xingu *r.* Brazil 61 1.40S 52.15W
Xinhe Xin. Uygur China 24 41.34N 82.38E
Xining China 24 36.35N 101.55E
Xinjiang Uygur Zizhiqu *d.* China 24 41.15N 87.00E
Xinjin Liaoning China 25 39.25N 121.58E
Xin Xian China 25 38.24N 112.47E
Xinxiang China 25 35.16N 113.51E
Xinyu China 25 27.48N 114.56E
Xinzhu Taiwan 25 24.48N 120.59E
Xique Xique Brazil 61 10.47S 42.44W
Xixabangma Feng *mtn.* China 29 28.21N 85.47E
Xizang Zizhiqu *d.* China 29 32.20N 86.00E
Xorkol China 24 39.04N 91.05E
Xuanhua China 25 40.36N 115.01E
Xuchang China 25 34.03N 113.48E
Xueshuiwen China 25 49.15N 129.39E
Xugou China 25 34.42N 119.28E
Xuyong China 24 28.10N 105.24E
Xuzhou China 25 34.17N 117.18E

Y

Ya'an China 29 30.00N 102.59E
Yaapeet Australia 46 35.48S 142.07E
Yabassi Cameroon 38 4.30N 9.55E
Yablonovyy Khrebet *mts.* Russian Fed. 21 53.20N 115.00E
Yabrūd Syria 32 33.58N 36.40E
Yacheng China 25 18.30N 109.12E
Yacuiba Bolivia 62 22.00S 63.25W
Yādgīr India 28 16.46N 77.08E
Yagaba Ghana 38 10.13N 1.14W
Yagoua Cameroon 38 10.23N 15.13E
Yahagi *r.* Japan 23 34.50N 136.59E
Yaizu Japan 23 34.52N 138.20E
Yajua Nigeria 38 11.27N 12.49E
Yakima U.S.A. 54 46.36N 120.31W
Yaksha Russian Fed. 18 61.51N 56.59E
Yakutat U.S.A. 50 59.33N 139.44W
Yakutsk Russian Fed. 21 62.10N 129.20E
Yala Thailand 29 6.32N 101.19E
Yalgoo Australia 43 28.20S 116.41E
Yalinga C.A.R. 35 6.31N 23.15E
Yallourn Australia 47 38.09S 146.22E
Yalong Jiang *r.* China 24 26.35N 101.44E
Yalta Ukraine 19 44.30N 34.09E
Yalutorovsk Russian Fed. 20 56.41N 66.12E
Yamal, Poluostrov *pen.* Russian Fed. 20 70.20N 70.00E
Yamanashi Japan 23 35.40N 138.40E
Yamanashi *d.* Japan 23 35.30N 138.35E
Yaman Tau *mtn.* Russian Fed. 19 54.20N 58.10E
Yamato Japan 23 35.29N 139.29E
Yamato-takada Japan 23 34.31N 135.45E
Yamba N.S.W. Australia 47 29.26S 153.22E
Yamba S.A. Australia 46 34.15S 140.54E
Yambio Sudan 35 4.34N 28.23E
Yambol Bulgaria 13 42.28N 26.30E
Yamdena *i.* Indonesia 27 7.30S 131.00E
Yamethin Myanmar 29 20.24N 96.08E
Yam Kinneret *l.* Israel 32 32.49N 35.36E
Yamma Yamma, L. Australia 44 26.20S 141.25E
Yamoussoukro Côte d'Ivoire 38 6.51N 5.18W
Yampi Sound Australia 42 16.11S 123.30E
Yampol Ukraine 15 48.13N 28.12E
Yamuna *r.* India 29 25.20N 81.49E
Yan Nigeria 38 10.05N 12.11E
Yana *r.* Russian Fed. 21 71.30N 135.00E
Yanac Australia 46 36.09S 141.29E
Yanbu'al Baḩr Saudi Arabia 30 24.07N 38.04E
Yancannia Australia 46 30.16S 142.50E
Yancheng China 25 33.23N 120.10E
Yanchep Australia 43 31.32S 115.33E
Yanchuan China 25 36.55N 110.04E
Yanco Australia 47 34.36S 146.25E
Yanco Glen *town* Australia 46 31.43S 141.39E
Yanda *r.* Australia 47 30.22S 145.38E
Yangarey Russian Fed. 18 68.46N 61.29E
Yangjiang China 25 21.51N 111.58E
Yangon Myanmar 29 16.45N 96.20E
Yangquan China 25 37.52N 113.29E
Yangtze *r. see* Chang Jiang *r.* China 25
Yanji China 25 42.45N 129.25E
Yanko Creek *r.* Australia 47 35.25S 145.27E
Yanqi China 24 42.00N 86.30E
Yanshan China 29 23.36N 104.20E
Yanskiy Zaliv *g.* Russian Fed. 21 72.00N 136.10E
Yantabulla Australia 47 29.13S 145.01E
Yantai China 25 37.30N 121.22E
Yao Chad 34 12.52N 17.34E
Yao Japan 23 34.37N 135.36E
Yaoundé Cameroon 38 3.51N 11.31E
Yap *i.* Federated States of Micronesia 27 9.30N 138.09E
Yapen *i.* Indonesia 27 1.45S 136.10E
Yaqui *r.* Mexico 56 27.37N 110.39W
Yar Russian Fed. 18 58.13N 52.08E
Yaraka Australia 44 24.53S 144.04E
Yaransk Russian Fed. 18 57.22N 47.49E
Yardea Australia 46 32.23S 135.32E
Yare *r.* U.K. 5 52.34N 1.45E
Yaremcha Ukraine 15 48.26N 24.29E
Yarensk Russian Fed. 18 62.10N 49.07E

Yargora Moldova **15** 46.25N 28.20E
Yaritagua Venezuela **60** 10.05N 69.07W
Yarkant He *r.* China **24** 40.30N 80.55E
Yarlung Zangbo Jiang *r.* China *See* Brahmaputra *r.* Asia **29**
Yarmouth Canada **55** 43.50N 66.08W
Yaroslavl Russian Fed. **18** 57.34N 39.52E
Yarra *r.* Australia **47** 37.51S 144.54E
Yarram Australia **47** 38.30S 146.41E
Yarrawonga Australia **47** 36.02S 145.59E
Yarrow *r.* U.K. **6** 55.32N 2.51W
Yar Sale Russian Fed. **20** 66.50N 70.48E
Yartsevo Russian Fed. **18** 55.06N 32.43E
Yartsevo Russian Fed. **21** 60.17N 90.02E
Yarumal Colombia **60** 6.59N 75.25W
Yaselda *r.* Belarus **15** 52.07N 26.28E
Yasen Belarus **15** 53.10N 28.55E
Yashi Nigeria **38** 12.23N 7.54E
Yashkul Russian Fed. **19** 46.10N 45.20E
Yasinya Ukraine **15** 48.12N 24.20E
Yasothon Thailand **29** 15.46N 104.12E
Yass Australia **47** 34.51S 148.55E
Yatakala Niger **38** 14.52N 0.22E
Yaví, Cerro *mtn.* Venezuela **60** 5.32N 65.59W
Yavorov Ukraine **15** 49.59N 23.20E
Ya Xian *see* Sanya China **25**
Yazd Iran **31** 31.54N 54.22E
Ybbs Austria **14** 48.11N 15.05E
Ye Myanmar **29** 15.15N 97.50E
Yea Australia **47** 37.12S 145.25E
Yecla Spain **10** 38.35N 1.05W
Yedintsy Moldova **19** 48.09N 27.18E
Yeeda Australia **42** 17.36S 123.39E
Yefremov Russian Fed. **18** 53.08N 38.08E
Yegorlyk *r.* Russian Fed. **19** 46.30N 41.52E
Yegoryevsk Russian Fed. **18** 55.21N 39.01E
Yegros Paraguay **59** 26.24S 56.25W
Yei Sudan **35** 4.05N 30.40E
Yei *r.* Sudan **35** 7.40N 30.13E
Yekaterinburg Russian Fed. **18** 56.52N 60.35E
Yelets Russian Fed. **18** 52.36N 38.30E
Yeletskiy Russian Fed. **18** 67.04N 64.00E
Yell *i.* U.K. **6** 60.35N 1.05W
Yellowdine Australia **43** 31.19S 119.36E
Yellowhead Pass Canada **50** 52.53N 118.28W
Yellowknife Canada **50** 62.30N 114.29W
Yellow Mt. Australia **47** 32.19S 146.50E
Yellowstone *r.* U.S.A. **52** 47.55N 103.45W
Yellowstone *r.* U.S.A. **54** 47.58N 103.59W
Yellowstone L. U.S.A. **54** 44.25N 110.38W
Yellowstone Nat. Park U.S.A. **54** 44.30N 110.35W
Yell Sd. U.K. **6** 60.30N 1.11W
Yelma Australia **42** 26.30S 121.40E
Yelsk Belarus **15** 51.50N 29.10E
Yelwa Nigeria **38** 10.48N 4.42E
Yemen Asia **35** 14.20N 45.50E
Yemilchino Ukraine **15** 50.58N 27.40E
Yenagoa Nigeria **38** 4.59N 6.15E
Yenda Australia **47** 34.15S 146.13E
Yendi Ghana **38** 9.29N 0.01W
Yenisey *r.* Russian Fed. **21** 69.00N 86.00E
Yeniseysk Russian Fed. **21** 58.27N 92.13E
Yeniseyskiy Zaliv *g.* Russian Fed. **20** 73.00N 79.00E
Yenyuka Russian Fed. **21** 57.57N 121.15E
Yeo L. Australia **43** 28.04S 124.23E
Yeoval Australia **47** 32.44S 148.39E
Yeovil U.K. **5** 50.57N 2.38W
Yeppoon Australia **44** 23.08S 150.45E
Yerbent Turkmenistan **31** 39.23N 58.35E
Yercha Russian Fed. **21** 69.34N 147.30E
Yerda Australia **46** 31.05S 135.04E
Yerepol Russian Fed. **21** 65.15N 168.43E
Yerevan Armenia **31** 40.10N 44.31E
Yerington U.S.A. **54** 38.59N 119.10W
Yermak Kazakhstan **20** 52.03N 76.55E
Yermitsa Russian Fed. **18** 66.56N 52.20E
Yermo U.S.A. **54** 34.54N 116.50W
Yershov Russian Fed. **19** 51.22N 48.16E
Yertom Russian Fed. **18** 63.31N 47.51E
Yerushalayim Israel/Jordan **32** 31.47N 35.13E
Yeşil *r.* Turkey **30** 41.22N 36.37E
Yessey Russian Fed. **21** 68.29N 102.15E
Yetman Australia **47** 28.55S 150.49E
Yeu Myanmar **29** 22.49N 95.26E
Yeu, Île d' *i.* France **11** 46.43N 2.20W
Yevpatoriya Ukraine **19** 45.12N 33.20E
Yevstratovskiy Russian Fed. **19** 50.07N 39.45E
Yeysk Russian Fed. **19** 46.43N 38.17E
Yi *r.* Uruguay **63** 33.17S 58.08W
Yiannitsá Greece **13** 40.48N 22.25E
Yibin China **24** 28.50N 104.35E
Yichang China **25** 30.43N 111.22E
Yilan China **25** 46.22N 129.31E
Yilehuli Shan *mts.* China **25** 51.20N 124.20E
Yilliminning Australia **43** 32.54S 117.22E
Yinchuan China **24** 38.30N 106.19E
Yindarlgooda, L. Australia **43** 30.45S 121.55E
Yingde China **25** 24.20N 113.20E
Yingkou China **25** 40.40N 122.17E
Yingtan China **25** 28.14N 117.00E
Yinkanie Australia **46** 34.21S 140.20E
Yinning China **24** 43.57N 81.23E
Yíthion Greece **13** 36.46N 22.34E
Yiyang Hunan China **25** 28.36N 112.20E
Ylitornio Finland **16** 66.19N 23.40E
Ylivieska Finland **16** 64.05N 24.33E
Yobe *d.* Nigeria **38** 12.30N 11.45E
Yodo *r.* Japan **23** 34.41N 135.25E
Yogyakarta Indonesia **26** 7.48S 110.24E
Yokadouma Cameroon **38** 3.26N 15.06E
Yokkaichi Japan **23** 34.58N 136.37E
Yoko Cameroon **38** 5.29N 12.19E
Yokohama Japan **23** 35.27N 139.39E
Yokosuka Japan **23** 35.18N 139.40E
Yola Nigeria **38** 9.14N 12.32E
Yongxiu China **25** 29.03N 115.49E
Yonkers U.S.A. **55** 40.56N 73.54W
Yonne *d.* France **9** 47.55N 3.45E
Yonne *r.* France **9** 48.22N 2.57E
York Australia **43** 31.55S 116.45E
York U.K. **4** 53.58N 1.07W
York Penn. U.S.A. **55** 39.58N 76.44W
York, C. Australia **44** 10.42S 142.31E
Yorke Pen. Australia **46** 35.00S 137.30E
Yorketown Australia **46** 35.02S 137.35E
York Factory *town* Canada **51** 57.08N 92.25W
Yorkshire Wolds *hills* U.K. **4** 54.00N 0.39W
Yorkton Canada **50** 51.12N 102.29W
Yoro Honduras **57** 15.09N 87.07W
Yōrō Japan **23** 35.32N 140.04E
Yosemite Nat. Park U.S.A. **54** 37.45N 119.35W
Yoshino *r.* Japan **23** 34.22N 135.40E
Yoshkar Ola Russian Fed. **18** 56.38N 47.52E
Yos Sudarsa, Pulau *i.* Indonesia **27** 8.00S 138.30E
Yōsu S. Korea **25** 34.46N 127.45E
Youghal Rep. of Ire. **7** 51.58N 7.51W
You Jiang *r.* Guang. Zhuang. China **25** 23.25N 110.00E
Young Australia **47** 34.19S 148.20E
Young *r.* Australia **43** 33.45S 121.12E
Young Uruguay **63** 32.41S 57.38W
Young U.S.A. **54** 34.06N 110.57W
Younghusband, L. Australia **46** 30.51S 136.05E
Younghusband Pen. Australia **46** 36.00S 139.15E
Youngstown U.S.A. **55** 41.05N 80.40W
Yoxford U.K. **5** 52.16N 1.30E
Yozgat Turkey **30** 39.50N 34.48E
Yreka U.S.A. **54** 41.44N 122.38W
Ystad Sweden **17** 55.25N 13.49E
Ythan *r.* U.K. **6** 57.21N 2.01W
Ytterhogdal Sweden **17** 62.12N 14.51E
Yu'alliq, Jabal *mtn.* Egypt **32** 30.21N 33.31E
Yuan Jiang *r.* Hunan China **25** 29.00N 112.12E
Yuan Jiang *r.* Yunnan China *see* Hong Hà *r.* Vietnam **24**
Yuba City U.S.A. **54** 39.08N 121.27W
Yucatán *d.* Mexico **57** 19.30N 89.00W
Yucatan Channel Carib. Sea **57** 21.30N 86.00W
Yucatan Pen. Mexico **56** 19.00N 90.00W
Yucca U.S.A. **54** 34.52N 114.09W
Yuci China **25** 37.40N 112.44E
Yudino Russian Fed. **20** 55.05N 67.55E
Yuendumu Australia **44** 22.14S 131.47E
Yuexi China **24** 28.36N 102.35E
Yugorskiy Poluostrov *pen.* Russian Fed. **18** 69.00N 62.30E
Yugoslavia Europe **13** 44.00N 20.00E
Yukon *r.* U.S.A. **50** 62.35N 164.20W
Yukon Territory *d.* Canada **50** 65.00N 135.00W
Yulara Australia **44** 25.14S 131.02E
Yule *r.* Australia **42** 20.19S 118.08E
Yuleba Australia **44** 26.37S 149.20E
Yuma Ariz. U.S.A. **54** 32.43N 114.37W
Yumen China **24** 40.19N 97.12E
Yungas *f.* Bolivia **62** 16.20S 65.00W
Yungera Australia **46** 34.48S 143.10E
Yunnan *d.* China **24** 24.30N 101.30E
Yunta Australia **46** 32.37S 139.34E
Yuribey Russian Fed. **20** 71.02N 77.02E
Yurimaguas Peru **60** 5.54S 76.07W
Yuryuzan Russian Fed. **18** 54.51N 58.25E
Yushkozero Russian Fed. **18** 64.45N 32.03E
Yushu China **24** 33.06N 96.48E
Yūtō Japan **23** 34.42N 137.38E
Yuzhno Sakhalinsk Russian Fed. **25** 46.58N 142.45E
Yuzhnyy Bug *r.* Ukraine **15** 46.55N 31.59E
Yvelines *d.* France **9** 48.50N 1.50E
Yvetot France **9** 49.37N 0.45E

Z

Zaandam Neth. **8** 52.27N 4.49E
Zābol Iran **31** 31.00N 61.32E
Zābolī Iran **31** 27.08N 61.36E
Zabrze Poland **15** 50.18N 18.47E
Zacapa Guatemala **57** 15.00N 89.30W
Zacatecas Mexico **56** 22.48N 102.33W
Zacatecas *d.* Mexico **56** 24.00N 103.00W
Zadar Croatia **12** 44.08N 15.14E
Zafra Spain **10** 38.25N 6.25W
Zagreb Croatia **12** 45.49N 15.58E
Zāgros, Kūhhā-ye *mts.* Iran **31** 32.00N 51.00E
Zagros Mts. *see* Zāgros, Kūhhā-ye *mts.* Iran **31**
Zāhedān Iran **31** 29.32N 60.54E
Zaḩlah Lebanon **32** 33.50N 35.55E
Zaindeh *r.* Iran **31** 32.40N 52.50E
Zaïre Africa **36** 2.00S 22.00E
Zaïre *r.* Zaïre **36** 6.00S 12.30E
Zaječar Yugo. **13** 43.55N 22.15E
Zakataly Azerbaijan **31** 41.39N 46.40E
Zákinthos *i.* Greece **13** 37.46N 20.46E
Zakopane Poland **15** 49.19N 19.57E
Zalaegerszeg Hungary **14** 46.51N 16.51E
Zalău Romania **15** 47.11N 23.03E
Zaleshchiki Ukraine **15** 48.39N 25.50E
Zalim Saudi Arabia **30** 22.43N 42.11E
Zambezi *r.* Mozambique/Zambia **36** 18.15S 35.55E
Zambezi Zambia **36** 13.33S 23.09E
Zambezia *d.* Mozambique **37** 16.30S 37.30E
Zambia Africa **36** 14.00S 28.00E
Zamboanga Phil. **27** 6.55N 122.05E
Zambrów Poland **15** 53.00N 22.15E
Zambue Mozambique **37** 15.09S 30.47E
Zamfara *r.* Nigeria **38** 12.04N 4.00E
Zamora Mexico **56** 20.00N 102.18W
Zamora Spain **10** 41.30N 5.45W
Zamość Poland **15** 50.43N 23.15E
Zamtang China **29** 32.26N 101.06E
Zaña Peru **60** 7.00S 79.30W
Záncara *r.* Spain **10** 38.55N 4.07W
Zanda China **29** 31.32N 79.50E
Zanesville U.S.A. **55** 39.55N 82.02W
Zanjān Iran **31** 36.40N 48.30E
Zanthus Australia **43** 31.02S 123.34E
Zanzibar Tanzania **37** 6.10S 39.16E
Zanzibar I. Tanzania **37** 6.00S 39.20E
Zaozhuang China **25** 34.40N 117.30E
Zapadno-Sibirskaya Ravnina *f.* Russian Fed. **20** 60.00N 75.00E
Zapadnyy Sayan *mts.* Russian Fed. **21** 53.00N 92.00E
Zapala Argentina **63** 38.55S 70.05W
Zaporozhye Ukraine **19** 47.50N 35.10E
Zara Turkey **30** 39.55N 37.44E
Zaragoza Spain **10** 41.39N 0.54W
Zarand Iran **31** 30.50N 56.35E
Zárate Argentina **63** 34.05S 59.02W
Zaraza Venezuela **60** 9.23N 65.20W
Zard Kūh *mtn.* Iran **31** 32.21N 50.04E
Zarghūn Shahr Afghan. **28** 32.51N 68.25E
Zari Nigeria **38** 13.03N 12.46E
Zaria Nigeria **38** 11.01N 7.44E
Zaruma Ecuador **60** 3.40S 79.30W
Żary Poland **14** 51.40N 15.10E
Zarzal Colombia **60** 4.24N 76.01W
Zaslavl Belarus **15** 54.00N 27.15E
Zatishye Ukraine **15** 47.20N 29.58E
Zave Zimbabwe **37** 17.14S 30.02E
Zavitinsk Russian Fed. **25** 50.08N 129.24E
Zāwiyat al Amwāt Egypt **32** 28.04N 30.50E
Zāyandeh *r.* Iran **31** 32.40N 52.50E
Zaysan Kazakhstan **24** 47.30N 84.57E
Zaysan, Ozero *l.* Kazakhstan **24** 48.00N 83.30E
Zbarazh Ukraine **15** 49.40N 25.49E
Zborov Ukraine **15** 49.40N 25.09E
Zdolbunov Ukraine **15** 50.30N 26.10E
Zduńska Wola Poland **15** 51.36N 18.57E
Zebediela R.S.A. **39** 24.19S 29.17E
Zeebrugge Belgium **8** 51.20N 3.13E
Zeehan Australia **45** 41.55S 145.21E
Zeeland *d.* Neth. **8** 51.30N 3.45E
Zeerust R.S.A. **39** 25.32S 26.04E
Zefa' Israel **32** 31.07N 35.12E
Zefat Israel **32** 32.57N 35.27E
Zeist Neth. **8** 52.03N 5.16E
Zeitz Germany **14** 51.03N 12.08E
Zelechów Poland **15** 51.49N 21.54E
Zelenodolsk Russian Fed. **18** 55.50N 48.30E
Zelenogorsk Russian Fed. **18** 60.15N 29.31E
Zelenokumsk Russian Fed. **19** 44.25N 43.54E
Zelentsovo Russian Fed. **18** 59.51N 44.59E
Zell Germany **8** 50.02N 7.11E
Zelts Ukraine **15** 46.38N 30.00E
Zelzate Belgium **8** 51.12N 3.49E
Zemio C.A.R. **35** 5.00N 25.09E
Zemun Yugo. **13** 44.51N 20.23E
Zenica Bosnia-Herzegovina **15** 44.12N 17.55E
Zenne *r.* Belgium **8** 51.04N 4.25E
Zetel Germany **8** 53.28N 7.57E
Zeven Germany **14** 53.18N 9.16E
Zevenaar Neth. **8** 51.57N 6.04E
Zevenbergen Neth. **8** 51.41N 4.42E
Zeya Russian Fed. **21** 53.48N 127.14E
Zeya *r.* Russian Fed. **21** 50.20N 127.30E
Zêzere *r.* Portugal **10** 39.28N 8.20W
Zgierz Poland **15** 51.52N 19.25E
Zgorzelec Poland **14** 51.12N 15.01E
Zhailma Kazakhstan **20** 51.37N 61.33E
Zhambyl Kazakhstan **24** 42.50N 71.25E
Zhanatas Kazakhstan **24** 43.11N 69.35E
Zhanghua Taiwan **25** 24.06N 120.31E
Zhangjiakou China **25** 41.00N 114.50E
Zhangye China **24** 38.56N 100.27E
Zhangzhou China **25** 24.57N 118.36E
Zhanjiang China **25** 21.05N 110.12E
Zharkent Kazakhstan **24** 44.10N 80.01E
Zhashkov Ukraine **15** 49.12N 30.05E
Zhejiang *d.* China **25** 29.15N 120.00E
Zheleznodorozhnyy Russian Fed. **18** 62.39N 50.59E
Zheleznodorozhnyy Russian Fed. **18** 67.59N 64.47E
Zhengzhou China **25** 34.35N 113.38E
Zhenjiang China **25** 32.05N 119.30E
Zherdnoye Belarus **15** 51.40N 30.11E
Zhezkazgan Kazakhstan **20** 47.48N 67.24E
Zhidachov Ukraine **15** 49.20N 24.22E
Zhigansk Russian Fed. **21** 66.48N 123.27E
Zhitkovichi Belarus **15** 52.12N 27.49E
Zhitomir Ukraine **15** 50.18N 28.40E
Zhlobin Belarus **15** 52.50N 30.00E
Zhmerinka Ukraine **15** 49.00N 28.02E
Zhob *r.* Pakistan **28** 31.40N 70.54E
Zhongba China **29** 29.56N 84.20E
Zhongdian China **29** 28.00N 99.30E
Zhupanovo Russian Fed. **21** 53.40N 159.52E
Zhuzhou China **25** 27.53N 113.07E
Žiar nad Hronom Slovakia **15** 48.36N 18.52E
Zibo China **25** 36.50N 118.00E
Ziel, Mt. Australia **42** 23.24S 132.23E
Zielona Góra Poland **14** 51.57N 15.30E
Ziftā Egypt **32** 30.43N 31.14E
Zigong China **29** 29.18N 104.45E
Zile Turkey **30** 40.18N 35.52E
Žilina Slovakia **15** 49.14N 18.46E
Zillah Libya **34** 28.33N 17.35E
Zima Russian Fed. **21** 53.58N 102.02E
Zimatlán Mexico **56** 16.52N 96.45W
Zimba Zambia **39** 17.19S 26.12E
Zimbabwe Africa **36** 18.55S 30.00E
Zimbor Romania **15** 47.00N 23.16E
Zimnicea Romania **15** 43.38N 25.22E
Zimniy Bereg *f.* Russian Fed. **18** 65.50N 41.30E
Zinder Niger **38** 13.46N 8.58E
Zinder *d.* Niger **38** 14.20N 9.30E
Zinga Mtwara Tanzania **37** 9.01S 38.47E
Ziniaré Burkina **38** 12.34N 1.12W
Ziro India **29** 27.38N 93.42E
Zitundo Mozambique **39** 26.45S 32.49E
Ziway Hāyk' *l.* Ethiopia **35** 8.00N 38.50E
Zlatograd Bulgaria **13** 41.23N 25.06E
Zlatoust Russian Fed. **18** 55.10N 59.38E
Zlín Czech Republic **15** 49.13N 17.41E
Złoczew Poland **15** 51.25N 18.36E
Złotów Poland **15** 53.22N 17.02E
Zlynka Russian Fed. **15** 52.24N 31.45E
Zmeinogorsk Russian Fed. **20** 51.11N 82.14E
Zmiyevka Russian Fed. **18** 52.40N 36.22E
Znamenka Ukraine **19** 48.42N 32.40E
Znin Poland **15** 52.52N 17.43E
Znojmo Czech Republic **14** 48.52N 16.05E
Zobia Zaïre **36** 2.58N 25.56E
Zobue Mozambique **37** 15.35S 34.26E
Zoétélé Cameroon **38** 3.17N 11.54E
Zogno Italy **9** 45.48N 9.40E
Zohreh *r.* Iran **31** 30.04N 49.32E
Zolochev Ukraine **15** 49.48N 24.51E
Zolotonosha Ukraine **19** 49.39N 32.05E
Zomba Malaŵi **37** 15.22S 35.22E
Zonguldak Turkey **30** 41.26N 31.47E
Zorritos Peru **60** 3.50S 80.40W
Zouar Chad **34** 20.27N 16.32E
Zoutkamp Neth. **8** 53.21N 6.18E
Zrenjanin Yugo. **13** 45.22N 20.23E
Zuénoula Côte d'Ivoire **38** 7.34N 6.03W
Zug Switz. **14** 47.10N 8.31E
Zuid Beveland *f.* Neth. **8** 51.30N 3.50E
Zuidelijk-Flevoland *f.* Neth. **8** 52.22N 5.22E
Zuid Holland *d.* Neth. **8** 52.00N 4.30E
Zuidhorn Neth. **8** 53.16N 6.25E
Zújar *r.* Spain **10** 38.58N 5.40W
Zújar, Embalse del *resr.* Spain **10** 38.57N 5.30W
Zülpich Germany **8** 50.42N 6.36E
Zululand *see* Kwa Zulu *f.* R.S.A. **39**
Zumbo Mozambique **37** 15.36S 30.24E
Zungeru Nigeria **38** 9.48N 6.03E
Zunyi China **29** 27.41N 106.50E
Zurich Neth. **8** 53.08N 5.25E
Zürich Switz. **14** 47.23N 8.33E
Zuru Nigeria **38** 11.26N 5.16E
Zushi Japan **23** 35.18N 139.35E
Zutphen Neth. **8** 52.08N 6.12E
Zuwārah Libya **34** 32.56N 12.06E
Zvenigorodka Ukraine **15** 49.05N 30.58E
Zverinogolovskoye Kazakhstan **20** 54.23N 64.47E
Zvishavane Zimbabwe **39** 20.20S 30.05E
Zvolen Slovakia **15** 48.35N 19.08E
Zwettl Austria **14** 48.37N 15.10E
Zwickau Germany **14** 50.43N 12.30E
Zwischenahn Germany **8** 53.13N 7.59E
Zwoleń Poland **15** 51.22N 21.35E
Zwolle Neth. **8** 52.31N 6.06E
Zyryanovsk Kazakhstan **20** 49.45N 84.16E
Żywiec Poland **15** 49.41N 19.12E

THE WORLD : Physical

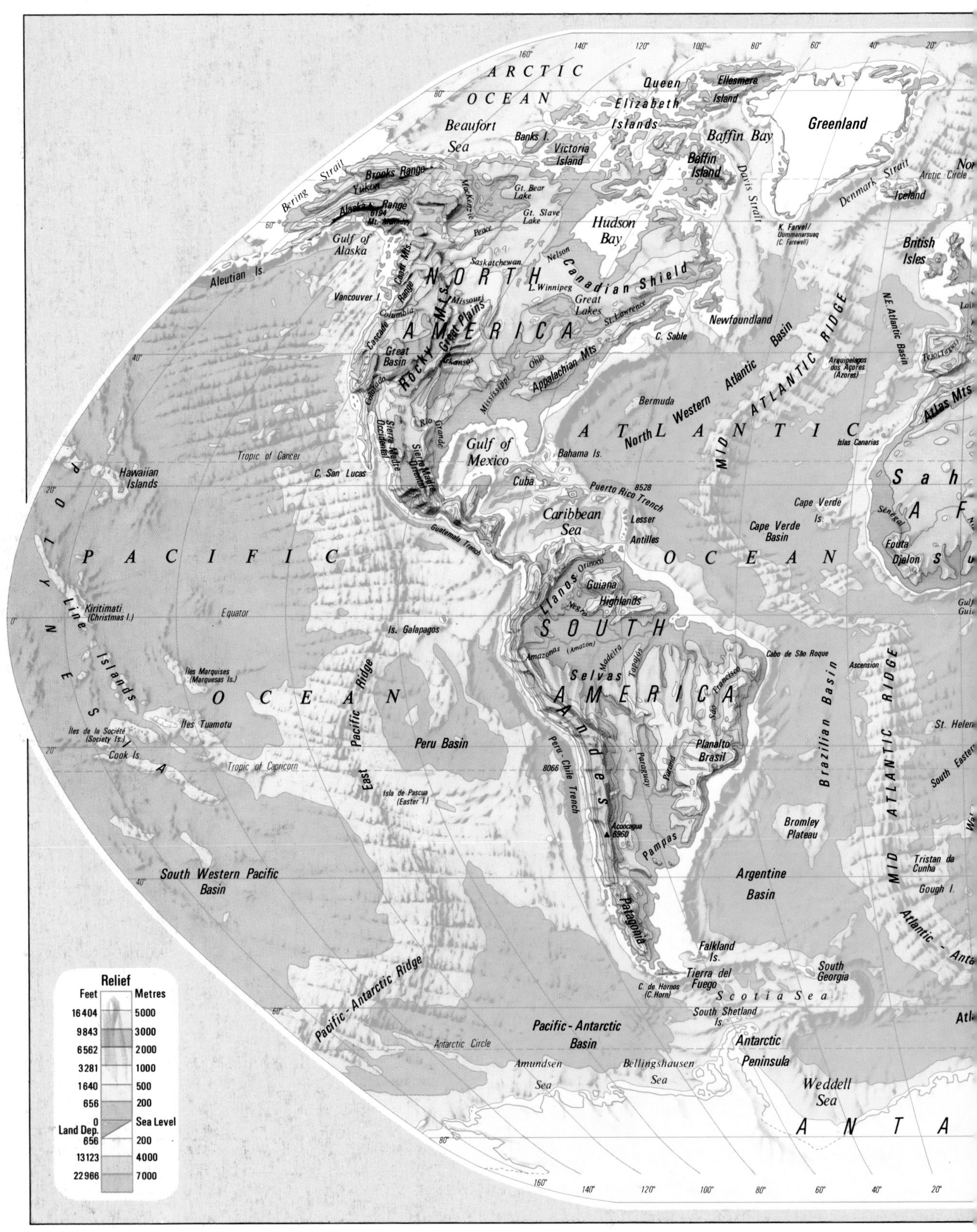

Relief

Feet		Metres
16 404		5000
9843		3000
6562		2000
3281		1000
1640		500
656		200
0		Sea Level
Land Dep.		200
656		
13 123		4000
22 966		7000